SMITHSONIAN INSTITUTION
BUREAU OF ETHNOLOGY: J. W. POWELL, DIRECTOR

I0120097

CHINOOK TEXTS

BY

FRANZ BOAS

WASHINGTON
GOVERNMENT PRINTING OFFICE
1894

IARLES CULTEE.

CONTENTS.

ILLUSTRATION.

CHINOOK TEXTS

Told by

CHARLES CULTEE

Recorded and translated by

FRANZ BOAS

INTRODUCTION.

HISTORICAL ACCOUNT.

The following texts were collected in the summers of 1890 and 1891. While studying the Salishan languages of Washington and Oregon I learned that the dialects of the lower Chinook were on the verge of disappearing, and that only a few individuals survived who remembered the languages of the once powerful tribes of the Clatsop and Chinook. This fact determined me to make an effort to collect what little remained of these languages.

I first went to Clatsop, where a small band of Indians are located near Seaside, Clatsop county, Oregon. Although a number of them belonged to the Clatsop tribe, they had all adopted the Nehelim language, a dialect of the Salishan Tillamook. This change of language was brought about by frequent intermarriages with the Nehelim. I found one middle-aged man and two old women who still remembered the Clatsop language, but it was impossible to obtain more than a vocabulary and a few sentences. The man had forgotten a great part of the language, while the women were not able to grasp what I wanted; they claimed to have forgotten their myths and traditions, and could not or would not give me any connected texts. One old Clatsop woman, who had been married to a Mr. Smith, was too sick to be seen, and died soon after my visit. The few remaining Clatsop had totally forgotten the history of their tribe, and even maintained that no allied dialect was spoken north of Columbia river and on Shoalwater bay. They assured me that the whole country was occupied by the Chehalis, another Salishan tribe. They told me, however, that a few of their relatives, who still continued to speak Clatsop, lived on Shoalwater bay among the Chehalis.

5

I went to search for this remnant of the Clatsop and Chinook peoples, and found them located at Bay Center, Pacific county, Washington. They proved to be the last survivors of the Chinook, who at one time occupied the greater part of Shoalwater bay and the northern bank of Columbia river as far as Greys Harbor. The tribe has adopted the Chehalis language in the same way in which the Clatsop have adopted the Nehelim. The only individuals who spoke Chinook were Charles Cultee and Catherine. While I was unable to obtain anything from the latter, Cultee (or more properly Q¡Eltē′) proved to be a veritable storehouse of information. His mother's mother was a Katlamat, and his mother's father a Quilā′pax; his father's mother was a Clatsop, and his father's father a Tinneh of the interior. His wife is a Chehalis, and at present he speaks Chehalis almost exclusively, this being also the language of his children. He has lived for a long time in Katlamat, on the southern bank of Columbia river, his mother's town, and for this reason speaks the Katlamat dialect as well as the Chinook dialect. He uses the former dialect in conversing with Samson, a Katlamat Indian, who is also located at Bay Center. Until a few years ago he spoke Chinook with one of his relatives, while he uses it now only rarely when conversing with Catherine, who lives a few miles from Bay Center. Possibly this Chinook is to a certain extent mixed with Katlamat expressions, but from a close study of the material I conclude that it is on the whole pure and trustworthy.

I have obtained from Cultee a series of Katlamat texts also, which appear to me not quite so good as the Chinook texts, but nevertheless give a good insight into the differences of the two dialects. It may be possible to obtain material in this dialect from other sources.

My work of translating and explaining the texts was greatly facilitated by Cultee's remarkable intelligence. After he had once grasped what I wanted, he explained to me the grammatical structure of the sentences by means of examples, and elucidated the sense of difficult periods. This work was the more difficult as we conversed only by means of the Chinook jargon.

The following pages contain nothing but the texts and translations. The grammar and dictionary of the language will contain a comparison of all the dialects of the Chinookan stock. I have translated the first text almost verbatim, while in the later texts I endeavored only to render the sense accurately, for which reason short sentences have been inserted, others omitted. Still, the form of the Chinook sentences has been preserved as nearly as possible.

ALPHABET.

a, e, i, o, u	have their continental sounds (short).
ā, ĕ, ĭ, ō, ū	long vowels.
A, E, I, O, U	obscure vowels.
ᵃ, ᵉ, ⁱ, ᵒ, ᵘ	vowels not articulated but indicated by position of the mouth.
ä	in German *Bär*.
â	aw in law.
ŏ	o in German *roll*.
ê	e in bell.
–	separates vowels which do not form diphthongs.
ai	i in island.
au	ow in how.
l	as in English.
ll	very long, slightly palatized by allowing a greater portion of the back of the tongue to touch the palate.
ᴛ	posterior palatal l; the tip of the tongue touches the alveoli of the lower jaw, the back of the tongue is pressed against the hard palate, sonans.
L	the same, short and exploded (surd; Lepsius's ţ).
Lᵢ	the same with very great stress of explosion.
q	velar k.
k	English k.
k·	palatized k (Lepsius's k′), almost ky.
kX	might be better defined as a posterior palatal k, between k and k·.
x	ch in German *Bach*.
X	x pronounced at posterior border of hard palate.
x·	palatal x as in German *ich*.
s, c	are evidently the same sound and might be written s· or c·, both being palatized; c (English sh) is pronounced with open teeth, the tongue almost touching the palate immediately behind the alveoli; s is modified in the same manner.
d, t b, p g, k	as in English, but surd and sonant are difficult to distinguish.
h	as in English.
y	as in year.
w	as in English.
m	is pronounced with semiclausure of the nose and with very slight compression of the lips; it partakes, therefore, of the character of b and w.
n	is pronounced with semiclausure of the nose; it partakes, therefore, of the character of d.

¡	designates increased stress of articulation.
!	designates increased stress of articulation due to the elision of q.
ᶜ	is a very deep laryngeal intonation, due to the elision of q.
2, 4	designate excessive length of vowels, representing approximately the double and fourfold mora.

Words ending with a short vowel must be contracted with the first vowel of the next word. When a word ends with a long vowel and the next begins with a vowel, a euphonic -y- is inserted. The last consonant of a word is united with the first vowel of the next word to one syllable.

TK¡ANĀ′MUKC.
MYTHS.

1. CIKʇA ICTA′KXANAM.
CIKʇA THEIR MYTH.

Lqui′numiks Lxĕlā′-itx Lā′wuX ăĕXa′t Lo·c̯ō′kuil neq¡′ĕlā′wilX. **1**
Five / there were, / their younger sister / one / a woman / menstruating the first time.

Atcunkō′mit icā′yim. ĔXt iqĕ′tak nikct Lap aLE′kxax. Ā′yō **2**
He carried her away / the grizzly bear. / One / year / not / find / he did it. / He went

iLā′xk′un. Atcō′xtkinEba Liā′wuX. Ā′yo mank kulā′i. Lap **3**
its elder brother. / He went to search for her / his younger sister. / He went / a little / far. / Find

ā′tcax ōni′ctXuic. Itcā′maᶜ atciā′lax; atcupō′nit. Ā′yō4; kulā′2i **4**
he did her / a pheasant. / Hitting her / he did her with it; / he hung her up. / He went; / far

ā′yō. Lap atci′tax t!′ŏʇ. Atcixā′laqʇ. A′lta Lōc Lq¡′ēyō′qxut k¡a **5**
he went. / Find / he did / a house. / He opened the door. / Now / there was / an old man / and

LēXā′t Lg′ā′cgc. Ayū′p!ŏm. ALxā′latck Lg′ā′cgc. TakE aLsŏ′pEna **6**
one / child. / He entered. / It rose / the child. / Then / it jumped up

Lg′ā′cgc. "O′quaqct, tā′ta," takE LE′k·im. TakE atcLō′skam, takE **7**
the child. / "Louse me, uncle," / then / it said. / Then / he took it, / then

atcLgē′qsta. TakE Lap ā′tcaq ō′Laqst. TakE L¡k·!ŏp ā′tcax. **8**
he loused it. / Then / find / he did her / its louse. / Then / squeeze / he did her.

TakE ātcā′yaqc gō iā′tuk. TakE L¡q¡ŏp ā′tcax iā′tuk. TakE **9**
Then / he bit him / at / his neck. / Then / cut / he did him / his neck. / Then

acgiō′Lata k¡a Liā′mama. TakE acgiō′pcut mā′Lxōlē. A′lta k·¡′ĕ **10**
they two hauled him / and / his father. / Then / they two hid him / inland. / Now / nothing

cmŏkct cᶜā′kil ckulā′pamam tā′lalX. **11**
two / women / they two went digging them / gamass.

A′lta LEla′ktikcka txĕ′lā-it. TakE nĕ′ktcuktē. A′lta wext ē′Xat **12**
Now / four only / remained. / Then / it got day. / Now / more / one

ā′yō. Ā′yō 4. TakE weXt Lap ā′tcax ōni′ctXuic. TakE itcā′maᶜ **13**
he went. / He went. / Then / again / find / he did her / a pheasant. / Then / hitting her

atciā′lax. TakE atcupō′nit weXt iā′xkatē. TakE ā′yō, kulā′i ā′yo **14**
he did her. / Then / he hung her up / again / there. / Then / he went, / far / he went

weXt. TakE Lap atci′tax t¡′ōL. TakE atcixā′laqʇē. A′lta Lōc **15**
again. / Then / find / he did them / a house. / Then / he opened the door. / Now / there was

Lq¡′ēyō′qxut k¡a Lg′ā′cgc. TakE ayū′p!ŏm. "Tā′ta, ō′quaqct!" **16**
an old man / and / a child. / Then / he entered. / "Uncle, / louse me!"

TakE Lap ā′tcax ō′yuqct. TakE L¡k¡′ŏp ā′tcax ō′yuqct. TakE **17**
Then / find / he did her / his louse. / Then / squeeze / he did her / his louse. / Then

atcā′yaqc gō iā′tuk; takE L¡q¡ŏp nĕ′xax iā′tuk. TakE acgiō′Lata **18**
he bit him / at / his neck; / then / cut / was / his neck. / Then / they two hauled him

k¡a Liā′mama. TakE acgiō′pcut gō mā′Lxōlē. TakE nā′k·ēm: **19**
and / his father. / Then / they two hid him / at / inland. / Then / she said:

"Tca txgō′ya! LgūLē′lXEmk gō tE′lxaoqL aLtĕ′mam." TakE **20**
"Come, let us two go! / A person / at / our house / has arrived." / Then

9

1 agō'lXam   Lgă'naa: "Ālqē   tcax."   Lē'le   ka   aci'xkō   k¡a
    she spoke to   her mother: "Later on   come."   A long time   then   they two   and
    her   went home

2 Lgă'naa.   A'lta   akLiLă'kux   Lᵉă'owilkt   gō   wē'wuLē.   A'lta
    her mother.   Now   she smelled it   blood   in   interior of   Then
                                                             house.

3 naXE'LXa.   A'lta   ōᶜō'lEptckiX   agacgE'ltcim.
    she became angry.   Now   [with] firebrand   she hit them two.

4 A'lta   Lō'nikcka   Lxē'lă-it.   TakE   nē'ktcuktē.   "NiXua   nai'ka
    Now   three only   remained.   Then   it got day.   "Well!   I

5 weXt   nō'ya!"   TakE   ă'yō4,   kulā'i   ā'yō.   TakE   weXt   Lap   ă'tcax
    also   I shall go!"   Then   he went,   far   he went.   Then   again   find   he did her

6 ōni'ctXuic.   TakE   itcă'maᶜ   atciă'lax.   Atcupō'nit   weXt   ia'xka.
    a pheasant.   Then   hitting her   he did her with   He hung her up   also   he.
                                             it.

7 TakE   weXt   ă'yō,   kulā'2i   ā'yō.   TakE   Lap   atci'tax   t!'ōL.   TakE
    Then   also   he went,   far   he went.   Then   find   he did them   a house.   Then

8 atcixă'laqᴛ;   Lōc   Lq¡'ēyō'qxut   k¡a   Lg'ă'cgc.   TakE   ayū'p!ōm.
    he opened the   there was   an old man   and   a child.   Then   he entered.
    door;

9 · · · [as above] · · ·   TakE   nă'k·im   kaX   ōk'ō'sks: "Tca   txgō'ya!
    · · · [as above] · · ·   Then   she said   that   girl: "Come   let us two go!

10 ALtē'mam   LgōLē'lXEmk   gō   tE'lxaôqL."   TakE   agō'lXam   Lgă'naa:
    It arrived   a person   at   our house."   Then   she spoke to   her mother;
                                                                 her

11 "Ā'Lqē, tcax!   ă'Lqē, tcax!"   TakE   agō'lXam: "Nēkct   na   LEmă'icX?"
    "Later on, come! Later on, come!"   Then   she spoke to   "Not [interrog-   thy relative?"
                                                     her: ative particle]

12 TakE   agō'lXam: "Lqui'numiks   LEmē'tata-iks."   TakE   aci'xkō
    Then   she spoke to her: "Five   thy uncles."   Then   they two
                                                                  went home

13 k¡a   Lgă'naa.   TakE   naXE'LXa;   takE   akcō'tEna   Lgă'mama
    and   her mother.   Then   she became angry;   then   she struck them two   her father

14 k¡a   Lgă'wuX.
    and   her younger brother.

15 A'lta   weXt   nē'ktcuktē.   A'lta   weXt   ē'Xat   niXE'ltXuitck.   Atc-
    Now   again   it got day.   Now   again   one   he made himself ready.   He

16 to'ckam   tiă'xalaitanEma.   TakE   ă'yō   weXt.   Kulā'i   ā'yō4,   ă'yō.   TakE
    took them   his arrows.   Then   he went   also.   Far   he went, be went.   Then

17 Lap   ă'tcax   ōni'ctXuic.   TakE   itcă'maᶜ   atciă'lax.   TakE   atcupō'nit
    find   he did her   a pheasant.   Then   hitting her   he did her   Then   he hung her up
                                                  with one.

18 iă'xkatē   weXt.   TakE   ă'yō   weXt.   Kulā'4i   ā'yō.   TakE   Lap   atci'tax
    there   also.   Then   he went   also.   Far   he went.   Then   find   he did them

19 t!'ōL.   TakE   atcixă'laqᴛē.   Lōc   Lq¡'ēyō'qxut   k¡a   Lg'ăcgc.   TakE
    a house.   Then   he opened the door.   There   an old man   and   a child.   Then
                                             was

20 ayū'p!ōm.   TakE   aLxă'latck   Lg'ă'ᶜgc.   TakE   aLksō'pEna: "Ō'quaqct
    he entered.   Then   it rose   the child.   Then   it jumped up: "Louse me.

21 tă'ta!"   TakE   akLgE'kXiks.   TakE   Lap   aqā'x   ō'Laqst.   TakE
    uncle!"   Then   he loused him.   Then   found   it was   its louse.   Then

22 L¡k¡ōp   ā'qāx.   TakE   atcă'yaqc   Liă'tata   gō   iă'tuk.   TakE   L¡q¡'ōp
    squeezed   it was.   Then   he bit him   his uncle   at   his neck.   Then   cut

23 atcē'xax   iă'tuk.   TakE   acgiō'Lata   maʼLxôlē;   acgiō'pcut.   TakE
    he did it   his neck.   Then   they two hauled him   inland;   they two hid him.   Then

24 nă'k·im   qaX   ōk'ō'sks: "Ai'aq,   ai'aq,   txgō'ya!"   TakE: "ALtē'mam
    she said   that   girl: "Quick,   quick, let us two go!"   Then: "It came

25 LgōLē'lXEmk   gō   tE'lxaôkL."   TakE   agō'lXam   Lgă'naa: "Ā'Lqē,
    a person   to   our house."   Then   she said to her   her mother: "Later on,

26 ă'Lqē."   TakE   aci'xko;   takE   acixă'laqᴛē.   A'lta   iLă'kux   Lᵉă'owilkt.
    later on."   Then   they two went   then   they two opened   Then   its smell   blood.
                        home;   the door.

27 A'lta   naXE'LXa.   A'lta   akcō'tena   Lgă'mama   k¡a   Lgă'wuX.
    Now   she became angry.   Now   she struck   her father   and   her younger
                         them two   brother.

A'lta smôkst cxēlā'-itX. Nĕ'ktcuktē. ··· [as before] ···   1
Now   two   remained.   It got day.   ··· [as before] ···

A'lta ēXā'tka ayukō'ētiXt. A'lta nigE'tsax, nigE'tsax, nigE'tsax   2
Now   one only   he was left.   Now   he cried,   he cried,   he cried

ka'nauwē ō'pull. Qꜟoā'p iktcō'ktīya, takE ayaō'ptit. TakE   3
all   night.   Nearly   it was going to get day,   then   he fell asleep.   Then

niXgē'qauwakō: "Manix Lap mā'xō ōni'ctXuic, nĕ'kct itcā'maᶜ   4
he dreamt: "When   find   you will do her   a pheasant,   not   hitting her

mialā'xō. Ēqctxē'Lau atcungō'mit LEmciā'wuX kꞏa ia'xka   5
you will do her   A monster   he carried her away   your younger sister   and   he
with him

atctōtē'na ka'nauwē LEmē'xk'uniks. Manix mō'ya, Lap mtā'xō   6
he killed them   all   your elder brothers.   When   you will go,   find   you will do them

tꞏ'ōL. Nēkct ai'aq amō'p!ꞏa ! Manix mōikElā'ya amō'kctikc   7
a house.   Not   quick   enter!   When   you will see them   two persons

ōxo-ēlā'-itX, amō'La-it gō-y-iqē'p!al !" A'lta nē'ktcukte. NixE'l'ōkō.   8
being there   stay   at the doorway!"   Now   it got day.   He awoke.

Ō, a'lta weXt nigE'tsax. TakE atctō'ckam tiā'xalaitan, takE ā'yō.   9
Oh, now   more   he cried.   Then   he took them   his arrows,   then   he went.

Āyō4, kulā'i ā'yō. TakE Lap ā'tcax ōni'ctXuic. Nēkct Ꞌitcā'maᶜ   10
He went,   far   he went.   Then   find   he did her   a pheasant.   Not   hitting her

atciā'lax. A'lta ā'yō, ā'yō, ā'yō, kulā'i ā'yō. Lap atci'tax   11
he did her with one.   Now   he went,   he went,   he went,   far   he went.   Find   he did them

tꞏ'ōL. TakE atcixā'lakꞆē. A'lta Lōc Lqꞏꞌēyō'qxut kꞏa LgꞋā'cgc.   12
a house.   Then   he opened the door.   Then   there was   an old man   and   a child.

TakE ayō'La-it gō-y-iqē'p!al. Lē'2lē takE ayō'La-it gō-y-iqē'p!al.   13
Then   he stayed   in   the doorway.   Long   then   he stayed   in   the doorway.

TakE nā'kꞏēm ōk'ō'sks; takE agō'lXam Lgā'naa: "Ai'aq, ai'aq,   14
Then   she spoke   the girl;   then   she said to her   to her mother: "Quick,   quick,

tXgō'ya. TakE aLtē'mam LgōLē'lXEmk gō tE'lxaôkL." TakE   15
we two go home.   Then   it came   a person   to   our house."   Then

agō'lXam Lgā'naa: "Tcā tXE'Xatgō!" TakE aci'xkō.   16
she said to her   her mother: "Come, let us turn back!"   Then   they two went home.

TakE acxkō'mam, takE ackixā'lakLē. A'lta LgōLē'lEXEmk   17
Then   they two reached   then   they two opened the   Now   a person
their house,   door.

Lōc. TakE ā'ctōp!. A'lta naXE'LXa kaX ōk'ō'sks. A'lta   18
there was.   Then   they two entered.   Now   she grew angry   that   girl.   Now

nō'ponEm. A'lta ayaxalgu'Litck Liā'wuX: "Ka'nauwē LtXa'xk'-   19
it grew dark.   Now   he told her   his younger sister: "All   our two selves'

unikc aLE'tē." A'lta naxalgu'Litck gō ōgō'xō: "LEmē'tata-ikc   20
elder   they came."   Now   she told her   to   her daughter: "Your uncles
brothers

ka'nauwē aLE'tē." "Mai'kꞏa mcni'luat." "Qa'da kcā'xoꜟ   21
all!   they came."   "You   you disbelieved me."   "How   they two shall
be done?

Txcōte'nanaꜟ" "Ā, tgtꞏꞌō'kti qcLXawā'ya!" A'lta: "Tgtꞏō'kti   22
Shall we kill them   "Ah!   good   they two are killed!"   Now: "Good
two?"

nLgElō'ya Lkckuī'!" TakE atcLi'tkLam Lkckuī' gō wē'wuLē.   23
I go to get it   pitchwood!"   Then   he went and carried   pitchwood   to   interior of
   it   house.

TakE nē'kꞏim ēqꞏꞌēyō'qxut: "I'kta miLgElā'xō LaLkckuī'ꟷꞏ" "A'Lqē   24
Then   he said   the old man: "What will you do with it   its pitchwood?"   "Later on

tcā'xElkꞆē LElxElgē'Lxaē." A'lta aLxē'la-it. Lē'lē aLxē'la-it. A'lta   25
winter   we make fire with it."   Now   they stayed.   Long   they stayed.   Now

nixē'llkulil lē'lē. Qꞏoā'p iktcō'ktiya, ka ayaō'ptit. A'lta   26
he spoke much   a long time.   Nearly   it was going to   then   he fell asleep.   Now
to him   get day,

atcō'lXam Liā'wuX: "Mxā'latck! Ai'āq a'lta cilxElgē'Lxaē!"   27
he said to her   to his younger   "Rise!   Quick   now   we will burn them
     sister: two!"

A'lta naxā'latck Liā'wuX, a'lta nō'pa. A'lta naxā'latck ōgō'Xō,   28
Now   she rose   his younger sister,   now   she went out.   Now   she rose   her daughter,

1 a′lta nō′pa. A′lta tuwā′x atci′Lax Lkckuī′. A′lta ayō′pa. A′lta
now she went out.   Now   light   he did it   the pitchwood.   Now   he went out.   Now

2 nō xō′LXa qō′ta t!ō̆L. TakE nĕ′k·im: "He! ē′qxiX! Mxā′latck
it [they] burnt   those   house.   Then   he said: "Heh!   brother-in-law!   Rise

3 ē′qxiX! lxLXa!" A′lta nixā′latck ēq¡′ēyō′qxut, a′lta ixpō′tē. A′lta
brother-   We burn!"   Now   he rose   the old one,   now   it was locked.   Now
in-law!

4 aci′xLXa, iā′Xa k¡a ia′xka.
they two burnt,   his son   and   he.

A′lta akLō′Xtkin Lgā′tata-iks. A′lta Lap agE′Lax gō mā′Lxộle,
Now she searched for them   her uncles.   Now   find   she did them   at   inland,

6 a′lta agE′Luk⸀ gō Ltcuq°. A′lta a′xka pō′pō agE′Lax gō Ltcuq°.
now she carried them   to water.   Now   she   blew   she did them   on the water.

7 A′lta ka′nauwē aLxulā′yutck. A′lta aLi′xkō; kulā′i ā′Lō̆. Lap
Now   all   they rose.   Now   they went home;   far   they went.   Find

8 aLgā′yax ikak¡′ō′LitX. A′lta ia′xkati aLx′ō′yut gō qīX ikak¡′ō′LitX.
they did him   lake.   Now   there   they bathed   in   that   lake.

9 A′lta nakL¡′ē′mEn kaX ō̆ō′kuil: "TcuX t′ayā′ na qiā′ nkL¡′ē′mEn?"
Now   she dived   that   woman: "Ha!   good [inter-   if   I dive!"
                                              rogative
                                              particle]

10 "Ā, t′ayā′ qiā′ mkL¡′ē′mEn." "Nikō′s⸝uit x·iau ikak¡′ō′LitX?" "Ā,
"Ah,   good   if   you dive."   Does it fit me in   this   lake!"   "Yes,
                                               water

11 mkō′s⸝uit." WeXt nakL¡ē′mEn. "TcuX t′ayā′ na qiā nkL¡ē′mEn?"
it fits you in   Again   she dived.   "Ha!   good [inter-   if   I dive!"
water."   rogative
                                              particle]

12 "Ā, t′ayā′ qiā′ mkL¡ ē′mEn." "Nikō′s⸝uit x·iau ikak¡′ō′LitX?" "Ā,
"Ah,   good   if   you dive."   "Does it fit me in water   this   lake?"   "Ah,

13 mkō′s⸝uit." A′lta weXt nakL¡′ē′mEn. Lō̆′ni nakL¡′ē′mEn; a′lta
it fits you in water."   Now   again   she dived.   Three times   she dived;   now

14 ī′tcaqcō ayaxā′lax. "TcuX nikō′s⸝uit ikak¡′ō′LitX?" "Ā, k·!ē nikct
her hair   began to grow   "Ha!   does it fit me   the lake?"   "Ah! no!   not
on her.   in water

15 mkō′s⸝uit." "Ē, qa′daqa nikct ā′nqate anicgEnō′lXam?" A′lta
it fits you in water."   "Eh,   why   not   before   you spoke to me!"   Now

16 qui′numē nakL¡′ē′mEn, a′lta kwā′nisum nō′ya. A′lta aLE′kXuk⸀
five times   she dived,   now   for always   she went.   Now   they carried her

17 ā′mkXa ōLā′LatXEn. A′lta aLXkō′mam gō tE′LaqL. A′lta aLxē′la-it.
only her   their niece.   Now   they arrived at   at their house.   Now   they stayed.
                                 their house

18 A′lta ēwā′ qē′xtcē aqaLxamElā′lEmX. K·¡ē, nēkct aLgō′tx. Ā′2lta
Now   thus   intending   they went repeatedly to buy   No,   not   they gave her   Now
                                       her.   away.

19 LēXat Lkā′nax aLgōmEl. A′lta ia′xkati nō′La-it.
one   chief   he bought her.   Now   there   she stayed.

A′lta ka′nauwē L⸝aLā′ma iq¡ē′sqēs nikct it¡′ō′kti ā′yamxtc, qēwa
Now   all   days   blue-jay   not   good   his heart,   because

21 nikct qā′utsix hē′hē nā′xax. A′lta lē′lē, ka nā′k·im: "Â, takE tEll
never   laugh   she did.   Now   a long   then   she said: "Ah,   then   tired
                                     time,

22 nē′xax ē′tcamxtc. TgEt¡′ō′kti mō′ ya kulā′i; a′lta hē′hē nxā′xō."
gets   my heart.   Good   you go   far;   now   laugh   I shall do."

23 "K·¡ä, k·¡ä, nikct hē′hē mxā′xō." Lē 2lē weXt kawit nā′k·im: "Â,
"No,   no,   not   laugh   you shall do."   A long   again and more   she said: "Oh,
                                               time

24 takE tEll nē′xax ē′tcamxtc." TakE atcō′lXam itcā′k·ikala:
then   tired   gets   my heart."   Then   he spoke to her   her husband:

25 "GEt¡′ō′kti a′lta hē′hē mxā′xo." A′lta agiō′lXam: "GEt¡′ō′kti a′lta
"Good   now   laugh   you do."   Now   she spoke to him: "Good   now

26 hē′hē nxā′xō. TakE tEll atcā′yax ē′tcamxtc iq¡ē′sqēs. Mō′ya
laugh   I shall do.   Then   tired   he makes him   my heart   blue-jay.   Go

mā'2Lxȯlē   gō.   MEci'n'ūyā'yai;   tEmē'utiks   mEtȯckā'mai!"   Ai'aq   **1**
inland   there.   Lie down on knees and elbows;   your ears   hold them!"   Quick

kawē'X   nax'ō'tam.   AkLō'skam   Lqō'tcamētē.   A'lta   aLaxa'ltciam;   **2**
early   she went to bathe.   She took it   a comb.   Now   she combed herself;

a'lta   nō'pa.   A'lta   nā'k·im: "Qaxē'4   mȯc,   iq¡ē'sqēs;   ā'uLEL   a'lta   **3**
now   she went out.   Now   she said: "Where   are you,   blue-jay;   well   now

hē'hē   nxā'xō.   Hahahē!   iq¡ē'sq¡ēs."   A'lta   aktā'wilᶜ   kanauwē'4   **4**
laugh   I shall do.   Hahahē!   blue-jay."   Now   she ate them   all

tē'lXim,   tiā'lEXam   itcā'k·ik·a.   A'lta   gō-y-ȯᶜ   ō'Lax,   a'lta   L¡'păkᶜ   **5**
people,   his people   her husband's.   Now   there   the sun,   now   recovered

nā'xax,   a'lta   nagE'm'aa.   Aktō'm'a   ka'nauwē4   tgā'Xamōkuk.   A'lta   **6**
she got,   now   she vomited.   She vomited them   all   their bones.   Now

agiō'XtkinEma   itcā'k·ika.   A'lta   k·¡ē,   nikct   Lap   agā'yax.   A'lta   **7**
she searched for him   her husband.   Now   nothing,   not   find   she did him.   Now

agiō'Xtkin   gō   qōtac   tē'lXim   tgā'Xamōkuk.   A'lta   Lap   agā'yax,   **8**
she searched for him   at   those   people   their bones.   Now   find   she did him,

yukpE't   k·¡ē   tiā'ᶜōwit.   A'lta   agē'lgitk   gō   iqō'mxōm.   A'lta   nakLā'yñ   **9**
up to here   nothing   his legs.   Now   she put him into   in   a basket.   Now   she moved

mank   kulā'i.   A'lta   t¡'ȯL   agE'tax.   A'lta   iā'xkati   nō'La-it.   **10**
a little   far.   Now   a house   she made them.   Now   there   she stayed.

A'lta   lē'lē   ē'tcatc¡a   ayaxā'lax.   A'lta   nakxa'tō.   Aktaxu'tō   **11**
Now   a long time,   her sickness   was on her.   Now   she gave birth.   She gave birth to them

amȯ'kstiks   tkā'la-uks.   A'lta   tEqoā'-iLa   nō'xȯx   tga'a.   A'lta   **12**
two   males.   Now   large   they got   her children.   Now

akcō'lXam: "Nēkct   yau'a   mtō'iX!   Iā'ma   yau'ā2   mai'ēmē   mto'iX!"   **13**
she said to them two: "Not   there   you two go!   Only   there   down river   you two go!"

A'lta   nau'itka.   Ctā'qoa-iL   aci'xȯx.   A'lta   atciō'lXam   Liā'wuX: **14**
Now   indeed.   Large [dual]   they two got.   Now   he said to him   to his younger brother:

"Tgt¡'ō'kti   qōi   atgō'iX   yau'a!"   A'lta   aē'Xt   oᶜō'Lax,   a'lta   a'cto.   **15**
"Good   will   we two go   there!"   Now   one   day,   now   they two went.

Ā'4lta   Lap   acgE'tax   tē'lXim   tgā'Xamōkuk   qᴀ̆   nō'Xuc.   "Ō,   ai'aq   **16**
Now   find   they did them   people   their bones   where   they were on ground.   "Oh,   quick

mE'tē,   txkō'ya!"   Acxkō'mam   gō   t¡'ȯL.   A'lta   atciōlXam   Liā'wuX: **17**
come,   let us two go home!"   They reached their house   at   house.   Now   he spoke to him   to his younger brother:

"O,   Lgā'xauyamtiks   qō'tac   tē'lXim.   Qa'daLx   nuxō'La-it?"   **18**
"Oh!   the poor ones   those   people.   How may be   they died?"

A'lta   cta'qoa-iL   aci'xȯx.   A'lta   acx'ō'yut;   a'lta   lax   aci'xax   **19**
Now   large [dual]   they two got.   Now   they two bathed;   now   miss   they two did it

Lqētcamē'te.   "Ō,   ā'u!   Lō'nas   gō   Lqētcamē'tē   Lkēx   gō   qiX   **20**
a comb.   "Oh,   my younger brother!   perhaps   there   a comb   it is   in   that

iqō'mxōm."   "Ō,   ai'aq   Laqᵒ   tgiā'xō   qiX   iqō'mxōm."   A'lta   Laqᵒ   **21**
basket."   "Oh,   quick   take out him   we will do   that   basket."   Now   take out

acgāyax   x·ix·   iqō'mxōm.   Laqᵒ   aLgi'ctax   LēXt   Lqoa'q.   A'lta   **22**
they did him   that   basket.   Take out   they did it   one   mountain goat blanket.   Now

LgōLē'lEXEmk   Lap   aLgE'ctax   gō   x·ix·   iqō'mxōm.   "O2   cgE'Xa!   O   **23**
a person   find   they two did it   in   this   basket.   "O   my two children!   O

cgE'Xa!   LEmtā'naa   itcā'q¡'atxal.   MtgEnā'gamit   a'lta   nci'tkum   **24**
my two children!   Your mother   her badness.   You two see me   now   I am half

1 k·¡ē. Ai'aq, ai'aq, mtgEuupō'nit! Ā'Lqī Ltē'mama LEmtā'naa,
nothing. Quick, quick, you two bang me up! Later on she will come your two selves' mother,

2 gElxawi'lᶜaya."
she will eat us."

   A'lta acgiō'ckam Lcta'mama, a'lta ackupōnit. Pō'lakli
Now they two took him their two selves' father, now they two hung him up. At dark

4 naxatkō'ma Lctā'naa. A'lta cgā'Xa aciXE'LXa. A'lta
she came home their mother. Now her two children they two were angry. Now

5 cq¡'ōā'lipX aci'xax cgā'Xa. A'lta acgiōlXam Lcta'mama:
two youths they two got her two children. Now they two said to their two selves' father:
       to him

6 "TgEt¡'ō'kti iō'LEma qEmā'xō." A'lta nē'k·im: "Â tgEt¡'ōkti!"
"Good curing by supernatural means we do you." Now he said: "Ah, good!"

7 A'lta acgiō'skam Lctā'mama, acgā'yukᴛ gō Ltcuqᵒ. A'lta
Now they two took him their father, they two carried him to the water. Now

8 L¡'Eli'p acgā'yax. A'lta acgō'skam Lctā'naa. Lkē'wucX
under water they two did him. Now they two took her their two selves' mother. A dog

9 aci'kxax.
they two made her.

   A'lta ā'ctō2. Āctō'4, kulā'i ā'ctō. A'lta actiga'ĩm
Now they two went. They two went, far they two went. Now they two reached him

11 iqēlō'q gō ikak¡'ō'LitX. Cmôkct cā'yaqtq qiX iqēlō'q. "TgEt¡'ō'kti
a swan in a lake. Two his two heads that swan. "Good

12 iā'maᶜ nila'xō x·ix· iqēlō'q." "Â, nikct iā'maᶜ mlā'xō.
shooting I do him with that one swan." "Oh! not shooting him you do him with one.

13 Ō'xuit tqctxēLā'wuks gō x·ix· ikak¡'ō'LitX." A'lta atctō'skam
Many monsters in this lake." Now he took them

14 tiā'xalaitan, a'lta iā'maᶜ atcē'lax. "TgEt¡'ō'kti nukuē'Xa
his arrows, now shooting him he did him with one. "Good I swim

15 niugō'lEmama." A'lta atci'Lxalukctgō Liā'ok. A'lta ayō'kuēXa,
I shall go to take him." Now he threw it off his blanket. Now he swam,

16 a'lta atciu'skam qix· iqēlō'q. A'lta L¡Ela'p ā'yō. A'lta nigE'tcax
now he took him that swan. Now under water he went. Now he cried

17 iā'xk'un. A'lta lō'Elō atci'Lax Lqā'nakc. A'lta na-ixE'lgiLx.
his elder brother. Now pile up he did them stones. Now he made a fire.

18 A'lta aLē'XEltuq. Ā'lta aLo's-ko-it Lqā'nakc. A'lta atciō'tcXEm
Now he heated them. Now they got hot the stones. Now he made it boil

19 ikak¡'ō'LitX. A'lta q¡'E'cq¡Ec nē'xax ikak¡'ō'LitX. A'lta atciō'lXam:
the lake. Now dry he got the lake. Now he said to him:

20 "Adē'! ō'xuit tqctxēLā'wuks!" A'lta atcō'ckam ōyā'qēwiqē. A'lta
"Adē'! many monsters!" Now he took her his knife. Now

21 LE'XLEX atci'tax tgā'wanaks. Ā'²lta ka'nauwē LEX atci'tax
cut he did them their bellies. Now all cut he did them

22 tgā'wanaks. A'lta atciō'lXam: "Ō2, qxā'oqaLx Lap niā'xō
their bellies. Now he said to him: "Oh, I cannot may be find I shall do him

23 Lgā'wuX." A'lta nigE'tcax. Ō2, a'lta ēXtka ianu'kstX iqctxē'Lau.
my younger brother." Now he cried. Oh, now one only small monster.

24 A'lta LEX atcā'yax iā'wan ianu'kstX iqctxē'Lau. A'lta Lap atcā'yax
Now cut he did him his belly small monster. Now find he did him

25 Liā'wuX. Atciā'ktcan iā'qēloq. A'lta atcā'yukᴛ Liā'wuX
his younger brother. He held him in hand his swan. Now he carried him his younger brother

26 gō Ltcuqᵒ. A'lta pō'pō atcā'yax Liā'wuX. A'lta nixā'latck
to water. Now blow he did him his younger brother. Now he rose

27 Liā'wuX: "Ō, ayāmō'lXam nikct mukuē'Xa! Qamāwu'lᶜaya!"
his younger brother: "Oh! I said to you not swim! You will be swallowed!"

A'lta weXt a'ctō. A'2cto, kulā'i a'ctō. A'lta Lap aLgE'ctax   1
Now again they two They two far they two Now find they two did
went. went. it

LgōLē'lEXEmk. ALgiō'ktcan i'Lạsiki. A'lta aLā'owil. "Ō, i'kta   2
a person. He held him his paddle. Now he danced. "Oh, what

mxē'lxalō?" "Ō2, tEmē'n'a ntā'owil." "NiXua mE'te! Ōmē'tso-itk   3
are you going "Oh, flounders I catch." "Well, come! Your dipnet
to do?"

na-y- akē'x?" "Ōgni'tsō-itk akē'x." "NiXua ā'tkⁿɪa! Ai'aq   4
[interro- there is?" "My dipnet there is." "Well! carry her Quick,
gative here!"
particle]

mE'tXuit iō'-kuk! NiXua gE'cgEc mtā'xo x·itik tEmē'n'a! Iō'kuk   5
stand here! Well, drive do them those flounders! Here

mE'tXuit! Lị Ela'p ā'xa-y ōinē'tsō-itk." A'lta Lị Eli'p ā'tcax.   6
stand! Under water do her thy dipnet." Now under water he did her.

Lē'lē Lị Eli'p ā'tcax. "NiXua ā'latck!" Ō4, qị oa'p pāL   7
Long under water he did her. "Well, lift her!" Oh, nearly full

ōyā'tsō-itk. "Ō, ē'ka ōguē' kuā'nEsum qtūpiā'Lxaē tEmē'n'a."   8
his dipnet. "Oh, thus thus always they will be caught flounders."

A'lta weXt a'ctō. Kulā'i a'cto. Lap aLgE'stax LgōLē'lEXEmk.   9
Now again they two Far they two Find they two did it a person.
went. went.

Wa2ā'2! Wa2ā2! Lxā'xo-il. "I'kta atcuwa! ēmxē'lXalEm?" "Ō,   10
Waà! Waà! it always did. "What [exclamation] are you doing? "Oh,

iLa'maᶜ niLi'Lxo-il x·ictik c'ē'Lxatct." "Ō2, tgEtị'ō'kti cka   11
shooting it, I always do it those two rain [dual]." "Oh, good and

mE'La-it!" A'lta aqtō'skam tā'yaqL; aqōXō'kXuē. A'lta aqE'tax   12
you stay!" Now it was taken his house; it was thrown away. Now they were
made

tā'yaqL; t'ayā' aqtē'lax. Aqiō'lXam: "NiXua mE'La-it!" A'lta   13
his house, good they were made He was told: "Well, stay!" Now
for him.

nikct qctomā'qta c'ē'Lxatct."   14
not they two will be rain [dual]."
killed

A'lta weXt a'ctō. Kulā'i a'ctō. A'lta Lap acgā'yax ilē'ē. A'lta   15
Now again they two Far they two Now find they two a coun- Now
went. went. did him try.

acx'ō'yut. A'lta gōyē'2 atcE'tax tiā'pōtē. A'lta ō2xuit têlXEm   16
they two bathed. Now thus he did them his arms. Now many people

x·itikc. A'lta pō atcE'tax. Ō2 nōXō-inā'Xit tê'lXEm.   17
these. Now blow he did them. Oh, they stood up people.

A'lta ā'citē2; actē'mam Kwi'naiūL. "Ō2, tgEtị'ō'kti iā'xkayuk   18
Now they two came; they came to Quinaielt. "Oh, good here

o'tsōyēha qōpiāLxa."   19
blue-back sal- she will be caught."
mon

A'lta weXt a'cto. Kulā'2i a'cto. Lap aLgE'ctax LgōLēlEXEmk.   20
Now again they two Far they two Find they two did a person.
went. went. it

"NLōkulā'ya Lqēwē'qē, manix ctē'mama qō'cta tê'lXEm t'ayā'   21
"I shall sharpen knives, when they two will those people good
them come,

kcktaxō'-il, a'lta x·iLē'k Lqēwē'qē ncgEltcē'ma." Ā, a'lta actigā'om.   22
the two always now these knives I shall strike them Ah, now they two met
making them, two." him.

"O2, i'kta miā'xo-il, iqị ēyō'qxut?" "A2, ctāxka qō'cta tê'lXEm   23
"Oh, what are you doing old man?" "Ah, they two those two people
him always,

t'ayā' kcktā'xo-il ncgEltcē'ma." "Ni'Xua, ā'tkɪā!" TakE ā'tcutX.   24
good the two always I shall strike them "Well, carry her Then he gave her
making them two." here!" away.

"WeXt aēXt ā'tkɪa!" TakE ā'tcutX weXt. "NiXua lā'X° mE'xax!"   25
"Again one carry her Then he gave her again. "Well head side- do!"
here!" away ways

1 LäX° nē'xax; aqa-ēlgā'mit a'ēXt. "Ni'Xua weXt läX° mE'xax!"
   Head he did; she was fastened one. "Well, again head side-do!"
   sideways   to him   ways

2 LäX° nē'xax, weXt ēXt aqēlgā'mit. Gō Lā'yaqtEq mô'ksti
   Head he did, again one was fastened to At his head twice
   sideways   him.

3 aqtilgā'mit; gō iā'putc ēXt aqilgā'mit. "Ni'Xua sE'pEna!"
   they were fas- at his backside one was fastened to him. "Well jump!"
   tened to him;

4 aqiō'lXam; atcō'pEna. Aqiō'lXam: "NiXua mēxē'Lxēgo! Ēmā'cEn
   was said to him; he jumped. It was said to him: "Well, turn round! Deer

5 ēmē'xal. Nēkct qa'ntsiX mtōtē'nax tê'lXEm."
   thy name. Never you will kill people."
                        them repeatedly

6 A'ctō, actiga'ōm Uq¡'ō'nExōn. "I'kta mxē'lXalEm?" "Ō,
   They two they two Uq¡'ō'nExōn. "What are you doing?" "Oh,
   went, reached her

7 nExEmō'sXEm." TakE aklō'skam Lē'Xat Lk'ā'ckc gō Lā'pōtitk.
   I play." Then she took it one child at its forearm.

8 TakE agē'Lxalukctgō iau'a kē'kXulē. "Ai'aq tcu'qoa cXE'lkayuwa
   Then she threw it away there below. "Quick let them they two will fight
                                                               together

9 ctxā'xamuks." TakE nā'k·ēm Uq¡'ō'nExōn: "Ō aqctxē'Lau
   our two selves' two dogs." Then she said Uq¡'ō'nExōn: "Oh, a monster

10 ōstā'xamukc. Ā'lta itcā'kXikala iā'lXam aqiā'wulᶜ, taua'lta
   their two selves' bitch. Even her husband his town she ate him, else

11 aqā'waᶜuX ōgu'xamukc." "Qa'da itcā'xal omē'xamukc?" "Ō, itcā'xal
   she will eat her my bitch." "How her name your bitch?" "Oh, her name

12 tqtqakc itcā'LxalEmax. Qa'da itcā'xal ōmtā'xamukc?" "Ō, itcā'xal
   heads eater. How her name your two selves' bitch?" "Oh, her name

13 ōguē'lEXtcut itcā'LxalEmax." A'lta acXE'lkayū takE.
   flint eater." Now they two fought together then.

14 A'lta Lq¡'ōp aqēā'xax itcā'tuk Uq¡'ō'nExōn ōgō'xōmukc. TakE
   Now cut it was done her neck Uq¡'ō'nExōn her bitch. Then

15 atcō'lxam qiX ē'Xat: "Tca a'lta mEnxalukctgō'ya." TakE
   he said to her that one: "Now you will throw me down." Then

16 atctō'lXam tqā'sōsiniks: "Manix gEnExalukctgō'ya a'lta mcgē'ina:
   he said to them the boys: "When she throws me down now you will say
                                                               so:

17 'MXata'kōmX wēlX!' Mcgē'ina." A'lta agiō'skam, a'lta
   'Return to land!' You will say so." Now she took him, now

18 agā'xēnayuX ōguē'lEXtcutk. A'lta agiō'skam gō tiā'pōtitk.
   she [they] stood flint-pieces [f.]. Now she took him at his forearms.
   upright

19 Qui'numī gō'yē agā'yax. TakE agē'xalukctgō. TakE agtō'lXam
   Five times thus she did to him. Then she threw him down. Then she said to them

20 tqā'sōsiniks: "Mxiq¡'EmLEmā'ōX wēlX!" TakE atctō'lXam
   to the boys: "Go and stay always away [in] land!" Then he said to them

21 tqā'sōsiniks: "MXatā'kōmX wēlX! mci'k·im! mci'k·im!" "Nā
   to the boys: "Return to land! say! say!" "Nä!

22 xiXō'Lac, a'lta Lō'itt LEmcā'mama-ikc!" TakE ā'yō gēkXulā'
   these people, now they come your fathers!" Then he went down

23 ayuqunā'ititam. Nixā'latck ka'nauwē, näkct LEkⁿ nä'xax. A'lta
   he went and lay. He rose whole, not broken he got. Now

24 Lap atci'tax tqā'cōciniks.
   find he did them the boys.

25 Ō, pāL gē'kXulē. A'lta atcLō'skam Ltcuqᵒ. A'lta pō'pō atci'tax
   O, full below. Now he took it water. Now blow he did them

26 ka'nauwē. A'lta nōxo-ina'Xit ka'nauwē a'lta. TakE atctō'lXam:
   all. Now they stood up all now. Then he said to them:

27 "TgEt¡'ō'kti mcgiEkEnā'-oi." A'lta aLklō'skam Lqā'nakc. A'lta
   "Good you watch her." Now they took them stones. Now

ayōē'wilX. Ayō'yam kᵘcā'xalē. A'lta atcō'lXam Uqᵢ'ō'nExōn: "Ō⌣, 1
he went up.   He arrived   above.   Now   he said to her   to Uqᵢ'ō'nExōn':   "Oh,

gā'Lak, daLᵢ nĕkct ōXō'La-it tikc tē'lXɛm, ēka mtāx. Nxē'lutcX 2
aunt,   look!   not   they are dead   those   people,   thus   you did   I saw them them.

gō gē'kXulē, ē'ka a'lta lē'lē gē'kXulē nkäx. OXuiwā'yul 3
at   below,   thus   now   long   below   I was.   They dance

ka'nauwē, ōkulā'lam; ēLukuma ōxusgā'liL; iqā'lExal ōxusgā'liL. 4
all,   they sing;   itlukum   they play;   disks   they play.

Tca, a'lta mai'ka yamxalukctgō'ya!" A'lta atcā'xēna ia'koa 5
Well,   now   you   I throw you down!"   Now   he placed them   there
upright [f.]

ōyā'kXilXtcutk. A'lta atcō'skam gō LE'kxakcō. A'lta qui'nɛmī 6
his flint-pieces.   Now   he took her   at   her hair.   Now   five times

gō'yē ā'tcax. A'lta Laxᵃ nē'xax itcā'wan. A'lta atcā'xalukctgō. 7
thus   he did her.   Now   break   did   her belly.   Now   he threw her down.

A'lta nuqunā'-ititam gē'kXulē. A'lta atkLō'skam Lqā'naqc. 8
Now   she went and lay   below.   Now   they took them   stones.

A'lta LEmE'nLEmEn ā'qxax. A'lta aqiXE'kXuē ē'tc'aLᶜa 9
Now   in small pieces   she was done.   Now   it was thrown away   her flesh

ka'nauwē qā. Aqē'xalukctgō itcā'ᶜowit iaua' Nafē'lim; aqē'xalukctgō 10
every   where.   It was thrown away   her leg   here [to]   Nehelim;   it was thrown away

LE'kxakcō, aqōXō'kXuē tqā'lēwanɛma iaua' kᵘcāla'. 11
her hair,   they were thrown   her ribs   there   up river.
away

Translation.

There were five brothers who had one younger sister. When she was grown up the grizzly bear carried her away. One year her brothers did not find her. Then her elder brother went to search for his younger sister. He went some distance and met a pheasant (?). He shot it and hung it on to the branch of a tree. He went on and found a house. He opened the door and saw an old man and a boy inside. He entered. Then the child jumped up and said: "Louse me, uncle!" He took the child and loused it. He found a louse and squeezed it. Immediately the old man bit his neck and cut off his head. Then the old man and the boy carried his body into the woods and hid it. The bear's wife and his daughter had gone digging gamass (camass) at that time.

Now four [brothers] only remained. One day the next eldest went. He also found a pheasant. He shot it and hung it on to the branch of a tree. He went a long distance and found a house. He opened the door and saw an old man and a boy inside. Then he entered. The boy jumped up and said: "Uncle, louse me!" He did so and found a louse. He squeezed it; then the old man bit his neck and cut off his head. Then the old man and the boy carried his body into the woods and hid it. The two women had again gone digging gamass. Then the daughter said to her mother: "Come, let us go home; somebody arrived at our house." The mother replied: "Wait a while." After some time the two women went home. Then the girl smelled blood in the house and knew at once what had happened. She grew angry and struck her father and her brother with a firebrand.

Now three [brothers] only remained. One day the next brother said: "I will go next." He went a long distance and he also found a pheasant. He shot it and hung it on to the branch of a tree. He went on and found a house. He opened the door and found an old man and a boy inside. He entered and shared the fate of his brothers. Then the girl said: "Come, let us go home; somebody arrived at our house." Her mother replied: "Wait a while." Then she said to her: "Have you no relatives?" She replied: "You have five uncles." Then the two women went home. She became angry and struck her father and her brother.

Now it became day and one more made himself ready. He took his arrows and he also went. He went a long distance; then he found a pheasant. He shot it and hung it on to the branch of a tree. He went on and found a house. Then he opened the door and saw an old man and a boy inside. He entered. The boy jumped and said: "Louse me, uncle." He did so and found a louse. He squeezed it. Then the old man bit his neck and cut off his head. Then they carried the body inland and hid it. The girl [who was digging gamass with her mother] said: "Come, let us go home; somebody arrived at our house." But her mother replied: "Wait a while." Then they went home. They opened the door and she smelled the blood. She became angry and struck her father and her brother.

Now one only remained. He cried the whole night. When it became nearly daylight he fell asleep. He dreamt: "When you will go you will meet a pheasant. Do not shoot it. A monster carried away your younger sister and killed all your elder brothers. When you will go you will find a house. Do not enter at once. When you see two persons in there stay at the door." Now it became day. He awoke and continued to cry. Then he took his arrows and went. He went a long distance and saw a pheasant. He did not shoot it. He went on and found a house. He opened the door. There was an old man and a boy inside. Then he stayed at the door. He remained there a long time. Then the girl spoke and said to her mother: "Come, let us go home; somebody arrived at our house." Her mother replied: "Let us turn back!" Then they went home. They reached their house and opened the door. Now there was a person. They entered. Then the girl grew angry. In the evening the man said to his younger sister: "All our brothers came here;" and she told her daughter: "All your uncles came here." [The daughter replied:] "You did not believe me." [Her uncle asked:] "What shall we do with the old man and the boy? Shall we kill them? [She replied:] "Yes; they shall die." Then the man said: "I will go and get pitchwood." He went and brought pitchwood into the house. Then the old man said: "What do you intend to do with that pitchwood?" "We shall use it to make fire in winter." Now they remained there a long time. [One night] he spoke to the old man a long time. When it became nearly day [the old man] fell asleep. Then he said to his sister: "Arise! now we will burn them." She arose and left the house. Her daughter also arose and went out. Then he set fire to the pitchwood. He went out. Now the house began to burn The old man said: "Heh! brother-in-law! Rise! We are going to be burnt." He arose and found that the door was locked. Now he himself and his son were burnt.

Then she searched for her uncles. She found them in the woods and carried them to the water. She blew some water on the bodies. Then they all arose. They went home. They went a long distance and came to a lake. They bathed in the lake. Now the woman [their sister] dived and said: "Shall I dive?" The brothers replied: "Yes, dive!" "Do I look pretty in this lake?" "Yes, you look pretty in the lake." She dived again. "Shall I dive?" "Yes, dive." "Do I look pretty in this lake?" "Yes, you look pretty in the lake." Then she dived again. After she had dived three times hair began to grow on her. She said again: "Do I look pretty in this lake?" "Oh, no! you do not look pretty in this lake." "Eh, why did you not tell me before?" Now she had dived five times, and she remained always in the lake and became a monster. They took only their niece along. They arrived at their house and stayed there. Now all the people wanted to marry the girl, but the brothers did not give her away. Finally a chief married her and she remained with him.

Now, Blue-jay was discontented because she never laughed. After a time she said [to her husband]: "I am getting tired. Go far away, then I shall laugh." "No, no, don't laugh!" After some time she said again: "I am getting tired." Then her husband replied: "Well, then laugh now." She said: "I will laugh because Blue-jay makes me tired. Go into the woods! Lie down on your knees and elbows and close your ears." Then early in the morning she went to bathe. She took a comb and combed herself. Then she went out. Now she said: "Where are you, Blue-jay? Now I shall laugh. Hahaheh! Blue-jay!" Then she devoured all her husband's people. In the afternoon she came to herself and vomited all the bones. She searched for her husband but did not find him. Then she searched for him among the bones of all these people. She found him, but his legs up to the knees were gone. Then she put him into a basket and moved a short distance. She made a house and lived there. After some time she fell sick and gave birth to two boys. When her children became older she said to them: "Do not go there up the river; you must go only down the river." They obeyed. When they became older the elder one said to his brother: "Let us go there [up the river]." One day they went and found the ground strewn with bones of people. "Oh, come, let us go home!" They reached their home and the elder one said: "These poor people! How may they have died?" Now they grew up. One day they bathed; now they missed a comb. The elder one said: "O, brother! Perhaps we shall find a comb in that basket." "Let us take down that basket." Now they took down the basket and took out a mountain-goat blanket. Now they

found a person in that basket. [The person said:] "O my children!
Your mother is bad. You see me. I am only half now! Quick! Hang
me up again, else your mother will come and devour us!" They took
their father and hung him up again. In the evening their mother
came back. Now the boys were angry. They became young men;
then they said to their father: "We will cure you." "Well," he
replied. Now they took him and carried him to the river. They put
him under water. Then they took their mother and transformed her
into a dog.

Now the two young men [who were now called Cikṭa] traveled on.
They came to a lake in which they saw a swan with two heads. "I
will shoot that swan." "Oh, don't shoot it. Many monsters are in
that lake." He, however, took his arrows and shot the swan. "I will
swim across the lake and get it." He threw off his blanket, swam, and
took hold of the swan. Then he disappeared under water. His elder
brother cried. He picked up stones and made a fire in which he heated
the stones. When they were hot he threw them into the lake and
made it boil. Then the lake became dry. Then he said: "Oh, how
many monsters there are!" Then he took his knife and opened their
bellies. When he opened them all he said: "Oh, I cannot find my
brother." He cried. Now only one small monster remained. He cut
its belly and found his brother who held the swan in his hand. He
carried him to the water and blew on him. Then he arose: "Oh, I told
you not to swim! [I thought] you would be swallowed!"

They went on. They met a person who held his paddle in his hand
and danced. "What are you doing there?" "I catch flounders."
[The flounders jumped into his canoe while he was dancing.] "Come
here; have you no dipnet?" "I have one." "Bring it here! Step
near! Drive the flounders. Stand here! Put your dipnet into the
water!" He did so and held the net under water a very long time.
"Now lift it." It was nearly full. "Thus people shall always catch
flounders."

Now they went on. They met a person who always made waā′waā′!
"What are you doing?" "I shoot the rain." "Stay here!" Now
they took his house, threw it away, and made a good house for him.[1]
They said: "Stay here; henceforth people will not shoot the rain."

Then they went on. They found a country. There they bathed.
Then they rubbed their arms and made people [of the dirt that they
rubbed from their skin]. They blew upon them and they arose.

Now they came to Quinaielt. "Here people shall catch blue-back
salmon."

They went on and found a person. [He said:] "I will sharpen my
knives. When these people come who make everything good I shall
kill them with these knives." Now they met him. "What are you
doing, old man?" they said. "I shall kill those who make everything

---
[1] His house had no roof, and he protected himself by shooting at the rain.

good." "Give me your knife." He gave it. "Give me the other one." He gave it also. "Now put your head sideways." He put his head sideways. Now they fastened one knife to one side of his head. "Put your head to the other side." He did so, and they fastened the other knife to the other side. They fastened two to his head and one to his backside. "Now jump!" they said to him, and he jumped. "Turn round! You shall be called deer. You will not kill man!"

They went on and came to Uqᵢō′nexōn. "What are you doing?" they said. "I play." Then she took a child at its forearm and threw it into the depth. "Let our dogs fight together," said the two men. She replied: "Oh, their bitch is a monster. She devoured even her husband's people. She will certainly kill my bitch." "What is the name of your bitch," they said. "Her name is Head-eater. What is the name of your bitch?" "Her name is Flint-eater." Now the two dogs fought together and Cikla's bitch cut off the head of Uqᵢ′ō′nexōn's bitch. Then one of the young men said to her: "Now throw me down the precipice." He had said to the boys [down below]: "When she throws me down you must say 'Return to the land.'" She took him. Flint pieces stood upright [at the foot of the precipice]. She took him at his forearms. She swung him around five times; then she threw him down. She said to the boys: "Say 'Stay always away from the land.'" He, however, said to the boys: "Say 'Return to the land.'" [When throwing him down Uqᵢ′ō′nexōn said:] "Now come these two people, your fathers!" He fell down and lay there [at the foot of the precipice]. He arose whole. He was not hurt. He saw that down below there was a multitude of boys. He took water and blew it on all of them. Then they all arose. He said: "Watch her [when she comes down]." They took stones. He went up and arrived on the top of the rock. Then he said to Uqᵢ′ō′nexōn: "O, aunt, look! These people whom you threw down are not dead. I saw them down there. I was there a while. They dance and sing; they play itlukum and disks. Now I shall throw you down." Now he placed his pieces of flint upright. He took her at her hair and swung her around five times. Her belly burst. Now he threw her down. She fell and lay there. Then the boys pelted her with stones and cut her to pieces. Her body was scattered in all directions. Her legs were thrown to Nehelim, her hair was thrown inland, her ribs were thrown up the river [therefore the Nehelim have strong legs, the Cowlitz have long hair, and the tribes of the upper river have bandy legs].

2. ŌKULĀ'M ITCĀ'KXANAM.

OKULĀ'M HER MYTH.

Txēlā' itX Lquinumiks. WăX aLEᴸē'taqʟ Lā'wuX. ALxō'kumak·¡'-
There were five men. Every they left him their younger They always
morning brother.

2 auwăkuX; imō'lekuma aLkiā'wul. Pā2L tE'LaqL L!'ōlē'ma, pāL
went hunting; elks they [hunted] Full their house meats, full
always made.

3 ō'pXil tE'LaqL. Ta'kE ă'yamxtc lāx° nē'xax Lā'wuX. TakE
grease their house. Then his heart lonesome he got their younger Then
brother.

4 nē'k·im: "Anā'! Lō'yam ta'yax nēkct giLā'qctit k¡a Lgōxoē'lax
he said: "Ana'! he arrive oh! that not the one satiated and he eats them

5 tik L!'ōlē'ma." A'lta la'kti ayā'qxoya nē'k·im; kā iō'c ka cix
these meats." Now four times his sleeps he said; where he is then noise
of
rattles

6 nē'xau gō iqē'pal. A'lta Lāx aLi'xax LgōLē'lEXEmk. A'lta môkst
got at doorway. Now visible it got a person. Now two

7 imō'lEkuma iLā'nk iyā'ck·¡upXEla. K·¡au'k·¡au ai'kawit ōᶜnā'LaLa.
elks his blanket his curried elkskins. Tied was to it hoofs.

8 A'lta aLō'p!'am LgōLē'lEXEmk. ALō'La-it. "Ō qăc! ō'lō gEua'xt."
Now he entered the person. He remained. "Oh, grand- hungry I am."
son!

9 Ayō'tXuit. TakE atcLE'lᶜēm L!'ōlē'ma; nēkct pāt ō'Xuit.
He stood up. Then he gave it to him meat; not very much
to eat

10 L!'ōlē'ma; ō'pXil atcLE'lᶜēm. Ayō'La-it. Nē'kXikct, ā'nqatē k·¡ē
meat; grease he gave it to him He remained. He looked, long ago nothing
to eat.

11 qō'ta ktcLE'lᶜēm. WeXt atcLE'lᶜēm, a'lta mank ō'Xuit. WeXt
that what he had given Again he gave him to now a little much. Again
him to eat. eat,

12 nē'kXikct, ā'nqatē k·¡ē; weXt aLktā'wilᶜ. AtcLElᶜē'mEniL aēXt
he looked, long ago nothing; again he ate it all. He gave him to eat one
often

13 ōᶜō'Lax. A'lta tsō'yustē nē'xauē. A'lta aLXkō'mam Liā'xkunikc.
day. Now evening it got. Now they got home his elder brothers.

14 A'lta aLktō'k¡am ōxōkuē'wall L!'ōlē'ma. A'lta aLgio'lXam
Now they carried them home fresh meats. Now they said to him

15 Lʇā'wux: "Qa'da amE'k·im? Qa'daqa L'Elxgā'tōm Lqctxē'Lau?"
their younger "How did you say? Whence it came to us the monster?"
brother:

16 "Ā-y-ītcāmxtc lāx° nē'xax k¡a anE'k·im nikct tayax giLā'qctit
"Ah! my heart lonesome it got and I said not oh! that the one satiated

17 Lō'yamt, k¡a Lgōxoē'lax L!'ōlē'ma. AnE'k·im." "Ō mE'L¡ala,
he would ar- and he would eat them meats. I said." "Oh, you fool,
rive,

18 LkElxuwi'lᶜaya Lqctxē'Lau!" A'lta aLkl·ᶜēmEniL cka wăx nē'ktcuktē.
he will eat us the monster!" Now they gave him and next it got day.
always to eat morning

19 A'lta aLkl'ē'mEniL cka nō'pōuEm. TakE nōxō'tctXum L¡ōlē'ma.
Now they gave him and it got dark. Then they were at an end the meats.
always to eat

20 TakE nē'k·im Lʇā'wuX: "Ē'kta Lx Lgiā'xō Lutcā'xgacgac?
Then he said their younger "What may he [will] eat it our grandfather?
brother:

21 A'lta iā'mkXa ē'ᶜcō'ma." "Ē'kta Lx niā'xo qā'cōma. A'lta iā'mkXa
Now only skins." "What may I shall grandchild- Now only
eat it ren!

22

ēᶜcō'ma ka mī'ca." "Qa'daXī aLE'k·im!" "'A'lta iā'mkXa ēᶜcōma 1
skins and you." "How he said?" "·Now only skins

ka mī'ca,' aLE'k·im." "NiXua weXt LElXam!" "Ē'kta LX 2
and you,' he said." "Well again speak to him!" "What may

Lgiā'xō Lntcā'xgacgac" [etc., as above five times]. 3
he will eat it our grandfather" [etc., as above five times].

A'lta aLkLxtcā'maa. ALgiō'tcXEm ēᶜcō'ma. ALgilᶜē'mEniL 4
Now they understood him. They boiled them the skins. They gave them
always to him to eat

ēᶜcō'ma. Lē2 nō'pōnEm. A'lta Lxoa'p aLgā'yax ilē'ē. ALgiō'lEXtcum 5
skins. Some it got dark. Now dig they did it ground. They sharpened it
time

itcxā'ma. A'lta aLgē'xēna gō qigō akL'ā'yuit. A'lta ā'Lō iau'a 6
arrowwood. Now they placed it at where they lay down Now they there
upright to sleep. went

Xigō naLxoa'p aLgā'yax ilē'ē. Qā'xē gō kulā'i ka Lāx aLxā'xō. 7
where hole they made it ground. Where at far and visible they became.

A'lta aLaē'taqᴛ ōLā'xēwicX qigō' naLxoa'p ilē'ē. ALgō'lXam 8
Now they left her their bitch where hole ground. They said to her

ōLā'xēwicX: "Manix tcimuā'amtcxōkō, wō̄ mxā'xoyē." TakE 9
their bitch: "When he asks you, wō̄, do." Then

aLa'xuwa. 10
they ran away.

A'lta qᵢoa'p iktcō'ktiya takE atcLckpā'ua. TakE atilgā'yuXuit 11
Now nearly it will get day then he jumped at them. Then they stuck in him

qōta tE'mᶜEcX gō iā'wan. TakE ka'nauwē La'qLaqᵒ atē'xax, 12
those sticks in his belly. Then all take out he did them,

LE'kLekᵘ atci'tax. TakE atcLgE'ta. Lāxᵃ nē'xax. TakE Lap ā'tcax 13
break he did them. Then he pursued them. Visible he got. Then find he did her

ōLā'xēwicX: "Qā'xēwa ā'Lō LEmē'Xana-xē'mct!" TakE wō̄ nā'xax. 14
their bitch: "Whither went thy masters?" Then wō̄ she did.

TakE nē'xankō iā'xkēwa. NēXata'kō, nēkct Lap ā'tcax ōLā'ēXatk. 15
Then he ran there. He returned, not find he did their tracks.
them

TakE weXt atcō'lXam ōLā'xēwicX: "Qā'xēwa ā'Lō 16
Then again he said to her their bitch: "Whither they went

LEmē'Xanaxē'mct!" TakE weXt wō̄ nā'xax. Iā'xkēwa nē'xankō. 17
thy masters?" Then again wō̄ she did. Then he ran.

Näkct Lap ā'tcax ōLā'ēXatk. Lō'ni nē'xankō. TakE Lap ā'tcax 18
Not find he did them their tracks. Three times he ran. Then find he did
them

ōLā'ēXatk. TakE atcLgE'ta. AtcLgE'ta, kulā'i atcLgE'ta. TakE 19
their tracks. Then he pursued He pursued far he pursued Then
them. them, them.

atciktā'ōm iLā'xkun. Atciā'waᶜ. WeXt nē'xanko. WeXt ē'Xat 20
he reached him the eldest one. He killed him. Again he ran. Again one

atcikta'ōm. WeXt atciā'waᶜ. WeXt nē'xankō, weXt ē'Xat atcikta'ōm. 21
he reached him. Again he killed him. Again he ran. again one he reached him.

Llä'ktiks atcLō'tēna. A'lta iā'mkXa Lā'wuX ayukō'ētiXt. A'lta 22
Four he killed them. Now only he the youngest remained. Now
one

nē'qankō2. TakE ayō'Lxam. A'lta Lap atci'Lax Lqᵢ'ēyō'qxut 23
he ran. Then he arrived at water. Now find he did him an old man

Lxā'xp!aōt. "Wāx nā'xa iau'a ēnatai; ēqctxē'Lau tcEnₐ'wat. 24
he fished with "Pour do me there to other side; the monster it pursues me.
dipnet.

Ai'aq, qā'qacqac." "Hōhū! qā'xēwaL amEnā'qacqac!" "Ai'aq, 25
Quick, grandfather." "Hōhū! where may be I your grandfather!" "Quick,

wax nā'xa, gā'tata!" "Ō, qā'xēwaL amEnā'tata!" "Wāx nā'xa 26
pour do me, uncle!" "Oh, where may be I your uncle!" "Pour do me

1 kāpxō!" "Hōhū′! qā′xēwaL amEnä′pxō?" LE′kxēamit Lkēx Lᶜa′kil
  elder brother!" "Hōhū! where may be I your elder bro- In stern of there a woman
                                ther?" canoe was

2 gō qiX ēq¡′ēyō′qxut. PāL tEpôqc ī′LaLa. "Â wuska′ wäx nä′xa
  at that old man. Full boils her body. "Â [exclamation] pour do me

3 ē′qsiX!" "Hō qada nikct ā′nqatē amEnō′lXam?" A′lta wax
  father-in-law!" "Hō why not before you said to me?" Now pour

4 atcā′yax iau′a ē′natai IkEnuwakcō′m. "Ai′aq māya gō tE′kXuqL.
  he did him there to other side the thunderer. "Quick go to my house.

5 Iā′xkati mō′p¡′aya!" TakE ā′yup!, ka ma′nXi aLE′Lxam qōLa
  There enter!" Then he entered, then a little it arrived at water that

6 Lq¡ēyō′qxut. "TcōXoa amE′LᶜElkEl iLā′anLā′wat, qitq¡′ēyō′qxut?"
  old man. "Well! did you see him the one whom I together old men?"
                                    pursue,

7 "Näkct anE′LᶜElkEl." "Ai′aq, wäx nä′xa iau′a ē′natai!
  "Not I saw him." "Quick, pour do me then the other side!

8 LamgEmō′ktia LgE′ciapōL." "Ē′kta niLgElä′xō Lciä′pōL?"
  I shall pay it to you my hat!" "What shall I do with it a hat?"

9 "IamkEmō′ktia ōgu′xolē." "Ē′kta niagElä′Xo ukō′lē?" "IamgE-
  "I shall pay it to you my cane." "What shall I do with it a cane?" "I shall

10 mō′ktia x·ig itcā′ok." "Ē′kta nigElä′xō-y-iōk?" "TcōXoa
  pay it to you this my blanket." "What shall I do with it a blanket?" "Well,

11 camkEmō′ktiä x·itik cLā′nict." A′lta atciē′lōt cLā′nict. A′lta gō′yē
  I pay it to you this twine." Now he gave it the twine. Now thus
                                    to him

12 atcā′yax iä′ᶜauwit. Wôk·¡ atcā′yax iä′ᶜauwit. A′lta atciō′lXam:
  he did it his leg. Straight he made it his leg. Now he said to him:

13 "Nekct mankō′tXumita Xak ōmē′Xolē." A′lta nē′katē iä′ᶜauwit.
  'Not make stand on me that your cane." Now he came walk-his leg.
                                    ing across

14 Kā′tsêk qiX ē′qxēl a′lta atca-ikō′tXumit uyā′Xolē gō iä′ᶜauwit.
  Middle that creek now he made it stand on him his cane on his leg.

15 TakE atcE′xumq¡′ōya iä′ᶜauwit. A′lta ayō′Xunē ēqctxē′Lau iau′a
  Then he bent it his leg. Now he drifted the monster there

16 mä′ēmē. ALō′Xunē Liä′siapōL. "Ō2kulä′m ēmē′xala! Iä′xkēwa
  down stream. It drifted his hat. "Okulä′m [waves] will be your There
                                  name!

17 ikxalēLa-itx, iä′xkēwa qamEltci′mlētima. Ma′nix iä′q¡′atxal ixElä′xō
  storm, there you will be heard. When bad it will get

18 igō′cax, ka LEmē′siapōL qLtcE′mlētima.
  the sky, then your hat will be heard.

  A′lta aci′xkō k¡a uyä′xa IkEnuwakcō′m. Acxkō′mam, a′lta
  Now they two went and his daughter the thunderer's. They two reached now
            home their house,

20 aLxē′la-it. A′lta nikct tq¡′ēx ä′tcax uyä′k·ikala. A′lta Lōnas
  they stayed. Now not like he did her his wife. Now I do not
                                  know

21 qa′nsix aLā′qxōya, a′lta kawē′X naxā′latck. Näx′ō′tōm. Qē′xtcē
  how many their sleeps, now early she arose. She went to bathe. Intend

22 akLq¡′ä′x Lctā′ok. ALixaniä′kuX. LēXt Liä′ok, LēXt Lga′ok
  she pulled it their two's blanket. He rolled it around One his blanket, one her blanket
                      himself.

23 ā′xka. A′lta qansi′X nixä′latck, a′lta Lōc Lᶜā′kil, ō2, t¡ō′kti
  her. Now how often he arose, now there was a woman, oh, a pretty

24 Lᶜā′kil. A′lta asxē′la-it. Nō′pōnEm. A′lta qē′xtcē atcLq¡′ä′x
  woman. Now they two stayed. It got dark. Now intend he pulled it

25 Lctā′ok. A′lta nēkct akLē′lutx. Agē′nk¡ēmenakō. A′lta lē′lē
  their two's Now not she gave it to him. She took revenge on him. Now a long time
  blanket.

26 t′ayā′ atxē′la-it. A′lta tq¡ēx agä′yax itcā′k·ikala.
  good they stayed. Now like she did him her husband.

  A′lta qa′nsix ē′kolē nēkElō′ya qiX eq¡′ēyō′qxut. Nē′k·im:
  Now how often whale he went to take that old man. He said:

"Nixēlō'tcxa   ētciqsiX!"   "Näkct,   näkct,   näkct   qa'nsıx   1
"I shall look at him   my father-in-law."   "No,   no   never

aqixē'lōtcxax."   Kalā'lkuilē nē'xax.   "Qā'toXui nixēlō'tcxa!" A'lta 2
he is looked at."   Scold   he did.   "Must   I look at him!" Now

ayō'La-it; atcixē'lōtcx, ska ma'nx·i ka atcē'ᶜElkEl ēXt ē'kolē. 3
he stayed; he looked at him, and a little then he saw him one whale.

A'lta aya-i'La-it uyā'nXcin, ska ma'nx·i qē'xtcē atciō'latck, takE 4
Now he went into net his dipnet, and a little intend he lifted it, then

atsō'pEna x·iX ē'kolē, atcā'kpEnakō uyā'nXcin. Nē'kXikct 5
he jumped that whale, he jumped out of it his dipnet. He looked

iau'a mā'Lxolē. Nau'i·y·ī'gilgct nē'xax. ALōitXuā'yutcō Lqā'kxul. 6
there inland. At once lightning it got. It rained down hail.

WeXt ē'kun nē'tē ē'kolē. TakE weXt atciō'tipa. Take weXt 7
Again one more came whale. Then again he dipped him up. Then again

qē'xtcē atciō'latck. TakE weXt atcā'kpEnakō uyā'nXcin. A'lta 8
intend he lifted him. Then again he jumped out of ıt his dipnet. Now

niXE'LXa, a'lta Lqā'kxul aLi'xax. A'lta nē'xkō, nēXkō'mam. 9
he grew angry, now hail ıt did. Now he went home, he reached his home.

Nau'i atcā'xaluketgō uyā'nXcin. Atcō'pa iā'qsiX, atcō'skam 10
At once he threw it down his dipnet. He went out his son-in-law, he took it

uqō'LXatsX. A'lta ā'yō gō tqā'nakc. A'lta Lē'el ā'tcax 11
coal. Now he went to a rock. Now black he made it

ōyā'tspux. A'lta itcxā'x nē'xax, ikā'amtq nē'xax. À2lta 12
his forehead. Now wind it got, southwest wind it got. Now

atctō'pēwē tā'yaqL iqᴸ'ēyō'qxut. Qē'xtcē atctūkolā'kux, ā'nqatē 13
he blew them away his house the old man's. Intend he fastened them on roof, long ago

atctupē'XoXoē. "Ō, āc, ē'XtkinEmam imē'k·ikal. Miōlā'ma 14
he had blown them away. "O, daughter, go and look for your husband. Tell him

wu'xē a'lta tcinxēlā'tcaya." A'lta nō'ya uyā'xa. Lap agā'yax 15
to-morrow now he shall look at me." Now she went his daughter. Find she did him

itcā'kXikala: "O, imē'qsiX tā'yaqL LE'kLEkᵘ nē'xax. Ixā'xo-il 16
her husband: "Oh, your father-in-law his house broken became. He said much

wu'xē a'lta mixēlā'tcxaya." A'lta atcLō'skam Ltcuq°, nixEmē'nakō. 17
to-morrow now you shall look at him." Now he took it water, he washed his face.

A'lta Lō nē'xauē. A'lta aci'xkō -y-uyā'kXikal. A'lta ackLukōlā'kō 18
Now calm it got. Now, they two went home his wife. Now they two fastened boards on roof

tE'LaqL. "Wu'xē nai'ka·y·i'qsiX nō'Lxaiē. MEnxēlō'toxaiē." 19
their house. "To-morrow I father-in-law! I shall go to water. You shall look at me."

Nē'ktcnktē, takE ā'yuLx ēiā'qsiX, ska ma'nx·i ka nē'tē ēXt 20
It got day, then he went to water his son-in-law, and a little then he came one

ē'kolē. TakE ayayi'La-it uyā'nXcin. A'lta atciō'latck. A'lta 21
whale. Then he went into net his dipnet. Now he lifted him. Now

atcē'xaluketgō mā'Lxôlē qiX ē'kolē. "Hōhō'! itci'qsiX, t'ā'qēa 22
he threw him down inland that whale. "Hōhō! my son-in-law, just as

nai'ka itci'qsiX." TakE nē'Xkō iā'qsiX. "Ē'ka nai'ka itci'qsiX 23
I my son-in-law." Then he went home his father-in-law. "Thus as I my son-in-law

ka ā'nqatē ngoLē'lEXEmk." 24
then long ago I got a person."
[when]

A'lta agā'wan naxā'lax uyā'kXikal. Lē'lē ka nakxa'tō. Smôkst 25
Now pregnant she got his wife. Long then she gave birth. To two

aksaxu'to. A'lta atciō'lXam iā'qsiX: "Ai'aq, ai'aq, Lgā'lEmam 26
she gave birth to two. Now he said to him his father-in-law: "Quick, quick, go to take them

Llēqᴸ'am; ka nitsEnō'kstX atgE'yēmōcXam." Ā'2yōptck 27
wolves: when I small they played with me." He went inland

1 atcugō'lEmam smō'kst cLē'q̣'am.   Atci'ctitkᵘᵢ smō'kst cLē'q̣'am.
he went to take them   two   wolves.   He carried them   two   wolves.
two   two here

2 Aci'tkᵘLᵢ am gō tE'LaqL, atcilXā'kXuē qiX iq̣'ēyō'qxut.   A'lta
He carried them   to   his house,   he threw them down   that   old man.   Now
home   before him

3 acgiā'qcimEnīL, acgixḳayō'kux.   "AtgEnxLE'lXta-it! ai'aq, ai'aq,
they two bit him much,   they two pulled him   "They forgot me!   quick,   quick,
               often.

4 cE'kⁿᵢa!"   TakE atci'ctukᵘᵢ; weXt atcalō'kctxam.   A'lta weXt
carry them   Then   he carried them two;   again   he went and carried   Now   again
two!"   them two back.

5 aLxē'la-it. IūLqtē aLxē'la-it.   "Ai'aq, ai'aq, skā'lEmam s'i'ʟsxut
he stayed.   A long time   he stayed.   "Quick,   quick, go and take them two   two black
                                            bears

6 sgE'xēmusXEma."   TakE ā'yū iā'qsiX.   TakE atci'kᵢam ēi'tsxut.
my two playfellows."   Then   he went   his son-   Then   he carried   the black
                         in-law.   him   bear.

7 À'yup!, atcilXā'kXuē.   TakE atciū'cgam ēq̣'ēyō'qxut qōcta
He entered,   he threw him down.   Then   he took him   the old man   those
                                                  two

8 s'i'tsxut.   A'lta tE'qtEq asgā'yax iau'a, acgixa'lukctgux, iau'a
two black   Now   clap   they two did   there,   they two threw him   there
bears.   him   down,

9 acgixa'lukctgux.   "Ai'aq, ci'kᵘᵢa, ci'kᵘᵢa; a'lta ckinXE'LEluX."
they two threw him   "Quick,   carry them   carry them two;   now   they two do not know
down.   two,   me."

10 A'lta atcalō'kctxam iā'qsiX atci'ctukᵘL.   NiXkō'mam iā'qsiX.
Now   he carried them two   his son-   he carried them   He arrived at his   his son-in-
     on his back   in-law   two.   house   law.

11 A'lta weXt aLxē'la-it.   A'lta atciō'lXam iā'qsiX: "Ai'aq,
Now   again   they stayed.   Now   he said to him   to his son-in-   "Quick,
                                                law:

12 ai'aq, skā'lEmam scā'yim."   A'lta a'yō iā'qsiX atcikō'lEmam
quick,   go and take them two   two grizzly   Now   he went   his son-in-   he went and took
                    bears."   law   them two

13 scā'yim.   A'lta ā'yō iā'qsiX: "Ayamtgā'lemam!"   A'lta
two grizzly bears.   Now   he went   his son-in-law: "I come to fetch you two!"   Now

14 atci'ctukᵢ atcō'kᵘᵢam gō tE'LaqL.   Aia'skōp!.   TakE
he carried them two   he carried them   to   his house.   He entered.   Then
           to the house

15 atcilXā'kXuē iā'qsiX.   Â! a'lta ackiō'pēqLa iā'qsiX. PāL ka'nauwē
he threw them   his father-   Â!   now they two scratched   his father-   Full   all
down to   in-law   him   in-law.

16 ā'yaLᶜa Lᶜā'owilkt.   "Â, ci'kᵘᵢa i'qsiX! A'lta ckinxE'LElux."
his body   blood.   "Â,   carry them two   son-in-law!   Now   they two do not
                                              know me."

17 A'lta atci'ctukᵢ iā'qsiX atcaalō'kctqam.   A'lta weXt aLxē'la-it.
Now   he carried them   his son-in-   he carried them two   Now   again   he stayed.
     two   law   on his back.

18 Lē'lē ka weXt atciō'lXam iā'qsiX: "Ai'aq, skā'lEmam skoāyawa'."
A long   then   again   he said to nim   his son-in-   "Quick,   go and take   two panthers!"
time   law: them two

19 TakE ā'yō iā'qsiX. Ayū'2ptck, takE atcō'lXam: "Iamtkā'lEmam!"
Then   he went   his son-   He went inland,   then   he said to them   "I came to take you
         in-law.   two: two!"

20 A'lta atci'ctōkᵘᵢ, atcō'kᵘᵢam gō tE'LaqL.   Atcixā'lakLē, aya'skōp!.
Now   he carried them   he carried them   to   his house.   He opened the door.   he entered.
     two   to house

21 TakE atcilXā'kxue iā'qsiX.   A'lta acgiōpē'qLa.   PāL nē'xax
Then   he threw them   his father-   Now   they two scratched   Full   got
     down to   in-law.   him.   him.

22 Lᶜā'owilkt iā'qsiX ā'yaLᶜa.   "Â, ci'kᵘᵢa, ī'qsiX. A'lta ckinxE'LElux."
blood   his father-   his body.   "Â, carry them   son-in-   Now   they two do not
        in-law   two,   law.   know me."

23 A'lta atci'ctōkᵘᵢ iā'qsiX. Acalō'kctxam.
Now   he carried them   his son-in-   He carried them on
     two   law.   his back.

"Tca, ĕ'qsiX! LEX txkcalā'xōma ŏ'mᶜEcX." A'lta ā'cto 1
" Well, son-in-law! split we two will go and a tree." Now they two
do it for us two went

iā'qsiX. A'lta tsEX askcā'lax ŏ'mᶜEcX. TsEX acxā'lax ŏ'mᶜEcX 2
his son-in-law. Now split they two did it a tree. Split they two did it a tree
for them two

aci'tkum. AtciṓlXam iā'qsiX: "Ni'Xua mxal'ā'yakŏ. 3
half. He said to him to his son-in-law: " Well, put yourself between
them.

Ayi'La-it kᵢa mxal'ā'yakuē!" TakE ayayi'La-it iā'qsiX. 4
Sit down in and put yourself between them!" Then he sat down his son-in-
there law.

TakE atctā'wilx·t ctā'xatcaôx. TakE Lu'XLuX atci'tax ka'nauwē. 5
Then he pushed aside the two wedges. Then break he did them all.

Ayauwĕā'yakuit iā'qsiX. TakE atciḗ'taqL, nēxkō. Iū'Lqtē 6
He enclosed him his son-in-law. Then he left him, he went home. Long

ā'yŏ. A'lta gō'yĕ atci'tax tiā'pōtē. TakE tsEX atcxā'lax 7
he went. Now thus he did them his arms. Then break he did it for him

kaX ŏ'mᶜEcX. TakE atcā'kxōnē ā'natai, ga-y-iō'yam gō 8
that tree. Then he carried it on one side, then he arrived at
his shoulder

tE'LaqL, takE atcā'xkaluktgō. Gō2m nē'xau. TakE ayō'pa 9
their house, then he threw it down. Gum it made. Then he went out

iā'qsiX: "Ohō! ītci'qsiX, t'ā'qē nai'ka itci'qsiX." A'lta 10
his father- "Oho! my son-in-law, just as I my son-in-law." Now
in-law:

aLxĕ'la-it. TakE ctā'qo-iL aci'xax ciā'xa. 11
they stayed. Then large [dual] they two his two sons.
became

TakE atciṓlXam iā'qsiX: "Ai'aq ikṓlEmam ē'tcipkᵢala gō 12
Then he said to him to his son-in-law: "Quick, go and take it the hoops at

tiō'LEma ikḗ'x." TakE ā'yō iā'qsiX; kulā'i ā'yō. TakE ayō'yam. 13
supernatural it is." Then he went his son-in- far he went. Then he arrived.
beings law;

A'lta gōyĕ' tixLā'kōt tê'lXEm. A'lta kā'tsEk qExukskoā'liL 14
Now thus they stood in people. Now in middle it was rolled often
circle to and fro

gō qō'tac tê'lXEm. A'lta ayō'La-it, txap nē'xax. NâpōnEm. TakE 15
at those people. Now he stayed, hesitating he was. It grew dark. Then

atcikpā'na; qxuL atcē'lax iā'pōtē. A'lta nē'xenakō atciunkō'mit. 16
he jumped at it; hang he did it on it his arm. Now he ran, he carried it away.

A'lta atigE'ta ka'nauwē; a'lta tkᵢēwaXE'ma atgE'tax. Qaxē'Ltxa 17
Now they pursued all; now torches they made them. How
him

kulā'i aqigE'ta, takE naxa'nkikEna uyā'k·ikal. TakE akcṓlXam 18
far he was pursued, then she thought his wife. Then she said to them
two

cgā'Xa: "Ai'aq, Lā'qLāq mtgE'Lax LEmtā'xqacqac." A'lta 19
her two children: "Quick, strike you two do him your grandfather." Now

acktō'cgam tE'mᶜEcX, a'lta Lā'qLāq acgE'ctax Lstā'xqacqac. A'lta 20
they two took them sticks, now strike they did him their grandfather. Now

aLxElgē'Lxal Lctā'xqacqac. Alā'xti aLxa'wīyuc. A'lta actā'auwiLxt. 21
he cried their two's grandfather. Then he urinated. Now it rained.

TakE tcXE'ptcXEp nōxôx tiō'LEma tgā'kᵢēwaXEma. TakE 22
Then extinguished got the supernatural their torches. Then
beings

nēXatgō'mam. 23
he came home.

A'lta weXt aLxēla-it iō'Lqte. A'lta weXt nē'k·im iqᵢ'ēyō'qxut: 24
Now again they stayed long. Now again he said the old man:

"Ai'aq, ai'aq, tkā'lEmam tiō'LEma tE'gaqᵢpas." A'lta nixa'lt- 25
" Quick, quick, go to take them the supernatu- their targets." Now he made
ral beings

Xuitck. A'lta ā'yō. A'yō2; ayō'yam gō tiō'LEma. A'lta wā'qᵢpas 26
himself Now he went. He went; he arrived at supernatural Now target
ready. beings.

1 ugō′kXuiX. A′lta tcXEp nē′xax. NâpōnEm ka atctō′cgam.
they played.   Now hesitating he got.   It got dark then he took them.

2 Nixa′tEnkō. A′lta atgētaa tiō′LEma. Wax atgE′tax tgā′kᵢēwaXEma.
He came running. Now they pur- the supernat- Light they did their torches.
sued him ural beings. them

3 A′lta nixatE′nkō hēi2! A′lta aqē′tuwa. Qaxē′2 ka naxa′nkikEna-y-
Now he came running hēi! Now he was pursued. Sometime then she thought

4 ūyā′k·ikala. Akcō′lXam cgā′xa: "Ai′aq, Lā′qLaq mtE′qxax
his wife. She said to them her two children: "Quick, strike you two do
him

5 mtā′xqacqac. A′lta actō′cgam tE′mᶜEcX. A′lta Lā′qLāq acgā′yax
your two selves' Now they two took sticks. Now strike they two did
grandfather." them him

6 Lctā′xqacqac. A′lta acixElgē′Lxala Lctā′xqacqac. A′lta akcElgē′cgam
their two selves' Now they hurt him their [dual] grand- Now she helped them
grandfather. father [dual]

7 Lctā′naa. Ā′2lta nixa′wiyuc iqᵢ′ēyō′qxut. A′lta acta′auwilXt.
their [dual] Now he urinated the old man. Now it rained.
mother.

8 TcXE′ptcXEp nō′xôx tgā′kᵢēwaXEma tiō′LEma. A′lta
Extinguished they got their torches the supernatural beings. Now

9 nixatEnkō′mam. AtctE′tkᵘɪa tE′gaqᵢpas.
he came home. He carried them the targets.

A′lta aLxē′la·it iō′Lqtē. Atcō′lXam uyā′k·ilala: "A′lta nō′ya.
Now he stayed long time. He said to her to his wife: "Now I shall go.

11 Nō′ya, kulā′i nō′ya." A′lta nixa′ltXuitck. Aktō′cgam tiā′ktēma.
I shall go, far I shall go." Now he made himself ready. He took them his ornaments.

12 Atixā′lax ka′nauwē2. Atctō′cgam tiā′xalaitan mô′kcti nauwē′kᵢc.
He put them all. He took them his arrows two [quivers] full.
on himself

13 A′lta ā′yō. A′yō2, kulā′i ā′yō. A′lta atcika′ōm ē′lXam, qui′num
Now he went. He went, far he went. Now he reached it a town, five

14 ciā′xilxē ē′lXam. Ā′yūp! kē′mk·itē gō gitānō′kstX t!ō′L. A′lta
its blocks town. He entered the last at having smallness house. Now
[pl.]

15 amô′kctiks ōxoēlā′itX tqᵢ′ēyō′qtiks. A′lta ā′yop! gō qôcta
two there were old ones. Now he entered at those
[dual]

16 cqᵢēyō′qxut. "Ō, kulE′ts tcLXgō′mita iqᵢē′sqēs Lkā′nax." TakE
two old ones. "Oh, once more he will make him blue-jay a chief." Then
unhappy

17 nēxa′nkikEna iqᵢē′sqēs: "LgōLē′lEXEmk Ltē′mam gō-y-ukō′lXul
he thought blue-jay: "A person he arrived at mice

18 tE′ctaqL." TakE ā′yō iqᵢē′sqēs nigē′kctam. A′lta nau′itka
their [dual] Then he went blue-jay he went to see him. Now indeed!
house."

19 Lkā′nax Lōc. TakE nē′Xtakō iqᵢē′sqēs. TakE atciō′lXam
a chief there was. Then he returned blue-jay. Then he said to him

20 iā′xakᵢEmāna iqᵢē′sqēs: "Lkā′nax Ltē′mam. LEmgē′tiam.
his chief blue-jay: "A chief came. He came to play
with you.

21 Wā′qᵢpas mtxcgā′ma." TakE weXt nē′Xtakō iqᵢē′sqēs: "Ā
Target you two will play Then again he returned blue-jay: "Ah
together."

22 tcimaXuē′mut ntcā′xakᵢEmana. Wā′qᵢpas mtxcgā′ma." TakE
he wishes to play our chief. Target you two will Then
with you play together."

23 nē′k·im: "O." Nē′Xtakō iqᵢē′sqēs. "qiX ikā′nax nē′k·im:
he said: "Oh." He returned blue-jay. "That chief he said:

24 "O.'" TakE weXt nē′Xtakō iqᵢē′sqēs: "Ai′aq, ai′aq, mō′Lxa
'Oh!'" Then again he returned blue-jay: "Quick, quick, go to the
beach

25 Lgmā′xo-ilL kā′nax." TakE atctō′cgam tiā′xalaitanEma iqᵢē′sqēs
he said often to the chief." Then he took them his arrows blue-jay
you

iā́xak¡Emana. TakE ā́yuLx iq¡ḗsqēs iā́xak¡Emana. TakE weXt   **1**
his chief.   Then   he went to the beach   blue-jay   his chief.   Then   again

nḗxaukō iq¡ḗsqēs: "Ā́ takE ā́yuLx ntcā́xak¡Emana." TakE ā́yuLx   **2**
he ran   blue-jay: "Ah   then   he went to the beach   our chief."   Then   he went to the beach

qiX ikā́nax. A′lta acxE′cgam wūq¡ pas. A′lta aqā́yuL x·ix· ḗXat   **3**
that   chief.   Now   they two played together   target.   Now   it was won   that   one from him

ikā́nax. Nḗk·iL iq¡ḗsqēs iā́xak¡Emana. AqtḗxoL tiā́ktēma   **4**
chief.   He won   blue-jay   his chief.   They were won from him   his ornaments

ka′nauwē2. AqtḗxoL tiā́xalaitanEma. AqLḗxoL Lā́yaqsō, aqḗxoL   **5**
all.   They were won from him   his arrows.   It was won from him   his hair,   it was won

ā́yaqtq, aqḗxoL iā́potē, kā́namôkst tiā́pōtē aqtḗxoL. AqtḗxoL   **6**
his head,   it was won from him   his arm,   both   his arms were won from him.   They were won from him

tiā́ᶜwit ka′namôkst. A′lta aqiXgṓmit. Laq° aqLḗxax Lā́yaqsō.   **7**
his legs   both.   Now   he was made unhappy.   Cut off   it was done   his hair.

A′lta aqiupṓnit gō tXut. A′lta pṓlakli actṓiX qṓcta ckṓlXōl.   **8**
Now   he was hung   in   smoke.   Now   dark   they went [dual] always   those [dual]   mice [dual].

AckLḗlōk꜀xax Ltcuq. Acgilᶜḗmaιnx ka′nauwē-y- ṓpol ḗka.   **9**
They two brought it to him   water.   They two gave him to eat   every   night   thus.

ĒXt iqḗtāk k¡ā́ya nḗxax. AcE′k·im ciā́xa: "Qōi   **10**
One   year   nothing   he got.   They two said   his two sons: "Let us

atxōgiṓxtkiuEmam I′txam." A′lta acxā́ltXuitck. Acktṓcgam   **11**
we two go to look for him   our [dual] father."   Now   they two made themselves ready.   They two took them

tctā́ktēma. Acktṓcgam tE′ctaq¡ pas. Acktṓcgam ctā́xalaitau. A′lta   **12**
their [dual] ornaments.   They two took them   their targets.   They two took them   their [dual] arrows.   Now

ā′ctō. Ā́ctō, kulā́i ā́ctō. Lap acgā́yax ḗlXam. Adḗ2 ia′aitᴄLx   **13**
they two went.   They two went,   far   they two went.   Find   they did it   a town.   Ah,   large

x·ik ḗlXam. "Lṓnas yaXkṓk Ltxū́mama Lōc." A′ctop! gō qṓgō   **14**
that   town.   "Perhaps   there   our [dual] father is."   They two entered   at that [pl.]

gitanṓkstX t¡′ōL. A′lta amốkctiks ōxoēlā́-itX tq¡′ēyṓqtiks.   **15**
having smallness   house.   Now   two   there were   old ones.

"Anā́2 qēXanā́Xēmct! qā́xēwa amtḗmam?" "Ā́, ḗntam   **16**
"Anah!   our [dual] two chiefs!   whence   did you [dual] come?"   "Ah,   our [dual] father

ntgiṓxtkin." "Kulḗtc tcuXgṓmita tkanā́Xēmct iq¡′ḗsqēs.   **17**
we two search for him."   "Once more   he will make two unhappy   chiefs   blue-jay.

Ā́nqatē LḗXat Lkā́uax aLtḗmaιn. AqLXgṓmit; gō tXut aLupṓnit.   **18**
Long ago   one   a chief   he came.   He was made unhappy;   in   smoke   he put him up.

QēnḗqctxEn nE′tāika; ntkLElᶜḗmEniL· Ltcuq; nLgilᶜḗmEniL   **19**
We two made him happy   we two;   we two give it to him   water;   we two give it to him to eat

iLxā́lEmax. A′lta k¡ē siā́xôst; Lk¡′ṓpLk¡ōp aci′xax." Lä2 ka   **20**
food.   Now   nothing   his eyes;   sunk   they got."   Some time   then

nixa′nkikEna iq¡ḗsqēs: "TakE aLtḗmam Lkā́nax gō-y-ukṓlXul   **21**
he thought   blue-jay: "Then   it came   a chief   at the mice

tE′ctaqL." TakE nḗxaukō, nigḗkctam iq¡ḗsqēs. A′lta amốkctikc   **22**
their [dual] house.   Then   he ran,   he went to see   blue-jay.   Now   two

tkanā́xēmct ōxoēlā́itX. TakE nḗXtakō iqḗsqēs. TakE atciṓlXam   **23**
chiefs   there were.   Then   he returned   blue-jay.   Then   he said to him

iā́Xak¡Emana: "Amốkctikc ōxoēlā́itX tkanā́xēmct gō ckṓlXul   **24**
to his chief: "Two   there are   chiefs   at   the two mice

1 tE'ctaqL.   Cogē'tiam."   "O,"   nē'k·im   iā'xak¡Emana   iq¡ē'sqēs.   TakE
their [dual] house.   They two came to play."   "Oh,"   said   his chief   blue-jay's.   Then

2 weXt   nē'Xtakō   iq¡ē'sqēs.   "Ā   tcimtaXuē'muL   ntcā'xak¡Emana.
again   he returned   blue-jay.   "Ah,   he wishes to play with you two   our chief.

3 Wā'q¡pas   mcxcgā'ma."   Nēkct   qā'da   acgiō'lXam.   TakE   weXt
Target   you will play together."   Not   [any] how   they two spoke to him.   Then   again

4 nē'xankō   iqē'sqēs.   Atciō'lXam   iā'xak¡Emana: "Mō'Lxa!"   Lō'ni
he ran   blue-jay.   He said to him   his chief: "Go to the beach!"   Three times

5 nē'Xtakō   iqē'sqēs.   Nēkct   qa'da   aqiō'lXam.   Gō   la'kti   nē'Xtakō
he returned   blue-jay.   Not   [any] how   was spoken to him.   There   four times   he returned

6 ka   atcā'yukct   qiX   iXgE'cᶜax.   Aqā'yukct   iqē'sqēs.
then   he looked at him   that   youngest one.   He was looked at   blue-jay.

Nau'i   aLE'XLXa   ka'nauwē   Lā'yaqsō.   Nē'Xtakō,   nixilkʇē'tckō
At once   it caught fire   all   his hair.   He returned   he told him

8 iā'xak¡Emana: "A,   ōxoē'ma   tkanā'ximct   tgatē'mam.   Aqā'nukct
his chief: "Ah,   others   the chiefs   they came.   I was looked at

9 x·ix·   ō'kuk,   kā'nauwē   aLE'XLXa   LE'kxaksō.   Mä'Lxa   acgEnō'lXam."
that   there,   all   it caught fire   my hair.   Go [dual] to the beach   they two said to me."

10 Lä2,   a'lta   a'ctōLx.   A'lta   ōxoē'neXat   tā'yaq¡pas: "Q'axtcī'Lx
Some time   now   they two went to the beach.   Now   they stood in the ground   his targets: "How bad

11 tik   tE'q¡pas!"   Lu'XLuX   acgE'tax   qō'ta   tE'q¡pas.   Acguxō'kXuē.
these   targets!"   Pull out   they two did them   those   targets.   They two threw them away.

12 "x·itē'k   tE'ntaq¡pas   nE'taika   tgt¡ō'kti."   Acgō'Xuina   tE'ctaq¡pas.
"These   our [dual] targets   our [dual]   good."   They two placed them in ground   their [dual] targets.

13 Lgā'kt¡'ōma   qō'ta   tE'q¡pas.   A'lta   aLXE'cgam   wā'q¡pas.   A'lta
They shone   those   targets.   Now   they played   target.   Now

14 aqā'yuL   iq¡ē'sqēs   iā'xak¡Emana.   Aqtē'xoL   iā'xak¡Emana   iq¡ē'sqēs
it was won from him   blue-jay   his chief.   They were won from him   his chief   blue-jay

15 tiā'ktēma   ka'nauwē.   A'lta   aqtē'xoL   tiā'lXama   ka'nauwē2.   Acgā'yuL
his ornaments   all.   Now   they were won from him   his people   all.   They two won from him

16 Lctā'mama.   Aqā'yuL   iqē'sqēs.   A'lta   aLiXā'mōtk   Lā'yaqsō.
their [dual] father.   He was won from him   blue-jay.   Now   he betted it   his hair.

17 AqLē'xoL   Lā'yēqsō.   NiXā'mōtk   ā'yaqtq,   niXā'mōtk   tiā'pōtē.
It was won from him   his hair.   He betted it   his head,   he betted him [them]   his arms.

18 Aqtē'xoL   tiā'pōtē.   AtiXā'mōtk   tiā'ᶜōwit.   Aqtē'xoL   ka'nauwē.
They were won from him   his arms.   They betted them   his legs.   They were won from him   all.

19 A'lta   aqō'cgam   lakt   uk¡unā'tan.   Aqa-ilā'wit   gō-y-uyā'ts¡puX
Now   they were taken   four   potentilla roots.   They were put into him   at his forehead

20 uk¡unā'tan.   Aqō'cgam   uguē'luXtcutk,   aqa-ilā'wit   ya'kwa   ka'nauwē
the potentilla roots.   They were taken   pieces of flint,   they were put into him   here   all

21 ā'yaLᶜa.   AqLō'cgam   ptciX   LE'LuwElkLuwElk.   PtciX   aqā'yax
his body.   It was taken   green   mud.   Green   it was made

22 iā'wan;   ptciX   aqā'yax   iā'kōtcX.
his belly;   green   it was made   his back.

A'lta   aqiuXtkē'mit: "IkaLē'nax   imē'xala.   Nä'kct   muXugō'mita
Now   he was thrown into the water and he swam: "Green sturgeon   your name will be.   Not   you will make them unhappy

24 tkanā'xēmct."   Aqiū'cgam   iqē'sqes.   Aqē'xalukctgō: "Iq¡'ē'sqēs
chiefs."   He was taken   blue-jay.   He was thrown away: "Blue-jay

imḗxala.	Näkct	qa′nsiX	muXugō′mita	tkanā′xĕmct.	Ka′nauwē	1
your name will be	Not	ever	you will make them unhappy	chiefs.	Every	

i′kta,	ma′nix	i′kta	iā́qᵢ atxala	ixā́xō,	mxā́xo-ilma	wa′tsEtsEtsE·	2
thing,	if	thing	bad	will get,	you will always say	wa′tsetsetse·	

tsEtsEtsE!	Ŏ	LEmtā′xauyam!	Ka′nauwē	i′kta	ā́Lqī	mtgiā́xo	3
tsetsetse!	Oh,	your [dual] pity!	Every	thing	later on	you two will eat it	

itᵢ′ō′kti.	Ka′nauwē	tkōxoē′ma	mtkta′xō."	TakE	aciū́cgam	4
good.	All	berries	you two will eat them."	Then	they two took him	

Lctā′mama.	A′lta	acgā́yukᵘᵢ	gō	Ltcuq.	A′lta	pō′pō	acgā́yax;	5
their [dual] father.	Now	they two carried him	to	water.	Now	blow	they two did him;	

nē′k·ikct.	A′lta	aLi′xkō.	6
he saw.	Now	they went home.	

Translation.

Once upon a time there were five brothers. The four older ones went hunting elk every day and left the youngest one at home. Their house was full of meat and of tallow. Once upon a time the youngest brother felt lonesome, and said: "O, I wish he would come, the Glutton, and eat all the meat." Four days he continued to say so, then he heard a noise like the shaking of rattles at the door. Now a person appeared who was so large that his blanket consisted of two elk-skins. It had a fringe of elk-hoofs. He entered, sat down, and said: "O, grandson, I am hungry." The boy arose and gave him some meat and tallow. When he looked the stranger had eaten it all. He gave him more, and when he looked again it had all disappeared. The whole day long he gave him meat and tallow. In the evening his brothers came home and brought a fresh supply of meat. When they saw what had happened they said to him: "What did you do? How did the evil spirit come here?" The boy replied, "I felt lonesome, and said: 'O, I wish he would come, the Glutton, and eat all the meat.'" "Oh, you fool, certainly the monster will eat us." They fed him all night until sunrise. They continued to feed him the whole day. Then the meat was at an end. The youngest brother said to the monster: "What will our grandfather eat next? There are only skins left." The monster replied: "What shall I eat, grandchildren, now there are only skins and you." "What does he say?" "'Now there are only skins and you,' he says." "Speak to him again." "What will our grandfather eat next? There are only skins left." The monster replied: "What shall I eat, grandchildren, now there are only skins and you." "What does he say?" "'Now there are only skins and you,' he says." "Speak to him again." "What will our grandfather eat next? There are only skins left." The monster replied: "What shall I eat, grandchildren, now there are only skins and you." "What does he say?" "'Now there are only skins and you,' he says." Now they began to understand him. They boiled skins and gave them to him. For a long time he continued to eat and it grew dark again. Then they dug a hole in the ground, sharpened some arrow-wood, which they placed upright at the place where they used to sleep, and then escaped through the hole which they had dug. At a distance from the house they came out of the hole. They left their bitch at the entrance to the hole and said to her: "If the monster asks you which way we have gone, point with your head another way and call 'Wo'." Then they ran away.

When the day began to dawn the monster awoke and made a jump at where he believed the brothers to be; then he fell on the sharp sticks which pierced his belly. He pulled them out of his body, broke them, and saw that the brothers had escaped through the hole. He followed them, and when he came to the outlet of the hole, he found the bitch. He asked: "Which way went your masters?" She replied: "Wo," pointing with her head in a direction which they had not taken. He pursued them. But after a while, when he did not find their tracks, he turned back. Then again he said to the bitch: "Which way went your masters?" She replied: "Wo," pointing with her head in a direction which they had not taken. He pursued them, but he did not find their tracks and turned back. Three times he pursued them, then he found their tracks which he followed. He followed them a long distance, and finally overtook the eldest brother. He killed him. He ran on and overtook the next one, whom he also killed. He ran on and killed one more. Thus he overtook and killed the four eldest brothers. Now the youngest only was left. He fled, and arrived at a river where he found an old man, the Thunderer, who was fishing with a dipnet. He said, "Take me across; the monster pursues me. Quick, quick, grandfather!" "Hoboo, who is your grandfather?" "Quick, quick, take me across, uncle." "Hohoo, who is your uncle?" "Take me across, elder brother." "Hohoo, who is your elder brother?" In the stern of the canoe there was an old woman whose body was full of scabs. Now the young man said, "O, please take me across, father-in-law." "Ho, why did you not say so before?" Then he took him across. "Quick, quick, go to my house and enter!" Then he entered and the old man stayed in his canoe. After a little while the monster arrived at the river and said to the old man, "Did you see the one whom I pursue?" "I did not see him." "Quick, quick, take me across; I will give you my hat in payment." "What shall I do with a hat?" "I will give you my cane." "What shall I do with a cane?" "I will pay you with my blanket." "What shall I do with a blanket?" "I will give you this twine." This he accepted. Then the Thunderer stretched his leg across the river, and said: "Walk across over my leg, but take care that you do not strike it with your cane." Now the monster walked over his leg. When he was in the middle of the river he struck it with his cane. Then the Thunderer bent his leg, the monster fell into the water and drifted down toward the sea. His hat fell down, and drifted down after him. Then the Thunderer said: "Ōkulā'm (noise of surf) will be thy name; only when the storm is raging you will be heard. When the weather is very bad your hat will also be heard."

Now the Thunderer and his daughter went home. They lived there for some time. The young man did not like his wife. After several days she arose early and went to bathe. When she tried to touch her husband he rolled his blanket about himself. They had each a separate blanket. After several days he rose, then he saw that she had become a beautiful woman. Now they continued to live there. It grew dark. Now when he tried to touch her she rolled her blanket around herself. She took revenge on him. But after awhile they began to like each other.

The Thunderer used to go whaling every day, and the young man said: "I shall look on when my father-in-law goes whaling." "No, no; nobody ever looks at him when he goes whaling." He got angry and said: "I must see him." Now after awhile he looked at him. Soon he saw a whale which went into the dipnet which the Thunderer held. The latter lifted it, but the whale jumped over the rim of the net. The Thunderer looked toward the land, and at once there was thunder, lightning, and hail. Another whale entered his dipnet and he lifted it, but when he did so the whale jumped out of the net. Then the Thunderer got angry, and it began to hail and to storm. He went home and threw down his dipnet. Then his son-in-law left the house, took some coal, and went to a rock. He blackened his forehead and soon a southwest wind arose which blew away the old man's house. He tried to fasten the boards to the roof, but was unable to do so. Then the Thunderer said to his daughter: "Oh, child, go and look for your husband. Tell him to-morrow he may look at me when I go whaling." His daughter went and found her husband. She said: "Oh you destroyed your father-in-law's house. He says to-morrow you may look at him when he catches whales." Then the young man took some water and washed his face. It became calm. He went home with his wife and helped the old man fasten the boards to the roof. He said to his father-in-law: "To-morrow I shall go down to the beach and you shall see me catching whales." On the following morning they went down to the beach together. After a little while a whale entered the dipnet. The young man lifted it and threw the whale ashore. Then the Thunderer said: "Hohoo, my son-in-law, you are just as I was when I was a young man."

Now the Thunderer's daughter became pregnant. After awhile she gave birth to two children. Then the old man said to his son-in-law: "Quick, quick, go and catch two wolves; I used to play with them when I was young." He went to the woods and caught two wolves which he carried to his father-in-law's house. He threw them down at his father-in-law's feet and they bit him all over and hauled him about. He cried: "Oh they have forgotten me; quick, quick, carry them back." The young man took them and carried them back. After awhile the Thunderer said: "Go quick and catch two bears; I used to play with them when I was young." Then his son-in-law went and caught two black bears. He carried them to the house of his father-in-law and threw them at his feet. Then they took hold of him, struck him with their paws, and threw him about in the house. "Oh," he cried, "carry them back, carry them back, they do not remember me." The young man carried them back. Again after awhile the Thunderer said: "Go quick and catch two grizzly bears; I used to play with them when I was young." The young man went into the woods, and when he found the grizzly bears he said: "I came to carry you along." He carried two of them to his father-in-law's house. He entered and threw them at the feet of his father-in-law. Oh, now they scratched him all over so that his body was full of blood. "Oh, carry them back, carry them back, my son-in-law, they have forgotten me." Then his son-in-law carried them back. Then after some time the old man said: "Go quick and catch two panthers; I used to play with them when I was young." Then the young man went into the woods and [when he met the panthers] he said: "I come to take you along." And he carried two of them to his father-in-law's house. He opened the door, entered, and threw them at his father-in-law's feet, Then they scratched him all over, and his whole body was full of blood. "Oh," cried he, "carry them back, carry them back, they do not know me any more." Then the young man carried them back.

[After awhile the Thunderer said:] "Come, son-in-law, let us go and split a log." They went and split a log in half. He said to his son-in-law, "Crawl in there and stem your arms against the log." The young man sat down in there. Then the old man knocked aside the wedges and broke them all. The tree closed over his son-in-law. He left him and went home. He went a long distance. The young man, however, kept the log apart with his elbows and broke it. He carried it home on his shoulder. He came home and threw it down in front of the house. When his father-in-law heard the noise he went out and [on seeing the young man] said: "Oh, my son-in-law, you are just as I was when I was young." They remained there and the children grew up.

Then his father-in-law said to him: "Oh, go to the supernatural people and bring me their hoops." The young man went, a long time he went, and finally he reached the country of the supernatural people. They stood in a circle, the hoop was being rolled to and fro in the circle. He was afraid to approach them any nearer and stood aside. But when it grew dark he made a jump and caught the hoop by pushing his arm through it. Then he ran away, carrying the hoop. The supernatural people lit their torches and pursued him. They pursued him a long distance; then his wife thought of him and told her children, "Now whip your graudfather." They took a stick and whipped him; then he cried and urinated. It began to rain and the torches of the supernatural people were extinguished. Thus he reached home.

After a while the old man said again, "Now go and bring the targets of the supernatural people." He made himself ready and went. After a long time he reached the country of the supernatural people. They were shooting at targets. He was afraid, but when it was dark he took the targets and ran away. Then the supernatural people lit their torches and pursued him. He came running, heh! He was pursued. After some time his wife thought of him and told her children, "Now whip your grandfather." They took a stick and whipped him; their mother helped them. Then the old man urinated, and it began to rain. Thus the torches of the supernatural people were extinguished, and the young man reached home carrying the targets.

After awhile he said to his wife, " Now I shall leave you." He made himself ready, put on all his dentalia and took two quivers full of arrows. Then he went. After awhile he reached a large town which consisted of five rows of houses. The last house was very small. This he entered and found two old women [the mice. When they saw him they said:] "Oh, now Blue-Jay will make another chief unhappy." Then Blue-Jay thought, "A person came to the house of the mice." He went to see and, indeed, there was a chief in the house. Then Blue-Jay went back to his chief and said: "A chief has arrived; he wants to have a shooting match with you." Then he went back to the stranger and said: "Our chief wants to play with you. You will have a shooting match." He said: "Oh." Blue-Jay ran back [to his chief and said]: "That chief said 'Oh.'" He went back again: "The chief says to you you shall come down to the beach quickly." Then Blue-Jay's chief took his arrows and went down to the beach. Blue-Jay ran back [to the stranger and said]: "Our chief went down to the beach." Then the other chief went down to the beach Now they shot at the targets. The other chief lost and Blue-Jay's chief won. He lost all his dentalia. He lost his arrows. He lost his hair. He lost his head. He lost both his arms. He lost both his legs. Then they made him miserable. They cut off his hair and hung him up in the smoke. But at night the two mice always went and gave him water and gave him to eat. Every night they did so.

One year he had been away. Then his sons said, " Let us look for our father." They made themselves ready, put on their dentalia, took their targets and their arrows. Then they went, they went a long distance; they found a town, oh, a large town. [They said:] " Perhaps here we shall find our father." They entered that small house. There were two old women [who said]: "Oh, chiefs, where did you come from ?" "We search for our father." "Oh, Blue-Jay will make miserable two more chiefs. A long time ago a chief came and they made him miserable and put him into the smoke. But we always gave him water; we always gave him food. He has lost his eyes."

After some time Blue-Jay thought that a chief must have arrived at the house of the mice. He ran there to look and he found two chiefs. Then he went back and said to his chief: "Two chiefs have arrived; they stay at the house of the mice; they came to play with you." "Oh," replied Blue-Jay's chief. He ran back [to the house of the mice, and said to the strangers]: "Our chief wants to play with you. You will have a shooting match." They did not say anything. Then Blue-Jay ran back and said to his chief: "Go down to the beach!" Three times Blue-Jay went back. But they did not speak to him. When he went there the fourth time the younger brother looked at him. He looked at Blue-Jay. At once all his hair began to burn. Then he returned and told his chief, "O, these strangers are more powerful than we are. They looked at me and my hair caught fire. They tell you to come down to the beach." After a little while they went down to the beach. Two targets were stuck into the ground. [They said:] "How bad are these targets!" and they pulled them out and threw them away. "Here, our targets are good." They put their targets into the ground. Their targets were shining. Then they began to shoot. Now Blue-Jay's chief lost. He lost all his dentalia. He lost all his people. They won their father from him. They won Blue-Jay. Now they staked his hair and they won it. They staked his head, they staked his arms. They won his head and his arms. They staked his legs; they won it all. Then they took four potentilla roots and put them on to the forehead [of Blue-Jay's chief]. They took pieces of flint and put them all over his body. They took green mud and painted his belly and his back green. Then they threw him into the water, and said: "Green Sturgeon shall be your name; henceforth you shall not make chiefs miserable." They took Blue-Jay, threw him away, and said: "Blue-Jay shall be your name; henceforth you shall not make chiefs miserable. You shall sing 'Watsetsetse-tsetse,' and it shall be a bad omen." [Then they turned to the mice and said:] "Oh, you pitiful ones, you shall eat everything that is good. You shall eat berries." Then they took their father and carried him to the water. They blew on him and he recovered his eyesight. Then they returned home.

3. ANĒKTCXŌ'LEMIX ITCĀ'KXANAM.

ANĒKTCXŌ'LEMIX HER MYTH.

Cxēlä'-itX ēXt iLā'lXam. Ayō'maqt iLā'xak¡Emana. TakE **1**
There were two one their town. He was dead their chief. Then

ctā'qoaiL ciā'xa, ā'ēXat ōᶜō'kuil, ē'Xat ē'kXala. Wāx ēlagē'tEma **2**
largᵉ [dual] his two one a girl, one a boy. Every sea-otters
children, morning

tgiā'wul tē'lXEm. A'qxēamē Liā'wuX guā'nEsum. Pō'lakli **3**
they always did the people. In stern of canoe his younger always. At dark
[hunted] them sister

tsXī acgō'mamX. Qui'nEmī ā'cto mā'Luē ka pōXᵘ nē'xauē. **4**
then they two arrived Five times they two sea-ward then foggy it became.
at their house. went

AkLuwā'luqL qō'La Ltcuq. MEL¡ aLE'xax LE'kxaksō ka **5**
She swallowed it that water. Wet it got her hair and
often

akLuwā'luqL qō'La Ltcuq. Iō'Lqte· nōxoē'la-it qōtac tē'lXEm. **6**
she swallowed it that water. Long time they stayed those people.
often

Ā'ᵉlta agā'wan naxā'lax. Iā'nēwa iq¡ē'sqēs ka xāx ā'tcax. **7**
Now pregnant she became. First blue-jay and observe he did her.

"Wu'ska! nēkct nā mcā'xaxōmē? TakE agā'wan atcā'lax **8**
"Heh! not [interroga- you observe her? Then her pregnancy he made it
tive particle] on her

Liā'wuX." "Hō'ntcin! k·¡ā ixā'xoiē, iq¡ē'sqēs," nē'k·im skā'sa-it. **9**
his younger "Don't! quiet become, blue-jay," he said robin.
sister."

Mcōk¡'uē'mactā'mita cilxā'xak¡Emana." "Hō'ntcin! ia'xka **10**
You make them [dual] ashamed our two chiefs." "Don't! he

iLalē'xgEqun. Iā'nēwa ka i'kta ilā'xo-ita." Lä2 ka iā'qoa-iL **11**
the eldest one. First then every- he will know." Some- then largᵉ
thing time

itcā'wan nixā'lax. "Wu'ska! lxkᴛā'yōwa!" nē'k·im iq¡ē'sqēs. "TakE **12**
her belly became. "Heh! We will move!" he said blue-jay. "Then

anxEmā'tcta-itck. TakE agā'wan atcā'lax itcā'lē. Lxkc'itā'qᴛa, **13**
I got ashamed. Then her pregnancy he made it her brother. We will leave them
on her [dual],

lxkᴛā'yōwa." Alā'xti ka'nauwē nau'itka aqigEmiLō'lExa-it iq¡ē'sqes. **14**
we will move." Then all indeed he was believed blue-jay.

Wext ā'cto Liā'wuX. Pō'2lakli acgō'mam. A'lta k¡am tē'lXEm, **15**
Again they his younger At dark they two came Now nothing people,
[dual] sister. home.
went

k¡am t!'ōLē'ma ka'nauwē. "Ō takE taL¡ aqE'txLayū. Ia'xka **16**
nothing houses all. "Oh, then look! we are deserted. He

iq¡ē'sqēs iā'xaqamt. Wu'ska, ōxanigu'Litck! La'ksta amē'wan **17**
blue-jay his advice. He! tell me! who your pregnancy

aLgamā'lax?"- "K·¡ē nikct tEnē'txix. Iā'ma qēa ē'Xti ā'txō, ka **18**
made it on you?" "Nothing not I know. Only when once we two then
went,

qēā pōXᵘ nē'xau, ka anLuwā'luqL qōLa Ltcuq. Ia'xkatik ē'mᶜalqᴛ **19**
when foggy it was. then I swallowed it that water. That this qualmish
often

atcā'nax." TakE acgō'xtkin ōᶜō'lEptckiX. Ka'nauwē Ltcuq **20**
he made me." Then they two searched fire. All water
for it

wā'xwax aqLā'kxax ōᶜō'lEptckiX. Gō kE'mk·itE tē'kXaqL **21**
pour it was done the fire. Then last her house

ōctā'Laq ōk¡unō' ka ā'xka ka wiXt k·¡ē tE'kXaqL. Ka **22**
their [dual] aunt the crow then her then also nothing her house. Then

37

1 cxuwā'yul ka L¡äk nā'xax ō'ᵋō'lEptckiX. "Qāxē x·iau L¡äk
they two walked about / and / crackle / it did / the fire. / "Where / this / crackle

2 nā'xax!" atcō'lXam Liā'wuX. Lä2 ka weXt L¡äk nā'xax. Mô'kcti
it does!" / he said to her / his younger sister. / Some time / then / again / crackle / it did. / Twice

3 L¡äk nā'xax ōᵋō'lEptckiX. A'lta LE'kLEk acgā'yax ilē'ē. A'lta
crackle / it did / the fire. / Now / burrow / they two did it / the ground. / Now

4 Lap acE'kxax ō'otcō. A'lta kā'tsEk gō-y- ō'otcō-y akē'x
find / they two did it / a shell. / Now / in middle / in / the shell / was

5 ōᵋō'lEptckiX. "Ŏ Lā'xauyam txā'Lak. Ā'qka taL¡ a'kXotk Xak
fire. / "Oh, / pitiful she / our [dual] aunt. / She / look! / she put into / that

6 ōᵋō'lEptckiX." A'lta nacXE'lgiLx. Wäx nē'ktcuktē.
fire." / Now / they [dual] made fire. / Next morning / it got day.

A'lta acgE'tax t¡'ōL. ALksō'kxōL! t¡'ōL, itanū'kstX t¡'ōL. A'lta
Now / they two made it / a house. / They finished it, / the house, / its smallness / house. / Now

8 ia'xkati asxē'la-it. Lä2 asxē'la-it ia'xkatē; ka nē'katxa, maLnā'
there / they two stayed. / Some time / they two stayed / there; / then / it grew windy, / from sea

9 nē'katxa. Kawē'X ka nixā'latck. Ā'yōLx. A'lta x·itik tE'cgan
it grew windy. / Early / then / he rose. / He went to the beach. / Now / there / ᵋcedar planks

10 tgE'xEniptcgEt; itca'LElam kaX ōmā'p; iLā'LElXamE'mtga
they drifted ashore; / ten / these / planks; / ten each

11 Lgå'nEXama. Ā'yōptck. Atcō'lXam Liā'wuX: "Lap anE'tax
fathoms. / He went up from the beach. / He said to her / his younger sister: / "Find / I did them

12 tE'cgaɴ, iLaLElXamE'mtga Lgā'nEXama." A'lta a'ctōLx Liā'wuX.
boards, / ten each / fathoms." / Now / they two went to the beach / his younger sister.

13 Ā'lta acktōLā'taptck, ka'nauwē acktōLā'taptck. Ā'lta acgE'tax
Now / they [dual] pulled them ashore, / all / they [dual] pulled them ashore. / Now / they two made it

14 tā'qoa-iL t¡'ōL. A'lta acxē'la-it ia'xkate. A'lta ē'tcatc!a ayaxā'lax
a large [pl.] house. / Now / they two stayed / there. / Now / her sickness / came on her

15 Liā'wuX. A'lta nakxa'tōm; LE'kXala akLaxô'tom.
his younger sister. / Now / she gave birth; / a male / she gave birth to it.

A'lta nē'k·im itcā'xk¡un: "Ē'ktaLx ēō'k Lgiā'xō!" Kawē'X
Now / he said / her elder brother: / "What may / blanket / she will make it!" / Early

17 ā'yuLx. Lap ɛtcā'yax môkct ilagē'tEma, kEnE'm ilagē'tEma. "Ŏ
he went to the beach. / Find / he did them / two / sea-otters, / small / sea-otters. / "Oh,

18 Lā'xauyam LgE'LatXEn ēō'k Lgiā'xō." Atcio'kctEptck gō
his poverty / my nephew / blanket / she will make it." / He carried them up from the beach / to

19 mā'Lxôlē. Atcō'lXam Liā'wuX: "Lap anā'yax ilagē'tEma." Ŏ
inland. / He said to her / his younger sister: / "Find / I did them / sea-otters." / Oh,

20 k¡wa'nk¡wan nā'xax Liā'wuX.
glad / she became / his younger sister.

"Ē'ktaLx agiā'xoLk LE'tcx·imcq Lgā'wuX!" Kawē'X nixā'latck.
"What may / she makes / soup / my younger sister!" / Early / he rose.

22 Ā'yōLx. A'lta igē'pix·L iuqunā'-itX. Atcā'yaxc, hē! ka'nauwē
He went to the beach. / Now / a sea-lion / it lay there. / He cut it, / heh! / all

23 atcā'yaxc. A'lta acgiutcXā'mal. A'lta ka'nauwē Lᵋalā'ma ayō'Lx,
he cut it. / Now / they two boiled it. / Now / all / days / he went to the beach,

mȯkct   ēlagē'tEma   Lⁱap   atciā'x.   A'lta   pāL   nȯ'xȯx   tE'ctaqL   **1**
two   sea-otters   find   he did them.   Now   full   it became   their [dual] house

ēlagē'tEma.   Wāx   nĕ'ktcuktē   ā'yōLx.   **2**
sea-otters.   Every morning   it got day   he went to the beach.

A'lta   yuqunā'-itX   ē'kōlē.   Nĕ'xankō   mā'L'xȯlē: "Ā,   ē'kolĕ'   x·ix·ī'x·   **3**
Now   there lay   a whale.   He ran   inland: "Ah,   a whale   this

yuqunā'-itX!"   "Ō,   aqtxēt!'ē'mam   pō'lakli.   E'wa   ē'natai   x·ik   **4**
lies there!"   "Oh,   food is sent to us   at night.   Thus   on the other side   this

ē'maL   x·i   aqtxet!'ē'mam.   Ia'xkēwa   taLⁱ   Xȯk   qⁱ'at   aqā'nax   ēwa   **5**
ocean   this   food is sent to us.   There   look!   those   love   I am done   thus

tiō'LEma.   Nitē'mam   Liā'mama   x·ix·ī'k   ik'ā'sks.   Ai'aq   ē'xca   **6**
the supernatural beings.   He came   his father   this   boy.   Quick   cut it

ka'nauwē   x·iau   ē'kōlē!"   TakE   atcā'yaxc,   ka'nauwē   atcā'yaxc   **7**
all   this   whale!"   Then   he cut it,   all   he cut it

itcā'xq'un.   TakE   acgiō'kXuiptck.   Ka'nauwē   acgiō'kXuiptck.   **8**
her elder brother.   Then   they two pulled it ashore.   All   they two pulled it ashore.

A'lta   naxE'ltXuitck   ōkⁱu'nō.   Kcūkctama   cgā'tgĕu.   A'lta   **9**
Now   she made herself ready   the crow.   She wanted to go to see them   her sister's children.   Now

nai'kōtcti   ō'kⁱu'nō.   Ā2qxulkt   ōkⁱu'nō.   Qⁱ'oā'p   naigō'tctamē;   a'lta   **10**
she went across   the crow.   She cried   the crow.   Nearly   she got across;   now

agō'ēkEl   t!'ōL.   Agō'ēkEl   tXut.   Nō'ya,   nō'ya,   nō'ya.   Qⁱ'oā'p   **11**
she saw it   a house.   She saw it   smoke.   She went,   she went,   she went.   Nearly

naxā'-ikElai.   Kᵘcā'xali   Lōc   Lkā'nax   gō   tE'LaqL   Lō'kōc.   "Ō   **12**
she landed.   Above   there was   a chief   on   his house   he was on it.   "O,

Lgā'xanyam   Ltxā'Lak."   TakE   naigā'tctamē.   Ayaxalgu'Litck   **13**
pitiful [f.]   our [dual] aunt."   Then   she came across.   He told her

Liā'wuX.   TakE   agē'ElkEl   ē'kolē   ōkⁱu'nō,   ē'kolē   tiā'Lᶜulēma.   **14**
his younger sister.   Then   she saw it   the whale   the crow,   a whale   its meats.

Iā'xkēwa   nōya   ōkⁱ'u'nō.   Agixkⁱ'ā'kux   a'lta   ē'Lᶜulē.   "Mä2t,"   takE   **15**
Then   she went   the crow.   She pulled it   now   the meat.   "Come,"   then

atcō'lXam   itcā'tgeu.   "Mä'tptcga,   mä'tptcga.   I'kta   migElā'xō   **16**
he said to her   her nephew.   "Come inland,   come inland.   What   are you going to do with it

iā'atcEkc!"   TakE   nā'k·im: "Ō   kā'ltac   niō'kuman."   TakE   nō'ptcga   **17**
its stench?"   Then she said: "O,   to no purpose   I look at it."   Then   she went inland

ōkⁱu'nō!   Nō'ptcga;   a'lta   pāL   ē'kolē   i'Xuc   gō   wē'wuLē.   Nau'i   **18**
the crow!   She went inland;   now   full   whale   it was on ground   in   interior of house.   Immediately

gō   qōLa   Lk'āsks   qē'xtce   akLō'cgam.   ALgE'tsax   qōLa   Lk'āsks.   **19**
to   that   boy   intending   she took it.   He cried   that   boy.

"Lmē'laqst   x·iLa   kⁱ'oa's   tLxā'Lxaut."   TakE   aqLā'lot   Ltcuq.   **20**
"Your tears   these   afraid   they make him."   Then   she was given   water.

TakE   naxEmē'nakō.   TakE   weXt   qē'xtcē   akLō'cgam.   WeXt   **21**
Then   she washed her face.   Then   again   intending   she took him.   Again

aLgE'tsax: "Āyō   ōmē'Lōtk   Xau   kⁱ'oa'c   qLxā'xau."   AkLō'cgam   **22**
he cried: "Ayo   your breath   that   afraid   makes him."   She took it

Ltcuq,   agā'yutcktc   i'tcacqL.   WeXt   akLō'cgam,   weXt   aLgE'tcax.   **23**
water,   she washed inside   her mouth.   Again   she took him,   again   he cried.

TakE   agō'lXam   ugō'tgeu: "Mxä'LōX   na   LgōLē'lEXEmk!   **24**
Then   she said to her   her niece: "You think   [int. part.]   a person?

Ēwa   taLⁱ   tiō'LEma   Lk'āsks.   Ia'xkēwa   weXt   aqēntā'lot,   **25**
Thus   look   the supernatural being's   child.   There   also   it was given to us [dual],

ia'xkēwa   x·ix·   ē'kōlē   āqentE'lᶜēm."   TakE   nā'k·im   ō'kⁱ'unō':   **26**
there   that   whale   it was given to us to eat."   Then   she said   the crow:

"Haᶜ-ōm!"   Aqā'2-lEqēx   ōkⁱ'unō'.   Aqā'lᶜēm,   naxLxā'l'Em.   ALā'xōLx.   **27**
"Oh!"   It was boiled for her   the crow.   She was given to eat,   she ate.   She finished.

1 A'lta na'xkō.   AgE'tōkᵘ₁ môkct tgitē'tcxala.   Agauwē'k·itk gō
  Now   she went home.   She carried them   two   pieces of blubber.   She put them into   in

2 Lgā'cguic.   Nō'ya,   nō'ya,   nō'ya;   nai'kōtctē.   Q¡'oa'p agiā'xōm
  her mat.   She went,   she went,   she went;   she went across.   Nearly   she reached it

3 ē'lXam;   a'lta nagE'tsax.   A'lta akcX₁ā'tal cgā'tgēu.
  the town;   now   she cried.   Now   she wailed for   her sister's children.

  "cEgEtgē'u,   cEgē'tgēu,   cEgē'tgēu!   Lalā'Xuks nōxō-ilā'wulXLE'mX!
  " My sister's chil-   my sister's   my sister's   Birds   fly up often!
  dren,   children,   children!

5 Utcaktcā'ktcinikc namᶜē'mō!
  Eagles   chew you!

  "cEgEtgē'u,   cEgē'tgēu,   cEgē'tgēu!   Iqonēqonē'tcinikc nā'mᶜēmōm!
  " My sister's chil-   my sister's   my sister's   Gulls   chew you!
  dren,   children,   children!

  "cEgEtgē'u,   cEgē'tgēu,   cEgē'tgēu!   Iqoalē'Xoatcinikc nāmᶜēmō'm!
  " My sister's chil·   my sister's   my sister's   Ravens   chew you!
  dren,   children,   children!

8 cEgEtgē'u, cEgē'tgēu!"
  My sister's   my sister's
  children,   children!"

  Q¡'oā'p agiā'xōmē.   Iō2c iq¡'ē'sqēs kᵘLā'xanē.   Q¡'oā'p agiā'xōmē
  Nearly   she arrived.   There was   blue-jay   outside.   Nearly   she arrived

10 ka wiXt nagE'tsax:
   then again   she cried:

   "cEgEtgē'u,   cEgē'tgēu,   cEgē'tgēu!   Lalā'Xuks nōxō-ilā'wulXLE'mX!
   " My sister's chil·   my sister's   my sister's   Birds   fly up often!
   dren,   children,   children!

12 Uk¡'ōnō'tcinikc nā'mᶜēmō'm!"
   Crows   chew you!"

   TakE nēxE'lqamX iqē'sqēs: "Ā -y·ā'xp!Ena uk¡'ōnō'ya.   Nēkct tc̣ī
   Then   he shouted   blue-jay: "Ah,   she named   the crow.   Not [int. part.]

14 nimcā'xaxōmē?   Iā!   Āxp!Ena-y ōk¡'u'nō!"   TakE naxkō'mam,
   you notice?   Iā!   She named   the crow!"   Then   she came home,

15 naxā'ēgilaē.   TakE nōptcga.   A'lta ā'tgep! tê'lx·Em ka'nauwē gō-y-
   she landed.   Then   she went up   Now   they entered   the people   all   at the
   from water.

16 ōk¡'unō' tE'kXaqL.   AqaXuā'tcagā'lEmam.   A'lta naxkᵘ₁ē'l ōk¡'unō'.
   crow   her house.   The people went to ask her.   Now   she said much   the crow.

17 Nā'k·im ōk¡'unō': "Anigō'tctamē;   pāL tElalā'Xukc kcxē'lax cgā'tgēu.
   She said   the crow: " I got across;   full   birds   eating them   my [dual] sis-
   two   ter's children.

18 Ka'nauwē tElalā'Xukc ō'tāmᶜō." · Iā'nēwa ka iqē'sqēs ayō'pa.
   All   birds   chewed them."   First   then   blue-jay   went out.

19 Ayoxō'La gō t!'ōL.   Iā'xkati ayō'la-it.   K'ā nā'xax ōk¡'unō'.
   He went around   at   house.   There   he stayed.   Silent   she became   the crow.

20 CXā'lak itcā'p₁'au kā'sa-it.   Tqui'numiks tga'a ōk¡'unō'.   A'lta
   They sat at   her dead hus-   robin.   Five   her chil-   the crow.   Now
   opposite sides   band's brother   dren
   of fire

21 naxa-iyi'lkᵘ₁ē itcā'p₁'au.   Cau'cau naxayi'llkᵘ₁ē.   Iqauwē'tsEtk
   she told him much   her dead hus-   Low voice   she told him much.   He listened
   band's brother.

22 iqē'sqēs; gō kᵘLā'xanī iō'c q¡'oāp t!'ōL.   TakE Laqu agā'yax
   blue-jay;   there   outside   he was   near   house.   Then   take out   she did it

23 tgākᵘtca-it.   A'lta Lqō'pLqōp agā'yax.   AgiLE'lᶜēm tga'a.   Agēlᶜēm
   the food she car-   Now   cut to pieces   she did it.   She fed them   her chil-   She fed him
   ried home.   dren.

24 itcā'p₁ᶜau.   TakE ayanᶜō'LuXuit ugō'xō, axgē'sax ugō'xō.   TakE
   her dead hus-   Then   it choked her   her daughter,   the youngest   her daughter.   Then
   band's brother.

25 ā'yōp! iqē'sqēs.   T¡'Eq atci'Lax Lgā'paa.   L¡'ōx ayuLā'taxit qix.
   he entered   blue-jay.   Slap   he did it   her nape.   Coming out   it flew out   that

ē′kolē.   Atciŏ′cgam   iqē′sqēs.   Ayō′pa iqē′sqēs: "Ā̆, nikct tcĕ   1
whale   He took it   blue-jay.   He went out blue-jay: "Ah, not [int.
[meat].   part.]

nimcā′xaxomē? GEnE′lcēm okᵢ'unōyā′!" Atcixōnēman qōtac tê′lx·Em   2
do you notice?   She fed me   the crow!"   He showed it to those people
                                                          them

qix· ē′kolē. Tlō′nkXa t!'ōlē′ma atcixō′nēma, ka atciā′owilc. Lä 2   3
that whale. Three only houses he showed it to then he ate it. Some
                                  them,   time

nō′pōnEm. Ŏ′lo getā′xt kā′nauwĕ qōtac tê′lX·Em. A′lta nixkᵘτē′l   4
it got dark. Hungry they were all   those people. Now he said much

iqē′sqēs: "Ŏ̄ ilxā′xakᵢEmāna ē′kolē pāL tā′yaqL. E′wa taLᵢ   5
blue-jay: "Oh, our chief   whale full his house. Thus look

tiō′LEma qᵢ'ät ā′xkax Liā′wuX kᵢa atcinE′t!'euL ilxā′xakᵢEmana."   6
the supernat- love they did his younger and he invited me   our chief."
ural beings   her sister

Aqā′t!'euL ōkᵢ'unō′ kᵢa kā′sa-it. A′lta nō′pōnEm, ka mE′nx·i ka   7
She was invited crow and robin. Now it grew dark, then a little then
                                                                while

Lāx nē′xax iqē′sqēs. Atciū′ktcan iā′lEkōtitk. "Txō′kst'itā kā′sa-it!   8
visible he became blue-jay. He took in hand his quilt. "We two will sleep robin!

Kwa′nEsum tsEs anE′xax pō′laklī." TakE nē′k·im kā′sa-it: "Yä2,   9
Always   cold I get at night."   Then he said robin: "Yä,

x·ĭx·ē′kik. Tcx·ä nā′mkXa· anxō′kstitX, ka wiXt aqangā′t!'ōm.   10
this one. Then I alone I sleep, then again people come home.

Ia′xkati x·ia mxō′kctit gō tgE′uit!" A′lta nixō′kstit iqē′sqēs gō   11
There here sleep at my feet!" Now he slept blue-jay at

tiā′ōwit, gō nuXumā′kXit tiā′ōwit kā′sa-it. A′lta nixEllkτā′ta-it   12
his feet, at their end [of] his feet robin. Now he was awake

iqē′sqēs. Ā′lta ikā′nim acgā′yax kā′sa-it kᵢ'a ōyā′pτ'au. Qᵢ'oāp   13
blue-jay. Now canoe they two made it robin and his dead bro- Nearly
                                                       ther's wife

iktcō′ktiya ka iaō′ptit iqᵢē′sqēs. A′lta aLā′kilōya ā′llta. ALktō′kuē   14
it got daylight then he slept blue-jay. Now they went to now. They carried to
                                               the canoe   the canoe

Lā′xamōt. A′lta atcō′cgam itsā′kᵢ'esiL ōē′kᵘtEqlix·, atcō′cgam   15
their property. Now he took it a sharp branch, he took it

kā′sa-it. Atcuqoā′na-it ēwa tiā′owit iqē′sqēs ōē′kᵘtEqlix·. A′lta   16
robin. He put it into the thus his feet blue-jay's the branch. Now
        ground

aLē′kXōtctē kā′sa-it kᵢa ōyā′pτ'au ōkᵢ'unō′. ALᴵcē′taqL iqē′sqēs.   17
they went across robin and his dead bro- the crow. They left him blue-jay.
                              ther's wife

Nixa′ll'ōkō iqē′sqēs kawī′X: "Mxa′ll'ōkō kā′sa-it!" Atcē′kτtuq.   18
He awoke blue-jay early: " Awake robin!" He kicked him.

Nau′i Lxoā′p ā′Lix Lā′yapc iqē′sqēs. Na-ilgā′Xit kaX ōē′kᵘtᵢEqlix·:   19
At once hole became his foot blue-jay's. He struck it that branch:

"Anā′! LEkXEpsā′! Ā′nqatē tāLᵢ Xūk aLEncē′taqL." A′lta   20
"Ana! my foot! Long ago see! here they left me." Now

nē′Xkō iqē′sqēs gō tiā′ā.   21
he went home blue-jay to his children.

ALigō′tctamē ōkᵢ'unō′. Nau′i ā′Lōptck gō t!'ōL. "Ai′aq,   22
They got across the crow. At once they went up to the house. "Quick,
                                       from the beach

lxigō′tctaē," nē′k·im iqē′sqēs. A′ltā nōxuē′tXuitck tigō′tctaē   23
we will go across," he said blue-jay. Now they made themselves they wanted
                                               ready   to go across

ka′nauwē. TakE atē′kXōkctē. Kā′tcEk qix· ē′maL ka nē′katxa;   24
all. Then they went across. Middle that bay then it grew windy;

hEmm. Lĕqs nuxō′La-it tê′lx·Em. TakE w·iXt nuXō′takō.   25
humm. Almost they died the people. Then again they returned.

Qoā′nEmi LᶜaLā′ma nuXōtā′lEkτ ka takE atigō′tctamē. A′lta   26
Five times days they always turned and then they got across. Now

1 atci'Lōtk,   Lkā'pa   aLi'xax.   ALōgōtgē'kxo-it   tê'lx·Em;   takE   tsEs
  it snowed,   snow   it became.   They were covered   the people;   then   cold

2 nō'xôx   tê'lx·Em.   AcLE'nk¡'ēmEnakō   iLā'Xak¡Emāna.   TakE
  they became   the people.   He took revenge on them   their chief.   Then

3 ā'yuptck   iq¡ē'sq¡ēs.   Qē'xtcē   atciō'lXam   kā'sa-it: "Anxatā'laqɪ,
  he went up   blue-jay.   Intending   he said to him   [to] robin: "Open me,
  from shore

4 kā'sa-it.   TakE   tsEs   anE'xax.   Nē't!'ēm,   kā'sa-it;   takE   ō'lō
  robin.   Then   cold   I got.   Bring me food,   robin;   then   hunger

5 anō'mEqt."   K¡ē   kā'sa-it,   "Ai'aq,   kā'sa-it,   sE'tk^utpa   c'E'mtgict."
  I die."   Nothing   robin.   "Quick,   robin,   put them two   the tongs."
                  out of house

  IxEltcXā'mal   kā'sa-it.   Ikolē'   atciutcXā'mal.   "Wu'ska,   kā'sa-it,
  He boiled much   robin.   Whale   he boiled it much.   "Oh!   robin,

7 sE'tk^utpa   cta   c'E'mtgict."   TakE   atcō'cgam   s'E'mtgEst   kā'sa-it.
  put them two   those   tongs."   Then   he took them   tongs   robin.
  out of house   [dual]

8 TakE   L¡'EmE'n   atci'ctax.   TakE   atcō'ktpa.   A'lta   atsō'mēqL   iqē'sqēs
  Then   soft   he made them   Then   he put them   Now   he licked them   blue-jay
        [dual].   out of house.

9 qō'cta   c'E'mtgict.   "Kā'sa-it,   kā'sa-it,   ē'lXam   ilxā'Xak¡Emāna,
  those   tongs.   "Robin,   robin,   say to him   our chief,

10 na-ilō'ta-y-ōgE'xa.   TcEnxElā'qɪa."   "Yä2,   i'kta   qtciēgElā'xō,
  I shall give him my   He shall open me."   "Yä,   what   shall be done with
  daughter.   her,

11 imcā'xak¡Emāna   ūyā'xa   x·au   aqā'uXuwā'kuX¡"   TakE   nē'xanko
  your chief   his daughter   that one   she is demanded¡"   Then   he ran

12 iqē'sqēs   mā'Lnē.   TakE   atciō'lXam   iLā'xak¡Emāna: "ĀqāuXuwā'kuX
  blue-jay   to the beach.   Then   he said to him   their chief: "She is demanded

13 ōmē'Xa,   k¡a   nai'ka   weXt   ōgu'xa   aqāuXuwā'kuX."   Näkct
  your daughter,   and   my   also   my daughter   she is demanded."   Not

14 qa'da   nē'k·'im   iLā'Xak¡Emāna   iqē'sqēs.   WēXt   nē'xankō   mā'Lxôlē
  anyhow   spoke   their chief   blue-jay's.   Again   he ran   upland

15 iqē'sqēs: "Kā'sa-it!   Tcinā'xo-il   intsā'Xak¡Emāna,   tca-ilō'ota-y-uyā'xa."
  blue-jay: "Robin!   He says   our chief,   he will give   his
                                    her to him   daughter."

16 Qoä'nEmi   ā'yūL   iqē'sqēs.   TakE   nē'k·im   iLā'Xak¡Emāna.   A'lta
  Five times   he always   blue-jay.   Then   he spoke   their chief.   Now
        went

17 atcō'tXuitck   uyā'Xa.   Atctā'lax   tgā'ktēma   ka'nauwē2·   Atsō'tXuitck
  he made her   his daughter.   He put them   her dentalia   all.   He made her ready
  ready   on her

18 uyā'Xa   iqē'sqēs.   Nē'xankō   wiXt   mā'Lxôlē   iqē'sqēs: "Kā'sa-it,
  his daughter   blue-jay.   He ran   again   upland   blue-jay: "Robin,

19 takE   anō'tXuitck   ōmē'wulx."   "Yä2,"   nē'k·im   kā'sa-it,   "Qādoxo-y-
  then   I made her ready   thy niece."   "Yä,"   said   robin,   "Shall

20 ōyū'sEmat   giakEna'oi."   TakE   ā'tcukɪ   iLā'Xak¡Emāna   uyā'xa.
  her chamber   she will look after it."   Then   he carried her   their chief   his daughter.

21 A'lta   aqaLxā'laqɪ.
  Now   it was opened.

  Nē'ktcuktē;   a'ltā   k¡ä   kaX   ōc̄ō'kuil   iLā'Xak¡Emāna   uyā'lē.   "TaL¡
  It got day;   now   nothing   that   woman   their chief   his sister.   "Look,

23 aqatgā'lEmam,   ē'wa   tiō'LEma   kāx   qōLa   Lk¡āsks."   TakE   aLxLē'la-it,
  they came and took   thus   the super-   where   that   child."   Then   they stayed,
  her,   natural beings

24 t!'ōLē'ma   aLgE'tax   ā'llta.
  houses   they made them   now.

  TakE   agiupā'yaLx   ik¡Enā'tan   ōk¡'u'nō.   Ē'xo-ē   agiupā'yaLx.   A'lta
  Then   she gathered them   potentilla   the crow.   Many   she gathered them.   Now
          much   roots

26 nai'kōtctē.   TakE   nō'yam   gō   tiō'LEma.   TakE   ā'tgaLx   ka'nauwē,
  she went across.   Then   she arrived at   supernatural   Then   they went to   all,
            beings.   the beach

27 aqēyō'kuman   itcā'k¡anatan.   Ā'ēXt   ōguē'mEskōtit   tgā'kciū,   LēXt
  they were searched   her potentilla roots.   One   [a plant]   its root,   one

LE'mōksin Lā'ksiū Lįap aqLā'x iā'xkatix·; ka aqLElā'tcax. TakE 1
[a plant]   its root find it was done   there;   then   it was eaten.   Then

wa'xwax aqā'yax itcā'kį Enatan ōkį'u'nō. Nōptcga-y- ōkį'u'nō. A'lta 2
pour out they were her potentilla roots the crow's. She went up   the crow.   Now
         done

agō'lXam ugō'tgēu: "Mxä'LuX na tê'lx·Em ka ä'mitkⁿį ikį'Enä'tan¶ 3
she said to her her niece: "You think [int.   people then you bring   potentilla roots¶
                                  part.]   them

MLōpia'Lxa Lmō'ksin. Mōpiā'Lxa ōguē'mskōtit tgä'kciū. Ka'nauwē 4
Gather it   [a plant].   Gather it   [a plant]   their roots.   All

gē'taqį Esema mtōpiā'Lxa. Manix weXt mtiā'ya itsanō'kstX 5
good smelling ones gather them.   When again you will come a small [f.]

ōLkį E'nLkįEn nai'ka mani'tkⁿįa, ōkįōnä'tan ä'luc." A'lta agō'lXam 6
oyster basket   me   bring her [it]   potentilla root it is in   Now she said to
                    to me.   it."   her

ugō'tgēu okį'u'nō: "MLō'kⁿįa XōLa Lgē'wisX; Lä'mitkEn 7
her niece   the crow's: "Take it   this   dog;   thy granddaughter

Lä'XēwusX. Ma'nix qį'oä'p mxigē'layaiē ka mLōlä'ma: 'Ē'cgam 8
her dog.   When   nearly   your land   then say to it: 'Take it

ē'kolē, Qį'aci'nEmicLx!'" Nä'k·im ōkį'unō': "Ha''ō." TakE nä'xkō-y- 9
a whale, Qį'aci'nEmicLx!'" She said   the crow: "Yes."   Then she went home

ōkį'unō'. Nō'ya, nō'ya-y· okį'u'nō. Ka kulä'yi agLō'lXam 10
the crow.   She went,   she went   the crow.   Then far   she said to it

Lgä'XēwisX: "Ē'cgam ē'kolē, Qį'aci'nEmicLx. Nau'itka na 11
her dog: "Take it a whale, Qį'aci'nEmicLx.   Indeed   [int.
                                                              part.]

imē'kickElēL ē'kolē¶" TakE aLxä'latck, ōgō'qxoiam Laqanä'itX. 12
you a catcher [of] whale¶"   Then   it rose,   in stern of canoe it stood.

TakE Läxa nē'xax ē'kolē. TakE aLgä'yaqs. A'lta lä'xElax nē'xax 13
Then   visible became a whale.   Then it bit him.   Now   roll   it did

itcā'xEnēma. "Qį'uL ē'cgam, qį'uL ē'cgam, ē'kolē, Qį'aci'nEmicLx!" 14
her canoe.   "Fast   take it,   fast   take it,   the whale, Qį'aci'nEmicLx!"

A'lta kwac nä'xax ōkį'u'nō: "Yä2c ē'xa ē'kolē, Qį'aci'nEmicLx!" 15
Now   afraid she became the crow: "Let alone do it the whale, Qį'aci'nEmicLx!"

A'lta yāc aLgä'yax ē'kolē. A'lta aLxagō'kctit. Naxä'ēgēlai 16
Now   let alone it did it the whale.   Now it lay down to sleep.   She landed

ōkį'u'no. TakE akLōnä'xLatck Lgä'xēwisX. NaxE'nkōn, kä'nauwē 17
the crow.   Then   she lost it   her dog.   She ran about,   all

t!ōLē'ma akLō'xtkin. Näkct Lįap agE'Lax. Näkct naxLxä'lEm 18
houses she searched for it.   Not   find she did it.   Not   she ate

ka naō'pōnEm. Tqįēx agE'Lax Lgä'XēwisX. 19
then it got dark.   Like   she did it   her dog.

Qoä'nEmi tiayä'kXōyaē, a'lta weXt naxa'lkįēwul. Agōpä'yaLx 20
Five times   their sleeps,   now   again   she dug many things.   She gathered it

ōguē'mskotit tgä'kcēu. AkLōpä'yaLx LEmō'ktcin Lä'kcēu. Ka'nauwē 21
[a plant]   its roots.   She gathered it   [a plant]   its roots.   All

aktōpä'yaLx gē'taqį sEma. A'lta itsanō'kstX ōLkį'E'nLkįEn agiä'lōtk 22
she gathered   good smelling ones.   Now   its smallness   an oyster basket she put into
them   it

ikį'Enä'tan. WēXt nai'kutctē ēwa tiō'LEma. Nō'yam gō tiō'LEma. 23
potentilla roots.   Again she crossed thus supernatural   She arrived at   the supernat-
                                          beings.   ural beings.

Atagä'luLX tiō'LEma ka'nauwē. A'lta aLE'tax ka'nauwē; aLE'tax 24
They went to the the supernat- all.   Now   they were   all;   they were
beach   ural beings   eaten   eaten

a'lta. Iä'xkatē mä'Lnē ka aqtä'wulᶜ. A'lta yä'mkXa ikį'Enä'tan 25
now.   There   at beach   then they were   Now   only they   potentilla roots
                                  eaten.

agä'yustX. AgE'LᶜElkEl Lgä'XEwucX. Ā'nqatē iä'xkatē wē'wuLē 26
she carried them.   She saw it   her dog.   Long ago   then   in house

Lkēx: "Mxä'LuX na tê'lx·Em Lgä'XēwisX¶ ALE'xatgō, aLE'xatgō," 27
it was: "You think   [int. people   their dog¶   It returned,   it returned,"
                       part.]

1 ago'lXam ugō'tgĕu: "Qa'daqa amLō'lXam ka mā'Lnē ka
she said to her   to her niece: "Why   did you say do it   when   at sea   then

2 Lgiŭsgā'ma ē'kolē! Gō'nitci kwac amE'xax. Qiā'X q̣oā'p ilē'ē tcx·ī
it shall take it the whale? Therefore afraid you became.   If   near   land   then

3 pōs amLō'lXam aLgiō'cgam. MxE'LaX na guā'nEsum aqLEmā'lōt?
[if]   you say to it   it takes it.   You think [int. part.] always   it was given to you?

4 ALE'xatgō, aLE'xatgō. Tatc̣ amLō'Xtkin. WĕXt mLō'k^u̧a
It returns,   it returns.   See!   you searched for it.   Again   you will carry it

5 mXgō'ya. Manĕx amLōnā'xLatcgō, näkct mLō'xtkinEma. Kaltā'2c
you will go   When   you have lost it   not   you shall search for   Only
home.   it.

6 aqamE'l^cĕm ka amE'Lok^u̧." Nā'k·im ōḳ'u'nō: "Ha''ō." TakE nā'xkō
you were given then you carried it."   She said   the crow: "Yes."   Then   she went
food   home

7 wiXt ōḳ'u'nō. AgE'Luk^u̧ qōLa Lgē'wisX. "Manix mLō'k^u̧a
again   the crow.   She carried it   that   dog.   "When   you will carry it

8 qiā'X q̣'oā'p ilē'ē tcXī amLō'lXam: 'E'cgam ē'kolē, Q̣aci'nEmicLx!'"
if   near   land   then   you say to it: 'Take it   the whale,   Q̣aci'nEmicLx!'"

9 TakE nā'xkō. Gō'qxóiam akLaqā'na-it Lgā'xĕwucX. Ā'ctō2; q̣oā'p
Then   she went   In stern   it lay   her dog.   They two   near
home   went;

10 ē'lXam! "E'cgam ē'kolē, Q̣aci'nEmicLx!" Näkct aLgiō'cgam.
the town!   'Take it   the whale,   Q̣aci'nEmicLx!'   Not   it took it.

11 AkLō'cgam Ltcuq. Wäx akLE'Lgax: "E'cgam ē'kolē, Q̣aci'nEmicLx!
She took it   water.   Pour she did it on it: "Take it   the whale,   Q̣aci'nEmicLx!

12 Nau'itka na nēmē'kickEliL!" Q̣oā'p ilē'ē takE wiXt akLo'lXam:
Indeed [int. part.] you a catcher?   Near   land   then   again   she said to it:

13 "E'cgam ē'kolē, Q̣'aci'nEmicLx!" ALxā'latck q̣'oā'p ilē'ē. A'lta
"Take it   the whale,   Q̣aci'nEmicLx!"   It rose   near   the land.   Now

14 aLgiō'cgam ē'kolē. A'lta wiXt lā'xElaxu nē'xax itcā'xEnēma.
it took it   the whale.   Now   again   rock   it did   her canoe.

15 "E2ṭ'ō'cgam ē'kolē, Q̣aci'nEmicLx. Q̣'uL ē'cgam ē'kolē,
"Hold it fast   the whale,   Q̣aci'nEmicLx.   Fast   hold it   the whale,

16 Q̣'aci'nEmicLx." E'XtEmaē ayā'xElEmamakuX: "Yāc ē'xa ē'kolē,
Q̣aci'nEmicLx."   Sometimes   she did not say to it right: "Left   do it   the whale,
                                                   alone

17 Q̣'aci'nEmicLx!" A'lta ayū'Xtkē ē'kolē iau'a mā'Lxôlē. Tca!
Q̣aci'nEmicLx!"   Now   it swam   the whale   then   landward.   Ah!

18 a'lta ā'tgELx tê'lx·Em. Ka'nauwē ā'tgELx. Aqā'yaxs ē kolē.
now   they went   the people.   All   they went to   It was cut   the whale.
to the beach   the beach.

19 Atgā'yaxs tgā'cōlal ōḳ'u'no. A'lta aqiō'Xuiptck ka'nauwē ē'kolē.
They cut it   her relatives   the crow's.   Now   it was carried up   the whole   the whale.
                                     from the shore

Iō'Lqtē aLxē'la it. TakE uē'k·im iLā'xaḳ Emāna: "Ā'nlaxta nō'ya.
A long time they stayed.   Then   he said   their chief: "I desire   I go.

21 Nō'kctama Lgā'wuX." A'lta nōxuitXuitck tiā'lXam, pāL ēXt
I shall go to see   my younger   Now   they made them-   his people.   full   one
her   sister."   selves ready

22 iā'qoa-iL ikani'm. A'lta ā'tgē. Atigō'tctamē gō tiō'LEma. TakE
large   canoe.   Now they went.   They came across   to   the supernat-   Then
                                      ural beings.

23 nē'k·im iLā'xaḳ Emāna: "Qā'ṭ ucXEm! qElxuk'uwā'kcta." Nau'itka·y-
he said   their chief: "Take care!   we shall be tried."   Indeed!

24 a'lta ikā'pa; pāL ikā'pa qīgō mā'Lnē. Atctō'lXam tiā'cōlal: "A'Lqī
now   ice;   full ice   there   at sea.   He said to them   his relatives: "Later on

25 tcaX lxaalō'Lxax." A'lta tsEs ikē'x iqē'sqēs. Nē'k·im iqē'sqēs:
we go up."   Now   cold   he was   blue-jay.   He said   blue-jay:

26 "Ka näkct tsEs nkā'tkēX. A'lta wiXt naḳā'-ita." Atcō'pEna
"Then   not   cold   I got.   Now   again I stay in the canoe."   He jumped

27 iqē'sqēs. ḶLE'pḶLEp ā'yū. TakE naLxE'lqamx LgōLē'lEXEmk
blue-jay.   Under water   he went.   Then   it shouted   a person

ē'wa   mā'Lxôlē: "Ē2hēhiū!   Lxuwā'ᵋ   ōᵋē'cᵋēc."   TakE   ayaā'lōLx   1
thus   landward: "Ehehiu!   he killed   himself   Then   he went up
                       blue-jay."

iLā'xakⱼEmāna.   Atciū'cgam   qix·   ikā'pa   ka   atciXE'kXuē.   "Ēhēhiū'4,"   2
their chief.   He took it   that   ice   then   he threw it away.   "Ehehiu!"

takE   naLxē'tqamX   LgōLē'leXEmk,   "qantsi'x·   tiō'LEma   itā'Xaqa   3
then   it shouted   a person,   "how   the supernatural   their ice
                               beings

qax·iXE'kXuē."   "'Ä'2hēhēio'2,'   msE'xatx.   AniXE'kXuē   qēwā   4
it is thrown away."   "'Ehehiu!'   you say.   I throw it away   that

anuqunā'itix·it."   A'lta   ā'Lōptck.   AcLō'lXam   iLā'xakⱼEmāna: 5
making me fall."   Now   they went up.   He said to them   their chief:

"Näkct   ai'aq   mcō'p!a!   Ā'Lqē   qixEta'qLa."   A'lta   -y-ēXt   iōc   6
"Not   quick   enter!   Later on   it will be opened."   Now   one   there
                                         was

igē'piXL   kⱼa   ē'nōL.   A'lta   ia'koa   ē'natai   igē'piXL   iōc.   ALxēnā'xit   7
sea-lion   and   sea-cow (?).   Now   here   on one side   sea-lion   there was.   They stood

gō   iqē'pal.   A'lta   tsEs   ikē'x   iqē'sqēs.   Atcō'pEna,   nē'skōp!   iqē'sqes.   8
in the doorway.   Now   cold   he got   blue-jay.   He jumped,   he ran into   blue-jay.
                                               the house

Wā4,   acgā'yaqs;   qalā'tcx·i   Laq   aqē'cxax.   A'lta   aya'ckōp!   9
Wa,   they two bit him;   almost not   take out   he was done.   Now   he entered

iLā'xakⱼEmāna.   Atciō'cgam   ia'koa-y-   ēXt,   ia'koa-y-   ēXt   kanā'mtEma.   10
their chief.   He took him   here   one,   here   one   in both hands.

A'lta   atcXE'kXuē.   "Ēhēhiū',"   naLxē'lqEmX   LgōLē'leXEmk.   11
Now   he threw them away,   "Ehehiu,"   it shouted   a person.

"'Ä'2hēhiō','   msE'xatx.   AntcXE'kXuē   acgā'naqs."   A'lta   ā'Lōp!   12
"'Ehehiu','   you say.   I throw them two   them two who   Now   they en-
                         away   bit me."   tered

ka'nauwē,   gō   wē'wuLē   aLxē'la-it.   Kⱼam   tē'lx·Em.   A'mkXa   kaX   13
all,   in interior of house   they stayed.   No   people.   Only she   that

uyā'lē   iLā'xakⱼEmāna.   "I'kta   Lx   āqilxangē'waLⱼ'amita,   kā'sa-it?"   14
his sister   their chief.   "What   may   be given to us to eat,   robin!"

"Hō'ntcin   ēmilqⱼ'ēlatcXita,"   nē'k·im   kā'sa-it.   TakE   nē'k·im   iqē'sqēs: 15
"Don't!   be quiet!"   he said   robin.   Then   he said   blue-jay:

"Ä'kaLx   ntcā'xakⱼEmāna   guā'nEsum   tumm   uyā'qXalEptckiX."   16
"Thus may   our chief   always   noise   his fire."

ĒXtka-y-   ē'mᵋEcX   yuqunā'itX   gō   wē'wuLē.   TakE   naLxE'lqamX   17
One only   log   there lay   in   the interior of   Then   it shouted
                                     the house.

LgōLē'leXEmk: "SEkEmā'Lx   siā'mist   asx·Elā'qs."   A'lta   aLa'cgEmaLx   18
a person: "Come down to the   his mouth   splitting wood   Now   it came down to
           fire   [dual.]"   the fire

iLā'mict   iū'ktⱼit.   A'lta   tsⱼE'xtsⱼEx   aLgā'yax   x·ix·   ē'mᵋEcX.   19
its mouth   long.   Now   split   it did it   that   log.

"Kā'sa-it,"   takE   nē'k·im   iqē'sqēs,   "qē'wa   itxā'qacqac   kⱼa   wiXt   20
"Robin,"   then   he said   blue-jay,   "that   our grandfather   and   again

iā'qacqac   iā'laitix·."   "TEnlā'xo-ix   na   tgE'eltgēu?   Mā'mka   21
his grandfather   his slave."   "I know them   [int. part.]   my slaves?   You only

tEmē'ltgēu."   TakE   nacxE'lgiLx.   A'lta   tXut   nō'xôx.   "CikEmā'Lx,   22
your slaves."   Then   they made fire.   Now   smoke   it got.   "Come down to the
                                            fire.

eXtē'kc."   "Kā'sa-it,"   take   atciō'lXam   iqⱼ'ē'sqⱼēs,   "ia'xka   qēwa   23
smoke-eater."   "Robin,"   then   he said to him   blue-jay.   "he   that

itxā'laitix·.   Qēwa   nai'ka   atcnō'stXulalEma-itx,   kⱼa   mai'ka   24
our [dual] slave.   That   me   he always carried me,   and   you

ktcmōptcā'lalEma-itx."   "Tenlā'xo·ix   na   tgE'eltgēu?   Mā'mka   25
he always led you by the hand."   "I know   [int. part.]   my slaves?   You only

tEmē'eltgēu."   TakE   ā'LELx,   gōyē'   iā'qa-iL   iLā'wan.   TakE   aLō'La-itX   26
your slaves."   Then   he went down   thus   large   his belly.   Then   he stayed
                     to the fire.

gō   kā'tcEk   t!'ōL.   TakE   ā'Lax   llll,   aLktā'wulᵋ   tXut.   Tuwā'X   nō'xôx   27
in   middle of   the house.   Then   he did   llll,   he ate it   the smoke.   Light   it became

1 t!ōL. TakE aqcō'cgam c^came̅'kcucX. A'ltā iaqkEnā'itX ēXt-
the house. Then it was taken a small canoe. Now there lay one

2 iā'kiLqḁ"p. "Kā'sa-it," takE nē'k·im iqē'sqēs, "qḁ'axtsē-y- i'kta
cut. "Robin," then he said blue-jay, "too little what

3 x·ix· aqĭlxElā'xō. Ā'Lqē LxEnukstā'ya." "CikEmā'Lx siā'mEstk
this we shall eat. Later on I shall not have "Come down to his mouth
enough." the fire [dual]

4 sxElgē'xs." Ā'LiLx LgōLē'lEXEmk. Iā'kḁēsiL iLā'mict. A'lta
cutting meat." He went down a person. Sharp [m.] its mouth. Now
to the fire

5 aLxa'lgixc, aLxa'lgixc, aLxa'lgixc. Pā2L acE'xax qōcta s^came̅'kcuc.
it cut meat, it cut meat, it cut meat. Full got [dual] that [dual] small canoe.

6 TakE pō aqE'ctāx qōcta s^came̅'kcuc. TakE ayūgō'Litx·it iā'qoa·iL
Then blown it was on that [dual] small canoe. Then he made it stay large
them [dual]

7 x·ix· ikanĭ'm; pāL ē'kolē. A'lta aqiō'tcXam ē'kolē. A'lta qḁoā'p
that canoe; full whale. Now it was boiled the whale. Now nearly

8 ayō'ktcikt ē'kolē. TakE aLō'pa ka'nauwē, takE atcō'cgam ō'pakuē.
it was finished the whale. Then they went all, then he took them reeds.
out

9 TakE atcaLā'lax gō-y- L'LaLqL ēwā'-y- ōLā'pōtc Lāx ō'pakuē
Then he put into them in their mouths thus their anus out reeds

10 kanauwē'tiks k!a iqē'sqēs. TakE aLō'p!am, a'Lōp! weXt. Iā'xkati
all persons and blue-jay. Then they came in, they entered again. There

11 aLō'La-itX, ia'xkati LE'kLEk aLgiā'x ilē'ē. A'lta aLxLxā'lEm.
they remained, there burrow they did it the Now they ate.
ground.

12 ALgiā'wul^ax, nau'i yawa Lā'xa nē'xax ēwa-y- uLā'pōtc, ka'nauwē-y-
They swallowed it, immedi- there visible it became thus their anus, all
ately

13 ē'ka. Atciā'wul^ iqē'sqēs. Ayō'tXuit. Iawā' yuqunā'itX uyā'potc.
thus. He swallowed it blue-jay. He stood up. There it lay its anus.

14 "Tca! kā'sa-it! x·ix·ĭ'x· ēwa-y- ōgu'pōtc ayō'lEktcū." Aqiō'cgam
"Look! robin! this thus my anus it fell down." He was taken

15 iqē'sqēs iā'potē, aqā'yuk^uI k^uLā'xani. Laq aqā'ēxax kaX ō'pakuē.
blue-jay his arm, he was carried outside. Out they were done these reeds.

16 A'lta wiXt a'ctōp! iā'xakḁEmāna. Gōnitsē Lōni atcLō'tipa ka
Now again they two his chief. Therefore [?] three he dipped and
went in times

17 ayā'qstē. A'lta nōxo-iLxā'lEm qōtac tê'lx·Em. MEnnx· nē'xax qix·
he was satia- Now they ate those people. Little got that
ted.

18 ē'kolē. TakE atctō'ktcpa tiā'lEXam. A'lta Lu'XLuX atcō'xōx
whale. Then he took them outside his people. Now pull out he did them

19 ka'nauwē'2 ō'pakuē. A'lta wiXt ā'tgEp!. A'lta weXt noxo-iLxā'lEm,
all the reeds. Now again they entered. Now again they ate,

20 cka qḁ'oē'L atgE'qcte, ka atgiā'wul^ itā'tcXemal. TakE
and in right way they became then they ate all what they had Then
satiated, cooked.

21 naLxE'lqamX LgōLē'lEXEmk! "Ē2hēhiũ'2! qantsī'2x·Lx· tiō'LEma
it shouted a person! "Ēhēhiu! how then the supernat-
ural beings

22 itā'tcXEmal kḁa aqē'tctXōm." A'lta iqē'sqēs nē'k·im: "Qa'da Lx
what they had and it is finished." Now blue-jay he said: "How then
boiled

23 pōs nēkst aniō'tctXōm qix· aqēnEl^cē'm!"
if not I finish it that I was given to eat!"

A'lta aLxē'la-it gō wē'wuLē. A'lta ayō'pa iqē'sqēs, kḁ'Ex ikē'x.
Now they stayed in the interior of Now he went blue-jay, over- he was.
the house. out satiated

25 A'lta gō'yi nē'xax iqē'sqēs. A'lta L^cē'caLx acLpā'Ll. A'lta
Now thus he did blue-jay. Now [a berry] all red. Now

26 nixLxā'lEm iqē'sqēs. "LXuā'2, ōcē'scēs, qantsī'2xLx tiō'LEma
he ate it blue-jay. "Lxuā! blue-jay, how then the supernat-
ural beings

itā'ētitk kᵢa agxē'tx." A'lta nē'k·inı iqᵢē'sqēs: "'Ä2hähähäyō''   1
their excrements   and   he eats them."   Now   he said   blue-jay   "'Ehehiu!'

msE'xatx. Lnxä'lax na! Ka'ltas nLō'kuman Lik Lᶜē'caLx."   2
you say.   I eat [int. part.]?   Only   I look at them   these   berries."

Kā aLxēlā'-it. TakE Lāx aLi'xax LgōLē'lEXEmk. "Ā,   3
Then   they remained.   Then   visible   it became   a person.   "Ah,

mcktē'mEnᶜa. Qamcaxoē'mōL." "TcXä2, antcktē'mEnᶜa-itx gō   4
you dive!   It is desired a game with you."   "Tcxä2,   we always dive   in

intcā'lEXam," nē'k·im iqē'sqēs. "Ka'nauwē Lᶜ̣aLā'ma   5
our town,"   he said   blue-jay.   "All   days

anktctē'mEnᶜa-itx." "Mxä'LuX na-y- ē'ka gō ilxä'lEXam?" akLō'lXam   6
we always dive."   "You think [int. part.]   thus as   in   our town?"   she said to them

uLā'cinEma-iL, "mxä'LuX na-y- ē'ka lxai'ka? NōguLᵢē'mEnᶜax   7
their woman married among a foreign tribe,   "you think [int. part.]   thus as   we?   They dive

amō'kctiks, Lā'xka aLō'mEqtx, Lā'xka aqLō'Lᶜax." TakE agiō'lXam   8
two,   that one   is dead,   that one   he has lost."   Then   she said to him

iqē'sqēs: "Ā, iqē'sqēs, ikLe'mEnᶜ." TakE ā'yuLx, iqᵢ'ē'sqēs,   9
blue-jay: "Ā   blue-jay,   he is a diver."   Then   he went to the beach,   blue-jay,

atcuXō'kXuē tLā'Xilkuē gō Ltcuq. A'lta cXumgē'tga   10
he threw them away   their bushes in the bottom of the canoe   into   water.   Now   they two played together

ōkᵢ'ōnasi'si kᵢa iqē'sqēs. A'lta ackLᵢē'mEnᶜ. Atcō'pcut uyā'tamqᵢ'aL   11
[a bird; diver]   and   blue-jay.   Now   they two dived.   He hid it   his club

iqē'sqēs. A'lta ackLᵢē'mEnᶜ, ē 4. Nē'ntctXōm iqᵢ'ē'sqēs. Lāxa   12
blue-jay.   Now   they two dived,   eh!   His breath gave out   blue-jay.   Visible

nē'xax gō qō'ta tLā'Xilkuē. Nige'Lōtk gō qō'ta tgē'lEkuēl;   13
he became   at   those   their bushes in the bottom of the canoe.   He breathed   at   those   bushes in the bottom of the canoe;

weXt niktē'mEnᶜ. Atcō'lXam ō'kᵢ'ōnasi'si: "Mōc na?" "Nōc,"   14
again   he dived.   He said to her   the diver: "You are there   [int. part.]?"   "I am,"

agiō'lXam. Lē'lē ka wiXt nē'ntctXōm. WiXt Lāxa nē'xax   15
she said to him.   Long   then   again   his breath gave out.   Again   visible   he became

gō qōta tLā'Xilkuē. TakE la'kti Lāxa nē'xax. A'lta tEll   16
at   those   their bushes in the bottom of the canoe.   Then   four times   visible   he became.   Now   tired

nē'xax iqē'sqēs. A'lta atcō'kctam ōkᵢ'ōnasi'si. A'lta agiä'qct ilē'ē,   17
he became   blue-jay.   Now   he went to look for her   the diver.   Now   she bit it   the ground.

A'lta sänpōt. Lāqᵘ ä'tcax ōyā'tamqᵢ'aL. AtcagE'lltcim yukpā'.   18
Now   she closed her eyes.   Out   he did it   his club.   He struck her   right here!

Kā ōxoēlā'-itix· tē'lx·Em ka aLuXuä'nitck LgōLē'lEXEmk: "La'xka   19
Where   they were   people   then   it drifted   a person: "That one

ēcᶜē'c," nELxE'lqamX LgōLē'lEXEmk. Iâ2c gō tgē'lEkuē, Mank   20
blue-jay,"   shouted   a person.   He was   at   the bushes in the bottom of the canoe.   A little

lē'lē ka atcō'pEna iqē'sqēs mā'Lxôlē "Ēhēhiū'2, qantsī'2x·Lx   21
long while   then   he jumped   blue-jay   ashore.   "Ehehiu!   how then

tiō'LEma ō'takᵢ'anasi'si ka aqaxā'tkakō!" "'Ä2hähähiū'2'   22
the supernatural beings   their diver   then   he is beaten!"   "'Ehehiū''

msE'xax, tcx·ī antskLᵢē'mEnᶜax gō intsā'lEXam," nē'k·im iqē'sqēs.   23
you say,   then   we dive   in   our town,"   he said   blue-jay.

TakE wiXt Lāx aLi'xax LgōLē'lEXEmk. "Qamcaxoē'mōL, mcō-   24
Then   again   visible   it became   a person.   "It is desired a game with you,   you

ē'walx·tEma." TakE nē'k·im iqē'sqēs: "Ka'nauwē Lᶜ̣aLā'ma   25
will climb up."   Then   he said   blue-jay: "All   days

1 antcō-ē'walx·tema-itx   gō   intcā'lEXam."   TakE   akLō'lXam
we always climb up   in   our town."   Then   she said to them

2 uLā'cinEma-iL: "Mcxä'Lax   na   -y-ē'ka   natē'tanuē?   Ikā'pa
their woman married   "You think   [int. part.] thus as   Indians?   Ice
to a foreign tribe·

3 aqexē'nxax   ka   ya'xka   aqik͇Xēwulxax.   Manix   aLuē'luktcax
is placed upright and   that   they climb it.   When   one falls down

4 Lu'kLuk   aLxā'x   ka   aqLō'LᶜAx."   TakE   aqiō'lXam   iqē'sqĕs:
broken   he gets   and   he has lost."   Then   he was spoken to   blue-jay:

5 "Qā'doXuē   iqē'qĕs   iō'iwulx·ta."   TakE   aqiō'tXEmt   ikā'pa,   gō
"Must   blue-jay   he goes up."   Then   it was placed upright the ice,   to

6 igō'cax   qoā't   ā'yaLqt.   TakE   nēXE'k·il   iqē'sqēs;   nix·Lx·ā'nakō
sky   thus   long.   Then   he tied the blan- blue-jay;   he put it on
                                                            ket around his waist

7 iā'itcxōt.   TakE   naxE'ltXuitck   ō'tṣ'ikin.   Ā'lta   actōiLxē'wulx·.
his bearskin   Then   she made herself   the chipmunk.   Now   they [dual] went
blanket.   ready   climbing up.

8 A'ctō,   ā'ctō,   ā'ctō,   ā'ctō.   Kulā'yi   kᵘcā'xali   actō'yam.   TakE   tEll
They   they went, they went, they went.   Far   up   they [dual] ar-   Then   tired
[dual] went,   rived.

9 nē'xax   iqē'sqēs.   Ayō'kux   mank   kᵘsā'xali   ka   wiXt   atciucgā'maxē.
he became   blue-jay.   He flew   a little   up   and   again   he took hold of it.

10 TakE   tEll   nē'xax.   AtciagEnā'nakō-y-   ōyā'tuwanXa.   A'lta   sā'npōt,
Then   tired   he got.   He looked back to her   the one he was   Now   she closed
                                                                      racing against.   her eyes,

11 guā'nEsum   ō'itEt,   ka   nikct   tEll   agā'tkax.   Atcō'gam   takE
always   she came,   and   not   tired   she became.   He took it   then

12 uyā'tamqi̭'aL,   yukpā'   atcā'owilX.   TakE   nōē'luktcū   ō'tṣl'ikin.   Ka
his club,   right here   he struck her.   Then   she fell down   the chipmunk.   And

13 yukuguē'kxamt   tê'lx·Em.   TakE   aqā'LᶜElkEl   LgōLē'lEXEmk
they looked up   the people.   Then   it was seen   a person

14 Lōē'luktcūt.   "Lā'xka   ē'cᶜĕc.   TakE   naLkᵘtcuwā'mam."   TakE
falling down.   "That one   blue-jay.   Then   she fell down."   Then

15 naLxE'lqamX   LgōLē'lEXEmk: "Ē2hēhiū'2,   qantsi'2x·Lx   tiō'LEma
it shouted   a person: "Ehehiû!   how then   the supernat-
                                                                                       ural beings

16 ō'tatṣl'ikin   aqaxā'tgagō."   "'Ē2hēhiū','   msE'xatx.   Tcx·ī   na
their chipmunk   is beaten."   "'Ehehiû!,'   you say.   Then   [int.
                                                                                                part.]

17 antcukuLxē'wulx·La-itx   gō   intcā'lEXam?"   TakE   môkct   ēlā'kētēma
we climb always   in   our town?"   Then   two   sea-otters

18 atcā'yul   iLā'Xakᵢ̭Emāna.
he won them   their chief.

A'lta   wiXt   mankx   aLxē'la-it.   TakE   wiXt   aLtē'mam
Now   again   a little   they stayed.   Then   again   it came

20 Lgō'Lē'lEXEmk: "Qamcaxoē'mōL.   Wā'qi̭pas   qamcaxoē'mōL."
a person: "It is desired a game   Target   it is desired a game
                          with you.   with you."

21 "Tcx·ī   na   wā'qi̭pas   ntsxcgā'liL   gō   intcā'lEXam   ka'nauwē
"Then   [int. part.] target   we always play   in   our town   all

22 LᶜaLā'ma,"   nē'k·im   iqē'sqĕs.   TakE   akLō'lXam   uLā'cinEma-iL:
days,"   he said   blue-jay.   Then   she said to them   their woman married
                                                                                          among a foreign tribe:

23 "Mcxä'2LuX   na   -y-ē'ka   natē'tanuē?   Têlx·ā'm   aqōxoēlā'-itEmitx
"You think   [int. part.] thus as   Indians?   People   are placed

24 amô'kctiks,   ē'wa   ē'natai   Lē'Xat,   ēwa   ē'natai   Lē'Xat.   Lā'xka
two,   thus   at one side   one,   thus   at other side one.   That one

25 Lā'nēwa   aLō'mEqt,   Lā'xka   aqLō'Li̭Eq."   Aqiō'lXam   iqoa-inē'nē:
first   dead,   that one   has lost."   He was spoken to   the beaver:

26 "Mai'ka   qEmuLā'ētEmita."   Aqō'cgam   utcā'la,   aqa-igē'kxōl.
"You   you are made to stand up."   It was taken   a grindstone.   it was put on him

27 iā'wan   utcā'la.   Ē'wa   iā'kōtcX   aēXt,   ē'wa   iā'wan   aē'Xt.
his belly   the grindstone.   Thus   his back   one,   thus   his belly   one.

AqēuLā'ētamit   ē'wa   ē'natai   iqō'Lqōlalē.   A'lta   acktō'cgam   1
He was made to stand up   thus   on one side   loon.   Now   they two took them

ctā'xalaitan.   Iā'maɛ   aqē'lax   iqoa-inē'nē.   LuX   nuLā'tax·it   ōkulai'tan.   2
their [dual] ar-   Shooting   he was   the beaver.   Broken   it fell down   the arrow.
rows.   him   done

Iā'maɛ   aqē'lax   iqō'Lqōlalē.   Ūhū'2   uē'xax.   WiXt   iā'maɛ   3
Shooting   he was done   the loon.   Ūhū'2   he made.   Again   shooting him
him

aqē'lax   iqoa-inē'nē.   Hä   nē'xax.   LuX   nuLā'taXit   kaX   ōkulai'tan.   4
he was done   the beaver.   Hä   he made.   Broken   it fell down   that   arrow.

Iā'maɛ   aqē'lax   iqō'Lqōlalē.   Ūhū'2   nē'xax.   Iā'xkēwa   ka   nicilgā'kxo-it   5
Shooting   he was   the loon.   Ūhū'2   he made.   There   then   he fell on his
him   done   back

ayō'maqt.   "Ēhēhiū'2,   qantsī'x·Lx   tiō'LEma   Lgā'lalax   aqLxā'tgagō!"   6
he was dead.   "Ebehiū',   how then   the supernat-   their bird   he is beaten!"
    ural beings

"'Ēhēhiū'2,'   msE'xatx,"   nē'k·im   iqē'sqēs;   "tcx·ī   na   wā'qɪ'pas   7
"'Ebehiū'',   you say,"   he said   blue-jay;   "recently   [int.   target
    part.]

ntsxsgā'liL   gō   intcā'lExam?"   8
we always play   in   our town?"

A'lta   wiXt   aLxē'la-it,   mank   iō'Lqtē   aLxēla-it.   TakE   wiXt   Lāx   9
Now   again   they stayed,   a little   long   they stayed.   Then   again   come
    out

aLi'xax   Lgōlē'lEXEmk.   TakE,   "Āqamcaxoē'mōl,   mcxalō'tga   10
it did   a person.   Then,   "It is desired a game   you will sweat
    with you,

ōqolō'tqan."   TakE   nē'k·im   iqē'sqēs: "Ka'nauwē   Lɛalā'ma   11
sweat house."   Then   he said   blue-jay: "All   days

antcxalō'tcElxēma-itx   gō   intcā'lExam."   TakE   akLō'lXam   12
we always sweat   in   our town."   Then   she said to them

uLā'cinEma-iL: "Tqānā'ks   aqauwē'kiLXaX.   AtgE'ckō-itxax   ka   13
their woman married   "Rocks   are heated.   They get warm   and
among a foreign tribe:

yā'xkati   atgE'p!x.   Tā'cka   nuxō'La-itx   tā'cka   aqtō'Lɛax."   A'lta   14
there   they enter.   Those   they are dead   those   have lost."   Now

nē'k·im   iLā'xakɪEmāna: "Qa'doXuē   lxō'Lxaiō."   A'lta   aqauwē'kiLX   15
he said   their chief: "Must   we go into the   Now   they were heated
    cave."

qō'tā   tqā'naks.   TakE   atqE'cko-itx.   Môkct   Lxoa'p   qō'ta   tqā'naks.   16
those   rocks.   Then   they got warm.   Two   holes   those   rocks.

A'lta   ēXti   naLxoa'p   ā'Lōp!   La'ska.   A'lta   ēXti   naLxoa'p   ā'Lōp!   17
Now   one   hole   they en-   they.   Now   one   hole   they en-
    tered   tered

tiō'LEma.   A'lta   aqiō'xōpō.   TakE   atciō'cgam   ikā'pa   atciōtcē'na   gō   18
the supernat-   Now   it was shut.   Then   he took it   ice   he laid it under   in
ural beings.   them

qō'ta   tqā'naks.   A'lta   ia'xka   aLigā'la-it.   Cka   ma'nx·i   ka   dEll, dEll,   19
those   rocks.   Now   it   they stood on it.   And   a little   and   noise of burst-
    ing,

qoä'nEmi   dEll   nē'xau.   TakE   aqiuxō'laqɪ   tqā'naks.   AqiLxā'laqL   20
five times   noise of   it was.   Then   they were opened   the rocks.   It was opened
    bursting

iqē'sqēs   Lā'nēwatiks;   Lka'nauwētiks   iLā'Xanatē.   Aqiōxō'laqL   21
blue-jay   first;   all of them   they were alive.   It was opened

tiō'LEma.   Aqoä'nEmiks   nuxō'Lā-it.   WeXt   nē'k·iL.   "Ēhēhiū'2!   22
the supernat-   Five of them   were dead.   Again   they won.   "Ehehiū'
ural beings.

qantsi'x·Lx   tiō'LEma   aqōxō'tgagō!"   "'Ēhēhiū','   msE'xatx!   Tcx·i   23
how then   the supernat-   are beaten!"   "'Ebehiū','   you say.   Then
    ural people

antsxalō'tElkEma-itx   gō   intcā'lEXam."   24
we always sweat   in   our town."

TakE atciō'lXam iā'kxix: "Tca! ikolē'ma wax lxLigElā'xō."
Then he said to him to his brother-in-law: "Come! whales pour we will do them."

2 TakE aklō'lXam uLā'cinEma-iL: " Qā'd'ōcXEm, mcXEna'oi.
Then she said to them their woman married among a foreign tribe: "Take care, look out!

3 Amcgiūk¡'oē'masamita imcā'xak¡'Emāna ka mcā'k¡ lEmatckō-y- a'lta."
You will make him ashamed your chief and you do the last now."

4 Agiō'lXam itcā'xk¡'un: "A'lta pō'2lakli, wāx aqE'Lax." Iō'kuk
She said to him her elder brother: "Now dark, pour it is done." Then

5 agā'yutk iqē'sqēs gō itcā'XEmalap!iX. Ia'koa ē'natai agā'yutk
she put him blue-jay in her armpit. There on other side she put him

6 kā'sa-it, ia'koa tc¡iqi'nk¡ēama agā'yutk. "Nēkct qa'nsix
robin, there on right side she put him. "Not [any] how

7 mgē'ma 'Ēhēhiū'!' Manix yamō'tga, nēkct qa'nsix mtgē'kcta
you say 'Ēhehiū!' When I hold you, not [any] how you [dual] look

8 amtkanamtEmō'kct." A'lta ā'LōLx pō'lakli gō qix· ē'maL.
both of you." Now they went to the beach at dark to that bay.

9 Agiō'lXam itcā'xk¡'un: "La'kt ēkolē'ma iō'ya, näkct milkē'kᵘca.
She said to him her elder brother: "Four whales they go, not harpoon them.

10 Ē'Laquinum ē'kolē iō'ya, tcx·ī amLē'lukc̓ax." TakE nōxuinā'Xit
The fifth whale goes, then harpoon him." Then they stood

11 tiō'LEma. AkLō'cgam Lk¡ē'wax kaX uyā'lē, agigElgē'cgam
the supernatural beings. She took it a torch that his sister, she helped him

12 itcā'xk¡'un. TakE nELxE'lqamX LgōLē'LEXEmk: " Yūyayūyā'4!
her elder brother. Then it shouted a person: "Yuyayuyā!

13 Ē'minᶜa ē'kolē x·iau iō'ya," Lē'Xat qō'La LgōLēlEXEmk nELxElqamX.
[A fish] whale that he goes," one that person shouted.

14 Lä'lē ka weXt nELxE'lqamX: "Yūyayuyā',·y· itā'mEla-y-
Sometime then again it shouted: "Yuyayuyā', albatross

15 ē'kōlē x·iau iōyā'! AmckLxē'latck LEmcātcō'L." Qē'xtcē nē'k·ikst
whale that he goes! Raise them your harpoon shafts!" Intend he looked

16 iqē'sqēs. TcXup tcXup tcXup tcXup tcXup aLE'xax Lā'k¡ēwax.
blue-jay. Flicker it did the torch.

17 Gōyi' agā'yax iqē'sqēs: "Nēkct Lgā'tgilkct." TakE weXt
Thus she did him blue-jay: "Not look." Then again

18 nELxE'lqamX LgōLē'lEXEmk: "Yuyayuyā', ēmō'lak ē'kolē
it shouted a person: "Yuyayuyā', elk whale

19 x·iau iōyā! MckLxē'latck LEmcātcō'L." WēXt naLxE'lqamX
that he goes! Raise them your harpoon shafts!" Again it shouted

20 LgōLē'lEXEmk: "Yūyayuyā', imō'kᵘtXi-y- ē'kolē x·iau iōyā'.
a person: "Yūyayuyā', sperm whale whale that he goes!

21 MckLxē'latck LEmcātcō'L." TakE agiō'lXam uyā'lē:
Raise them your harpoon shafts!" Then she said to him his elder sister:

22 "Qā't'ōcXEm! A'lta ia'xka itiā'ya." TakE wiXt nELxE'lqamx
"Look out! Now he he will come." Then again it shouted

23 LgōLē'lEXEmk: "Yūyayūyā', tiō'LEma itā'kolē x·iau iōyā'!"
a person: "Yuyayuyā, the supernatural beings their whale that goes!"

24 Qē'xtcē nē'ki·kst iqē'sqēs; tcXup tcXup tcXup tcXup aLE'xax
Intend he looked blue-jay; flicker it did

25 Lā'k¡'ēwax. "Qantsī'x·Lx AnēktcXō'lEmiX Lgā'k¡'ēwax ka
the torch. "How may AnēktcXō'lEmiX her torch and

26 aLxatᶜmā'nEnuk⊣." A'lta nē'k·im qō'La LgōLē'lEXEmk:
it always flickers." Now he said that person:

27 "Yūyayuyā'; tiō'LEma itā'kolE x·iau iōyā'!" Agiō'lXam
"Yuyayuyā; the supernatural beings their whale that goes!" She said to him

28 itcā'xk¡'un: "A'lta ia'xka itiā'ya." AtcLē'lukc itcā'xk¡'un.
her elder brother: "Now that one he will come." He harpooned it her elder brother.

Atcē′xaluketgō mǎ′Lxôlē: "Ēhehiū′2, qantsī′x·Lx tiō′LEma itǎ′kolē 1
He threw it down landward: "Ehēhiū, how then the supernatural beings their whale

ka aqēLxatēmǎ′ptck." TakE nē′k·im iqē′sqēs: "Ēhēhiū′!" TcXup 2
and it is thrown ashore." Then he said blue-jay: "Ehēhiū." Extinguished

ǎ′Lax Lǎ′k¡ēwax. L¡la′pL¡lap ǎ′yō iqē′sqēs. TakE ayō′Xōnē 3
it became the torch. Under water he went blue-jay. Then he drifted away

iqē′sqēs WeXt aLE′k·iL. Nǎ′k·iL weXt iLǎ′xak¡′Emǎna. 4
blue-jay. Again they won. He won again their chief.

A′lta aLi′xkō. AkLō′lXam uLǎ′cinEma-iL: "x·ix·ī′k ē′Lan 5
Now they went home. She said to them their woman married among a foreign tribe: "This rope

mcgīakXat¡′ō′ya! Manix mcigō′tctamai, k¡′au mcgiǎ′xo kǎ′sa-it 6
coil up in canoe! When you will get across, tie do to it robin

iǎ′ōk." A′ltā aqē′Lgax ēitcxǎ′x qigō aLi′xkō. A′lta aqcǎ′kXatEq 7
his blanket." Now it was made against them a storm where they went home. Now it was put on the edge of the canoe

gō Liǎ′aLxap′ukc ikanī′m, ka aqē′Lgax ēitcxǎ′x; Lē2qc puc aLxE′la-it 8
on its gunwale canoe, and it was made against them a storm; almost if they were dead

ka aLigō′tctam. 9
and they came across.

Translation.

There was a town the chief of which had died. His two children were grown up; one was a girl and one a boy. Early every morning the people went out to hunt sea-otters. The girl was always in the stern of the canoe. At dark they returned home. Five times they had gone hunting, then it grew foggy. Her hair became wet and she swallowed the water which dripped down from her hair. A long time the people remained there. Then she became pregnant. Blue-Jay was the first to observe it. He said: "Don't you notice it? He made his sister pregnant." Robin said: "Be quiet, Blue-Jay, you will make our chief's children ashamed." "Ha, he is the elder of us two and he ought to know better than I." After some time she became stouter. "Heh, we will run," said Blue-Jay. "I am ashamed because her brother made her pregnant. We will leave them; we will move!" Then, indeed, the people believed Blue-Jay. Again the brother and sister went hunting sea-otters. In the evening they came home. Now there were no people and no houses. "Lo, they deserted us. Blue-Jay advised them to do so." Then the brother continued: "Tell me who made you pregnant?" She replied, "I do not know. Once when we went out hunting sea-otters a mist came up and I swallowed the water which made me qualmish." Then they searched for fire. But the people had poured water into all the fires. The last house was that of their aunt, the Crow. It also was taken away. They walked about and there they heard the crackling of fire. The brother said to his sister: "Do you hear the fire?" After awhile it crackled again. They found the place from where the sound appeared to come. They dug into the ground and found a shell. In the shell there was burning coal. "Oh," they said to each other, "our aunt pitied us; she put the fire into the shell for us." Now they started a fire. The next day they built a small house. There they lived for a long time. One day a sea breeze arose. Early in the morning the man rose and went down to the beach. There he found ten cedar planks, each ten fathoms long, which had drifted ashore. He went up to the house and said to his sister: "I have found ten planks, each ten fathoms long." They went to the beach, hauled them up to their house, and the brother made a large house. Then the brother said: "What kind of a blanket will you make for your son?" In the morning he went down to the beach and there he found two small sea-otters. He said: "Oh, my poor nephew, this will be your blanket." He took them up to the house and said to his sister: "I found these sea-otters." Then she was very glad. The brother said: "What soup are you going to make for your son?" In the morning he arose and went down to the beach. There he found a sea-lion. He skinned it and cut it, and then they boiled it. Every day he went down to the beach, and every time he found two sea-otters. And their house was full of sea-otter skins. One morning he went to the beach; there was a whale. Then he ran back to his sister and cried: "A whale is on the beach!" His sister said in reply: "Every night the people on the other side of the ocean send us food. Those supernatural people love me. My boy's father came. Now cut the whale." Then he skinned it and cut it and they carried up the meat.

Now the Crow made herself ready to look for her nephew and her niece. She launched her canoe and paddled across, wailing all the time. When she had almost crossed the bay she discovered a house and saw smoke rising. She went on. When she was near the shore she saw a chief sitting on the roof of the house. [The latter said to his sister, when he saw the Crow coming:] "Our aunt who pitied us is coming there." She arrived and saw the whale on the beach. She [was very hungry,] went to the whale and pulled at the meat. Then her nephew said: "Come up to the house; why do you touch that rotten meat?" She replied: "Oh, I only looked at it," and went up to the house. She entered and saw that it was full of whale meat. She went right up to the child [and wanted to take it in her arms], but the child began to cry. The sister said: "Oh, he is afraid of your tears." They gave her water and she washed her face. Then she tried again to take him, but still he cried. The sister said: "He is afraid of your breath." Then she took water, cleaned her mouth and took him again, but still he cried. Then the sister said to her aunt: "Do you think he is a human being? Look here, he is the son of a supernatural being. They gave us that whale to eat." "Oh," said the Crow. They boiled whale meat for her and she ate it. After she had finished eating she went home. They gave her two pieces of blubber which she put into her mat.

The Crow went across the bay; and when she approached the town she cried: "O, my sister's children, my sister's children, birds flew up from you many times; eagles were eating you. O, my sister's children, my sister's children, gulls were eating you. Ravens were eating you, O, my sister's children." Now she came still nearer the town. Blue-Jay was sitting outside and saw her coming. When she had nearly arrived she cried again: "O, my sister's children, my sister's children, birds flew up from you; crows were eating you." Then Blue-Jay shouted: "Do you not notice? She names the Crow; she names the Crow." Now she landed and went up to the house. Now all the people came into the Crow's house. They asked her how she had found her sister's children. She replied and told much. "I went across and I found their bodies full of birds which ate them. All kinds of birds ate them." After she had finished, Blue-Jay was the first to leave the house. He went to the rear of the house, where he stayed. Now, the Crow was silent. Robin, who was her deceased husband's brother, remained with her. They sat on opposite sides of the fire. She had five children. Then she told him everything in a low voice, and Blue-Jay listened outside. She pulled out the food which she had carried home, cut it to pieces, and gave it to her children and to Robin. Her youngest daughter choked [when eating the blubber]. Then Blue-Jay, who had been peeping through the chinks of the wall, entered and slapped her nape. The piece of whale meat flew out of her mouth. Blue-Jay took it up, went out, showed it to the people, and said: "Do you see? The Crow fed me." He went to three houses showing it around, then he ate it. After some time it grew dark. The people were very hungry.

Then Blue-Jay said to the chief of the town: "O, chief, the house [of the young man whom we deserted] is full of whale meat. A supernatural being loved his sister. He invites me, and he has invited the Crow and Robin." Late in the evening Blue-Jay came out of the house, took his large blanket [and went to his elder brother, Robin,] saying, "Robin, let us sleep under one blanket; I always get cold." Robin replied: "Ya-a, I always sleep alone, and do not want anyone with me; sleep there at my feet." Now Blue-Jay lay down at Robin's feet. Blue-Jay remained awake. When it was nearly morning Blue-Jay fell asleep. Now Robin and Crow made a canoe [ready]. Then Robin and the Crow went to their canoe and carried their property into it. Now Robin took a sharp stick and put it in the ground at Blue-Jay's feet. Then Robin and the Crow went across to the young man and to his sister, and left Blue-Jay alone. Early in the morning when he awoke, he said: "Wake up, Robin," and kicked him; but his feet struck the stick, and he hurt himself. "O, my feet!" he cried. "They left me here alone." Then he went home to his children. Crow and Robin crossed the bay and went up to the house of the young man.

Early next morning Blue-Jay said: "Now, let us all go across." They made themselves ready and went across. When they were in the middle of the bay a heavy gale arose, and the people almost died. They

had to turn back. Five days [they tried to cross the bay], but every
time they were driven back. Then they got across. Now it began to
snow, and the people were covered with snow. They became very cold.
Thus their chief took revenge upon them. Then Blue-Jay went up to
the house. [He found a knothole and called to Robin, who was in the
house:] "Robin, open for me, I am cold. Bring me food, Robin, I am
starving." Robin did not reply. "Robin, take the tongs and put
some food through this hole." Robin was boiling meat. Then he took
the tongs and put them into the boiling kettle. He pushed the tongs
through the knothole. Blue-Jay [was so hungry that he] licked the
fat off from the tongs. He said: "Robin, Robin, tell the chief that I
will give him my daughter in marriage, but let him open the door."
"Ya-a," said Robin; "What shall he do with her? He wants your
chief's daughter [not yours]." Then Blue-Jay ran down to the beach
and said to his chief: "The young man asks for your daughter and for
my daughter." The chief did not reply, and Blue-Jay ran back to the
house and said: "Robin, the chief says he will give him his daughter."
Five times Blue-Jay ran down to the beach and back to the house. Then
his chief spoke; he made his daughter ready, and put on her dentalia,
and so did Blue-Jay. Once more he ran up to the house and said:
"Robin, I have made my daughter ready." "Ya," replied Robin; "She
shall look after the chamber." Now they brought the chief's daughter
up to the house and they opened the door.

On the following morning the sister had disappeared. Lo! The supernatural beings had taken her and her child away. The people remained
in this place and made new houses.

Once upon a time the Crow gathered many potentilla roots [put them
into her canoe] and crossed the sea. When she arrived at the country
of the supernatural beings they all came down to the beach. They
searched among her roots and found one ōguē′mEskōtit and one
LE′mōksin among them. These they ate, and threw away the Crow's
potentilla roots. Then she went up to the house and met her niece,
who said: "Do you think they are men, that you bring them potentilla
roots? Gather ōguē′mEskōtit and LE′mōksin. When you come again
bring all kinds of nice smelling roots, and bring one small basket of
potentilla roots for me." Then she said to her: "Take this bitch along;
it belongs to your grandson. When you come near the shore say:
'Catch a whale, Q¡acī′nEmicLX.'" "Yes," said the Crow, and then she
went home. When she was in the middle of the ocean she said to the
dog: "Catch a whale, Q¡acī′nEmicLX. Do you know indeed how to
catch whales?" Then the bitch who lay in the stern of the boat arose.
A whale came up. She bit it. Then the canoe rocked violently.
"Hold it fast, Q¡acī′nEmicLX." Then the Crow became afraid and
said: "Let go, let go, Q¡acī′nEmicLX." Then she let go the whale and
lay down to sleep. The Crow landed [and when she arrived], she had

lost her dog. She ran about and searched for it in all the houses, but did not find it. Then she [was very sad and] did not eat because she liked her dog.

The Crow stayed here five days, and then again she gathered many roots of plants. She gathered ōguē′mɛskōtit and ʟɛ′mōksin. She gathered all kinds of nice smelling roots. She put potentilla roots into one small basket. Then she crossed again to the country of the super-natural beings. Then they all came down to the beach. They [took the nice smelling roots and] ate them right there at the beach. She carried the potentilla roots up to her niece. Now she saw her dog, which was in the house. [Her niece said:] "Do you think this is a com-mon bitch? She returns. Why did you say in the middle of the ocean: 'Take the whale?' Therefore you became afraid. You must not say so until you are near the shore. Do you think they gave her to you as a present? She always returns. You will take her again when you go home. Do not search for her when you have lost her. She provides you with food when you are going." The Crow replied: "Yes." And when she went back she carried that bitch along. "When you approach the land say: 'Catch a whale, Qᵢacī′nɛmicʟX.'" Then she went home. The dog lay in the stern of the canoe. When they were near the town the Crow said: "Catch a whale, Qᵢacī′nɛmicʟX." She did not move. Then the Crow took some water, poured it over her and said: "Catch a whale; are you indeed able to catch a whale?" When they were quite near the shore she said again: "Catch a whale, Qᵢacī′nɛmicʟX." Then she arose and caught a whale. Again the canoe rocked. She said: "Hold it fast, Qᵢacī′nɛmicʟX." Sometimes she did not say it right and cried: "Let go the whale, Qᵢacī′nɛmicʟX." Then the whale drifted ashore. The people went down to the beach and cut the whale. They carried the meat up to house.

After some time the chief said: "I desire to go and see my sister." Now the people made themselves ready and started in a large canoe. When they came near the country of the supernatural beings their chief said: "Take care, they will test us." [When they had gone a little far-ther] the whole sea was covered with ice. He said to his people: "We will land after a while." Now Blue-Jay became very cold, but he said: "I never get cold, I will stay in the canoe." He jumped into the water and sank out of sight at once. Then a person shouted on shore: "Ehehiu, [Blue-Jay] killed himself." Then the chief arose in the canoe; he took the ice and threw it away. Then that person shouted: "Ehe-hiu, how he threw away the ice of the supernatural beings." "'Ehehiu,' you say, I threw it away; what made me fall down?" [said Blue-Jay]. Then they went up to the house. The chief said: "Do not enter at once. After a while they will open their house." Now there was a sea-lion and a sea-cow (?), one at each side of the door. They stood in the doorway. Now Blue-Jay became very cold. He tried to jump into the house and the animals bit him. They had almost been unable to recover him.   Then the chief stepped up and he took one sea monster in each hand and threw them away. "Ehehiu," shouted the person ["how he throws away the sea lions of the supernatural people"]. "'Ehehiu', you say; I threw away those who bit me," said Blue-Jay. Then they all entered the house and stayed there.   There were no people in it except the chief's sister. [Blue-Jay said to his brother Robin:] "What will they give us to eat, Robin?" "Oh, be quiet," replied Robin.   Then said Blue-Jay: "Our chief's fire makes noise just as this here."   There was only one log in the house.   Then the person shouted: "Come down to the fire you who splits wood with his beak."   Then a being came out [from under the bed] with a long beak who split the log.   "Robin," said Blue-Jay, "that was our great-great-grandfather's slave."   "I do not know that he was our slave; you alone have slaves."   Then a fire was made and the whole house was full of smoke.   The person shouted: "Come down to the fire, Smoke-eater." "Robin," said Blue-Jay, "he also was our (great-great-grandfather's) slave; he always carried me on his back and led you by the hand." "I do not know that he was our slave; you alone have slaves."   Then the smoke man came down and [they saw that] he had an enormous belly.   He stepped into the middle of the house and swallowed all the smoke.   The house became light.   Then they brought a small dish and one cut of meat was in it.   "Robin," said Blue-Jay, "that is too little; that is not enough for all of us; I certainly shall not get enough."   Then a person shouted: "Come down to the fire you who cuts whale with his beak."   Then a person came to the fire with a very sharp beak, who began to cut meat.   He cut and cut until the whole dish was full.   Then he blew upon it and it became a large canoe full of meat.   They boiled it, and when it was nearly done they all went out and their chief took reeds.   These he put into their mouths [and pushed them right through them] so that they came out at the anus. They all did so, also Blue-Jay.   Then they entered again and sat down. They made small holes where they sat and began to eat.   They swallowed the meat and it went right out at the anus.   Blue-Jay arose and there lay his anus.   "Look here, Robin, my anus fell down right here!"   Then the people took him by his arms, carried him out of the house, and pulled the reed out of his mouth.   Then the chief and Blue-Jay entered again; he took three spoonfuls and he had enough.   Then the people continued to eat and the whale meat became less and less. Then they went out, took out the reeds and reentered.   They continued to eat.   Now they ate in the right way and finished all they had boiled. Then a person cried: "Ehehiu, how they eat all the meat of the supernatural beings!"   Then Blue-Jay said: "Did you think I could not finish what you gave me to eat?"

Now they stayed in the house.   Blue-Jay went out.   He was oversatiated.   He looked and saw a patch of kinnikinnik berries.   He began to eat them, when a person called: "Oh, Blue-Jay eats the excrements of the supernatural people;" whereupon Blue-Jay said: "'Ehehiu', you say; do you think I eat them? I merely look at your kinnikinnik berries."

They stayed there. After awhile a person came out of the house and said: "They wish to play with you; you will dive." Blue Jay said: "We always dive in our country." "Do you think they do as you are accustomed to?" said the woman. "When they dive the one dies and the other one has won." She said to them: "Blue-Jay shall dive." Blue-Jay went down to the water and threw the bushes out of his canoe into the water. Then he and the diver fought against each other. They dived. Blue-Jay hid his club under his blanket. They jumped into the water and after awhile Blue-Jay's breath gave out. He came up and hid under the bushes which he had thrown out of his canoe. There he breathed and dived again. He said to the diver: "Where are you?" "Here I am," she replied. After awhile his breath gave out again. Once more he came up under the bushes. Four times he did so, and then he became tired. He went to look for the diver. He found her biting the bottom of the sea. She had her eyes closed. Blue-Jay took his club and hit her on the nape. The people saw something floating on the water and then a person said: "There is Blue-Jay." He was, however, in the bushes which he had thrown out of his canoe. After a little while Blue-Jay jumped ashore and a person shouted: "Ehehiu, how Blue-Jay won over the diver of the supernatral beings." "'Ehehiu', you say; we always dive so in our country," said Blue Jay.

Then again a person stepped out and said: "They want to play with you; you will climb up a tree together." Then Blue-Jay said: "We climb every day in our country." But the young woman remarked: "Do you think they are just like Indians? They will place a piece of ice upright, then you will have to climb up the ice. When a climber falls down he breaks to pieces and the other one wins." Then they said to Blue-Jay: "You shall climb up." They placed upright a piece of ice which was so long that it reached to the sky. Blue-Jay made himself ready and tied his bearskin blanket around his belly. [The supernatural beings sent a] chipmunk who made himself ready [to climb up the ice]. They began to climb, and when they had reached a certain height Blue-Jay grew tired. [Then he let go of the ice] and flew upward. [When he had rested] he again took hold of the ice. Then he grew tired again. He looked back to the one with whom he was racing and saw her climbing up with her eyes shut. She did not grow tired. Then Blue-Jay took his club [from under his blanket] and struck her on the nape. The chipmunk fell down. The people looked up and saw a person falling down. "Ah, that is Blue-Jay! There he falls down." [But when they saw the chipmunk] a person shouted: "Ehehiu, how they won over the chipmunk of the supernatural beings."

"'Eheh̓iu', you say; we always climb in our country." Then their chief won two sea-otters.

Then they stayed awhile longer. Then again a person came out and said: "They want to have a shooting match with you." Blue-Jay said: "We have shooting matches every day in our country." The young woman said: "Do you think they are like Indians? They place people against each other. One stands on one side, the other on the other. [They shoot at each other,] the one dies, and the other wins." Then they said to the Beaver: "You stand up [on our side]." They took a grindstone and tied it to his belly. They took another one and tied it to his back. The supernatural beings made the loon stand up on their side. Then [the beaver and the loon] took their arrows and the loon shot at the beaver. The arrow broke and fell down. Then the beaver shot at the loon. "Uhū," said he when he was struck by the arrow. Then the loon shot again. "Ha," he said, and the arrow broke and fell down. Then he shot again at the loon. "Uhū," he said, then fell on his back and died. "Eh̓eh̓iu! How they won over the bird of the supernatural people." Blue-Jay spoke: "You say 'eh̓eh̓iu'; we have shooting matches in our country every day."

They stayed there some time longer. Then again a person came out of the house and said: "They want to play with you; you will sweat in the sweat house." Blue-Jay spoke: "We always sweat in our country." Then the young woman said: "They always heat caves, and when they are hot, they enter them. The one party will die, the other will win." Then their chief said: "We must go into the cave." Now the supernatural beings heated the caves. They got hot. There were two caves in a rock. [The chief and some of his people] went into one, the supernatural beings went into the other. Then the caves were closed. The chief, however, took some ice and put it under their feet. They stood on it. After a little while a sound was heard like the bursting of a shell that is being roasted. Five times that sound was heard. Then the caves were opened; first that of Blue Jay's people—they were all alive; next that of the supernatural beings—five of them were dead. They had won again. "Eh̓eh̓iu! How they won over the supernatural beings." "'Eh̓eh̓iu', you say," replied Blue-Jay, "we use the sweat house every day in our country."

Now the chief's brother-in-law said: "Let us catch whales." The sister told him: "Take care; they will try to put you to shame. This is their last attempt at you." In the evening they went to catch whales. She took Blue-Jay and put him into her right armpit. Then she took Robin and put him into her left armpit [and told them]: "Now I shall keep you here; do not say 'eh̓eh̓iu,' do not look!" Then in the evening they all went down to the beach. She said to her elder brother: "Four whales will pass you, but do not throw your harpoon; when the fifth comes, then harpoon it." Now the supernatural people stood there. The young woman took a torch in order to help her brother.

After a while a person shouted: "Yuyayuya, a flatfish whale comes."
[The chief did not stir.]   After a while a person shouted: "Yuyayuya, an albatross whale comes; raise your harpoons." Blue-Jay tried
to look [from under the arms of the woman].   At once her torch
began to flicker, and she pressed Blue-Jay, saying: "Do not look!"
Then again a person shouted: "Yuyayuya, an elk whale comes; raise
your harpoons." [The chief did not stir.]   Next a person shouted:
"Yuyayuya, a sperm-whale comes; raise your harpoons." Then the
sister said to him: "Now, look out; now the real whale will come."
Then a person shouted: "Yuyayuya, the whale of the supernatural
people comes." Blue-Jay tried to look [from his hiding place].   Then
the torch of the young woman began to flicker and was almost extinguished. The people said: "Why does AnēktcXō'lɛmiX's torch always
flicker?" The person shouted once more: "Yuyayuya, the whale of
the supernatural people comes." Then AnēktcXō'lɛmiX said to her
brother: "Now the real whale will come." The chief harpooned it and
threw it ashore. "Ehehiu! How they threw ashore the whale of the
supernatural people." Blue-Jay replied: "Ehehiu," and at once the
torch was extinguished, and Blue-Jay [fell down from the armpit of the
woman and] was drowned. He drifted away. Thus they won again.
Their chief won again. Then they went home. AnēktcXō'lɛmiX said:
"Coil up this rope in your canoe; when you get across tie Robin's
blanket to it." [Then they started.   When they were in the middle of
the ocean the supernatural people] created a strong gale against those
going home. Now they tied [Mink] on to the gunwale of their canoe
[thus making it higher and preventing its being swamped]. They
almost perished; finally they reached their home [safely.   Then they
tied Robin's blanket to the rope. AnētcXō'lɛmiX pulled it back, and
when she found the blanket at the end of the rope she knew that her
brother had reached home safely].

4. IGUĀ'NAT IĀ'KXANAM.

THE SALMON HIS MYTH.

Iŏ'c ē'Xat iLā'Xak¡'Emāna, ŏⁱŏ'kuil uyā'Xa. Ēwā' qē'xtcē
There one   their chief,   a woman his daughter. Thus intending
was

2 aqēxEmElā'luX. Näkct atsō'tx. A'lta atcLuqoā'na-it imŏ'lak
they wanted to buy   Not   he gave her Now   he put down   elk
her.   away.

3 Liā'atcam: "Ma'nix La'ksta tc¡Ex LkLā'xō Lik LᶜE'tcam, Lgucgā'ma
its antlers: "When   who   break he will do it these antlers, he shall take her

4 ōgu'Xa." A'lta aqō'xōqtc tê'lXEm, tā'nēwatikc ōxōwā'yŏl.
my daughter." Now they were invited the people, first the walkers.

5 Ka'nauwē aqō'xōqtc. Ā'tElaxtikc ktgE'kal. Ka'nauwē2 aqō'xōqtc
All   they were in- Then they   the fliers.   All   they were invited.   vited.

6 ktgE'kal. TakE aqō'lXam ōts!Emŏ'ëkXan. "Mā'nēwa ts¡Ex
the fliers. Then she was told the snail.   "You first break

7 LE'xa!" Nō'ya ōts!Emē'nkXan. Qē'xtcē akLō'cgam. Nēkct ts¡Ex
do it!" She went the snail.   Intending she took it. Not break

8 aLE'xax. Aqiō'lXam ik¡ā'ōtEn! "Ā'mElaxta tc¡Ex LE'xa!"
it did. He was told squirrel: "You next break do it!"

9 A'lta tc¡Ex atci'Lax ik¡ā'ōtEn cka mEnk aLxElE'l. Aqiō'lXam
Now break he did it squirrel and a little it moved. He was told

10 ēnanā'muks: "Ā'mElaxta tc¡Ex LE'xa!" Ā'yuLx ēnanā'muks.
the otter: "You next break do it!" He went to the the otter.
                                         middle of the house.

11 NaxLō'lExa-it kaX ŏⁱŏ'kuil: "Â, qō iā'xka tc¡Ex tclEtx!" Q¡āt
She thought that woman: "Â, will he break he does it." Love

12 agā'yax. AtcLō'cgam, qē'xtcē tc¡Ex atci'Lax. Näkct tc¡Ex aLE'x.
she did him. He took it, intending break he did it. Not break it did.

13 Āyō'ptck weXt. A'lta a'ēlaxta ēᶜē'na ā'yuLx. Gōyä'2 iā'qa-iL
He went up again. Now he next the beaver he went to Thus large
                                      the middle of
                                      the house.

14 iā'wan. TakE nē'k·im iqē'sqēs: "LE ia'xka x·ix·ī'x· giā'ts¡axan
his belly. Then he said blue-jay: "LE he this with large belly

15 ts¡Ex tclā'xō." AtcLō'cgam ēᶜē'na qō'La Lᶜatcā'ma. Lēqs tc¡Ex
break he will do it." He took them the beaver those antlers. Almost break

16 atcE'Lax ka weXt tEll nē'xax. Ā'yuptck ēᶜē'na. A'ēlaxta
he did it and again tired he got. He went up the beaver. Next

17 ēlē'q¡am ā'yuLx. AtcLō'cgam, Lēqs ts¡Ex aLE'xax. TakE
the wolf went to the mid- He took it, almost break it did. Then
            dle of the house.

18 wiXt tEll nē'xax. Ā'yuptck ēlē'q¡am. Ā'ēlaxta ii'tcxōt ā'yuLx.
again tired he got. He went up the wolf. Next he the bear went to the
                                                                   middle of
                                                                   the house.

19 AtcLō'cgam qō'La Lᶜatcā'ma ii'tsxōt. Lēqs ts¡Ex atci'Lax. Tä2ll
He took them those antlers the bear. Almost break he did them. Tired

20 nē'xax ii'tsxōt.
he got the bear.

Gō Lē'Xat Lōc LgōLē'lExEmk; ka'nauwē iō'L¡aqLa ē'LᶜaLᶜa;
There one it was a person;   all   sore   his body;

60

LE'Laqcō ka'nauwē LōL¡aqLa. TakE nē'k·im iqē'sqēs: "Ē'kta 1
his hair all sore. Then he said blue-jay: "What

qtcē'tuwa x·ix·ī'x· ka'nauwē ā'yaLᵉa giā'tcikc?" A'lta a'ēlaxta 2
can he do this all his body stinking?' Now next

icā'yim ā'yuLx. Lēqs pus tc¡Ex atci'Lax. Ā'lta weXt tä2ll nē'xax. 3
the grizzly he went to Almost break he did it. Now again tired he got.
bear the middle of the house.

A'lta iLā'xak¡Emăna a'ēlaxta ā'yuLx ik¡oayawa'. A'lta ka'nauwē 4
Now their chief he next he went to the panther. Now all
the middle of the house.

nōxō'tctXom ōxōwā'yul. A'lta ā'tElaxta tgE'kal. A'lta ā'yō 5
they were at an end the walkers. Now next they the fliers. Now he went

yā'nēwa-y-ēntsᵘX. Qē'xtcē atcLō'cgam. Lēqs ts¡Ex atci'Lax. A'lta 6
first Ents·X. Intending he took it. Almost break he did it. Now

wiXt täll nē'xax. A'lta ā'ēlaXta ipō'ēpoē ā'yuLx. NxLō'lExa-it 7
again tired he got. Now he next ipō'ēpoē he went to She thought
the middle of the house.

qaX ōᵉō'kuil: "Ō ia'xka taya'x ts¡Ex tsLEtx." A'lta atcLō'cgam; 8
that woman: "Oh, he if break he would do it." Now he took it;

näkct qa'da aLE'x. Ā'yōptck. Ā'cElaXta cE'nqētqēt ā'ctōLx. 9
not [any] how it did. He went up. Next he [dual] the sparrow he went
hawk [dual] [dual] to the middle of the house.

Lēqs ts¡Ex aLgE'ctax. A'lta ā'ctōptck cE'nqētqēt. A'lta ā'ēlaxta 10
Almost break he did it. Now he [dual] the sparrow Now he next
went up hawk.

it'ē't'ē ā'yōLx. Lēqs tc¡Ex atcE'Lax, ka weXt tEll nē'xax. Ā'lta 11
the hawk he went Almost break he did it, and also tired he got. Now
down.

āᵉlaxta ō'npitc nō'Lxa. Qē'xtcē tc¡Ex agE'Lax. Näkct aLElE'll. 12
next she the chick- she went to Intending break she did it. Not it moved.
en hawk the middle of the house

Ā'ēlaxta iqoē'lqoēl ā'yuLx. Näkct aLxElE'll. Ā'yōptck iqoē'lqoēl. 13
Next he the owl he went down. Not it moved. He went up the owl.

A'lta ā'ᵉlaxta ūtcaktcā'k nō'Lxa. AkLō'cgam, Lēqs ts¡Ex agE'Lax. 14
Now next she the eagle she went down. She took it, almost break she did it.

A'lta ka'nauwē qtgE'kal nōxō'tctXōm; ka'nauwē ōXōwā'yul 15
Now all the fliers they were at an end; all walkers

nōxō'tctXōm. 16
they were at an end.

TakE nē'k·im iqē'sqēs: "AmckLē'lot x·ix· tiā'L¡k¡ēnEma. 17
Then he said blue-jay: "You give it to him that his sores.

Ē'kta qtsē'tūwa?" TakE tā'mEnua nō'xôx tê'lx·Em. 18
What can he do?" Then giving it up they became the people.

"Ai'aq, ai'aq, mE'tXu-it," nē'k·im iqē'sqēs; "Ē'kta amē'tuwa? 19
"Quick, quick, stand up!" he said blue-jay; "What can you do?

Ts¡Ex LE'xax Xōla LᵉEtcā'ma." Qoä'nEmi atciō'lXam. TakE 20
Break do them these antlers!" Five times he spoke to him. Then

aLō'tXuit qō'La LgōLē'lEXEmk. TakE tō'tō nē'xax. TakE tō'tō 21
he stood up that person. Then shaking he became. Then shake

atcā'yax iā'ōk. CEll, tō'tō nē'xax iā'ōk. TakE tō'tō 22
he did it his blanket. Noise shaking it became his blanket. Then shake
of rattles,

atci'Lax Lā'yaqcō. TakE ā'yuLx gō kā'tsEk t!'ōL. TakE 23
he did it his hair. Then he went down to the middle of the house. Then

atcLō'cgam Lᵉatcā'ma. AcLō'cgam, tc¡Ex atcE'Lax. WeXt 24
he took them the antlers. He took them, break he did them. Again

atcLō'cgam, tc¡Ex atcE'Lax. Qoä'nEmī tc¡Ex atcE'Lax, ka 25
he took them, break he did them. Five times break he did them, and

1 atcLXE′kXuē.   TakE   nē′xankō   cka   nuguguē′qxamt   tê′lx·Em.
he threw them down.   Then   he ran   and   they looked at him   the people.

2 Atgiā′qamt.   Mank   iŏ′Lqtē   ka   nē′k·im   iqē′sqēs: "A2,   Lōwatskā′
They looked at   A little   long   and   he said   blue-jay: "Āh,   they pursue
him   her

3 Lkā′nax   ā′kē."   TakE   aktō′cgam   tgā′ktēma.   Nā′xanko.   A′lta
the chief's niece."   Then   she took them   her dentalia.   She ran.   Now

4 aqcgE′ta.   Ka′nauwē   tê′lx·Em   a′lta   atcgE′ta.   Kulā′i   aqcgE′ta.
they were pur-   All   people   now   pursued them.   Far   they were
sued.   pursued.

5 Ē′maL   atcā′yax.   TakE   atiga′ōm   ē′maL.   Iawā′2   iā′qoa-iL   ē′maL.
A bay   he made it.   Then   they reached it   the bay.   There   a large   bay.

6 TakE   atigā′ōm   ē′maL   tê′lx·Em.   A′nqatē   iau′a   ē′natai   actō′yam.
Then   they reached it   the bay   the people.   Long ago   there   on the other   they [dual]
                                                                             side   arrived.

7 Cka   mä′2nx·i   ka   wiXt   atigō′ptckam   ē′maL.   TakE   wiXt   aqcgE′ta.
And   a little   and   again   they came land-   the bay.   Then   again   they were
                              ward of   pursued.

8 Kulā′2i   weXt   aqcgE′ta.   Gō′yi   nē′xax,   nix·enā′nakō.   A′lta   weXt
Far   again   they were   Thus   he did,   he looked back.   Now   again
              pursued.

9 qᵢ′oā′p   tkcāxt   tê′lx·Em.   WeXt   ē′maL   atcā′yax.   A′lta   mank
near   they over-   the people.   Again   a bay   he made it.   Now   a little
        took them

10 Lᵢ′āp   iā′qaiL   ē′maL.   TakE   weXt   atiga′ōm   ē′maL   tê′lx·Em.
fitting (?)   large   bay.   Then   again   · they   the bay   the people.
middle   reached
size

11 TakE   kulā′i   weXt   actōē′taqᴛ.   WeXt   ka′nauwē   atigō′ptckam
Then   far   again   they two left them.   Again   all   they came landward

12 tê′lx·Em.   WeXt   aqcā′wa.   Qoä′nEma   LEmä′LEma   atci′Lax   ka
the people.   Again   they were   Five   bays   he made them   and
                      pursued.

13 tä′mEnua   nē′xax.   Ka′nauwē   aqLgō′ptckam   qō′La   qoä′nEm
giving up   he got.   All   they came landward   those   five

14 LEmä′LEma.   TakE   tEll   nē′xax   itᵢā′lapas   ka-y-   ī′pEnpEn
bays.   Then   tired   he got   coyote   and   badger

15 kēamtᵢā′m   koä′nsum.   TakE   atciō′lXam   iā′cikc.   "TakE   tEll
after   always.   Then   he said to him   to his friend: "Then   tired

16 ani′xax,   cīkc!   Qa′da   tEmē′x·ataqux   tkipā′lau   ntalā′xō   XaXā′k
I got,   friend!   How   your thought   bewitched   I shall make   that
                                                                them on her

17 ōgu′Xalaitan."   Ta′kE   nē′k·im   ē′pEnpEn: "Ā′yipē."   TakE   pō′pō
my arrow."   Then   he said   badger: "Well!"   Then   blow

18 ā′tcax   uyä′Xalaitan   itᵢ′ā′lapas: "Gō   ia′yaqtq   mō′ya!   gō   iä′yaqtq
he did on it   his arrow ·   coyote: "At   his head   go!   at   his head

19 mō′ya!"   Lō′nī   atcō′lXam   uyä′Xalaitan: "Gō   iä′yaqtq   mō′ya!"
go!"   Three times   he said to it   his arrow: "At   his head   go!"

20 Qoä′nEmi   pō′pō   ā′tcax   ūyä′Xalaitan.   TakE   atcō′Lata   uyä′Xalaitan.
Five times   blow   he did it   his arrow.   Then   he shot it   his arrow.

21 Kᵘcā′xalē   atcō′Lata.   TakE   nō′ya   uyä′Xalaitan   ha′lElElElElE.
Up   he shot it.   Then   it went   his arrow   halelelelele.

22 Yukpā′   iä′maᶜ   atcē′lax   gō   Liä′paa.   Iä′xkēwa   ayuqunā′ētix·t·
Right here   shooting   he did him   in   his Lape.   There   he fell down.
            him   on him

23 Lā′nēwatikc   LIēqᵢ′ā′muks   gaaLxuwā′ma.   Lä′cka   aLgō′cgam   kaX
First they   the wolves   pursuers.   They   they took her   that

24 ōᶜō′kuil.   A′lta   atgā′yax   ka′nauwē   qō′tac   tê′lx·Em.   Atgiā′wulᶜ.
woman.   Now   they ate him   all   those   people.   They ate all.

25 TakE   aqayā′lot   itᵢ′ā′lapas   ō′pLᵢikē,   ōyä′′pLᵢ′ikē   iguä′nat.   TakE
Then   it was given   to coyote   the bow,   his bow   the salmon's.   Then
      to him

26 aLōē′luktcū   LeXt   Liä′apta;   gō   Lqā′naks   kä′tsEk   aLawiä′yakuit
it fell down   one   his egg;   in   stone   middle   it fell into a hole

Lia'apta gō Lqā'naks. TakE nō'Xukō tê'lx·Em, ka'nauwĕ   1
his egg   in   stone.   Then   they went home   the people,   all

nō'Xukō tê'lx·Em ka takE naxEltcā'ma ōk¡'unō'. "Aqiā'waᶜ   2
they went   the people,   and   then   she heard about it   the crow.   "He is killed
home

ēmē'tgĕu." Nō'ya-y- ōk¡'uno', ayaxa'nEx·Enēmai nagE'tsax. A'lta   3
your nephew."   She went   the crow,   she cried while walking   she cried.   Now

nō'yam qīgō kaXē' aqiā'waᶜ. A'lta Lā'qLāq agE'Lax Lqā'naks.   4
she arrived   where   where   he was killed.   Now   turn over   she did them   stones.

Ā'qxulqt. Lā'qLaq kLāxt Lqā'nakc, kLik¡'elā'lEplē. TakE Lap   5
She cried.   Turn over   she did   stones,   she turned them over   Then   find
        them   often.

agE'Lax LĕXt LgEmā'k·ikct. TakE agE'Lukᵘɪ gō-y- ē'qxĕL.   6
she did it   one   salmon egg.   Then   she carried it   to   a creek.

LE'kLEk agā'yau. TakE akLaLᶜEnqā'na·it gō Ltcuq. Tsō'yustē   7
Dig   she did it.   Then   she put it into   in   water.   Evening

ka nā'Xkō. NaXkō'mam gō tE'kXaqL.   8
and   she went home.   She got home   to   her house.

Kawī'X ka wiXt nō'ya. AkLō'qstam qō'La Lᶜā'pta.   9
Early in the   and   again   she went.   She went to see it   that   salmon egg.
morning

A'lta Lā'qoa-iL qō'La Lᶜā'pta, mank Lō'Lqat. A'lta LE'kLEk agā'yax   10
Now   large   that   salmon egg,   a little   long.   Now   dig   she did it

mank iā'qoa-iLē. Tsō'yustē weXt nā'Xkō. NaXkō'mam. Näkct   11
a little   large.   Evening   again   she went home.   She got home.   Not

naō'ptit ka nä'ktcuktē. Kawī'X ka weXt nō'ya. Ā'qxulqt, nō'ya.   12
she slept   and   it got day.   Early   and   again   she went.   She cried,   she went.

Nō'yam gō qō'La Lᶜā'pta. A'lta-y- ū'LElō yuXtkē'l. Ā'lta yūL¡ mank   13
She arrived at   that   salmon egg.   Now   a small trout   there swam.   Now   glad   a little

nā'xax. A'ltā iā'qoa-iL LE'kLEk agā'yau. Tsō'yustē nā'Xkō. ME'nx·'i   14
she became.   Now   large   dig   she did it.   Evening   she went home.   A little

naō'ptit ka nē'ktcuktē. WiXt nō'ya iLā'lakt. TakE nō'yam gō qō'La   15
she slept   and   it got day.   Again   she went   the fourth   Then   she arrived at   that
                                      time.

Lᶜā'pta. A'lta-y- ōp¡ā'lō yuXtkē'l. TakE kwa'nkwan nā'xax   16
salmon egg.   Now a   trout   swam there.   Then   happy   she became

ōk¡'u'nō! LE'kLEk agā'yau, iā'2qo-iL iLE'kLEk agā'yau. Cka mEnx·   17
the crow!   Dig   she did it,   a large   dug hole   she made it.   And   a little

lāx ōᶜō'Lax ka nā'Xkō. NäXko'mam. Tcx·ī nō'pōnEm   18
afternoon   sun   and   she went home.   She got home.   Just   it grew dark,

ka naō'ptit. Kawī'x· naxE'l'ōkō. Naxā'latck. Nō'ya wiXt;   19
then   she slept.   Early   she awoke.   She rose.   She went   again;

ayō'kctam kaX ōp¡!ā'lō. Nō'2yam. A'lta ianō'kstX iguā'nat   20
she went to see it   that   trout.   She arrived.   Now   a small   salmon

yuXtkē'l. A'lta LE'kLEk agā'yau, iā'2qoa-iL LE'kLĕk agā'yau.   21
swam there.   Now   dig   she did it,   a large   dig   she did it.

WiXt naiē'taqɪ. Pāt ōᶜō'Lax ka nā'Xkō. NaXkō'mam. Iā'miaXkēwa   22
Again   she left him.   Noon   sun   and   she went   She got home.   Only of that
                            home.

tgā'XatakôX. Nō'pōnEm. Kawī'X ka nō'ya. Nō'yam, a'lta iā'qoa-iL   23
her thoughts.   It grew dark.   Early   then   she went.   She arrived,   now   a large

iguā'nat yuXtkē'l. Agiō'cgam, agē'xalukctgō mā'Lxôlē. A'lta   24
salmon   swam there.   She took him,   she threw him down   on shore.   Now

Lk¡'āsks aLō'La-it, Lā'qoa-iL Lk¡'āsks. A'lta k¡wa'nk¡wan nā'xax   25
a boy   there was,   a large   boy.   Now   happy   she got

ōk¡'u'nō. A'lta aci'Xkō. AcXkō'mam. TakE agiō'lXam itcā'kXen   26
the crow.   Now   they [dual]   They [dual] got   Then   she said to him   her grandson
               went home.   home.

ōk¡'unō': "Amx'ō'tōL. Iō'LEma mēElkElā'ya." A'lta nix'ō'tōL,   27
the crow: "Bathe.   Supernatural   you shall see them."   Now   he bathed,
                    beings

nix'ō'tōL, nix'ō'toL. Iā'nēwatē gō Lctuq nix'ō'tōL. ALē'Lx·ōL¡, gō-y-   28
he bathed,   he bathed.   The first time   in   water   he bathed.   He finished,   in

1 ē'maL nix'ō'toL. Ka'nauwē Lpō'lEma nix'ō'tōL. ALE'x·ōL̨ nix'ō'tōL
   bay   he bathed.   All   nights   he bathed.   He finished   he bathed

2 gō-y· ē'maL. A'lta gō Lpakā'lEma nix'ō'tōL. A'lta-y· iq̨'oā'lipx·
   in   bay.   Now   on   mountains   he bathed.   Now   a youth

3 nē'xax.
   he became.

   A'lta naxa-iyi'lkⁿ̨Tēl uyā'k̨ik̨ē. Agiō'lXam: "It̨ā'lapas
   Now   she told him much   his grandmother.   She said to him: "Coyote

5 atciā'waᶜ LEmē'mama, iā'cikc ē'pEnpEn. Qia näkct kaX ōᶜō'kuil
   they two killed him   your father,   his friend   badger.   If   not   that   woman

6 pōc näkct aqiā'waᶜ. Gō Llǟq̨am aLgō'cgam kaX ōᶜō'kuil."
   [if]   not   he was killed.   To   wolves   they took her   that   woman."

7 TakE atcō'lXam uyā'k̨ik̨ē: "Nō'ya. Niō'XtkinEmama
   Then   he said to her   his grandmother: "I shall go.   I shall go and search for him

8 it̨ā'lapas." "Näkct mō'ya, taua'lta aqema'wòòx." TakE wiXt
   coyote."   "Not   go,   else   you will be killed."   Then   again

9 acxē'la-it uyā'k̨ik̨ē. Iō'Lqtē acxē'la-it, ka weXt naxa-ilgu'Litck:
   they two stayed   his grand-mother.   Long time   they two stayed,   then   again   she told him:

10 "Go it̨ā'lapas aqō'cgam uyā'pL̨ikē LEmē'mama." "Â, nō'yaya
   "To   coyote   it was taken   his bow   your father's."   "Â,   I shall go.

11 Niu'XtkinEma it̨ā'lapas. TakE ō'Xuit tiō'Lema anō'ikEl."
   I shall search for him   coyote.   Then   many   supernatural beings   I saw them."

12 "Ni'Xua amxānitgu'Litck, ē'kta imē'yōLEma?" TakE atcō'lXam
   "Well,   tell me,   what   your supernatural beings?"   Then   he said to her

13 uyā'k̨ik̨ē: "Ni'Xua mE'tpa!" TakE nō'pa-y· ōk̨'u'nō. Atcō'Lata-y·
   to his grand-mother: "Well,   come outside."   Then   she went out   the crow.   He shot it

14 uyā'xalaitan iau'a mā'Lxôlē. Ia'xkēwa nē'xLx·aē. Atcō'Lata
   his arrow   then   inland.   There   it caught fire.   He shot it

15 uyā'xalaitan ē'wa tEmᶜā'ēma. Ia'xkēwa nēXLXaē. TakE nā'k·im
   his arrow   then   to prairie.   There   it caught fire.   Then   she said

16 ōk̨'u'nō: "Ō nau'itka taL̨ iō'LEma amē'ElkEl." Agiō'lXam:
   the crow: "Oh   indeed   lo!   supernatu-ral being   you saw it."   She said to him:

17 "Qā'doxē mō'ya. Qā't'ocx·Em, ēmx·Enā'oyē." Agō'n ōᶜō'Lax ka
   "Must   you go.   Take care,   take care of yourself."   One   more day   and

18 nixE'ltXuitck. Atctō'cgam tiā'ktēma, atixā'lax ka'nauwē. Atcto'cgam
   he made himself ready.   He took them   his dentalia,   he put them on to himself   all.   He took them

19 tiā'xalaitanEma. A'lta acxē'lagux igō'cax. A'lta ā'yō. Ayō'ēpa
   his arrows.   Now   it thundered from clear sky   the sky.   Now   he went.   He went out to it

20 tEmᶜā'ēma. Qoā'nEm tEmᶜā'ēma ayō'ēpa.
   to a prairie.   Five   prairies   he went out to them.

   A'lta atcō'ikEl t!'ōL. Ā'yō, ā'yō, ā'yō. Q̨'oa'p atci'tax t!'ōL.
   Now   he saw it   a house.   He went, he went, he went.   Near   he got to it   a house.

22 A'lta iLXgulā'magux LgōLē'lEXEmk. Ayō'tXuit gō kⁿLā'xanē t!'ōL.
   Now   singing song of vic-tory   a person.   He stood   at the outside of   the house.

23 A'lta ēwa' gu'latā Lē'Xat iLXgulā'magux. Lāwā'2 atcixā'laq̨Tē,
   Now   thus   at the end of the house   one   singing song of victory.   Slowly   he opened the door.

24 ayō'La-it gō iqē'p!al. KⁿtcXä nē'xax it̨'ā'lapas. "Ia'xkayuk ayō'yam
   he stood   in the doorway.   Sneeze   he did   coyote.   To here   he arrived

25 iguā'nat iā'xa. "Tcintuwa'ᶜōmx qiqō'q antsauwīp'Enā'nanma-itx
   the salmon   his son.   "He will kill me   that   I always jump inside

26 tE'kXEqL. Tcintuwa'ᶜōmx." Lqā'LXatc Lē'lauit gō ciā'xôct. TakE
   in house.   He will kill me."   Coal   it was put   on   his face.   Then

ā'yamɛnukᵘt. Ē'pɛnpɛn wiXt ā'yamɛnukᵘt. Qᵢ'ē nē'xax iqamō'tĕ.   1
his face was black-ened.   Badger   also   his face was black-ened.   Squeak   did   the door.

Nē'k·ikct ē'wa iqē'p!al itᵢ'ā'lapas. A'lta ia'xka ikē'x, qtciyā'uwaᶜ   2
He looked at   thus   the door-way   coyote.   Now   he   he was,   whom he had killed

iŏc gŏ iqē'p!al. TakE nigɛ'tsax: "Anā' itsɛsta'mXa, anā   3
there was   at   the doorway.   Then   he cried: "Anah,   my dear,   anah,

itsɛsta'mXa;" itᵢ'ā'lapas nē'k·im, "Aqētā'waᶜ qēau itsɛ'stamX.   4
my dear;"   coyote   said,   "He was killed   that   my dear.

Nɛxōwā'yuɪɛma-itx kʟxɛlgā'yutsXa." TakE ā'yup!. TakE ā'yup,   5
They go from place to place   those looking just like him."   Then   he entered.   Then   he entered,

iguā'nat iā'xa. Ayŏ'La-it gŏ iɪɛmē'tk. Â cka kᵢ'ā mɛʳxax   6
the salmon   his son.   He stayed   at   the settee.   Â,   and   silent   become

itᵢ'ā'lapas. "Näkct na tnē'txiX amiā'waᶜ ʟgɛ'mama?" TakE   7
coyote.   "Not   [int. part.]   I know   you killed him   my father?"   Then

kᵢ'ā nē'xax itᵢ'ā'lapas. TakE ē'wa mā'Lxōlē nēxɛ'Lxēkŏ ēpɛnpɛn.   8
silent he became   coyote.   Then   thus   from fire   he turned his face   badger.

A'lta ciā'xŏct Xā'Xa atci'ctax. "Ā'nēt ʟgɛ'mama ōyā'pʟᵢikē,"   9
Now   his face   rub   he did it.   "Give it to me   my father   his bow,"

nē'k·im iguā'nat iā'xa. Nē'k·im itᵢ'ā'lapas: "IamɛLō'ta qēstamX!"   10
he said   the salmon   his son.   He said   coyote: "I shall give it to you   my dear!"

TakE ayŏ'tXuit itᵢ'ā'lapas. Lāqᵒ ā'tcax aē'Xt ōpʟᵢikē. Atcō'gam,   11
Then   he stood up   coyote.   Take out   he did it   one   bow.   He took it,

gŏyī' ā'tcax. ɪɛkᵘ nā'xax. Atca-igɛ'ltcim, aqiā'auwilx· ō'pʟᵢikē.   12
thus   he did it.   Break   it did.   He struck him,   he was hit with it   the bow.

Acē'kᵢ ēlapx·it. Qu'l qul qul qul tiā'ᶜwit nō'xuita. Nixā'latck   13
He fell down head-long.   Qul   qul   qul   qul   his legs   they shook.   He rose

itᵢ'ā'lapas. "Ā'nēt ʟgɛ'mama uyā'pʟᵢikē," nē'k·im iguā'nat iā'xa.   14
coyote.   "Give it to me,   my father,   his bow,"   he said   the salmon   his son.

TakE nē'k·im itᵢ'ā'lapas: "IamɛLō'tā qē'stamX." Lāqᵒ ā'tcax aē'Xt   15
Then   he said   coyote: "I shall give it to you   my dear."   Take out   he did it   one

ō'pʟᵢikē wiXt. Atcayā'lot. WiXt aqa-igɛ'ltcim gŏ ciā'xŏst. L'ŏx   16
bow   more.   He gave it to him.   Again   he was struck with it   on   his face.   Falling

nĭcilgā'kXo-it itᵢ'ā'lapas. Qul qul qul qul tiā'ᶜwit nō'xŏx. WiXt   17
he fell on his back   coyote.   Qul   qul   qul   qul   his legs   they did.   Again

nixā'latck. "Ā'nēt, ʟgɛ'mama uyā'pʟᵢikē, itᵢ'ā'lapas! QadaXē'   18
he rose.   "Give it to me,   my father   his bow,   coyote!   Why

lā'xlax amɛnā'xt?" Atcayā'lot a'lta iqstō'kōnkōn ā'yaqtq   19
deceive   you do me?"   He gave him   now   woodpecker   its head

iakᵢ'ō'yuʟᵢɛma qaX ōpʟᵢikē'. TakE gŏyē' ā'tcax; näkct ɪɛkᵘ nā'xax.   20
glued on   that   bow.   Then   thus   he did it;   not   break   it did.

Ia'kwa' gŏyē' ā'tcax qinkᵢēama', ɪɛkᵘ nā'xax. Aqa-igɛ'ltcim   21
Here   thus   he did it   right hand,   break   it did.   He was struck with it

wiXt. TakE wiXt nĭcilgā'kXo-it itᵢ'ā'lapas. Lä2kt ɪpʟᵢi'kē   22
again.   Then   again   he fell on his back   coyote.   Four   bows

atci'Lōt itᵢ'ā'lapas. Ka'nauwē ɪɛ'kɪɛk ā'Lax. Ā'Laquiɴɛm a'lta   23
he gave him   coyote.   All   broken   they became.   The fifth   now

ā'xka iguā'nat ōyā'pʟᵢikē atcayā'lŏt. Gŏ'yē ā'tcax iauwa'   24
that   the salmon   his bow   he gave it to him.   Thus   he did it   there

tcaqᵢ'ɛtckta, Lŏ'nī gŏ'yē ā'tcax; ala'xti ya'kwa tcixqinqᵢēa'ma   25
his left hand,   three times   thus   he did it;   then   here   his right hand

Lōni gŏ'yē ā'tcax; näkct ɪɛkᵘ ā'tcax. Ŏ'kXuʟpa ʟgā'patsēu   26
three times   thus   he did it;   not   break   he did it.   Red shafted woodpecker   its red heads

1 akXā'cama qaX ōpʟ̣ikē! TakE aqiō'lXam ē'pEnpEn: "Ā cka kị'ā
  put on by twos that bow! Then he was told badger: "Ah, and quiet

2 mE'xax. Nĕkct na tnē'txiX ka mai'ka amē'kị̣aukị̣au!" Nĕ'k·im
  be. Not [int. I know and you you a murderer?" He said
      part.]

3 ē'pEnpEn: "Näkct agE'kị̣aukị̣au. Ka'ltas ē'tcEmEnukᵘt aqēnā'lax."
  badger: "Not I murderer. Only my blackened face was made me."

4 TakE aqiō'cgam gō Liā'paa. A'lta aqcō'ktcpa. A'lta aqcXE'ltcim.
  Then he was taken at his nape. Now they were hauled Now they were struck
      out.   together.

5 AqcXE'ltcim, aqcXE'ltcim. AcXE'ʟa-it. Aqē'xalukctgō itị̣'ā'lapas:
  They were struck they were struck They were dead. He was thrown away coyote:
  together, together.

6 "Itị̣'ā'lapas imē'xal. Näkct tkanā'Ximct mtōtē'na." Aqē'xalukctgō
  "Coyote your name. Not chiefs you will kill He was thrown away
      them."

7 ē'pEnpEn: "Ē'pEnpEn imē'xal. Näkct tkanā'Ximct mtōtē'na. Ā'mka
  badger: "Badger your name. Not chiefs you will kill Only
      them.

8 ōmē'wicqc kị̣oa'c xaxā'xō. Näkct qị̣'oā'p amʟi'tx ʟgōlē'lEXEmk."
  your farts afraid they will be of Not near you will get a person."
      them.   him

9 TakE aqcx·E'kXuē itị̣'ā'lapas kị̣a-y· ·ē'pEnpEn. TakE aqōxō'lXama
  Then they were thrown coyote and badger. Then it was burnt
      away

10 tE'ctaqʟ.
  their house.

11 TakE wiXt ā'yō. Ayō'ēpa wiXt tēXt tEmᶜā'ēma. Atcō'ēkEl
  Then again he went. He went out to again one prairie. He saw it

12 tXut gō kE'mk·itē tEmᶜā'ēma. TakE ā'yō, ā'yō, ā'yō. Qị̣'oā'p
  smoke on end of the prairie. Then he went, he went, he went. Nearly

13 atctā'xom t!'ōʟ. A'lta ʟā'qXulqt ʟᶜā'kil. Atcixā'laqᴛ ʟawā'4.
  he reached it a house. Now it cried a woman. He opened the door slowly.

14 Qị̣'ō nē'xax iqamō'tē. Nā'k·ikst qaX ōᶜō'kuil. Agē'ElkEl, ia'xka
  Squeak it did the door. She looked that woman. She saw him, he

15 qix· itcā'kikala qix· aqiā'waᶜ. Aia'skōp!. Pāʟ ʟᶜōlē'ma qō'ta t!'ōʟ.
  that her husband that he was killed. He entered. Full meat that house.

16 "Ā, iamEtXtki'nEmam; tXgō'ya. Nai'ka ʟgE'mama qiau aqitā'waᶜ."
  "Ah, I came to search for you; we two will My my father that he was killed."
      go home.

17 TakE agiō'lXam: "TqctxēLā'wuks tgEmuwa'ᶜō." "Qā'doXoē
  Then she said to him: "Monsters they will kill you." "Shall

18 tgEmuwa'ᶜō." NixʟLxā'lEm, agiugē'waʟị̣'am. Gō'yē ōᶜō'Lax, lāx
  they shall kill me." He ate. she fed him in her house. Thus the sun, after-
      noon

19 ōᶜō'Lax ka yō'pa. Lqị̣ōp atci'Lax Liā'paa. Qui'nEmi Lqị̣up
  the sun and he went out. Cut he did it his nape. Five times cut

20 atci'Lax. Atcuxukị̣'uē'niyanukᴛ qō'ta tiā'ʟwulē. A'lta ā'tcax kaX
  he did it. He made bundles that meat. Now be ate it that

21 ōpXa; pāʟ iā'wan nē'xax. A'lta ayō'p!am. Atctā'lot kaX ōᶜō'kuil
  alder- full his belly got. Now he came in. He gave that woman
  bark;   them to her

22 kanEm qoā'nEm nōxōkị̣oē'nēyak. "Manix Ltē'mama, ēXt
  together five bundles. "When they come, one

23 inixkị̣'ē'niyak Lē'Xat mitElō'ta. Manix Lktawu'lᶜa x·itē'k, ka
  bundle to one give it to them. When they will eat it this, then

24 nʟō'ʟ'aya. Ma'nix xāx ʟgEnā'xoyē ēXt Lē'Xat mitElō'ta." A'lta
  I shall win When notice they will do me, one to one give it to them." Now
  over them.

25 lā'xlax atci'Lax. Pō ā'tcax ōᶜō'lEptckiX. Pāʟ tE'kEmōm nē'xax;
  deceive he did them. Blow he did the fire. Full ashes he got;
      on it

26 iqị̣'ēyō'qxōt nē'xax.
  an old man he got.

Tsō'yustē ka qull nē'xau. ALā'cgatp! LgōLē'lEXEmk. Kā'tsEk 1
Evening and noise of became. It entered a person. In middle of
falling
objects

t!ōL aLE'tē. "Hômm, iguā'nat ēniLā'kux; iguā'nat ēniLā'kux; 2
house he came. "Hômm, salmon I smell it; salmon I smell it;

hômm, iguā'nat ēniLā'kux." TakE atci'LkLtuq qō'La Lqı'ēyō'qxōt; 3
hômm, salmon I smell it." Then he kicked him that old man;

ē'xauwitē aqē'kLtuq. Wāx aLi'xax L̯ā'owilqt gō iā'yacqL. TakE 4
often he was kicked. Pour out it came the blood in his mouth. Then

nō'tXuit ōᶜō'kuil. Lāq° agā'yax ēXt inē'xkı'ēniak. "NgōLā'lEXEmk 5
she stood up the woman. Take out she did it one bundle. "I am a person

anE'xax. Lxpōc nēkct aLgā'icX! x·ix·ē'k aLgē'tkᵘɪam x·iLa 6
I am. Do you think not my relative? This he brought it this

Lqı'ēyō'qxōt." "Hō! itci'kōkcin! Qa'daqa nēkct ā'nqatē amiō'lXam! 7
old man." "Hō! My sister-in-law's Why not long ago you told me!
relative!

TsE'xtsEX anE'Lax LgE'kōkcin." WiXt qul nē'xau. WiXt ē'Xat 8
Hurt I did him my sister-in-law's Again noise of there was. Again one
relative." falling
objects

Lā'qo nē'xax. Nē'tp!a. Iō'kuk qı'oā'p kā'tsEk tı'ōL: "HEmm, iguā'nat 9
visible he became. He came in. There near middle of house: "HEmm, salmon

iā'tsEks iniLā'kux. HEmm, iguā'nat iniLā'kux." Ēwā' atci'LqLtuq. 10
his smell I smell. HEmm, salmon I smell." Thus he kicked him.

Ēwā' ayuLā'tax·it, ē'xoēt ayuLā'tax·it aqē'qLtuq. Wāx ā'Lxax 11
Thus he flew about, much he flew about he was kicked. Pour out it did

L̯ā'owilqt ēwā yā'yackL. "NgōLā'lEXEmk anE'xax. Lxpōc nikct 12
the blood thus his mouth. "I am a person I am. Do you think not

aLgā'icX! x·ix·ē'k aLgē'tkᵘɪam x·iLa Lqı'ēyō'qxōt." Agē'lōt eXt 13
my relative! This he brought it this old man." She gave it one
to him

inixkı'ē'niak. "Ohō', itci'kōkcin! Qa'daqa nikct ā'nqatē amEnō'lXam! 14
bundle. "Oho, my sister-in-law's Why not long ago you told me!
relative!

TsE'xtsEX anE'Lax LgE'kōksin." WiXt qul nē'xau. WiXt 15
Hurt I did him my sister-in-law's Again noise of became. Again
relative." falling
objects

ē'Xat Lāqo nē'xax LgōLē'lEXEmk. Nē'tp!a. Kā'koa kulā'i 16
one visible he became a person. He entered. Thus far

kā'tsEk nē'k·im: "HEmm, iguā'nat iā'tsEks iniLā'kux. HEmm, 17
in middle he said: "HEmm, salmon his smell I smell it. HEmm,

iguā'nat iniLā'kux." Ēwā' atci'LqLtuq. Ēwā' ayuLā'tax·it, ē'xoēt 18
salmon I smell it." Thus he kicked him. Thus he flew about, much

ayuLā'tax·it aqē'qLtuq. L̯ā'owiqt wāx ā'Lxax ē'wa yi'LackL gō 19
he flew about he was kicked. Blood pour out it did thus his mouth at

qō'La Lqēyō'qxōt. Iō'Lqtē tcaX nō'tXuit. Lāq agā'yax ēXt 20
that old man. Some time then she stood up. Take she did it one
out

inixkıē'niak. Agē'lōt itcā'pōtcxan. "Ohō' itci'qōqcin Liā'xauyam! 21
bundle. She gave it her brother-in- "Ohō! my sister-in- the poor one!
to him law. law's relative

Qa'daqa nikct ā'nqatē amEnō'lXam! TsE'xtsEX anE'Lax 22
Why not before you told me! Hurt I did him

LgE'qōqcin." WiXt qul nē'xau. WiXt ē'Xat Lā'qo nē'xax 23
my sister-in-law's Again noise of there Again one visible became
relative." falling was.
objects

LgōLē'lEXEmk. Cka mEnx· cka nē'cgatp! ka nā'yiLa: "HEmm, 24
a person. And a little and he entered and he smelled it: "Hemm,

iguā'nat iā'tsEks iniLā'kux. HEmm, iguā'nat iniLā'kux." Ēwā' 25
salmon his smell I smell. HEmm, salmon I smell." Thus

atci'LqLtuq. Ēwā' ayuLā'tax·it, ē'xoēt ayuLā'tax·it aqē'qLtuq. 26
he kicked him. Thus he flew about, much he flew about he was kicked.

1 Wāx   ā′Lxax   Lᵉā′owilqt   ē′wa   iā′yackL.   Iō′Lqtē   nō′tXuit.
   Pour out it did   blood   thus   his mouth.   Long time   he stood up.

2 "NgōLä′lEXEmk anE′xax. Lxpōc nikct aLgā′icX! x·ix·ē′k aLgē′tkᵘɴam
   "I am a person   I am.   Do you not my relative? This   he brought it
                                         think

3 x·i′La Lq¡′ēyō′qxōt." Agē′lōt ēXt inixk¡′ē′niak: "Ohō′ itci′qōqcin!
   this   old man."   She gave it one   bundle: "Ohō! my sister-in-
                           to him   law's relative!

4 Qā′daqa nikct ā′nqatē amEnō′lXam? TsE′xtsEx anE′Lax LgE′qōqcin."
   Why   not   before   you told me? Hurt   I did him my sister-in-
                                                                law's relative."

5 Atciā′wulᵉ qix· iguā′nat. A′lta iā′mkXa itcā′k·ikal. Ka mE′nx·i ka
   He ate it   that   salmon.   Now   only he   her husband. And a little and
                                                                         while

6 qull nē′xau. Tcx·ī atcixā′laqɴē, ka nä′yiLa: "HEmm, iguā′nat
   noise there was. Just   he opened the   and   he smelled it: "HEmm,   salmon
   of fall-   door,
   ing objects

7 iā′tsEks iniLä′kux. HEmm, iguā′nat iniLä′kux." Ēwä′ atci′LqLtuq.
   his smell I smell.   HEmm, salmon I smell."   Thus   he kicked him.

8 Ēwä′ ayuLä′tax·it, ē′xoēt ayuLä′tax·it aqē′qLtuq. Wāx ā′Lxax
   Thus   he flew about,   much   he flew about   he was kicked. Pour out it did

9 Lᵉā′owilqt ē′wa iā′yackL. Iō′Lqtē tcXep nä′xax, iō′Lqtē aqLqLtu′qo-im
   blood   thus his mouth.   Long hesitating she was, long   he was kicked much

10 qō′La Lq¡ēyō′qxōt. Nō′tXuit qaX ōᶜō′kuil: "NLgōLä′lEXEmk
   that   old man.   She stood up that   woman: "I am a person

11 anE′xax. Lxpōc nikct aLgā′icX! x·ix·-ē′k aLgē′tkᵘɴam x·iLa
   I am.   Do you think not my relative? This   he brought it   this

12 Lq¡ēyō′qxōt." Agē′lōt ēXt inixk¡′ē′niak. "Ohō′ itci′qsiX, qa′daqa
   old man."   She gave it that bundle.   "Ohō! my brother- why
                   to him   in-law,

13 nēkct ā′nqatē amEnō′lXam? TsE′xtsEx anä′yax itci′qsiX."
   not   before   you told me?   Hurt   I did him my brother-in-law."

   A′lta aLxE′lgixc, aLgā′yaxc imō′lEkuma. A′lta qē′xtcē
   Now   they cut open,   they cut them   the elks.   Now   intending

15 aLgilᶜē′mEniL qix· ēq¡ēyō′qxōt. Näkct nixLxä′lEm. TakE nä′k·im
   they gave him food that old man.   Not   he ate.   Then   she said

16 qaX ōᶜō′kuil: "Lō′nas LE′kLEk nō′xôx Lä′lēwanEma,
   that   woman: "Perhaps broken   are   his ribs,

17 qä nēkct aLxēLxE′lEmax." Wāx nē′ktcuktē. Kawī′X ka
   there- not   he eats."   Next morn- it got day.   Early   and
   fore   ing

18 aLxE′ltXuitck Llē′q¡′am. ALxō′kumak¡′auwa. A′lta nixä′latck
   they made them- the wolves.   They went hunting.   Now   he rose
   selves ready

19 iguā′nat iā′xa. Nix′ō′tam. A′lta agilgē′xo-il qaX ōᶜō′kuil. A′lta
   the salmon his son. He went to bathe. Now   she boiled much that   woman.   Now

20 nixLxä′lEm. ALē′XōL¡ iā′LxElEmax ka ackɴā′yōit gō ilEmē′tk.
   he ate.   He finished   his eating   and they two lay   in   bed.
                                                       down

21 Lāx ōᶜō′Lax, takE wiXt pō′pō ā′tcax ōᶜō′lEptckiX. TakE wiXt
   After- sun,   then   again   blow   he did it   the fire.   Then   again
   noon

22 ēq¡ēyō′qxōt nē′xax. Tsō′yustē aLXatgō′mam; Lkanauwē′tikc
   the old man   he got.   Evening   they arrived at home;   all

23 aLXatgō′mam. ALgē′tkᵘɴam imō′lEkuma. A′lta näkct
   they arrived at home. They brought   elks.   Now   not

24 aLgEqLtu′qo-im. Nâ′2-pōnEm ka aLktō′kuman tiā′xalaitanEma.
   they kicked him.   It grew dark   and they looked at them his arrows.

25 "Masā′tsiLx tik tiā′xalaitanEma, x·ik ilxā′qōqcin!" TakE nē′k·im
   "Pretty   these   his arrows,   this   our sister-in-law's Then   he said
                                               relative's!"

26 qix· iq¡ēyō′qxōt: "Nai′ka itci′xōtckin." "Ā, tgEt¡′ō′kti mtEnlä′xō!
   that   old man: "My   my work."   "Ah,   good   you make them
                                                                       for me!

Mēnlā'xō igē'lEXtcutk." "Mai'ka imē'Xakamit. E'XtEmaē 1
You will make a flint arrow head." "Your your mind. Sometimes
it for me

mâkct LEmE'nLEmEn nixā'nēxax, ē'XtEmaē ēXt LEmE'nLEmEn 2
two broken they get, sometimes one broken

nixā'nēxax." TakE atcayā'lōt ōguē'luXtcutk, qoā'nEm nats¡E'x 3
it gets." Then he gave them to flint pieces, five pieces
him

ōguē'luXtcutk. 4
flint.

Nē'ktcuktē a'lta. Kawī'X wiXt ā'Lo Llēq¡ā'muks. Ā'Lo ka wiXt 5
It got day now. Early again they the wolves. They and again
went went

nix'ō'tam iguā'nat iā'xa. Atciā'xōtckē igē'luXtcutk. AtcLē'kXuL¡ 6
he went to the salmon his son. He worked on them the arrow heads. He finished them
bathe

ka'nauwē'2, atciā'xōtck qiX igē'luXtcutk. ĒXt Lăqⁿ atcā'yax, 7
all, he made them these arrow heads. One take out he did it,

nixilē'maᶜ. Tsō'yustē ka wiXt aLXatgō'mam Lkanauwē'tiks. 8
he kept it. Evening and again they arrived at home all.

ALgē'Lkⁿ₁am imō'lEkuma. ALgā'yaxc ka'nauwē imō'lEkuma. A'lta 9
They brought home elks. They cut them all the elks. Now

aLgiō'kuman qix· igē'luXtcutk. Ō, it¡ō'kti x·ik igē'luXtcutk. 10
they looked at these arrow heads. Oh, good these arrow heads.

"Ā'nqatē ka aⁿgōLē'lEXEmk," nē'k·im iq¡ēyō'qxōt "itsE't¡ōxōtskin 11
"Formerly and I was a man," he said the old one, "I a good worker

igē'luXtcutk." "Wuxī'k ā'nlaxtā minlā'xō," atciō'lXam ē'Xat: 12
arrow heads." "To-morrow me next you will make he said to him one:
them for me,"

"Mai'ka imē'Xakamit." TakE wiXt aqayi'ltatkc qoā'nEm 13
"Your your mind." Then again were left for him five

ōguē'lⁿXtcutk. 14
flint-pieces.

Kawī'X ka wiXt ā'Lō Llē'q¡'am. ALxō'kumak¡aua. 15
Early and again they went the wolves. They went hunting.

Lä ka nixā'latck. A'lta atciā'xôtck igē'luXtcutk. Ka'nauwē 16
Some- and he rose. Now he made them the arrow heads. All
time

atcLē'kXōL¡. ĒXt nixelē'maᶜ. Tsō'yustē aLXatgō'mam. Nâ'pōnEm. 17
he finished them. One he kept. In the evening they arrived at home. It grew dark.

ALgiō'kuman igē'luXtcutk iā'xōtskin qix· iq¡ēyō'qxōt. La'ktka 18
They looked at them the arrow heads his work that old man. Four only

atcē'tElōtxax. ĒXt nixēlē'maᶜx. Nē'k·im wiXt ē'Xat: "WuXi 19
he gave them to him. One he kept. He said again one: "To-morrow

ā'nlaxta tcinlā'xoya, itci'qōqcin." WēXt atcē'ltatck qui'nEmi 20
me next he will make my sister-in-law's Again he left them to five times
them for me, relative." him

nats¡E'x. Kauwī'X ka ā'Lō wiXt. ALxō'kumak¡auwa. A'lta wiXt 21
pieces. Early then they again. They went hunting. Now again
went

atciā'xotckē qix· igē'luXtcutk. Ka'nauwē atcLē'kXōL¡. ĒXt 22
he worked at them those arrow heads. All he finished them. One

nixilē'maᶜ. Tsō'yustē aLXatgō'mam. Nâ'pōnEm. ALgiō'kuman 23
he kept. In the evening they arrived at home. It grew dark. They looked at it

iā'xōtckin qix· iq¡ēyō'qxōt. Ō it¡'ōkti x·ig igē'luXtcutk. "WuXī 24
his work this old man. Oh, good these arrow heads. "To-morrow

ā'nlaxta mēnlā'xo qē'qōqcin!" Aqayā'lōt quā'num nāts¡Ex 25
me next you will make my sister-in-law's They were five pieces
it for me, relative." given to him

ōguē'luXtcutk. 26
flint.

Kawī'X   ka   aLxE'lXuitck   Llē'q¡am.   A'lta   aLxō'kumak¡auwa.
Early   and   they made them-   the wolves.   Now   they went hunting.
                  selves ready

2   Nixā'latck   iguā'nat   iā'xa.   Atciā'xotskē   qix·   igē'luXtcutk.
     He arose   the salmon   his son   He worked at them   these   arrow heads.

3   AtcLē'kXōL¡   ka'nauwē   qix·   igē'luXtcutk.   ĒXt   nigilē'maᶜ.   Tsō'yustē
     He finished them   all   these   arrow heads.   One   he kept.   In the evening

4   aLXatgō'mam.   Nâ'pōnEm.   AtciLā'lōt   la'ktka,   ēXt   nixilē'maᶜ.
     they arrived at home.   It grew dark.   He gave them   four only,   one   he kept.
                                            to him

5   O   it¡'ō'kti   x·ig   igē'luXtcutk.   "WuXī'   ā'nlaxta   itci·qciX
     Oh,   good   these   arrow heads.   "To-morrow   me next   my brother-
                                                                            in-law

6   tcinlā'xō,"   nē'k·im   qix·   ixgē's'ax,   itcā'k·ikal   qaX   ōᶜō'kuil.   "Mai'ka
     he will make   he said   that   youngest one,   her husband   that   woman.   "Your
     them for me,"

7   imē'Xakamt,"   atciō'lXam.   Atcayi'ltātkc   qoā'nEm   nats¡E'x
     your mind,"   he said to him.   He left them for him   five   pieces

8   ōgnē'luXtcutk.
     flint.

     Kawī'X   ka   aLxE'ltXuitck   Llēq¡'ā'mukc.   Nixā'latck
     Early   and   they made themselves ready   the wolves.   He rose

9   iguā'nat   iā'xa.   A'lta   atciā'xôtckē   igē'luXtcutk.   Ka'nauwē
     the salmon   his son.   Now   he worked at   the arrow heads.   All
                              them

11   atcLē'kXuL¡.   ĒXt   nixēlē'maᶜ.   Tsō'yustē   aLXatgō'mam.
      he finished them.   One   he kept.   In the evening   they arrived at home.

12   ALgē'tkᵘʇam   ēmō'lEkuma.   Pā2L   takE   tE'LaqL   imō'lEkuma.
      They brought home   elks.   Full   then   their house   elks.

13   Pō'laklī   aLXatgō'mam.   A'lta   aLgiō'kuman   iā'xōtckin   qix·
      At dark   they arrived at home.   Now   they looked at it   his work   those

14   igē'luXtcutk: "O,   itsi'qsiX!   Masā'tsiLx   igē'luXtcutk,   it¡ō'kti
      arrow heads: "Oh, my brother-in-law!"   Pretty   arrow heads,   good

15   x·ik   igē'luXtcutk."   Kawī'X   ka   wiXt   aLxē'lagutck.   Ā'Lō
      these   arrow heads."   Early   and   again   they rose.   They
                                                                      went

16   aLxō'kumak¡aua.   Nixā'latck   iguā'nat   iā'xa.   Atcō'lXam   qaX
      they went hunting.   He rose   the salmon   his son.   He said to her   that

17   ōᶜō'kuil: "Mxā'latck.   A'lta   nLōtē'naya."   Naxā'latck   qaX   ōᶜō'kuil.
      woman: "Rise.   Now   I shall kill them."   She rose   that   woman.

18   "Qā't¡'ōcXEm!"   atcō'lXam.   TakE   acxE'ltXuitck.
      "Take care!"   he said to her.   Then   they made themselves ready.

      Lqui'numiks   qō'Lac   Llē'q¡'amuks,   qoā'nEm   qō'La   Lā'pLxuma.
      Five   those   wolves,   five   those   their wells.

20   TakE   actō'paē   ōyā'pʇ'au.   Atcō'cgam   ōyā'pL¡'ikē.   Atcā'Eltē
      Then   they went out   his dead father's   He took it   his bow.   He spanned it
                              wife.

21   ōyā'pL¡ike.   Gōyē'   ā'tcax   uyā'xalaitan   ē'wa   Lpakā'lēma.   A'lta   ē'tōL
      his bow.   Thus   he made it   his arrow   thus   mountains.   Now   hot

22   nē'xax.   Q'E'cq'Ec   atci'Lax   lakt   qō'La   LpLxoa'ks.   Ā'mka   qix·
      it became.   Dry   he made them   four   those   wells.   Only   that

23   ixgē's'ax   ōyā'pLx   mEnx·   LElgā'-itX   qō'La   Ltcuq.
      youngest one   his well   a little   there was   that   water.

      Ka   igō'cgēwal   iLā'xk'un.   TakE   LE'ku   nā'xax   uyā'pL¡ikē.
      And   he went much   the eldest one.   Then   break   it did   his bow.

25   TakE   atcixE'llqLēLx: "TaL¡   ia'xka,   taL¡   ia'xka   igua'nat   iā'xa
      Then   he cried much: "Lo   he,   lo   he,   the salmon   his son

      exā'ntsēlōlā'mit."   Ā'yōLx,   nē'Xkō,   Ā'yuLx,   ā'yuLx,   ā'yuLx.
26   he disguised himself   He went to   he went   He went to-   he went to-   he went to-
      before us."   the water,   home.   ward the   ward the   ward the
                                          beach,   beach,   beach.

A′lta qı̣′E′cqı̣Ec ikē′x ā′yāmxtc. Ltcuq iō′mEqtit. Ayō′yam gō·y·   **1**
Now   dry   became   his heart.   Water   he was thirsty.   He arrived   at

ōyā′pLx. Nē′k·ikst, ā′tcukct ōyā′pLx. A′lta qı̣′E′cqı̣Ec, axā′lōtX.   **2**
his well.   He looked,   he looked   his well.   Now   dry,   it was empty.
            down into

Ā′tcukct kcx·ꞁEmā′t Liā′wuX ōyā′pLx. Qı̣′E′cqı̣Ec, axā′lōtX.   **3**
He looked   the next one   his younger   his well.   Dry,   it was empty.
down into   brother

ĒkXatsak Liā′wuX ā′tcukct uyā′pLx. Qı̣′E′cqı̣Ec, axā′lōtX. Qı̣oā′p   **4**
The middle   his younger   he looked   his well.   Dry,   it was empty.   Near
one   brother   down into

ixgE′sᶜax kcx·ꞁEmā′t Liā′wuX uyā′pLx ā′tcukct; axā′lōtX. Ā′tcukct   **5**
youngest one   the next one   his younger   his well   he looked   it was empty.   He looked
         brother   down into;   down into

Lā′2wuX ōyā′pLx. A′lta mEnx· Lā′lōc. Atcō′pEna iau′a kē′kXulē.   **6**
the youngest   his well.   Now   a little   was in it.   He jumped   then   down.
brother

Atcꞁā′kXamct, atcꞁā′kXamct, atcꞁā′kXamct. Pā2L nē′xax iā′wan.   **7**
He drank,   he drank,   he drank.   Full   got   his belly.

Iā′maᶜ atcē′lax iguā′nat iā′xa; iā′maᶜ aqē′lax ilē′qı̣am, ac iā′xkatē   **8**
Shooting   he did him   the salmon   his son;   shooting   he was   the wolf,   and   there
him   him   done

ayuqunā′ētix·. Acgiō′Lata, acgiō′pcut.   **9**
he fell down.   They hauled him   they hid him.
        out,

Ka igō′cgēwal weXt ē′Xat [etc., as before]. . . . . A′lta mEnx· **10**
And   he went much   more   one   [etc., as before]. . . . .   Now   a little

Lā′lōc. Atci′Lukct qō′La Ltcuq. Nigē′kxamt, nigē′kxamt, nigē′kxamt. **11**
was in it.   He looked at it   that   water.   He looked,   he looked,   he looked.

Näkct i′kta atcē′ElkEl. TakE ayō′itcō gō qaX ōpLx. A′lta **12**
Not   anything   he saw it.   Then   he went down   to   that   well.   Now

atcꞁā′kXamct, atcaꞁā′kXamct. Pā2L nē′xax iā′wan. Iā′maᶜ atcē′lax **13**
he drank,   he drank.   Full   got   his belly.   Shooting   he did him
                                          him

iguā′nat iā′xa. Ia′xkatē ayuqunā′ētix·. Acgiō′Lata, atciō′pcut.   **14**
the salmon   his son.   There   he fell down.   They hauled   he hid him.
                              him out,

Ka igō′cgēwal wiXt ē′Xat [etc., as before]. . . . . A′lta mEnx· **15**
And   he went much   more   one   [etc., as before]. . . . .   Now   a little

Lā′lōc. Nigē′kxamt, nigē′kxamt, nigē′kxamt. Qē′xtcē pōc ayō′itcō. **16**
was in it.   He looked,   he looked,   he looked.   Intending   if   he went
                                             down.

A′lta wiXt nigē′kxamt, nigē′kxamt, nigē′kxamt. Ayā′xLakō qaX **17**
Now   again   he looked,   he looked,   he looked.   He went around it   that

ōpLx. Ē′Xtī ayā′xLakō. A′lta ayā′lEtcō, ayō′itcō. Atcꞁā′kXamct, **18**
well.   Once   he went around   Now   he went into   he went   He drank,
         it.   the hole,   down.

mEnx· atcꞁā′kXamct, ka wiXt nigē′kxamt. WiXt atcꞁā′kXamct, **19**
a little   he drank,   and   again   he looked.   Again   he drank,

atcꞁā′kxamct. PāL nē′xax iā′wan. Iā′maᶜ atcē′lax iguā′nat iā′xa. **20**
he drank.   Full   got   his belly.   Shooting   he did him   the salmon   his son.
                                him

Iā′xkatē ayuqunā′ētix·. Acgiō′Lata, acgiō′pcut.   **21**
There   he fell down.   They hauled   they hid him.
                  him out,

Ka igō′cgēwal wiXt ē′Xat [etc., as before]. . . . . A′lta mEnx· **22**
And   he went much   more   one   [etc., as before]. . . . .   Now   a little

Lā′lōc. Nigē′kxamt, nigē′kxamt, nigē′kxamt. Xā′xa nē′xax, xāx **23**
was in it.   He looked,   he looked,   he looked.   Observing   he   observe
                                             became,

atci′ctax. Qē′xtcē pōc ayōē′tcax. A′lta wiXt ayaxLā′nukL qaX **24**
he did them.   Intending   if   he went down.   Now   again   he went often around   that

ōpLx. Alā′Xti ka ayō′itcō, lē′2lē ka ayō′itcō. Atcꞁā′kXamct, **25**
well.   At last   and   he went   a long   and   he went   He drank,
                 down.   time   down.

1 mEnx· atcʇā′kXamct, wiXt ayō-iʟxē′wulx. Alā′Xti ayō′itco wiXt
  a little   he drank,   again   he went up.   At last   he went down again

2 ka atcʇā′kXamct, atcʇā′kXamct, atcʇā′kXamct. Pāʟ nē′xax iā′wan.
  and   he drank,   he drank,   he drank.   Full   got   his belly.

3 Iā′maᶜ atcē′lax iguā′nat iā′xa. Iā′xkatē ayuqunā′ētix·. Acgīō′ʟata,
  Shooting he did him the salmon his son.   There   he fell down.   They hauled
  him   him out,

4 acgiō′pcut.
  they hid him.

  Ka igō′cgēwal ixgē′sᶜax. TakE ʟEkᵘ nā′xax uyā′pʟ¡′ikē.
  And   he went much the youngest one.   Then break it did   his bow.

6 TakE atcixE′llqēlx: "Taʟ¡ iā′xka, taʟ¡ iā′xka iguā′nat iā′xa
  Then   he cried much: "Lo he,   lo   he,   the salmon his son

7 ēxā′ntselōlā′mit." A′lta nē′ʟxa; neʟxamm. Ā′tcukct ēgun ē′Xat
  he disguised himself   Now he went out he came out of   He looked   more   one
  before us."   of the woods;   the woods.   down into

8 iā′Xkun. Q¡′E′cq¡′Ec akē′x, axā′lōtX. ʟkE′nam ʟlā′ktiks
  his elder   Dry   it was,   it was empty.   Together   four
  brother.

9 Liā′xk¡uniks ʟxā′lōtX ʟā′pʟxoakc. A′lta-y- āmka-y- uyā′pʟx mEnx·
  his elder brothers were empty   their wells.   Now   only   his well   a little

10 ʟā′luc. AtcE′ʟ′Elkel mEnx· ʟᶜā′wulqt. A′lta ayaxʟā′nukʟ
  was in it.   He saw it   a little   blood.   Now   he went often around

11 uyā′pʟx, ayaxʟā′nukʟ uyā′pʟx. A′lta atcō′Xtkin, nik¡′ē′x·tkin.
  his well,   he went often around his well.   Now   he searched for them, he looked about.

12 Lēqspus atcgō′tXuitX. Atcō′pEna kē′kXulē. Atcʇā′kXamct,
  Almost   he stepped on them.   He jumped   down.   He drank,

13 atcʇā′kXamct, atcʇā′kXamct. TakE wiXt atcō′pEna kᵘcā′xalī. A′lta
  he drank,   he drank.   Then again he jumped   up.   Now

14 wiXt nik¡ē′x·tkin, nik¡ē′x·tkin, nik¡ē′x·tkin. WiXt atcō′pEna
  again he looked about, he looked about, he looked about.   Again   he jumped

15 kē′kXulē. Qoä′nēmi atcō′pEna kē′kXulē. A′lta atcʇā′kxamct.
  down.   Five times   he jumped   down.   Now   he drank.

16 Pā2ʟ nē′xax iā′wan. Iā′maᶜ atcē′lax. Atciā′k¡ ʟEmatsk atciā′waᶜ.
  Full   got   his belly.   Shooting he did.   His last one   he killed him.
                            him

  A′lta a′ctōʟx. Atcōxō′ʟXam tE′ʟaqʟ. A′lta a′ctō, aci′xko.
  Now they went down   He burnt it   their house.   Now they went, they went
  to the water.   home.

18 Ā′tcōkᵘɪ qaX ōᶜō′kuil. Actigā′ōm ikani′m. A′lta actō′tctcō
  He carried   that   woman.   They reached a canoe.   Now   they went down
  her   it   the river.

19 Kaxē′2 kulā′yi actō′yam atcō′lXam: "Ēē′wam tcinā′xt.
  Where   far   they arrived he said to her: "Sleepy   I get.

20 NExagō′kctita. A′lta qoā′nEm ʟᶜaʟā′ma nēkct mEna′ōtc!a."
  I shall lie down in   Now   five   days   not   you will awake
  canoe.   me."

21 Ayiaxagō′kctit. A′lta ā′k¡aya nō′ya qaX ōᶜō′kuil. Ayā′qxoyē,
  He lay down in canoe.   Now   alone   she went that   woman.   He slept,

22 mô′kctē ayā′qxoyē, a′lta pEmm tEmōtsgā′nuks gō iā′yacqʟ.
  twice   he slept,   now noise of flying   flies   at   his mouth.

23 Ayā′qxoyē, ʟō′nē ayā′qxoyē. A′lta pāʟ acxE′ʟ′uicā′yū. ʟā′kti
  He slept,   three he slept.   Now   full   fly-blows.   Four times
          times

24 ayā′qxoyē ka naxElā′yō-y- ō′yamōa. A′lta agiā′qxōtc!. Agiō′ʟEl,
  he slept   and they moved much his maggots.   Now   she awoke him.   She shook
                                                                         him,

25 agiō′ʟEl. Nixa′l′ōkō. Atcō′cgam: "Qa′daqa amēnā′qxōtc!?
  she shook him.   He awoke.   He took her: "Why   did you awake me?

26 Ayamō′lXam na mEna-ō′tc!a?" Atcā′xalukctgō. "O′omEn imē′xal.
  I told you   [int.   you shall awake   He threw her away.   "Pigeon   your name.
             part.]   me?"

27 Näkct ʟmē′k·ikal ā′ʟqē ʟkā′nax. Manix tcā′ko-i ka mxtcā′xa-itx."
  Not   your husband   later on chief.   When summer   and you will cry much."

TakE nikʟⱼ'ē'mEn iguā'nat. Nŏ'xunitak ŏ'omEn, qaxē'ʟx ka 1
Then   he dived   the salmon.   She drifted away   the pigeon,   where may be   and

nuXuā'niptck. A'lta ʟⱼap aci'kxax cmŏkst ckoalē'x·oa. Nē'k·im 2
she drifted ashore.   Now   find   they did her   two   ravens.   He said

qix· ē'Xat: "ĒXt itcā'xotk, ēXt itcā'melqtan. Kā'tsek ʟqⱼup 3
that   one: "One   her eye,   one   her cheek.   Middle   cut

tgā'amcukc, tqcauwē'xa." Nē'k·im qiX ē'Xat: "K·ⱼē, k·ⱼē, k·ⱼē, 4
her intestines,   we cut them in two."   He said   that one: "No,   no,   no,

k·ⱼē; nai'ka ka'namŏkst sgā'xost ka ēXt itcā'melqtan, ka kā'tsek 5
no;   I   both   her eyes   and one   her cheek,   and   middle

ʟqⱼōp tgā'amcukc tqcauwē'xa." "Imē'mElaXaqamē," atciŏ'lXam; 6
cut   her intestines,   we cut them in two."   "You are wrong,"   he said to him;

"ĒXt itcā'xot mai'ka, ēXt itcā'xot nai'ka. ĒXt itcā'melqtan 7
"One   her eye   you,   one   her eye   I.   One   her cheek

nai'ka, ēXt itcā'mElqtan mai'ka. Kā'tsek ʟqⱼōp tgā'amcukc." 8
I,   one   her cheek   you.   Middle   cut   her intestines."

KăyeX ackē'x ka naxā'latck. Nŏ'ko, akc'ē'taqʟ. 9
Thus   they did   and   she rose.   She flew away.   she left them.

A'lta ā'yo, nikᵘʟⱼē'mEn iguā'nat. Ayū'Xtki a'lta. Nigŏ'ptcgam 10
Now   he went.   he dived   the salmon.   He swam   now.   He came ashore

ēXt ilē'ē. TakE ā'yŏptck. Ā'2yŏ kulā'yi. TakE nigā'ōm ē'qxēʟ. 11
one   land.   Then   he went inland.   He went   far.   Then   he reached it   a creek.

TakE atcŏ'ikEl tXut iau'a ē'natai. TakE niXxagŏ'mit. TakE 12
Then   he saw it   smoke   there   on the other side.   Then   he made himself poor.   Then

iqⱼēyŏ'qxōt nē'xax, ka'nauwē ā'yaʟ'a iā'atcikc, ʟā'yaqtq ka'nauwē 13
an old man   he became,   all   his body   stinking,   his head   all

ʟā'tcikc. TakE naēxE'lqamX. "Ā, ʟā'ksta x·ix·ŏ'ʟa‽ Lgā'lEmam;" 14
stinking.   Then   he shouted.   "Ah,   who   that?   Go to take him;"

aʟgŏ'lXam uʟā'xk'un. Lqui'nEmiks Lxā'mEXutctikc iʟā'qula. 15
they said to her   their eldest sister.   Five   sisters   their camp.

A'lta nai'kutetē uʟā'xk'un. Naikŏ'tctam. A'lta mā'Lxôlē Lŏc. "Ā, 16
Now   she crossed   the eldest sister.   She got across.   Now   inland   he was.   "Ah,

iamtgā'lEmam; mE'Lxa." "Ā, cka aqanŏctXuē'l." Nā'Xtakō, 17
I came to fetch you;   come down to the water."   "Ah,   and   carry me on your back."   She returned,

nā'Xtakō. NaxaLEngu'Litck Lgā'mEXutctiks: "Ā, ʟqⱼēyŏ'qxot, 18
she returned.   She told them   her sisters: "Ah,   an old man,

ka'nauwē ēLaʟ'a iā'atcikc. ALgEnā'xo-il cka aqLŏ'ctXux. 19
all   his body   stinking.   He said to me much   and   I should carry him on back.

Ka'nauwē'2 pāʟ LEmŏ'ckikc ēLaʟ'a." Nā'k·im kcx·ⱼEmā't: "Nai'ka 20
All   full   pus   his body."   She said   the next eldest one: "I

nLugŏ'lEmam. Olxā'qxalptckix· LgiakEnā'oi." TakE nai'kutetē 21
go to fetch him.   Our fire   he shall look after."   Then   she crossed

akLugŏ'lEmam. "Ā, iamtgā'lEmam," akcŏ'lXam. "Ā, cka 22
she went to fetch him.   "Ah,   I came to fetch you,"   she said to him.   "Ah,   and

aqEnŏctxŏ'x." TakE nŏ'ptcga. AkLŏ'cgam gŏ iLā'potē. Qē'xtcē 23
carry me on back."   Then   she went up.   She took him   at   his arm.   Intending

agē'xk'a iLā'potē. Nau'i La'qxauwilqt wāx aLi'xax. AkL'ē'taqʟ, 24
she pulled it   his arm.   Immediately   his blood   pour out   it did.   She left him,

nā'Xko. "Maniqⱼ'ä' taʟⱼ iqⱼēyŏ'qxot. Qē'xtcē aniŏ'cgam gŏ 25
she went home.   "Too!   lo!   old.   Intending   I took him   at

iLā'potē. Nau'i Lā'qxauwilqt wāx aLi'xax." TakE agŏ'lXam 26
his arm.   Immediately   blood   pour out   it did."   Then   she said to her

Lgā'wuX: "Mai'ka Lgā'lEmam." TakE nŏ'ya ā'kXatsak. 27
her younger sister: "You   go and fetch him."   Then   she went   the middle one.

1 Naigō′tctam. "Ā iamtgā′lEmam, mE′Lxa." "Ā, cka aqanōctxō′x."
She got across. "Ah, I came to fetch you, come down." "Ah, and carry me on your back."

2 TakE nō′ptcga. Agiō′cgam iLā′pōtitk, akLō′latck. Ka′nauwē′2 wāx
Then she went up. She took it his forearm, she lifted him. All pour out

3 aLi′x[ax] Lā′qxauwilqt k¡a Lā′mōckikc. AkL′ē′taqL wiXt. TakE
it did his blood and his pus. She left him also. Then

4 nā′k·im q¡′oā′p ōxgē′sax kcx·LEmā′t: "K′c nai′ka nLugō′lEmam;
she said near the youngest the next: "And I go to fetch him;

5 ōlxā′qxalptckix· LgīakEna′oi." TakE nai′kōtctē. Naigō′tctam.
our fire he shall look after it." Then she crossed. She came across.

6 "Ā, mE′Lxa, iq¡ēyō′qxōt; iamtgā′lEmam." "Ā, cka aqanō′ctxōx."
"Ah, go down to old man; I came to fetch you." "Ah, and carry m· on your back."

7 TakE nō′ptcga. A′lta ayaxalō′ctxamt. Mank kulā′yi agāyukᵘ¡.
Then she went up. Now she carried him on her back. A little far she carried him.

8 PāL nā′xax Lɛā′owilqt; pāL nā′xax LEmō′ckikc. AgEē′taqL:
Full she got blood; full she got pus. She left him:

9 "Maniq¡ā′ taL¡ ka′nauwē iLā′atcikc. Yū′L¡aqL′Et ka′nauwē ē′LaL′a."
"Too! lo! all· stinking. Full of sores all his body."

10 TakE ōc Lā′wuX cka k¡ā ka nō′tXuit. Näkct qa′da nā′k·im. TakE
Then there their younger and silent and she stood up. Not [any] how she spoke. Then
sister

11 nai′kōtctē. TakE aLgō′lXam Lā′wuX: "Ā′xka XaX nikct itcā′yuL¡ᴛ
she crossed. Then they said to her their younger "She that not proud
sister:

12 ka kᴛōctxō." ALgā′qxamt Lā′wuX ka naigō′tctamē. TakE nā′k·im
and she will carry They looked at their younger and she got across. Then she said
him." her sister

13 uLā′xk'un: "Tc¡a." TakE ayō′tXuit. A′lta ayagā′lōLx. Tō′tō
their eldest "Look." Then he stood up. Now he went to the Shake
sister: canoe.

14 nē′xax. CEll iā′ok, taL¡ īēlā′kē iā′ok. AyagE′La-it. Actigō′tctamē.
he did. Rattling his lo! sea-otter his He was in the They two came
blanket. blanket. canoe. across.

15 Ō, masā′tsiLx Lkā′nax! A′lta atcō′cgam qaX ōxgē′s'ax,
Oh, pretty chief! Now he took her that youngest one,

16 uyā′tcinkikala na-ēxā′lax. AtcLō′mitckiL Lkanauwē′tikc, Liā′nemckc
his head wife she was to him. He took them all, his wives

17 aLixā′lax. Altā′2 ā′mka ōxgē′s'ax tq¡′ēx ā′tcax.
he made them Now only the youngest like he did her.
to him. one

A′lta aLxē′la-it iā′xkatē. Ka′nauwē Lɛalā′ma aLkᴛōlā′lEpᴛā-itx.
Now he stayed there. All days they went always digging roots.

19 Iā′mka aLEē′taqLax. Tcä2xLx Lɛalā′ma aLEē′taqL, ka nā′Xko
Him alone they left him. Several days they left him, and she went home

20 ā′nēwa-y· uLā′xk'un. NaXkō′mam. A′lta k¡ē gō Lā′o-imatk. Nō′Lxa
first she the eldest one. She came home. Now nothing at their camp. She went to the beach

21 mā′Lnē. A′lta iā′qxoyō gō iLā′xanīma. Iakqauā′itx·. Lawā′
seaward. Now he slept in their canoe. He lay down. Slowly

22 agiō′tctEmt iLā′xanīma. MaLxolā′-y· ē′kxāt. A′lta atciō′pēwē
she pushed it their canoe. From land wind. Now it drifted

23 mā′Lnē. Mā2′Lnē ka nēxE′l'ōkō. Atciō′latck iā′ok. A′lta k¡ē-y·
seaward. Seaward and he awoke. He lifted it his blanket. Now no

24 ilē′ē. Nēkct atcē′ElkEl. WeXt nixk¡ē′nyakō. Ayā′qxoya, mō′kcti
land. Not he saw it. Again he tied blanket He slept, twice
around himself.

25 ayā′qxoya. NixE′l'ōkō, a′lta t¡ā′qē lā′xlax ikē′x iā′xanīm.
he slept. He awoke, now just as rock it did his canoe.

NēElkĕ'Elakō.   A'lta gō ʟux iūgō'ōX.   Ayĕā'lōʟx.   Atciusgē'wulX   **1**
He took off his   Now   at island   it was on the   He went ashore.   He hauled it up
blanket.   beach.

iā'xanīm.   Lāx atcā'yax iā'xanīm.   A'lta iā'xkatĕ kē'kXulē nixō'kctē.   **2**
his canoe.   Turned   he made it   his canoe.   Now   there   below   he lay down.
            over

Kawī'X ka LgōLē'lEXEmk aLE'tĕ gō Lkamēlā'lEq, tcx tcx tcx tcx   **3**
Early   and   a person   came   on   the sand,   noise of footsteps

gō Lkamēlā'lEq.   Nā'wi aLigā'luptck qaxē' qigō' nikē'x.   TakE   **4**
on   the sand.   Immediately   she went up   where there   where   he was.   Then

aLgiō'lXam: "Amxā'latck, txgō'ya." TakE nixā'latck. AcgiucgēʼwulX   **5**
she said to him: "Rise,   let us go!"   Then   he rose.   They pulled up

iā'xanīm ka cā'cā acgā'yax.   A'lta aci'Xkō.   AcXgō'mam gō qō'ta   **6**
his canoe   and   break   they did it.   Now   they went   They arrived at   at   that
        to pieces   home.   home

t!'ōL.   A'lta pāL ēlagē'tEma qō'ta t!'ōL.   A'lta agiō'pcut.   Lä2   **7**
house.   Now   full   sea-otters   that   house.   Now   she hid him.   Some-
                                                      time

ka naxatgō'mam ugō'xk'un. Môkct itcā'ctxōl ēlagē'tEma. Kawī'X   **8**
and   she came home   her elder sister.   Two   her load   sea-otters.   Early

ka wiXt a'ctō. Ā'nēwa naxatgō'mam qaX uXgē's'ax. ĒXtka   **9**
and   again   they went.   First   she came home   that   youngest one.   One only

ēlā'kē ʟ‚ap agā'yax. TakE agō'lXam Lgā'wuX qaX uxkE'kxun: **10**
sea-otter   find   she did.   Then   she said to her   her younger   that   eldest one:
                                            sister

"Ā'nqatē taʟ‚ amxatgō'mam." "Aiā'q anE'Xatkō qē'wa nikct ē'kta   **11**
"Long ago,   lo!   you came home."   "Quick   I returned   as   not   anything

ʟ‚ap anā'yax." TakE naxLōlExa-it ugō'xk'un: "Qa'da ā'Lqē nakē'x,   **12**
find   I did it."   Then   she thought   her elder sister: "How   later on she will be,

ka nikct ē'kta ʟ‚ap agā'yax, axā'xo-il." Wāx kawī'X ka a'ctō,   **13**
and   not   anything   find   she did it,   she always   Next morn-   early   and   they
                                  says."   ing   went,

iLā'môkctē a'ctō. Actā'ckta, actuxōLā'kux qō'La Lux. Iā'kwa nō'ix   **14**
the second time   they   They searched   they went around   that   island.   Here   always
               went.   on the beach,   it,   went

qaX ā'ēXat, iau'a ta'nata qō'ta Lux nō'ix qaX ā'ēXat qaX   **15**
that   one,   there   to the other   that   island   always   that   one   that
                   side   went

ōxgi'c'ax. Gō ku'mk·itē qō'ta Lux ka acXā'ōmX. A'lta kulā'yi   **16**
youngest one.   At   the end of   that   island   and   they met.   Now   far

qī'gō acXā'omEniLx, a'lta naxtā'kōx qaX uxgE'c'ax. A'lta xāx   **17**
where   they always met,   now   she returned   that   youngest one.   Now   observe

ā'kxax qaX Lgā'wuX qaX ōxgE'kXun. Ā'nēwa qaX uqgE'c'ax   **18**
she did her   that   her younger   that   eldest one.   First   that   youngest one
               sister

naxgō'mam. Wāx kawī'X weXt ā'ctō. Nō'ya qāxē qīgō   **19**
came home.   The next   early   again   they went.   She went   where   there
        morning   where

acXā'omEniLx. K·‚ē tgā'xatk qaX Lgā'wuX. Gō kulā'yi a'lta   **20**
they always met.   Nothing   her tracks   that   her younger   At   far   now
                                   sister's.

ōXutā'kot tgā'xatk. TakE pāt xāx ā'kxax. Nā'xkō, Lōn ʟ‚ap   **21**
they turned   her tracks.   Then   really   observe   she did   She went   those   find
back   her.   home,

agā'yax ēlagē'tEma. AgE'tukct ctā'Xti. A'lta ōxoē'Lk‚ik tgā'Xti   **22**
she did them   sea-otters.   She saw it   their smoke.   Now   crooked   her smoke

qaX Lgā'wuX. AgE'tukc ā'xka tgā'Xti. A'lta wuk‚ qōta tgā'Xti   **23**
that   her younger   She saw it   her own   her smoke.   Now   straight   that   her smoke
       sister.

ā'xka. A'lta pāt xāx ā'kxax. Wāx iLā'laktē ā'ctō, cka mank   **24**
her.   Now   really   observe   she did   The next   the fourth   they   and   a little
                         her.   morning   time   went,

kulā'yi nō'ya qaX uxgE'c'ax ka naXā'takō. Nō'ya qaX ōxgE'kXun   **25**
far   she went   that   youngest one   and   she turned back.   She went   that   eldest one

1 nōxo'Lakō qōta LuX. A'lta kulā'yi, a'lta aXLā'kōt, tgā'kipLaXat
she went around that island. Now far, now she had returned, her tracks

2 uxōtā'kōt. WiXt agE'tōkct ctā'Xti. A'lta pät ōxuē'Lkĭik ctā'Xti.
had returned. Again she saw it their smoke. Now really crooked their smoke.

3 TakE nā'xkō qaX ōxgE'kXun. Naxgō'mam. Ā'nqatē iō'c Lgā'wuX.
Then she went home that eldest one. She arrived at home. Already there was her younger sister.

4 Agō'lXam: "Ā'nqatē taLĭ amXatgō'mam." "Näkct ē'kta Lĭap
She said to her: "Already behold you came home." "Not anything find

5 anā'yax ka aiā'q anE'Xatkō." Wäx kawī'X ka wiXt ā'ctō
I did it and quick I returned." The next morning early and again they went

6 ē'LaquinEmē. A'nēwa nō'ya qaX ōxXE'kXun. Naxā'pcut,
the fifth time. First she went that eldest one. She hid herself,

7 agā'qxamt Lgā'wuX. Kĭimtā' ka nō'ya. Nā'Xtakō. Nakĭ'ē'Xtkin
she watched her her younger sister. Afterward and she went. She returned. She searched

8 gō Lgā'wuX itcā'lEXamitk. Lĭap agE'Lax LE'kXala, Lō'ktik.
at her younger sister her bed. Find she did him a man, he lay down.

9 "Mxā'latck," agiō'lXam, "mxā'latck. Nau'itka amtE'Lĭāla. Qa'daqa
"Rise," she said to him, "rise! Indeed you two are foolish. Why

10 agEmupcō'lit?" NaXkō'mam Lgā'wuX. A'lta iō'c itcā'k·ikal.
did she hide you?" She came home her younger sister. Now there was her husband.

11 A'lta agō'lXam ugō'Xkun: "Ō nau'itka mE'Lĭāla, nēkct
Now she said to her her elder sister: "Oh, indeed you are foolish, not

12 tEmē'Xatakux. Qa'daqa amīupcō'lit itxā'k·ikala? Qēc nai'ka Lĭap
your mind. Why did you hide him our husband always? If I find

13 anā'yax, pōc nikct aiamxa'pcut." A'lta atcō'cgam; ckanacmō'kct
I did him, [if] not I hid him." Now he took her; together both

14 ciā'k·ikal acixā'lax. Iō'2Lqtē iā'xkatē ayō'La-it. A'lta nē'k·im:
his wives they became. A long time there he stayed. Now he said:

15 "ikā'kXuL tcinā'xt." A'lta acgiō'lXam ciā'k·ikal cē'iuwall. A'lta
"Homesick I get." Now they two spoke to him his wives [birds]. Now

16 acgiō'tXuitck. Qoā'nEm ē'tElōc agē'lōt ā'eXat; ō'xqun'a, wiXt
they made him ready. Five baskets full she gave the one; the eldest one, also

17 quā'nEm ē'tElōc agē'lot; ōxgE'c'ax wiXt qoā'nEm ē'tElōc agē'lōt.
five baskets full she gave them to him; the youngest also one five baskets full she gave them to him.

18 TakE acgiō'lXam: "Wu'xi a'lta qamō'kᵘ Tai." Nä'ktcuktē, a'lta
Then they said to him: "To-morrow now you will be carried." It got day, now

19 yuqunā'-itX gō mā'Lnē ē'kōlē, LpE'lpEl ē'kōlē. A'lta aqēā'kElkoē
there lay on the beach a whale, a red whale. Now they were carried to the canoe

20 ēelagē'tEma. A'lta aqiō'lXam: "Amxō'kctit! Nēkct mgē'kcta!"
sea-otters. Now he was told: "Lie down! Not look!"

21 Qoä'nEmī ayā'qxoyē ka nēElgē'lakō. A'lta mā'Lxolē yuqunā'-itX
Five times his sleeps and he took off his blanket. Now on shore it lay

22 qix· ē'kōlē. Lqĭōp atcā'yax qoä'nEmi iā'kiLqĭp. A'lta atciō'kXuiptck
that whale. Cut he did it five times its cuts. Now he carried them from the shore upward

23 qix· ēelagē'tEma. A'lta wiXt nē'Xtakō qix· ē'kōlē.
those sea-otters. Now again it returned that whale.

24 Lä 2, ka Lĭap aLgā'yax Lgō'Lē'lEXEmk. Iōc gō mā'Lnē. IgE'lxac
Some time and find he did him a person. He was at at beach. It lay near him

25 iā'kōlē, igE'lxac ēelagē'tEma. TakE atcLō'lXam LgōLē'lEXEmk:
his whale, they lay near him his sea-otters. Then he said to him to that person:

26 "Qāxē Lgā'nEmcks aLxēlā'itix·?" "Ā Lxēlā'-itix· gō tE'LaqL."
"Where my wives are they?" "Ah, they are in their house."

"Ai'aq amᴌōlā'ma ᴌE'ʟxa."   TakE ā'ʟōptck qō'ʟa ʟgōʟē'lEXEmk.   **1**
"Quick tell them they come to the beach."   Then he went up that person. from the beach

"Ā īmcā'k·ikal iXatgō'mam.   TcEmcā'xo-il mcō'ʟxa."   Qōcta   **2**
"Ah, your husband he has come home.   He says to you you come to the beach."   Those

cmȯkct nēkct ʟE'ctaqcō.   Lqɩ'ōp aʟgE'ctax ʟE'ctaqcō.   AʟE'ʟxam   **3**
two not their hair.   Cut they did it their hair.   They came down to the beach

a'lta ʟʟā'ktikcka.   K·ɩē-y- ūʟā'xk'un, nēkct nā'ʟxam.   Aqiō'Xuptck   **4**
now four only.   Not their elder sister, not she came down to the beach   It was carried up from the beach

qix· ē'kōlē.   Aqiō'Xuptck qix· ēelagē'tEma.   "Ai'aq mcgōlā'ma   **5**
that whale.   They were carried up those sea-otters.   "Quick tell her

umcā'xk'un ā'ʟxa.   Gitgā'lEmama x·ix· ē'kōlē."   Aʟgō'lXam   **6**
your elder sister she shall come to the beach.   She shall fetch it this whale."   They said to her

uʟā'xk'un: "ME'ʟxa, mE'ʟxa, igā'lEmam x·iau ē'kōlē."   A'lta   **7**
their elder sister: "Go to the beach, go to the beach, fetch it this whale."   Now

aʟaxEl'E'tcam, akʟō'cgam ʟᵋā'tcau, aʟaxa'lltigō.   Agō'cgam   **8**
she combed herself, she took it grease, she greased herself.   She took it

unuā'lEma.   A'lta naxgē'matsk.   A'lta nō'ʟxa.   TakE nō'yam.   **9**
paint.   Now she painted her face.   Now she went to the beach.   Then she arrived.

TakE atciō'latck qix· ē'kōlē.   NaxE'ʟxēkō iau'a mā'ʟxolē.   "Iau'a   **10**
Then he lifted it that whale.   She turned round here landward.   "Here

mā'ʟnē mxE'ʟxēkō," atcō'lXam.   NaxE'ʟxēkō iau'a mā'ʟnē.   **11**
seaward turn," he said to her.   She turned round here seaward.

Aqēalō'ctxamt qix· ē'kōlē.   Naui yukpä't natlō'tXuit Ltcuq. WiXt   **12**
It was put on her back that whale.   At once up to here she stood in the water.   Again

aqiō'latck qix· ē'kōlē.   Naui yukpä't natlō'tXuit.   Qoä'nEmī   **13**
it was lifted that whale.   At once up to here she stood in the water.   Five times

aqiō'latck.   TakE nō'kuiXa.   TakE nō'ya, gō'yē agE'tax tgā'potē.   **14**
it was lifted.   Then she swam.   Then she went, thus she did them her arms.

A'lta nō'kō.   "O'waniō imē'xal.   Manix tEllō' ixā'xoēlEmxē   **15**
Now she flew.   "Coatch your name.   When calm it gets

ka wulElElE mugō'ya.   Näkct muXugō'mit tkanā'ximc."   **16**
and wulElElE you will fly.   Not you will make them poor chiefs."

A'lta ā'yuptck, a'lta niXgō'mam gō Lia'nEmckc.   AtciʟE'lEmak,   **17**
Now he went up, now he came home to his wives.   He gave each food,

kanauwē' atciʟE'lEmak, qix· ēelagē'tEma, ēXt iā'kiʟqɩp ē'kōlē   **18**
all he gave them food, those sea-otters, one its cut whale

Lē'Xat Liā'k·ikal LkanEmElō'ktikc Lɩā'nEmckc.   **19**
one his wife all his wives.

Translation.

Once upon a time there was a chief who had a daughter. Many people wanted to marry her, but he was unwilling to part with her. [Finally he arranged for a contest.] He put [a pair of] elk antlers [in the middle of the house and said]: "Whosoever breaks these antlers shall have my daughter." He invited all the people. First the quadrupeds, then the birds. [When all were assembled] the people said to the snail: "You try first to break them." The snail went down to the middle of the house and tried to break the antlers, but did not succeed.

Then they said to the squirrel: "You try next to break them." The squirrel bent the antlers a little, but was not able to break them. Then they said to the otter: "Now you try to break them." When the otter went down the girl thought: "I wish he would break them." She liked him [because he was so pretty]. He tried to break them, but did not succeed. He went up again. Next the beaver went down. He was very stout, and Blue-Jay said: "Oh, certainly, he with his big belly, he will break them." He took up the antlers and almost succeeded in breaking them, but he grew tired and went back. Then the wolf went down and almost succeeded in breaking the antlers, but he grew tired and went up. Then the bear went down and almost succeeded in breaking the antlers.

Now there was one person in the house whose body was full of sores and boils. Then Blue-Jay said: "Let him try what he can do, the one whose body is sore all over." But next the grizzly bear went down. He almost broke it, when he also grew tired. Next the panther, the chief of all, went down, but he did not succeed. Then Ipo'ĕpoē went down. Then the girl thought: "O, if he would break them." He took them up, but did not succeed at all. He went up. After that the sparrow-hawk went down. He almost broke them, and went up; then another hawk went down. He almost broke them, but then he grew tired. Now next the chicken-hawk went down. He tried to move them, but they did not move. Then the owl went down. They did not move. Then he went back. Then the eagle went down. He bent them and almost broke them. Now all the quadrupeds and all the birds had tried.

Then Blue-Jay said: "Give the antlers to that one who is full of sores; let him try what he can do." All the people had given it up. He continued: "Quick, stand up; [let us see] what can you accomplish? Break those antlers." Five times he said so. Then that person arose, shook his body, and shook his blanket. He shook his hair. [Then his body became clean, his hair long and full of dentalia, and he was very beautiful. They saw that he was the salmon.] Then he went to the middle of the house, took up the antlers and broke them. He broke them into five pieces and threw them down. Then he ran away. The people stared at him. After a little while Blue-Jay said: "Let us pursue our chief's niece." Then she took her dentalia and ran also. "Ah," said the wolf, "we will pursue them." Then all the people went in pursuit. They followed them a long distance. Then the man created a bay behind them. The people reached it, but the couple was already on the other side. After a while the people reached the other side of the bay. They continued to pursue them. Again they pursued them a long distance. He looked back and saw that the people were near overtaking them. Then he made a middle-sized bay. Again the people reached the bay and saw the two far away on the other side. Again the people reached the other side of the bay and continued their pursuit.

He made five bays, then he gave it up. The people crossed all five bays. Coyote and Badger, who were among the pursuers, became tired, and Coyote said to his friend: "My friend, I am getting tired. What do you think if I enchant my arrow?" Badger replied: "All right." Then Coyote blew on his arrow [singing]: "Strike his head, strike his head." Three times he sang to his arrow: "Strike his head, strike his head." And five times he blew on it. Then he shot upward and the arrow went "Halululululululu." The arrow struck the young man right in the nape and he fell down dead. The wolves were first among the pursuers, and they took the woman. The people devoured the salmon. They gave coyote the salmon's bow. Then an egg fell down from him into a hole in the rock. Then the people went home. Now the Crow learned that her nephew had been killed. She went away and cried. She cried. Now she arrived at the place where he had been killed. She [looked for his remains,] turned over the stones, cried, and turned them again. Then she found one salmon egg. She carried it to the river, made a small hole [in the bank of the river] and put the egg into the water. In the evening she went home.

Early next morning the Crow went again to look after that egg. It had grown a little. Then she made a larger hole [and put the egg into it]. In the evening she went home again. She reached her house. She did not sleep at all, and it grew day again. Early in the morning she went again [to look after the egg]. She cried while going. She arrived at that salmon egg. Now a small trout was swimming [in the hole]. This gladdened her a little. She made a still larger hole. In the evening she went home and slept a little. Early in the morning she went out again the fourth time. She arrived at that salmon egg and saw a large trout swimming there. Then the Crow was really glad. She made a large hole. Early in the afternoon she went home. She arrived at home. When it grew dark she fell asleep. Early in the morning she awoke, arose, and went to look after the trout. She arrived and saw a small salmon swimming there. Now she made a still larger hole and left it again. At noon she went home. She arrived at home. She thought only of the salmon. It grew dark. Early the next morning she went again. She arrived and now there swam a large salmon. She took it, threw it ashore, and it was transformed into a tall boy. Now the Crow was happy. They went home together. She said to her grandnephew: "Bathe, that you may see spirits." He bathed. First he bathed in the river and after that in the sea. Every night he bathed. After he had finished bathing in the sea, he bathed in [ponds on] the mountains. Now he became a young man.

Then his grandaunt told him: "Coyote and his friend Badger killed your father. If it had not been for that woman they would not have killed him. They took her to the wolves." He replied: "I will go and search for Coyote." "Do not go, else they will kill you." After a while the Crow told him: "They gave your father's bow to Coyote."

"I will go and search for Coyote; I have seen enough spirits." "Oh, tell me who is your spirit?" Then he said to his grandaunt: "Let us go outside." The Crow went out with him. Then he shot his arrow toward the forest and it caught fire. He shot his arrow toward the prairie and it caught fire. Then the Crow said: "Indeed you have seen spirits." She said: "You must go, but take care of yourself." The next day he made himself ready. He put on his dentalia and took his arrows. Then it thundered, although the sky was clear. He went on and crossed five prairies.

Then he saw a house [a long way off]. He went on and when he came near the house he heard a person singing songs of victory. He stayed outside. Somebody was singing there at the end of the house. Slowly he opened the door and stood in the doorway. Then Coyote sneezed and sang jestingly: "Salmon's son came; certainly he will kill me. But I jump about much in my house; certainly he will kill me." He had put black paint on his face. His face was blackened, and so was Badger's face. At that moment the door made a noise and he looked back to the doorway. Verily there stood the one in the door whom they had killed. "O, my dear, my dear!" said Coyote, "they killed him whom I loved so well. Somebody who looks just like him is walking about." Then the salmon's son entered. He sat down on the bed and said: "Be quiet, Coyote! I know that you killed my father." Then Coyote was quiet. Badger meanwhile turned his face toward the wall and was rubbing it [in order to remove the paint]. The salmon's son said: "Give me my father's bow." Coyote replied: "I will give it to you, my dear!" He arose and took a bow out [of a box]. [The young man] took it and spanned it. It broke to pieces, and he struck Coyote with the pieces so that he fell down headlong. His feet quivered. Then Coyote arose again. The salmon's son said: "Give me my father's bow." Coyote replied: "I will give it to you, my dear." He took out another bow and gave it to him. [When the young man tried to span it it broke and] he struck Coyote's face with the pieces. He fell on his back and his feet quivered. Again he arose [and the salmon's son said once more]: "Give me my father's bow! Why do you deceive me?" Then Coyote gave him another bow to the back of which heads of woodpeckers were glued. The young man spanned it with his left hand. It did not break. Then he spanned it with his right hand and it broke to pieces. He struck Coyote with the pieces and he fell on his back. Then Coyote had given him four bows; and they all broke. The fifth one which he gave him was his father's bow. Three times he spanned it with his left hand; three times he spanned it with his right hand. It did not break. The heads of red-headed woodpeckers were put by twos on the back of that bow. Then the young man said to Badger: "Be quiet, Badger, I know that you are a murderer." Badger replied: "I am no murderer; I merely blackened my face for fun." Then the young man took hold of Coyote and Badger at their napes, hauled them out of the house, struck them together and killed them. He threw down Coyote and said: "Coyote will be your name; henceforth you will not kill chiefs." He threw down Badger and said: "Badger will be your name; henceforth you will not kill chiefs. People will fear only your winds. You will never go near men." He threw them away and burned their house.

He went on. [After traveling sometime] he came to a prairie. He crossed it and saw smoke arising at its end. He went on. He almost reached a house, and heard a woman crying inside. He opened the door slowly, but it made a noise. The woman looked up and saw him; [he looked like] her husband whom they had killed. He entered. The house was full of meat. He said: "I came to look for you; let us go home. The one who was killed was my father." Then she replied: "The monsters will kill you." "Let them kill me," he said. She gave him to eat and he ate. In the afternoon he went outside and cut five pieces of flesh from his nape. He tied them up. Then he ate alder-bark until his stomach became full. He re-entered the house and gave the woman the five bundles of meat, saying: "When the monsters come home give each one of them a bundle of meat. If they eat it I shall be able to win over them. Give it to them when they notice me." Now he deceived them. He blew on the fire until he was covered with ashes and looked like an old man.

In the evening the noise of falling objects was heard. A person entered and when he came to the middle of the house he cried: "I smell salmon; I smell salmon." When he saw the old man he kicked him many times, until blood came out of his mouth.* Then the woman arose and gave him one bundle of meat, saying: "I am a human being; do you think I have no relatives? This old man [is one of my family]; he brought this for you." "O, my sister-in-law's relative, why did you not tell me before, I should not have hurt my sister-in-law's relative." After a little while a noise was heard again. Another person appeared. He entered. When he was near the middle of the house he cried: "I smell salmon; I smell salmon." When he noticed the old man he kicked him many times, so that he flew about and blood came out of his mouth. Then the woman arose and said: "I am a human being; do you think I have no relatives? This old man brought this for you." And she gave him one bundle of meat. "O, my sister-in-law's relative, why did you not tell me before, I should not have hurt my sister-in-law's relative." Again a noise was heard outside and a person appeared. He entered. Some distance before he reached the middle of the house he said: "I smell salmon; I smell salmon." When he saw the old man he kicked him and he flew about in the house and blood came out of his mouth. The woman waited a little while, then she arose and took a bundle of meat and gave it to her brother-in-law, saying: "I am a human being; do you think I have no relatives? This

---

*In fact he was expectorating the juice of the alder bark which he had chewed.

old man brought this for you." "O, my sister-in-law's relative, poor man, why did you not tell me long ago? I should not have hurt my sister-in-law's relative." Again a noise was heard and one more person appeared. He had hardly entered the house when he said: "I smell salmon; I smell salmon." When he saw the old man he kicked him so that he flew about and blood came from his mouth. The woman waited a long time. Then she said: "I am a human being. Do you think I have no relatives? This old man brought this for you;" and she gave him one bundle of meat. "O, my sister-in-law's relative, why did you not tell me long ago, I should not have hurt my sister-in-law's relative." And he ate the piece of salmon. Now only her husband remained [outside]. After a little while a noise was heard and one more person appeared. He just opened the door when he noticed the smell of salmon and said: "I smell salmon; I smell salmon." When he saw the old man he kicked him many times, so that he flew about and blood came from his mouth. The woman hesitated, and the old man was kicked much. Then she arose and said: "I am a human being. Do you think I have no relatives? This old man brought this for you." She gave him that bundle. "O, my brother-in-law, why did you not tell me long ago? I should not have hurt my brother-in-law."

Now they skinned and carved the elks and wanted to give some of the meat to the old man, but he did not eat it. The woman said: "Perhaps you have broken his ribs, so that he can not eat." Early the following morning the wolves made themselves ready and went hunting. Then the young salmon arose and went bathing. The woman boiled food for him, which he ate. After he had finished they went to bed. In the afternoon he again blew into the fire [so that he was covered with ashes] and became an old man. In the evening the wolves arrived at home and brought elks. This time they did not kick him. In the evening they looked at his arrows and said: "How pretty are the arrows of our sister-in-law's relative!" He replied: "I made them." "Make one for me; make me a flint arrowhead," said the eldest brother. The young salmon replied: "Willingly; but sometimes I will break a piece or two of flint." Then he gave him five pieces of flint. Early the next morning the wolves went hunting again. When they had gone the salmon's son went to bathe and then worked at the arrowheads. He finished them all. He took one and kept it for himself. In the evening the wolves returned and brought home elks. After they had carved them they looked at the arrowheads and said: "How pretty are these arrowheads." The salmon replied: "[That is nothing,] when I was a young man I knew how to make arrowheads." The second wolf said: "To-morrow you must make some for me." "Willingly." Then he gave him five pieces of flint. Early the next morning the wolves went hunting. After some time he arose and made the arrowheads. He finished them all, but kept one for himself. In the evening they arrived at home. When it had become dark they looked at the arrowheads which the old man had made. He gave him four and kept one for himself. Then the next said: "To-morrow you must make some for me, my sister-in-law's relative." He also left five pieces of flint. Early the next morning they left and went hunting. Now he worked again at the arrowheads and finished all. He kept one for himself. In the evening the wolves arrived at home. When it grew dark they looked at the old man's work. "Oh, how pretty are these arrowheads," they said. Then the fourth wolf said: "To-morrow you must make some for me, my sister-in-law's relative." He gave him five pieces of flint. Early the next morning the wolves made themselves ready and went hunting. Then the salmon's son arose. He worked at the arrowheads and finished them all. One he kept for himself. In the evening the wolves arrived at home. It grew dark and he gave them four arrowheads, one he kept for himself. "Oh, how pretty are these arrowheads." "To-morrow my brother-in-law will make some for me," said the youngest wolf, the husband of that woman. "Willingly," replied he. He left five pieces of flint for him. Early the next morning the wolves made themselves ready and went hunting. Then the salmon's son arose; he worked at the arrowheads and finished them; one he kept for himself. In the evening they arrived at home and brought elks. Their house was full of elk meat. When it grew dark they looked at the arrowheads. which he had made: "Oh, my brother-in-law, your arrowheads are pretty, they are good." Early the next morning they arose again and went hunting. Then the salmon said to the woman: "Arise, now I shall kill them." The woman arose. "Take care," she said. Then they made themselves ready.

The five wolves had each a well. The salmon's son and his widow went out of the house. He took his bow and spanned it; he pointed his arrow to the mountains. Then it became hot and the wells dried up, except that of the youngest wolf, in which a little water remained.

The eldest one was on his hunt; [the heat dried the bows of the hunters and when the eldest wolf spanned] his bow it broke. Then he cried: "O, certainly the salmon's son came in disguise." He went to the beach. He became very thirsty and came to his well; he looked into it and it was dry and empty. He looked into that of his younger brother; it was also dry and empty. Then he looked into the well of the middle one; it was dry and empty. He looked into the well of the next brother; it was dry and empty. Then he looked into the well of his youngest brother, and there he found a little water. He jumped down and began to drink. He drank, and drank, and drank until he had enough. Then the salmon's son shot him. He fell right where he stood. They hauled out the body and hid it.

And the second brother was on his hunt [etc., as before]. He found a little water. He looked at it. He looked and looked, but he did not see anything and went into the well and began to drink. He drank, and drank, and drank, until he had enough. Then the salmon's son shot him and he fell right where he stood. They hauled out the body and hid it.

And one more went out to hunt [etc., as before]. He found a little water. He looked, and looked, and looked. He intended to go down, but looked again. He went around the well once. Then he jumped down into it. He drank a little and looked again. Then he drank again. He drank, and drank, and drank, until he had enough. Then the salmon's son shot him. He fell down right where he stood. They hauled out the body and hid it.

And still another went out to hunt [etc., as before]. A little water was in the well. He looked, and looked, and looked. He observed something suspicious, but decided to go down. He went around the well many times, and waited a long time; then he went down. He drank a little, then came up. At last he went down again, and drank, and drank, and drank until he was full. Then the salmon's son shot him and he fell. They hauled him out and hid him.

And the youngest one went out to hunt. Then he broke his bow. He cried: "Oh, the salmon's son came to us in disguise." Then he went out of the woods and looked into the wells of his elder brothers. They were dry and empty. The wells of his four elder brothers were dry, but a little water was in his own well. He saw a little blood. Then he went often around his well and he searched for them. He looked about. He almost stepped on them. Then he jumped down and drank. He jumped up again. Now he looked up again and looked about. He jumped down again. Five times he jumped up and down. Then he drank and got enough. Then the salmon's son shot him. He killed the last one.

Now the man and the woman went down to the water and burnt their house. He went home and took the woman along. They came to their canoe and went down the river. When they had gone a distance he said: "I am getting sleepy. I shall lie down in the canoe; you shall not awake me until after five days." He lay down in the canoe, and they traveled on. He slept two nights; then the woman noticed flies on his mouth. After three nights she saw that he was full of fly-blows, and after four nights she saw maggots crawling around his mouth. Then she [became afraid] and awoke him. She shook him. He awoke, took hold of her and said: "Why did you awake me? Did I tell you to awake me?" He flung her into the water and said: "Your name will be Pigeon; henceforth you will not be the wife of a chief. Your cry will be heard in summer." Then the salmon jumped into the water. The pigeon drifted away and somewhere she drifted ashore. After awhile two ravens found her. One of them said: "I will take one of her eyes and I will take one of her cheeks; we will divide the intestines." "No," said the other, "I will take both her eyes and one of her cheeks; we will divide the intestines." "You are wrong," replied the other, "one eye for you, one eye for me, one cheek for me, and one cheek for you; we will divide the intestines." While they were talking she arose, flew away and left them.

Now the salmon swam away. After awhile he came to a country and went ashore. He went a long way and came to a creek. He saw smoke arising on the other side. Then he assumed the form of an old man. His whole body and his head were full of scabs. He shouted. Five sisters were camping there. [When they heard him they said to the eldest one:] "Who is that? Go and fetch him." She went across the creek and when she saw him she said: "Come down to the water, I came to fetch you." "Oh," he replied, "carry me on your back." She returned and said to her sisters, "It is an old man; he told me that I should carry him on my back, but his body is all full of scabs." The next younger sister said: "I will go and fetch him. He shall look after our fire." She went across the creek and said: "I come to fetch you." "Oh, carry me on your back." She went up and took him by his arm and was going to take him, but blood came out at once. Therefore she left him and went home. She said: "He is too old, I touched his arm and blood came out at once." Then she said to her younger sister: "Go and fetch him." The middle one went across the creek. She arrived on the other side and said: "I come to fetch you, come down to the water." "Oh, carry me on your back." Then she went up and took hold of his arm. She lifted him and blood and matter came out at once. Then she also left him. Then the next sister said: "I will go and fetch him; he shall take care of our fire." She went across, and when she arrived on the other side said: "Come down, old man, I came to fetch you." "Oh, carry me on your back." She went up and took him on her back. She carried him a short distance, and became full of blood and matter. She left him. [When she came back to her sisters she said:] "He is indeed too full of scabs and sores." Then the youngest sister arose and went across the creek without saying a word. They said to her: "You are not proud, you will certainly be willing to carry him." They saw how their younger sister went across. Then the eldest one said: "Look!" The old man came and went to the canoe. He shook himself. Then [his scabs fell off and] he had a fine sea-otter blanket on. He went into the canoe and the girl carried him across. He was a beautiful chief. He married the sisters and the youngest one became his head wife. He married them all; but he loved only the youngest one.

Now they lived there for some time and the women went digging roots every day. They left him alone. After several days the eldest sister came home first. She did not find him in the camp, and when she went down to the beach she saw him asleep in their canoe. He lay there. She pushed the canoe slowly from the shore. There was a land-breeze and the wind drifted it seaward. When the man

awoke he lifted his blanket and saw no land. Then he covered his
face again. He slept for two days. Then he awoke; he felt as though
the canoe was rocking. He took off his blanket and saw that he was
on the beach of an island. He went ashore. He hauled his canoe up,
turned it over, and lay down beneath it. In the morning he heard the
noise of steps on the beach, and he saw a woman coming. She stepped
right up to where he lay and said: "Rise! Let us go home." He arose.
They hauled up his canoe and she broke it to pieces. Now they went
home. They reached a house which was full of sea-otters. She hid
him. After awhile [another woman] her elder sister entered the house.
She carried two sea-otters on her back. Early the following morning
they went again and the youngest one came home before the other.
She carried one sea-otter only. Then the elder one said to her: " Lo!
You are home already!" [The younger one replied:] " Yes I came
home because I did not find anything." Then the elder sister thought:
" What is the matter with her? She says that she does not find anything." On the following morning they went the second time. They
always searched on the beach going around the island. The one always
went on one side of the island, the other on the other. At the farther
end of the island they used to meet. Now the younger one returned
long before she reached the place where they always met. The elder
one observed her. Again she came home first. Early the next morning they went again. When the elder one got to the place where they
always met, she found no tracks of her younger sister. [She went on
and saw] she had turned back long ago. Then she observed her more
closely. She came home; she had found three sea-otters. She saw
their smoke. Now her younger sister's smoke did not arise straight,
while her own smoke arose straight. Then she noticed that something
had happened. On the fourth morning the two sisters started again.
The youngest went a short distance and returned. The eldest went
around the island and saw that her sister had turned back far from
where they used to meet. Again she saw their smoke, and saw that her
sister's did not rise straight. Then she went home. The younger sister
was already there. She said: " You are at home already." " Yes," she
replied, " I did not find anything and turned back." On the fifth morning they started again. Now the eldest one went first. She hid herself
and watched her younger sister who went later. [When she had left]
she returned and searched in her sister's bed. She found a man lying
down, and said: "Arise! indeed, you two are foolish. Why did she
hide you?" Soon her sister returned home and saw that her [sister had
found her] husband. Then the elder sister said: "Indeed, you are
foolish, you have no sense. Why did you always hide our husband?
If I had found him I should not have hid him." Then he married both
the sisters.

He stayed there a long time; then he said: "I am homesick." Then
his wives made him ready. They each gave him five baskets. Then

they told him: "To-morrow you will be taken home." The next morning he saw a whale on the beach; it was a red whale. Now they carried sea-otter skins to the canoe [i. e., the whale], and they said to him: "Now lie down [in the whale] and do not look." After five nights he took off his blanket. The whale lay on the beach. He cut five pieces of blubber from the whale and carried his sea-otters and his baskets to the shore. Then the whale returned.

After awhile a person met him on the beach. Near him lay the whale meat and the sea-otters. He asked that person: "Where are my wives?" "They are in their house." "Tell them to come down here." Then that person went up to the house and said: "Oh, your husband has come home; he tells you to come down to the beach." Two of the women had cut their hair. Four of his wives went down to the beach. Only the eldest one did not come. They carried up the whale and the sea-otter skins. He said: "Tell your eldest sister to come down; she shall carry this whale." They went up to the house and said to their sister: "Come down and fetch that whale." Then she combed herself, greased her hair, and painted her face. She went down to the beach and lifted the whale. When she turned to go home the man said: "Turn toward the sea." She turned seaward. He put the whale meat on her back. The water reached up to her knees. They put another piece of whale meat on her and the water reached to her hips. Five times they did so, then [the water reached up to her neck and] she began to swim. She moved her arms up and down. Now she began to fly [and the man said]: "Coatch shall be your name; when it is calm you will fly about. Henceforth you will not make chiefs miserable." Then he went home to his wives. He gave them everything, the sea-otters and a piece of whale meat each.

5. IKOALĒ'X·OA K¡A IQONĒ'QONĒ ICTĀ'KXANAM.

RAVEN AND GULL THEIR MYTH.

Iō'c iqonē'qonē. Ka'nauwē ᴸᵉaᴸā'ma nicktā'kutsgō-itx. PāL
There   the gull.   All   days   he searched all over the   Full
was   beach.

2 Lī'cku-ic. Atctōmē'tckëx tqalXtᴇ'mX k¡a tᴇlā'ta-is k¡a tpkē'cXiks.
his mat.   He found always   poggies   and   codfish   and   flounders.

3 Qā'xʟx naᶜā'ʟax nē'ckta. A'lta LgōLē'lᴇXᴇmk Lā'gipʟaxa ōXōtā'kut.
One   day   he searched   Now   a person   his tracks   turned back.
            on the beach.

4 Kulā'yi ā'yō, nē'ckta. Nä2kct i'kta L¡ap atcā'yax. Nē'Xkō,
Far   he went,   he searched   Not   anything   find   he did it.   He went
        on the beach.   home,

5 nēXkō'mam. NixLō'lᴇXa-it, wuXī' kawī'X nō'ya. Nē'ktcuktē
he reached his house.   He thought,   to-morrow   early   I shall go.   It got day

6 kawī'2X ka ā'yō. Kulā'yi ā'yō. L¡ap wiXt atci'tax Lā'gipʟaxa
early   and he went.   Far   he went.   Find   again   he did them   his tracks

7 LgōLē'lᴇXᴇmk. Ā'nqatē ōxōtā'kut. NēXᴇ'ʟXa. Mank kulā'yi
a person's.   Already   they had turned   He got angry.   A little   far
                         back.

8 ā'yō. Näkct i'ktā L¡ap atcā'yax. Nē'Xtakō, nēXkō'mam. Kalā'lkuilē
he went.   Not   any-   find   he did it.   He went home,   he got home.   Scold
               thing

9 ikē'X. Kawī2X nixā'latck, ā'yō. Mank kulā'yi ā'yō. L¡ap atci'tax
he did.   Early   he rose,   he went.   A little   far   he went.   Find   he did them

10 Lā'gipʟaxa LgōLē'lᴇXᴇmk. Ā'nqatē ōXōtā'kōt. NiXᴇ'ʟXa. Oka
his tracks   a person.   Already   they had returned.   He became angry.   And

11 ma'nx·i kulā'yi ā'yō. K¡ē, nēkct ē'kta L¡ap atcā'yax. NiXkō'mam.
a little   far   he went.   Noth-   not   any-   find   he did it.   He came home.
          ing,   thing

12 Kalā'lkuilē nē'xax gō wē'wuʟē. Ia'xka tiā'xētatkc qōta tkamēlā'lᴇq.
Scold   he did   In interior of house.   He   his inheritance   that   beach.

13 WuXī' kawī'2X ka ā'yū iʟā'laktē. Ayō'2, mank kulā'yi ā'yō.
To-morrow   early   and he went   the fourth time.   He went,   a little   far   he went.

14 L¡ap atci'tax Lā'gipʟaxa LgōLē'lᴇXᴇmk. Kalā'lkuilē nē'xax;
Find   he did them   his tracks   a person's.   Scold   he did;

15 niXᴇ'ʟXa. Nē'Xtakō. NiXkō'mam gō tā'yaqʟ. Atcō'kōla -y·ōya'-
he became angry.   He returned.   He came home   to   his house.   He sharpened   his

16 q¡ēwīqē. "WuXī' ā'Lqī mxᴇltcᴇmā'o Lākcta qʟgᴇnxgā'lukʟ."
knife.   "To-morrow   later on   I shall show you   who   the one always before
                                                  me."

17 Näkct nixʟxā'lᴇm ka nō'pōnᴇm Kawī'X ka pō'lakli ka ā'yō.
Not   he ate   and   it grew dark.   Early   and   dark   and he went.

18 Kulā'yi ā'yō ka-y· ē'kᵘtᴇliʟ nē'tē. A'lta Lō'itt LgōLē'lᴇXᴇmk.
Far   he went   and   the morning   came.   Now   it came   a person.
                               star

19 Atci'ʟᵉᴇlkᴇl. Lä2 nixatᴇlgē'taqtamit. Atciugoā'laqʟ a'lta ikoalē'x·oa.
He saw him.   Some-   they met each other.   He recognized him   now   the raven.
          time

20 A'lta iyā'ctxul ikoalē'x·oa gō Li'cguic, gō Lā'qoa-iʟ Lic'guic. "Ē'kta
Now   his load   the raven   in   a mat,   in   a large   mat.   "What

21 ē'lōc imē'ʟkuiʟX, qā'nauwulᴇwulᴇwulᴇwulᴇ?" "Tkna'paâyōyucX
is in it   your mat basket,   qa'nauwulᴇwulᴇwulᴇwulᴇ?"   "Crab's claws

22 antᴇ'tᴇlukᵘɪ Lmē'wulXnana." Nē'xʟakō wiXt. WiXt atciō'lXam:
I carry them to   your nephews."   He went around   more.   Again   he said to him:
them   him

23 "Ē'kta ē'lōc imē'ʟkuiʟX, qa'nauwulᴇwulᴇ wulᴇwulᴇ?" "Tknā'pa-
"What   is in it   your mat basket,   qa'nauwulᴇwulᴇwulᴇwulᴇ?"   "Crab's

24 â'yōyucX antᴇ'tukᵘɪ Lmē'wulXnana." Qoā'nᴇmī nē'xʟakō,
claws   I carry them to them   your nephews."   Five times   he went around him,

88

atcigge′LqᴛA.　　Iā′xkati　ayuqunā′itix·it　ikoalē′x·oa.　　Ayō′mEqt.　　1
he stabbed him.　Right there　he fell down　　　the raven.　　He was dead.

AtcLō′cgam　Liā′ckuic　ikoalē′x·oa.　Wax atci′tax iqonēqōnē′.　A′lta　2
He took it　his mat　the raven's.　Pour out he did them　the gull.　Now

wax　nō′xôx　tqalx·tE′mx·　uxoēxē′lak　qamx　tpkē′cXEkc　qamx　3
poured　they　poggies　mixed with　partly　flounders　partly
out　became

tElā′ta-is.　Atcawē′k·itk　gō　Liā′cguc.　A′lta　nē′Xko.　"Kuc! ta′kE　4
codfish.　He put them into　in　his mat.　Now　he went home.　"Well!　then

aniā′waᶜ　qiqiā′ôx　qtcEnxgā′lukᴛ."　NiXgō′mam　iqonēqonē′.　5
I killed him　that one　who always went first."　He came home　the gull.

　　　Lᵢ ap aqā′yax ikoalē′x·oa.　A′lta iō′mEqtEt.　"Ai′aq amcxalkLē′tcgōm　6
　　　Find he was done　the raven.　Now he was dead.　"Quick　tell her

Liā′wuX!"　TakE ā′Lō Lqᵢ oā′lipX.　ALE′xangō aqugō′ōm tE′kXaqL　7
his younger sis-　Then he went　a youth.　He ran　he reached　her house
ter!"

ōkᵢ′unō′.　Aiā′cgōp! qix·　iqᵢ oā′lipX.　A′lta akxō′tckin ōkᵢ′unō′;　8
the crow's.　He entered　that　youth.　Now　she was working　the crow;

ī′LkuiL giā′xo-il.　"Qiā′waᶜ ēmē′lē, Laqᵢ′ō′!"　Kᵢômm, nēkct qa′da　9
a large mat she was work-　"He is killed your brother, crow!"　No noise, not (any) how
ing at it.

nā′k·im.　"Iqonēqonē′ atciā′waᶜ　ēmē′lē."　Kᵢômm　nēkct　qa′da　10
she spoke.　"The gull　he killed him　your brother."　No noise　not　(any) how

nā′k·im.　WeXt aqō′lXam:　"Qiā′waᶜ ēmē′lē, Laqᵢ′ō′!"　Qoä′nEmi　11
she spoke.　Again　she was told:　'He killed your brother,　crow!"　Five times

aqō′lXam.　Nō′tXuit　ō′kᵢ′unō′.　Laq agE′Lax Lᶜuē′luL.　Kᵢau　12
she was told.　She stood up　the crow.　Take out she did it　cedar bark.　Tle

aLExā′lax,　gō-y·　i′tcaqtq, ōkukᵢ ētik agE′Lax.　ALExE′llgēl Lᶜuē′lōL.　13
she did it to it　to　her head, cedar bark she made it.　She tied around　cedar bark.
　　　　　　　　　　　head ring　　　　　　　her waist

Agiō′cgam　itcā′kilx·EmalālEma.　A′lta　aLax·ilā′ᶜlama.　A′lta　14
She took them　her shells [rattle].　Now　she sang and shook rattle.　Now

agō′xuqtcᵢ　tgā′lEXam,　x·itik　mā′Lxôlē　tElalā′xukc;　agE′LXaqtcᵢ　15
she called　her town,　these　inland　birds;　she called them
together　　　　　　　　　　　　　　　　　　together

Ltcaqtcā′qkc;　agE′LXaqtcᵢ　Lqoēlqo-ē′lEkc;　agō′xuqtcᵢ tqoacqoä′cEkc;　16
the eagles;　she called them　the owls;　she called them　the cranes;
　　　　　together　　　　　　　　　together

agE′LXaqtcᵢ　LEnpE′tckc;　agE′LXaqtcᵢ　LE′t′ēt′ē;　agō′Xuqtcᵢ　17
she called them　the chicken-hawks;　she called them　the fish-hawks;　she called them
together　　　　　　　　　together　　　　　　　together

tE′nqētqēt;　ka′nauwē　tgō′LxēwulXEma　tgā′lEXam.　Atcō′Xuqtcᵢ　18
the duck-hawks　all　strong people　her town.　He called them
[?];　　　　　　　　　　　　　　　　　together

tiā′lEXam　iqonēqonē′.　Tgoēxoē′xokc,　tEmônts′ikts′ē′kuks,　19
his town　the gull.　The ducks,　the tail ducks,

tqᵢ ē′ptcxEntcxEn,　Ltcuyā′mukc,　Ltamēlā′yikc,　Lqō′Lqōlalē,　20
the sprit-tail ducks [?],　pelicans [?],　albatross　loons,

Lpā′qxo ikc,　ō′Lqēkc; ka′nauwē　itā′xalx·tE　tE′kXapc tiā′lEXam　21
shags,　coatches;　all　flat　their feet　his people

iqonēqonē′.　A′lta　stāqᵢ　agā′yax　iqonēqonē′-y-　ōkᵢ′unō′.　22
the gull's.　Now　war　she made on　(on) the gull　the crow.

"Aniō′goatuwā′　wu tē′acgEtē′, Tacmō′L, Tacmō′L, hē, hē, hē, hē·　23
"I shall make them　on　the sand,　Gull,　Gull,　heh, heh, heh, heh.
frighten him away

"Aniō′goatuwā′　wu tē′acgEtē′, Tacmō′L, Tacmō′L hē, hē, hē, hē·　24
"I shall make them　on　the sand,　Gull,　Gull,　heh, heh, heh, heh.
frighten him away

AqcEkpā′na　ōmuntsᵢ ē′ktsᵢ ik,　ā′nqatē　kᵢ ut　aqeā′x　ē′tcaqtq.　25
She was jumped　the tail duck [?],　long ago　tear off　it was done　her head.
upon

AckcEkpā′na　cE′nqētqēt.　A′lta　aqtō′tēna tiā′lEXam iqonēqonē′.　26
He jumped on her　the duck hawk [?].　Now　they were killed　his people　the gull's.

1 Aqā'mXikc aqtō'tEna tiā'lEXam iqonēqonē', ta'kE k¡wac nō'xôx
Part of them   were killed   his people   the gull's,   then   afraid   they got

tiā'lXam.   Nā'k·im ōk¡'unō': "Qēyalō'ta-y- i'kXaktē qō q¡ul
his people.   She said   the crow: "He shall give us   ebb tide   it shall   low be water

3 niktcō'ktixē."   "Ya'xkē ageowā'kux ōk¡unō'. Q¡ul niktcōktixē
it gets day."   "This   she asks for it   the crow.   Low water   it gets daylight

4 k¡a Lā'witckut.   Ō'Xuit tā'nEma atgEmē'ptEga-itx."   Aqēā'lōt
and   it begins to be flood.   Many   things   drift ashore."   It was given to her

5 qē'xtcē qō qoē't niktcō'ktixē.   Näkct tq¡ēx agā'yax.   Ta'kE k¡wac
intending   it will be water   low   it gets day.   Not   like   she did it.   Then   afraid

6 nō'xôx tiā'lEXam iqonēqonē'.   "Iā'lōt, iā'lōt ka'nauwē gElxōtē'na."
they became   his people   the gull's.   "Give it to her   give it to her   all   she will kill us."

7 Atciā'lōt qē'xtcē qōq mank q¡ul niktcō'ktixē.   Tcē'tkum tiā'lEXam
He gave it to her   intending   it will be   a little   low   water   it gets daylight.   One half   his people

8 aqtō'tena iqonēqonē'.   Lā'ktē qēxtcē-y- i'kXaktē atciā'lōt.   Näkct
were killed   the gull's.   Four   intending   ebb tide   he gave it to her.   Not

9 agiō'cgam.   Atgiō'lEXam tiā'lEXam iqonēqonē': "Tgt!'ō'kti mīalō'ta.
she took it.   They said to him   his people   the gull's: "Good   you give it to her.

10 GElxōtē'nai.   Itcā'xiq˥atEna.   Mā'nēwa mxElcō'lakuLx, k¡'imtā'
She will kill us!   She is one who cannot rise early.   You first   you will probably awake,   later

11 axElcō'lakuLx.   Mā'nēwa mactā'kutskō, k·¡imtā' a'xka actā'kutskō."
she will probably awake.   You first   you will go to search on the beach,   later   she   she will go to search on the beach."

12 Ta'kE nē'k·im iqonēqonē': "Amcgā'lXam ta'kE aniā'lōt."   Ta'kE
Then   he said   the gull: "Tell her   then   I give it to her."   Then

13 aqō'lXam ōk¡'unō': "Ā, takE atcimā'lōt ya'xka qix· amiXuwā'kok."
she was told   the crow: "Ah, then   he gave it to you   he   that   what you asked for."

14 Ta'kE it¡'ō'kti nē'xax ē'tcamxtc ōk¡'unō'.   Ta'kE aLi'xkō ok¡'unō'
Then   good   became   her heart   the crow's.   Then   they went home   the crow

15 k¡a tgā'lEXam.
and   her people.

Translation.

There was the gull. Every day he went on the beach to search for food, and filled his bag with poggies and codfish and flounders. One day he went to search on the beach and saw tracks of a person which had come towards him and turned back again. He went all over the beach, but he did not find anything. He went home and thought: "To-morrow I will start earlier." The next morning he went again. He went a long distance. He found tracks of a person who had already returned home [before he came to the beach]. He grew angry. He went some distance, but did not find anything. Then he went home. He scolded. Early the next morning he arose and went. He went a short distance and found tracks of a person who had already returned. He was very angry. He went a short way, but did not find anything. He went home. Then he scolded. He had inherited the beach. On the following morning he went out the fourth time. He went a short distance and found tracks of a person. He became very angry and scolded. He returned home, sharpened his knife, and said: "To-morrow I will discover who is always earlier than I." He did not eat, and when

it was still quite dark he started. He had gone quite a distance when
the morning star rose. Now he saw a person, and after some time
they met. He recognized the raven. He carried a large mat on his
back. "What is in your mat, Kanauwulewulewulewule?" "I carry
crabs' claws to my children." The gull went around him and said to
the man: "What is in your mat, Kanauwulewulewulewule?" "I carry
crabs' claws to my children." Five times he went around him and
then he stabbed [the raven with his knife]. He fell down and died.
Then he took the raven's mat and poured it out. Then poggies mixed
with codfish and flounders fell out. He put them into his own mat and
went home. [While he was walking he sang:] "Now I have killed the
one who always went out first." He got home.

After a little while some people found the raven dead on the beach.
[They said to a young man:] "Quick, go and tell his sister." He ran
to the house of the crow and entered. He found the crow at work
making a large mat. "Your brother has been killed, crow," he shouted.
She remained silent. He repeated, "The gull has killed your brother."
She remained silent. Again he said: "Your brother has been killed,
crow." Five times he repeated it. Then the crow arose, took some
cedar bark, and tied it around her head as a head ring, and tied some
around her waist. Then she took a rattle and began to sing and to shake
her rattle. She called together all her people, the land birds. She called
the eagles, the owls, the cranes, the chicken-hawks, the large hawks, the
duck-hawks. All her people were strong. The gull called together
his people, the ducks, the tail ducks [?], sprit-tail ducks [?], pelicans,
albatross, loons, shags, and coatches. All his people were flat footed.
Now the crow made war against the gull. [They sang their war song:]
"I shall frighten him away from the beach, Tasmō'tl Tasmō'tl hē hē hē
hē [Tasmō'tl is the mythical name of the gull]. The duck-hawk jumped
at the tail duck and tore off its head and they killed part of the gull's
people. They became afraid. The crow said: "Let it be low water early
in the morning." They said: "The crow asks for low water in the morning. Then the flood tide shall begin. Many things will drift ashore."
The gull wanted to give her high water early in the morning, but the
crow did not accept it. The gull's people were afraid and said: "Give
her what she wants, give her what she wants, or she will kill us."
Then he wanted to give her half-tide early in the morning. But the
crow did not accept it. One-half of the gull's people were killed by
that time. Then he offered her ebb tide late in the morning, but she
did not accept it. Then the gull's people said: "Give her what she
wants, else she will kill us. She can not rise early, you will always be
the first to wake up and she will awake after you. You will first go
to the beach and she will go after you." Then the gull said: "Tell her
that I will give her what she wants." They went to the crow and said:
"Now he gives you what you have asked for." Then the crow was
glad, and she and her people went home.

6. IT¡Ā′LAPAS IĀ′KXANAM.

COYOTE HIS MYTH.

Nĕ′tē it¡ā′lapas, nitĕ′mam Gôt¡′ā′t. A′lta āqoā′-iL ugō′lal akē′x.
He came   coyote,   he came to   Gôt¡′a′t.   Now   large   surf   there was.

2 Nŏ′ptcgEx nau′i gŏ tEmā′ktcXEma. A′lta k¡oa′s nĕ′xax it¡′ā′lapas
He went up   at once   to   spruce trees.   Now   afraid   he became   coyote

3 yuXunā′ya. lŏ′Lqtē ayŏ′La-it Got¡′ā′t. AtcLŏ′cgam Lkamilā′lEq,
he might drift   Long time   he stayed at   Got¡′a′t.   He took it   sand
away.

4 atcLXE′kXuē gŏ qaX ugō′lal. "TEmᶜā′ēma ŏxō′xŏ, näkct ugō′lal
he threw it   on   that   surf.   "Prairie   it shall be,   not   surf

5 āxā′tx. UxonāʼXEnitEma tê′lx·Em ugō′cgēwakEma gŏ x·itĭk
it will be.   Generations   people   they will walk   on   this

6 tEmᶜā′ēma." A′lta tEmᶜā′ēma nŏ′xôx Tiā′k¡ēlakē. TEmᶜā′ēma
prairie."   Now   prairie   it became   Clatsop.   A prairie

7 nŏ′xôx qaX ugō′lal.
became   that   surf.

A′lta-y- ē′qxēL nĕ′xax Niā′xaqcē. Ā′yŏ, t¡′ōL atci′tax it¡ā′lapas
Now   a creek   became   Niā′xaqcē.   He went,   a house   he made it   coyote

9 gŏ Niā′xaqcē. Nixŏ′tXuitamē gŏ ciā′mict Niā′xaqcē. AtcLā′lukc
at   Niā′xaqcē.   He went and stood   at   its mouth   Niā′xaqcē.   He speared them

10 môkct ŏ′owun; atcLē′lukc iguā′nat, atcLē′lukc ē′qalEma.
two   silver-side   he speared it   a salmon,   he speared it   a fall salmon.
salmon;

Atcē′xaluktgŏ qix· iguā′nat; atcē′xaluktgŏ qix· ē′qalEma.
He threw it away   that   salmon;   he threw it away   that   fall salmon.

12 "TuXul ka ianu′kstX ē′qxēL. Nēkct tq¡ēx antE′tx tiā′kunat,
"Too   and   small   creek.   Not   like   I do them   its salmon,

13 nēkct tq¡ēx antE′tx tē′qalEma. TuXul ka ianu′kstX ē′qxēL.
not   like   I do them   fall salmon.   Too   and   small   creek.

14 Qiā′x tcLa-uwē′LxōLxa, tcx·ī Lgiāwa′ᶜō-y- ē′qalEma LgōLē′lEXEmk
If   it is bad omen,   then   they kill him   a fall salmon   a person

15 Lŏ′mEqtēmx. Ä′ka iguā′nat. Ma′nix ēā′kil iguā′nat qēwā′qxēmEnīLx
will die.   Likewise   a salmon.   When   a female   salmon   it will be killed

16 ka Lᶜā′gil Lŏ′mEqtEmx, ma′nix ē′k·ala qēwā′qxēmEnīLx ka LE′k·ala
and a woman   will die;   when   a male   it will be killed   and   a man

17 Lŏ′mEqtEmx. Ē′ka-y- iguā′nat, ē′ka-y- ē′qalEma." A′lta ā′tcukⁿᴛ
will die.   Thus   salmon,   thus   fall salmon."   Now   he carried it

18 ā′mkXa qaX ŏ′owun. Nē′Xkŏ. Nāu′i Lq¡u′pLq¡up atcā′lax.
only   that   silver-side   He went home.   At once   cut   he did it.
salmon.

19 Nāu′i atcā′qxōpk, nixLxā′lEm. Nē′ktcuktē. Atciŏ′cgam iā′tcōL,
At once   he steamed it on   he ate it.   It got day.   He took it   his harpoon,
stones,

20 nixŏ′tXuitamē gŏ ciā′mict Niā′xaqcē. Nēkct i′kta atcē′ElkEl
he went and stood   at   its mouth   Niā′xaqcē.   Not   anything   he saw it

21 ka aLtuwē′tcgōm. Nē′Xkŏ. Nē′ktcuktē wiXt, wiXt ā′yo.
and   it became flood-tide.   He went home.   It got day   again,   again   he went.

22 Nixŏ′tXuitamē. Näkct i′kta wiXt atcē′ElkEl. NiXE′LXa, nē′Xkŏ.
He went and stood   Not   anything   again   he saw it.   He became angry,   he went
there.   home.

23 AtcLa′auwitcXa. Atciŏ′lXam iā′ēlitk: "Mxanigu′Litck, qa′daqa
He defecated.   He said to them   his excrements: "Tell me   why

24 k¡ā′ya nā′xax qaX ŏ′owun?" "Ē nikct tEmē′XatakôX, tiā′ᶜwit
nothing   became   those   silver-side   "Ē   not   your mind,   his legs
salmon?"

25 ŏxoīLk¡′a′yukta. Ma′nix aqā′waᶜox ŏ′owun, q¡atsE′n aqā′waᶜox,
bandy.   When   it is killed   a silver-side   first   it is killed,
salmon,

26 näkct Lq¡u′pLq¡up aqā′x. Ka′nauwē aqā′xcx ka aqō′lEktcX.
not   cut   it is done.   Whole   it is split along   and   it is roasted.
back

92

Näkct aqä'opgux. Qiä'x gō kᵘca'la t!'a'ʟEma nō'ix, tcx·ī aqä'opgux."   1
Not   it is steamed.   If   at   up river   creeks   they go,   then   they are steamed."

Nē'Xkō it̢'ā'lapas. Nē'ktcuktē. WiXt ä'yō. AtcLä'lukc ʟōn.   2
He went   coyote.   It got day.   Again   he went.   He speared them   three.
home

Nē'Xko; atci'tax ʟōn t!Emtk. Atcō'lEktc ctēXt cga'amtkct ā'ēXt   3
He went   he made   three   spits.   He roasted it   one   spit   one
home;   them

qaX ō'owun. ʟōn qaX ō'owun, ʟōn tga'amtk. Nē'ktcuktē, wiXt   4
that   silver-side   Three those   silver-side   three   their spits.   It got day,   again
    salmon.   salmon,

ä'yō, nixō'tXuitamē. Nēkct i'kta atcē'ElkEl ka actuwē'tcgōm.   5
he went, he went and stood there.   Not [any] thing   he saw it   and   it became flood-tide.

Nē'Xkō, niXE'LXa. AtcLa'auwitcXa. Atciō'lXam, atciwa'amtcxōkō   6
He went   he was angry.   He defecated.   He said to them,   he asked them
home,

iä'ēlitk: "Qa'da nä'xax qaX ō'owun?" AtciōlXam, nē'k·im iä'ēlitk: 7
his excre-   "How   became   these   silver-side   They said to him,   they spoke   his excrements: salmon?"   ments:

"Ayamō'lXam, x·ik tiä'ᶜwit ōxo-iLk̢'ayō'kuima; ma'nix tcx·ī   8
"I said to you,   this   his legs   bandy;   when   first

aqä'waᶜox ō'owun, ctēXt cga'amtkct ugō'k'ultcin, ctēXt cga'amtkct   9
they are killed   silver-side   one   its spit   its head,   one   its spit
          salmon,

ugō'kōtcX, ctēXt cLä'amtkct Lga'apta, ctēXt cga'amtkct ō'gōLᶜa.   10
its back.   one   its spit   its roe,   one   its spit   its meat.

Ōgō'qxoēmōpa nacxE'lgiLxax." Nē'k·im it̢'ā'lapas: haō'!   11
Its gills   are burnt."   He said   coyote: yes!

Nē'ktcuktē, wiXt ä'yō. Atcō'tēna wiXt ʟōn ō'owun. AtcLä'lukc.   12
It got day,   again he went.   He killed them   again   three   silver-side   He speared them.
                                  salmon.

Nē'Xkō wiXt. NiXkō'mam. Ā'tcaxc ka'nauwē. A'lta t̢'Emtk   13
He went home again.   He got home.   He cut it   all.   Now   spits

atci'tax. Ō'xau-it t̢'Emtk atci'tax. A'lta atcō'lEktc, ka'nauwe   14
he made them.   Many   spits   he made them.   Now   he roasted it,   all

tEnō'Xuma tga'amtk. Kulä'yi ō'gōᶜLa cga'amtkct, kulä'yi ugō'k'ultcin,   15
apart   their spits.   Far   its flesh   its spit   far   its head,

kulä'yi ugō'gōtcX cga'amtkct; kulä'yi Lga'apta Lcta'amtkct·   16
far   its back   its spit;   far   its roe   its spit.

Nē'xilktc it̢'ā'lapas. Nē'ktcuktē wiXt. Ā'yō. AtcLä'lukc itcä'ʟēlam   17
He roasted it   coyote.   It got day   again.   He went.   He speared them   ten

ō'owun. YuL̢l nē'xax it̢'ā'lapas. NiXkō'mam. NixE'lgixc.   18
silver-side   Glad   he got   coyote.   He got home.   He split it.
salmon.

Qä'mxka ä'tcaxc, nä'qxoya. QaX qāmx axgē'wal nä'qxoya.   19
Part only   he cut it,   he slept.   That   part   fresh   he slept.

Nē'ktcuktē, tcx·ī wiXt atcō'lEktc. WiXt ä'yō, nixō'tXuitamē.   20
It got day,   then   again   he roasted it.   Again   he went,   he went and stood
                                        there.

Nikct i'kta atcē'ᶜElkEl. ALtuwē'tcgōm. Nē'Xkō. WiXt nē'ktcuktē,   21
Not   anything   he saw.   It became flood-tide.   He went home.   Again   it got day,

wiXt ä'yō. WiXt näkct i'kta atcē'ᶜElkEl. Nē'Xkō niXE'LXa.   22
again   he went.   Again   not   anything   he saw it.   He went home,   he became
                                         angry.

AtcLä'auwitcXa it̢'ā'lapas. Atciwa'amtcxōkō iä'ēlitk: "Qa'daqa   23
He defecated   coyote.   He asked them   his excrements: "Why

k̢ä'ya nä'xax qaX ō'owun?" Atciō'mēla iä'ēlitk. Aqiō'mēla   24
nothing   became   these   silver-side   They scolded him   his excre-   He was scolded
                 salmon?   ments.

it̢'ā'lapas. "Ma'nix tcx·ī aqōtē'nax ō'owun, q̢atsE'n aqōtē'nax,   25
coyote.   "When   first   they are killed   silver-side   first   they are killed,
                             salmon,

näkct aqaō'yamitx auwē'ᶜ; ka'nauwē aqō'ktciktamitx. Qē'xtcē   26
not   they are left   raw;   all   they are made (roasted).   Intending

1 ā′xauwē aqōtē′nax, tatc¡a ka′nauwē aqō′ktciktamitx. Näkct nā′o-ix.”
  many   they are killed, look!   all   they are made (roasted). Not he sleeps.”

2 WiXt nē′ktcuktē. Ā′yō it¡ā′lapas, nixō′tXuitamē. AtcLā′lukc
  Again it got day. He went coyote,   he went and stood there. He speared

3 itcā′Lēlam. A′lta atci′tax t¡Emtk, ō′xuē atci′tax t¡Emtk. A′lta
  ten.   Now he made them spits, many he made them spits.   Now

4 nixElq¡āta-it, ka′nauwē atcō′ktcktamit qaX iā′k¡ētēnâx. A′lta
  he was awake, all   he made them (roasted) those what he had caught. Now

5 ka′nauwē atci′tōL¡ tgē′Lau, tgā′k·iLau ō′owun q¡atsE′n nō′yamx gō
  all   he finished taboos, their taboos the silver- first   they arrive at
           them   side salmon

6 Niā′xaqcē. Ia′xkatē ayō′La-it. Nē′k·im it¡ā′lapas: “Ē′ka-y· ōxō′xō
  Niā′xaqcē. Then   he stayed. He said coyote: “Thus   they will do

7 Natē′tanuē, manix Lmē′mElōst kLkLōcgā′liL Lgā′xō-y· ō′owun, nau′i
  the Indians, when   corpses who takes them (pre- he eats them silver-side at once
                                pares for burial)   salmon

8 k¡aya′-y· axā′xō. Ma′nix gaLā′k¡auk¡au Lgā′Xō-y· ō′owun, nau′i
  nothing   they will When   a murderer   he eats them silver-side at once
            become.   salmon,

9 k¡aya′-y· axā′xō. Ē′ka Lqēlā′wulX, ē′ka LqLā′xit. A′la nai′ka,
  nothing   they will get. Thus a girl menstruating thus a menstruating Even I,
                            the first time,   woman.

10 ā′la tEll anE′xax.”
   even tired I became.”

   A′lta nē′tē, kaxā′ nitē′mâm ayugō′t¡ōm tā′nEmckc tk¡olā′lipL·
   Now he came, where he arrived he met them women   digging much
                        coming   with sticks.

12 Atctuwa′amtcxōkō: “Ē′kta amcgiā′wul?” “Ā tā′lalX ntcktā′wul.”
   He asked them: “What are you doing?” “Ah gamass we make.”

13 “Qantsī′x· Lx Tiā′k¡ēlakē pōc tā′lalX aqta′wul, amcgiupā′yaLx
   “How may be Clatsop   if gamass is made,   you dig

14 iq¡aLxoē′ma k¡a ēcanā′tauc, iā′mkXa qiupiā′Lxa gō x·ik ilē′ē.
   beets (?)   and thistles (?), only they will be dug in this land.

15 Nēkct tā′lalX qtE′tpiaLxax.” A′lta atgiupā′yaLx iq¡aLxoē′ma k¡a
   Not gamass it is dug.”   Now they dig   beets (?)   and

16 ēcanā′tauc. Ayōē′taqL qō′tac tā′nEmckc. AtcuXugō′mē qō′ta tā′lalX.
   thistles (?). He left them those women.   He made poor that gamass.

17 Lcē′Lpatē nō′xôx qō′ta tā′lalX.
   Scylla   became that gamass.

   Nitē′mam Tiā′k¡ēlakē. A′lta tcā′ēpaē. L¡ap atcā′yax Liā′wuX
   He came to Clatsop.   Now it was spring. Find he did him his younger
                                                               brother

19 iā′xkatē itcā′yau. Atciō′lXam Liā′wuX: “Tgt¡ō′kti tEnauä′itk
   there   the snake. He said to him to his younger “Good   net
                                     brother:

20 txqtā′xō.” Nē′k·im itcā′yau: “Mai′ka imē′Xaqamit.” A′lta acgō′mEl
   we two make He said the snake: “Your your mind.”   Now they two
   it.”   bought it

21 ōmō′tan. A′lta aqcgē′mgīktē ōcuē′ēē k¡a-y· ōqōsā′na. AcE′ktgEm.
   material for Now they were paid the frog and the newt. They span.
   twine.

22 A′lta nixElā′ya-itx, atciāgElā′ya-itx ōmō′tan. A′lta itcā′yau cka
   Now he always cleaned, he cleaned it much the material Now the snake and
                                              for twine.

23 nik¡xē′laLEma-itx. A′lta acktgEmā′ya-itx ōcuē′ēē k¡a-y· ōqosā′na.
   he crawled about much. Now they two span much frog and newt.

24 A′lta atciō′lXam Liā′wuX: “Ē′mx·Ela-y· ē′mx·Ela! Ka′nauwē
   Now he said to him to his younger “Clean it,   clean it! All
                        brother:

25 Lcalā′ma cka mLxē′l,” aqiō′lXam itcā′yau. Atciō′lXam it¡ā′lapas:
   days   and you always he was told the snake. He said to him coyote:
            crawl about,”

26 “Mai′ka tā′nata mtā′xō, nai′ka tā′nata,” nē′k·im it¡ā′lapas.
   “You one side you will make I   the other he said coyote.
           it.   side.”

AqLō′kXuL‚ Lanē′ctukc, tiā′Lanēctukc it‚ā′lapas: "Ai′aq, ai′aq,
It was finished   the twine,   his twine   coyote's: "Quick,   quick,   **1**

ai′aq!" aqiō′lXam itcā′yau. Amcinguwā′kōt, mxE′lgēkᵘtck." Nē′k·im
quick!"   he was told   the snake.   You let me wait,   make net."   He said   **2**

itcā′yau: "Mai′ka amcinguwā′kōt," aqiō′lXam it‚ā′lapas. A′lta
the snake: "You,   you let me wait,"   he was told   coyote.   Now   **3**

nixE′lgēkᵘtck it‚ā′lapas. AtcLō′kXuL‚ ka′nauwē atci′tōkᵘtck. TE′pa-it
he made net   coyote.   He finished it   all   he made net.   Rope   **4**

cktā′xo-il qō′cta cᶜā′kil. Atci′Lax LE′qXun it‚ā′lapas. Ia′xkatē
they two made   those   two women.   He made it   net-buoy   coyote.   There   **5**
it

nikᴛxē′lalEma-itx itcā′yau. Nē′k·im it‚ā′lapas: "LE′kXun LE′Xa!"
he crawled about much   the snake.   He said   coyote: "Net-buoy   make!"   **6**

aqiō′lXam itcā′yau. "Amcinguwā′kōt." Nē′k·im itcā′yau: "Ai′aq,
he was told   the snake.   "You let me wait."   He said   the snake: "Quick,   **7**

ai′aq, āmxElEXulā′ma! Amcinguwā′kōt." AtcLä′LgōL‚ LE′qXun
quick,   make haste!   You let me wait."   He finished it   the net-buoy   **8**

it‚ā′lapas. Lqā′nakc atci′LgElōyē. NixE′ltōm itcā′yau. Gō
coyote.   Stones   he went to take them.   He accompanied the snake.   At   **9**
    him

Sōguamē′ts‚iak Lqā′nakc aLgE′cgElōya. NēkLxē′l qix· itcā′yau gō
Tongue Point   stones   they two went to   He crawled   that   snake   at   **10**
   take them.   about much

qō′La Lqā′nakc. TcLō′guiLxat it‚ā′lapas Lqā′nakc. Acē′Xkō.
those   stones.   He carried them down   coyote   the stones.   They went   **11**
   often   home.

AcXkō′mam. Ā′yō tE′kcēu it‚ā′lapas, ayō′kuiya tE′kcēu. NixE′ltōm
They arrived at   He went   spruce roots   coyote,   he went to get   spruce roots.   He accompa-   **12**
home.   them   nied him

itcā′yau. Iā′xkatē LE′kᴌEk ā′tciax ilē′ē it‚ā′lapas. Iā′xkatē itcā′yau
the snake.   There   dig   he did it   the ground   coyote.   There   the snake   **13**

nikLxē′l. Acē′Xkō. Tc‚E′xtc‚Ex atci′tax tE′kcēu it‚ā′lapas.
crawled about   They went home.   Split   he did them   the spruce roots   coyote.   **14**
much.

"Wu′ska mE′kxōtckē," aqiō′lXam itcā′yau, "amcinguwā′kōt." Nē′k·im
"Go on,   work,"   he was told   the snake,   "you let me wait."   He said   **15**

itcā′yau: "Ai′aq, ai′aq, mE′kxōtckē!" aqiō′lXam it‚ā′lapas,
the snake: "Quick,   quick,   work!"   he was told   coyote,   **16**

"amcinguwā′kōt." A′lta atcLauwē′xētEq tiā′nauwa-itk it‚ā′lapas.
"you let me wait."   Now   he tied it to the buoys   his net   coyote.   **17**

Wuk‚ atcā′yax icō′Eltc. A′lta iā′xkati atcLauwē′xētEq tiā′nauwa-itk.
Straight   he made it   a mat.   Now   there   he tied it to the buoys   his net.   **18**

Ia′xkatē nikᴛxē′lalEma-itx itcā′yau. AtcLō′kXuL‚ tiā′nauwa-itk
There   he crawled around much   the snake.   He finished it   his net   **19**

it‚′ā′lapas. QuL atctā′wix kᵘLā′xanē. Kawī′X ayō′pa it‚ā′lapas.
coyote.   Hang up   he did it   outside.   Early   he went out   coyote.   **20**

Ā′nqatē quL tā′wēwut itcā′yau tiā′nauwa-itk. "Ē Lgā′wuX,"
Already   hang up   it did   the snake   his net.   "Eh   younger bro-   **21**
    ther,"

atciō′lXam "tci′ᴅxgakō." NixEmā′tcta-itk it‚ā′lapas. Atcā′yuL
he said to him   "he got the better   He was ashamed   coyote.   He won over   **22**
   of me."   him

itcā′yau. Aqā′yuL it‚ā′lapas. Nē′k·im it‚ā′lapas: "Ma′nix nauā′itk
the snake.   He lost   coyote.   He said   coyote: "When   net   **23**

Lktā′xō LgōLē′lEXEmk, a′lta tä2ll Lxā′xo-ilEmx, tcx·ī aLkLō′kōLax.
makes   a person,   now   tired   he shall always get,   then   he shall finish it.   **24**

Näkct tgt‚ō′kti qīgō nikct tEll amE′xax." Nē′k·im itcā′yau:
Not   good   when   not   tired   you get."   He said   the snake: **25**

"Ayamō′lXam amcinguwā′kōt;" aqiō′lXam it‚ā′lapas.
"I told you,   you let me wait;"   he was told   coyote.   **26**

Nē′ktcuktē. ALxēnauwā′itgēmam. Aci′xanXa. Nau′i mōkct
It got day.   They went to catch salmon in   They laid the   At once   two   **27**
    net.   net.

1 atce′La-it. Nau′i atcugō′pEna tctā′nauwa-itk itჯā′lapas. A′lta qē′xtcē
they caught. At once he jumped their net coyote. Now intending
across it

2 aci′xēnauā-itgē; aLtuwä′tcgōm. Tä′mka môkct ka ictä′kჯ ētēnax. A′lta
they caught salmon in it got flood tide. Only two only their catch. Now
their net;

3 aLtuwä′tcgōm. A′lta aci′Xkō. Ō′lō gia′xt itჯā′lapas. Nē′k·im, nau′i
it got flood-tide. Now they went Hun- he got coyote. He spoke, at once
home. gry

4 nixE′lgixc aci′xēlEktc. ALxgē′ktcik aLxLxä′lEm. Ōcoē′ēē kჯa-y-
he split it they roasted it. It was roasted he ate. The frog and

5 ōqჯōsä′na ctä′lē. Nē′ktcuktē, wiXt aLxēnauwä′itgēma. Itcä′paēt
the newt their It got day, again they went to catch salmon Looking after
cousins. in the net. the rope

6 ōqჯōsä′na; tä′yacaxala itcä′yau, ayä′ckuiLx itჯā′lapas.
the newt; the one at the upper the snake, the one at the lower coyote.
end of the net end of the net

7 ALE′xēnauw-äitgē qē′xtcē, acuwä′tka ka aLtuwä′tcgōm. ALi′Xkō.
They caught salmon in intending, they did not get and it became flood-tide. They went
the net anything home.

8 Ē′x·LXa-ūt itჯā′lapas. AtcLä′auwitcXa. Atciuwä′amtcxōkō iä′ēlitk.
He was angry coyote. He defecated. He asked them his excrements.

9 Nē′k·im iä′ēlitk itჯā′lapas: "imē′Lჯ EmēnXut." "x·ik tiä′ᶜwit
They said his excrements coyote: "you lied." "This his legs

10 ōxo-iLkჯā′yōkōma. Manix atgiä′waᶜox iguä′nat, näkct aLkcugupE-
bandy. When they catch it salmon, not they jump

11 nä′kux La′nauwa-itk. Näkct mcugō′tkakō tEmē′nauwa-itk. Manix
across it, their net. Not you step across your net. When

12 qჯ'atsE′n aqtōtē′nax tguä′nat, gō′yē ōᶜō′Lax tcx·ī aqtä′xs." Nē′k·im
first they are killed salmon, thus the sun then they are cut." He said

13 itჯā′lapas: "Ō, ta′kE kopE′t amxanlgu′Litck." Nē′ktcuktē wiXt
coyote: "Oh, then enough you told me." It got day again

14 aLxēnauwa′-itgēmam. Ma′nix aLgiä′waᶜox iguä′nat, näkct atcugōpE-
they went to catch salmon in When they killed him a salmon, not he jumped
the net.

15 nä′kux tiä′nauwa-itk. Mô′kcti aLE′xana kopä′ti aLē′Lჯa-it tguä′nat.
across it his net. Twice they laid that many went into the salmon.
the net net

16 Atcō′kō qaX ōqჯōsä′na: "La′xtēwa, takE päL nē′xax Ltcuq x·iau
He ordered that newt. "Bail out, then full it got water that
her

17 ikanī′m. AkLä′xtēwa-y- ōqჯōsä′na. Qē′xtcē aLExē′nauwä-itgē
canoe. She bailed it out the newt. Intending they caught salmon in
the net,

18 aLuwē′tcgōm. ALE′Xkō. ALgō′xōtEq iLä′kჯētēnax gō wē′wuLē.
it became flood-tide. They went home. They put it down what they had caught in the interior of
the house.

19 Gō nō′yam ōᶜō′Lax ka nixE′lgixc itჯā′lapas. Ä2 ka qaX ō′ōwEn
There arrived the sun and he split it coyote. Thus that silver-side
salmon

20 ä′tcaxc, ä′ka atci′taxc qō′ta tkuä′nat. Kulä′yi-y- uyä′kჯEltcin
he cut it, thus he cut them those salmon. Far its head

21 cga′amtkct, kulä′yi-y- uyä′kōtcX, kulä′yi-y- ä′yaLᶜa ciä′amtkct,
its spit, far its back, far its meat its spit,

22 kulä′yi Liä′apta Lctä′amtkct. ALxgē′ktcikt. Nē′ktcuktē, wiXt
far its roe its spit. They were done. It got day, again

23 aLxēnauwa′-itgēmam. Nēkct i′kta aLgiä′waᶜ, aLi′cxᴇmgEna.
they went to catch salmon in net. Not anything they killed it, they got nothing.

24 NiXE′LXa itჯā′lapas. AtcLa′auwitcXa. Atciō′lXam iä′ēlitk:
He became angry coyote. He defecated. He said to them his excrements:

25 "MxanElgu′Litck, qa′daqa k·ჯē nō′xôx tik tguä′nat?" Atciō′mēla
"Tell me, why nothing they be- these salmon?" They scolded
came him

iā'ēlitk: "AmXE'LōXu na ä'ka qaX ō'owun! Oxoä'ēma tgä'k·iLau
his excre-   "You think [int. thus as those silver-side Others   its taboos
ments: part.]   salmon!   1

ō'ōwun; ixElôi'ma iguā'nat tiä'k·iLau. Manix mcxēnauwa'-itgēmama,
the silver- other   the salmon its taboo. When you go out to catch salmon in net,   2
side salmon;

ma'nix ēauwiLä'-ita tEmcä'nauwa-itk, Lō'ni mcxēnä'ya; kopä't
when   he goes into the net   your net,   three times you lay net; enough   3

mcēLä'-ita iguā'nat. Kopä't; nēkct qa'nsix· mckLextēwä'ya. Manix
you will take in   salmon. Enough; never bail out your canoe. When   4
the net

mc·Xgō'mama ka miä'xca iguā'nat, yukpä' tc·Ex miä'xō, kulä'yi
you get home and you cut it salmon, here [at sides] cut do it, far   5

iä'wan ciä'amtkct, kulä'yi iä'kōtcX ciä'amtkct; a'lta tE'mcEcX
its belly, its spit,   far   its back its spit; now sticks   6

mōxo inä'ya lakt. A'lta ctcē'lEqL mcä'xo. A'lta ia'xkati
place them in the four. Now two parallel sticks do. Now there   7
ground vertically   over the others

Lgä'kōtcX mLōkōXut·ō'ya ka-y· uyä'k·Eltcin k·au gō-y· uyä'kōtcX
its back lay [m. obj.] on top of it and its head fast to its back   8

ci'Xa-ōt ka Liä'lict k·au ci'Xa-ōt." Atciō'lXam iä'ēlitk: "Ta'kE
it is and its tail fast it is." He said to them his excre- "Then   9
                                                                    ments:

kopE't amxanElgu'Litck." Nē'ktcuktē aLxēnauwä'itgēmam,
enough you told me."   It got day they went to catch salmon in   10
                                                                 the net,

aLktō'tēna Lōn tguā'nat. Näkct aLkLä'xtēwa. Atcō'lXam ōq·osä'na:
they killed them three salmon. Not they bailed it out. He said to her the newt: 11

"Igä'lEmam ē'mcEcX mä'Lxolē. Oqōgu'nkꞇat lxgiä'xo." Nō'ya-y-
'Go and take it a stick inland. A club we shall make it." She went   12

oq·ōsä'na, agiōgō'lEmam ē'mcEcX wiXt aLE'xana. WiXt ēXt
the newt, she took it a stick again they laid the net. Again one   13

niLē'La-it, atcLixE'gunk. Qē'xtcē aLixēnauwa'-itgē, aLixēnauwa'-itgē;
was in there, he clubbed it. Intending they caught salmon in they caught salmon in   14
                                           the net,   the net:

aLtuwē'tcgōm, la'ktka iLä'k·ētēnax. ALgō'xntEq Lä'kunat.
it became flood-tide, four only what they had caught. They put them down their salmon.   15

Gō nō'yam ōcō'Lax ka nixE'lgixc it·ä'lapas. A'lta atcō'xo-ina
There he arrived the sun and he split them coyote. Now he placed in   16
                                                              ground

lakt tE'mcEcX. A'lta ä'ka atci'taxc qō'ta tguā'nat, ä'ka qigō
four sticks. Now thus he cut them those salmon, as where   17

atciō'lXam iä'ēlitk. ALxgē'ktcikt. Nä'wi LE'kLEk atci'Lax qō'La
they told him his excre- They got done. Immedi- break he did it that   18
               ments.   ately

LE'kXutcX qix· it·ä'lapas. Nē'ktcuktē aLxēnauwa'itgēmam. Näkct
backbone that coyote. It got day they went to catch salmon in Not   19
                                                                 the net.

i'kta aLgiä'waꞔ ka aLtuwē'tcgōm. ALE'Xko. NiXE'LXa it·ä'lapas;
any- they killed it and it became flood-tide. They went home. He was angry coyote;   20
thing

atcLa'auwitcXa. "Qa'daqa k·äya nō'xòx tik tguā'nat!"
he defecated. "Why nothing they became these salmon!"   21

atciuwa'amtcxōkō iä'ēlitk. "Ayamō'lXam," aqiō'lXam it·ä'lapas;
he asked them his excrements. "I told you," he was told coyote;   22

atciō'lXam iä'ēlitk, "MxE'LōXuna-ya- ē'ka-y- ō'ōwun tgä'k·ilau!
they said to him his excre- "You think [int. part.] thus as silver-side their taboo!   23
                  ments,   salmon

Ōxoē'ma tgä'k·iLau tguā'nat. Ma'nix mcgēwaꞔō-y- iguā'nat, näkct
Other their taboo the salmon. When you will kill it a salmon, not   24

qa'nsix· ē'mcEcX amcgixgu'ncEkō. Qiä'x qiaō'pko, tcx·ī-y-ē'mcEcX
[any] how [with a] stick you strike it. If it is steamed, then [with a] stick   25

qiXgu'nEkō. Qiä'x q·ōä'p LE'taLxē, tcx·ī aqiä'ōpkux iguā'nat.
it is struck. If nearly autumn, then it is struck the salmon.   26

1. Näkct LE'kLEkᵘ qLEtxt Liä'kōtcX iguä'nat q¡atsE'n ayō'yamx.
Not   break   it is done   its back   the salmon   first   it arrives.

2. Manix aqiä'waᵋox iguä'nat ka Lkamilä'lEq aqLō'cgamx. AqLik·ä'tqoax
When   it is killed   the salmon   and   sand   it is taken.   It is strewn

3. gō iä'xot ka aqixtcē'na-ox gō iä'xot. Nēkct aqLē'xkungux." Nē'k·im
on his eye   and it is pressed with   on his eye.   Not   it is clubbed."   He said
          the fist

4. it¡ä'lapas: "Ta'kE kapE't amxanElgu'Litck." ALxēnauwa'itgēmam,
coyote: "Then   enough   you told me."   They went to catch salmon in net,

5. nē'ktcuktē. ALē'La-it tguä'nat. Nau'i Lōn alē'La-it. Ka'nauwē
it got day.   They were in the   salmon.   Immedi-   three   were in the   All
       net   ately   net.

6. Lkamilä'lEq atcLEkuXōtE'qo-imx, atcuXōtcē'nan'Emx. Ō'xoē
sand   he strewed on each,   he pressed with his fist on each.   Many

7. aLktō'tēna tguä'nat. ALE'Xko ka aLE'xēluktc. ALxgē'ktcikt. A'lta
he killed them   salmon.   They went home and   they roasted them.   They got done.   Now

8. aLktō'mak gō kᵘca'la -y-ē'lXam. A'lta ōk¡uē'lak aLE'kxax.
he distributed it   to   upstream   town.   Now   dried salmon   they made.

9. Nä'ktcuktē, aLxēnauwä'itgemam. Qē'xtcē aLixēnauä'-itgē, acuwä'tka;
It got day,   they went to catch salmon in   Intending   they caught salmon   they got noth-
       the net.   in net,   ing:

10. aLtuwē'tcgōm, aLE'Xkō. NiXE'LXa it¡ä'lapas. AtcLä'auwitcXa.
it became flood-tide,   they went   He became angry   coyote.   He defecated.
       home.

11. "Qa'daqa k¡ä'ya nō'xôx tik tguä'nat." "Ayamō'lXam x·ig
"Why   nothing   they became these   salmon."   "I told you   this

12. iō'L¡ElEx, tiä'ᶜwit ōxoē'Lk¡ayōkōma. Ō'xoē tgä'k·iLau qē'wa
lean one,   his legs   bandy.   Many   their taboos   those

13. tguä'nat. Ma'nix aqtōtē'nax ō'xoē tguä'nat, nēkct qa'nsix·
salmon.   If   they are killed   many   salmon,   not   [any] how

14. aqiō'ktcpax, iä'xkatē aqiō'lEktcX, iä'xkatē aqiä'x. Ma'nix
they are carried   then   they are roasted,   then   they are eaten.   When
outside,

15. nicxgä'ētix·itx, iä'xkatē iqiō'tgEx. Manēx ok¡uē'lak aqä'x, qiä'x
he leaves some of it,   there   it is put.   When   dry salmon   are made,   if

16. aLuwē'tcgōmx agō'n ôᶜō'Lax, tcx·ī-y- ok¡uē'lak aqä'x." Atciō'lXam:
it gets flood-tide   next   day   then   dry salmon   it is made."   He said to them:

17. "KapE't amxanElgu'Litck." Nē'ktcuktē wiXt. ALxēnäuwä'-itgēmam,
"Enough   you told me.'   It got day   again.   They went to catch salmon in
                                   the net,

18. aLktō'tēna tguä'nät, ō'xoē aLktō'tēna tguä'nät. ALktō'lEktc
they killed them   the salmon,   many   they killed them   salmon.   They roasted them

19. ka'nauwē, aLxgē'ktcikt. A'lta aLguguixē'mam tê'lx·Em, aqō'gō-y-
all,   they got done.   Now   they invited them   the people,   she was sent

20. ōq¡'ōsä'na. Nōxo-iLxE'lEmam gō tä'yaqL it¡ä'lapas. Alō'XoL¡
the newt.   They went to eat   at   his house   coyote's   They finished

21. nōxō-iLxä'lEm tê'lx·Em. Iä'xkate atoē'takᵧ qtoxōgō'itix·it. A'lta·y-
they ate   the people.   Then   they left it   what they had left   Now
                                  over.

22. ē'kXakᵘtē nē'xax. Kawī'2X ka ä'LōLx, aLE'xana. K·¡ē, nēkct
low water in   it was.   Early   and   they went to   they laid the   Nothing.   not
the morning   the beach,   net.

23. ē'kta, aLE'xēnaua-itgē cka aLtuwä'tcgōm. Näkct ē'kta aLgiä'waᵋ;
anything   they caught salmon   and   it became flood-tide.   Not   anything   they killed it;
in the net

24. aLi'cXumgEna. Mâ'kcti qē'xtcē aLxēnauwä'itgēmam kawī'X,
they did not get anything.   Twice   intending   they went to catch salmon in   early,
                           the net

25. acuwä'tka, aLcXE'mugEnax. AtcLä'auwitcXa it¡ä'lapas. Atciō'lXam
they did not get   they did not get any·   He defecated   coyote.   He said to
anything.   thing.   them

26. iä'ēlitk: "Qa'daqa k¡ä'ya nō'xôx tguä'nat?" Aqiō'lXam it¡ä'lapas:
his excre-   "Why   nothing   they be-   the salmon?"   He was told   coyote:
ments: came

"Ayamō'lXam　x·ik　iō'L! ElEx,　ō'xoē　tgā'k·iLau　qē'wa　tguā'nat.
"I told you　　this　　lean one,　　many　　their taboo　　those　　salmon.　　　1

Ma'nix ē'kXakᵘtē　mxēnauwa'itgēmam,　qiā'x　Lāx　axā'xō　ōᶜō'Lax,
If　low water in the　you go to catch salmon in the　if　out　comes　the sun,　　2
　　morning　　　　net,

tcx·ī amxE'nXax.　Näkct mxEnXā'ya manix ka　nikct Lāx ōᶜō'Lax.
then　lay net.　　Not　lay net　when then　not　out the sun.　　3

Näkct qiutctpā'ya iguā'nat.　Qiā'x　ōk!u'nō　gīuktcpā'ya　tcx·ī
Not　they are carried out　salmon.　If　a crow　she will carry it out　then　　4

aqiō'ktcpax,　tcx·ī aqtō'magux　tguwē'ᶜ.　Nēkct　qā'nsiX　tcagō'ktia
it is carried out,　then　it is distributed　raw.　Not　[any] how　it will get day-　　5
　　　　　　　　　　　　　　　　　　　　　　　　　　　　　　light

ōᶜō'lEptckiX,　näkct qa'nsiX qcā'xō ciā'tckunict,　qiā'x ctaō'ya tcx·ī
fire,　not　[any] how　it is eaten　its breast,　if　they sleep then　　6

aqcā'x. Ma'nix aqiō'lEktcx iguā'nat gō·y·　ōᶜō'lEptckiX,　ayō'ktcEktx,
it is eaten.　When　it is roasted　salmon at　the fire,　it gets done,　　7

nā'u'i wāx aqLā'kax Ltcuq qaX ōᶜō'lEptckiX." Atciō'lXam ia'ēlitk:
immedi-　pour　it is done water that　fire."　He said to them his excre-　　8
ately　into　　　　　　　　　　　　　　　　　　　　　　　　　　ments:

"KapE't　ta'kE　amxanElgu'Litck.　Ē'ka-y-　ōxō'xō　Natē'tanuē,
"Enough　then　you told me.　Thus　they will do　the Indians,　　9

uxōuā'XEnitEma Natē'tanuē.　Ē'ka　tgā'k·iLau.　Ā'la　nai'ka　tEll
the generations of　Indians.　Thus　their taboo.　Even　I　tired　　10

anE'xax," nē'k·im it! ā'lapas gō Tiā'k! ēlakē tgā'k·iLau. Atckō'lXam
I became,"　he said　coyote　at Clatsop　their taboos.　He said to them　　11

ctā'lē: "lxk꜀ā'yuwa iau'a ē'natai." NaxE'ltXuitcgō ōq! ōsā'na.
his cousins: ' We will move　there to the other side." She made herself ready　the newt.　　12

Ā'tcukct itcꜗyau ōcuē'ēē. A'lta a'xLXaōt,　cā'uca-u　agē'x. Ayaga'ōm
He looked　the snake [at] the frog. Now　she [the frog]　growling with　she did. He reached　　13
at her　　　　　　　　　　　　　was angry,　closed mouth　　her

itcā'yau, a'lta atcā'waᶜ. Aqā'waᶜ ōcuē'ēē; itcā'yau atcā'waᶜ.
the snake,　now　he killed her. She was killed the frog; the snake　killed her.　　14

ALtē'mam ya'koa ē'natai. ALE'xēnaua-itgē. ALktō'tēna tguā'nat.
They arrived　here　on the other They caught salmon in They killed them　salmon.　　15
　　　　　side.　the net.

Ē'ka atci'tax Tiā'k! ēlak, Lkamilā'lEq atcLē'kXatq gō iā'xōt qix·
Thus as they made　Clatsop,　sand　he strewed on them in　his eye　that　　16
them

iguā'nat. Gōyē' atcā'yax, atcix·tcē'na. Qē'xtcē aLE'xēnaua-itgē
salmon.　Thus　he did him,　he pressed him with Intending　they caught salmon　　17
　　　　　　　　　　　　　　　　　his fist.　　　　　　　　　　in net

wiXt, näkct aLgiā'waᶜ. ALE'Xkō. Nē'ktcuktē. ALxēnauā'·itgēmam,
again,　not　they killed him. They went　It got day.　They went to catch sal-　　18
　　　　　　　　　　　home.　　　　　　　　　　　　　　mon in the net,

näkct i'kta aLgiā'waᶜ. Nē'ktcuktē wiXt, aLixē'naua-itk. Nēkct
not　anything they killed it. It got day　again,　they caught salmon in　Not　　19
　　　　　　　　　　　　　　　　　　　　　　　the net.

i'kta aLgiā'waᶜ. Kalā'lkuilē nē'xax. AtcLa'auwitcX: "Qa'daqa
anything they killed it. Scold　he did.　He defecated:　"Why　　20

k·!ē nō'xôx tik tguā'nat?" "Ē, mē'L! ala, it! ā'lapas. Ma'nix
nothing they be-　these　salmon?"　"Oh,　you fool,　coyote.　When　　21
came

mēuwa'ᶜō iguā'nat cka mik꜀tu'qoēma! MXa'LōXEna-y-　ē'ka
you will kill　a salmon and　you kick him! You think [int. part.]　thus as　　22

Tiā'k! ēlakē?" Nē'k·im it! ā'lapas: "ō!" Nē'ktcuktē, wiXt aLxēnauwa'-
Clatsop?"　He said　coyote:　"Oh!" It got day,　again they went to catch　　23

itgēmam. ALE'xāna. Môkct aLktō'tēna tguā'nat. WiXt aLE'xana,
salmon in the They laid the Two　they killed them　salmon.　Again　they laid net,　　24
net.　net.

Lōn aLktō'tēna tguā'nat. Atcē'xalukctgō eXt mā'Lxolē. Nēlgā'Xit
three they killed them salmon. He threw it ashore　one　upland.　He fell down　　25
　　　　　　　　　　　　　　　　　　　　　　　　　　　　　　headlong

ā'yacq꜀ gō Lqamēlā'lEq qix· iguā'nat. Qē'xtcē wiXt aLE'xana.
his mouth　in　the sand　that　salmon.　Intending　again　he laid the net.　　26

1 K¡ē   nēkct   i′kta   aLgiā′waꜬ.   ALixē′naua-itgē   qē′xtcē   cka
   Nothing not   anything he killed it. He caught salmon in net intending and

2 aLtuwä′tcgōm.   Näkct   i′kta   aLgiā′waꜬ.   Qoā′nEmka   iLā′k¡ētēnax.
   it became flood-tide. Not anything they killed it. Five only what they caught.

3 Āli′Xkō.   Tsō′yustē   nixE′lgixc   it¡ā′lapas.   ALe′xēluktc,   aLxgē′ktcEkt.
   They went   In the even- he split them coyote.   They roasted them, they were done.
   home.   ing

4 Nē′ktcuktē   aLxēnauwa′itgēmam,   näkct   i′kta   aLgiā′waꜬ.   Kalā′lkuilē
   It got day   they went to catch salmon in not anything they killed it.   Scold
                 the net,

5 nē′xax   it¡ā′lapas.   AtcLā′auwitcXa: "Qa′daqa   k¡ā′ya   nō′xôx   tik
   he did   coyote.   He defecated: "Why   nothing   they be-   these
                                                                        came

6 tguā′nat?"   "Ē,   mE′L¡ala,   it¡ā′lapas!   MxE′LōXEna·y-   ē′ka
   salmon?"   "Oh,   you fool,   coyote!   You think [int. part.]   thus as

7 Tiä′k¡ēlakē?   Näkct   qix·itkctguā′liL   iguā′nat,   ē′wa   kē′kXulē
   Clatsop?   Not   he is thrown ashore   salmon,   thus   down

8 a′yaqtq,   tgā′k·iLau.   Manix   mēwa′Ꜭo   iguā′nat,   a′lta   amLgElō′ya
   his head,   it is their taboo.   When   you kill him   a salmon,   now   go and take them

9 Lä′lēlē,   ma′nix   ō′xoē   tguā′nat   amtōtē′na,   ka′nauwē   amLauwē′qcamita
   salmon-   when   many   salmon   you have killed   all   you put into their mouths
   berries,   them.

10 Lä′lēlē."   "Ō,   takE   kopE′t   amxanElgu′Litck,"   atciō′lXam   iä′ēlitk.
   salmon-ber-   "Oh,   then   enough   you told me,"   he said to them   his excre-
   ries."   ments.

11 Nē′ktcuktē.   WiXt   aLxēnauwa′itgēmam.   Ō′xoē   aLktō′tēna   tguā′nat.
   It got day.   Again   they went to catch salmon in Many   they killed them   salmon.
                          the net.

12 Atcō′kō   oq¡ōsā′na,   Lä′lēlē   agE′LgElōya.   AkLE′Lkᵘ¡am   Lä′lēlē
   He sent her   the newt,   salmon-   she shall go to take   She brought them   salmon-
                              berries   them.   berries

13 ōq¡ōsā′na.   A′lta   aqLauwē′qcEmt   qō′La   Lä′lēlē   qō′ta   tguā′nat.
   the newt.   Now   they were put into their   those   salmon-   those   salmon.
                       mouths   berries

14 Nē′ktcuktē,   wiXt   aLxēnaua′itgēmam.
   It got day,   again   they went to catch salmon
                          in the net.

   ALōgō′ōm   ōxoēnauwä′-itgē   gō   mä′Lnē.   Mank   mā′ēma   aLe′xana,
   They met   men fishing salmon   at   on water.   A little   seaward   they laid net,
              with net

16 tcä′xēL   aLe′xana,   ka   aLō′tctuwilX,   mank   kᵘcalā′.   ALe′Xkō   qix·
   several   they laid the net,   and   they ascended the   a little   up the river.   They passed   that
   times   river,   it

17 ikanī′m,   itä′xēnim   qō′tac   ōxoēnauā′itgē.   ALe′xana.   ALexē′naua-itgē
   canoe,   their canoe   these   men fishing salmon   They laid their   They caught salmon in
                                    with net.   net.   the net

18 qē′xtcē,   nēkct   i′kta   aLgiā′waꜬ.   ALe′cXumgEna.   ALe′Xkō;
   intending,   not   anything   they killed it.   They did not catch anything.   They went
                                                                                    home;

19 kalā′lkuilē   nē′xax   it¡ā′lapas.   AtcLā′auwitcXa: "Qa′daqa   k¡ā′ya
   scold   he did   coyote.   He defecated: "Why   nothing

20 nō′xôx   tik   tguā′nat?"   "Yä2,   x·ik   iō′L¡′ElEx,   ma′nix   mēwa′Ꜭo
   became   these   salmon?"   "Yä,   this   lean one,   when   you kill him

21 iguā′nat,   iä′xkatē   mxEnxä′ya.   WiXt   ēXt   mēwa′Ꜭō,   wiXt   iä′xkatē
   a salmon,   there   you lay net.   Again   one   you kill him,   again   there

22 mxEnxä′ya.   Näkct   mxgō′ya   ikanī′m,   ma′nix   ōxoēnauā′-itgē   tē′lx·Em.
   lay net.   Not   pass   a canoe,   when   they put salmon in   people.
                                                a net

23 Tgä′k·iLau."   "Haō′,"   nē′k·im   it¡ā′lapas.   Nē′ktcuktē,   wiXt
   It is their taboo."   "Haō,"   he said   coyote.   It got day,   again

24 aLxēnauā′-itgēmam.   Nē′k·im   it¡ā′lapas: "Ā′la   nai′ka   ä′la   tEll
   they went to catch salmon in   He said   coyote: "Even   I   even   tired
   net.

25 nE′xax;   ē′ka-y-   ōxō′xō   Natē′tanuē.   Nēkct   Lgiä′xō   iguā′nat
   I become;   thus they   will do   the Indians.   Not   it will eat him   salmon

gaLā′k¡auk¡au,   ē′ka   Lmē′mɛlōct   k˥k˥ōcgā′liL,   ē′ka   Lqēlā′wulX,   **1**

a murderer,   thus   corpses   who takes [them]   thus   girl first men-

                                       always,   struating,

ē′ka   LqLɛ′Xit,   ē′ka   Lɛ′pL’au.   Ka′nauᵂā·v·   ē′ka   tgā′k·iLau   tē′lx·ɛm   **2**

thus   menstruated   thus   widow and   All   thus   their taboo   people

      woman.   widower·

nuxunā′xɛnitɛma   tē′lx·ɛm.   **3**

generations of   people.

Translation

Coyote was coming. He came to Gōt'a′t. There he met a heavy surf. He was afraid that he might be drifted away and went up to the spruce trees. He stayed there a long time. Then he took some sand and threw it upon that surf: "This shall be a prairie and no surf. The future generations shall walk on this prairie." Thus Clatsop became a prairie. The surf became a prairie.

At Niā′xaqcē a creek originated. He went and built a house at Niā′xaqcē. He went out and stayed at the mouth of Niā′xaqcē. Then he speared two silver-side salmon, a steel-head salmon, and a fall salmon. Then he threw the salmon and the fall salmon away, saying: "This creek is too small. I do not like to see here salmon and fall salmon. It shall be a bad omen when a fall salmon is killed here; somebody shall die; also when a salmon is killed. When a female salmon or fall salmon is killed a woman shall die; when a male is killed a man shall die." Now he carried only the silver-side salmon to his house. When he arrived there he cut it at once, steamed it and ate it. On the next day he took his harpoon and went again to the mouth of Niā′xaqcē. He did not see anything, and the flood tide set in. He went home. On the next day he went again and did not see anything. Then he became angry and went home. He defecated and said to his excrements: "Why have these silver-side salmon disappeared?" "Oh, you with your bandy legs, you have no sense. When the first silver-side salmon is killed it must not be cut. It must be split along its back and roasted. It must not be steamed. Only when they go up river then they may be steamed." Coyote went home. On the next day he went again and speared three. He went home and made three spits. He roasted each salmon on a spit. He had three salmon and three spits. On the next day he went again and stood at the mouth of the creek. He did not see anything until the flood tide set in. Then he became angry and went home. He defecated. He spoke and asked his excrements: "Why have these silver-side salmon disappeared?" His excrements said to him: "I told you, you with your bandy legs, when the first silver-side salmon are killed spits must be made, one for the head, one for the back, one for the roe, one for the body. The gills must be burnt." "Yes," said Coyote. On the next day he went again. He killed again three silver-side salmon. When he arrived at home he cut them all and made many spits. He roasted them all separately. The spits of the breast, body, head, back, and roe

were at separate places. Coyote roasted them. On the next morning
he went again. He speared ten silver-side salmon. Coyote was very
glad. He came home and split part of the fish. The other part he
left and went to sleep. On the next morning he roasted the rest.
Then he went again and stood at the mouth of the river. He did not
see anything before the flood tide set in. He went home. On the next
morning he went again, but again he did not see anything. He went
home angry. He defecated and asked his excrements: "Why have
these silver-side salmon disappeared?" His excrements scolded him:
"When the first silver-side salmon are killed, they are not left raw.
All must be roasted. When many are caught, they must all be roasted
before you go to sleep." On the next morning Coyote went and stood
at the mouth of the river. He speared ten. Then he made many double
spits, and remained awake until all were roasted that he had caught.
Now he had learned all that is forbidden in regard to silver-side salmon
when they arrive first at Niā′xaqcē. He remained there and said:
"The Indians shall always do as I had to do. If a man who prepares
corpses eats a silver-side salmon, they shall disappear at once. If a
murderer eats silver-side salmon, they shall at once disappear. They
shall also disappear when a girl who has just reached maturity or when
a menstruating woman eats them. Even I got tired."

Now he came this way. At some distance he met a number of women
who were digging roots. He asked them: "What are you doing?"
"We are digging gamass." "How can you dig gamass at Clatsop?
You shall dig [a root, species?] and thistle [?] roots in this country.
No gamass will be dug here." Now they gathered [a root, species?]
and thistle [?] roots. He left these women and spoiled that land. He
transformed the gamass into small onions.

Then he came to Clatsop. It was the spring of the year. Then he
met his younger brother the snake. He said to him: "Let us make
nets." The snake replied: "As you wish." Now they bought material
for twine, and paid the frog and the newt to spin it. Now Coyote
cleaned all the material for twine while the snake was crawling about.
Then the frog and the newt spun it. Then Coyote said to his younger
brother: "Clean it, clean it. You crawl about all day." Thus he spoke
to the snake. Coyote continued: "You shall make one side of the net,
I make the other." Coyote finished his twine and said to the snake:
"Quick! quick! you let me wait. Make your net." The snake replied:
"You let me wait." Thus he spoke to Coyote. Now, Coyote made his
net. He finished it all. The two women made the ropes, Coyote made
the net buoys; while the snake crawled about. Coyote said: "Make
your net buoys; you let me wait." Thus he said to the snake. The
snake replied: "Make haste! you let me wait." Coyote finished his
net buoys. Then he went to look for stones, and the snake accompanied
him. They went for stones to Tongue point. The snake crawled about
among the stones, while Coyote carried them down. They went home.

After they reached home Coyote went to gather spruce roots. The
snake accompanied him. Coyote dug up the ground and the snake
crawled about at the same place. They went home. Coyote split the
spruce roots. "Go on; work," he spoke to the snake; "you let me wait."
The snake replied: "Quick, quick; work! you let me wait." Now
Coyote tied his net to the buoys and laid it down flat on a large mat.
Then he tied it to the buoys. The snake crawled about at the same
place. Coyote finished his net and hung it up outside. Early the next
morning he stepped out of the house, and there hung already the net
of the snake. "Oh, brother," he said, "you got the better of me."
Coyote was ashamed. The snake had won over him. Coyote said:
"When a person makes a net, he shall get tired before he finishes it.
It would not be well if he would not get tired." The snake said to him:
"I told you that you would let me wait."

It got day. Then they went to catch salmon in their net. They laid
the net and caught two in it. Coyote jumped over the net. Now they
intended to catch more salmon, but the flood-tide set in. They had
caught only two before the flood-tide set in. Now they went home.
Coyote said that he was hungry, and he split the salmon at once. They
roasted them. When they were done they ate. The frog and the newt
were their cousins. The next morning they went fishing with their net.
The newt looked after the rope, the snake stood at the upper end of
the net, Coyote at the lower end. They intended to catch salmon, but
they did not get anything until the flood-tide set in. They went home.
Coyote was angry. He defecated and spoke to his excrements: "You
are a liar." They said to him: "You with your bandy-legs. When people
kill a salmon they do not jump over the net. You must not step over
your net. When the first salmon are killed, they are not cut until the
afternoon." "Oh," said Coyote, "You told me enough." On the next
morning they went fishing. When they had killed a salmon they did
not jump over the net. They laid their net twice. Enough salmon
were in the net. Then he ordered the newt: "Bail out the canoe, it
is full of water." She bailed it out. Then they intended to fish again,
but the flood-tide set in. They went home and put down what they
had caught in the house. In the afternoon Coyote split the salmon.
He split them in the same way as the silver-side salmon. He placed
the head, the back, the body, and the roe in separate places and on
separate double spits. They were done. The next morning they went
fishing. They did not kill anything. Coyote became angry and defecated. He said to his excrements: "Tell me, why have these salmon
disappeared?" His excrements scolded him: "Do you think their
taboo is the same as that of the silver-side salmon? It is different.
When you go fishing salmon and they go into your net, you may lay it
three times. No more salmon will go into it. It is enough then. Never
bail out your canoe. When you come home and cut the salmon, you
must split it at the sides and roast belly and back on separate double

spits. Then put four sticks vertically into the ground [so that they form a square] and lay two horizontal sticks across them. On top of this frame place the back with the head and the tail attached to it." He said to his excrements: "You told me enough." On the next morning they went fishing and killed three salmon. They did not bail out their canoe. Then he said to the newt: "Fetch a stick from the woods. We will make a club." She went and brought a stick. Then they laid their net again. Again a salmon was in it and he killed it with his club. They intended to continue fishing, but the flood-tide set in. They killed four only. They put down their salmon. In the afternoon Coyote cut them and put four sticks into the ground. Now he did as his excrements had told him. When they were done he broke the backbone at once. On the next morning they went fishing. They did not kill anything before the flood-tide set in. They went home. Coyote was angry and defecated. "Why have these salmon disappeared?" he asked his excrements. "I told you," they said to Coyote; "do you think their taboo is the same as that of the silver-side salmon? It is different. When you kill a salmon you must never strike it with a stick. When they may be boiled, then you may strike them with a stick. When it is almost autumn you may strike them with a stick. Do not break a salmon's backbone when they just begin to come. When you have killed a salmon take sand, strew it on its eye, and press it with your fist. Do not club it." Coyote said: "You have told me enough." On the next morning they went fishing. Salmon went into the net; three went into the net immediately. He strewed sand on each and pressed each. He killed many salmon. They went home and roasted them. When they were done he distributed them among the people of the town above Clatsop. Now they dried them. On the next morning they went fishing. They tried to fish but did not catch anything before the flood-tide set in. They went home. Coyote was angry. He defecated: "Why have these salmon disappeared?" "I told you, you lean one, with your bandy-legs. There are many taboos relating to the salmon. When you have killed many salmon you must never carry them outside the house. You must roast and eat them at the same place. When part is left they must stay at the same place. When you want to dry them you must do so when the flood-tide sets in on the day after you have caught them." He said to them: "You have told me enough." On the next morning they went fishing again. They killed many salmon. They roasted them all. When they were done he invited the people. The newt was sent out. They came to eat in Coyote's house. They finished eating. Then they left there what they had not eaten. Now it was low water in the morning. They went out early to lay their net, but they did not catch anything. They fished until the flood-tide set in. They did not kill anything. They were unsuccessful. Twice they tried to go fishing early in the morning, but they were unsuccessful; they did not catch anything. Coyote defecated and said to his excrements: "Why have the salmon disappeared?" Coyote received the answer: "I told you, you lean one, that the salmon has many taboos. When you go fishing and it is ebb-tide early in the morning, you must not lay your net before sunrise. The salmon must not be carried outside until a crow takes one and carries it outside. Then it must be distributed raw. No fire must be made until daylight; the breast must not be eaten before the next day. When salmon are roasted at a fire and they are done, water must be poured into the fire." He said to his excrements: "You have told me enough. The Indians shall always do this way. Thus shall be the taboos for all generations of Indians. Even I got tired."

Thus spoke Coyote about the taboos of Clatsop. He said to his cousins: "We will move to the other side." The newt made herself ready. Then the snake looked at the frog, who was growling. The snake reached her, struck, and killed her.

Now they arrived here on this side. They went fishing and killed salmon. He did the same way as in Clatsop. He strewed sand on the eye of that salmon. He pressed its eye. Then they intended to fish again, but they did not kill anything. They went home. On the following morning they went again fishing, but they did not kill anything. On the next morning they went fishing again, but they did not kill anything. Coyote scolded. He defecated: "Why have these salmon disappeared?" "Oh, you foolish Coyote. When you kill a salmon you must kick it. Do you think it is the same here as at Clatsop?" "Oh," said Coyote. On the next morning they went fishing again. They laid their net and caught two salmon. They laid their net again and caught three salmon. He threw one ashore. It fell down head first, so that the mouth struck the sand. They tried to lay their net again, but they did not kill anything. They tried to fish until the flood tide set in. They had not killed anything. They had caught five only. They went home. In the evening Coyote cut the salmon and roasted them. They were done. The following morning they went fishing, but did not kill anything. Coyote scolded. He defecated: "Why have these salmon disappeared?" "Oh, you foolish Coyote. Do you think it is the same here as at Clatsop? Do not throw salmon ashore so that the head is downward. It is taboo. When you kill a salmon go and pick salmonberries. When you have caught many salmon put salmonberries into the mouth of each." "Oh, you have told me enough," he said to his excrements. The next morning they again went fishing. They killed many salmon. He sent the newt to pick salmonberries. The newt brought the salmonberries. Now they put those berries into the mouths of those salmon. It got day and they went fishing again. They met fishermen on the water. A short distance down river they laid their net. They laid it several times and went up the river a short distance. They passed the canoes of those fishermen. They laid their net and intended to fish, but they did not kill anything. They were unsuccessful. They went home. Coyote scolded. He defecated: "Why have these salmon disappeared?" "You lean one! When you kill a salmon, and you have laid your net at one place and you kill one more, you must lay your net at the same place. You must not pass a canoe with fishermen in it. It is taboo." "Yes," said Coyote. On the next day they went again fishing. Coyote said: "Even I got tired. The Indians shall always do in the same manner. Murderers, those who prepare corpses, girls who are just mature, menstruating women, widows and widowers shall not eat salmon. Thus shall be the taboos for all generations of people."

7. IQOĀ'CQOAC IĀ'KXANAM.

THE CRANE HIS MYTH.

LxĕlӐ'ĕtix· iqoā'cqoac k¡a it¡ā'lapas k¡a ixoā'ck¡oai. Ka'nauwĕ 1
There were   the crane   and   coyote   and   the heron.   All

Lᶜalā'ma Lĕ'iĕ aLkᴛupiā'Lxa-it. ALuwĕ'tcgōmx. A'lta nĕ'k·imx 2
days   mud clams   they gathered.   It became flood tide.   Now   he said

it¡ā'lapas: "Qantsī'X tq¡ō'xōL tEmē'qolĕyū?" Nĕ'k·imx iqoā'cqoac: 3
coyote: "How many   Ōq¡ō'xōL   are your sweethearts?"   He said   the crane:

'Mȯkct ōkunī'm pӐ'LEma k¡a qā'mxikc pEnka'." Nĕ'k·imx it¡ā'lapas: 4
"Two   canoes   full   and   part   afoot."   He said   coyote:

"ME'nx· ka Lmĕ'qolĕyū. Nai'ka qoā'nEm ōkunī'm pӐ'LEma k¡a 5
"Few   only   your sweethearts.   I have   five   canoes   full   and

qā'mxikc pEnka';" cka k¡ā nixā'xo-itx ixoā'ck¡oai. Qoā'nEmē 6
part   afoot;"   and   silent   he always was   the heron   Five times

tĕaLō'Lx aLkᴛō'piatx Lĕ'iĕ ka aLkᴛ'Ӑ'yō-itx gō mӐ'Lxȯlĕ gō 7
their sleeps   they gathered   mud clams   then   they always slept   at   inland   on

tEmᶜā'ĕma. Ĕŏ'wam atcī'ax iqoā'cqoac. Nĕ'xElatckō it¡ā'lapas: 8
a prairie.   Sleepy   he made him   the crane.   He rose   coyote:

"Ōq¡ō'xōL XaXaw ō'Lxat." AtcixElqĕ'Lxalem iqoā'cqoac; ayoō'ptitx. 9
"Ōq¡ō'xōL   she   comes down to the beach."   He shouted   the crane;   he had slept.

Nĕ'k·im it¡ā'lapas: "Ka'ltas lā'xlax aiamtā'x." Ē'xoĕti lā'xlax atcā'x. 10
He said   coyote: "Only   deceive   I did you."   Often   deceive   he did him.

A'lta aLk¡ĕ'witox·itx. NōLx Oq¡ō'xōL, akLE'lgitgax; ĕgi'gula aqiā'x 11
Now   they fell asleep.   She came   Ōq¡ō'xōL,   she put them into [basket]   below   he was put

it¡ā'lapas, kā'tsEk aqĕ'lgītgax iqoā'sqoas, ĕ'kᵘcaxala aqiā'x 12
coyote,   in middle   he was put   the crane,   on top   he was made

ixoā'cqoai. MӐ'Lxolĕ aqLō'kᵘᴛamx. NixEl'ō'gux ixoā'cqoai. 13
the heron.   Inland   she arrived carrying them.   He awoke   the heron.

Atcō'cgamx ōĕ'kᵘtEqᴛ'ix·. Iā'xkatĕ nixpō'nitx. Kulā'yi nō'yamx 14
He took it   a branch.   There   he hung.   Far   she arrived

uqcxĕ'Lau. NixEl'ō'gux it¡ā'lapas. Nĕ'k·imqac pEt nixā'x. NixEl'ō'kux 15
the monster.   He awoke   coyote.   He looked [??]   quiet   he was.   He awoke

iqoā'cqoac. AtcixE'lqĕLxax. "K¡ā amE'x, k¡ā amE'x," nĕ'k·imx 16
the crane.   He shouted.   "Silent   be,   silent   be,"   he said

it¡ā'lapas. "GElxō'ctxōt uqctxĕ'Lau." Akcō'kᵘᴛamx gō tE'kXaqL 17
coyote.   'She carries us   the monster."   She carried them two   to   her house

gō tga'a uqctxĕ'Lau. Agiŏnā'xLatcgox qix· ĕ'Xat. Agō'lXam 18
to   her children   the monster.   She lost him   that   one.   She said to her

uxgE'kxun ugō'xō: "Ē'qxamctk ĕ'kElōya. Mȯkct mtE'Lkᵘᴛa 19
the eldest one   her daughter: "A spit   go and take it.   Two   carry

wuk¡Ema' itĕ'la-itqE'q." Nō'ix ugō'xo. Atciō'lXamx iā'cikc 20
straight   huckleberry sticks."   She went   her daughter.   He said to him   to his friend

it¡ā'lapas: "MixEnLk¡ā'yōgō imĕ'tuk ma'nix aqEmō'lEktca." 21
coyote: ·'Bend   your neck   when   it is intended to roast you."

Aqiŏ'kᵘᴛamx qix· ĕ'qxamctk. AtcixEnLk¡ā'yugux iā'tuk iqoā'cqoac. 22
It was brought   that   spit.   He bent it   his neck   the crane.

Agō'lXamx ugō'xō: "Ē'kElōya ixEnLk¡ā'yukta -y-ĕ'qxamctk. 23
She said to her   her daughter: "Bring   a crooked   spit.

Nĕ'k·imx it¡ā'lapas: "Manix qĕ'tkᵘᴛama ixEmk¡ā'yukta, wuk¡ amiā'x 24
He said   coyote: "When   it is brought   a crooked one,   straight make

107

1 imē'tuk." Agē'tkuᴵam ugō'xō ixEnLk¡ā'yukta. Wuk¡ atcā'yax
 your neck." She brought it her daughter a crooked one. Straight he made it

2 iā'tuk. Qoä'nEmi nōya qaX uk'ō'ckc ugō'xō-y-Ōq¡ō'xōL ka aLā'x
 his neck. Five times she went that girl her daughter Ōq¡ō'xōL's and she became

3 q¡'am. Nā'k·im Ōq¡ō'xōl: "Cka cELā'ētix qcā'xō." Ciyi'q¡'Ema
 lazy. She said Ōq¡ō'xōL: "And slaves we will make them." Half a fathom

4 iLā'Lqta Liā'itcX iqoā'cqoac. Nē'k·im it¡ā'lapas, aqiō'lXam iqoā'cqoac:
 long his tail crane. He said coyote, he was told the crane:

5 "Qā't¡'ōcXEm! lā'xlax tgā'xo. AnEktcxEmä'ya, mEnGEnō'tēnEma."
 "Look out! deceive her we will do I shall sing my conjurer's song, you will help me sing."

6 ALkcupā'yaLx Lkuckuē' pāL qō'ta t!'ōL, ka nē'ktcxEm it¡ā'lapas.
 They gathered it pitchwood full that house, and he sang the conjurer's song coyote.

7 Ō'kuk¡'uētik atcā'yax itcā'yau. Qē'xtcē atciō'lXam iqoā'cqoac:
 Headband he put on him the snake. Intending he said to him [to] the crane:

8 "Okuk!uē'tik iamELā'xo x·ik itcā'yau." AcixElqē'Lxal iqoā'cqoac,
 "Headband I shall put on you this snake." He shouted the crane.

9 k¡oa'c nē'xax. A'lta nē'ktcxEm it¡ā'lapas. Lā'kti ayā'qxoya
 afraid he was. Now he sang the conjurer's song coyote. Four times sleeps

10 nixElkᴵā'ta-it, ō'LaquinEm ō'pōl ka nōō'ptit Ōq¡ō'xōL k¡a tgā'a.
 he remained awake, the fifth night and she slept Ōq¡ō'xōL and her children.

11 Atciō'cgam ēLq. Atcilgā'mētē gō-y- ilē'ē. Ā'mka uyā'makul
 He took it a digging stick. He placed it upright in the ground. Only its handle

12 Lāx. K¡au atci'Lax LE'kXakcō gō qix· ēLq; k¡au'k¡au atctō'kXux
 visible. Tie he did it their hair at that digging stick: tie he did them

13 qō'tac tga'a Ōq¡ō'xōL. Actō'pa. WaX acgE'tax, waX qō'ta t!'ōL.
 those her children Ōq¡ō'xōL. They went out. Light they did it, light that house.

14 Nē'xLXa iqoā'cqoac gō Liā'itcX. Atciō'lXam: "ME'La-it gō x·ita
 He burnt the crane at his tail. He said to him: "Stay in this

15 tEmᶜā'ēma!" Ayō'La-it iqoā'cqoac. Nō'xōLXa gō qō'ta tEmᶜā'ēma.
 prairie." He stayed the crane. It burnt at that prairie.

16 "ME'La-it gō Xau ūcā'qca!" Ayō'La-it gō qaX ucā'qca. Nā'xLXa
 "Stay in this Pteris aquilina." He stayed at that Pteris aquilina. It burnt

17 qaX ucā'qca. "ME'La-it gō Xiau ē'Xca-ōt ē'mᶜEcX!" Ayō'La-it.
 that Pteris aquilina. "Stay at this dry wood!" He stayed.

18 Nē'xLXa qix· ē'Xca-ōt ē'mᶜEcX. Alā'xti aLxE'tcXōm qō'La
 It burnt that dry wood. At last it was finished that

19 Liā'itcX iqoā'cqoac. Tcx·ī atciō'lXam: "ME'La-it gō x·iLa Ltcuq,"
 his tail the crane's. Then he said to him: "Stay in this water."

20 nixLō'lEXa-it it¡ā'lapas. Ta'kE aLxE'tcXōm Liā'itcX iqoā'cqoac.
 he thought coyote. Then it was finished his tail the crane's.

21 A'lta nā'xLXa-y- ōqctxē'Lau. NaxE'l'ōkō, a'lta ōxō'LXa tE'kXaqL.
 Now she burnt the monster. She awoke, now it burnt her house.

22 Aktō'lXam tga'a "McxELā'yutck! Tcūxō'LElama tE'lxaqL it¡ā'lapas."
 She said to them her children "Rise! He will burn it our house coyote.

23 Qē'xtcē naxā'latck. Naxk¡ā'Xit. ALE'XLXa Lkanauwä'tiks k¡a tgā'a.
 Intending she rose. It pulled her. They burnt all and her children.

 A'lta ā'ctc it¡ā'lapas ē'wa Nix·kELā'x. Kuca'la ac'tō gō iā'Xakatck
 Now they two coyote thus went Nix·kELā'x. Up river they went to its cataract

25 Nix·kELā'x. T!'ōL acgE'tax. Lxoa'p atci'tax tqā'nakc it¡ā'lapas:
 Nix·kELā'x A house they made it. Dig he did them stones coyote.

26 "K¡ō'ma tssōpEnā'ya ē'qaLEma qigō naLxoā'pē; Ō'owun ksōpEnā'ya
 "Perhaps they will jump the fall salmon where the hole; silver-side salmon will jump

27 qigō naLxoā'pē; ō'la-atcX ksōpEnā'ya qigō naLxoā'pē; ka'nauwē
 where the hole; calico salmon will jump where the hole; all

tḳᵢ'ē'wulElqL tksopEnā'ya qigō naLxoa'pē." A'lta atcā'yax ē'tcōL 1
fish   will jump   where   the hole."   Now   he made it   a harpoon shaft

iqoā'cqoac, atcī'ctax ckulkulō'L. Ayō'tXuita-itx gō mā'Lnē iqoā'cqoac. 2
the crane,   he made it   a harpoon.   He always stood   at   toward the water   the crane.

Qiā'x ē'k·ala ē'qalEma, tcx·ī atcᴦē'lukc'ax; qia'x ō'kXōla-y· ō'owun 3
If   a male   fall salmon,   then   he speared it;   if   a male   silver-side salmon

tcx·ī atcᴦā'lukc'ax. Ō'xoē atctō'piaLxax tḳᵢē'wulElqᴦ iqoā'cqoac. 4
then   he speared it.   Many   he gathered them   fish   the crane.

Ala'xti atctā'xcx; ka'nauwē L꞊alā'mā·y· ē'ka. Itᵢā'lapas, qiā'x 5
At last   he split them;   all   days   thus.   Coyote,   if

iā'q̣ᵢ'atxala ē'qalEma, tcx·ī atssō'pEnax qigō naLxoā'pē, qiā'x 6
a bad   fall salmon,   then   it jumped   where   the hole,   if

ō꞊ō'kuil ō'owun, tcx·ī aksō'pEnax qigō naLxoā'pē. Ä2'XtEmaē tcx·ī 7
a female   silver-side salmon,   then   it jumped   where   the hole.   Sometimes   then

itᵢ'ō'ktē atssōpEnā'x. PāL nō'xôx tE'ctaqL. Lgā'kxatcau pāL 8
a good one   jumped.   Full   got   their house.   Its grease   full

iā'kⁿcEmal iqoā'cqoac. Atctō'kctx iā'kⁿcEmal itᵢā'lapas; ka'nauwē 9
his dry salmon   the crane.   He looked up to   his dry salmon   coyote;   all

cpE'qEma, nēkct Lgā'kxatcau. NixLō'lEXa-it itᵢā'lapas: "Niuwa'ꞓō. 10
gray,   not   its grease.   He thought   coyote: "I shall kill him.

Mtucgā'ma Xō'ta iā'kⁿcEmal." A'lta nē'ktcxEmx itᵢā'lapas. 11
I shall take them   these   his dry salmon."   Now   he sang his conjuror's song   coyote.

Nix·ēnō'tēnEmx iqoā'cqoac. Ā'qoa·iL uyā'xōlē itᵢā'lapas. Ayōpē'Lax 12
He helped him sing   the crane.   Large   his baton   coyote's.   He stretched it out

iā'tuk iqoā'cqoac. Nix·ēnō'tēnEmx. Atciā'ōwilX gō iā'tuk, 13
his neck   the crane.   He helped him singing.   He struck him   at   his neck,

atcē'XEmq̣ᵢ'ōya iā'tuk iqoā'cqoac. Aqiō'kLpa ka nixEmā'tcta-itck 14
he bent it   his neck   the crane.   He was missed   and   he was ashamed

itᵢā'lapas. Atcawē'k·itk tiā'ḳᵢewalElqᴦ iqoā'cqoac, ka'nauwē qix· 15
coyote.   He put them into [basket]   his fish   the crane,   all   that

ia'kⁿcEmal. Atcawē'k·itk itᵢā'lapas iā'kⁿcEmal. A'lta cx·Lx·ā'yoōt. 16
his dry salmon.   He put them into [basket]   coyote   his dry salmon.   Now   they were angry against each other.

Ē'x·LXaōt iqoā'cqoac, ē'x·LXaōt itᵢā'lapas. Atctō'ctxōniLtck 17
He was angry,   the crane,   he was angry   coyote.   He carried them on his head

iā'kⁿcEmal iqoā'cqoac. Tcē'xēLx nē'Xtakō ka ka'nauwē nōxō'tctXōm. 18
his dry salmon   the crane.   Several times may be   he turned back   and   all   he finished them.

Q̣ᵢ'am nē'xax itᵢā'lapas igē'ctxō. Atcō'Xuina qō'ta tiā'ḳᵢēwulElqᴦ. 19
Lazy   he was   coyote   he carried them on back.   He placed them in a row   those   his fish.

Aēkgō'tē qaX uē'Xatk gō Nix·kElā'·x. NixLō'lEXa-it itᵢā'lapas: 20
It led across the hill   that   trail   to   Nix·kElā'·x.   He thought   coyote:

"Ntukᵢ'uwā'kcta nuXuwā'ya." AtcLE'lgitk lēXt Lꞓā'pta gō 21
"I shall try   I shall drive them."   He put into   one   roe   in

tiā'xalaitanEma nauē'gic, ate'xLxō tiā'xalaitanEma. A'lta ātcō'Xuwa 22
his arrows   where they were in,   he hung them over his shoulder   his arrows.   Now   he drove them

qō'ta tiā'ḳᵢēwulElqᴦ. Ā'nqatē ayō'tctcō iqoā'cqoac. Goyē' mank 23
those   his fish.   Already   he went down river   the crane.   Thus   a little

akā'x qaX ō'ēXatk qĩgō nō'Lxamtt. A'lta nōXuwa', nōXuwa' qō'ta 24
did   that   trail   where it came down to the water.   Now   he drove them,   he drove them   those

tiā'ḳᵢēwulElqᴦ gō Lqā'giltk auwigē'ca, gō Lqōmqō'mukc auwigē'ca. 25
his fish   in   baskets   they were in,   in   large baskets   they were in.

1 Q̣ioä'p atgE'Lxam, a'lta tcịpāk atkxtā'mXit. Ayō'Lxam qix· iā'něwa
Nearly they came to the now really they rolled. He arrived at that first
water, the water

2 iqā'giltk. Nau'i gō Ltcuq Lịlap ně'xax; wiXt ěXt ayō'Lxam, nau'i
basket. At once in water under it got; again one arrived at the at once
water, water,

3 gō Ltcuq Lịlap ně'xax. Ka'nauwě ā'tgě. Ně'xankō; qě'xtcě
in the water under water it got. All they went. He ran; intending

4 atciō'cgam ěXt, Lịlap ā'cto. ALgě'xkịa qō'La Lᶜā'pta. Lịlap
he took it one, under water they two It pulled him that roe. Under
went. water

5 ā'yō. Lā'qo atě'xax qō'ta tiā'xalaitanEma. Ā'yoptck. K·ē ka'nauwě
he went. Take he did them those arrows. He went ashore. Noth- all
off ing

6 qō'ta tiā'kịěwulElqʇ. Ně'k·im itịā'lapas: "AnxE'LuX tcịa ě'ka
those fish. He said coyote: "I think thus

7 ōxō'xō tê'lx·Em. Ma'nix ōgōLā'yuwa ka cka tgōXuwä'ya tgā'cxělax;
they will the people. When they move then and they will drive it their food;
do

8 ā'la nai'ka, ā'la tgE'nxgakō. Qā'doxoē ato'xqiäxtEl, tEll xā'xo-ilEmx
even I, even they got the bet- Must they always work, tired they always get
ter of me.

9 LgōLě'lEXEmk Lgě'ctxoniLx, ma'nix aLkLā'yuwa. Kịoně'kịoně!;
person he carries much when they are going to The story;
on back move.

10 wu'xi ickagā'p.
to-mor- it is fair weather.
row

Translation.

Crane, Coyote, and Heron lived together. Every day they went digging clams until the flood-tide set in. One day Coyote said: "How many Oqịō'xōL have you for your sweethearts?" Crane replied: "Two canoes full and some must walk." Coyote said: "How few sweethearts you have! I have five canoes full and some must walk." Heron remained silent. Five days they dug clams, and the nights they slept on a prairie. When Crane was sleepy Coyote rose and cried: "An Oq'ō'xoL comes down to the beach!" Crane shouted; he had fallen asleep. Then Coyote said: "I have only deceived you." He did so often. Now they fell asleep. Then Oq'ō'xōL came to the beach and put them into her basket. She put Coyote at the bottom, Crane in the middle, and Heron on top. She carried them inland. Now Heron awoke. He took hold of a branch and hung there. When the monster had gone a long distance Coyote awoke. He looked around but remained quiet. Then Crane awoke. He shouted, but Coyote said: "Be quiet, be quiet, the monster carries us away." She brought them to her house and to her children. One she had lost. Then she said to her eldest daughter: "Go and get two spits; bring straight huckleberry sticks." Her daughter went out. Then Coyote said to his friend: "Bend your neck when she is about to roast you." When the spit was brought Crane bent his neck. Then she said to her daughter: "Bring a crooked spit." Coyote said: "When a crooked spit is brought stretch out your neck." The girl brought a crooked spit, then Crane stretched out his neck." Five times the girl, the daughter of Oqịō'xōL, went; then she became tired. Oqịō'xōL said: "We will make them our slaves." At that time Crane's tail was half a fathom long. Coyote said to him: "Look here! We will deceive her. I shall sing my conjurer's song and you will help me." They gathered pitchwood and when the house was full Coyote sang his conjurer's song. He put the snake on as a headband. He said to Crane: "I will put the snake on your head as a headband." Then Crane shouted; he was afraid. Now Coyote sang his conjurer's song. Four nights they remained awake; on the fifth night Oq̣ṓ'xŏꞮ and her children fell asleep. Then he took a digging stick and rammed it into the ground so that only the handle remained visible. He tied the hair of Oq'ṓ'xŏꞮ and of her children to the digging stick. Then they went out and lit the house. Crane's tail caught fire. Then Coyote said to him: "Stay on this prairie." Crane did so and the prairie caught fire. "Stay in this fern." He did so and it caught fire. "Stay in this dry wood." He did so and it caught fire. At last Crane's tail was wholly burnt. Then Coyote thought: "Stay in the water." Thus Crane's tail was burnt. Now the monster caught fire. She awoke and saw her house burning. She said to her children: "Rise, Coyote will burn our house." She wanted to rise, but her hair pulled her back. She and her children were all burnt.

Now Coyote and Crane went to Nix·kꞮlā'x. They went up the river to its rapids. Then they built a house. Coyote made holes in the stones and said: "Perhaps fall salmon will jump into my hole. Silver-side salmon will jump into my hole. Calico salmon will jump into my hole. All kinds of fish will jump into my hole." Crane made a harpoon shaft and a harpoon and stood near the water. When a male fall salmon or a silver-side salmon passed him, he speared them. He caught many fish. Then he split them. Every day he did so. Bad fall salmon and female silver-side salmon jumped into Coyote's hole. Sometimes a good one would jump into it. Now their house was full of fish. The dry salmon of Crane was fat. When Coyote looked up his salmon was all grey and no fat was on it. Coyote thought: "I will kill him and take his dry salmon." Now he sang his conjurer's song and Crane helped him. Coyote had a large baton. Crane stretched out his neck when he helped Coyote. Then he struck at his neck, but Crane bent it. Coyote was ashamed because he had missed him. Crane put all his dry fish into a basket. So did Coyote. They were angry with one another. Crane and Coyote were angry. Crane carried his dry salmon on his back. He came back several times until he had carried them all. Coyote, however, was too lazy to carry them on his back. He placed all those fish in a row. The trail led across the hill to Nix·kꞮlā'x. Coyote thought: "I shall try to drive them." He put a roe into his quiver which he hung over his shoulder. Then he drove his fish. Crane had already gone down the river. The trail went a little down hill when it approached the river. Now Coyote drove the baskets in which his fish were. When they came near the water, they

began to roll rapidly. The first basket arrived at the river and rolled
into it. The next one arrived at the river and rolled into it. All rolled
into the river. He ran after them in order to hold them. He took hold
of his fish, but he was pulled into the water by the roe in his quiver.
Then he took off his arrows and went ashore. All his fish had disappeared. Then he said: "I think the people shall do thus: When they
move from one place to the other they shall not drive their food. Even
I could not do it. They shall work and become tired, carrying it on
their backs when they move." That is the story; to-morrow it will be
good weather.

ĒNTS¡X HIS MYTH.

Ēnts¡X ōyä'k¡ikē Ūpē'qciuc. A'ltä agiō'kXul imō'lak tcikElō'ya.
Ēnts¡X his grandmother Ūpē'qciuc. Now she always said elk he shall go and
to him take it.   **1**

Wäx qē'xtcĕ ayō'yix; ä'mka ō'tsikin atcā'woᶜôx; iā'mka ik¡'ä'ōtEn
Every intending he went; only chipmunks he killed them; only squirrels
morning   **2**

atciä'woᶜôx; anä'-y- ōkō'lXul atcā'woᶜôx. Tcä'xĕ Lx ä'yō.
he killed them; sometimes mice he killed them. Several times maybe he went.   **3**

Ē'xauwitē ä'yō ka ayō'tXuit gō tEmᶜä'ēma. Na'ixE'lqamx:
Often. he went and he stayed on the prairie. He shouted: **4**

"Ok¡uitkapä'2-y- imōlä'2k. AtxElkä'yō walalE'muX, atxEluwē'yō
"Come down to the prairie, elk. We will fight, we will dance."   **5**

walalE'muX!" L¡äq, L¡äq, L¡äq, Lä'xa nē'xax iskē'epXoa; "Ia'xka
Out, out, out, out it became a rabbit; "Him   **6**

aniqElxē'mōLx, tiä'utcakc t'a'qĕ LkalkE'mstk." TakE nigE'tsax
I called him, his ears just as spoons with long Then it cried
handles."   **7**

iskē'epXoa, takE ä'yuptsk. NigE'tsax. WiXt nä-ixE'lqamx:
the rabbit, then it went into It cried. Again he shouted: **8**
the woods.

"Ok¡uitkapä'2-y- imōlä'2k. AtxElkä'yō walalE'muX, atxEluwē'yō
"Come down to the prairie, elk. We will fight, we will dance!"   **9**

walalE'muX!" TakE wiXt L¡äq, L¡äq, L¡äq, Läxa nē'xax ēmä'cEn.
Then again out, out, out, out it became a deer.   **10**

"Ia'xka aniqElxē'mōLx, ciä'xòst qē'ta tE'ptō-ix·ē." TakE nigE'tsax
"Him I called him, his eyes the same huckleberries." Then it cried
as   **11**

ēmä'cEn. Ā'yuptck. WeXt na-ixE'lqamx:
the deer. It went into the Again he shouted: **12**
woods.

"Ok¡uitkapä'2-y- imōlä'2k. AtxElkä'yō wä'lalEmä'mm. AtxEluwē'yō
"Come down to the prairie, elk. We will fight. We will dance!"   **13**

wä'lalEmä'mm." TakE wiXt L¡äq, L¡äq, L¡äq nē'xau, Läxa nē'xax
Then again out, out, out it became, out it became   **14**

ē'nEmckc imō'lak. "Ia'xka x·ix· nēqētxēmō'L." WiXt na-ixE'lqamX:
a female elk. "Her this one I called her." Again he shouted: **15**

"Ōk¡uitkapä'2-y- imōlä'2k. AtxElkä'yō walalEmä'mm. AtxEluwē'yō
"Come down to the prairie, elk. We will fight. We will   **16**

wä'lalEma'mm!" TakE wiXt L¡äq, L¡äq, L¡äq nē'xau; Läxa nē'xax
dance!" Then again out, out, out it became; out became   **17**

imō'lak; I'k·ala imō'lak. A'lta ayä'owitck Ēnts¡X:
an elk; a male elk. Now he danced Ēnts¡X: **18**

"Qä'xpa yä'2mEllk¡'apkä'? Lō'nas gō-y- ē'micqL yä'milk¡'apkä'!
"Where shall I go into you? Perhaps in your mouth I will go into you!   **19**

x,x,x, mxä'xoiĕ; tä'mka tEmXtē'mam nxä'xoiē. Lō'nas gō cmē'ktcXict
x,x,x, you will make; only saliva I shall be- Perhaps in your nostrils   **20**
come.

yä'milk¡'apkä'. Xui, mxä'xō. L¡ōx nuLä'taXita. Ā'mka ō'qxotck
I shall go into you. Xui, you will do. Falling I shall fall. Only mucus   **21**
down

ɒxä'xoiē. Lōnas gō y- ō'mēutca yä'milk¡apqä'. Tō'tō mxä'xoie. L¡ōx
I shall become. Perhaps in your ear I shall go into you. Shake you will do. Falling   **22**
down

1 nuLā′taXita. Lōnas gō-y- ōmē′putc yā′milk¡apqā′. MLawē′tcXa, pāL
I shall fall.　Perhaps in　your anus　I shall go into you!　You will defecate,　full

2 ē′xalitk nxā′xo.″ Lä2 ka nē′lkXaʟ! gō-y- uyā′putc. A′lta
excrements I shall be-　Sometime and　he entered him　at　his anus.　Now
come.″

3 Lq¡ō′pLq¡ōp atcā′yax iā′yamxtcX. Lä2 ka ayūqunā′itix·t ka ayō′mEqt.
cut to pieces　he did it　his stomach.　Some-and　he fell down　and　he was dead.
time

4 A′lta atcā′yaxc, Lāq° atcē′xax iā′sk¡ōpx·El; Lāq° atctē′xax tiā′ᶜōwit;
Now　he cut it,　off　he made it　its skin;　off　he made them　its legs;

5 Lāq° atctē′xax tiā′pōtē; Lāq° atcē′xax ā′yaqtq; iā′tuk Lāq° atcē′xax;
off　he made them its forelegs;　off　he made it　its head;　its neck off　he made it;

6 tiā′lēwanEma, ciā′kxalauct atcē′xax. Ka′nauwē atcā′yaxc. A′lta
its ribs,　its rump bone　he made it.　All　he cut it.　Now

7 nē′Xkō. NēXkō′mam. ″Imō′lak aniā′waᶜ, gā′k¡′ē!″ ″Atcuwā′-y-
he went　He arrived at home.　″An elk　I killed it,　grandmother!″　″Certainly
home.

8 ukō′lXul.″ ″Liā′atcam, Liā′atcam, imō′lak.″ ″Atcuwā′-y- utsEmē′nxan.″
a mouse.″　″It has horns,　it has horns,　an elk.″　″Certainly　a snail.″

9 ″Imōlā′2k, imō′lak aniā′waᶜ.″ ″Atcuwā′-y- ō′tsikin.″ ″Imōlā′2k,
″An elk,　an elk　I killed it.″　″Certainly　a chipmunk.″　″An elk,

10 imō′lak aniā′waᶜ.″ ″Atcuwā′-y- ik¡ā′ētEn.″ Al′ta tEll ā′tcax. A′lta
an elk,　I killed it.″　″Certainly　a squirrel.″　Now　tired he made her.　Now

11 ā′ctōptck. Actigā′ōm, a′lta imō′lak· yuqunā′itX. ″Ē′kta amiō′ctxō,
they went in-　They reached it,　now　an elk　lay there.　″What　will you carry
land.　it,

12 gā′k¡ē! Ā′yaqtq amiō′ctxō.″ ″Acē′nk¡amukʟpax, kā′ēkaē!″ ″Ē′kta
grand-　Its head　you will carry it.″　″It pulls me down headlong,　grandson!″　″What
mother!

13 amiō′ctxō! Tcuxō iā′tuk miō′ctxo.″ ″Acē′nk¡amukʟpax, kā′ēkaē!″
will you carry it?　Then　its neck　will you carry it.″　″It pulls me down headlong,　grandson!″

14 ″Tcuxō ōpō′titk mō′ctxō.″ ″Acē′nk¡amukʟpax.″ ″Tcuxō iāᶜowit
″Then　the forelegs you will carry　″They pull me down headlong.″　″Then　its leg
them.″

15 miō′ctxo.″ ″Acē′nk¡amukʟpax.″ ″I′ktaʟx miō′ctxō! Tcuxō
you will carry　″It will pull me down headlong.″　″What may　you will carry　Then
it.″　be　it?

16 iā′atcX miō′ctXō.″ ″Acē′nk¡amukʟpax.″ ″I′ktaʟx miō′ctxō! Tcuxō
its breast　will you·carry it.″　″It pulls me down headlong.″　″What may　will you carry　Then
be　it?

17 tElēwā′nEma mtō′ctXō.″ ″Acē′nk¡amukʟpax.″ ″Tcuxō iā′kutcX
the ribs　you will carry them.″　″They pull me down head-　″Then　its back
long.″

18 miō′ctXō.″ ″Acē′nk¡amukʟpax.″ ″Tcuxō cqalā′auwictX miō′ctxō.″
you will carry　″It pulls me down headlong.″　″Then　its rump bone　you will carry
it.″　it.″

19 ″Cici′lax, cici′lax, kā′ēkaē! Cici′lax, cici′lax, kā′ēkaē!″ A′lta
″Tie it up,　tie it up,　grandson!　Tie it up,　tie it up,　grandson!″　Now

20 atccā′lax, a′ltā agE′ctuctx. Nā′xankō ā′nēu. Nō′ya, ā′nēu nō′ya.
he tied it up,　now　she carried it on　She ran　ahead.　She went,　ahead she went.
her back.

21 A′lta atctō′cgam, ka′nauwē atci′tōctx. Ā′yū a′lta nē′Xkō. Qaxä′ʟ
Now　he took them,　all　he carried them　He went　now,　he went　Somewhere
on his back.　home.

22 ayakta′ōm ūyā′k¡ik¡ē. A′lta gi′cguc itcā′ctxul kcō′tctEmalt: ″Ē′Xt
he reached her　his grandmother.　Now　kneeling on　her load　he pushed it to and　″One
it　fro:

23 ilā′xElax, ē′Xt imō′yEmōyE; e′Xt ilā′xElax, ē′Xt imō′yEmōyē.″
[?],　one　[?];　one　[?],　one　[?].″

24 TakE ayaga′ōm. ″Qa′da amE′xax gā′k¡ē!″ ″Acē′nk¡amukʟpax,
Then　he reached her.　″How　are you doing, grandmother!′　″It pulled me down headlong,

25 kā′ēkae.″ TakE wiXt atcalō′tcXam, takE nā′xankō. A′yō, ā′yō,
grandson.″　Then　again　he carried it on his　then　she ran.　He went, he went,
back,

ā'yō;   kulā'yi   ā'yō.   TakE   wiXt   atca'ɛalkEl.   Ōc,   kcō'tctEmal   1
he went;   far   he went.   Then   again   he saw her.   She was there,   she pulled it to and fro

itcā'ctxul.   "Qa'da amE'xax gā'k¡ē!"   WiXt akēx: 2
her load.   "How   are you doing, grandmother?"   Again   she made:

"Ē'Xt ilā'xElax, ēXt imō'yEmōyē; ēXt ilā'xElax, ēXt imō'yEmōyē."   3
"One   [?],   one   [?];   one   [?],   one   [?]."

"Qa'da amE'xax, gā'k¡ē!"   "Acē'nkamukLpax, kā'ekaē."   QoänEmite   4
"How   are you doing,   grand-mother?"   "It pulled me down head-long,   grandson."   Five times

ayaga'ōm   ka   acXgō'mam.   5
he reached her   and   they arrived at home.

"Ai'aq   Ltcuq   mā'ya;   gā'k¡ē,   txEltcXEmā'ya."   TakE   nō'ya   6
"Quick   water   go;   grandmother,   we will boil it."   Then   she went

uyā'k¡ik¡ē.   AkLō'cgam   quā'nEm   LcgE'nEma.   Nō'ya mank kulā'yi.   7
his grandmother.   She took them   five   buckets.   She went   a little   far.

Naxk¡anwā'pa,   ka'nauwē   pāL   aLE'xax   Lgā'cgEnEma.   A'lta   8
She urinated,   all   full   she made them   her buckets.   Now

nā'Xkō.   NaXkō'mam.   TakE   atcō'lXam,   itcā'kXēn: "Qa'xeä Lik   9
she went home.   She arrived at house.   Then   he said to her,   his grand-mother: "Where   this

Ltcuq   nEgā'k¡ē!"   TakE   agiō'p!Ena   gō   ēXt   ē'qēL.   WiXt aē'Xt   10
water,   grandmother?"   Then   she named it   at   one   creek.   Again   one

atcō'cgam ugō'cgan.   "Qaxē x·iLik Ltcuq, nEgā'k¡ē!"   "Ik¡Emō'ikᵘtiX   11
he took it   her bucket.   "Where   this   water, grandmother?"   "Upper fork of Bear creek

Ltcuq."   Qoä'nEm   Lgā'cgEnEma   atcLō'cgam.   12
water."   Five   her buckets   he took them.

A'lta   acE'xEltcxEm.   TakE   naxa'Lxēkō   iau'a   mā'Lxolē.   A'lta   13
Now   they cooked.   Then   she turned round   there   from fire.   Now

Lxoa'pLxoap   agE'Lax   Lcta'amua.   Ka'nauwē2   Lxoa'pLxoap   agE'Lax,   14
holes   she made into them   the shell spoons.   All   holes   she made into them,

kā2   LE'ts¡EmEnō   Lxoa'pLxoap   agE'Lax,   kā2   Li'c'ō   Lxoa'pLxoap   15
and   wooden spoons   holes   she made into them,   and   mountain-sheep-horn dishes,   holes

agE'Lax.   TakE   acxgē'ktcikt.   TakE   acgiō'kXuiptck   ictā'tcXEmal.   16
she made into them.   Then   their food was done.   Then   they hauled out of fire   what they had boiled.

"A'tkᵘ┌a-y· ō'kuk ōgoa'namua.   Qā'xqēa nitsEnō'kctX nāga'amua!"   17
"Bring me   that   my shell-spoon.   Where when   I was young   my shell-spoon?"

"Itca'ē naLxoa'p kā'ēka-ē!"   "Qäx itcE'ts¡EmEnō qēa nitsEnō'kstX   18
"It has   a hole,   grandson!"   "Where   my wooden spoon   when   I was young

nētsE'ts¡EmEnō!"   "Iā'ē naLxqa'p kā'ē-ka-e."   Qā'xqēa ī'tcic'ō qēa   19
my wooden-spoon!"   "It has   a hole,   grandson."   Where   my mount-ain-sheep-horn dish   when

nitsEnō'kstX   ī'tcic'ō!"   "Iā'ē naLxoa'p   kā'ēka-e!"   "Qā'xqēa   20
I was young   my mountain-sheep-horn dish?"   "It has   a hole,   grandson!"   "Where

stasgE'xEnim qēa nitsEnō'kstX asgE'XEnim; cka qēa nitsEnō'kstX   21
my toy canoe   when   I was young   my toy canoe;   and when   I was young

asga'amiksōs."   "Icta'ē naLxoa'p,   ka'ēka-ē."   "Tā'mka tcī stā'2ē   22
my toy canoe (of another shape)."   "They have   holes,   grandson."   "Only   [int. part.] they

naLxoa'p!"   TakE atciō'cgam ictā'tcXEmal,   wax atciä'kXax.   TakE   23
have holes!"   Then   he took it,   what they had boiled,   pour   he did it on her.   Then

naxa'Lxaiō,   tgā'pōtē nōxoē'Lxēyō.   TakE   atciaxa'n'iakō   ā'yaqcō   24
she shrivelled up,   her arms   became bent.   Then   he rolled her up   [in] its skin

ictā'mō┌ak.   TakE   atcalē'maLx.   Nō'Xunit   mā'ēmē   qā   asxā'xp!aōt   25
their elk's.   Then   he threw her into the water.   She drifted   down the river   where   they fished in dipnet

kā'sa-it   k¡a   iq¡ē'sq¡ēs.
robin   and   blue-jay.

TakE atcē'ᶜElkEl imō'lak kā'sa-it. YuXunē't: "Ā̆ itsumō'lak
Then   he saw it   an elk   robin.   It drifted: "Ah,   my elk

2 itgatsuwā'4." TakE nē'k·im iq¡ē'sq¡ēs: "Kā'sa-it, mxEltca'maana?
is coming down   Then   he said   blue-jay: "robin,   do you hear?
stream."

3 qatxE'lqEmxia." TakE wiXt nē'k·im kā'sa-it. "Ā̆ itsumō'lak
We are called."   Then   again   he said   robin: "Ah,   my elk

4 itgatsuwā'4." TakE nē'k·im iq¡ē'sqēs:
coming down river."   Then   he said   Blue-jay:

"Ā̆' hahaha'haha'."

5
"A   hahaha'haha'."

6 Quä'nEmī nē'k·im kā'sa-it, ka tak atcixtcā'ma: "Ā̆, itcumō'lak
Five times   he said   robin,   and then   he heard it: "Ah,   my elk

7 itgatsuwā'4," wiXt nē'k·im kā'sa-it. Ta'kE nē'k·im iq¡ē'sq¡ēs: "Ā̆
is coming down   again   he said   robin.   Then   he said   blue-jay: "Ah,
stream,"

8 itsumō'lak itgatsuwā'4." "Qā'xēyaX, qā'xēyaX?" "AXiXū'yaX,
my elk   is coming down stream."   "Where,   where?"   "Here,

9 aXiXū'yaX." TakE acgē'ᶜElkEl imō'lak, acgiū'cgam. TakE
here!"   Then   they saw it   the elk,   they took it.   Then

10 acgiakqā'na-it. A'lta k·¡au'k¡au ikē'x ā'yaqcō. TakE stu'XstuX
they put it into their   Now   tied   it was   the skin.   Then   untie
canoe.

11 acgā'yax. A'lta uctā'Lak. "Ō̆, utxā'Lak taL¡ XaXā'k." "Qa'da
they did it.   Now   their aunt.   "Oh,   our aunt   look   that."   "How

12 itxā'alqt qtgiā'xō, kā'sa-it?" TakE nē'k·im kā'sa-it:
our crying   we shall make,   robin?"   Then   he said   robin:

"Tsā'ntxawa, tsäntxawā', än'xaxa, änxaxā', a'ntaLak, äntaLā'k."

"He killed her,   he killed her,   Ênts¡'X,   Ênts¡X,   our aunt,   our aunt."

14 "Ksta q¡oä'L amE'k·im, kā'sa-it." A'lta aci'Xko. Q¡ᶜoä'p
"And   all right   you said,   robin."   Now   they went home.   Nearly

15 acgiā'xōm ē'lXam, a'lta cxē'nim: "Nǟ Lctā'xauyam. Qā'da
they reached it   the town,   now   they cried: "Oh,   the unhappy ones.   How

16 aci'xax?" Cxē'nim kā'sa-it:
they do?"   They cry   robin:

"Tsā'ntxawa, tsäntxawā', ä'nxaxa, anxaxā', ä'ntaLak, antaLā'k."
"He killed her,   he killed her,   Ênts¡x,   Ênts¡x,   our aunt,   our aunt.'

18 Acxē'gela-ē. A'lta aqcgā'lōLx. Ā̆, a'lta aqō'kctiptck mā'Lxôlē.
They landed.   Now   the people went   Ah,   now   she was carried up   inland.
down to the beach   from the beach
to them.

19 A'lta aqagē'la-it. Lä2, t¡ayā' ā'qxax. A'lta aqauwā'amtcxoko:
Now   they tried to   Some-   well   she became.   Now   she was asked:
cure her.   time,

20 "I'kta iā'laqL aqEmē'lōtk?" "Pē'ckan," nä'k·im: "Aqiō'p!Ena
"What [which way did you place it]?"   "Pē'ckan   she said: "He is named
[a bird,"]

21 iL¡'alē'xqEkun." "Amcgā'cgiLx uyā'xEnima." WiXt aqanwā'amtcxōko.
the eldest one."   "Pull down to water   his canoes."   Again   she was asked.

22 Aqiōp!Ena skā'sa-it. Lä: "Aqiōp!Ena iL¡'alē'xqEkun," nē'k·im
He was named   Robin.   Some-   "He is named   the eldest one,"   he said
time:

23 iq¡ē'sqēs. Ka'nauwē aktōp!Enā'yam tē'lx·Em. K·imtā', a'lta
blue-jay.   All   she named them   the people.   Last   now

24 aqiō'p!Ena iqē'sqēs. A'lta aqō'cgiLx uyā'xEnīma iqē'sqēs. A'lta
he was named   blue-jay.   Now   they were pulled   his canoes   blue-jay's.   Now
down to the water

25 staq¡ giā'xō, Ênts¡X. A'lta ā'tgi tē'lx·Em mōkct ōkunī'm pāL.
war   she made   Ênts¡X.   Now   they   the people   two   canoes   full.
on him,   went

1 Ā'tgī, ā'tgī, ā'tgī tê'lx·Em. Qaxē kulā'yi atgā'yam, aqugō'ōm
They went, / they went, / they went / the people. / When / far / they arrived, / they reached them

2 amô'kctikc ugō'L'ayū. Lē'Xat Lē'k·ala, Lē'Xat Lᵉā'kil. TakE
two / sleepers. / One / man, / one / woman. / Then

3 ayā'lnLx iq¡ē'sqēs. AtcLē'nxokti ia'koa tcexē'nk¡iama, atcLā'nxokti
he went ashore / blue-jay. / He took him at his head / there / in his right hand, / he took her at her head

4 qaX oᶜō'kuil ia'koa tciq¡ē'tcqta. Atcī'ctukᵘ₁ gō ikanī'm. TakE
that / woman / then / in his left hand. / He carried them / to / the canoe. / Then

5 atciak₁ā'itEm. TakE wiXt ā'tgī tê'lx·Em. Kulā'yi ā'tgi, ka
he made them his slaves. / Then / again / they went / the people. / Far / they then went,

6 acXEluwā'yutck qō'ctac cgōlē'lEXEmk. TakE nē'k·im iqē'sqēs:
they danced / those / people. / Then / he said / blue-jay:

7 "Kā'sa-it! Qi'sta ciā'laitix· itxā'qacqac. Qi'sta ā'nqatē
"Robin! / These / his slaves / our grandfather's. / These / long ago

8 qsgEmō'stxula'lEma-itx k¡a mai'ka qsgEmōptcā'lalEma-itx. Qē'au
they carried me always on their backs / and / you / they always led you by the hand. / Those

9 itxā'qacqac k¡a wiXt ē'wa iā'qacqac ciā'laitix·." "Iä', x·ix·ī'k
our grandfather / and' / again / thus / his grandfather / his slaves." / "Iä, / this one

10 mā'mka tEmē'eltkĕu. TEnlā'xo-ixna tgE'ĕltgeu?" nē'k·im
you only / your slaves. / I know [int. part.] / my slaves?' / he said

11 skā'sa-it. "Hō'ntcin, ia'xka ikta ēlā'xō-iX x·ix·ī'k iL¡alē'xqEkun!"
robin. / "Oh, / he / what / he knows / this / the eldest one!"

12 A'lta a'ctō, ā'tgī, qō'tac tê'lx·Em, a'lta acXEluwā'yutck:
Now / they went, / they went, / those / people, / now / they danced:

13 "Q¡oā'p tuwē'x·ilak intā'owila, q¡oā'p tuwē'x·ilak intā'owila. Wā'

♩ ♫♪ ♫ ♪ ♫♪♪ ♫♪⁊ ♩ ♫♪ ♫ ♪ ♫♪♪ ♫♪⁊ ♩.♩

"Near / fallen trees / we dance, / near / fallen trees / we dance. / Wā'

14 Lā'la guyū', guyū', guyū' guyū'. Wā La'la guyū', guyū', guyū' guyū'.

♪♪ ♫♪ ♩ ♫♪ ♩ ♫♩ ♫♩⁊ ♩.♩ ♪ ♪ ♫♩ ♫♩ ♫♩ ♫♩⁊

Lā'la / guyū', / guyū', / guyū', / guyū'. / Wā / Lāla / guyū', / guyū', / guyū', / guyū'.

15 TakE nē'k·im iqē'sqēs: "Q¡oā'p kati x·iau ilē'ē x·iau sxā'xo-il."
Then / he said / blue-jay: / "Near / this / land / this / they always say."

16 "Iä'," nē'k·im skā'sa-it, "iä' x·ix" ē'kta! kawatka cimxp!ē'Xaiyaii'ta."
"Iä," / said / robin, / "iä / this / thing! / soon / they will run away from you."

17 Nau'itka gō x·ix· ikē'x, ayā'lukLx ē'mᶜcX. TakE aci'xauwa,
Indeed / there / this / was, / it lay over water / a tree. / Then / they ran,

18 takE acksō'pEna. TakE nē'xankō iqē'sqēs, takE atcgE'ta.
then / they jumped. / Then / he ran / blue-jay, / then / he pursued them.

19 Mā'Lxôlē nēxantkō'mam. TakE atcixalqē'tqal iqē'sqēs: Anā'2, anā'2.
Inland / he arrived running. / Then / he called much / blue-jay: / Anah, / anah.

20 TakE nitē'mam, nē'Lxam iqē'sqēs. Lā'mka Lᵉā'owilkt ia'ᶜōwit.
Then / he came, / he came to the water / blue-jay. / Only / blood / his leg.

21 "Qa'daqa nikct ā'mōptck kā'sa-it! CkEna'ᶜowa. AtcLnE'nxōkti
"Why / not / you went inland / robin? / They struck me. / He took hold of my head

22 qix· ē'kXala, a'lta agEna'ōwilXLx· gō itcE'ᶜōwit." "Iä', ia'xka
that / man, / now / she struck me / at / my leg." / "Iä, / he

23 x·ix·ī'x·Lx ik¡ā'·utEn ka tciusgā'ma. Ia'xka Lx ō'tsikin ka
this may be / squirrels / and / he will take them. / He / may be / chipmunks / and

24 tcūsgā'ma." A'lta wiXt ā'tgi tê'lx·Em. Ē2, kulā'yi ā'tgi. AqLga'ōm
he will take them." / Now / again / they went / the people. / Eh, / far / they went. / They reached him

25 Lā'k¡aya. Lxā'xp!aōt. "Masā'tsiLx ēmē'xEnim, āt," nē'k·im
one man in a canoe. / He fished with a dipnet. / "Pretty / your canoe, / nephew," / said

1 iqē'sqēs.   "TEkEmē'ctx."   "Masā'tsiʟx imē'ski, āt."   "TEkEmē'ctx."
   blue-jay.   "They loaned it to me."   "Pretty   your   nephew."   "They loaned it to me."
                                                                paddle.

2 "Masā'tsiʟx   ōmē'etewaʟxti,   āt."   "TEkEmē'ctx."   "Masā'tsiʟx
   "Pretty   your bailer,   nephew."   "They loaned it to me."   "Pretty

3 ōmē'nuXcin,   āt."   "TEkEmē'ctx."   "Masā'tsiʟx   LEmē'x·ilkuē,
   your dipnet,   nephew."   "They loaned it to me."   "Pretty   your mat in your
                                                                canoe,

4 āt."   "TEkEmē'ctx."   "TāmokXā'tsit   tä'2kEmēctx."   TakE
   nephew."   "They loaned it to me."   "Your things   they loaned them to you."   Then

5 atcLē'nxokti.   TakE   atcē'xaluktcgō   gō   iʟā'xanīm.   "Mcktā'nit   x·i'ta
   he took hold of his   Then   he threw him down   in   their canoe.   "Give me   this
   head.

6 tE'pa-it!   k¡au'k¡au   niā'xō."   "TēnXpēqʟā'!"   "Mcktā'nit   x·i'ta
   rope!   tie   I shall do him."   "I shall scratch it."   "Give me   these

7 tpē'naʟX."   "TēnXpēqʟā'."   "K¡a   ē'ktaʟx   aqēlā'xo¡   Mcktā'nit
   spruce twigs."   "I shall scratch them."   "And   what may be is done with him¡   Give me

8 x·i'ta   tqōqoā'-iʟax."   TēnXpēqʟā'!"   "Hä, hä, hä,"   takE   nigE'tsax;
   these   short dentalia."   "I shall scratch them."   "Hä,   hä,   hä,"   then   he cried;

                    "Ō'qômôm ōqômä'm."

                    "Sea grass,   sea grass."

10· "Ai'aq, kā'sa-it, ā'tkᵘLa Xau ō'qomum."   A'lta k¡au'k¡au atcayā'lax
   "Quick,   robin,   bring   that   sea grass."   Now   tie   he did him
                                                                with it

11 gō   tiā'kcia   gō   tiā'ᶜōwit.   A'lta   atcialē'maʟx.   A'lta   lEp   nē'xax
   at   his hands   at   his legs.   Now   he threw him into   Now   boiling   it became
                                        the water.

12 qīgo   atcialē'maʟx.   "Ō,   itci'LatXEn.   Ia'xka   ikalā'lkuilē,
   when   he had thrown him into   "Oh,   my nephew.   He   scolds,
          the water.

13 ninxElō'yamit   itci'LatXEn."   "Iä',   x·ix·ī'x·   tcimaō'nim   x·igō'."
   I killed my relative   my nephew."   "Iä,   this one,   he laughed at you   here.'

14 "Ia'xka qialē'maʟxa kā'sa-it ka hē'hē ixā'xō."
   "He   is thrown into the   robin   and laugh   he does."
         water

   A'lta   wiXt ā'tgi tê'lx·Em.   Lä2, aqā'ᴸcElkEl   LgōLē'lExEmk.
   Now   again they went the people.   Some time   he was seen   a person.

16 Lktō'ktcan tkalai'tan.   "Sau'atsa, sau'atsā', iqē'sqēs!"   "Ēkta Lx
   He held in his   arrows.   "The news,   the news,   blue-jay!"   "What   may
   hand   be

17 aqēmilkᵀē'tcgō¡ Iā'mka-y- ō'kuk mā'ema ilqā'icX anialā'maʟx."   "Tō
   is told to you¡   Only   down stream our rela-   I threw him into   "Am
                                        tive   the water."

18 nai'kXa tc¡a gō," aLE'k·im Xō'La LgōLē'lExEmk.   "Iä', x·ix·ī'k k¡a
   I   look! that,"   he said   that   person.   "Iä,   this one   and

19 ia'xka x·ix·ī'x· amialä'maʟx!"
   he   this one   you threw him into the water!"

   A'lta   wiXt ā'Lō, ā'Lo gō tā'yaqL Ēnts¡X.   TakE aqōxō'Lakō
   Now   again they they to his house ĒntsiX's.   Then   it was surrounded
         went, went

21 tā'yaqL   ĒntsiX.   TakE atcXE'lgiLX.   TakE nō'xōLXa   tā'yaqL
   his house   ĒntsiX's.   Then   he set fire to it.   Then   it burnt   his house

22 ĒntsiX. Ayō'pa ĒntsiX gō naLxoā'pē gō-y- ō'ēkᵘtEql'ix·. Nō'xōLXa
   ĒntsiX's. He went out ĒntsiX at hole at knot hole.   It burnt

23 tā'yaqL, ka'nauwē tā'yaqL.   TakE Lap atcā'yax ēqtq iqē'sqēs.   "Ō,
   his house,   the whole   his house.   Then   find   he did it   a head   blue-jay.   "Oh,

24 ĒntsiX ā'yaqtq x·ix·ī'k."   TakE nē'k·im skā'sa-it: "Iä', x·ix·ī'kik¡
   ĒntsiX   his head   this."   Then   he said   robin: "Iä,   this one.

25 Ā'nqatē ayō'pa."   A'lta nō'xōkō têlx·Em, aqēē'taqL ĒntsiX.
   Already   he went out."   Now   they went the people,   he was left   ĒntsiX.

Translation.

Ents¡x's grandmother was Upē'qciuc. She always asked him to go elk hunting. Early every morning he started, but he killed only chipmunks and squirrels; sometimes he killed mice. Oftentimes he went and stayed on a prairie. He shouted: "Come down from the woods, elk! we will fight, we will dance." Down came the rabbit. "You are the one I have called, your ears are like spoons with long handles." Then the rabbit cried and went back. Then he called again: "Come down from the woods, elk! we will fight, we will dance." Down came a deer. "You are the one I have called, your eyes are like huckleberries." Then the deer cried and went back. He called again: "Come down from the woods, elk! we will fight, we will dance." Down came a female elk. "You are the one whom I have called!" He called again: "Come down from the woods, elk! we will fight, we will dance." Then a male elk came down. Now Ēntsx danced and sang: "Where shall I go into him? Where shall I go into him? I think I will go into his mouth. No, he will spit and I shall get full of saliva. I think I will go into his nostrils. No he will snort and I shall get full of mucus. I think I will go into his ear. No, he will shake himself and I shall fall down. I think I shall go into his anus. No, he will defecate and I shall get full of excrements." After some time he entered his anus. Now he cut his stomach to pieces. After a little while the elk fell down and died. Then Ēntsx skinned and dissected it. He cut off the hind-legs; he cut off the fore-legs. He cut off the head, the neck, the ribs, and the rump bone. Then he went home. When he came to his grandmother he said: "I killed an elk, grandmother!" "Perhaps it was a mouse." "No, it has horns, it has horns, it is an elk." "Then perhaps it was a snail." "No, no, I killed an elk, an elk." "Perhaps it was a chipmunk." "No, no, I killed an elk, an elk." "Perhaps it was a squirrel." Then she got tired and they went into the woods. They arrived at the place where the elk lay. Ēntsx asked: "What do you want to carry, grandmother? Do you want to carry its head?" "It will pull me down headlong, grandson." "What do you want to carry, grandmother? Do you want to carry its neck?" "It will pull me down headlong, grandson." "What do you want to carry, grandmother? Do you want to carry its hind-legs?" "They will pull me down headlong, grandson." "What do you want to carry, grandmother? Do you want to carry its fore-legs?" "They will pull me down headlong, grandson." "What do you want to carry, grandmother? Do you want to carry its breast?" "It will pull me down headlong, grandson." "What do you want to carry, grandmother? Do you want to carry its back?" "It will pull me down headlong, grandson." "What do you want to carry, grandmother? Do you want to carry its rump bone?" "Tie it up, tie it up, grandson." Then he tied it up, she put it up, she raised it on her back. The old woman ran ahead of her grandson, who carried the rest of the elk. They went home. After a little while he came near his grandmother, who had put her load on the ground and pushed it to and fro, singing at the same time [page 114, line 23].

He reached her and asked: "What are you doing there, grandmother?" "It pulled me down headlong, grandson." Then she took it again on her back and ran. He went on. Then he saw her again sitting down and pushing her load to and fro and singing [page 115, lines 3]. [He asked:] "What are you doing there, grandmother?" "It pulled me down headlong, grandson." Five times he overtook her, when they reached home.

[Ēntsx said:] "Now go and bring some water, grandmother, we will boil the elk." His grandmother took five buckets and went out. She went a short distance, urinated and filled all the buckets. Then she went home. Her grandson asked her: "Where did you get that water, grandmother?" She named a river. Then he took up another bucket and asked: Where did you get this water, grandmother? "This I took from the upper fork of Bear creek," she replied. Thus she named a new creek for each bucket.

Now they boiled the elk. The old woman turned her back toward the fire and made holes in Ēntsx's shell spoons, wooden spoons, and horn dishes. When the food was done they took it away from the fire. Ēntsx said: "Bring me my shell spoon which I used when I was a child." "There is a hole in it, grandson." "Then give me my wooden spoon which I used when I was a child." "There is a hole in it, grandson." "Then give me the spoon made of mountain-sheep horn." "There is a hole in it, grandson." "Then give me my toy canoes which I used when I was a child." "There are holes in them, grandson." "Have they all holes?" he said. Then he took the boiling food and poured it over his grandmother. She was scalded and her legs and arms became doubled up. Then he rolled her up in the elk skin, threw her into the river and she drifted down to a place where Winter Robin and Blue-Jay were fishing with a dipnet.

Robin saw an elk skin drifting down and said: "Ah! an elk comes down to me." Then Blue-Jay said: "Robin, do you hear? they call us?" Then Robin said: "Ah! an elk comes down to me." Then Blue-Jay said: "Ah! hahahaha." Five times Robin said: "An elk comes down to me." Then Blue-Jay understood what he said and called himself: "Ah! an elk comes down to me." "Where does it come?" [Blue-jay pointed out.] "Here, here, here" [pointing in all directions because he did not see it]. Then they saw the elk and took it. They put it into their canoe [and saw that] it was tied up. They unfastened the strings and [out came] their aunt. "Oh, behold our aunt!" "How shall we wail for her, Robin?" Then Robin sung: "O, Ēntsx, Ēntsx, he killed her, he killed her, our aunt, our aunt." "That is a good song," said Blue-Jay. Now they went home, and when they came near their town they began to wail. " Oh, the poor ones, how they do wail?" said the people. They sang: " Ēntsx, Ēntsx, he killed her, he killed her, our aunt, our aunt." They landed and the people went down to see them. Then they carried the body of Upē'qciuc up to the house. They tried to cure her. After a while she recovered. Then they asked her: " What [?]." She named [a bird]. " She named the eldest one," said Blue-Jay. " Pull his canoes into the water." Again they asked her. She named Robin. " She named the eldest one," said Blue-Jay. She named all the people. Last of all she named Blue-Jay. Now they launched his canoes and they went to make war upon Ēnts¡x. Two canoes full of people went.

They went a long distance and met two people asleep, a man and a woman. Blue-Jay went ashore. He took the man by his hair in his right hand and he took the woman in his left. Then he took them to his canoe and made them his slaves. When they traveled along these two persons were dancing [in Blue-Jay's canoe]. The latter said: " Robin! These two persons were our grandfather's slaves; they always carried me on the back and led you by the hand. They were our great-great-grandfather's slaves." " Iä-a, they are only your slaves. Do you think that I do not know my slaves?" replied Robin. " Pshaw! he is older than I am and does not remember it!" Now the two persons danced and sang: " Near the trees we always dance, watlala guyu, guyu, guyu, guyu."

Then Blue-Jay said: " They always say: 'Close to the trees, close to the trees'". " Iä" replied Robin, " thus they will run away from you." And indeed so it happened. [When they got a little farther they came to] a tree which hung over the water. [The man and the woman] jumped up and escaped by running [over the tree]. Blue-Jay ran in pursuit. He came inland. Then he called anah, anah. When he came back to the canoe his legs were full of blood [and he said to his brother Robin]: " Why did you not go inland? They nearly killed me. That man took hold of my head and the woman struck my legs." [Robin laughed and replied:] " Iä, they were the squirrel and chipmunk whom you caught."

They traveled on. They went a long distance and met one man who was sitting in his canoe. He fished with a dipnet. Blue-Jay said: " My nephew, you have a pretty canoe." " I borrowed it." " My nephew, you have a pretty paddle." " I borrowed it." " My nephew, you have a pretty bailer." " I borrowed it." " My nephew, you have a pretty dip-net." " I borrowed it." " My nephew, you have a pretty mat in your canoe." " I borrowed it." [Then Blue-Jay got angry and said:] " Do you borrow everything?" He took hold of his head and threw him into his canoe. He said: " Give me that rope and I will tie him." [The man whom he had caught replied:] " I shall scratch your ropes to pieces." [Then Blue-Jay said:] " Give me a rope of spruce limbs." " I shall scratch it to pieces." " What shall I take to tie him with!   Give me strings of dentalia."   "I shall scratch them to pieces."   "Ha, ha, ha," he cried then; "sea-grass, sea-grass!"   "Give me sea-grass, give me sea-grass, quick Robin."   Now he tied the hands and the feet of that man.   Then he threw him into the water.   The water began to boil where they had thrown him down.   [Blue-Jay cried:]   "O, my nephew, he scolds.   I killed my nephew."   [Robin remarked:]   "Iä, he is laughing at you here."   "Pshaw, a man does not laugh when he is thrown into the water" [said Blue-Jay].

Now the people went on, and after awhile they saw a person who held arrows in his hands.   [He said:]   "Tell me the news, Blue-Jay!"   "I have nothing to tell you, only that I threw my relative down there into the water."   "I am the one," said that person.   "Iä," cried Robin, "that is the one whom you threw into the water."

They went on to Ēnts¡x's house.   They surrounded it and set it on fire.   When it began to burn Ēnts¡x flew out through a knothole. When the whole house was burnt, Blue-Jay found a [mink's] head. "Oh that is Ēnts¡x's head!" he shouted.   But Robin said: "Iä, he went out already."   Now the people went home and left Ēnts¡x.

9. ŌK¡UNŌ' ITCĀ'KXANAM.

THE CROW HER STORY.

Lxēlā'itiX ōk¡unō' Lqui'numikc tga'a. Gōlata' gō iō'c ikoalēx·oa   1
There was   the crow   five   her children.   At the end of the house   there   there was   the raven

itca'lē ōk¡unō'. Ō'lo kLāx. Ā'gōn ōᶜō'Lax nō'ya-y· ōk¡unō'.   2
her cousin   the crow.   Hungry they were.   The next   day   she went   the crow.

Nā'ckta.   3
She searched on the beach.

"NE'cxatk¡a' ē'maL ciā'xak'agō'x. Qulqulqulqul ē'qulqul   4
"I haul them [dual]   the bay   its [?].   [Noise of empty vessels being struck]

tcinō'- Lawatckut." L¡ap agE'xax ōkulXtE'mX. Agā'kLtEq. WiXt   5
he   [?]. me."   Find   she did it   a poggy.   She kicked it.   Again

nō'ya kulā'yi. WiXt aktō'pEna tgā'ēwam.   6
she went   far.   Again   she named it   her song.

"NE'cxatk¡ā' e'maL ciā'xak'agō'x. Qulqulqulqul ē'qulqul   7
'I haul them [dual]   the bay   its [?]   [Noise of empty vessels being struck]

tcinō'Lawatckut." L¡ap akxā'x upkī'cX. Agā'kLtEq. WiXt nō'ya.   8
he   [?]. me."   Find   she did it   a flounder.   She kicked it.   Again   she went

WiXt aktō'pEnā tgā'ēwam [as above]. L¡ap agE'xax ukō'tckōtc.   9
Again   she named it   her song   [as above].   Find   she did it   a porpoise.

Agā'kLtEq. WiXt nō'ya. WiXt aktō'cgam tgā'ēwam [as above].   10
She kicked it.   Again   she went.   Again   she took it   her song   [as above].

L¡ap akxā'x ō'lXaiū. Agā'kLtEq. WiXt nō'ya, wiXt aktō'cgam   11
Find   she did it   a seal.   She kicked it.   Again   she went,   again   she took it

tgā'ēwam [as above]. WiXt L¡ap agā'yax ēnā'kxōn. Mô'kctī   12
her song   [as above].   Again   find   she did it   a sturgeon.   Twice

nā'ixLakō. Agiē'taqL, agē'kLtEq. WiXt nō'ya, hē4. Aktō'cgam   13
she went around it.   She left it,   she kicked it.   Again   she went,   hē.   She took it

tgā'ēwam [as above]. L¡ap agā'yax igē'pix·L. Agē'xLakō, Lō'ni   14
her song   [as above].   Find   she did it   a sealion.   She went around it,   three times

agē'xLakō. Agē'kLtEq; agiE'ltaqL. WiXt aktō'cgam tgā'ēwam   15
she went around it.   She kicked it;   she left it.   Again   she took it   her song

[as above]. Nō'ya kulā'i, L¡ap agā'yax ē'kolē. AgExLā'nukL;   16
[as above].   She went   far,   find   she did it   a whale.   She went often around it;

la'ktē agē'xLako. Agē'kLtEq. WiXt agē'kLtEq, wiXt agē'kLtEq.   17
four times   she went around it.   She kicked it.   Again   she kicked it,   again   she kicked it.

LEkⁿ nē'xax itca'ᶜowit. "Anā'3, itcuwitā'3!" acaxa'lqiLx. Nō'ptcga-y·   18
Break   it did   her leg.   "Anah,   my leg!"   she cried.   She went inland

a'lta. Q¡u'tq¡ut agE'Lax Lgē'wan. K·¡au agā'yax itca'ᶜowit. A'lta   19
now.   Pull out   she did it   grass.   Tie   she did it   her leg.   Now

wiXt nō'ya. Mank kulā'ı nō'ya. L¡ap agā'yax iguā'nat. "Anā'-y·   20
again   she went.   A little   far   she went.   Find   she did it   a salmon.   "Anah

itcukunā't, anā' itcukunā't." Nau'itck, k¡oa'nk¡oan nā'xoa.   21
my salmon,   anah   my salmon."   She danced,   glad   she was.

Agē'lgitk gō Lgā'cgo-ic. A'lta nā'Xkō. Q¡oā'2p naXkō'mam ka   22
She put it into   in   her mat.   Now   she went home.   Nearly   she arrived at house   and

agE'LᵉElkEl Lᵉā'kil. Q¡oā'p kat ē'ka agōqoā'lakL. "Ā-y· utcaktcā'k   23
she saw her   a woman.   Nearly   there   she recognized her.   "Ah,   the eagle

taL¡!" Lä nagā'tōm. "Ē'kta amiō'ctxul?" "Ā, iguā'nat."   24
behold!"   Sometime   she met her.   "What   do you carry?"   "Ah,   a salmon."

1 "Tcōxo iamxEmElāˈlEma. IamElōˈta Xak ugEˈqⱼˈēLxam." "TinLāˈ-
"Well   I wish to buy it from you.   I shall give you   that   my coat."   "They

2 utama-ē LqⱼˈēLxāˈpukc." "Kⱼa tcōxō, iamElōˈta igicaˈōk."
are lying about   coats."   "And   well,   I shall give you   my blanket."

3 "Ēˈkta nigElāˈxō ēōˈk. Ōˈxu-ē tgaˈōkc." "Tcōxō, iamElōˈta
"What   shall I do with it   blanket.   Many   my blankets."   "Well,   I shall give you

4 itcEˈmctaa." "Ēˈkta nigElāˈxō iEˈmctaa. Lōˈnas āˈxaui-y- ōˈmiqctit
my hat."   "What   shall I do with it   a hat.   Perhaps   many   your lice

5 gō imēˈmcta." "Tcux, tamElōˈta tgEˈkcia." "Ēˈkta anigukuēˈxa
in   your hat."   "Well,   I shall give them   my hands."   "What   shall I do with them
to you

6 tEmēˈkcia. x·itēˈk naiˈka wiXt tgEˈkcia." "Niˈxua, āˈxkⱼa XaX
your hands.   These   I   also   my hands."   "Well,   pull it out   this

7 ōpāˈowil!" Nōˈyā-y- utcⱼaktcⱼāˈk, agāˈxkⱼa qaX ōpāˈowil. Nauˈi
bunch of grass!"   She went   the eagle,   she pulled it out   that   bunch of grass.   At once

8 Lāq āˈqxax. "Tca! āˈmElaxta āˈxkⱼax." Nōˈya-y- ōkⱼunōˈ, qēˈxtcē
come out   it did.   "Now   you next   pull it out."   She went   the crow   intending;

9 qēˈxtcē ayāˈxkⱼa. Näkct Lāq āˈqxax. "Tcōxō, cgEˈxōst ctamElōˈta;
intending   she pulled it out.   Not   come out   it did.   "Well,   my eyes   I shall give them
to you;

10 gō2 kulāˈi, āˈnqatē iˈktu amiāˈqxamt." "Ēˈkta nicgElāˈxo cqōct.
then   tar   already   something   you see it."   "What   shall I do with them   eyes.

11 x·ictēˈk wiXt naiˈka cgEˈxōkct." "Kⱼa tcōxō, mLEngēˈqsta." Näqⱼ
These   also   I   my eyes."   "And   well,   louse me."   Näqⱼ

12 ōˈqXukcti Lgāˈqamē. "Tcōx maiˈka Lamgēˈqsta." Aˈlta LagEˈkXēqst
her lice   her plate full.   "Well   you   I louse you."   Now   she loused her

13 ōkⱼunōˈ. Aˈlta ēˈēwam āˈtcax ōkⱼunōˈ. Alāˈxti naōˈptit. Aqiūˈcgam
the crow.   Now   sleepy   she became   the crow.   At last   she fell asleep.   It was taken

14 itcāˈkunat ōkⱼunōˈ. Agiōˈcgam utcⱼaktcⱼāˈk. AqāˈlEgitk upāˈowil gō
her salmon   the crow's.   She took it   the eagle.   It was put into   a bunch of   in
grass

15 Lgāˈcgo-ic. AqāˈyukuꞮ itcāˈkunat kⁿcāˈxalē gō-y- ēˈmaktc. NaxEˈTˈōkō,
her mat.   It was carried   her salmon   up   on   spruce tree.   She awoke,

16 aˈlta kⁿcāˈxālē itcāˈkunat aqixēˈlax. Iaˈxkati ka nuqunāˈ-itix·.
now   up   her salmon   it was eaten.   There   then   she fell down.

17 "Qānāˈxtcī ōēˈmōpⱼa manitˈōˈLa," ka acilgaˈox. AqaqLⱼuwāˈēma
"Please   the gills   throw them down to   and   she lay on her   They were thrown [soft
me,"   back.   things] down to her

18 ōēˈmōpⱼa kⱼa LgāˈxEmakikct. Āˈ2lta nāˈXkō, nagEˈtsax ōkⱼunōˈ.
the gills   and   its roe.   Now   she went home,   she cried   the crow.

19 NaXkōˈmam gō tEˈLaqL. Nōˈpⱼam. Lxēlāˈētix·Lgaˈa. AkꞮōˈlEktc qōˈLa
She arrived at   at   their house.   She came in.   There were   her chil-   She roasted it   that
home   dren.

20 LgEmāˈkikct: "Aiˈaq māˈya Ltcuq," axgEˈqxun ugōˈxo. "Ōmēˈxa-y- ōc."
roe: "Quick,   go for water,"   the eldest one   her   "The next is there."
daughter.   one

21 WiXt agōˈlXam aēˈXat ugōˈxō: "Māˈya Ltcuq." "Ōmēˈxa-y· ōc."
Again   she said to her   one   her daughter: "Go for   water."   "The next one   is there."

22 WiXt agōˈlXam aēˈXat ugōˈxō: "Māˈya Ltcuq." "Ōmēˈxa -y-ōc."
Again   she said to her   one   her daughter: "Go for   water."   "The next one   is there."

23 LElaˈktikc akLōˈlXam qēˈxtcē. Aˈlta qaX oguēˈsˈax ugōˈxō nōˈya
Four   she said to them   intending.   Now   that   youngest one   her   she went
daughter   for

24 Ltcuq. AkLEˈtkuꞮam Ltcuq. Aˈlta qⱼoāˈp Lōˈktcikta itcāˈlEktcala.
water.   She arrived bringing   water.   Now   nearly   it was done   what she roasted.

25 Aˈlta naxEmēˈ2nakō. "TakE na tkⱼōp anEˈxax!" "Ēˈka Läl."
Now   she washed her face.   "Then [int. part.]   white   I became!"   "Thus   black."

26 WiXt naxEmēˈnakō. WiXt akLuwaˈamtcxōkō tgaˈa. ALgōˈlXam:
Again   she washed her face.   Again   she asked them   her children.   They said to her:

27 "ēka Läl." TakE atcōˈpEna ikoalēˈx·oa, atcLōˈcgam itcāˈlEktcal.
"Thus   black."   Then   he jumped   the raven,   he took it   what she roasted.

AtciaxE'cgam, atcLā'wilᶜ ka'nauwē. Ā'lta wixt nagE'tsax ōkᵢunō'. 1
He took it away, he ate it all. Now again she cried the crow.

A'lta nixō'kcti ikoalē'x·oa. NixEmā'tsta-itck. Nâ'pōnEm ka takE 2
Now he lay down the raven. He was ashamed of himself. It grew dark and then

ā'yatcᵢa nixā'lax ikoalē'x·oa. A'lta nē'ktcxam: 3
his sickness came to be the raven. Now he sang his conjuror's song:
on him

"Ō'kualä'pka'n qau āyi'tkᵢa' itcē'ē'yā'xōta' qau Lē'yaLa'm. 4
"A brass pin qau hit it my eye qau its pupil became opaque.

Qoā'qoaxqoä', qoā'qoaxqoä', qoā'qoaxqoä'." 5
Qoā'qoaxqoä', qoā'qoaxqoä', qoā'qoaxqoä'."

Lä2, aqLugō'lEmam ōqōLxē'la. Ka'nauwē aqLugō'lEmam ka 6
Some time, the people went to the crabs. All the people went to and
fetch them fetch them

tga'a ōqōLxē'la. A'lta aLē'xEltEq ikoalē'x·oa. TakE aLō'cko-it 7
their the crabs'. Now he heated stones the raven. Then they were hot
children

Lqā'nakc. A'lta aqā'ixpoē. TakE aLxLō'lExa-it LqaLxē'la: 8
the stones. Now the door was Then he thought a crab:
locked.

"QElxElxē'ya." Ā'2lta aqā'LXatuq ka'nauwē ka tga'a. AqLā'kXōpk 9
"It is cooked for us." Now they were thrown all and their They were steamed
on the stones young ones.

ālta. Anō'ktcikt ōquLxē'la: "Āi'aq mcLxā'lEm," aqLō'lXam 10
now. They got done the crabs: "Quick eat," they were told

ōkᵢ'unō' kᵢa tga'a. TakE itᵢō'kti nē'xax ē'tcamxtc ōkᵢ'unō'. 11
the crow and her children. Then good became her heart the crow's.

ĀLxLxā'lEm kᵢa tga'a. 12
They ate and her children.

Translation.

There were the Crow and her five children. At the end of their house lived her cousin the Raven. They were hungry, and one day she went to look for food on the beach. She sang [page 123, line 4]. She found a poggy, kicked it and went on. She repeated her song. Soon she found a flounder. Again she sang her song. Then she found a seal; she kicked it and went on. Again she sang her song. Then she found a sturgeon. She went around it twice, then she left it and kicked it. She went on and repeated her song. Then she found a sealion; three times she went around it. She kicked it and left it. She repeated her song. She went a long distance and found a whale. Four times she went around it, then she kicked it and kicked it again. She broke her leg. "Oh, my leg," she cried. She went up to the woods, pulled out some grass and tied it on to her leg. She went on and after a little while she found a salmon. "Oh! my salmon," she said. She was very glad and danced. She put it into her mat and went home. When she had almost arrived at her house she saw a woman. When she came nearer she recognized her. "Behold! the eagle," she said. The latter said: "What do you carry there?" "Oh," she replied, "A salmon." "I wish to buy it; I will give you my coat." "Plenty of coats are lying about in my house." "I will give you my blanket." "What shall I do with your blanket? I have many blankets." "I will give you my hat." "What shall I do with your hat? May be it is full of lice." "I will give you my hands." "What shall I do with your hands? I have hands as well." "Pull out that bunch of grass." The eagle went and pulled out the bunch of grass, which gave way at once. Then she said, "Now you try to pull it out." The Crow went and tried to pull it out. It did not give way. "I will give you my eyes; you will be able to see a long distance." "What shall I do with your eyes? I have eyes as well." The eagle said: "Louse me." She did so and found a plate full of lice. [After she had finished the eagle said:] "Now I will louse you." She loused the Crow, who became sleepy and finally fell asleep. Then the eagle took the salmon and put a bunch of grass in her mat. She carried it to the top of a spruce tree. When the Crow awoke she saw the eagle sitting on top [of the spruce tree] eating her salmon. Then [she was so much grieved that she fell down at once. She asked the eagle]: "Please give me the gills." The Crow lay on her back and the eagle threw down the gills and the roe. The Crow went home angry. She arrived there. Her children were in the house. She came to her children. She roasted the salmon roe. [She asked] her eldest daughter: "Go and get some water." [She replied:] "The next younger one is there." She asked another one of her daughters: "Go and get some water." [She replied:] "The next younger one is there." She asked four of them. Now her youngest daughter brought her some water. When the salmon roe was nearly done she washed her face. [She asked her daughters:] "Is my face white now?" "No, it is still black." She washed it again and asked her children once more: "Is my face white?" "No, it is still black." Then the raven jumped up and took what she was roasting. He took it away and ate it all. Then the Crow cried again and the raven lay down. He was ashamed of himself. In the evening he fell sick and sang his conjurer's song: "O, my brass pin hit my eye and it got blind, qoāqoaxqoiĭ', qoāqoaxqoä', qoāqoaxqoä' !"

After a while they went and asked the crabs and their young ones to come. The raven heated stones and when they were hot he shut the door. Then a crab thought: "He is cooking for us." But they threw all of them on the stones, old and young. They were steamed. When they were done he said to the Crow and her children: "Come eat!" Now she was glad, and she ate, together with her children.

10. CĀ'XAL IĀ'KXANAM.

CĀ'XAL   HIS MYTH.

Cā'xaL ayō'mEqt iā'xa, ixgE'kXun iā'xa. Wāx iā'qxulqt. Kulā'i **1**
"Cā'xaL   he was dead   his son,   the oldest   his son.   Every   he wailed.   Far
                                                                    morning

gō mā'Lnē ayōLā'-ita-itx. Iō'2Lqtē guā'nsum nēXEnXEnē'max, **2**
at   seaward   he always stayed.   A long time   always   he went to wail on
                                                              the beach,

nēXEnXEnēmā'-itx. QāxLxauaā'Lax atci'cᶜElkEl ckoalē'x·oa. Yau'a **3**
he always went to wail on   One day   he saw them   two ravens.   Then
the beach.

mā'Lnē aci'tptcgam. Q¡oā'p acgē'txam yauā' actik¡ēlā'pXuitxē, yauā' **4**
seaward   they reached the   Nearly   they reached there   they turned over each other,   there
land.   him

actik¡ēlā'pXuitxē. Q¡oā'p acgē'txam ka nicxE'luktcō. Lō'2lō i'ktā **5**
they turned over each other.   Nearly   they reached him and   they let it fall.   A round   thing

nicxE'luktcō. Ayuqunā'ētix·t gō Lkamilā'lEq. Ā'yōLx atciugō'lEmam. **6**
they let it fall.   It lay there   on   the sand.   He went   he went to take it.
                                                       down to the beach,

Atciō'cgam, a'lta iktē'lōwa-itk. Tsō'yustē ka nē'Xkō. TakE atcō'lXam **7**
He took it,   now   an abalone shell.   In the evening and   he went   Then   he said to her
home.

uyā'k·ikala: "UguExē'mam qō'tac tē'lx·Em ka'nauwē." TakE **8**
his wife: "Invite them   those   people   all."   Then

nō'ya-y- ūyā'k·ikala. Ā2, atcEmcgElē'mōL qēauq Liā'xauyam." **9**
she went   his wife.   Ā,   he invites you much   that   poor one."

TakE ā'tgē tiā'lXam ka'nauwē. TakE ā'tgEp! gō tä'yaqL ka'nauwē. **10**
Then they went   his people   all.   Then they entered   in   his house   all.

"Ā, x·ix·ī'k qcgingē'tkcptcgam. x·ix·ī'k mcgiō'kumanEma. Iakpā' **11**
"Ah,   this   they brought it up to the shore   This   you will see it.   Just there
to me.

aci'tptcgam." TakE nē'k·im iq¡ē'sq¡ēs. "WuXi lxō'yaya; **12**
they came ashore."   Then   he said   blue-jay.   "To-morrow   we will go;

lxyō'xtkinEmama qaxē' gō acE'k·itkᵘᴵ." Kawī'2x· ka nixE'nkōn **13**
we will search for it   where   from   they brought it."   Early   and   he ran

iqē'sqēs. "Ai'aq, ai'aq, ai'aq amcxElā'yutck." TakE nuxulā'yutck **14**
blue-jay.   "Quick,   quick,   quick   rise."   Then   they arose

tē'lx·Em kanauwē'. TakE aqō'icgiLx môkct ōkunī'm. A'lta ā'tgē **15**
the people   all.   Then   they hauled   two   canoes.   Now   they
down to the   went
water

mā'Lnē tē'lx·Em a'lta. TakE kulā'i ā'tgē. A'lta cka LEll **16**
seaward   the people   now.   Then   far   they went.   Now   and   almost
disap-
peared

Lpakā'lEma. TakE atgē'cElkEl ēlē'ē. Take nē'k·im iqē'sqēs: **17**
the mountains.   Then   they saw it   a land.   Then   he said   blue-jay:

"Ia'xkati taL¡ iktē'luwa-itk nē'xauē." Lä atxigēlā'mamē. A'lta **18**
"There   behold   the abalone shells   were."   Some   they landed.   Now
time

cka pā2L ē'Xōc iktē'luwa-itk. A'lta ataā'luLX tē'lx·Em. A'lta **19**
and   full   it was on   abalone shells.   Now   they went ashore   the people.   Now
ground

atgiomē'tckin qix·ī'x· iktē'luwa-itk; qiā'x ia'xka pāt qptciX **20**
they took them   these   abalone shells;   if   that   very   green

tcx·ī aLgiō'cgamX. Iqē'sqēs ia'xka gō q¡oā'p kat ikanī'm **21**
then   they took it.   Blue-jay   he   then   near   that   canoe

127

1 ka   atciupā'yaLx.   TakE   ā'yō;   niL'ē'taqL   iLā'xak¡Emana.
   and   he gathered them.   Then   he went;   he left them   their chief.

2 Ayuxō'Lakō   qō'ta   LEX.   Qiā'x   iā'qoa-iL,   tcx·ī   atciō'cgamx,   qiā'x
   He went around it   that   island.   If   a large one.   then   he took it,   if

3 pāt   qptciX   tcx·ī   atciō'cgam.   TakE   aLgiuLā'win   iLā'Xak¡Emana.
   really   green   then   he took it.   Then   they waited for him   their chief.

4 TakE   ō'lō   agā'yax   iqē'sqēs.   "Wu'ska   lxēelō'qLa."   Nugō'kXōm
   Then   hunger   acted upon him   blue-jay.   "Heh!   we will leave him."   They said

5 aqā'mXikc: "K¡ē,   qā'doXoē   lxēgumLā'ita.   Lō'nas   ayukō'om   tē'lx·Em."
   part of them: "No,   must   we wait for him.   Perhaps   he met them   people."

6 Nē'k·im   iqē'sqēs: "Tca   lxēeltā'qLa."   Tsō'yustē   nē'xauē,   takE
   He said   blue-jay: "Come   we will leave him."   Evening   it became   then

7 atEē'taqL   tiā'cōlal.   Iqē'sqēs   iā'Xaqamt.   Nō'Xōkō   tiā'cōla.   Tsō'yustē
   they left him   his relatives.   Blue-jay   his mind.   They went   his relatives.   In the evening
                                                                                  home

8 ka   ayōxō'Lakō   LEX.   A'lta   k¡ē   tiā'cōla;   atEē'taqL.   Ia'xkati
   and   he went around   the island.   Now   nothing   his relatives;   they left him.   There

9 kē'kXulē·y-   ē'mᶜEcX   nixō'kctē.   A'lta   nigE'tsax: "Ēktā'2   atgēnē'lōtk
   below   a tree   he lay down.   Now   he cried: "What   they deserted me

10 agE'lXam,   qā   tkLEnᶜē'taqL   agE'lXam."   A'lta   ia'xkatē   nē'xax
   my people,   where   they left me   my people."   Now   there   he was

11 iō'Lqatē.   A'lta   atciō'koē   ka'nauwē   x·ixī'x·   iktē'lauwa-itk.   QāxLxa-
   a long time.   Now   he carried them   all   those   abalone shells.   The
                                                            often

12 naā'Lax   ēlā'ki   L¡ap   atciā'x.   QāxLxanaā'Lax   kawī'X   nēxE'l'ōkō.
   next day   an otter   find   he did it.   The next day   early   he awoke.

13 A'lta   oxoī'tcōt   tē'lx·Em   gō   Liā'maLna.   Atciō'latck   iā'ōk.   Nē'k·ikst
   Now   they talked   people   at   seaward from him.   He lifted it   his blanket.   He looked

14 mā'Lnē.   Tā'mka   tqonēqonē'   ōxoēlā'itX.   WiXt   nēxEnk¡ē'Litso.
   seaward.   Only   gulls   there were.   Again   he pulled his blanket
                                                                over his head.

15 Wāx   wiXt   nē'ktcuktē.   WiXt   atcauitcā'ma   tē'lx·Em   oxoī'tcōt
   Every   again   it got day.   Again   he heard them   people.   they talked
   morning

16 gō   mā'Lnē.   Gōyē'   atci'Lax,   atcLō'latck.   A'lta   tā'mka   Ltamilā'ikc
   at   seaward.   Thus   he did it,   he lifted it.   Now   only   albatross

17 Lxēlā'itX.   Qoā'nEmi   ayā'qoyaē   atcawitcE'mElē   tē'lx·Em.   Kawī'X
   there were.   Five times   his sleeps   he heard them   people.   Early

18 ka   aLigEmō'tXu-it   LgōLē'lEXEmk.   AqLō'latck   Liā'ōk.   "Wu'Xē
   and   it stood near him   a person.   It was lifted   his blanket.   "To-morrow

19 a'lta   qamō'kᵘɪa;   qam'alō'kctxama."   Wāx   nē'ktcuktē.   TakE   wiXt
   now   you will be carried;   you will be carried   The next   it got day.   Then   again
                              on back."   morning

20 aLgEmō'tXu-it   LgōLē'lEXEmk.   ALgiō'lXam: "Mxā'latck!   A'lta
   it stood near him   a person.   He said to him: "Arise!   Now

21 qamō'kᵘɪa."   Nē'k·ikct   iau'a   mā'Lnē.   A'lta   ē'kolē   yuqunā'itX.
   you will be carried."   He looked   there   seaward.   Now   a whale   there lay.

22 A'lta   atciō'kXuiLx   iā'ktElauwa-itk.   A'lta   Lxoa'p   ikē'x   kā'tsEk   qiX
   Now   he carried to the   his abalone shells.   Now   a hole   was   in middle   that
       beach

23 ē'kolē.   A'lta   ia'xkatē   aqēiLā'ētamit: "Nēkct   mgē'kctaiē,   ma'nix
   whale.   Now   then   he was put into it: "Not   open your eyes,   when

24 aqamō'kᵘɪa."   A'lta   nixō'kctit,   a'lta   aqā'yukᵘɪ.   A'lta   atgā'yukᵘɪ
   you are carried."   Now   he lay down,   now   he was carried.   Now   they carried him

25 tē'lx·Em   ka'nauwē.   A'lta   nuguqLē'watck.   AqLō'lXam   Ltamilā'yikc,
   the people   all.   Now   they paddled.   They were told   the albatross,

26 aqLō'lXam   Lqat!ē'wuLala: "Kē'kXulē   LEmca'cgi."   AqLō'lXam
   they were told   the pelicans: "Down   your paddles."   They were told

27 Lqonē'qonē: "Kᵘcā'xalē   LEmca'cgi."   Aqō'lXam   ōē'Xsa: "Kᵘcā'xali
   the gulls: "Up   your paddles."   They were told   the snipes: "Up

28 LEmca'cgi."   Ka   mā'Lnē   aqā'mXikc   k¡ē   nō'xôx   qō'tac   tē'lx·Em.
   your paddles."   And   at sea   part of them   nothing   became   those   people.

Q̣ioā′p ilē′ě aqā′mXikc ḳē nō′xôx qō′tac têlx·Em. A′lta ā′mka-y-   1
Near land part of them nothing became those people. Now only

ōē′Xsa ḳa tqonēqonē′. Nix·gElā′kux ka lā′XlaX nē′xax. Ḳā   2
snipes and gulls. He felt and rock it did. Silent

nō′xôx qō′tac têlx·Em ka′nauwē ka atciā′latck iā′ōk. A′lta gō   3
they became those people all and he lifted it his blanket. Now there

mā′Lxôlē yuqunā′-itX. Nē′k·ikst a′lta, ā′mka-y- ōē′Xsa ka tqonēqonē′.   4
landward he lay. He looked now, only snipes and gulls.

A′lta nixā′latck. Atciō′kctEptck ka′nauwē iā′ktēlauwa-itk.   5
Now he rose. He carried inland all his abalone shells.

Atciō′kctEptck qix· ēlagē′tEma ka′nauwē. Qoä′nEm Lq̣iup   6
He carried inland those sea otters all. Five cut

atcā′yax qix· ē′kolē. Ä′2 ka aqiō′lXam, aLgiō′lXam qō′La   7
he did it that whale. Thus he was told, he said to him that

LgōLē′lXEmk. A′lta wiXt nē′Xtakō qix· ē′kolē. A′lta ā′yôptck   8
person. Now again he turned back that whale. Now he went up

q̣ioā′p gō tE′LaqL ka ayō′La-it. Iō′lqtē ayō′La-it ka atcE′LᶜElkEl   9
near at his house and he stayed. A long time he stayed and he saw it

Lḳā′ckc. ALE′tē, q̣ioā′p aLgē′txam.   10
a child. It came, near it came to him.

ALgā′Lata-y- uLā′xalaitan. Q̣ioā′p na-ikmō′tXu-it. Atcō′cgam,   11
It shot its arrow. Near it stuck in the ground. He took it,

atcaLxxa′pcôt. ALE′tē ka aLgō′xtkin uLā′xalaitan. Näkct Ḷap   12
he hid it. It came and it reached for it its arrow. Not find

aLi′kXaxa uLā′xalaitan ka aLgE′tcax: "Atcuwā′, mai′kXa iqē′sqēs   13
it did it its arrow and it cried: "Oh, you blue-jay,

mEnXi′pcūt ōgu′Xalaitan. AmLEnElxā′-uyam iqē′sqēs. Tātc̣au!   14
you hide from me my arrow. You make me poor blue-jay. See!

wiXt amEnx·EnEmō′sx·Ema-itx. Ā′nēt ōgu′xalaitan." Ḳē nēkct   15
again you tease me always. Give me my arrow." Nothing not

LE′Laqsō qō′La Lḳāsks. A′lta Lḳō′pLḳōp Lctā′xôs. Ēmā′sEn   16
its hair that child. Now sunken its eyes. Deer

ā′yäqsō iLā′ōq. TakE atcLō′cgam iLā′pôtē. TakE atcLō′lXam: 17
its skin its blanket. Then he took it at its arm. Then he said to it:

"La′kstama?" "Ā, nai′kXa," aLgiō′lXam. "AqēLā′taqL LgE′mama.   18
"Who are you?" "Ah, I," it said to him. "He was left my father.

Iqē′sqēs atcēeLā′qal." TakE atci′Lukᵘɪ gō Ltcuq qō′La Lḳāsks.   19
blue-jay he left him." Then he carried it to water that child.

TakE atcLōmē′nakō. A′lta pō′pō atci′Lax gō Lctā′xôs. A′lta   20
Then he washed its face. Now blow he did it on its eyes. Now

aLE′k·ikst. A′lta atcLō′lXam: "Nai′ka, nai′ka aqX. TakE   21
it saw. Now he said to it: "I, I, child. Then

anXatgō′mam." TakE atcē′xalukctgō iLā′ōk qō′La Liā′xa.   22
I came home." Then he threw it away its blanket that his child's.

AtciLkLXā′nakō ēlā′kē. "Ai′aq mxanē′tk꜔ēl t!ayā′na mcxēlā′·itix·?"   23
He put around it the sea otter. "Quick, tell me good [int. part.] you are?"

"Tcintcx·gō′mitīt iq̣ē′sqēs. Qi′ctac môkct cEmē′k·ikala   24
"He made us poor blue-jay. Those two your wives

kanasmō′kst a′lta ciā′k·ikala iq̣ē′sqēs. Manix L'ē′tcx·enīL aLgiā′x   25
both now his wives blue-jay's. When wanting to defecate he does

atcLāuwē′tcxamx gō tE′ntcaqL ka ia′xka itcā′ōk ka aniyē′nanLxax.   26
he goes to defecate in our house and this my blanket and I wipe him with it.

A′lta cmō′kctka nēkct tq̣ēx acgā′yax." "Ai′aq cgā′lEmam." "Â   27
Now two only not like they did him." "Quick bring them." "Ah,

nēkct ictā′kēqamt, Lḳō′pLḳōp ctā′xôs." A′lta nē′Xko iā′xa,   28
not they seeing, sunken their eyes." Now he went home his son

atciō′kō. Atcugō′lEmam Liā′naa. Atcō′lXam Liā′naa: "TakE   29
he sent him. He went to fetch her his mother. He said to her his mother: "Then

LgE′mama niXatgō′mam." TakE nagE′tsax Liā′naa. Acxē′nim   30
my father he came home." Then she cried his mother. They two wailed

1 qaX   ā'ēXat   ōᶜō'kuil.   "Iq̣ē'sq̣ēs   atcimaō'nima-itx.   Lā'XlaX
  that   one   woman.   "Blue-jay   always fools you.   Deceive

2 atcimā'xo-itx."   "Nau'itka,   nau'itka,   LgE'mama   aLtē'mam.   A'lta
  he always does you."   "Indeed,   indeed,   my father   he came.   Now

3 itci'kēqamt   Xōk.   AtcnE'tōkō   ayamtgā'lEmam.   Ni'Xua   i'skam
  I seeing   now.   He sent me   I came to fetch you.   Well   take

4 x·ik   itcā'ōk."   Agiō'sgam   Liā'naa.   A'lta   LEmE'n   qix·   iā'ōk.
  this   my blanket."   She took it   his mother.   Now   soft   that   his blanket.

5 "Tā'tc̣a!   mcEuE'luat."   TakE   atci'ctukᵘᵢ   Liā'naa   qaX   ā'ēXat
  "Look!   you did not believe me."   Then   he brought them to   his father   that   one

6 ōᶜō'kuil.   Atcō'ptca.   Atcō'kᵘᵢam   gō   ā'yam.   A'lta   atcumē'uakō.
  woman.   He led them.   He arrived bringing   at   his father.   Now   he washed their
                                       her   faces

7 A'lta   cE'k·ikst.   A'lta   atcō'lXam: "Ai'aq,   mcktūguē'xēyam   tE'lxaqL.
  Now   they saw.   Now   he said to them: "Quick,   go and sweep   our house.

8 Ka'uauwē2   mcktūguē'xēya.   TakE   ā'Lō.   A'lta   aLktō'guaxē   tE'LaqL,
  The whole   sweep it.   Then   they went.   Now   they swept it   their house,

9 ka'nauwē   aLktō'guēxē.   A'lta   aLgiō'kuē   ka'nauwē   wē'wuLē.   ALgiō'kuē
  the whole   they swept it.   Now   they carried   all   into the interior   They carried
                                                them much   of house.   much

10 qix·   ē'kolē   ka'nauwē   wē'wuLē.   ALgiō'kuē   qix·   ēlagē'tEma   wē'wuLē.
  that   whale   all   into the interior   They carried   those   sea-otters   into the inte-
                         of the house.   them much   rior of the house.

11 TakE   aya'ckōp!,   Cā'xaL   takE   aya'ckop!.   Ayā'qxôiē;   kawī'X   atcixā'laqL
  Then   he entered,   Cā'xaL   then   he entered.   One sleep;   early   he opened

12 iqē'p!al   iqē'sqēs.   A'lta   atcLā'auwitcXa   gō   iqē'p!al   iqē'sqēs.   "Ai'aq
  the door   blue-jay.   Now   he defecated   in   the door-way   blue-jay.   "Quick

13 Ē'npēyucX,   ntq̣ē'xEnapstam."   "A'ckam   Xau   oᶜō'lEptckiX.
  Ē'npēyucX,   wipe me!"   "Take it   that   fire-brand.

14 Ama-ilō'ktgutc   gō-y-   ūyā'putc."   TakE   atcō'cgam   qix·   iḳā'sks.   A'lta
  Push him   in   his anus."   Then   he took it   that   boy.   Now

15 atcā-ilō'ktgux   gō-y-   uyā'putc.   "Anā'"   takE   atcixE'lgiLx   īqē'sqēs.
  he pushed him   into   his anus.   "Anah!"   then   he cried   blue-jay.

16 "Anā'!   tEnxE'LElama.   TakE   Lx   nigā't!ōm   ā'yam   ka   atcnxE'Lama."
  "Anan!   they burnt me.   Then   maybe   he arrived   his father   and   he burnt me."

17 Nē'k·ikst   ē'wa   wē'wuLē   iqē'sqēs.   A'lta   iō'c   iLā'XaḳEmana   gō
  He looked   then   [into] the in-   blue-jay.   Now   there   their chief   at
                      terior of the house   was

18 wē'wuLē.   Nē'xaukō,   nēxkᵘLē'tcgōm: "Ā,   ilxā'XaḳEmana   takE
  the interior of   He ran,   he went to tell them: "Ah.   our chief   then
  the house.

19 nitē'mam."   A'lta   atktē'lōt   ka'nauwē   tgā'ktEma   tiā'lXam;   ka'nauwē
  he arrived."   Now   he gave to   all   his property   his people;   all
                       them

20 itā'ktēlauwa-itk   atgē'lōt.
  the abalone shells   he gave them.

Translation.

Cā'xaL's eldest was dead. Every morning he went to the beach
and wailed. Day by day he went to the beach and cried. Once upon
a time he discovered two ravens flying from the sea towards the shore.
When they came near him he saw that they turned [in the air] over
one another. [Sometimes the one was above, then the other.] When
they had almost reached him they let fall a round object, which fell on
the sand. He went down to the beach and took it. It was an abalone
shell. In the evening he went home. Then he said to his wife: "Invite
all the people." His wife went and said: "My poor husband invites
you." Then all the people came and entered the house. He said:

"This was carried up to me from the sea. You will see it. Just there
they came ashore." Blue-Jay said: "Let us go to-morrow and see
where they found it." Early he ran around [saying]: "Quick, quick,
arise!" All the people arose and launched two canoes. Then they
went out seaward. They traveled a long distance. When the mountains [of their own country] had almost disappeared they discovered
land. Blue-Jay said: "Certainly here are abalone shells." After awhile
they landed. The ground was full of abalone shells. The people went
ashore and picked up these abalone shells. They selected only the
very green ones. Blue-Jay gathered those which were near the canoe.
Then their chief [Cā'xaL] went away and left them. He went around
the island. He took only the large and very green ones. The people
waited for their chief. Then Blue-Jay became hungry, and said: "Let
us leave him." But part of the people said: "No; we must wait for
him; perhaps he met some people." [After awhile] Blue-Jay said:
"Come! Let us leave him." It grew dark; then his people left him.
They followed Blue Jay's advice and went home. In the evening the
chief had gone around the island. Now his people had disappeared;
they had left him. Then he lay down under a log and cried: "Why
did my people desert me; why did they leave me?" He stayed there
for a long time. He carried all the abalone shells [up to the log]. On
the next day he found a seaotter. On the following morning he awoke
and heard people talking on the beach below him. He lifted his
blanket and looked seaward, but he saw only gulls. He pulled his
blanket over his head again. On the next morning, when it grew daylight, he heard again people talking on the beach below. Again he
lifted his blanket, but there were only albatross. Five days he heard
people [talking on the beach]. On the next morning [he saw] a person
standing by him. He lifted his blanket [and the stranger said]: "To-
morrow you will be carried back." Early the next morning the person stood again near him, and said: "Arise; now you will be carried
back." He looked down to the beach and saw a whale. He carried
down his abalone shells. A hole was in the middle of the whale, into
which he was placed. [The person said:] "Do not open your eyes
while they are carrying you." Now he lay down and he was carried
away. All the people carried him. They paddled. The albatross and
pelicans were told: "Put down your paddles; put down your paddles."
The gulls were told: "Put up your paddles, put up your paddles."
The snipes were told: "Put up your paddles, put up your paddles."
Then when they were at sea, part of those people departed. When
they were near the land another part departed. Now only the snipes
and gulls remained. He felt [the whale] rock, then all was quiet and
he lifted his blanket. He lay on the beach. He looked and saw only
gulls and snipes. Now he arose. He went inland, carrying all his
abalone shells and the sea otters. He took five cuts of the whale.
That person had told him to do so. Then that whale returned. Now

he went up to his house and staid there. After awhile he saw a child.
It approached him, shooting an arrow. [The arrow] struck the ground
near him, and he took it and hid it. Then the child came searching
for his arrow. When he did not find it he cried: "O, Blue-Jay, you
have hidden my arrow. You make me feel miserable. You always
tease me; give me my arrow." The child had no hair, and his eyes
were sore. His blanket was made of deerskin. Then [Cā'xaL] took
him by his arm and said: "Who are you?" "Oh it is I. My father
was deserted. Blue-Jay deserted him." Then [Cā'xaL] took [the boy]
to the water and washed his face; he blew on his eyes and the boy
recovered his eyesight. He said: "Child! it is I; I have returned."
He threw away [the boy's] blanket and gave him a sea-otter blanket.
"Tell me," he continued, "are you all well?" The boy replied: "Blue-
Jay made us miserable; two of your wives are now his wives. He
always defecates in our house, and I must wipe him with my blanket.
Two only [of your wives] do not like him." "Bring them here." "Oh,
they can not see, for they have lost their eyes." Then the boy went
home. He sent him to fetch his mother. He said to her: "Father
has come home." Then his mother and the other woman began to cry:
"O, Blue-Jay has deceived you; he always deceives you." "No, indeed,
father has come. I have recovered my eyesight; he sent me to fetch you.
Just feel my blanket." Then his mother felt it. It was soft. [The boy
continued:] "See, you did not believe me!" Then he led them to his
father. He reached his father, who washed their faces. Then they
recovered their eyesight. Cā'xaL said to them: "Go and sweep our
house." They went back and swept the whole house. They carried
everything into the house, his whale, his sea otters, and his abalone
shells. Then Cā'xaL entered the house.

On the following morning Blue-Jay opened the door and defecated in
the doorway. [He called:] "Ē'npēyucX, wipe me!" "Take that fire-
brand and push his backside," said his father. The boy took it and
pushed him. "Heh," cried Blue-Jay: "Oh, he burnt me; certainly
his father has returned." Blue-Jay looked into the house and saw the
chief sitting in the house. Then he went and told the people: "Our
chief has arrived." [Cā'xaL] distributed all his property among his
people. He gave them all the abalone shells.

11. STIKUA' ITCĂ'KXANAM.

STIKUA' HER MYTH.

Gŏ Nakōt!ă't Lxēlă'-itX, LE'xo-itiks Lxēlă'itx. A'lta ayŏ'mEqt 1
At Seaside, they lived. many they lived. Now he was dead

iLă'xakĮ Emana. Iă'qoa-iL iă'xa. Ta'kE tcă'xilkᴛē nē'xauē, ta'kE 2
their chief. Large his son. Then winter it was, then

ŏ'lŏ agE'Lax. Ta'kE iă'ɪnka iniă'matk aLgiă'xo-itx kĮa-y- ŏgū'ican. 3
hungry they were. Then only mussels they ate them and roots.

KăxLxnaă'Lax ka nē'k·im ktiă'xēqLax: "AmcxE'ltXuitck." 4
One day and he said a hunter: "Make yourselves ready."

Nŏxui'tXuitck ka'nauwē2 qŏ'tac tkă'lamukc. Atagă'la-it mŏkct 5
They made themselves all those men. They were in the two
ready canoes

ōkunī'm. Ta'kE ă'tgē mă'Lnē. Ta'kE atcē'lkikc igē'pix·L qix· 6
canoes. Then they went seaward. Then he speared it a sealion that

ktiă'xēqLax, cka atcō'pEna ka ayuXuă'nitck qix· igē'pix·L. 7
hunter, and it jumped and he drifted that sealion.

ALgē'Elta-uī mă'Lxŏlē. Nē'k·im iqē'sqēs: "Iă'xkayuk 8
They hauled it up ashore. He said blue-jay: "Here

lxgīutsXEmă'ya." TakE iă'xkatē naLx·E'lgīLx. AgElkᴛikĮ'E'tsXēma. 9
we will boil it." Then there they made a fire. They singed it.

A'lta aLgă'yaxc. A'lta aLE'xalEtcXEm. Nē'k·im iqē'sqēs: 10
Now they cut it. Now they boiled it. He said blue-jay:

"Ia'xkayuk lxgēuwu'lᶜaya, lxgēutctXŏ'maya." Ta'kE nŏxuiLxă'lEm 11
"Here we will eat it, we will finish it." Then they ate

qŏ'tac tē'lx·Em. Atciō'pcut qē'xtcē ikoalē'x·oa gŏ Liă'cguc. Atcă'yukⁿL 12
those people. He hid it intending the raven in his mat. He carried it

gŏ-y- ikanī'm ēXt igitē'tsxal. Ā'nqatē nē'xankŏ iqĮē'sqēs, Lăqᵒ 13
to the canoe one piece. Already he ran blue-jay, take out

atcă'yax. Atcă'yukⁿᴛ gŏ- ŏᶜŏ'lEptckiX qix· igitē'tsxal. Nix·E'lgīLx. 14
he did it. He carried it to the fire that piece. He burnt it.

Ta'kE aLE'Xkŏ. ALkiupă'yaLx ēniă'matk kĮa itguē'ma. Tsŏ'yustē 15
Then they went They gathered them large mussels and small mussels. In the evening
home.

aLx·gŏ'mam. Na-ixE'lqamx iqĮē'sqēs: "Ā2, y imcă'niamatkā'2, 16
they arrived at home. He called blue-jay: "Ah, your mussels

Stikuayā'2!" Stikua' itcă'xal uyă'k·ikal iqĮē'sqēs. TEmm aLi'Xaua 17
Stikua'!" Stikua' her name his wife blue-jay's. Noise of they ran
feet

Stikua' mă'Lnē. ALgiugŏ'lEmam iniă'matk. Ā'tgELx ka'nauwē 18
Stikua' down to beach. They went to take the mussels. They came to all
the beach

qŏ'tac tă'nEmckc. Atgiŏ'kXuiptck itguē'matk kĮa iniă'matk. Gŏ 19
those women. They carried them up the small mussels and the large mussels. Theₙ

ikoalē'x·oa atcigE'nXaōtē iLă'xakĮ Emana iă'xa. Nē'k·im qix· ikĮă'ckc: 20
the raven he took care of him their chief his son. He said that boy:

"WăXi ka nxEltŏ'ma." Atciō'lXam iqĮē'sqēs: "Ē'kta amiuwă'ya! 21
"To-morrow and I go along." He said to him blue-jay: "What are you going
to do!

Ugŏ'lal gEmŏ'kⁿᴛa, muXună'ya. LEqs anŏ'Xunē nai'kXa;" nē'k·im 22
The waves will carry you you will drift away. Almost I drifted away I;" he said
away,

iqē'sqēs. Kawī'X wiXt nŏxui'tXuitck. Ată'kElōya. Ā'yuLx qix· 23
blue-jay. Early again they made themselves He went into He went to the that
ready. the canoe. beach

133

1 ik¡ā'sks,   ā'yuʟx qē'xtcē ixEltō'ma.   Qē'xtcē atciō'cgam ikanī'm
   boy,   he went to the intending he went along. Intending he took it the canoe
             beach

2 ixEltō'ma. "Mō'ptcga, mō'ptcga" atciō'lXam iq¡ē'sq¡ēs. Ā'yuptck
   he went along. "Go up,   go up."   he said to him blue-jay.   He went up

3 Lā'yaxax qix· ik¡ā'sks. Nē'k·im iq¡ē'sqēs: "Ai'aq, lxēē'taqʟ." TakE
   sad   that   boy.   He said   blue-jay: "Quick, we leave him." Then

4 nūguqʇē'watck tê'lx·Em. TakE atigā'ōm Lgipē'x·Lukc iLā'xanakc.
   they paddled the people. Then they arrived at the sealions their rock.

5 Ayaā'luʟx ktiā'xēkʇax. AtɔLē'lukc ēXt igē'pix·L, cka atcō'pEna;
   He went   the hunter.   He speared   one sealion, and it jumped;
   ashore

6 iā'xkati ayuXuā'nitck. ALgē'ltāuwē. ALgēgilā'mamē gō-y-īlē'ē.
   there   it drifted.   They hauled it up. They pulled it ashore to the land.

7 ALgiuLā'taptck. Nē'k·im iq¡ē'sqēs: "Iā'xkayuk lxgiuwu'lɔa
   They pulled it up from He said blue-jay: "Here   we will eat it
   the beach.

8 kā'nauwē; taua'lta k¡oa'n nēxā'x ilxā'xak¡Emāna iā'xa."
   all;   else   always desir- he becomes our chief   his son."
                        ing to go here

9 ALgiā'Lk¡tsx·ēma iā'xkatē. ALgā'yaxc. ALgiō'tcXum a'lta iā'xkatē.
   They singed it   there.   They cut it. They boiled it now   there.

10 Ta'kE ayō'ktcEkt iLā'tcXEmal. ALxLxā'lEm, aLxLxā'lEm. Qē'xtcē
   Then   it got done what they boiled. They ate,   they ate.   Intending

11 atciō'pcut ikoalē'x·oa ēXt igitē'tcxal. K·¡au atci'Lax Lā'yaqcō.
   he hid it   the raven   one piece.   Tie   he did it in his hair.

12 Ia'xkati qē'xtcē atciō'pcut. Ā'nqatē Laq° atcā'yax iq¡ē'sqēs.
   There   intending he hid it. Already take out he did it blue-jay.

13 AtcixE'lgiLx igitē'tcxal. Tsō'yustē itguē'ma aLgiupā'yaLx k¡a
   He burnt it   the piece.   In the evening small mussels they gathered them and

14 ēniā'mā ka aLi'Xkō. Q¡oāp aLxē'gilaē, naLxE'lqamx: "Ā2,
   large mussels and they went Nearly they landed, he shouted: "Ah,
            home.

15 Stikuayā' ēmcā'niamatgā'2." TEmm, āLi'xatoa ā'LiLx tga'a
   Stikua'   your mussels."   Noise of feet, they came they went to her
                                             running, the beach children

16 Stikua'. Ka'nauwē2 ā'tgELx qō'tac tā'nEmckc. Atgiō'kXuiptck
   Stikua'. All   they went to those women.   They carried up
                        the beach

17 itguē'ma k¡a ēniā'matk. Atctō'lXam qō'tac tê'lx·Em iq¡ē'sqēs:
   the small and the large mussels. He said to them those people blue-jay:
   mussels

18 "Nē2kct mcxqʇē'tcgōye mckanauwē'tikc, taua'lta iqētō'mEl atciā'x
   "Not   tell him   all of you,   else   accompany us he does

19 ilxā'xak¡Emana iā'xa." A'lta nē'k·im qix· ik¡ā'sks: "Wä2Xi ka
   our chief   his son." Now he said that boy: "To-morrow and

20 nxaltō'ma." TakE nē'k·im iq¡ē'sqēs. "Ē'kta miuwā'ya! Taua'lta
   I shall go along." Then he said blue-jay. "What are you going Else
                                                       to do?

21 amuXunē'x, itcā'aitcma-y· ugō'la." "Qā'dox nxEltō'ma," nē'k·im
   you drift away, confounded waves." "Must I go along," he said

22 ik¡ā'sks.
   the boy.

   Kawī'X nōxōlā'yutck ī'LaLonē. Ā'tgELx. Ā'yuLx qix· ik¡ā'sks.
   Early   they rose   the third time. They went He went to that boy.
                                        to the beach. the beach.

24 Atciō'cgam qix· ikanī'm qē'xtcē. Atciū'tctEmt iq¡ē'sqēs qix·
   He took it that canoe intending. He pushed him blue-jay that

25 ik¡ā'sks. "Ē'kta tcīuwā'ya x·ix·ē'kik! ME'ptcga." NigE'tsax qix·
   boy.   "What will he do this one! Go up from the He cried that
                                          beach."

26 ik¡ā'sks, ā'yuptck. "Ai'aq, amckLē'watck," nē'k·im iq¡ē'sqēs;
   boy,   he went up. "Quick, paddle,"   he said blue-jay;

"lxēitā'qLa." TakE nugukLĕ'watck tê'lx·Em. Ta'kE agatgō'yam gō 1
"we will leave him." Then they paddled the people. Then they arrived at

Lgipē'x·Lukc Lā'xanakc. TakE ayaā'luLx qix· ktiā'xke٦ax. AtcLĕ'luke 2
the sealions their rock. Then he went ashore that hunter. He speared it,

ēXt igē'pix·L, iā'qoa-iL igē'pix·L, cka atcō'pEna, ia'xkati ayuXuā'nitck. 3
one sealion, a large sealion, and it jumped, there it drifted.

TakE aLgē'lta-u mā'Lxolē. ALgē'kilaē gō-y· ilē'ē. ALgiuLā'taptck. 4
Then they hauled it up landward. They landed at the land. They pulled it up from the beach.

ALgieLk¡E'tsx·ēma. ALkLĕ'kXōL¡ aLgīeLk¡E'tsx·ēma. A'lta aLgā'yaxc, 5
They singed it. They finished it, they singed it. Now they cut it,

aLgiō'tcXEm ia'xkati. Ayō'ktcikt. Ta'kE aLxLxā'lEm. Nĕ'k·im 6
they boiled it there. It was done. Then they ate. He said

iq¡ē'sqēs: "Kanauwē'2 lxgēwu'l٢ai. Näkct La'ksta LxkLĕ'tcgō, 7
blue-jay: "All we will eat it. Not anyone tell,

taua'lta ēqitō'mEl atciā'x ilxā'xak¡Emana iā'xa." MEnx· niLgā'ētix·t 8
else accompany-ing us he makes our chief his son." A little he left over

ka aLaqctā'yū. Qē'xtcē atciō'cgam ēXt igitē'tcxal ikoalē'x·oa. K¡au 9
and they were satiated. Intending he took it one piece the raven. Tie

atcā'yax gō ia'٢owit. Nĕ'k·im LEkᵘ nĕ'xax iā'٢owit. Nix·E'lgiLx 10
he did it to his leg. He said broken it became his leg. He burnt it

qix· iLgā'ētix·t. Kanauwē' nix·E'lgiLx iq¡ē'sqēs. Atciō'lXam 11
that what he had left over. All he burnt it blue-jay. He said to him

ikoalē'x·oa iq¡ē'sqēs: "Ni'Xua niō'kumanEma imē'٢owit." Atcikpā'na, 12
[to] the raven blue-jay: "[Interjection] I want to see it your leg." He jumped at it,

stuX atcā'yax gō iā'٢owit. L¡ap atcā'yax ēXt igitē'tsxal gō 13
untie he did it at his leg. Find he did it one piece at

ikoalē'x·oa iā'٢owit. Atciō'cgam iq¡ē'sqēs nix·E'lgiLx. Tsō'yustē 14
the raven his leg. He took it blue-jay he burnt it. In the evening

aLgiupā'yaLx itguē'ma k¡a ēniā'matk. ALE'Xkō. Q¡oā'p 15
they gathered small mussels and large mussels. They went home. Nearly

aLXgō'mam, ta'kE nēxE'lqamx iq¡ē'sqēs: "Ā, imcā'tguēmatgā' 16
they arrived at home, then he shouted blue-jay: "Ah, your mussels

Stikuayā'!" TEmm, ā'LōLx Stikua'. A'lta aLgiō'kXuiptck 17
Stikua'." Noise of feet, they went to the beach Stikua'. Now they carried up from the beach

iLā'tguēma. A'lta atgā'yax qix· itguē'ma ka'nauwē -y-ō'pōl ka 18
their mussels. Now they ate those mussels all night and

qix· iLā'xak¡Emana iā'xa. Nĕ'k·im ik¡'ā'sks: "Wu'Xi a'lta 19
that their chief his son. He said the boy: "To-morrow now

nExEltō'ma." TakE nē'k·im iq¡ē'sqēs: "Ē'kta amiuwā'ya? 20
I shall go along." Then he said blue-jay: "What are you going to do?

MuXunā'ya. Mâ'kctē anō'Xunē qē nikctx ikanī'm aniō'cgam." 21
You will drift away. Twice I drifted away if not the canoe I took it."

'Kawī'X ka wiXt aLxE'ltXuitck ī'Lalakte. Nixā'latck qix· ik¡'ā'sks. 22
Early and again they made themselves ready the fourth time. He rose that boy.

NixE'ltXuitck. ALgō'cgiLx uLā'xanīm. ALagā'lait uLā'xanim. 23
He made himself ready. They hauled down to the water their canoes. They went into the canoes their canoes.

Qē'xtcē ayagE'La-it x·ix· ik¡'ā'sks. Atciō'cgam, iq¡ē'sqēs, 24
Intending he went into the canoe that boy. He took him, blue-jay,

atciaēlē'maLx. Yukpā't nitElō'tXuit gō Ltcuq. Qē'xtcē atciō'cgam 25
he threw him into the water. Up to here he stood in the water in water. Intending he took it

qix· ikanī'm. Atcta'-uwilx·L tiā'kcia qix· ik¡ā'sks iq¡ē'sqēs. Iā'2xkati 26
that canoe. He struck them his hands that boy's blue-jay. There

ayō'tXuit. NigE'tsax, nigE'tsax ka ā'yuptck. Ā'Lō, ā'Lō, 27
he stood. He cried, he cried and he went up. They went, they went,

1 ăLkⱦē′watck iq̣ē′sqēs. ALigā′ōm qix· iqā′nakc, Lgipē′x·Lukc
they paddled   blue-jay.   They reached it   that   rock,   the sealions

2 iLā′xanakc. Ayaā′LuLx qix· ktiā′xēkⱦax, atcLē′lukc ēXt igē′piXL,
their rock.   He went ashore   that   hunter,   he speared it   one   sealion,

3 cka atcō′pEna, ka ia′xkatē ayuXnā′nitck. TakE wiXt aLgē′Eltā-uwĕ.
and   it jumped,   and   there   it drifted.   Then   again   they pulled it to the
                                                                    shore.

4 ALgīgēl′ā′mam ēlē′ē. ALgiuLā′taptck. ALgēLk̥ E′tsx·Ema ia′xkatē.
They towed it to   the land.   They hauled it up from   They singed it   there.
                            the shore.

5 ALkLē′kXōL̥ aLgēLk̥ E′tsx·ēma. ALgā′yaxc; a′lta aLgiō′tcXEm
They finished it,   they singed it.   They cut it;   now   they boiled it

6 ia′xkati. Ayŏ′ktcikt. Nē′k·im iqē′sqēs: "Iā2′xkuktē lxgēwu′l̥aya."
there.   He finished it.   He said   blue-jay: "Here   we will eat it."

7 ALXLxā′lEm, aLXLxā′lEm. cka icē′tkum aLgiā′wul̥ ka aLaqctā′yū.
They ate,   they ate,   and   half   they ate it   and   they became
                                                                 satiated.

8 ALk̥ē′witx·it; k̥′E′xk̥Ex aLE′xax ka aLk̥ē′witx·it. NixE′l̥ōkō
They went to sleep;   overeaten   they became   and   they went to sleep.   He awoke

9 iq̣ē′sqēs, nix·E′lgiLx ka′nauwē qix· iLgā′ētix·it. Tsō′yustē
blue-jay,   he burnt   all   that   what they had left over.   In the evening

10 aLgiupā′yaLx itguē′ma k̥a ēniā′ma. A′lta aLXgō′mam. Q̣oā′p
they gathered   small mussels   and   large mussels.   Now   they came home.   Nearly

11 aLgiā′xomē: "A imcā′niamatgā′ Stikuayā′." TEmm, aLi′xaua mā′Lnē.
they came ashore: "Ah!   your mussels   Stikua′."   Noise of   they ran   seaward.
                                                                        feet,

12 ALgiō′kXuiptck ēniā′ma k̥a itguē′ma. Nē′k·im qix· ik̥ā′sks:
They carried up from the   the large   and   small mussels.   He said   that   boy:
beach   mussels

13 "Wä2x·i a′lta nxEltō′ma." Atciō′lXam iq̣ē′sqēs. "Ē′kta miuwā′ya?
"To-morrow   now   I go along."   He said to him   blue-jay: "What   are you going
                                                                                 to do?

14 Lxaxō′-ita. L̥ lap mō′ya."
We shall capsize. Under water   you will go."

15   Wäx kawī′X noxolā′yutck. Nixā′latck qix· ik̥′ā′sks.
     On the next   early   they made themselves ready.   He rose   that   boy.
     morning

16 NixE′ltXuitck. ALgō′cgiLx uLā′xanIma iqē′sqēs. Qē′xtcē ayagE′La-it
He made himself   They hauled   their canoes   blue-jay.   Intending   he went into the
ready.   down to the water   canoe

17 qix· ik̥ā′sks. Atciaēlē′maL iqē′sqēs. Atciō′cgam qē′xtcē qix·
that   boy.   He threw him into the   blue-jay.   He took it   intending   that
               water

18 ikanī′m. Yukpä′t tiā′xEmalap̣ix· nitElō′tXuit. Qe′xtcē atciō′cgam
canoe.   Up to here   his arm-pits   he stood in the water.   Intending   he took it

19 qix· ikanī′m, atc·ta′auwilx·L tia′kcia iqē′sqēs qix· ik̥′ā′sks.
that   canoe,   he struck   his hands   blue-jay   that   boy's.

20 NigE′tsax, nigE′tsax qix· ik̥′ā′sks. Ā′Lō· y-a′lta iq̣ē′sqēs.
He cried,   he cried   that   boy.   He went   now   blue-jay.

21   Lä2 ka ā′yuptck ik̥′ā′sks. Atctō′cgam tiā′xalaitanEma.
    Some time   and   he went up from the   the boy.   He took them   his arrows.
                    beach

22 A′lta ixLā′kōi pEnka′. Atcaga′ōm utcaktcā′k, Lē′el utcaktcā′k.
Now   he went   afoot.   He met it   an eagle.   a black   eagle.
     around the point   [young]

23 Itcā′maᵋ atciā′lax. Tc̥ux a′tcax, qē′xtcē quL naēxā′lax. Iō′kuk
Shooting it   he did it.   Skin   he did it,   intending   putting   he did it on   Here
                                                    on   to himself.

24 kⁿcaxala′ tiā′q̣ôxLEma ka na-igE′nkakō. Lāq° nā′ēxax. WiXt
above   his knees   and   it was too small.   Take off   he did it.   Again

25 ā′yō, wiXt aē′Xt utcaktcā′k ayagā′ōm. Itcā′maᵋ atciā′lax.
he went,   again   one   eagle   he met it.   Shooting it   he did it.

26 Nôē′luktcū. Tk̥ōp ē′tcEqtq utcaktcā′k. Tc̥ux ā′tcax, quL naēxā′lax.
It fell down.   White   its head   the eagle.   Skin   he did it,   put on   he did it on
                                                                 to himself.

1 Mank kĕkula' tiā'qˌ ôxLEma, na- igE'nkakō. Lāq° nā'ōxax, atcaē'taqL.
A little   below   his knees,   it was too small.   Take off he did it,   he left it.

2 WiXt ā'yō, kulā'yi ā'yō. Atcigā'ōm ininē'x·ō. Iā'maᶜ atcē'lax.
Again   he went,   far   he went.   He met it   a bald-headed eagle.   Shooting it he did it.

3 Mô'kctē iā'maᶜ atcē'lax; ayôē'luktcū. Tcˌux atcā'yax quL nēxā'lax.
Twice   shooting it he did it;   it fell down.   Skin   he did it   put on   he did it on to himself.

4 Qˌoā'p nēXE'kXa ka nigE'nkakō. Ayū'kō nixkˌ'ā'wakct. Kĕ'kXulē
Nearly   it fitted   and   it was too small.   He flew   he attempted.   Down

5 ayō'kō, nikct ayōlā'tckuix·t. ILā'môkct Lāq nē'xatx, a'lta t!'aya'
he flew,   not   he rose.   The second time   turn   he did,   now   good

6 ayō'kō. A'lta nē'xLakō-i ē'wa mā'Lnē Gôt!'ā't. Qˌoā'p nēxLā'komē.
he flew.   Now   he went around the point   thus   seaward from   Gôt!'a't.   Nearly   he came around the point.

7 Ta'kE atā'yiLa tXut; kˌEX qō'ta tXut. NēxLā'komē, atci'LᶜElkEl
Then   he smelled it   smoke;   smell of fat   that   smoke.   He came around the point,   he saw them

8 qō'tac giLā'lEXam. Gō kulā'yi ka ayugō'La-it. A'lta atcLā'qxamt
those   the people of his town.   There   far   and   he sat on top of a tree.   Now   he saw them

9 ē'wa kĕ'kXulē. ALxgē'ktcikt. A'lta aLxLxā'lEm atcLā'qxamt.
thus   below.   It was done.   Now   they ate   he saw them.

10 Qˌoā'p aLE'Lx·ōLˌ ka ayō'kō. NiXLō'lEXa-it: "Iqē'sqēs tayax
Nearly   they finished   and   he flew.   He thought: "Blue-jay: oh if

11 tcin'ē'tgElax!" Goyē' nē'xax iqē'sqēs, a'lta LElā'lax Lō'kōl. "Ā,
he would see me!"   Thus   he did   Blue-jay,   now   a bird   flew about.   "Ah,

12 LElā'lax qLgE'lxētuwā'Lam." WiXt Lāqᵃ nēxā'x. Qoä'nEmI Lāqᵃ
a bird   it comes to get food from us."   Again   turn   he did.   Five times   turn

13 nē'xax, a'lta kĕ'kXulē. Atciō'cgam ēXt igitē'tcxal iqē'sqēs. "x·iau
it did,   now   down.   He took it   one   piece   blue-jay.   "This

14 amE'lᶜēm," atciō'lXam qō'La LElā'lax. OXX aLE'tē qō'La LElā'lax.
I give you to eat," he said to it   that   bird.   CXX   it came   that   bird.

15 LkE'pLkEp atciō'cgam qix· igitē'tcxal. A'lta aLō'kō qō'La LElā'lax.
Grasping   it took it   that   piece.   Now   it flew   that   bird.

16 Nĕ'k·im iqē'sqēs: "Taqē LgōLē'lXEmk tE'Lapc." ALaqctā'yō iqē'sqēs,
He said   blue-jay: "Just as   a person   its feet."   They became   blue-jay,   satiated

17 aLkˌ'ē'witx·it. WiXt atciō'pcut ikoalē'x·oa ēXt igitē'tcxal.
they went to sleep.   Again   he hid it   the raven   one   piece.

18 ALxEl'ō'yōkō iqē'sqēs tsō'yustē. A'lta wiXt aLxLxā'lEm. A'lta
They awoke   blue-jay   in the evening.   Now   again   they ate.   Now

19 wiXt atix·E'lgiLx iqē'sqēs qō'ta Lxgā'itix·it. Tsō'yustē nē'xau,
again   he burnt it   blue-jay   that   what they had left.   Evening   it became,

20 aLgiupā'yaLx itguē'ma kˌa ēniā'matk, ka aLi'Xkō. NiXkō'mam
they gathered   small mussels   and   large mussels,   and they went home.   He came home

21 nau'i nixō'kctit. Qˌoā'p ē'lXam aLgiā'xom iqē'sqēs. Ta'kE nēxE'lqamX
at once   he lay down.   Near   the town   they arrived   blue-jay.   Then   he shouted

22 iqē'sqēs: "Ā, Stikuayā', imcā'niamatgā'!" TEmm aLi'Xaua. Ā'LōLx.
blue-jay: "Ah,   Stikua',   your mussels."   Noise of feet   they ran.   They went down to the beach.

23 A'lta aLgiō'kXuiptck itguē'ma kˌa ēniā'matk. Qē'xtcē aqiā'qxōtsˌ
Now   they carried them up   the small mussels   and   the large mussels.   Intending   he was roused

24 qix· ikˌ'ā'sks. Näkct nixā'latck.
that   boy.   Not   he rose.

25 Wāx wiXt nē'ktcuktē. Kawī'X ka nō'xuitXuitck. A'lta wiXt
On the next morning   again   it became day.   Early   and   they made themselves ready.   Now   again

26 atgō'cgiLx utā'Xanīma. Iō'ktik qix· ikˌ'ā'sks iLā'xakˌEmāna iā'xa.
they pushed the canoe into the water   their canoe.   He lay in bed   that   boy   their chief   his son.

1 Näkct iqētō′mEl atcā′yax. Lāx nā′xax oᶜō′Lax. TakE nixā′latck,
   Not   accompanying he did it. Visible became the sun. Then he rose,
   them

2 atcukuēxē′mam tā′nEmckc, ka′nauwē′2 atcukuēxē′mam kᵢa
   he called them together the women, all he called them together and

3 tqā′sōsinikc. "Ai′aq, amckLi′cgam Lō′yuc. Amcx′ō′yutx. Näkct
   the children. "Quick, take urine. Wash yourselves. Not

4 qᵢam mcxā′xō." A′lta atkLō′cgam Lō′yuc tā′nEmckc. Nuxoō′yut,
   lazy be." Now they took it urine the women. They washed
                                                     themselves,

5 ka′nauwē2 nuxoō′yut. "Ai′aq, LEmcxE′ltcam." Ta′kE atcuqoā′na-it
   all they washed "Quick, comb yourselves.' Then he put it down
       themselves,

6 ōmā′p. Laq atcā′yax igitē′tcxal. "TEmcā′nEmckc mckanauwē′tikc
   a plank. Take he did it the piece. "Your husbands your all
          out

7 x·ix·ē′k iōXuē′lax." Mâkct igitē′tcxal atcē′Xtuq gō qaX ōmā′p.
   this they eat it much." Two pieces he put them on that plank.
                                        side by side

8 A′lta Lqu′pLqup atcā′yax igitē′tcxal. A′lta atcLE′lltēkō Lkanauwē′tikc
   Now cut he did it a piece. Now he greased their all of them
                                    heads

9 qō′Lac Lā′nEmckc. AtcLawē′tikō qō′tac tqā′sōsinikc. A′lta Lu′xLux
   those women. He greased their those children. Now pull out of
                  heads   ground

10 atcā′yax ē′nXat. A′lta atcē′lEmēma. Manēx ā′yaxalx·t ē′nXat,
   he did them the wall Now he sharpened them. When wide a wall
             planks.   plank,

11 tcᵢEx atcē′lax. Ka′nauwē atcē′lEmēma. Kē′mk·iti tā′yaqL ikoalē′x·oa.
   split he did it. All he sharpened them. The last his house the raven.

12 Nä2kct Lu′xLux aqā′yax itā′nXat. A′lta atciauwigā′melt gō itā′kōtcX
   Not pull out they were its wall Now he put them into in their backs
          done planks.

13 qix· ē′nXat. Ka′nauwē atciauwigā′melt gō itā′kōtcX ka that!aunā′na.
   those wall planks. All he put them into in their backs those girls.

14 Atctō′lXam: "Tcā mci′Lxa! Manix qīa mcō′ya mā′Lnē, qoā′2nEmi
   He said to them: "Now, go to the When if you go seaward, five times
                          beach!

15 mcixLā′kō qix· iqā′nakc, tcx·ī amcō′Lx mā′Lnē. Manix Lāp
   go around that rock, then go seaward seaward. When find

16 amcgiā′xo-ilEmx igē′pix·L cka amckikLtā′2qo-imx. Qē′uwa Lᵢō′ya
   you will always do them sealions and you will always kill them. Those not giving
                                                                      to stingy
                                                                      people.

17 aqē′mcgax. Nai′ka ntō′kⁿꞀa x·iti′kc tqā′cōcinikc. Ē′wa mā′Lnē x·ik
   you do. I I carry them these children. Thus seaward this

18 ē′maL tgE′lXam tEnxElā′xō." A′lta tsᵢE′xtsᵢEx ā′tcax ō′ckꞀaX;
   sea my relatives they will be to me." Now split he did them sinews;

19 ā′xauē tsᵢE′xtsᵢEx ā′tcax ō′ckꞀax. A′lta ā′tgELx gō Ltcuq qō′tac
   many split he did them sinews. Now they went to water those
                                            down to the sea

20 tā′nEmckc. Lā′wa tcax gō′yē uoxō′xu·il. Qoā′nEmi Laqᶜ nō′xôx gō
   women. Slowly now thus they jumped. Five times turn they did at

21 qix· ē′lXam. Ā′lta ā′tgē yau′a mā′Lnē, a′lta cka aLx·um′ēlā′pXit
   that town. Now they went there seaward, now and it turned inside out

22 Ltcuq. A′lta ā′tgē iau′a mā′Lnē, kā2 Lxaltcx·ā′mal iqē′sqēs. A′lta
   the water. Now they went then seaward, where they always boiled blue-jay. Now
                                                                      food

23 nē′k·im iqē′sqēs: "I′kta x·ik iō′itEt?" A′lta aqixE′lōtcx qix· i′kta.
   he said blue-jay; "What that comes there?" Now the people looked that some-
                                                    at it   thing.

24 Aksō′pEnayux qaX ōhotaunā′na. Qoā′nEmi akē′xLakō iLā′xanakc
   They jumped often those girls. Five times they went around it their rock

25 iqē′sqēs. TakE ka nō′Lxa iau′a mā′Lnē; ka ma′nx·i ka aLE′tit
   blue-jay's. Then and they went there seaward; and a little and they came
                      seaward

LElā′lax aLE′tga; tᵢā′qēa Lᵉā′wulqt gō-y· i′LackႧ qō′La LElā′lax.   1
birds   they came flying;   just   as if blood   at   their bills   those   birds.

A′lta tgiä′wat qō′ta gEnE′mt Llalā′xukc. "Ā, nēkcttcē   2
Now   they followed them   those   small   birds.   "Ah,   not [int. part.]

nēmsā′xaxōmē?" nē′k·im iqē′sqēs: "Llā′laxukc x·itiks tgē′itEt,   3
do you observe it?"   he said   blue-jay: "The birds   then   they come,

qā′xēwa atgatē′mam ē′ka Lgā′pelatikc." TakE nē′k·im ikoalē′x·oa: 4
where   they came   thus   many."   Then   he said   the raven:

"Ia′xka x·ix·ī′x· ciā′kulqᵢ'ast. TEmēa xō′tac mōxoē′LEluXt.'   5
"He   this   his eyes squinting.   Your children   these   you do not recognize them,"

nē′k·im ikoalē′x·oa. Qoä′nEmi atē′xLakō qix· iqā′nakc. A′lta   6
he said   the raven.   Five times   they went around   that   rock.   Now

atciXE′kXuē qaX ōckႧX gō qō′La Lqā′nakc. AtcLō′lXam: "Manix   7
he threw them down   those   sinews   on   those   stones.   He said to them: "When

aLō′yima-itx iqē′sqēs itguē′ma aLigElō′yEma-itx ka qᵢ'E′lqᵢ'El   8
they always go   blue-jay   mussels   they always go to take them   then   fast

mxā′xo-ilEmx." Atcō′lXam qaX tā′nEmckc: "Ōkulā′ma imcā′xal, qiäx   9
you shall always be."   He said to them   those   women: "Killer-whales   your name   if

it!ö′kti ē′kolē tcx·ī mcgiā′xō. Manix igē′pix·Lx amcgēwä′kxemenīLx,   10
a good   whale   then   you will eat it.   When   a sealion   you kill it,

ka mcgē′xElukctguläLx. Qē′wa Lᵢō′ya aqē′mcgax."   11
then   you throw it away.   Those not giving to stingy people   you do."

A′lta aLXLxā′lEm, iqē′sqēs. Nē′k·im qix· ktiä′xēkႧax: "Ai′aq   12
Now   they ate,   blue-jay.   He said   that   hunter: "Quick

lxgō′ya, ka alxauwē′LxoLx. Nēkct qa′nsix ē′ka iā′lkō-ilē alxgēᶜE′lkElax   13
we will go   then   we became afraid at   Not   [any] how   thus   similar to it   we saw
home,   seeing spirits.

gō qix· iqā′nakc." A′lta aLgiupā′yaLx itguē′ma. A′lta atgā′yukⁿႧ   14
at   that   rock."   Now   they gathered them   mussles.   Now   they carried it

qix· iLxgā′ētix·t igē′pix·L. ALgā′yukⁿႧ a′lta. Tsō′yustē ka   15
that   what they had left over   the sealion.   They carried it   now.   In the evening   then

aLXgō′mam. "Ā-y- imcā′tguimatgā′ Stikuayā′!" Kᵢōmm tē′lx·Em.   16
they came home.   "Ah,   your mussels   Stikua′!"   No noise of   people.

Qoä′nEmi qē′xtcē aqaLE′lqamx. A′lta ā′tgEptck qō′tac tē′lx·Em.   17
Five times   intending   she was called.   Now   they went up from the beach   those   people.

A′lta kᵢ'ē-y· itā′nXat qō′ta t!ōLē′ma. A′lta nōxoē′nim tē′lx·Em.   18
Now   nothing   their wall planks   those   houses.   Now   they cried   the people.

NigE′tsax iqē′sqēs. Aqiō′lXam: "kᵢ'ä mE′xax, iqē′sqēs. Qē nēkctx   19
He cried   blue-jay.   He was told: "Silent   be,   blue-jay.   If   not

mai′kXa imē′qᵢ'atxala, pōc nēkct ē′ka atci′lxax ilxā′xakᵢ'Emäna,   20
you   you were bad,   [if]   not   thus   he did to us   our chief,

qē nēkctx mai′kXa imē′qᵢatxala." A′lta tē′Xtka t!ōL atgE′tax   21
if   not   you   you were bad."   Now   one only   house   they made it

kanauwē′tikc, iā′mka ikoalē′x·oa tēx·t tā′yaqL. Ayō′ix nēcktā′x,   22
all.   only he   the raven   one   his house.   He went often,   he searched often on the beach,

ēnā′qxon Lᵢap atciā′x. Ayō′ix nēcktā′x, ūkō′tskōts Lᵢap atcā′x.   23
a sturgeon   find   he did it.   He went often   he searched often on the beach,   porpoise   find   he did it.

Ayō′ix iqē′sqēs qē′xtcē nēcktā′x. Lkā′kXul aLxā′x. Gōyä′ iLā′qa-iLa   24
He went often   blue-jay   intending   he searched often on the beach.   Hail   it became.   Thus   large

Lkā′kXul. Qē′xtcē aLē′gElo-ix itguē′ma. Qē′xtcē tcᵢu′xtcᵢux aLgiā′x.   25
hail.   Intending   he gathered often   mussels.   Intending   breaking off   he did them.

Qxā′oxaL tcᵢux nēxā′x. Tā′mēnua aLxā′x aLXgō′x. Ayō′ix ikoalē′x·oa   26
Cannot   breaking off   he did.   Giving up   he became   he went home.   He went often   the raven

1 nĕcktā′x. Niktcā′xā-itx. Ŏ⌐1Xaiū L¡ap atcā′x. Ctā′mkXa cgē′san
 he searched   He cried much.   A seal   find   he did it.   Only   roots
 at the beach.

2 aLkcā′xo-itx. AtcLE′nk¡ēmEnakō iLā′xak¡Emāna.
 they ate them.   He took revenge on them   their chief.

Translation.

Many people were living at Nakot!ā′t. Now their chief died. He had [left] a son who was almost grown up. It was winter and the people were hungry. They had only mussels and roots to eat. Once upon a time a hunter said: "Make yourselves ready." All the men made themselves ready and went seaward in two canoes. Then the hunter speared a sealion. It jumped and drifted on the water [dead]. They hauled it ashore. Blue-Jay said: "Let us boil it here." They made a fire and singed it. They cut it and boiled it. Blue-Jay said: "Let us eat it here, let us eat all of it!" Then the people ate. Raven tried to hide a piece of meat in his mat and carried it to the canoe. [But] Blue-Jay [had already seen it]; he ran [after him], took it and threw it into the fire. He burned it. Then they went home. They gathered large and small mussels. In the evening they came home. Then Blue-Jay shouted : "Stikua', fetch your mussels!" Stikua' was the name of Blue Jay's wife. Then noise of many feet [was heard], and Stikua' and the other women came running down to the beach. They went to fetch mussels. The women came to the beach and carried the mussels to the house. Raven took care of the chief's son. The boy said: "To-morrow I shall accompany you." "Blue-Jay said to him: "What do you want to do? The waves will carry you away, you will drift away; even I almost drifted away."

The next morning they made themselves ready. They went into the canoe and the boy came down to the beach. He wanted to accompany them and held on to the canoe. "Go to the house; go to the house," said Blue-Jay. The boy went up, but he was very sad. Then Blue-Jay said: "Let us leave him." The people began to paddle. Then they arrived at the sealion island. The hunter went ashore and speared a sealion. It jumped and drifted on the water [dead]. They hauled it ashore and pulled it up from the water. Blue-Jay said: "Let us eat it here; let us eat all of it, else our chief's son would always want to come here." They singed it, carved it, and boiled it there. When it was done they ate it all. Raven tried to hide a piece in his hair, but Blue-Jay took it out immediately and burned it. In the evening they gathered large and small mussels and then they went home. When they approached the beach Blue-Jay shouted: "Stikua', fetch your mussels!" Then noise of many feet [was heard]. Stikua' and her children and all the other women came running down to the beach and carried the mussels up to the house. Blue-Jay had told all those people: "Don't tell our chief's son, else he will want to accompany us." In the evening the boy said: "To-morrow I shall accompany you."

But Blue-Jay said: "What do you want to do? The confounded waves will carry you away." But the boy replied: "I must go."

In the morning they made themselves ready for the third time. The boy went down to the beach and took hold of the canoe. But Blue-Jay pushed him aside and said: "What do you want here? Go to the house." The boy cried and went up to the house. [When he turned back] Blue-Jay said: "Now paddle away. We will leave him." The people began to paddle and soon they reached the sealion island. The hunter went ashore and speared one large sealion. It jumped and drifted on the water [dead]. They hauled it toward the shore, landed, pulled it up and singed it. They finished singeing it. Then they carved it and boiled it, and when it was done they began to eat. Blue-Jay said: "Let us eat it all, nobody must speak about it, else our chief's son will always want to accompany us." A little [meat] was still left when they had eaten enough. Raven tried to take a piece along. He tied it to his leg and said his leg was broken. Blue-Jay burned all that was left over. Then he said to Raven: "Let me see your leg." He jumped at it, untied it and found the piece of meat at Raven's leg. He took it and burned it. In the evening they gathered large and small mussels. Then they went home. When they were near home Blue-Jay shouted: "Stikua', fetch your mussels!" Then noise of many feet [was heard] and Stikua' [her children and the other women] came down to the beach and carried the mussels up to the house. The [women and children] and the chief's son ate the mussels all night. Then that boy said: "To-morrow I shall accompany you." Blue-Jay said: "What do you want to do? You will drift away. If I had not taken hold of the canoe I should have drifted away twice."

On the next morning they made themselves ready for the fourth time. The boy rose and made himself ready also. The people hauled their canoes into the water and went aboard. The boy tried to board the canoe also, but Blue-Jay took hold of him and threw him into the water. He stood in the water up to his waist. He held the canoe, but Blue-Jay struck his hands. There he stood. He cried, and cried, and went up to the house. The people went; they paddled and soon they reached the sealion island. The hunter went ashore and speared a sealion. It jumped and drifted on the water [dead]. Again they towed it to the island and pulled it ashore. They singed it. When they had finished singeing it they carved it and boiled it. When it was done Blue-Jay said: "Let us eat it here." They ate half of it and were satiated. They slept because they had eaten too much. Blue-Jay awoke first and burned all that was left. In the evening they gathered large and small mussels and went home. When they were near the shore he shouted: "Stikua', fetch your mussels!" Noise of many feet [was heard] and Stikua' [her children and the other women] came running down to the beach and carried up the mussels. The boy said: "To-morrow I shall accompany you." But Blue-Jay replied:

"What do you want to do? We might capsize and you would be drowned."

Early on the following morning the people made themselves ready. The boy arose and made himself ready also. Blue-Jay and the people hauled their canoes down to the water. The boy tried to board it, but Blue-Jay threw him into the water. He tried to hold the canoe. The water reached up to his armpits. Blue-Jay struck his hands [until he let go]. Then the boy cried and cried. Blue-Jay and the other people went away.

After some time the boy went up from the beach. He took his arrows and walked around a point of land. There he met a young eagle and shot it. He skinned it and tried to put the skin on. It was too small, it reached scarcely to his knees. Then he took it off and went on. After awhile he met another eagle. He shot it and it fell down. It was a white-headed eagle. He skinned it and tried the skin on, but it was too small. It reached a little below his knees. He took it off, left it, and went on. Soon he met a bald-headed eagle. He shot it twice and it fell down. He skinned it and put the skin on. It was nearly large enough for him, and he tried to fly. He could fly downward only. He did not rise. He turned back, and now he could fly. Now he went around the point seaward from Nakōt!ā't. When he had nearly gone around he smelled smoke of burning fat. When he came around the point he saw the people of his town. He alighted on top of a tree and looked down. [He saw that] they had boiled a sealion and that they ate it. When they had nearly finished eating he flew up. He thought: "O, I wish Blue-Jay would see me." Then Blue-Jay looked up [and saw] the bird flying about. "Ah, a bird came to get food from us." Five times the eagle gyrated over the fire, then it descended. Blue-Jay took a piece of blubber and said: "I will give you this to eat. The bird came down, grasped the piece of meat and flew away. "Ha!" said Blue-Jay, "that bird has feet like a man." When the people had eaten enough they slept. Raven hid again a piece of meat. Toward evening they awoke and ate again; then Blue-Jay burned the rest of their food. In the evening they gathered large and small mussels and went home. When the boy came home he lay down at once. They approached the village and Blue-Jay shouted: "Fetch your mussels, Stikua'!" Noise of many feet [was heard] and Stikua' [and the other women] ran down to the beach and carried up the mussels. They tried to rouse the boy, but he did not arise.

The next morning the people made themselves ready and launched their canoe. The chief's son stayed in bed and did not attempt to accompany them. After sunrise he rose and called the women and children and said: "Take urine and wash yourselves, be quick." The women obeyed and washed themselves. He continued: "Comb your hair." Then he put down a plank, took the piece of meat out [from under his blanket, showed it to the women and said|: "Every day your husbands eat this." He put two pieces side by side on the plank, cut them to pieces and greased the heads of all the women and children. Then he pulled the planks forming the walls of the houses out of the ground. He sharpened them [at one end and] those which were very wide he split in two. He sharpened all of them. The last house of the village was that of Raven. He did not pull out its wall-planks. He put the planks on to the backs of the women and children and said: "Go down to the beach, when you go seaward swim five times around that rock. Then go seaward. When you see sealions you shall kill them. But you shall not give anything to stingy people. I shall take these children down. They shall live on the sea and be my relatives."

Then he split sinews. The women went into the water and began to jump [out of the water]. They swam five times back and forth in front of the village. Then they went seaward plowing through the water Now they went seaward to the place where Blue-Jay and the men were boiling. Blue-Jay said to the men: "What is that?" The men looked and saw the girls jumping. Five times they swam around Blue-Jay's rock. Then they went seaward. After awhile birds came flying to the island. Their bills were [as red] as blood. They followed [the fish]. "Ah," said Blue-Jay: "Do you notice them? Whence come these numerous birds?" The Raven said: "Ha, squinteye, they are your children; do you not recognize them?" Five times they went around that rock. Now [the boy] threw the sinews down upon the stones and said: "When Blue-Jay comes to gather mussels they shall be fast [to the rocks]." And he said to the women, turning toward the sea: "Whale-Killer will be your name; when you catch a whale you will eat it, but when you catch a sealion you will throw it away, but you shall not give anything to stingy people."

Blue-Jay and the people were eating. Then that hunter said: "Let us go home. I am afraid we have seen evil spirits; we have never seen anything like that on this rock." Now they gathered mussels and carried along the meat which they had left over. In the evening they came near their home. [Blue-Jay shouted:] "Stikua', fetch your mussels!" There was no sound of people. Five times he called. Now the people went ashore and [they saw that] the walls of the houses had disap_peared. The people cried. Blue-Jay cried also, but somebody said to him: "Be quiet, Blue-Jay; if you had not been bad our chief's son would not have done so." Now they all made one house. Only Raven had one house [by himself]. He went and searched for food on the beach. He found a sturgeon. He went again to the beach and found a porpoise. Then Blue-Jay went to the beach and tried to search for food. [As soon as he went out] it began to hail; the hail-stones were so large [indicating]. He tried to gather mussels and wanted to break them off, but they did not come off. He could not break them off. He gave it up. Raven went to search on the beach and found a seal. The others ate roots only. Thus their chief took revenge on them.

12. Ō′PENPEN ITCĀ′KXANAM.

THE SKUNK HER STORY.

A′lta nä′ktcXEm qaX ukō′nax. A′lta t!ōL agE′tax, tä′qoa-iL
Now   she sang her con- that chieftainess. Now a house she made it, a large
      juror's song

2 t!ōL agE′tax. A′lta agō′xuqtc tê′lx·Em. Ta′kE atxē′gēla-i tê′lx·Em.
  house she made it. Now she invited them people. Then they landed the people.

3 Tciä′xuwaltck iqē′sqēs qaX ukō′nax. "Ā, akcEma x·itac
  He helped her singing blue-jay that chieftainess. "Ah, who   there

4 ōxuiwä′yutcgō?" "Ā-y- ō′mōa x·iLā′c kLx·iluwä′yutcgō." A′lta
  they dance?" "Ah, maggots these they dancing. Now

5 Lgitxtä′maē ō′mōa:
  they entered the the maggots:
  house to dance

"Antsgiō′lats, antsgiō′lats iqō′tEn, iqō′tEn. Antsgiō′lats, antsgiō′lats
"We make it move, we make it move [?] [?]. We make it move, we make it move,

7 iqō′tEn, iqō′tEn."
  [?]   [?]."

TakE nix·inō′tēn iqē′sqēs. AqLilgē′qxo-im LēXt Lqoä′k. Atcō′lXam
Then he joined their blue-jay, He was given in pay one mountain- He said to her
     song   for his help   goat blanket.

9 uyä′k·ikala: "LuXLXā′nagō′, ōq̣ōyō′qxōt!" TakE nä′k·im: "Ḷ lōp
  his wife: "Put it on,   old woman!"   Then she said: "[?]

10 Ḷ lōp nēx nēx tcū tcū!" "Ḳa nauē′tkaa," nē′k·im iqē′sqēs. "Lē′Xat
   [?] [?] [?] [?] [?]!" "And indeed,"   he said blue-jay, "oue

11 na qLä′qēwam LE′x·aōt, pōs namXLXā′nagō it!ō′ktē?" WiXt
   [int. conjuror assembles, if you put on   a good one?" Again
   part.]

12 atktō′pEna tgä′ēwam tê′lx·Em gō-y- icq iqē′p!al. "Ā, akcEma x·itac
   they uttered their song people at in front doorway. "Ah, who then
                            of house

13 ōxuiwä′yutcgō?" "Ā, LḳElaḳElä′max x·iLac kLx·Eluwä′yutcgō."
   they dance?" "Ah, the geese these they dancing."

14 A′lta aLgiō′xtamai LḳElaḳElä′ma:
   Now they entered the the geese:
        house to dance

‖: Antsgä′yilEmē′matsq ē′maL uyä′tstpa gū′tstpa gū′tspa: ‖
We pull it out and it drifts the bay its sea grass, grass, grass.

AqLē′luqL iqē′sqēs LḳElaḳElä′ma kLkēx L′ōk. NōXuinä′Xit gō
They carried to him blue-jay geese being blanket. They stood at

17 iqē′p!al tê′lx·Em: "Ā akcEma x·itac oxuiwä′yutcgō?" "Ā-y-
   the doorway people: "Ah, who then they dance?" "Ah,

18 imō′lEkuma:
   the elks:"

"‖: Nä′caikā′ antcgä′wicilä′ poqō′XumāX, acilä′ ci′lē, acilä′
We   we hiss [on] bluffs, hiss, zz, zz,

20 ci′lē.: ‖"
   zz."

TakE nix·Enō′tē iqē′sqēs:
Then he joined their song Blue-jay:

144

"‖: Nä´caikā´ antcgā´wicilä´ poqō´Xumä´X, acilä´, ci´lē acilä´ ci´lē:‖" 1
"We   we hiss   [on] bluffs,   hiss,   zz,   zz,   zz."

Aqē´lukꞬ imō´lEqan iqē´sqēs. Atcō´lXam uyā´k·ikala: 2
It was brought to him   a young elk   blue-jay.   He said to her   his wife:
[blanket]

"ĒmXLXā´nakō-y· ōqᵢōyō´qXut!" Agiō´lXam: "Lᵢlōp Lᵢlōp, nēx 3
"Put it on   old woman!"   She said to him: "[?]   [,?]   [?]

nēx tcū tcū." "Kᵢa nauē´tkaa Lē´Xat na qLā´qēwam LE´x·a-ōt, pōs 4
[?]   [?]   [?]."   "And   indeed   one   [int.   conjuror   assembles,   if
part.]

na mXLXā´nakō it!ō´ktē?" WiXt nōXo-inā´Xit tê´l·xEm gō iqē´p!al. 5
[int.   you put on   a good one?"   Again   they stood   people   in   the door-
part.]   way.

"Ā, akcEma x·itac ōXo-inä´Xit, ōxo-iwā´yutcgō?" "Ā, Llēqᵢā´mukc." 6
"Ah,   who   then   they stand   they dance?"   "Ah,   the wolves."

"Nē´saikā´ qLE´nsxit nä´tkankuē´l kᵢa cx·tä´mtx·ï´x. A, 7
"We   we haul with our   [?]   and   the deer fawn.   Ah,
           mouths

qLLEncā´nEmkōti´kcä kōti´kca kōti´kca." 8
we have our faces blackened,   blackened,   blackened."

Nix·nō´ti iqē´sqēs. AqLē´lukꞬ Llē´qᵢamL kLkēx L´ōk. 9
He helped   blue-jay.   It was carried   wolves   being   blanket.
singing   to him

Aktcxā´mal ō´pEnpEn tä´nox: 10
She sang much her   skunk   separate:
conjuror's song

"Axlā´wat, axlā´wat, untāmēwā´lEma qix· iqē´sqēs ā, qix· iqē´sqēs." 11
"Together,   together,   our dead people   that   blue-jay,   that   blue-jay."

A´lta nē´k·im iqē´sqēs: "Mō´pa kā´sa-it. Ngē´ma." "Nä2, hō´ntcin 12
Now   he said   blue-jay: "Go out   robin.   I shall speak."   "No,   do not

ēmilqᵢē´latcx·ita. Ā´xka xilgē´ma i´kta iaxagElā´xō. Qāna qēna 13
you will be a silent one   She   she will speak   what   she resolves it.   When   if [int.
                              to herself   [int. part.]   part.]

mōlā´ma?" 14
you say to her?"

Ta´kE wiXt nōXoinā´Xit tê´lx·Em. "Ā, akcEma x·itac 15
Then   again   they stood   people.   "Ah,   who   then

kLgūwā´yutckō?" "Lcayā´mukc." A´lta aLx·Eluwā´yutck Lcayā´mukc. 16
they dancing?"   "The grizzly bears."   Now   they danced   the grizzly bears.

Iō´Lqtē aLx·Eluwā´yutck gō wē´wuLē. Ta´kE aLE´k·im LgōLē´lEXEmk 17
Long   they danced   in the interior   Then   he said   a person
                             of the house.

gō kᵘLā´xanē: "Qantsī´x aLtpā´ya? LāmkXa tikcna? Kᵢa iō´Lqtē 18
at   outside: "When   they go out?   Only   these   And   long
                                    [int. part.]?

ta´kE aLx·Eluwāyul." TakE nē´k·im Lcayā´mukc iLā´XakᵢEmana: 19
then   they dance much."   Then   he said   the grizzly bears   their chief:

"La´kcta x·iLa-y- ē´ka qLxā´xo-il? Lᵢ E´xLᵢEx aniä´xō-y- ī´LaL´a. 20
"Who   that   thus   saying much?   Tear   I shall do it   his body.

NLuwu´lᵏaya." "Nai´kXa-y- ē´ka anxā´xo-il. E´natka giä´nEptēma. 21
I shall eat him."   "I   thus   I said much.   One side only   my braid.

Manix anLE´lgap!ax LgōLē´lXEmk, näkct naxl·´wulX ōᶜō´Lax, 22
When   I enter him   a person,   not   he gets high up   the sun,

ā´nqatē aLō´mEqtx." TakE atclō´lXam tiä´cōlal: "Ai´aq a´lta 23
already   he dies."   Then   he said to them   his relatives: "Quick   now

lxō´pa. Ā´tElaktikc Lx·Eluwā´yutcko. TaLᵢ ōkulaī´tanEma 24
we will go out.   They next   they dance.   Behold   the arrows

qExkcE´xtEna." Ta´kE ā´LElaktikc LEntsᵢE´xuks LxEluwa´yutckō. 25
they growl."   Then   they next   the Entsᵢxs   they danced.

A´lta LkcikEmuXulā´ma ilē´ē LEntsᵢE´xuks: 26
Now   they beat fast time   the ground   the Entsᵢxs:
         [made shake]

"Āntsgiō´layā´ ilē´ē qtEntsā´ēwē gEnE´ma," aLE´k·im 27
"We made it shake   the ground   our legs   small,"   they said

1 LEnts̯; E'xuks̯. A'lta nē'k·im iqē'sqēs: "LE, q̣i'axtsē'Lx Lā'ᶜowit,
the Ents; xs.   Now   he said   blue-jay: "Ha,   how bad   their legs,'

2 La'ska ā'Lqī aLgiōlā'ya-y- ilē'ē. Qōi ska ḳā aLXkē'x
they   later on   they will shake it   the ground.   Shall   and   silent   they are

3 giLā'q̣i atxalEma." A'lta aLx·Eluwā'yutck LEnts̯; E'xukc, ka mE'nx·i
the bad ones."   Now   they danced   the Ents; xs,   and   a little

4 ka nō'xōla qō'ta t!ōL ka nē'xela ilē'ē. Ayō'tXuita iqē'sqēs:
and   it shook   that   house   and   it shook   the ground.   He stood up   blue-jay:

5 "Lā'wa, Lā'wa, Lā'wa, Lā'wa ā'wima! TgEluktcuwā'ya tik t!ōL."
"Slowly,   slowly,   slowly,   slowly   younger   It will fall down   this   house."
                                         brothers!

6 ALā'LXuL̯; LEnts̯; E'xukc aLx·Eluwā'yul. A'lta ā'LElaXtikc
They finished   the Ents; xs   they danced.   Now   they next

7 Lq̣i acpalē' Lx·Eluwā'yutck. Lgīuxtā'mai. It̯iā'lapas ī'Lax·ala. A'lta
the gray cranes   they danced.   They entered to   Coyote   their husband.   Now
                                              dance.

8 nē'ktcxam it̯iā'lapas: "Nikct iLx·atuā'nᵘk̯ɪ ā'tsē. Amā'Lgum
he sang his con-   Coyote: "Not   look back often   younger   You will make
juror's song   sister.

9 ḳā'mitapa witxā'qôk." Ā'taqc ā'ēXat ugō'xō. Lq̣iōp atcī'ax
that they make a   our children."   He bit   one   her daughter.   Cut   he did it
mistake in their
dance

10 itcā'tuk. ALā'2LXuL̯; aLx·Eluwā'yutck. A'LElaktikc skē'pXoa
her neck.   They finished   they danced.   Next they   the rabbits

11 aLx·Eluwā'yutck:
    they danced:

"Lā'q mExā'nxala walā'patē' hēhâ' hēhâ'! Ēmē'maq ayā'mElax

"Going out   you do for me   post   hēhâ   hēhâ!   Shooting you I do it to you
of way

hēhâ' hēhâ.

13
hēhâ   hēhâ.

Tccalā'tit uyā'pL̯ik: TakE nē'k·im iqē'sqēs:
He spanned it   his bow.   Then   he said   blue-jay:

"Lāq mxē'xela witsō'Xuix· walā'patē, hēhâ; ēmē'maq
"Going out   you do for him   my younger brother   post,   hēhá;   shooting you
of way

16 tcimElō'xoax hēhâ!"
he does it to you   hēhá!"

AqLē'lukᵘɪ skē'pXoa kLkēx L'ōk. "LEmxLx·ā'nakō-y-
It was brought   rabbit   being   blanket.   "Put it on
to him

18 ōq̣ioyō'qxut!" "L̯iōp L̯iōp nēx nēx tcū tcū." "Tc̯a nalauwē'tkaa
old woman!"   "[ʔ]   [ʔ]   [ʔj   [ʔ]   [ʔ]   [ʔ]"   "Well   indeed

19 Lē'Xat na qLā'qēwam LE'x·ā-ōt, pōs na mXLXā'nakō it!ō'ktē?"
one [int.   conjuror   assembles,   if [int.   you put it on   a good one?"
part.]   part.]

Akä'2x qaX ukō'nax ā'ktcxEm:
Often   that   chieftainess   she sang her con-
                         juror's song:

"AxElā'wat, axElā'wat ntā'mēwalEma ā qix· iqē'sqēs, ā qix·
"Together,   together   our dead ones   ah   that   blue-jay,   ah   that

22 iqē'sqēs m-m."
blue-jay   m-m."

Ta'kE wiXt atciō'lXam ia'xk'un iqē'sqēs: "Mō'pa kā'sa-it. Ta'kE
Then   again   he said to him   his elder   blue-jay: "Go out   robin.   Then
                           brother

24 ō'lō agā'nax. Ai'aq iō'mEqta x·ix· ē'kōlē. Ngēmai." Ta'kE
hunger   it acts on   Quick   it will be dead   this   whale.   I shall speak."   Then
me.

nĕ'k·im kā'sa-it: "Iä x·ix· ĕ'kik. Mā'mkXa na mā'kxEmt? Ā'xka   1
he said   robin: "Iä   this   one.   You alone   [int.   you see it!   She
    part.]

xalgĕ'mai i'kta-y- axagElā'xō." Qoä'nEmi atciō'lXam iä'xk'un   2
she will say   what   she will do herself."   Five times   he said to him   his elder
herself   brother

iupā'ya. Näket ayō'pa skā'sa-it. A'lta na-ixa'lqamx iqē'sqēs: 3
he shall go   Not   he went out   robin.   Now   he shouted   blue-jay:
out.

"Ugô'ōicqc ō'pEnpEn. Ē'tcats; a agia'laut qa ik¡uanō'm agiä'xo il."   4
"She a farter   skunk.   Her sickness   she makes on   when   potlatch   she always
                 him   makes."

Pō naxE'lwicqc, ac iä'xkatē ac ĕ'k·¡ilapx·il nicilgā'kxo-it ĕ'kolē.   5
Blow-   she farts,   and   then   and   falling over   he lay on his back   the whale.
ing

Atciō'pēwē iqē'sqēs. Ayugōō'L¡ō it ayawēä'yakuit. A'lta aqā'yaxc   6
He blew him away   blue-jay.   He flew away and   he was squeezed into   Now   it was cut
                 stuck to it   a hole.

qix· ĕ'kolē. Kanauwē' tĕ'lx·Em atgā'yaxc. Qä2xtcē na-ixE'lqamx   7
that   whale.   All   people   they cut it.   Intending   he shouted

iqē'sqēs: "Laqⁿ nE'xa kā'sa-it." Aqiō'tctXum, ka'nauwē aqā'yaxc,   8
blue-jay: "Take out   do me   robin."   It was finished,   all   it was cut,

tcx·ī ayōĕ'wulXt kā'sa-it, tcx·ī Laqⁿ atcā'yax. A'lta iä'mkXa qix·   9
then   he went up   robin,   then   take out   he did him.   Now   only   that

ĕ'Lwulē atcā'yaxc iqē'sqēs.   10
its meat   he cut it   blue-jay.

Translation.

A chieftainess sang her conjurer's song. She made a large house and invited the people. The people landed. Blue-Jay was the chorus leader of the chieftainess. "Who are those outside who want to dance?" "Ah, the maggots; they will dance." Now the maggots entered; they sang: "We make move the rotten meat; we make move the rotten meat." Blue-Jay joined their song and they gave him a mountain goat blanket in payment. He said to his wife: "Put it on, old woman." But she replied; "Llop, Llop, nēq, nēq, tcu, tcu." "Certainly," said Blue-Jay, "when conjurers assemble it is better not to put on beautiful clothing." Now other people sang in front of the door. "Who are those who want to dance?" "Ah, the geese; they want to dance." Now the geese entered; they sang: "We pull out the sea-grass, the sea-grass, the sea-grass, and it drifts away." They gave Blue-Jay in payment a blanket made of geese skins. Other people stood at the door. "Who are those who want to dance?" "Ah, the elks; they want to dance." Now they entered and sang: "We hiss on bluffs; we make z-z-z on bluffs." Blue-Jay joined their song: "You hiss on bluffs." They gave him a blanket made of the skin of a young elk in payment. He said to his wife: "Put it on, old woman." She replied: "Llop, Llop, nēq, nēq, tcu, tcu." "Certainly," said Blue-Jay, "when conjurers assemble it is better not to put on beautiful clothing." Again people stood at the door. "Who are those who want to dance?" "The wolves; they want to dance." They entered and sang: "We carry deer-fawns in our mouths; we have our faces blackened." Blue-Jay joined their song and they gave him a wolf blanket in payment.

The chieftainess, the skunk, was singing by herself: "Blue-Jay's and my ancestors used to keep company." Blue-Jay said to his brother: "Robin, go out, I shall speak to her." Robin replied: "No, be quiet, do not speak to her, she will say herself what she resolves to do. Do not speak to her."

Then more people stood in front of the door. "Ah, who are those who want to dance?" "The grizzly bears." Now the grizzly bears danced. They danced a long time in the house. Then a person said outside: "When will they go out; do they think they alone want to dance?" Then the chief of the grizzly bears said: "Who is talking there? I shall tear him to pieces; I shall eat him." "I am talking; I have a braid on one side of my head only. When I enter a man in the morning he must die before noon." Then the grizzly bear said to his people: "Let us go out and let them dance. Behold the arrows are growling."

Next the birds Ēntsₗx danced. They sang in a rapid movement: "Our legs are small, but we make the ground shake." Blue-Jay said: "Ha, how miserable are your legs, they will make the ground shake! Be quiet, you bad people." The birds danced and after a little while the house began to shake. Blue-Jay arose and said: "Slowly, slowly, slowly, younger brothers, the house will fall." The birds finished dancing, and next the gray cranes began to dance. Coyote was their husband. He sang his shaman's song, "Do not look back, younger sister, because you cause our children to make mistakes." Then he bit one of the children and tore off his neck. After they finished dancing the rabbits came and sang: "Step aside, step aside, post, heha, heha, I will shoot you, heha, heha!" He spanned his bow and Blue-Jay said: "Step aside for my younger brother, post, heha, else he will shoot you, heha!" They gave him a blanket made of rabbit skins. [Blue-Jay gave it to his wife and said:] " _ut it on, old woman." She replied: "Llop, Llop, nēq, nēq, tcu, tcu." "O, yes," remarked Blue-Jay, "when conjurers assemble it is better not to put on beautiful clothing." Now the chieftainess continued to sing her conjurer's song: "Blue-Jay's and my ancestors used to keep company, m-m-m-m." Again Blue-Jay said to his brother: "Go out, Robin, I am hungry. She shall kill the whale quickly." Robin replied: "Iä, do you think you alone see this? She will say herself what she wants to do." Five times Blue-Jay said to his elder brother to go out, but Robin did not leave the house. Then Blue-Jay shouted: "The skunk is a wind-maker; she will make sick those whom she invited to the dance." She made wind and the whale fell down dead right there. Blue-Jay was blown away and he was caught in a knot-hole in the wall, in which he stuck. Now the people cut the whale. Blue-Jay cried: "Take me out, Robin, take me out." When the whale was all cut, Robin went up and took him out. Then Blue-Jay cut the meat only.

13. SKĀ'SA-IT ICTĀ'KXANAM K¡A IQĒ'SQĒS.

ROBIN THEIR MYTH AND BLUE-JAY'S.

Cxēlā'itX	ckā'sa it.	Ā'lta-y-ŏ'lŏ-y-	agE'ctax.	QãxLxnaᵋā'Lax:	1
There was	robin.	Now hunger	it did him.	One day:	

"Ai'aq,	mxE'ltXuitck	kā'sa·it,"	nē'k·im	iqē'sqēs.	A'lta	ā'cto	gō	2
' Quick,	make·yourself ready	robin,"	he said	blue·jay.	Now	they two	to went	

wē'kua.	Gŏ-y-ēnLē'x·atk	acxgā'mita.	TakE	naēxE'lqamx:	"Â,	3
the ocean.	In a slough	they were in canoe.	Then	he shouted:	"Ah,	

ınxātālā'ptck	gitsākxēwā'm!"	TakE	naxE'lqamx	gitsā'kxēwām.	4
come shoreward	sleeper."	Then	she shouted	the sleeper.	

Ē'maLna	nēLā'et.	TakE	wiXt	na-ēxE'lqamx	iqē'sqēs:	"Xoā'u	5
Seaward from him	she was.	Then	again	he shouted	blue·jay:	"Why	

mxaLē'Lx!	QtumgElŏ'kstxa,	iqsŏ'tElŏtElŏ	tiā'ᶜwit."	TakE	wiXt	6
do you go seaward?	Something is carried to you,	[a bird with long legs]	his legs."	Then	again	

naxE'lqamx	gitsa'kxēwam.	Q¡oā'p	ē'maLna	nēLā'-ēt.	WiXt	7
she shouted	the sleeper.	Nearly	seaward from him	she was.	Again	

atcŏ'lXam:	"Xoā'u	mxaLē'Lx!	QtumgElŏ'kstxa,	iqsŏ'tElŏtElŏ	8
he said to her:	" Why	do you go seaward?	Something is carried to you,	[a bird with long legs]	

tiā'ᶜwit."	Qoā'nEmi	atcā'lqamx.	Alā'xti	naxa-igE'cgiptck.	A'lta	9
his legs."	Five times	he called her.	Next	she swam shoreward.	Now	

atcā'lEk·ikc.	Aci'Xkŏ	a'lta.	Acgakqā'na-it	ictā'k¡ētēnax.	10
he speared her.	They two went home	now.	They put it into the canoe	what they had killed.	

AcXgŏ'mam;	ā'ctŏptck.	Atciŏ'lXam	iāXk'un:	"MxE'lgiLx,	11
They arrived at home;	they went inland.	He said to him	his elder brother:	"Make fire,	

kā'sa-it!"	Na-ixE'lgiLx	skā'sa-it.	A'yuLx	iqē'sqēs,	atcŏLā'taptck	12
robin!"	He made fire	robin.	He went seaward	blue·jay,	he carried it inland	

iā'k¡ētēnax.	A'lta	nixE'lgēxs	iqē'sqēs.	Ta'ke	nē'k·im	skā'sa-it:	13
what he had killed.	Now	he cut	blue·jay.	Then	he said	robin:	

"Nai'kXa	Lgā'lict,	nai'kXa	Lgā'mŏkuē,	nai'kXa	ūgŏ'k'ultcin."	14
"My	my tail,	my	my flesh under the chin,	my	my head."	

Ta'kE	nix·E'Lx·a	iqē'sqēs:	"MxElgē'x·ēalē,	mxElgē'x·ēalē.	Tgiā'xŏ	15
Then	he became angry	blue·Jay:	"You ask for it,	you ask for it.	They will eat it	

Q¡tē'nsē	x·ik	ē'kta	aqēmE'lua."	Ta'kE	nigE'tsax	kā'sa-it.	16
Q¡tē'nsē	this	that	it was killed for you."	Then	he cried	robin.	

Atciŏ'cgam	iā'xŏtckin.	Ayŏ'pa.	A'lta	nigE'tsax	kᵘLā'xanī.	17
He took it	his work.	He went out.	Now	he cried	outside.	

ALā'xŏL¡	nixE'lgixc	iqē'sqēs.	TakE	atcigE'lxēm	iā'xk¡un:	18
He finished	he cut	blue·jay.	Then	he called him	his elder brother:	

"Mä'tp!a,	mä'tp!a	Lmē'xauyam	Lmä'mŏkuē	mai'kXa,	Lmä'mŏkXuē	19
"Come in,	come in	you poor one,	your flesh under the chin	yours,	your flesh under the chin	

mai'kXa;	ōmä'k¡ultcin	mai'kXa;	LEmä'lēct	mai'kXa."	Ta'kE	ā'yŏp!	20
yours;	your head	yours;	your tail	yours."	Then	he entered	

skā'sa-it.	A'lta	acxgē'ktcikt	ictā'lEktcal;	ta'kE	acxLxā'lEm.	Iŏ'Lqtē	21
robin.	Now	it was done	what they roasted;	then	they ate.	A long time	

acxē'la-it.	Nix·gē'qauwakŏ	iqē'sqēs.	"Kā'sa-it,"	atciŏ'lXam	22
they stayed.	He dreamt	blue·jay.	"Robin,"	he said to him to	

iā'xk¡un,	"aqantgā'lEmam;	anx·gē'qauwakŏ	nuguilā'ita."	Ta'kE	23
his elder brother."	"people came to fetch us;	I dreamt	I shall cure by means of sorcery."	Then	

1 acxēlā'-it. · A'lta Lō'itEt iLxEnxEnē'mate.   Q¡oā'p aLxē'gēla-ē,
   'they two stayed. Now they came they who wailed while Nearly they landed,
                                        traveling.

2 ackugoā'laq⸱ a'lta ōgoē'xgoēx. Nexā'-ēgila-ē. Aqiō'lXam iqē'sqĕs:
   they two recognized now the ducks. They landed. He was told blue jay:

3 "Ā, ayin'uyā'xit imtā'qix·. Iamtgā'lEmam, mīgēlā'-ēta-ē." Nĕ'k·im
   "Ah, he chokes your brother- I came to fetch you, you shall cure him by He said
                    in-law.   means of sorcery."

4 iqē'sqĕs: "ntō'ya." A'lta acxE'ltXuitck iqē'sqĕs. A'lta ā'cto.
   blue-jay: "We will go." Now they made themselves blue-jay. Now they
                              ready   went.

5 Atciō'lXam iā'xk'un: "Mgē'ma kā'sa-it: 'ĔXt ikak¡ō'Litx·
   He said to him [to] his elder "Say robin: 'One lake
                        brother:

6 gitxalEmē'mtōma igō'n ē'nata.' Ē'ka mōlā'ma manix anigēlā'-ētaē."
   she will pay us for curing also one side' Thus you will say when I cure him by means
   him   of sorcery."

7 Nĕ'k·im skā'sa-it: "Ā'yipē!" Acxē'gila-ē. A'lta cka ci'llcill uya'Lutck
   He said robin: "Well!" They landed. Now and rattling his breath

8 itcā'k·ikal ōgoē'xgoēx. A'lta ayuguē'la-it iqē'sqĕs:
   her husband the duck's. Now he cured him by blue-jay:
                            means of sorcery

   Ka iaXā'lak, ka iaXā'lagE' kaxuntā'gEmēmtō'm agun ā'nata.

   And both sides, and both sides we are paid for curing him and its one side.

10 Kulā'yi tā'noxuē ōqoē'xqoēx axEnō'tēm: "Qoē'x ā'nata
   Far another (song) the female duck helped singing: "Qoē'x one side

11 LEmtăLtx·Enā'n!" Ā, Laq° atcā'ēxax qax ēn'ō'L¡ō-it. T!ayā'
   your nephews!" Ah, out he made it that what choked him. Well

12 atcā'yax, t!ayā' nē'xax. A'lta acktōpā'yaLx ctā'kemē'mtōm
   he made him, well he got. Now they gathered what they had received
                                                    in pay for curing him

13 môket ōkunī'm pāL. A'lta aci'Xgō acgE'tōkL. AcXgō'mam.
   two canoes full. Now they went they carried They came home.
                            home them.

14 Actō'kXuiptck tctā'at. Ka'nauwē actō'kXuiptck. A'lta acxē'la-it,
   They carried inland their roots. All they carried inland. Now they stayed,

15 acgE'tax tctā'at. Acktō'2tctXōm ka'nauwē qō'ta tctā'at.
   they ate their roots. They finished all those roots.

   Ta'kE wiXt nix·gē'qauwakō iqē'sqĕs: "Kā'sa-it," atciō'lXam
   Then again he dreamt blue-jay: "Robin," he said to him [to]

17 iā'xk¡'un, "Nix·gē'qauwakō aqEntgā'lEmam, nōguēlā'ētaē." Mank
   his elder brother, "I dreamt people came to fetch us, I shall cure him by A little
                                                            means of sorcery."

18 kⁿsā'xali nā'xax ōꜷō'Lax; acgē'ElkEl ikanī'm, ā'k¡amôkctikc.
   up became the sun; they saw a canoe, two in canoe.

19 Nixä'2gila-ē ikanī'm. Ā'tgatptck a'lta mô'kctikc tq¡'ulipXunā'yu.
   It landed the canoe. They came inland now two youths.

20 Acä'2tptcgam a'lta LlEq¡ā'mukc Lctā'q¡'olipx·. Aqiō'lXam iqē'sqĕs:
   They came inland now the wolves their youths. He was told blue-jay:

21 "Kamtgā'lEmam. Ōntcā'hat!au ayan'ō'L¡o-it." Nĕ'k·im iqē'sqĕs:
   "We came to fetch you. Our virgin is choking." He said blue-jay:

22 "Ntō'yaa." Lä2, a'lta acxE'ltXuitck iqē'sqĕs k¡a skā'sa-it.
   "We shall come." Some time now they made themselves blue-jay and robin.
                                      ready

23 Atciō'lXam iā'xk¡un iqē'sqĕs: "Ma'nix nūguilā'ita, ia'xka iā'qoa-iL
   He said to him [to] his elder blue-jay: "When I cure him by that large
                        brother means of sorcery,

24 iqō'mxōm, iā'xka mīgintciā'kᵘtia. Mgē'max: 'x·ix·ō'yax qē'La-it.'"
   basket. that point to it. Say: 'That there somebody is in
                                                    it [spirit of
                                                    disease].'"

25 Nĕ'k·im skā'sa-it: "A'yipē." Acxä'2gila-ē iqē'sqĕs. A'lta cka
   He said robin: "Well." They two landed blue-jay. Now and

tcᵢē′ktcᵢēk ugō′mokuē qaX ōhō′t!au. Take ayō′La-it iqē′sqēs. A′lta
almost out of   her throat   that   virgin.   Then   he stayed   blue-jay.   Now   **1**
breath

yuknēlā′ēta-i:
he cured her by means of sorcery: **2**

I′kta qia yā′lōc qau ōkᵢō′skEs ko nā′xumLxiō′gux ōgō′mokue.

                                                   3
"What   if   in there   that   girl   it gets curled up   her throat."

Ta′kE nē′k·im skā′sa-it: "x·ix·ō′yax qē′La-it." AtcigE′ntciaktē qix·
Then   he said   robin: "That there somebody is in."   He pointed to it·   that   **4**

iā′qoa-iL iqō′mxōm. Aqiō′ikⁿtcō iqō′mxōm. AqigElō′tx·Emit· ka′sa-it.
large   basket.   It was taken down   the basket.   It was placed near him·   robin.   **5**

A′lta· ē′ka nē′xax ka′sa-it; qiax iā′qoa-iL, tcx·ī atcigEntciā′qtxē
Now   thus   did   robin;   if   a large one,   then   he pointed at it   **6**

iqō′mxōm. Lāq° atcī′ax qix· ē′kta yan′ō′Lᵢōx. A′lta imō′lak
the basket.   Out   he made it   that   something   choking her.   Now   an elk   **7**

uyā′qᵢ′oxL. Aqcilgē′mēmtōm pāL môkct ōkunī′m LᵢōLē′ma cxē′lak
its knee.   He was paid for curing her   full   two   canoes   meats   mixed   **8**

kᵢa-y· ō′pXul. A′lta aci′Xkō. Iō′LᵢL aci′xax a′lta. AcXgō′mam
and   fat.   Now   they went home.   Glad   they became   now.   They came home   **·9**

gō tE′ctaqL; actō′kXuiptck qō′La LᵢōLē′ma. PāL nō′xôx tE′ctaqL. **10**
to   their house;   they carried inland   that   meat.   Full   became   their house.

Translation.

There were Blue-Jay and Robin. Once upon a time they were hungry. Blue-Jay said: "Make yourself ready, Robin." And they went to the sea where a slough was left by the receding tide. They were in their canoe. Blue-Jay called: "Come ashore, sleeper!" [name of a large fish]. The sleeper shouted [in reply], but it was far away from the shore. Blue-Jay called again: "Why do you stay far from the shore? Only the heron can carry [food] to you [if you stay that far from the shore]." Again the sleeper shouted; he was nearer the shore now. Blue-Jay repeated: "Why do you stay far from the shore? Only the heron can carry [food] to you [if you stay that far from the shore]." Blue-Jay called him five times; then he came ashore. Blue-Jay speared him and he and his brother went home after they had thrown the fish into their canoe. They reached their home and went ashore. Blue-Jay said to his brother, "Make a fire." Robin made a fire. Blue-Jay went and carried the fish up to the house. He cut it and Robin said: "I will have its tail, I will have its breast, I will have its head." Then Blue-Jay became angry: "You want to have everything for yourself; the Qᵢtē′nse* are going to eat what has been killed for you." Then Robin cried; he took his work and left the house. He cried outside. Blue-Jay finished cutting the fish. Then he called his elder brother [and said]: "Come in, come in, you poor one, you shall have the breast, you shall have the head, you shall have the tail." Then Robin came in. When the fish was roasted they began to eat.

After some time Blue-Jay dreamed, and he said to his elder brother: "Robin, I dreamed people sent for us; I was to cure a sick person." After some time people came in a canoe, wailing. When they had almost

---

*An imaginary tribe.

reached the shore they recognized the duck. She landed and said to
Blue-Jay: "O, your brother-in-law is choking. I came to fetch you;
you shall cure him." Blue-Jay replied: "We shall go." They made
themselves ready to go. They went, and he said to his elder brother:
"Robin, you must say, 'She shall give us in payment one lake and one-
half of another lake.' Thus you must say when I cure her." Robin said:
"All right." They landed. The duck's husband was breathing heav-
ily. Now Blue-Jay began to cure him and Robin sang: "You shall
pay us both sides of one lake and one side of another lake." One of
the ducks who sat at some distance sang differently: "Qoē'x, one side
shall be yours, my nephews." Then Blue Jay took out the morsel
which was choking the duck and made him well. He recovered. Now
[Robin and his brother] dug roots on the place which they had received
in payment. They gathered two canoes full and went home. They
arrived at home. They carried their roots up to the house. They
stayed there for some time. They ate all their roots. Then Blue-Jay
dreamed again. He said to his elder brother: "Robin, I dreamed that
people sent for us; I was to cure a sick person." In the afternoon
they saw a canoe coming; two persons were in it. They landed and
two young men came up to the house. They were the young wolves.
They said to Blue-Jay: "We come to call you; a girl of our family is
choking." Blue-Jay replied: "We shall go." After some time he
and his brother made themselves ready, and he said to his elder
brother: "When I cure her you must point to the largest basket and
say, 'There is the spirit of the disease.'" "All right," replied Robin.
They landed, and when they came to the house the girl was almost
suffocated. Then Blue-Jay began to cure her. He sang: "What is it
that is in this girl? Her throat is all twisted up." Then Robin said,
pointing to the largest basket: "It is in that large basket." The
wolves took it down and placed it near Robin. Robin continued to do
so, and pointed to all the large baskets. Then Blue-Jay took out what
had choked the girl; it was the kneepan of an elk. Then they gave
them in payment two canoes full of meat and grease. They went
home and now they were satisfied and carried the meat up to the
house. Their house became full.

14. IQĒ'SQĒS K¡A IŌ'I ICTĀ'KXANAM.

BLUE-JAY AND IŌ'I THEIR MYTH.

Cxēlā'-itx· iqē'sqes k¡a uyā'xk'un. Ka'nauwē Lᶜaлā'ma 1
There were blue-jay and his elder sister. All days

akлōlā'lEpта-itx ik¡Enā'tan. "Qō'i tkalai'tanEma mtāx," agiō'lXam 2
she always dug potentilla roots. "Shall arrows make," she said to him

uyā'xk'un. "Itci'pōtc atgiumē'qLa-itx tlalā'xukc, tqoēxqoē'xukc, 3
his elder sister. "My buttocks they always lick it the birds, ducks,

tk¡ElakElā'ma, tmōnts¡ikts¡ē'kuks." Nē'k·im iqē'sqēs: "Ä'ka 4
geese. tail ducks." He said blue-jay: "Thus

anxE'Lux." Nē'ktcuktē, wiXt nō'ya akлōlā'pam uyā'xk'un. Atci'tax 5
I think." It got day, again she went she dug his elder sister. He made

tkalai'tanEma atcлō'kXoL¡. A'lta ā'yō. Atcō'xtkinEmam uyā'xk'uń. 6
arrows he finished them. Now he went. He searched for her his elder sister.

Kā kлōlā'lEpт Iō'i, ā, LE'xLEx iлā'pōtc nē'xax. NaxE'Lxēgō, gōyē' 7
Where she always Iō'i. ah, noise of her anus became. She looked back, thus
dug scratching

nā'xax. A'lta cix·Elā'tit iqē'sqēs. Gō itcā'pōtc: "Anā'x, x·ix·ī'k 8
she did. Now he spanned his blue-jay. At her anus: "Anah, this
bow

kx·siā'kulq¡'ast!" Aga ēxE'cgam uyā'pL¡ikē. Agiō'lXam: "Xō'ta, 9
squint eye' She took it from him his bow. She said to him: "These,

Xō'ta tlalā'xukc ōxoēlā'-itx·." Itā'maᶜ agiā'wax. Iā'maᶜ agē'lax 10
these birds they are." Shooting she did them. Shooting she did him
them him

ēXt icimē'wat. Ayā'pXEla qix· icimē'wat. Agiō'lXam Liä'uX: 11
one male mallard His grease that male mallard She said to him her younger
duck. duck. brother:

"Ai'aq mE'Xkō. Manix mXgō'mama cEmä'lEq, cEmä'lEq, 12
"Quick go home." When you arrive at home nose ornament, nose ornament,

antElᶜē'ma. Iā'mqa iqā'naks mcgangElō'tka k¡a tgā'pa-it." 13
bring them to eat. Only a stone keep for me and its rope."

"Ä'ka anxE'Lux," nē'k·im iqē'sqēs. Nē'Xkō iqē'sqēs. A'lta atcē'klata 14
"Thus I think," he said blue-jay. He went blue-jay. Now he plucked it
home

qix· icimē'wat. AtcLä'2kXōL¡ atcē'klata. Lqui'nEmiks tga'a Iō'i. 15
that male mallard He finished he plucked it. Five her chil- Iō'i.
duck. dren.

Ta'kE Lq¡u'pLq¡up atcā'yax qix· ē'pXill; iä'pXEla icimē'wat. A'lta 16
Then cut he did it that grease: Its grease the male mal- Now
lard duck's.

k¡au'k·¡an atcē'Lgax qō'Lac Lkā'cōcinikc, Iō'i tga'a. Na-ixE'lgiLx: 17
tie he did it to them those children. Iō'i her chil- He made a fire:
dren.

"Ai'aq amcxā'nEmiL¡ ōᶜō'lEptckiX. Mckanauwē'tikc mcxLxē'gō 18
"Quick put your faces to the fire. You all look into the fire

iau'a mā'Lnē." A'lta atciupō'nit iqā'nakc, gōyē' iä'qa-iL. A'lta 19
there to the middle Now he put it up a stone, that large. Now
of the house."

aLxE'Lxēgō iau'a-y- ōᶜō'lEptckiX. A'lta ayō'sku-it qix· ē'pXill. 20
they looked into there the fire. Now it became warm that grease.
the fire

A'lta aLKлō'miqL Liä'qxatcau. Nā'Xkō Iō'i. Agixā'laqтē. AgE'LᶜElkEl 21
Now they licked it off it, fat. She went Iō'i. She opened the door. She saw them
home

tga'a. A'lta cxLā'llt ctā'xôst. Aksō'pEna iau'a wē'wuLē. Yukpā' 22
her chil- Now flushed their faces. She jumped then into the house. Right here
dren.

153

1 qix· iqā'naks ayagEltcē'mEx·it. Iā'xkatē nā'ēkĮElapXuitē. Iā'2Lqtē
   that   stone   it hit her.   There   she fell over. A long time

2 nuqunā'ētix·t; naxā'latck, atcalā'takō. "Nā2, x·ix· ksiā'qulqĮ'ast!
   she lay there; she arose,   she recovered. "Anah, that   squint eye!

3 Ē'ka   na   ayamō'lXam?"   AquXō'kXuit   tga'a   mā'Lxôlē.
   Thus [int. did I say to you?" She threw them her chil- from the mid-
         part.]   dren   dle to the sides
                                                              of the house.

4 "Ayamō'lXam: 'Mä'nx·E,   mä'nx·E   mitElEmā'kō.' Ayamō'lXam,
   "I said to you: 'A little,   a little   give them.'   I said to you,

5 'Ōqunā' amsgangElō'tka.'" "Ä'kā anxE'Lux," nē'k·im iqē'sqēs,
   'The stomach keep for me.'" "Thus I thought," he said   blue-jay,

6 kĮa mai'kXa tān tci tĮaya' amEnō'lXamx?"
   "and you   some- [int. good   you say to me?"
              thing part.]

   Agiō'lXam wiXt Lgā'uX Iō'i: "Qō'i ikanī'm amē'nElax, ē'ɛowitq
   She said to him again her younger Iō'i: "Shall a canoe you make it for me, a leg
                          brother

8 LĮ'ā'ap." "Ä'ka anxE'Lux," nē'k·im iqē'sqēs. Nā'k·im Iō'i: "Ta'kE
   fitting."   "Thus I think," he said blue-jay. She said Iō'i: "Then

9 kĮē x·ix· ik;Enā'tan; a'lta iau'a ē'natai nō'yima manix
   nothing these potentilla roots; now   then on the other side I shall go when
                                                                          often

10 mLigō'LĮa qix· ikanī'm." "Ä'ka anxE'Lux," nē'k·im iqē'sqēs.
   you finish that canoe."   "Thus I think,"   he said   blue-jay.

11 Kawī'X ā'yō iqē'sqēs. AtcLiE'ltgīpa ē'ckan. Atciō'quna-itx iā'ɛōwit;
   Early .o went blue-jay. He hollowed out a cedar. He put into it his leg;

12 atciā'kqana-itx.   AtcLē'kXōLĮ ikanī'm iqē'sqēs.   Atcio'lXam
   he put it into t..canoe.   He finished the canoe blue-jay.   He said to her

13 uyā'xk'un: "Ta'kE anLē'kXoLĮ qix· ikanī'm." Ā'ctō acgīusgē'Lxam.
   his elder sister: "Then I finished it that canoe." They went they took it to the
                                                                          water.

14 Actō'yam gō uyā'xk'un. Agē'ɛElkEl Iō'i qix· ikanī'm. A'lta ēɛwit
   They arrived at his elder sister. She saw it Iō'i tha: canoe. Now   a leg

15 LĮāp. "Nāx, x·ix· ksiā'kulqĮast! Ē'ka na ayamō'lXam?
   fitting. "Anah, that squint eye!   Thus [int. part.] did I say to you?

16 Ayamō'lXam Lā'k·Įayax Lgiō'ktELl." "Ä'ka anxE'Lux," nē'k·im
   I said to you one man in canoe carrying."   "Thus I thought," he said

17 iqē'sqēs, "kĮa mai'kXa tā'n tci wukĮ amEnō'lXam?"
   blue-jay,   "and   you   something [int. part.] straight you say to me!'

18 Nē'ktcuktē wiXt. A'lta ē'kūn wiXt atcā'yax iqē'sqēs ikanī'm.
   It got day again. Now another again he made it blue-jay canoe.

19 A'lta itĮō'kti ikanī'm, Lā'k·Įayax Lgiō'ktELl. A'lta agiō'ktEl
   Now a good canoe, one man in canoe carrying. Now she carried it

20 uyā'xk'un.
   his elder sister.

   Lē'lē aLxē'la-it. Agiō'lXam uyā'xk'un: "Qō'i amulē'mēxa-itx.
   Long they staid. She said to him his elder sister: "Shall you marry.

22 Lɛā'gil amLō'cgamx. ALgEugElgē'cgEliLx LElā'lipꞇ, kana'xtci
   A woman take her.   She shall help me   digging,   but

23 Lmē'mElōct." Nē'k·im iqē'sqēs: "Ä'ka anxE'Lux." Nō'mEqt
   a dead one." He said blue-jay: "Thus I think."   She was dead

24 iLā'xakĮ'Emāna-y- uyā'xa qō'Lac ēXt giLā'lXam. Ā'yō pō'lakli ka
   their chief his daughter those one people of town. He went at dark and

25 Lāqº atcā'xōm iqē'sqēs. Kawī'X nixē'gēla-i ka atcō'lXam uyā'xk'un:
   take out he did her blue-jay. Early he landed and he said to her his elder sister:

26 "A, Xō'La anLē'gēla-i Lmē'mElōct, äka qē amEnō'lXam." "Nāx,
   "Ah, that one I land here the dead one, thus as you said to me."   "Anah,

27 x·ix· ksiā'qulqĮast! LqĮēyō'qxot ayamō'lXam mLucgā'ma. Ai'aq
   that squint eye! an old one I said to you you shall take her. Quick

28 LE'kᵘLa iau'a tiō'LEma." A'lta ayō'tctcō iqē'sqēs. Lāqº aLē'xax
   carry her there to the supernat- Now he went out blue-jay. Cut off he did it
             ural beings."   to sea

Lā′yaqcō ka′nauwē2. Iā′qxulqt, ā′yō kā ŏxoēlā′itix· tiō′LEma.
his hair all. He cried, he went where they were the supernatural beings. **1**

Atgiltcā′ma aqixEnē′matē. AtgE′pa tiō′LEma. "Āk¡c, ˌLiā′xauyam
They heard him somebody cried They went the supernatural beings. "Oh, the poor one, **2**
while traveling. out

iqē′sqēs. Iā′xka x·ik ēxEnxEnē′matē. Lō′nas uyā′xk'un Xau
blue-jay. He that he cried traveling. Perhaps his elder sister that one **3**

ō′mEqt." Ixā′xo-il iqē′sqēs: "Ā-y- ōgu′k·ikala!" "Lō′nas uyā′lē
dead." He said much blue-jay: "Ah, my wife!" "Perhaps his sister **4**

Xauq, tcā′xo-il uyā′k·ikala." Nixä′gila-ē iqē′sqēs. Aqagē′la-it
that, he says his wife." He landed blue-jay. She was cured by **5**
means of sorcery

qēxtcē. Aqēwä′amtcxōkō: "Qantsi′x ka nō′mEqt?" Nē′k·im:
intending. He was asked: "How many [days] and she is dead?" He said: **6**

"Tā′anLkī nō′mEqt." "Ā, mō′ya gō-y- ēXt gitā′lXam, La′cka
"Yesterday she died." "Ah, go to one people of a town, they **7**

Lktō′kul L¡pāq aLkLā′x ē′Xtē k¡ā′o-itEt." Nē′k·im iqē′sqēs, ā′xka-y-
they know heal they do them one sleep." He said blue-jay, that **8**

ōꞓō′Lax atcō′mEl ka nō′mEqt. WiXt ā′yō iqē′sqēs. Qaxä′2 kulā′-i
day he bought her and she died. Again he went blue-jay When far **9**

ka ayā′kxoyē. Wāx nē′ktcuktē; wiXt ā′yō iqē′sqēs kā-y- ŏxoē-
then he slept. On the next it got day; again he went blue-jay where they **10**
morning

lā′itx· tiō′LEma. WiXt ē′qxElqt atgiltcā′ma. AtgE′pa tiō′LEma:
were the supernatural Again a crying one they heard him. They went out the supernat. **11**
beings. ural beings:

"Ā, iqē′sqēs Liā′xauyam x·ik ixEnxEnē′matē; Lōnas uya′xk'un
"Ah, blue-jay the poor one that he cries traveling; perhaps his elder sister **12**

nō′mEqt." Ixā′xo-il uyā′k·ikala ō′mEqt. Nixä′2gila-ē iqē′sqēs. Ā′tgELx
died." He always his wife was dead. He landed blue-jay. They went to **13**
said the beach

tiō′LEma. Aqigā′luLx iqē′sqēs. Ā, nēxgu′Litsk iqē′sqēs: "A′xka-y-
the supernat- They went down blue-jay. Ah, he told them blue-jay: "That **14**
ural beings. to him

ōꞓō′Lax anō′mEl ka nō′mEqt. Ayamcgē′tkᵘ¡am ıncagelā′ēta-i."
day I bought her and she died. I brought her to you you cure her." **15**

Aqō′kumam uyā′k·ikal iqē′sqēs. Aqiō′lXam: "Qantsi′x·ē ta′kE
She was looked at his wife blue-jay's. He was told: "How many then **16**

nō′mEqt nā′qxôiē?" "Ā, mô′ctī ta′kE nā′qxôiē." "Ā, mō′kᵘ¡a
she is dead sleeps?" "Ah, two then sleeps." "Oh, carry her **17**

gō-y- ēXt gilā′lXam; La′ska LkLō′kul mô′kcti qLā′o-itt L¡pāq
to one people of a town; they they know two sleeps heal **18**

aLkLā′x." WiXt ā′yō iqē′sqēs. Kulā′yi ā′yō; ayā′qxôiē. Kawī′x·
they do her." Again he went blue-jay. Far he went; he slept. Early **19**

wiXt nexE′l′ōkō. A′lta wiXt ā′yō. Ayō′yam gō-y- ēXt itā′lXam·
again he awoke. Now again he went He arrived at one their town. **20**

Aqiltcā′ma iqix·Enē′matē. Nō′xaua kᵘLā′xanē qō′tac tē′lx·Em:
He was heard he cried traveling. They ran outside those people: **21**

"Liā′xauyam iqē′sqēs; Lō′nas ūyā′lē ō′mEqt." Iā′qxulqt. Nixä′2gila-ē
"The poor blue-jay; perhaps his sister died." He cried. He landed **22**

iqē′sqēs. Ā′tgELx tiō′LEma. A′lta itcā′tcikc qaX ōꞓō′kuil. Aqiō′lXam:
blue-jay. They went the supernat- Now stinking that woman. He was told: **23**
down to the ural beings.
beach

"Tcē′xē ta′kE uā′qxôiē?" "Ā, ta′kE Lō′nē nā′qxôie." AqLō′cgam Ltcuq
"How many then her sleeps?" "Ah, then three her sleeps." It was taken water **24**

cka aqoniä′2nakō. Aqiō′lXam: "Mō′kᵘLa gō-y- ēXt gilā′lXam;
and her face was washed. He was told: "Carry her to one people of a town; **25**

La′cka t!aya′ aLkLā′x Lō′nē qLā′o-itt." Ā′yō iqē′sqēs. "Qaxē′
they good they make it three sleeps." He went blue-jay. "Where **26**

ayō′yam ka ayā′qxôya. Wāx nē′kctuktē. WiXt ā′yō. Q¡oā′p
he arrived and he slept. The next it got day. Again he went. Near **27**
morning

1 atciā'xōm ē'lXam. Aqiltcā'ma iqix·Enē'matē yō'itEt. AtgE'pa
he reached   the town.   He was heard   crying while traveling   he came.   They went out

2 tê'lx·Em: "Ā, Liā'xauyam iqē'sqēs, ixinxEnē'matē, Lō'nas Lgā'xauyam
the people: "Ah,   poor   blue-jay,   he cries while travel-   perhaps   poor
                                              ing,

3 uyā'lē ō'mEqt." Ixā'xo·il uyā'k·ikal nō'mEqt. Nixä'2gila-ē iqē'sqēs.
his sister   died."   He said much   his wife   died.   He landed   blue-jay.

4 "Ā-y- ōgu'k·ikal nō'mEqt." Aqiō'lXam: "Qantsī'x·ē ta'kE
"Ah,   my wife   died."   He was told: "How many   then

5 nā'qxôyē!" "Ā, ta'kE la'ktī nā'qxôiē." Ā'lta ā'qxôtcktc ka'nauwē
sleeps!"   "Ah,   then   four times   sleeps."   Now   she was washed   all

6 aqō'kxot. Nawi k·ɪē nē'xax itcā'tckē. "Mō'kuɪa gō Xō'Lac ēXt
she was   At once   nothing   became   her stench.   "Carry her   to   these   one
bathed.

7 gilā'lXam." Ā'yō iqē'sqēs; kulā'yi ayōyam; qįoā'p atciā'xōm
people of a town."   He went   blue-jay;   far   he arrived;   nearly   he reached it

8 ē'lXam ayā'qxôiē. Kawī'2x· nixE'lᶜōkō. A'lta wiXt ā'yō
the town   he slept.   Early   he awoke.   Now   again   he went

9 kā ōxoēlā'ētx· tiō'LEma. Iqix·Enē'mat atgiltcā'ma. AtgE'pa
where   they were   the supernatural   A crying one   they heard him.   They went
                        beings.   out

10 tiō'LEma. "Ā, Liā'xauyam iqē'sqēs. Lō'nas nō'mEqt uyā'xkį'un."
the supernat-   "Ah,   the poor one   blue-jay.   Perhaps   she died   his elder sister."
ural beings.

11 Nixä'gila-ē iqē'sqēs. Ā'tgELx tiō'LEma. Nē'k·im iqē'sqēs: "Ā'xka
He landed   blue-jay.   They went   the supernat-   He said   blue-jay·   "That
              down   ural beings.

12 ōᶜō'Lax anō'mEl, ā'xka ōᶜō'Lax ka nō'mEqt." "Ā, qantsi'xē ta'kE
day   I bought her,   that   day   and   she died."   "Ah,   how many   then

13 nā'qxôiē nō'mEqt!" "Ā ta'kE qui'nEmē nā'qxôiē." Ia'xkatē mā'Lnē
nights   she is dead!"   "Ah   then   five   nights."   There   seaward

14 ka aqagē'la-it. NixElE'l ē'tcamxtc. A'lta aqō'kctEptck. A'lta gō
and   she was cured.   It moved   her heart.   Now   she was carried from   Now   in
                                                        the water inland.

15 t!ōL aqagē'la-it. AtcalXā'takō uyā'k·ikala iqē'sqēs. Gē'gula itcā'pōtc
the   she was cured.   She got well   his wife   blue-jay's.   Below   her buttocks
house

16 LE'kXaqsō iLā'Lqta. A'lta aqia'cgōktc! iqē'sqēs gō ita'xkįun
her hair   long.   Now   he was brought into   blue-jay   to   the eldest
                        the house   brother of

17 tiō'LEma. A'lta aqiā'xōtcki iqē'sqēs. Yukpä't iā'pōtc Lā'yaqsō
the supernat-   Now   they worked on him   blue-jay.   To here   his buttocks   his hair
ural beings.

18 aqLē'lax iLā'Lqta. Aqiō'lXam iqē'sqēs: "Ia'xkayuk mɪā'-ita! Ē'ka
it was made   long.   He was told   blue-jay: "Here   stay.   Just as

19 nsai'ka mxā'xō. Qui'nEm iLaō'yiniLx alō'mEqtx LgōLē'lEXEmk
we   do.   Five   nights   dead   a person

20 Lįpāq amLā'xō-ilEmx." Kawī'2x· nē'xElatckō qix· iō'LEma.
well   you always make him."   Early   he rose   that   supernatural
                                                            being.

21 Aqiō'lXam iqē'sqēs: "Ni'Xua LE'mkxo-it!" Qē'xtcē atcLō'mEkxo-it
He was told   blue-jay: "Well   spit!"   Intending   he spit

22 iqē'sqēs, ac iā'xkayuk aLuqunā'ētix·t Xō'La Lia'muXtē.
blue-jay,   and   there   it fell down   that   saliva.

23 AtcLō'mEkxo-it qix· iō'LEma. LįEq ē'wa tā'nata t!ōL aLukucē'mx·it
He spit   that   supernatural   Striking thus   the other   the   it struck
              being.   side of house

24 qō'La Liā'mXtē. Qoā'nEmi ayā'qxôya iqē'sqēs. A'lta atcLō'mEkxo-it,
that   saliva.   Five times   his sleeps   blue-jay.   Now   he spit,

25 LįEq ē'wa tā'nata t!ōL aLukucē'mx·it. Ā'lta ikakįEmā'na nē'xax
striking thus   the other   the   it fell down.   Now   a chief   became
              side of house

26 iqē'sqēs. Iâ'Lqtē nē'xax iā'xkatē. A'lta ikā'kXuL atcā'yax. Aqiō'lXam
blue-jay.   Long time   he was   there.   Now   homesickness   affected him.   He was told

iqē'sqēs: "Ma'nix mxgō'mama, ma'nix ē'k·it miā'xō, nēkct qā'nsix **1**
blue-jay: "When you get home, when buying you do, not [any] how
a wife

Lā'miqcō ē'k·it mLā'xō." Ta'kE nē'xkō iqē'sqēs. NiXkō'mam iqē'sqēs **2**
your hair buying do it." Then he went blue-jay. He arrived at home blue-jay
a wife home

gō-y- uyā'xk̥un. Atcō'kᵘ˥am uyā'k·ikal. **3**
at his elder sister. He brought her his wife.
home

Lā'qoa-iL Lgā'wuX qaX ōᶜō'kuil. QāxLxnaᶜā'Lax ā'Lō iau'a kulū'i. **4**
Large her younger that woman. One day he went there far.
brother

ALō'yam gō iqē'sqēs tā'yaqL. ALgickXā'nap!ē gō naLxoā'pē. A'lta **5**
He arrived at blue-jay his house. He looked into the house at a hole. Now

atca'ᶜElkEl qaX uyā'xk̥un gō iqē'sqēs cxēlā'itx·. Yukpä'2tEma **6**
he saw her that his elder sister at blue-jay they two were. Down to here

Lā'yaqcō iqē'sqēs iLā'Lqta. NiXgō'mam qix· ik̥ā'sks. Näkct **7**
his hair blue-jay long. He arrived at home that boy. Not

nixgu'Litck. Kawī'2x· wiXt ā'yō. WiXt atcickXā'nap!ē. Ā'xka **8**
he told. Early again he went. Again he looked into the house. She

atcuguā'laqL uyā'xk̥un. Qoä'nEmī ā'yō qoä'nEm LᶜaLā'ma ka **9**
he recognized her his elder sister. Five times he went, five days and

agē'ᶜElkEl uyā'xk̥un. AgigE'lxēm: "Mä'tp!a, mä'tp!a, au!" **10**
she saw him his elder sister. She called him: "Come in, come in, younger
brother!"

agiō'lXam. Ā'yōp!; agē'lᶜēm. A'lta nē'Xkō. NiXkō'mam; atcō'lXam **11**
she said to him. He entered; she gave him Now he went He arrived at home; he said to her
to eat. home.

Liä'naa: "AgE'xk̥un gō iqē'sqēs ōc." Aqiō'cgam ē'mᶜEcX ka **12**
his mother: "My elder sister at blue-jay she·is." It was taken a stick and

aqixElgē'lEx·Lakō. NigE'tsax: "Nau'itka, nau'itka," nē'k·im, **13**
he was whipped. He cried: "Indeed, indeed," he said,

"agEnE'lᶜēm; agEngE'lxēm, ā'nōp! ka agEnE'lᶜēm." Aqō'kctam **14**
"she gave me to eat; she called me, I entered and she gave me to eat." Somebody went
to see

qaxē qigō ā'qxotk. A'lta k̥'ē, iā'mka ikanī'm iupō'nitX. AqLō'gō **15**
where where she had been Now nothing, only a canoe what was put He was sent
put up. up.

Lq̥oā'lipx· gō iqē'sqēs tā'yaqL. A'lta nau'itka-y- ōc iä'xkatē gō **16**
a youth to blue-jay his house. Now indeed there was there at

iqē'sqēs tā'yaqL iLā'Xak̥Emāna uyā'xa. A'lta nē'k·im iLā'Xak̥Emāna: **17**
blue-jay his house their chief his Now he said their chief:
daughter.

"Ai'aq amᴄgilXā'mam iqē'sqēs. Ka'nauwē x·i'La Lā'yaqcō tcLEnlō'ta." **18**
"Quick go and speak to him blue-jay. All this his hair he shall give it
to me."

Qē'xtcē aqiōlā'mam iqē'sqēs: "Ā, Lā'mēqcō qLE'mxuwākux." **19**
Intending somebody went to blue-jay: "Ah, your hair is asked from you."
say to him

Näkct qa'da nē'k·im iqē'sqēs. Qoä'nEmi qē'xtcē aqiō'lXam. A'lta **20**
Not at all he spoke blue-jay. Five times intending he was told. Now

nē'k·im qix· itā'Xak̥Emāna qō'tac tē'lx·Em: "Ai'aq, lxō'ya. **21**
he said that their chief those people: "Quick, we will go.

LxgōLā'ta." A'lta ā'tgi tē'lx·Em. Ia'kwa aqō'cgam ē'natai itcā'pōtitk. **22**
We will haul Now they the people. Here she was taken on one her forearm.
her." went side

Ia'kwa ē'natai itcā'pōtitk aqiō'cgam Lē'Xat, kanā'mtEma tgā'pōtitk **23**
Here on the other her forearm she was taken one, both her forearms
side

aqtō'cgam. Aqō'tx·Emt. Qoā'p iqē'p̥al ayō'kō iqē'sqēs. Nē'xax **24**
were taken. She was put on her feet. Near the doorway he flew blue-jay. He became

iqē'sqēs, wa'tsEtsEtsEtsE ayō'kō. Ia'xkatē nūL̥ōwai'ō-it qaX **25**
a blue-jay, wa'tsEtsEtsEtsE he flew. There she collapsed that

ōᶜō'kuil. Qē'xtcē aqiō'lXam iqē'sqēs: "Omē'k·ikal, iqē'sqēs **26**
woman. Intending he was told blue-jay: "Your wife, blue-jay

1 mXā'takō, ō'mēk·ikal iqē'sqēs!" Nĕkct nēXā'takō iqē'sqēs. A'lta
   turn back,   your wife   blue-jay!"   Not   he turned back   blue-jay.   Now

2 wiXt ā'qxōtk qaX ōᶜō'kuil. Nō'mEqt wiXt.
   again she was put by that   woman.   She was dead   again.

Translation.

There were Blue-Jay and his elder sister [Iō'i]. The latter went every day digging roots. [Once upon a time] she said to her brother: "Make some arrows; the ducks, the geese, the tail-ducks always lick my buttocks." "Yes, I will do so," said Blue-Jay. The next day she went again digging. Then Blue-Jay made the arrows. When he had finished them he went and searched for his elder sister. When he came to the place where Iō'i always dug roots he heard her scratching her anus. She looked back, turning her head over her shoulder. Now Blue-Jay spanned his bow and shot her in her buttocks. "Anah, Squint-eye" [she said]. She took away his bow and said: "These here are the birds," and she shot them. She killed a male mallard duck which was very fat. Then she said to her younger brother: "Go home, and when you get home give them the nose ornament to eat, keep for me only a stone and its rope." "I will do so," said Blue-Jay. Iō'i had five children. He went home. Now he plucked the duck. He finished plucking it. Now he cut the fat of the duck and tied it to the noses of Iō'i's children. He made a fire and said: "Go near the fire. Look into the fire in the middle of the house." Now he put a stone aside; a stone of that size. Now they looked into the fire and the fat became warm. Then they licked it off. Iō'i went home. She opened the door and saw her children. Their faces had become flushed by the heat. Then she jumped into the house. The stone [which Blue-Jay had put aside] hit her right on her forehead and she fell down. She lay there a long time; she recovered, arose [and said]: "Anah, Squint-eye, what did I tell you? I told you to give them a little and to keep the stomach for me." Then she took her children away from the fire. Blue-Jay replied: "I thought so; why do you not speak plainly when you speak to me?"

Another time Iō'i said to her brother: "Make me a canoe large enough for one leg." "I will do so," replied Blue-Jay. Iō'i said: "When there are no roots here I shall always go to the other side when you have finished the canoe." "I think so," replied Blue-Jay. Early next morning Blue-Jay went and hollowed out a piece of cedar wood. He put his leg into the canoe [to measure it and made it just as large as his leg]. He finished the canoe and went to his sister. He said: "I have finished the canoe." They carried it to the water and went to the canoe. When she saw it [and noticed that] it was just large enough for one leg she said: "Anah, Squint-eye, what did I tell you? I told you to make a canoe large enough for one man." Blue-Jay replied: "I thought so; why do you not speak plainly when you speak to me?" On the next day Blue-Jay made a large canoe. It was good, large enough to carry one person. He brought it to his sister.

After a while his sister said to him: "You ought to get married. Take a wife. She shall help me dig roots. But take a dead one." "I will do so," said Blue-Jay. Now the daughter of the chief of a town had died. Blue-Jay went to the grave at night and took her out. Early the next morning he landed and said to his elder sister. "Here, I bring the dead one ashore, as you told me." "Anah, Squint-eye, I told you to bring an old one. Quick! Take her to the supernatural beings [and ask them to cure your wife]." Now Blue-Jay went. He cut off all his hair and began to cry. He went to the place where the supernatural beings lived. They heard somebody crying and went outside. They spoke: "Oh, see; that is poor Blue-Jay who is crying there; perhaps his sister died." But he cried all the time: "O, my wife; O, my wife." "Perhaps his sister died, but he said his wife." He landed and they tried to cure her. They asked him: "How long has she been dead?" He replied: "She died yesterday." [Then the supernatural beings said:] "Then you must go to another town where they can cure those who have been dead one day." Blue-Jay said: "She died on the same day when I bought her." He traveled on, and when he had gone some distance he lay down to sleep. On the next morning he went on and came to the town of the supernatural beings. They heard some one crying and went outside. They spoke: "Oh, see; that is poor Blue-Jay who is crying there; perhaps his sister died." But he always said his wife died. Blue-Jay landed and the supernatural people went down to meet him. He told them: "She died on the same day when I bought her. I bring her to you to cure her." They looked at her and asked him: "When did she die?" He replied: "She died two days ago." "Then you must carry her to another town where they know how to cure people who have been dead two days." Then Blue-Jay traveled on, and after he had gone a distance he lay down to sleep. Early the next morning he awoke and traveled on. After some time he reached a town, and the people heard him crying. They ran outside and said: "Oh, see; that is poor Blue-Jay; perhaps his sister died." He cried. He landed, and the supernatural people came down to meet him. Now the body of that woman was stinking. They asked him: "When did she die?" "O," he replied, "three days ago." They took water and washed her face. Then they said: "You must carry her to another town where they know how to cure those who have been dead three days." Blue-Jay went on, and after some time he lay down to sleep. Early the next morning he started again, and reached the town of the supernatural people. They heard him crying and said: "Oh, that is poor Blue-Jay who is crying there; perhaps his sister died." But he always said his wife had died. He landed. "O, my wife has died." They said to him: "When did she die?" "O," he replied, "four days ago." Now they washed the whole body and bathed her. The bad smell disappeared. [They said:] "Carry her to another town." Blue-Jay went. When he had gone some distance and had almost reached the town he lay down to sleep. Early

the next morning he awoke and traveled on to the place of the supernatural beings. They heard somebody crying and went outside and
said: "Oh, see; that is poor Blue-Jay; perhaps his sister died." He
landed and the supernatural people went down. He said: "She died on
the same day when I bought her." "When did she die?" "Oh, five days
ago." They tried to cure her there on the beach. Her heart began
to move and they carried her up to the house. There they continued
to cure her. And Blue-Jay's wife resuscitated. Her hair was so long
that it hung down below her buttocks. Now they brought Blue-Jay
into the house of the oldest one of the supernatural people, they
worked over him and made his hair grow until it hung down to his
thighs. They said to him: "Remain here; you shall do as we do.
When a person has been dead five days you shall cure him." Early
the next morning the supernatural man arose. [He sat down with
Blue-Jay] and said: "Spit [as far as you can]." Blue-Jay tried to spit,
but his saliva fell down near by. Then the supernatural being spat,
and his saliva struck the other side of the house. Five days Blue-Jay
tried, then he spat, and his saliva struck the other side of the house.
Now he became a chief. He stayed there some time and then he
became homesick. The supernatural people told him: "When you go
home never give your hair in payment for a wife." Blue-Jay went
home. He arrived at his elder sister's house with his wife.

The younger brother of the woman had grown up. One day he
went some distance and reached Blue-Jay's house. He peeped into the
house through a hole and he saw his elder sister sitting with Blue-Jay.
Blue-Jay's hair reached down to his thighs. The boy came home, but
he did not tell anything. Early the next morning he went again to the
house and peeped into it, and again he recognized his sister. Five
times he went and then his elder sister saw him. She called him:
"Come in, come in, brother." He entered and she gave him to eat.
Then the boy went home and said to his mother: "My elder sister is
staying with Blue-Jay." The people took a stick and whipped him.
He cried: "Indeed, indeed, she gave me to eat. She called me; I went
into the house and she fed me." Then the people went to the burial-
ground and saw that she had disappeared. Only the canoe was there.
They sent a young man to Blue-Jay's house, and, indeed, there was the
chief's daughter. Then the chief said: "Go to Blue-Jay and tell him
that he must give me his hair in payment for his wife." The messengers went and said to Blue-Jay: "The chief wants your hair." Blue-Jay
did not reply. Five times they spoke to him. Then the chief said to
his people: "Let us go, we will take her back." Now the people went.
They took hold of her, one at each arm. They put her on her feet [and
dragged her out of the house]. Then Blue-Jay began to fly. He
became a blue-jay and flew away: wa'tsEtsEtsEtsEtsE. The woman
collapsed right there. Then they called him: "Blue-Jay, come back,
she shall be your wife." But he did not return. Now they buried her
again. She had died again.

15. IQḖ′SQḖS K̨A IŌ′I ICTĀ′KXANAM.

BLUE-JAY AND IŌ′I THEIR MYTH.

Cxēlā′·itx· Iō′i k̨a Lgā′wuX. QâxLx nā′pōl ē′k·it atgā′yax **1**
They were there Iō′i and her younger One night buying they did
                              brother.   a wife

tmēmElō′ctikc.· Aqŏ′mEl Iō′i. Aqä′2tutk tga′xamōta. Ia′xkatē **2**
the ghosts. She was bought Iō′i. They were kept their dentalia. There

pō′laklī aqā′xo-iktcgō. Nē′ktcuktē, a′lta k̨ē Iō′i. Iō′Lqtē nē′xax **3**
at night she was married. It got day, now nothing Iō′i. A long time he was

iqē′sqēs. ĒXt iqē′taq, a′lta nē′k·im: "Nu′xtkinEmama ōgu′xk·un." **4**
blue jay. One year, then he said: "I shall go to search her my elder sister."

A′lta qē′xtcē atctuwā′amtcxōgō ka′nauwē tE′mcEcX: "Qā′xēwa **5**
Now trying he asked them all trees: "Where

aLō′ix LgōLē′lEXEmk ma′nix aLō′mEqtx?" Atctuwā′amtcxōgō **6**
goes a person when he dies?" He asked them

ka′nauwē tElalā′xukc. Nä2kct atxElgu′Litck. Ā′laxta utcā′nix **7**
all birds. Not they told. Next the wedge

atcuwā′amtcxōkō. Agiō′lXam: "MEngEmgē′ktia! Iamō′kuꞮa." Qōgu **8**
he asked her [it]. She [it] said to him: "Pay me! I shall carry you." Where

itcā′q̨atxala ayā′xElax utcā′nix. A′lta atcagE′mEgiktē. A′lta **9**
her [its] badness came on her [it] the wedge. Now he paid it. Now

agā′yukuꞮ ē′wa tEmēwā′lEma. Actō′yam utcā′nix k̨a iqē′sqēs **10**
it carried him thus [to] the ghosts. They arrived the wedge and blue-jay

iā′2qo-iL ē′lXam. K̨ē tXut qiꞰ· ē′lXam. Gō kE′mk·iti tix· t̨ōL, **11**
[at] a large town. No smoke that town. At the last that house.

tā′qoa-iL t̨ōL, a′lta ia′xkatē tXut atcō′cēkEl. A′lta ia′xkatē ā′yup!. **12**
a large house; now there smoke he saw it. Now there he entered.

L̨ap ā′tcax uyā′xk'un ia′xkatē. "Ānā′ LgāwuXā′," agiō′lXam. **13**
Find he did her his elder sister there. "Ah, my younger brother," she said to him.

"Qā′xēwa amtē′mam? Mŏ′mEqtua?" "Ā, nēkct anō′mEqt. Utcā′nix **14**
"Whence did you come! Are you dead?" "Ah, not I am dead. The wedge

agEnaē′tkctXam. A′lta atciuxō′lalqꞮ qō′ta t̨ōLē′ma ka′nauwē‧. **15**
brought me here on its back. Now he opened them those houses all.

Tā′mkXa tkamō′kXuk pā′LEma qō′ta t̨ōLē′ma. IakEnqenā′·itx· **16**
Only bones full those houses. It lay near her

uyā′xk'un ēXt iauwā′qcta k̨a tkamō′kXuk. "I′kta atsuwa′ **17**
his elder sister one skull and bones. "What now

amiuguē′xa tik tkamō′kXuk k̨a x·ik iauwā′qcta?" Agiō′lXam **18**
will you do with these bones and this skull?" She said to him
them

uyā′xk'un: "Imē′qxiX, imē′qxiX." "Qu′ltci igō′LgEl itcā′Xt Iō′i. **19**
his elder sister: "Your brother- your brother- "Always lie she does Iō′i.
in-law, in-law."

Ētci′qxiX iauwā′qcta agEnā′xo-il." Nō′2pōnEm; a′lta noxulā′yutck **20**
My brother-in- a skull she always says to me." It got dark; now they arose
law

qō′tac tē′lx·Em, cka pāL nō′xôx qō′ta t̨ōL. ILā′Lēlam LE′kXana **21**
those people, and full became that house. Ten fathoms

qō′ta t̨ōL. Atcō′lXam uyā′xk'un: "Qā′xēwa atgatē′mam tikc **22**
that house. He said to her his elder sister: "Whence they came these

tē′lx·Em?" Agiō′lXam uyā′xk'un: "AmxE′LuxEna tē′lx·Em? **23**
people?" She said to him his elder sister: "Do you think people?

Tmē′mElōctikc; tmē′mElōctikc." Agiō′lXam uyā′xk'un. Iō′Lqtē **24**
Ghosts; ghosts." She said to him his elder sister. Long

1　ayō'La-it gō-y· uyā'xk'un. Agiō'lXam uyā'xk'un: "Qōi amxuxō'q̡ulax,
　　he stood　　at　his elder sister. She said to him his elder sister: "Future　imitate them,

2　amxaxp!a'ōmx." "Ä'ka anxE'Lux." Nō'ponEm ka nixE'ltXuitck.
　　fish in dipnet."　　"Thus　I think."　　It got dark　and he made himself ready.

3　ALxE'ltXuitck Lē'Xat Lk̡ãsks, cka wu-u-u-u, nōxo-itcuwā'ya-itx
　　He made himself ready　one　boy,　and　whispering　they spoke

4　qō'tac tê'lx·Em. Nä2kct atcuxōtcE'mElitEma-itx. Agiō'lXam
　　those　people.　Not　he understood them.　She said to him

5　uyā'xk'un: "LEmē'qoqcin Xō'La mtō'ya." Agiō'lXam: "Nēkct
　　his elder sister: "Your brother-in-　this　you two will go." She said to him: "Not
　　　　　　　law's relative

6　mLupalā'wulalEma; ac k̡ā mxā'xō." A'lta ā'ctō. Qoā'p acktā'xōm
　　speak much to him; and　silent　be."　Now they went. Nearly　they reached
　　　　　　　　　　　　　　　　　　　　　　　　　　　　　　them

7　tê'lx·Em ōgulā'lam tgE'tc̡ tcuwāma. A'lta atcugō-ēxō'tēn nigElā'lam.
　　people　singing going down river in canoe. Now　he helped them　he sang.

8　K̡ā nō'xōx. Nē'k·ikct ē'wa gō'qxôiama. Tā'mkXa tkamō'kXuk
　　Quiet　they were. He looked　thus　in stern of canoe.　Only　bones

9　tā'kXac gō'qxôiama. Ā'lta wiXt ayō'tctc!ō. A'lta k̡ā nē'xax,
　　they were in　in stern of canoe.　Now　again　he went down　Now　quiet　he was,
　　canoe　　　　　　　　　　　　　　　　　　　stream.

10　ayō'tctc!ō. Gō'yi nē'xax, nix·Enā'nakōc ē'wa gō'qxôiama. A'lta Lā'guc
　　he went down　Thus　he did,　he looked back　thus in stern of canoe. Now　he was in
　　stream.　　　　　　　　　　　　　　　　　　　　　　　　　　the canoe

11　wiXt qō'La Lk̡ãsks. AtcLō'lXam, cãu atcE'Lax. "Qā'xē-y· umcā'aL?"
　　again　that　boy.　He said to him,　low voice he made.　"Where　your weir?"

12　atcLō'lXam, Lawā'2 atcLō'lXam. ALgiō'lXam qō'La Lk̡ãsks: "Gō
　　he said to him,　slowly　he said to him.　He said to him　that　boy:　"There

13　mä'ēmē." Ā'ctō wiXt. AtcLō'lXam, tc!pāk atcLō'lXam: "Qaxē'gō-y-
　　down stream." They　again. He said to him,　loud　he said to him:　"Where
　　　　　　　went

14　umcā'aL?" Tā'mkXa tkamō'kXuk atakXā'La-it gō gō'qxôiama.
　　your weir?"　Only　bones　they were in the canoe at　the stern of the
　　　　　　　　　　　　　　　　　　　　　　　　　　canoe.

15　WiXt k̡ā nē'xax iqē'sqēs. Nē'k·ikst, a'lta wiXt Lā'guc Lk̡ãsks.
　　Again　silent he was　blue-jay.　He looked,　now　again　he was in　the boy.
　　　　　　　　　　　　　　　　　　　　　　　the canoe

16　WiXt cā'u atci'Lax, atcLō'lXam: "Qaxē'gō-y- umcā'aL?"
　　Again　low voice he made,　he said to him:　"Where is　your weir?"

17　ALgiō'lXam: "Iō'kuk." A'lta acxaxE'p!a. Nē'x·gEla i'kta nīyi'La-it
　　He said to him:　"Here."　Now　they fished in　He felt　some-　was in the net
　　　　　　　　　　　　　dipnet.　　　　　　　thing

18　gō-y· uyā'nuXcin. Atcō'Latck uyā'nuXcin. A'lta Lā'mkXa
　　in　his dipnet.　He lifted it　his dipnet.　Now　only

19　L'ē'k"tEqL'ix· mōkct aLayi'La-it. Wäx atci'Lax gō Ltcuq. Ka
　　branches　two　were in the net. Pour out he did them　into　water.　And

20　mä'nx·ī L̡EmE'n atcā'x uyā'nuXcin. Pāl naxā'x tE'kXōn. Wäx
　　after a little　into water　he did it　his dipnet.　Full　it got　leaves.　Pour out
　　while

21　atctā'x, qāmx atk̡ā'taXitx qō'ta tE'kXōn. ALktōmē'tckix qō'La
　　he did them,　part　they fell into [the　those　leaves.　He gathered them up　that
　　　　　　　　　　canoe]

22　Lk̡ãsks. L'ē'k"tEqL'ix· aLayi'La-it uyā'nuXcin. Wäx atciLā'x gō
　　boy.　A branch　was in the net　dipnet.　Pour out he did it　into

23　Ltcuq. Anā' tE'kXōn atayi'La-itx; wäx atctā'x. Qāmx wäx nō'xôx
　　the water. Some-　leaves　were in it;　pour he did them. Part　poured they be-
　　times　　　　　　　　　out　　　　　　　　out　　came

24　gō ikanī'm qō'ta tE'kXōn. ALktōmē'tcqix qō'La Lk̡ãsks. Môkct
　　in　canoe　those　leaves.　He gathered them up　that　boy.　Two

25　q̡āt atci'Lax qō'La L'ē'k"tEqL'ix· "x·iLē'k nLalō'kLa Iō'i;
　　like　he did them　those　branches.　"Those　I will take them　Iō'i;
　　　　　　　　　　　　　　　　　　　　　　to her

26　LaxElgē'Lxaya." Laqoā'iLa qō'La L'ē'k"tEqL'ix· AcXgō'mam.
　　she will make fire with　Large　those　branches.　They came home.
　　them."

Ā'ctŏptck.   E'XLXaut iqē'sqēs,   qē'wa   acē'XEmkEna   ALŏ'kcptcgam   **1**
They went up   He was angry   blue-jay,   because   he had not caught   He arrived carrying up
from the shore.   anything.

qō'La   Lk¡āsks   LE'cgo-ic   pāL   ŏp!ā'lŏ.   A'lta aqō'lEktc qaX ŏp!ā'lŏ.   **2**
that   boy   a mat   full   trout.   Now they were roasted those   trout.

A'lta axkฺē'l qō'La Lk¡āsks: "Ā, cka atcuXŏ'kXuē, atctaE'lguiLxax   **3**
Now   he told much that   boy: "Ah, and   he threw it away,   he threw it out of the
                                           canoe into the water

qō'ta intā'k¡ētēnax.   LXpŏc pāL nē'xax intā'xēnīm qē nēkctx cka   **4**
that   what we had caught.   Probably full   was   our canoe   if   not   and
then

atcuXŏ'kXuē."   Agiŏ'lXam uyā'xk'un: "Qa'daqa cka amuXŏ'kXuē   **5**
he threw it away."   She said to him his elder sister: "Why   and did you throw away

qō'ta imtā'k¡ētēnax."   "AnuXŏ'kXuē qē'wa L'ē'kᵘtEqL'ix·."   "Tā'Xka,   **6**
that   what you had caught."   "I threw it away   because   branches."   "That,

tā'Xka tk¡ē'wulElqL,"   agiŏ'lXam;   "MxE'LuXna L'ē'kᵘtEqL'ix·?   **7**
that   food,"   she said to him;   "Do you think   branches?

Ma'nix tE'kXōn, a'lta ŏp!ā'lŏ; manix L'ē'kᵘtEqL'ix·, a'lta LE'qaLEma."   **8**
When   leaves,   then   trout;   when   branches,   then   fall salmon."

Atcŏ'lXam   uyā'xk'un: "ILamŏ'kct   L'ē'kᵘtEqL'ix· anE'LEtkᵘฺ,   **9**
He said to her   his elder sister: "Two   branches   I brought here,

LEmxElgē'Lxaya."   Nŏ'Lxa uyā'xk'un.   A'lta mŏkct LE'qaLEma   **10**
you will make fire with   She went to his elder sister.   Now   two   fall salmon
them."   the beach

Lā'kXac. AkLŏ'kctEptck. Nŏ'p!am LE'qaLEma kLŏ'ktcan. Atcŏ'lXam   **11**
were in [the   She carried them up.   She entered   fall salmon   carrying in hand.   He said to her
canoe].

uyā'xk'un iqē'sqēs: "Qaxē'   atsuwa'   agE'Luxtk Iŏ'i   Xŏ'La   **12**
his elder sister   blue-jay: "Where   now   she stole them Iŏ'i   those

LE'qaLEma?"   Agiŏ'lXam uyā'xk'un: "K¡a Lā'xka imē'k¡ētēnax."   **13**
fall salmon?"   She said to him his elder sister: "And   this   what you caught."

"QulE'tci igŏ'LgEl itcā'xt Iŏ'i."   **14**
"Always   lie   she does Iŏ'i."

Nä'ktcuktē.   Ā'yuLx ē'wa mā'Lnē iqē'sqēs.   A'lta ŏlā'ox   **15**
It got day.   He went to thus   seaward   blue-jay.   Now   they were
      the water   on the beach

utā'xēnim qŏ'tac tEmēmElŏ'ctikc. Ka'nauwē Lxoa'pLxoap, qāmx a'lta   **16**
their canoes those   ghosts.   All   holes,   part   now

tgā'xamīūgax qaX utā'xēnim tmēmElŏ'stikc. Ā'yuptck iqēs'qēs.   **17**
their lichens   those   their canoes   the ghosts.   He went up   blue-jay.

Atcŏ'lXam uyā'xk'un iqē'sqēs: "QaxtsiˈLx uyā'xēnim itcā'k·ikal   **18**
He said to her   his elder sister   blue-jay: "How   his canoes   her husband

Iŏ'i!"   "Qŏi cka k¡ā mkē'x, tkcEminā'ya tē'lx·Em."   "Ka'nauwē   **19**
Iŏ'i!"   "Future and silent be,   they will become the people."   "All
                     tired of you

Lxoū'pLxoap uta'xanīm tikc tē'lx·Em."   Agiŏ'lXam uyā'xk'un: **20**
holes   their canoes those   people."   She said to him   his elder sister:

"Tē'lx·Em na, tē'lx·Em na? TEmēuwā'lEma."   WiXt nŏ'pōnEm,   **21**
"People [int. part.], people [int. part]?   Ghosts."   Again   it grew dark,

wiXt nixE'ltXuitck iqē'sqēs; wiXt aLxE'ltXuitck qō'La Lk¡āsks.   **22**
again he made himself ready blue-jay; again he made himself ready that   boy.

WiXt ā'ctŏ. A'lta aLiXEnEmŏ'cx·Em qō'La Lk¡āsks. Ka actŏ'yama   **23**
Again   he went. Now   he teased him   that   boy.   Where   they will
                                          arrive

ka atcaLE'lqamx, tā'mkXa tkamā'kXuk. Tcä'2xēL ē'ka atci'Lax   **24**
where he shouted,   only   bones.   Several times thus   he did

ka actŏ'yam. A'lta acxaxa'p!a. A'lta atcLōpā'yaLx L'ē'kᵘtEqL'ix·;   **25**
and they arrived. Now   they fished with Now   he gathered them   the branches;
                the dipnet.

atctōpā'yaLx tE'kXōn, ka Lxaluwēˈgŏt ka pāL nē'xax ictā'Xanīm.   **26**
he gathered them the leaves, and it became ebb-tide and full   was   their canoe.

Ta'kE aci'Xkŏ. A'lta atcuXuimŏ'cx·Em qō'tac tEmēuwā'lEma.   **27**
Then   they went Now   he teased them   those   ghosts.
home.

1 Ma'nix actauwitā'qtEtx, atcauwiqE'mxLoLx. Tā'mka tkamō'kXuk
   When   they met one,   he shouted.   Only   bones

2 atakXā'La-itx. AcXkō'mam. A'lta nagē'guiptck gō-y- uyā'xk'un.
   were in the canoe. They arrived at home. Now he carried them up to his elder sister.

3 AkLō'kXuiptck, LE'qalEma qāmx ō'ꞓōn.
   She carried them up, fall salmon · partly silver-side salmon.

      Wăx nĕ'ktcuktē. A'lta ā'yō iau'a qix· ē'lXam iqē'sqĕs. Ŏ,
      Next day it became day. Now he went there that town blue-jay. Oh,

5 ō'Xuit tkamō'kXuk gō qō'ta t!ōLē'ma. Nâ'pōnEm. "Ā, ē'kolē
   many   bones   in   those   houses. It got dark. "Ah, a whale

6 L¡ap aqā'yax." Agayā'lōt ōqoēwē'qxē uyā'xk'un. Agiō'lXam:
   find it is done." She gave it to him a knife his elder sister. She said to him:

7 "Ai'aq mE'xEnkō! Ē'kolē x·iau L¡ap aqā'yax." Nē'xankō ta'kE
   "Quick run!   A whale that find it is done." He ran then

8 iqē'sqĕs. Ayō'yam gō tkamilā'lEq. Ayukōtā'ōm qō'tac tē'lx·Em.
   blue-jay. He arrived at the beach. He met them those people.

9 Atctuwā'amtcxōkō. Tc¡pāk atctuwā'amtcxōkō; tc¡pāk atctō'lXam:
   He asked them. Loud he asked them; loud he said to them:

10 "Qaxē' x·ik ē'kolē nē'xax!" Tā'mkXa tkamō'kXuk noxō'La-it.
   "Where this whale is!" Only bones lay there.

11 AtcuguLtE'qo-im qō'tac t'auaqctā'akc. Ayōē'taqL. Kulā'yi nē'xankō.
   He kicked them much those skulls. He left them. Far he ran.

12 WiXt tgō'nikc ayugōtā'ōm. AtcauixqE'muXLōL Tā'mkXa
   Again others he met them. He shouted much. Only

13 tkamō'kXuk nuxō'La-it. Tcā'2xēL ē'ka atci'tax qō'tac tē'lx·Em.
   bones ·   lay there. Several times thus he did to them those people.

14 Ta'kE ayagā'ōm qaX ō'mꞓEcX; ā'qoa-iL qaX ō'mꞓEcX. Lō'nas
   Then he reached it that log; large that log. Perhaps

15 gōyē' itcā'xēLawunX qaX ugō'ElEm. A'lta cka pāL tē'lx·Em
   thus thick that its bark. Now and full people

16 tc¡u'Xtc¡uX tgăxt qaX ōolE'm. AtcauwiqE'muXLōL iqē'sqĕs.
   peel off they did it that bark. He shouted blue-jay.

17 Tā'mkXa tkamō'kXuk nuXō'La-it. Lā'mkXa Lkⁿckuē' qaX ōolE'm.
   Only   bones lay there. Only pitch that bark.

18 Tc¡u'Xtc¡uX ā'tcax Lō'nas qansi'x. Atca'kxōna môkct. Nē'Xkō.
   Peel off he did it I do not how much. He carried on his two. He went
                     know   shoulder   home.

19 NixLō'lEXa-it: "NxE'LuX qē nauē'tka-y- ē'kolē. TaL¡ umqci'ckan."
   He thought: "I thought if indeed a whale. Look a fir."

20 Nē'Xkō, niXkō'mam. KⁿLā'xanē atcaXE'kXuē uyā'alEm. Ā'yōp!.
   He went home, he arrived at home. Outside he threw it down his bark. He entered.

21 Atcō'lXam uyā'xk¡un: "NxE'Lux qē nauē'tka-y- ē'kolē, taL¡ ōolE'm.
   He said to her [to] his elder sister: "I thought if indeed a whale, look bark.

22 Agiō'lXam uyā'xk'un: "Ē'kolē-y-ē'kolē. MxE'Lux na-y- ōolE'm!"
   She said to him his elder sister: "A whale, a whale. You think [int part.] bark!"

23 Nō'pa-y- uyā'xk'un. A'lta môkct iā'qiLq¡ⁿp ē'kolē ē'Xōc. Nā'k·im
   She went his elder sister. Now two its cuts whale were on the She said
   outside   ground.

24 Iō'i: "Macā'tciLx ē'kolē. Qana'xL aLia'xELawEnX x·ik ē'kolē."
   Iō'i: "Good whale. Very thick this whale."

25 Atciā'qxamt iqē'sqĕs. A'lta-y- i'kolē-y-ē'Xōc. Nē'Xtakō iqē'sqĕs.
   He looked blue-jay. Now a whale was on the beach. He turned back blue-jay.

26 NiLE'lltaqt LgōLē'lXEmk iqē'sqĕs, Lgō'ctxōt ōolE'm. AtcaLE'lqamX.
   He met a person blue-jay, he carried on bark. He shouted.
                              his back

27 Tā'mkXa tkamâ'kXuk nuXō'La-it. Atciō'cgam qaX ōolE'm,
   Only bones lay there. He took it that bark,

28 atcā'qxōna, nē'Xkō. NiXkō'mam. A'lta ē'ka atci'tax qō'tac
   he carried it on he went He arrived at home. Now thus he did them those
   his shoulder, home.

29 tEmēuwā'lEma. Alā'xti ē'xoē-y- iā'kolē nixā'lax iqē'sqĕs.
   ghosts. In course of time much his whale became to him blue-jay.

A′lta wiXt ayō′La-it ia′xka iqē′sqēs. A′lta wiXt - ā′yō iau′a qiX 1
Now again he stayed that blue-jay. Now again he went there that

ē′lXain. A′lta ayō′p!am gō qō′ta t!ōL. Atciō′cgam iLā′awEqcta 2
town. Now he came in into that house. He took it its skull

Lk¡′ăckc, atciuqoā′na-it gō qō′ta taqoā′-iLa tkamō′kXuk. Atciō′cgam 3
a child, he put it on to those large bones. He took it

qix· iā′qoa-iL ēauwā′qcta, atciū′qona-itX gō qō′La Lk¡ăckc 4
that large skull, he put it on on that child's

Lā′XamōkXuk. Ka′nauwē′-y- ē′ka atci′tax qō′tac tê′lx·Em. 5
his bones. All thus he did them those people.

ALi′xElatcgux Lk¡ăckc qigō nōpō′nEmx. Qē′xtcē aLō′La-itx. 6
He rose to his feet the boy when it grew night. Intending he sat.

ALē′k·¡ēlapx·itxē. AtciLkɪā′-itx ē′Laqtq. ALE′xElatckō Lq¡ēyō′qxut. 7
He fell over. It threw him down his head. He rose the old man.

Kullku′ll ē′Laqtq. Wăx wiXt nēktcō′ktxē. A′lta wiXt 8
Light his head. On the next again it became day. Now again
morning

atctauwiXă′ktcgux tgā′qtqakc. Anā′ tga′ᶜowēt ē′ka atctā′x qō′tac 9
he replaced them their heads. Sometimes their legs thus he did them those

tmēmElō′ctikc. Ē′wa Lq¡ēyō′qxut gEnE′m Lā′ᶜowit nō′xôx; ē′wa 10
ghosts. Thus an old man small his legs he made; thus

Lk¡āsks Laqoā′iL Lā′ᶜowēt nôxôx. Anā′ Lᶜā′gil Lā′ᶜowit, ē′wa LE′k·ala 11
a boy large his legs he made. Some- a woman her legs, thus a man
times

Lā′ᶜowit atctE′LElax. Atcō′Xumak¡ E′nuapax LE′k·ala Lā′ᶜowit k¡a 12
his legs he made them to He exchanged them a man his legs and
them.

Lᶜā′gil. Alā′xti ka aqcā′yina. Atcō′lXam Iō′i itcā′k·ikal: "Ta′kE 13
a woman's. In course and he was disliked. He said to her Iō′i her husband: "Then
of time

atkcā′yina tikc tê′lx·Em, Xōgu ē′ka atctā′xt. Tgt!ō′kti miōlā′ma 14
they dislike him these people, because thus he does to them. Good you tell him

a′lta iXkō′ya. A′lta nēkct tq¡ēx tgētxt tikc tê′lx·Em." Qē′xtcē 15
now he will go home. Now not like they do him these people." Intending

giaxoē′wuniL Lgā′wuX Iō′i. xā′ōqxaL atcā′xtcimaôx. WiXt 16
she stopped him her younger Iō′i. Can not he understood her. Again
always brother

nē′ktcuktē. NixE′l′ōkō kawī′X. A′lta agiō′ktcan gō itcā′pōtitk 17
it got day. He arose early. Now she held it in her arm

ēuwā′qcta Iō′i. Atcē′xaluktcgō. "Ē′kta wiXt agiō′ktcan 18
a·skull Iō′i. He threw it away. "What again she holds it

Iō′i ēuwā′qcta?" "Anā′ imē′qxiX, ta′kE LEkᵘ mē′xax iā′tuk." 19
Iō′i a skull?" "Anah your brother- then break you did it his neck."
in-law

Nō′pōnEm. A′lta ā′yatc!a iā′qxiX. A′lta aqigē′la-it iā′qxiX. 20
It grew dark. Now his sickness his brother- Now he was cured by his brother-
in-law means of sorcery in-law

Atigē′la-it iā′cōlal, t!ayā′ nē′xax iā′qxiX. 21
They cured him his relatives, well he became his brother-in-law.

A′lta nē′Xkō, iqē′sqēs. Agiō′lXam uyā′xk′un: "Qā′t!ōcXEm, 22
Now he went home, blue-jay. She said to him his elder sister: "Take care,

imx·Enā′oyE. Manix ōxō′LXat tEmᶜā′ēma, năkct wa′xwax amLō′kōtx; 23
be careful. When it burns prairie, not pour out do it;

gō tLā′lakt tEmᶜā′ēma tcx·ī wăx′wax amLō′gux." "Ă′ka anxE′Lux," 24
at the fourth prairie then pour out do it." "Thus I think,"

nē′k·iin iqē′sqēs. A′lta nē′Xkō. Ayugō′om tēXt tEmᶜā′ēma. A′lta 25
he said blue-jay. Now he went home. He reached one prairie. Now

tgE′ckō-it qō′ta tEmᶜā′ēma. A′lta LpEl wax ikē′x ik¡ē′wax. Wa′xwax 26
it was hot that prairie. Now red blos- they did flowers. Pour out
som

atcLē′kxax qix· ik¡ē′wax. Nau′i Xuē′t nā′xax XaX uyā′ckan ā′ēXt. 27
he did it much those flowers. At once half full it became this his bucket one.
[on]

1 Ayugō'ptcgam. Qō'ta tEmᶜā'ēma gō kE'mk·itē ōxō'ʟXat. WiXt tēXt
He came up into the   That   prairie   at   end   burnt.   Again   one
woods.

2 ayūgō'om tEmᶜā'ēma. Atcō'ēkEl iau'a tcē'tkum ōxō'ʟXat a'lta.
he reached it   a prairie.   He saw it   there   half   it burnt   now.

3 "Tā'xka taʟ xitik aktEnxE'lXam agE'xk'un." Wa'xwax atcLō'kxux
"That   look!   this   to me about it   my elder sister."   Pour out   he did it

4 gō qaX uyā'ēXatk. Naxä'tctXōm ā'ēXt uyā'cgan. WiXt ā'gōn
on   that   his road.   He finished it   one   bucket.   Again   one more

5 atcō'cgam uyā'ckan, q¡oā'p Xuē't nā'xax ka nigō'ptcgamē. WiXt
he took it   his bucket,   nearly   half   it became   and   he came up to the   Again
woods.

6 tēXt ayugō'ōm tEmᶜā'ēma, Lā'Lōn tEmᶜā'ēma. A'lta tci'tkum pEt
one   he reached it   a prairie,   the third   prairie.   Now   half   really

7 ōxō'ʟXat. Atcō'cgam aē'Xt uyā'ckan. Naxä'tctXōm uyā'ckan;
it burnt.   He took it   one   his bucket.   He finished   his bucket;

8 atcō'cgam ā'gōn uyā'ckan. Xuē't nā'xax uyā'ckan ka nigō'ptcgamē.
he took it   one more   his bucket.   Half   it became   his bucket   and   he came up to the
woods.

9 A'lta mō'kctka Lia'ckanEma agō'n Xuē't. WiXt tēXt ayugō'ōm
Now   two only   his buckets   and more   a half.   Again   one   he reached it

10 tEmᶜā'ēma. LEqc ka'nauwē ōxō'ʟXat. Atcō'cgam qaX Xuē't uyā'ckan.
a prairie.   Almost   whole   it burnt.   He took it   that   half   bucket.

11 Naxä'tctXōm. Agō'n aē'Xt ō'cgan atcō'cgam, cka nigō'ptcgam ka
He finished it.   One more   one   bucket   he took it,   and   he came up to the   and
woods

12 naxE'tctXōm. A'lta aē'Xt ka uyā'ckan ugō'itX. Atcugō'ōm wiXt
he finished it.   Now   one   only   his bucket   was left.   He reached it   again

13 tēXt tEmᶜā'ēma. A'lta kā'²nauwē ōxō'ʟXat. Wa'xwax atcLō'kXuk.
one   prairie.   Now   the whole   burnt.   Pour out   he did it.

14 Q¡oā'p atctutctXō'mam qō'ta tEmᶜā'ēma, ka nExE'tctXōm uyā'ckan.
Nearly   he came finishing it   that   prairie,   and   he finished it   his bucket.

15 Laqⁿ uē'xax iā'itcxut. A'lta atciagE'ltcim qaX ōᶜō'lEptckiX. Nixē'tEla
Take off   he did   his bear-skin   Now   he struck it   that   fire.   It burnt
blanket.

16 ka'nauwē iā'itcxut. A'lta Lā'yaqtq ā'LElaxta, aLē'XLXa ka'nauwē
the whole   his bear-skin   Now   his head   last,   it burnt   all
blanket.

17 Lā'yaqcō. A'lta nē'xLXa.
his hair.   Now   he burnt.

Ayō'mEqt iqē'sqēs. Tcx·ī nō'ponEm. Ōc uya'xk'un:
He was dead   blue-jay.   Just   it grew dark.   There was   his elder sister:

19 "kukukukukuku Iō'i!" Acaxa'llqēLx uyā'xk'un: "Anā', LgawuXā',"
"Kukukukukuku   Iō'i!"   She cried   his elder sister: "Anah.   my younger
brother."

20 nā'k·im; "takE ayō'mEqt LgawuXā'." Ē'wa ē'natai qix· ē'qxēL
she said;   "then   he is dead   my younger   Thus   on the other   that   creek
brother."   side

21 qigō nō'Lxamit qaX uē'Xatk. Agiō'cgiLx ikanī'm, agiugō'lEmam
where   it led to the   that   road.   She launched   a canoe,   she went to fetch him
water

22 Lgā'wuX. Naiga'ōm Lgā'wuX. "Masā'tsiLx ikanī'm, Iō'i." Agiō'lXam
her younger   She reached   her younger   "Pretty   the canoe,   Iō'i."   She said to him
brother.   him   brother.

23 uyā'xk'un: "K'a ia'xka qē'wa amiō'lXam tiā'xamiuguX." "A, hā,
his elder sister: "And   that   when   you said to it   it had lichens."   "Ah, ha.

24 qulE'tc igō'Lgelē tcāxt Iō'i. Lxoā'p ikē'x tā'nuX XiauX,
always   lies   she makes   Iō'i.   Holes   were   the other ones   those.

25 tiā'xamiuguX." Agiō'lXam: "Amō'mEqt ta'kE." "Nu qulE'tc
they had lichens."   She said to him: "You are dead   now."   "Nu   always

26 igō'Lgelē tcāxt Iō'i." A'lta agā'yukL ē'wa ē'natai Lgā'wuX. A'lta
lies   she makes Iō'i."   Now   she carried him   thus   to the other   her younger   Now
side   brother.

atctā'qxam tê'lx·Em. Gō-y- ōkulā'lam, gō-y- i'Lukuma ōxocgā'liL 1
he saw them people. There they sang, there ihtlukum they played
much,

gō-y- ōōmE'nt!ō oxucgā'liL; gō tā'nEmckc ē'mEla-ē ōxucgā'liL; gō-y- 2
there beaver teeth they played there women's ihtlukum they played there
much; much;

i'pḳala ōxucgā'liL; gō iqā'lxal ōxucgā'liL; gō wā'cakoa-i ōxucgā'liL; 3
hoops they played there ten disks they played there wā'cakoa-i they played
much; much; much;

gō-y- ō'kōtcxEm iau'a kulā'yi ēXt ē'lXam. ItcauitcE'mElēt iqē'sqēs. 4
there they sang con- there far one town. He heard them blue-jay.
jurer's song

Oxuiwā'yuL kumm, kumm, kumm, kumm, ōXuiwā'yuL. Ā'yō qē'xtcē 5
They danced kumm, kumm, kumm, kumm, they danced He went intending
much. much.

gō qō'tac ugōlā'lam. Qē'xtcē nɪgElā'lam na-ixE'lqEmXLōL, cka 6
to those singers. Intending he sang he shouted, and

aqiaō'nim iqē'sqēs. Ēwā' qē'xtcē ayō'ix atcauiqE'mXLōLx, cka 7
he was laughed blue-jay. Thus intending he went he shouted always at them, and
at

aqiaō'nimx. Ā'yōp! gō tê'LaqL, gō tā'yaqL iā'qxix·. A'lta Lōu 8
he was laughed at. He entered in his house, in his house his brother-in- Now there
law's. was

Lkā'nax, masā'tsiLx Lgā'k·ikal Iō'i. Agiō'lXam: "Ḳa ia'xḳa qiau 9
a chief, pretty her husband Iō'i's. She said to him: "And he when

LEkᵘ mē'xax iā'tuk." "QulE'tc igō'LgEli tcāxt Iō'i. Qā'xēwa 10
break you did it his neck." "Always lies she makes Iō'i. Whence

natē'mam Xak ōkunī'm? Masā'tsiLx ōkunī'm." "Ḳa ia'xḳa qiau 11
they came those canoes? Pretty canoes." "And this when

mā'xo-il tgā'xamiuguX." "QulE'tc igō'LgEli tcāxt Iō'i. Ka'nauwē 12
you always they had lichens." "Always lies she makes Iō'i. All
said

tā'mak Lxoa'pLxoap, qāmq tga'xamiuguX." "Amō'mEqt, amō'mEqt," 13
the others holes, partly they had lichens." "You are dead, you are dead,"

agiō'lXam uyā'xk'un; "mm, amō'mEqt." "QulE'tc igō'LgEli tcāxt 14
she said to him his elder sister; "mm, you are dead." "Always lies she makes

Iō'i." Qē'xtcē atcauiqE'mXLuLX qō'tac tê'lx·Em, cka atgiaō'nimx. 15
Iō'i." Intending he shouted at them always those people, and they laughed at
him.

Tā'mēnua nēxā'x, ḳā nēxā'x. AyaxE'l'iōmEqt Lgā'wuX, 16
Give up he did, silent he became. She forgot him her younger
brother,

agiō'xtkinEmam. A'lta gō q̣oā'p atctā'x qō'tac ōXuiwā'yuL. 17
she went to look for him. Now then near he was them those dancers.

Qoā'nEmi ayā'qxoya-ē, alā'xti nē'ckōp! gō qō'tac ōXuiwā'yuL 18
Five nights, then he entered at those dancers

iqē'sqēs. Agixā'laqLē-y- uyā'xk'un. A'lta iā'wil ē'wa tE'kᵘcala 19
blue-jay. She opened the door his elder sister. Now he danced thus up

tiā'cowit, ē'wa ē'cḳēmatcx·. Nā'xtakō-y- uyā'xk'un, nagE'tsax. A'lta 20
his legs, thus head downward. She turned back his elder sister, she cried. Now

wiXt wuḳ ayō'mEqt. Ayō'mEqt ḳa wiXt iLā'môkctē ayō'mEqt. 21
again really he was dead. He died and again a second time he died.

Translation.

There were Blue-Jay and Iō'i. One night the ghosts went out to
buy a wife. They bought Iō'i. [Her family] kept the dentalia [which
they had given] and at night they were married. On the following
morning Iō'i had disappeared. Blue-Jay stayed at home for a year,
then he said: "I shall go and search for my sister." He asked all the
trees: "Where do people go when they die?" He asked all the birds,

but they did not tell him. Then he asked an old wedge. It said: "Pay me, and I shall carry you there." Then he paid it, and it carried him to the ghosts. The wedge and Blue-Jay arrived near a large town. There was no smoke [rising from the houses]. Only from the last house, which was very large, they saw smoke rising. Blue-Jay entered this house and found his elder sister. "Ah, my brother," said she, "where do you come from! Have you died?" "Oh, no, I am not dead. The wedge brought me hither on his back." Then he went and opened all those houses. They were full of bones. A skull and bones lay near his sister. "What are you doing with these bones and this skull?" [asked Blue-Jay]. His sister replied: "That is your brother-in-law; that is your brother-in-law." "Pshaw! Iŏ'i is lying all the time. She says a skull is my brother-in-law!" When it grew dark the people arose and the house was [quite] full. It was ten fathoms long. Then he said to his sister: "Where did these people come from?" She replied: "Do you think they are people? They are ghosts." He stayed with his sister a long time. She said to him: "Do as they do and go fishing with your dipnet." "I think I will do so" [replied he]. When it grew dark he made himself ready. A boy [whom he was to accompany] made himself ready also. Those people always spoke in whispers. He did not understand them. His elder sister said to him; "You will go with that boy; he is one of your brother-in-law's relations." She continued: "Do not speak to him, but keep quiet." Now they started. They almost reached a number of people who went down the river singing in their canoes. Then Blue-Jay joined their song. They became quiet at once. Blue-Jay looked back and saw that [in place of the boy] there were only bones in the stern of his canoe. They continued to go down the river and Blue-Jay was quiet. Then he looked back towards the stern of the canoe. The boy was sitting there again. He said to him in a low voice: "Where is your weir?" He spoke slowly. The boy replied: "It is down the river." They went on. Then he said to him in a loud voice: "Where is your weir?" And only a skeleton was in the stern of the canoe. Blue-Jay was again silent. He looked back and the boy was sitting again in the canoe. Then he said again in a low voice: "Where is your weir?" "Here," replied the boy. Now they fished with their dipnets. Blue-Jay felt something in his net. He lifted it and found only two branches in his net. He turned his net and threw them into the water. After a short while he put his net again into the water. It became full of leaves. He turned his net and threw them into the water, but part of the leaves fell into the canoe. The boy gathered them up. Then another branch came into [Blue-Jay's] net. He turned the net and threw it into the water. Some leaves came into it and he threw them into the water. Part of the leaves fell into the canoe. The boy gathered them up. [Blue-Jay] was pleased with two of the branches [which had caught in his net]. He thought: "I will carry them to Iō´i. She may use them for making fire." These branches were large. They arrived at home and went up to the house. Blue-Jay was angry, because he had not caught anything. The boy brought a mat full of trout up to the house and the people roasted them. Then the boy told them: "He threw out of the canoe what we had caught. Our canoe would have been full if he had not thrown it away." His sister said to him: "Why did you throw away what you had caught?" "I threw it away because we had nothing but branches." "That is our food," she replied. "Do you think they were branches? The leaves were trout, the branches fall salmon." He said to his sister: "I brought you two branches, you may use them for making fire." Then his sister went down to the beach. Now there were two fall-salmon in the canoe. She carried them up to the house and entered carrying them in her hands. Blue-Jay said to his elder sister: "Where did you steal these fall salmon?" She replied: "That is what you caught." "Iō´i is always lying."

On the next day Blue-Jay went to the beach. There lay the canoes of the ghosts. They had all holes and part of them were mossgrown. He went up to the house and said to his sister: "How bad are your husband's canoes, Iō´i." "Oh, be quiet," said she; "the people will become tired of you." "The canoes of these people are full of holes." Then his sister said to him: "Are they people? Are they people? They are ghosts." It grew dark again and Blue-Jay made himself ready. The boy made himself ready also. They went again. Now he teased the boy. When they were on their way he shouted, and only bones were there. Thus he did several times until finally they arrived. Now they fished with their dipnets. He gathered the branches and leaves [which they caught] and when the ebb-tide set in their canoe was full. Then they went home. Now he teased the ghosts. He shouted as soon as they met one, and only bones were in the canoe. They arrived at home. He went up to his sister. She carried up [what he had caught]; in part fall salmon, in part silver-side salmon.

On the next morning Blue-Jay went into the town. He found many bones in the houses. When it grew dark [somebody said]: "Ah, a whale has been found." His sister gave him a knife and said to him: "Run! a whale has been found." Blue-Jay ran and came to the beach. He met one of the people whom he asked, speaking loudly: "Where is that whale?" Only a skeleton lay there. He kicked the skull and left it. He ran some distance and met other people. He shouted loudly. Only skeletons lay there. Several times he acted this way toward the people. Then he came to a large log. Its bark was perhaps that thick. There was a crowd of people who peeled off the bark. Blue-Jay shouted and only skeletons lay there. The bark was full of pitch. He peeled off two pieces, I do not know how large. He carried them on his shoulder and went home. He thought: "I really believed it was a whale, and, behold, it is a fir." He went home. When he arrived he threw down the bark outside the house.   He entered and said to his sister: "I really thought it was a whale.   Look here, it is bark." His sister said: "It is whale meat, it is whale meat; do you think it is bark?"   His sister went out and two cuts of whale lay on the ground. Iō'i said: "It is a good whale; [its blubber] is very thick."   Blue-Jay looked.   A whale lay on the beach.   Then he turned back.   He met a person carrying bark on his back.   He shouted and nothing but a skeleton lay there.   He took that piece of bark and carried it home on his shoulder.   He came home.   Thus he did to the ghosts.   In course of time he had much whale meat.

Now he continued to stay there.   He went again to that town.   He entered a house and took a child's skull, which he put on a large skeleton.   And he took a large skull, which he put on that child's skeleton. Thus he did to all the people.   When it grew dark the child rose to its feet.   It wanted to sit up, but it fell down again because its head pulled it down.   The old man arose.   His head was light.   The next morning he replaced the heads.   Sometimes he did thus to the legs of the ghosts. He gave small legs to an old man, and large legs to a child.   Sometimes he exchanged a man's and a woman's legs.   In course of time they began to dislike him.   Iō'i's husband said: "These people dislike him because he maltreats them.   Tell him he shall go home.   These people do not like him."   Iō'i tried to stop her younger brother.   But he did not follow her.   On the next morning he awoke early.   Now Iō'i held a skull in her arms.   He threw it away: "Why do you hold that skull again, Iō'i?"   "Ah, you broke your brother-in-law's neck."   It grew dark.   Now his brother-in-law was sick.   A man tried to cure him and he became well again.

Now Blue-Jay went home.   His sister gave him five buckets full of water and said: "Take care!   When you come to burning prairies, do not pour it out until you come to the fourth prairie.   Then pour it out." "I think so," replied Blue-Jay.   Now he went home.   He reached a prairie.   It was hot.   Red flowers bloomed on the prairie.   Then he poured water on the prairie and one of his buckets was half empty. He reached the woods [and soon he came to a] prairie, which was burning at its end.   He reached another prairie which was half on fire. "That is what my sister spoke about."   He poured out on his road the rest of the bucket.   He took another bucket and when it was half empty he reached the woods on the other side of the prairie.   He reached still another prairie, the third one.   One half of it burned strongly.   He took one of his buckets and emptied it.   He took one more bucket and emptied one-half of it.   Then he reached the woods on the other side of the prairie.   Now he had only two buckets and a half left.   He reached another prairie which was almost totally on fire. He took that half bucket and emptied it.   He took one more bucket and when he reached the woods at the other side of the prairie he had emptied it.   Now only one bucket was left.   He reached another prairie which was all over on fire. He poured out his bucket. When he had come nearly across he had emptied his bucket. He took off his bear-skin blanket and beat the fire. The whole bearskin blanket was burnt. Then his head and his hair caught fire and he was burnt.

Now Blue-Jay was dead. When it was just growing dark he came to his sister. "Kukukukukuku, Iō'i," he said. His sister cried: "Ah, my brother is dead." His trail led to the water on the other side of the river. She launched her canoe and went to fetch him. She reached him. Iō'i's canoe was pretty. She said to him: "And you said that canoe was moss-grown." "Ah, Iō'i is always telling lies. The other ones had holes and were moss-grown." She said to him: "You are dead now [therefore you see them differently]." "Iō'i is always telling lies." Now she carried her brother across to the other side. He saw the people. They sang, they played ihtlukum, they played dice with beaver teeth; the women played their ihtlukum; they played hoops; they played dice with ten disks; they played wacakoa-i. Farther in the town they sang conjurers' songs. Blue-Jay heard them. They were dancing, kumm, kumm, kumm, kumm. He wanted to go to these singers. He tried to sing and to shout, but he was laughed at. He went and tried to shout but they all laughed at him. Then he entered his brother-in-law's house. There was a chief; Iō'i's husband was good looking. She said: "And you broke his neck." "Iō'i is always telling lies. Whence came these canoes? They are pretty." "And you said they were moss-grown." "Iō'i is always telling lies. The others had all holes. Part of them were moss-grown." "You are dead now [therefore you see everything differently]," said his sister. "Iō'i is always telling lies." He tried to shout at the people, but they laughed at him. Then he gave it up and became quiet. His sister forgot him [for a moment]. When she went to look for him, he stood near the dancers. After five nights he entered their house. His sister opened the door and saw him dancing on his head, his legs upward. She turned back and cried. Now he had again really died. He had died a second time

16. IQĒ'SQĒS K¡A IŌ'I ICTĀ'KXANAM.

BLUE-JAY AND IŌ'I THEIR MYTH.

Lgā'wuX Lxēlā'itx· iqē'sqēs, Iō'i itcā'xal uyā'xk¡'un.
Her younger brother there were blue-jay, Iō'i her name his elder sister.

2 "Txuwā'L¡ama Iō'i," atcō'lXam uyā'xk'un, "gō ipō'ēpōe." Kawī'x·
"We will go visiting Iō'i," he said to her his elder sister, "at magpie [?]" Early

3 ka ā'ctō. Qoā'p acgiā'xōm ipō'ēpōe. Iō'gōc tā'yaqL. Acxē'gela-i,
and they Nearly they reached magpie. He was on his house. They two landed,
went. top of

4 ā'ctōptck. Atctō'p!am. Iâc ipō'ēpōe gō tā'yaqL, cka mE'nx·ē
they went up. They came into There magpie in his house, and a little while
the house. was

5 ayō'La-it ka atciō'guixē. Atctō'guixē tā'yaqL. L¡äp ā'tcax aēXt
he stayed and he swept it. He swept it his house. Find he did it one

6 umō'ēkXux. Atcā'LEn'uya gō Liä'xEmalaptckix·. ALē'x·eltuq
salmon egg. He put it into in his topknot. He heated them

7 Lqā'nakc. ALō'ckō-it Lqā'nakc. Atcō'cgam ōōmᶜē'cX, atcLā'lōtk
stones. They were hot the stones. He took it a kettle, he poured into it

8 Ltcuq qaX ōōmᶜē'cX. A'lta atcanqā'na-it qaX ōmō'ikXux gō qaX
water that kettle. Now he threw them into that salmon egg in that
the water

9 ōōmᶜē'cX. A'lta atcLō'tcXEm, atcLō'tcXEm. PāL nā'xax ōōmᶜē'cX
kettle. Now he boiled it, he boiled it. Full became the kettle

10 qō'La Lmō'ikXūx. AqLcgElgō'Lit iqē'sqēs k¡a uyā'lē. A'lta
those salmon eggs. It was placed before blue-jay and his sister. Now
them

11 acxLxā'lEm, acxLxā'lEm, cka Xuē'te nā'xax qaX ōōmᶜē'cX ka
they ate, they ate, and half became that kettle and

12 actā'qtē. A'lta acgE'Lōkᵘ¡, aci'Xgō Agiō'lXam uyā'xk'un: "Ai'aq
they were Now they carried it, they went She said to him his elder sister: "Quick
satiated. home.

13 †xō'Lxa. Mā'nēwa mE'Lxa," nā'k·im qaX Iō'i. Nē'k·im iqē'sqēs:
let us go to You first go to the she said that Iō'i. He said blue-jay:
the beach. beach,"

14 "Mā'nēwa mE'Lxa." Nō'Lxa uyā'xk'un iqē'sqēs. Nē'k·im iqē'sqēs:
"You first go to the She went to his elder sister blue-jay's. He said blue-jay:
beach." the beach

15 "Wē'x·ē mEtgā'lEmam Xak ōōmᶜē'cX." Nē'k·im ipō'epōe: "nō'ya."
"To-morrow come and fetch this kettle." He said magpie: "I shall go."

16 AcXgō'mam iqē'sqēs. Kawī'X na-ixE'lgīLx iqē'sqēs. AyōLxē'wulX
They came home blue-jay. Early he made fire blue-jay. He went up

17 gō tE'ctaqL. A'lta ia'xkatē ayō'La-it. TakE atciō'lXam uyā'xk'un:
on their house. Now there he stayed. Then he said to her his elder sister:

18 "IkEnī'm iō'itEt." "Iō'itEt qē'wa amiō'lXam itiā'ya." Nixā'gēla-i
"A canoe is coming." "It is com- because you said to him he shall He landed
ing come."

19 a'lta ipō'ēpōe. Ā'yuptck ipō'epōe. Ayō'tXuit iqē'sqēs. Atctō'kuix·ē
now magpie. He went up magpie. He stood there blue-jay. He swept
to the house

20 tā'yaqL. L¡ap ā'tcax aē'Xt ōmō'-ikXux. Atcā'LEn'uya
his house. Find he did it one salmon egg. He put it into

21 Liä'xEmalaptckix·. AtcLō'kXuL¡ tā'yaqL atctō'kuixē. A'lta
his top-knot. He finished his house he swept it. Now

22 aLē'x·Eltuq Lqā'nakc. ALō'ckō-it Lqā'nakc. Atciō'cgam ōyā'amicX,
he heated them stones. They were hot the stones. He took it his kettle,

23 atcLā'lōtk Ltcuq. Atcō'cgam qaX ōmō'ikXux atcaLEnqā'na-it
he poured into it water. He took it that salmon egg he threw it into the
water

172

gō qō'La Ltcuq. A'lta atcLā'LElXatq qō'La Lqä'nakc kLō'cko-it. LEp
in that water. Now he threw them into it those stones hot ones. Boil — 1

nä'xax qaX ōōmᶜē'cX. A'lta atcakgē'tgē. Ä'2ka nē'xax ipō'epōe,
it did that kettle. Now he covered it. Thus he did magpie, — 2

ä'2ka wiXt nixē'xkᵢEla. Iō'Lqtē ka atcL'Elgē'lakō. K·ᵢē, nikct
thus also he imitated. Long time and he uncovered it. Nothing, not — 3

ē'kta gō qaX ōōmᶜē'cX. "Ē'Xtka tänLx ix·Elā'xō iqē'sqēs."
anything in that kettle. "One only what may be he did to him blue-jay." — 4

AtcLō'cgam qō'La Lqä'nakc ipō'epōe. Laq atcLā'xax qaX ōō'mᶜēcX.
He took them those stones magpie. Take out he did them that kettle. — 5

AtcaLEnqā'na-it aē'Xt ōmō'ikXux. AtcLā'LEXatk qō'La Lqä'nakc
He put into it one salmon egg. He put into it those stones — 6

kLō'ckō-it. LEp aLE'xax qō'La Ltcuq. Atcakgē'tgē qaX ōōmᶜē'cX.
hot ones. Boil it did that water. He covered it that kettle. — 7

Atca'Elgē'Elakō qaX ōōmᶜē'cX. A'lta pāL qō'La LEmō'ikXux.
He uncovered it that kettle. Now full those salmon eggs. — 8

A'lta atc'ē'taqL; nē'xkō ipō'epoē.
Now he left them; he went home magpie. — 9

Tcä'2xēL ayā'qxoia-ē, wiXt ō'lō agE'ctax. "Tcu'xō atxuwā'Lᵢamx,
Several nights, again hunger acted on "Come we will go visiting, — 10
them.

Iō'i, gō-y· ō'Lqikc." "Ā, wu'xi txō'ya;" nä'k·im Iō'i. Qui'nEmikct
Iō'i, at the duck." "Ah, to-morrow we will she said Iō'i. Five — 11
go;"

tga'a Iō'i. Nä'ktcukte. A'ctō-y· a'lta atcōwā'Lᵢam. Acxä'gila-ē gō
her chil- Iō'i. It got day. They went now they went visiting. They landed at — 12
dren

Lgä'maLna ō'Lqikc, ä'ctōptck. Actō'ptcgam. Ta'kE akLō'lXam
seaward from her the duck, they went up They arrived coming Then she said to them — 13
from the beach. up from the beach.

tga'a ō'Lqikc; qui'nEmikc tga'a: "lxᶜōyutä'ma." Ta'kE ä'LuLx
her chil- the duck; five her chil- "Let us go and bathe." Then they went to — 14
dren dren: the beach,

aLxᶜō'yutām, aLkLᵢē'mEn Lkauauwē'tikc, Lgä'qcit ōp!ä'lō. Iä'Lēlamē
they went to bathe, they dived all, they bit a trout. Ten times — 15

aLkLᵢē'mEn ka pāL aLi'xax LE'cgō-ic ōp!ä'lō. Ā'Lōptck. NaLxE'lgiLx
they dived and full became their mat trout. They went up She made a fire — 16
from the beach.

ōᶜō'lEptckiX. ALi'xēluktc, aqci'lgix a'lta iqē'sqēs kᵢa uyä'lē.
a fire. They roasted it, they were fed now blue-jay and his sister. — 17

Nō'ktcEkt iLä'lEktcal ō'Lqikc. Aqcingē'waLᵢamit a'lta iqē'sqēs.
It was done what she roasted the duck. She gave them to eat now blue-jay. — 18

AcxLxä'lEm a'lta iqē'sqēs kᵢa uyä'lē. Qä'mxka acgō'tctXōm ka
They ate now blue-jay and his sister. Part only they finished and — 19

actä'qctē. Agiō'lXam uyä'lē iqē'sqēs: "Mä'nēwa mE'Lxa, taua'lta
they were She said to him his sister blue-jay: "You first you go to the else — 20
satiated. beach,

atcuwa' qä'da amE'gimx." Atcō'lXam uyä'lē: "Atcuwa' kᵢoä'n
indeed how you always say." He said to her his sister: "Come always stay- — 21
ing here

mkēx. Mä'nēwa mE'Lxa," atcō'lXam uyä'lē. Nō'Lxa uyä'lē. Ā'nēwa
you are. You first you go to the he said to her his sister. She went to his sister. She first — 22
beach." the beach

nĭ'Lxa. "Wä2x· mcō'ya amckLugō'lEmam LEmcä'cguic." A'lta
she went to "To-morrow you go you fetch it your mat." Now — 23
the beach.

ä'yuLx iqē'sqēs. Nä'k·im ō'Lqikc: "Wäx· ntcō'ya." A'lta ä'ctō;
he went to blue-jay. She said the duck: "To-morrow we shall come." Now they — 24
the beach went;

aci'Xkō iqē'sqēs; acXkō'mam. Kawī'2x· nixä'latck iqē'sqēs.
they went blue-jay; they came home. Early he arose blue-jay. — 25
home

AyōLxē'wulXt gō tä'yaqL. Atcō'LXam uyä'xk'un: "Iō'itEt ikanī'm."
He went up on his house. He said to her his elder sister: "It comes a canoe." — 26

1 Agiō′lXam: "Iō′itEt qē′wa amia-uē′wuL." ALxä′gilaē-y- ō′tqikc.
She said to him: "It comes because you invited him." They landed the ducks.

2 Ā′Lōptck, aLxē′la-it. Nē′k·im iqē′sqēs, atctō′lXam tga′a uyä′xk′un:
They went up they remained He said blue-jay, he said to them her chil- his elder sister's:
from the beach, dren

3 "Tca lxcō′yutam." Ta′kE ä′LuLx iqē′sqēs k¡a tga′a uyä′xk′un.
"Come we will go to bathe." Then they went to blue-jay and her chil- his elder sister's.
the beach dren

4 Qē′xtcē aLkL¡ē′mEn, ē′ka Läx iLä′kötcX. Iä′LElamē aLkL¡ē′mEn,
Intending they dived, thus out their back. Ten times they dived,

5 LEqs aLXi′La-it itsä′tsa. Ā′Lōptck acuwä′tka. "Ē′gōn tän ix·Elä′xō
almost they died cold. They went up empty handed. "One more what he will do to
him

6 iqē′sqēs." AkLō′lXam tga′a-y- ō′Lqikc: "Ai′aq, amcxcō′yutam.
blue-jay." She said to him her children the duck: "Quick, go and bathe.

7 LxkLElgē′tatEkca." A′LōLx, ō′Lqikc tga′a aLx′ō′yut a′lta. Iä′LElamē
We will throw food before They went to the duck her chil- they bathed now. Ten times
them. the beach dren

8 aLkL¡ē′mEn. PäL aLi′xax Li′cgo-ic. Ā′Lōptck ō′Lqikc tga′a.
they dived. Full became their mat. They went up the duck her children.

9 "XaXä′q aqamci′lltatkc ōp!ä′lō." A′lta aLi′Xkō-y- ō′Lqikc.
"That is thrown at you trout." Now they went home the ducks.

10 Tcä′xEL ayä′qxoiē, ta′kE wiXt ō′lō agē′ctax iqē′sqēs k¡a uyä′lē.
Several nights then again hunger did them blue-jay and his sister.

11 "Ā, txauwä′L¡ama gō-y- ii′tcxut," nē′k·im iqē′sqēs. Wäx nē′ktcuktē
"Ah, we will go visiting at the bear," he said blue-jay. On the it got day
next morn-
ing

12 ka ä′ctō. Actō′yam gō-y- ii′tcXut tä′yaqL. ALē′XEltq il′tcxut;
and they went. They arrived at the bear his house. He heated them the bear;

13 atcō′lXam uyä′lē: "E′ktaLx aqitxEngē′lwaLamita, Iō′i!" ALō′cko-it
he said to her his sister: "What may be will be given to us to eat, Iō′i!" They were hot

14 Liä′xanakc. Atcō′kula-y- uyä′qēwēqē. Lq¡ōp atci′Lax Lä′yapc
his stones. He sharpened it his knife. Cut he did it his foot

15 iakwa′ ka′nauwē. Lq¡ōp atcä′yax iō′kuk iä′mElk. Gōyē′ nē′xax,
here [around all. Cut he did it here his thigh. Thus he did
the sole]

16 ka′nauwē ia′xka iä′lkō-ilē. Gōyē′ atci′Lax Lä′yapc, ka′nauwē ia′xka
all that well. Thus he did to them his feet, all that

17 iLä′lko-ilē. A′lta Lq¡u′pLq¡up atcä′yax, Lq¡u′pLq¡up atcä′yax. Ta′kE
well. Now cut he did it, cut he did it. Then

18 atciū′tcXEm. Ayō′ktcEkt iä′tcXEmam. Aqicgilcgō′Lit, cka mä2nx·
he boiled it. It was done what he boiled. It was placed before and a little
them,

19 acgiō′tctXōm, ka actä′qcti. Agiō′lXam uyä′xk′un: "ME′Lxa.
they finished, and they were satiated. She said to him his elder sister: "Go down to
the beach.

20 Mä′newa mE′Lxa, taua′lta atcuwa′ qä′da amE′gimx." Atcō′lXam
You first go down to else indeed how you always say." He said to her
the beach,

21 uyä′xk′un: "Mai′kXa mä′nēwa mE′Lxa." Nō′Lxa-y- uyä′xk′un
his elder sister: "You you first go down to She went down his elder sister
the beach."

22 ä′nēwa. Ta′kE nē′k·im iqē′sqēs, aqiō′lXam ii′tsxut: "Wē2x·
she first. Then he said blue-jay, he was told the bear: "To-morrow

23 mLugō′lEmam LEmē′cgo-ic." Aci′Xkō-y- a′lta iqē′sqēs k¡a uyä′lē.
go and fetch your mat." They went home now blue-jay and his sister.

24 AcXgō′mam. Kawī′2X nixä′latck iqē′sqēs, na-iXE′lgiLx.
They arrived at home. Early he rose blue-jay, he made a fire.

25 AyuuLxē′wulXt gō tä′yaqL. Atcō′lXam uyä′lē: "Ikanī′m iō′itEt."
He went up on his house. He said to her his sister: "A canoe it comes."

26 "Iō′itEt qē′wa amiä-uwē′wull." Nixē′gēla-i ii′tcxut. Nē′tptcgam
"It comes because you invited him." He landed the bear. He came up from
the shore

ii'tcxut. ALē'x·EltEq iqē'sqēs. ALō'cgu-it qō'La Lqā'nakc, Liā'xanakc 1
the bear.　He heated stones　blue-jay.　They were hot　those　stones,　his stones

iqē'sqēs. Atcō'kula-y· uyā'qēwēqē. Lqʲ ōp atci'Lax Lā'yapc, ac 2
blue-jay's.　He sharpened it　his knife.　Cut　he did it　his foot,　and

ia'xkēwa nē'kʲ ēlapx·itē, ayō'mEqt. Pâ, pâ, pâ aqā'yax, Lʲ pāq 3
then　he fell down headlong,　he fainted.　Blow, blow, blow he was done,　recover-
　　　　　　　　　　　　　　　　　　　　　　　　　　　　　　　　　　ing

atcilā'takō iqē'sqēs. Nē'k·im ii'tsxut: "ĒXt ka tān imx·ē'lEx·ala 4
he recovered　blue-jay.　He said　the bear:　"One　only　thing　you will do

iqē'sqēs." AtcLō'cgam Lā'yapc ii'tsxut, Lqʲ oä'2p atci'Lax, iā'mElk 5
blue-jay."　He took it,　his foot　the bear,　slowly cut　he did it,　his thigh

Lqʲ oä'2p atcā'yax. Lqʲ u'pLqʲ up atcā'yax gEnE'm ka'nauwē. A'lta 6
slowly cut　he did it.　Cut to pieces　he did it　small　all.　Now

atciō'tcXem. AtcLä'kXōLʲ atciōtcXem, ayō'qtcikt. Atcici'lltatkc. 7
he boiled it.　He finished,　he boiled it,　it was done.　He threw it before
　　　　　　　　　　　　　　　　　　　　　　　　　　　　　　　them.

Nē'Xkō ii'tsxut. A'lta ē'Latsʲa Lā'yapc iqē'sqēs. 8
He went　the bear.　Now　its sickness　his foot　blue-jay.
home

Tcä'xeL ayā'qxoyē, ta'kE wiXt ō'lō agE'ctax. Atcō'lXam 9
Several　nights,　then　again　hunger　acted on them.　He said to her

uyā'xk'un: "Wu'Xē txōwā'Lʲ ama gō ēᶜē'na." Wāx nē'ktcuktē. 10
his elder sister: "To-morrow　we will go visiting　at the beaver." On the next　it got day.
　　　　　　　　　　　　　　　　　　　　　　　　　　　　　　morning

A'lta ā'ctō actuwā'Lʲ am. Actō'yam gō ēᶜē'na. Iōc ēᶜē'na gō tā'yaqL, 11
Now　they　they went visiting.　They arrived　at the beaver. He the beaver on　his house,
　　went　　　　　　　　　　　　　　　　　　　　　　was

cka mE'nx·ē acxē'la-it, ayō'pa ēᶜē'na. Atci'tkutcʲam ēlā'ēma, 12
and　a little　they remained,　he went out　the beaver. He carried them to　willows,
　　　　　　　　　　　　　　　　　　　　　　　　the house

atcicgi'lxatEq. Atciō'cgam ē'am. Ayō'pa. Atcē'tkutcam pāL 13
he placed them before　He took it　a dish.　He went out.　He carried it to the　full
them.　　　　　　　　　　　　　　　　　　　　　house

ē'Lʲ uwalkLʲ uwalk gō qix· ē'am. Ā, näkct acgā'yax ka aci'Xkō· 14
mud　　　in　that　dish.　Ah,　not　they ate it　and　they went
　　　　　　　　　　　　　　　　　　　　　　　　　　　home.

Agiō'lXam uyā'xk'un: "Mā'nēwa mE'Lxa, taua'lta atcuwa' qä'da 15
She said to him　his elder sister:　"You first　you go to the　else　indeed　how
　　　　　　　　　　　　　　beach,

amE'kiinx." Atcō'lXam uyā'xk'un: "Mā'nēwa mE'Lxa." No'Lxa-y· 16
yon always say."　He said to her　his elder sister:　"You first　go to the beach." She went to
　　　　　　　　　　　　　　　　　　　　　　　　the beach

uyā'xk'un ā'nēwa. Nē'k·im iqē'sqēs: "Wē'x·ē miōgā'lEmama 17
his elder sister　she first.　He said　blue-jay:　"To-morrow　go and fetch

x·ig ē'am." Nē'k·im ēᶜē'na: "Nō'yaa. Nō'ya wu'Xē," nē'k·im ēᶜē'na. 18
the dish."　He said　the beaver:　"I shall go.　I go　to-morrow,"　he said the beaver.

Kawī'2X nēxE'lgiLx iqē'sqēs, ayuē'wulXt gō tā'yaqL. Atcō'lXam 19
Early　he made a fire　blue-jay,　he went up　on　his house.　He said to her

uyā'xk'un: "Ikanī'm iō'itEt." "Io'itEt qē'wa amiō'lXam itiā'ya." 20
his elder sister:　"A canoe　comes."　"It comes　because　you told him　he should
　　　　　　　　　　　　　　　　　　　　　　　　　　come."

Nixä'2 gila-ē -y· ēᶜē'na. Ayō'pʲam gō tE'ctaqL. Ayō'pa iqē'sqēs, cka 21
He landed　the beaver.　He came into　in their house. He went out blue-jay,　and

mE'nx·i kʲ ā'ya nē'xax. Atcē'tkuqam gōyä'2 Liā'pēla ēlā'ēma. 22
a little　nothing　he was.　He brought　thus　many　willows.

AqigE'lxatk ēᶜē'na. Atcā'yax tcxoa'ptcxoap, atciō'tctXum kanauwē'2. 23
He threw them　the beaver.　He did　gnaw,　he finished them　all.
before him

Nē'xaukō iqē'sqēs mā'Lnē, atcē'kElōya-y· ē'Lʲ uwalkLʲ uwalk. 24
He ran　blue-jay　sea-ward,　he went to take it　mud.

AqigElgō'Lēt ēᶜē'na. Atcā'yax, atcā'yax, ka'nauwē atciō'tctXum. 25
He placed it before　the beaver.　He ate it,　he ate it,　all　he finished it.
him

A'lta nē'Xkō ēᶜē'na. 26
Now　he went　the beaver.

WiXt atcō'lXam uyā'xk'un: "WuXĪ' txuā'Lₗama gō‧y‧ ō'lXaiŭ."
Again he said to her his elder sister: "To-morrow we will go visit- at the seal."
                                                              ing

2 Nä'2ktcuktē ka ā'ctō. Actō'yam gō‧y‧ ō'lXaiŭ tE'kXaqL. Qui'nEmiks
   It got day and they They arrived at the seal her house. Five
              went

3 tga'a‧y‧ ō'lXaiŭ. AkLō'lXam ō'lXaiŭ tga'a: "Amcō'ya gō mā'Lnĕ
   her children the seal. She said to them the seal her children: "Go to seaward

4 gō aLXE'muit Ltcuq. Ia'xkati mcXxatₗō'ya." A'LōLx tga'a ō'lXaiŭ
   to its edge the water. There lie down." They went her chil- the seal
                                                             to the beach dren

5 gō aLXE'muit Ltcuq. ALXxā'Xatq. Agiō'cgam ē'mᶜEcX ō'lXaiŭ,
   to its edge the water. They lay down. She took it a stick the seal,

6 nō'Lxa. AkLga'om tga'a, aga'owilx‧ qaX ōxgē's'ax gō ī'tcaqtq.
   she went to She reached her chil- she struck her that youngest one on her head.
   the beach. them dren,

7 ALkLₗĕ'wamEn tgā'a. Lāx aLi'xax, aLktā'yutck Lkanauwē'tikᶜ
   They dived her children. Come they did, they emerged all
                            out

8 tga'a ō'lXaiŭ Lkanam Lqoā'nEmiks. Agōlā'taptck qaX aĕ'Xt
   her chil- the seal together five. She hauled her ashore that one
   dren

9 agā'waᶜa. AgaLkₗE'tsXĕma. AkLā'kXuLₗ agaLkₗE'tsXĕma. A'lta
   she had killed She singed her. She finished, she singed her. Now
   her.

10 ā'kXaxc. Lōn kcī ōgō'pXula. Agō'tcXEm, agō'tcXEm. Nō'ktcikt.
    she cut her. Three fingers her blubber. She boiled her, she boiled her. She was done.

11 Aqacingĕ'waLₗamit iqē'sqēs kₗa uyā'xk'un qaX ō'lXaiŭ, cka qāmx
    They were given food blue-jay and his elder sister that seal, and part

12 aci'kXax ka actā'qcti. Agiō'lXam uyā'xk'un iqē'sqēs: "Ai'aq
    they ate it and they were satia- She said to him his elder sister blue-jay: "Quick
                      ted.

13 mE'Lxa, mā'nĕwa mE'Lxa." Atcō'lXam: "Mā'nĕwa mE'Lxa. Atcuwa'
    go to the you first go to the He said to her: "You first go to the Indeed
    beach, beach." beach.

14 kₗoā'n mkēx Xuk aqamElᶜē'mEniL," atcō'lXam uyā'xk'un: "Ai'aq
    always you are here you are given much to he said to her his elder sister: "Quick
    wanting eat,"
    to stay

15 mE'Lxa." Nō'Lxa‧y‧ uyā'xk'un. Nĕ'k‧im iqē'sqēs: "Wĕ'x‧i mugō'lEmama
    go to the She went to his elder sister. He said blue-jay: "To-mor- go and fetch it
    beach." the beach row

16 Xak ōmᶜē'micX." "Nō'yaa," nā'k‧im ō'lXaiŭ. Kawī'2X na-ixE'lgiLx
    this your kettle." "I shall go," she said the seal. Early he made a fire

17 iqē'sqēs. Ayō-iLxē'wulx‧t gō tā'yaqL. "Iō'itEt ikanī'm," atcō'lXam
    blue-jay. He went up on his house. "It comes a canoe," he said to her

18 uyā'xk'un. "Iō'itet qē'wa amiā'owĕwuт." Nixä'gila‧ē ikanī'm. Ā,
    his elder sister. "It comes because you told them often." It landed the canoe. Ah,

19 ō'lXaiŭ Lxē'gēla‧ē kₗa tga'a. Ā'Luptck ō'lXaiŭ. TakE nĕ'k‧im
    the seal landed and her children. They went up the seal. Then he said
                                        from the shore

20 iqē'sqēs, atcLō'lXam uyā'xk'un tga'a: "Amcō'ya gō aLXE'muit
    blue-jay, he said to them his elder sister her children: "Go to its edge

21 Ltcuq. Ia'xkati mcXxatₗō'ya." Ta'kE ā'LōLx Iō'i tga'a. ALE'Xxatq
    the water. There lie down." Then she went to Iō'i her chil- They lay down
                                                          the beach dren.

22 gō aLXE'muit Ltcuq. Ta'kE atciō'cgam ē'mᶜEcX iqē'sqēs. Ā'yōLx,
    at its edge the water. Then he took it a stick blue-jay. He went to
                                                                    the beach,

23 atca'owilx‧ qaX ōxgoē's'ax. Mô'kctē atcā'owilx‧. Ia'xkatē nō'mEqt.
    he struck her that youngest one. Twice he struck her. There she died.

24 Atctō'lXam uyā'xk'un tga'a: "Ai'aq, amckLₗĕ'mEn." ALkLₗĕ'mEn,
    He said to them his eldest sister her chil- "Quick, dive!" They dived,
                                        dren:

25 aLgE'tätck. Ā'ēXat kₗē. Qoā'nEmī aLkLₗĕ'mEn, goā'nsum nō'mEqt
    they emerged. One nothing. Five times they dived, always dead

qaX ā′ēXat. A′lta aLxē′ɪ.im Iō′i k¡a tga′a: "Ä." Nā′k·im ō′lXaiū: 1
that   one.   Now   they wailed   Iō′i   and her chil-   "Ah."   She said   the seal:
                             dren.

"Ēgun tān ix·Elā′xō iqē′sqēs." Aga′owilx· a′ēXat ugō′Xō. "Ai′aq   2
"One more thing he will do to blue-jay." She struck her   one   her daughter. "Quick,
               him

amckL¡ē′mEn," nā′k·im ō′lXaiū. ALgE′tatck Lka′nauwē Lqoä′nEmikc.   3
dive,"   she said   the seal.   They emerged   all   five.

Agā′Lk¡tcXēma ugō′xō. AkLā′kXuL¡ agā′Lk¡tsXēma. Ā′kXaxc   4
She singed her   her daughter. She finished   she singed her.   She cut her

agaLE′lltatkc. Akcō′lXam: "XaXā′k mtgā′xo." Ā′2lta aLkcxk¡ē′niakō,   5
she threw her be-   She said to them: "This   you will eat."   Now   they tied her up,
fore them.

aLgE′ctōtk Lmē′mElōct Iō′i Lgā′xa. ALi′Xkō-y- ō′lXaiū.   6
they put her up   the dead   Iō′i   her child.   They went home   the seal.

A′lta acxē′la·it iqē′sqēs k¡a uya′xk'un. WiXt ō′lō agE′ctax: 7
Now   they stayed   blue-jay   and   his elder sister.   Again hunger   acted on
                                               them:

"Tcu′xa txuwā′L¡amx, Iō′i, gō LE′qxaLa. Wux·ī′ txgō′ya."   8
"Well   we will go visiting,   Iō′i,   at   the shadows.   To-morrow   we will go."

Nē′ktcuktē, a′lta ā′ctō. Actō′yam gō LE′qxaLa tE′LaqL. Ā′ctōptck.   9
It got day,   now they went. They arrived at   the shadows   their house.   They went up
                                             from the beach.

PāL qō′ta tk¡ē′walElqᴛ qō′ta t!ōL. IXō′ca gō LElx·emē′tk   10
Full   those   provisions   that   house.   They lay about   on   the bed

iqauwik¡ē′Lē. ŌXō′ca tq¡ētxā′puke, ōXō′ca tpayi′xama, ōXō′ca   11
large dentalia.   They lay about   coats,   they lay about deer blankets   they lay
                                                       about

tqoā′qEma, ōXō′ca t·ōlā′l′ōma. Nē′k·im iqē′sqēs: "Qā′xēwa Lx ā′tgi   12
mountain-goat   they lay   ground-hog   He said   blue-jay: "Where   maybe they
blankets,   about   blankets.   went

tikc tē′lx·Em?" Agiō′lXām uyā′xk'un: "Ōxoēlā′itx· tē′lx·Em k¡a   13
those   people?"   She said to him   his elder sister: "They are there   the people   and

nēkct mtE′tqEmt." Atciō′cgam qix· iqauwik¡ē′Lē. "Hahaha ō′go-utca,   14
not   you see them."   He took them   those   large dentalia.   "Hahaha   my ear,

iqē′sqēs," aLE′xax LgōLē′lEXEmk. L¡L¡L¡L¡ nōxowā′-itx tē′lx·Em.   15
blue-jay,"   he did   a person.   Tittering   they laughed   people.

Atcō′cgam c·ōlā′l. Atci′cxk¡a: "Hahaha cgō′ulal iqē′sqēs.   16
He took it ·   a ground-hog He pulled at it: "Hahaha   my ground-hog   blue-jay.
           blanket.   blanket

Nik¡ē′x·tkin gō gē′kXulē ilEmē′tk. L¡L¡L¡L¡, hē′hē nō′xôx tē′lx·Em.   17
He searched for   at ·   under   the bed.   Tittering,   laugh   they did   people.
him

Atcō′cgam ōq¡oē′Lxap ōkunx·tā′m: "Qā′daqa wiXt amō′latck   18
He took it   a coat   a woman's coat of   "Why   again   you lift it
                   mountain-goat wool:

ōgu′q¡oēLxap, iqē′sqēs?" Atciō′cgam icā′mElᶜ. Atcē′xk¡a iqē′sqēs   19
my coat,   blue-jay?"   He took it   a nose ornament. He pulled at it   blue-jay

icā′mElᶜ. "Hahaha itci′cimElᶜ, iqē′sqēs." Ayuē′luktcū ēXt iqō′mxōm.   20
the nose or-   "Hahaha   my nose orna-   blue-jay."   It fell down   one   basket.
nament.   ment,

Atciō′cgam, atcē′xElukctgō mā′Lxôlē. ALo-ē′luktcu Lᶜā′pta.   21
He took it,   he put it up   at the side of the house.   It fell down   salmon-roe.

Atci′txaluktgō mā′Lxôlē. Nik¡ē′x·tkin ē′wa gēkXula′ ēlEmi′tk.   22
He put it up   at the side of the   He searched   thus   below   the bed.
                 house.

A′lta wiXt hē′hē nō′xôx. L¡L¡L¡L¡ aqiaō′nimx iqē′sqēs. Qē′xtcē   23
Now   again   laugh   they did.   Tittering   he was laughed at   blue-jay.   Intending

agiō′lXam uyā′xk'un: "Pɛt mE′xax. I′kta LEmē′kxal LE′qxaLa?   24
she said to him his elder sister: "Staying   be.   What   thy names   shadows?
                 quietly

Lx pōc nēkct ē′ka nugō′tkiX." Gōyē′ aci′xax, ā′nqatē ōtX ō′pXuē   25
Maybe if   not   thus   they do."   Thus [they   they did,   already   there salmon-roe.
                              looked]   stood

1 A'lta acxLxā'lEm. Nĕ'k·im iqē'sqĕs: "Qaxē'Lx noxoĕlā'-itX tikc
  Now   they ate.   He said   blue-jay: "Where may be they are   those

2 tĕ'lx·Em!" Agiŏ'lXam uyā'xk'un: "Ōxoĕlā'-itX, ōxo-ĕlā'itX kįa
  people!"   She said to him his elder sister: "They are there, they are there and

3 nikct mtE'tqamt." Nâ'pōnEm. Nĕ'k·im iqē'sqĕs: "Ia'xkuk txaō'ya."
  not you see them." It grew dark. He said blue-jay: "Here we will
                                                                    camp."

4 A'lta actā'qxoya pō'lakli. NixE'l'ōkō iqē'sqĕs, ayŏ'pa. Qē'xtcē
  Now   they slept   at night. He awoke blue-jay, he went out. Intending

5 ayŏ'tXu-it nixau'yus, cka iakwa' aLxō'gua gō tiāᶜowit. Nō'pa-y-
  he stood up he urinated, and here it ran down at his legs. She went out

6 uyā'xk'un iqē'sqĕs. Nō'La-it gō-y- ilē'ē nā'xkįauwapa. Gō aLō'tXuit
  his elder sister blue-jay. She sat down on ground she urinated. There stood

7 qō'La Lgā'xakįauwalpɪ. L'āk atci'tax tiā'ᶜowit iqē'sqĕs: "Tcįa'a!
  that   her urine. Spread he did them his legs blue-jay: "Look!

8 Iŏ'i, qa'da Xuku nE'xax. Atcxkįā'kux cia'kxo-itōc, acaxElaē'Lxal
  Iŏ'i, bow   here I became. He pulled them his groins, she cried

9 uyā'xk'un: "Ahaha'y- i'tcitc!a x·iq siā'kulqįast." "Ā'xka na itcā'Lᶜa
  his elder sister: "Hahaha my sickness that squint-eye." "She [int. her body
                                                                          part.]

10 Iŏ'i ka-y- i'tcatc!a atciā'laut!" Iŏ'Lqtē ka agĕ'nkįēmEnakō.
   Iŏ'i and her sickness is on her!" Some time and she took revenge on him.

11 Agē'xkįa qix· iā'kįalx·ix·. "Anā'2," nĕ'k·im iqē'sqĕs, "i'tcitc!a Iŏ'i."
   She pulled it that his penis. "Anah," he said blue-jay, "my sickness Iŏ'i."

12 "Ia'xka na ā'yaLᶜa ka-y- ā'yatc!a nĕ'laut!" WiXt ackįē'witx·it.
   "He   [int. his body and his sickness is on him!" Again they went to sleep.
         part.]

13 Kawī'2X nixE'l'ōkō iqē'sqĕs. Ia'xka iā'lko-ilē ē'k·ala qigō ā'nqatē.
   Early he awoke blue-jay. He the same man as formerly.

14 NixE'l'ōkō-y- uya'xk'un. A'lta wiXt ōᶜō'guil ē'ka qigō ā'nqatē.
   She awoke his elder sister. Now again a woman thus as before.

15 Nitcā'lakuilē. AqcEnkįē'mEnakō iqē'sqĕs qigō atcuXuimō'cXEm
   She was well. It was taken revenge on him blue-jay as he teased them

16 tĕ'lx·Em. "Tgt!ō'kti txgō'ya, taua'lta wiXt aqtXEnEmō'cXEmx."
   the people. "Good we go, else again they tease us."

17 Agiŏ'lXam uyā'lē: "Mai'ka nikct imē'xEtci'mElē ka
   She said to him his elder sister: "You not you believed me and

18 aqtxinEmō'cXEm." A'lta aci'Xkō, acXgō'mam. Nā'k·im uyā'lē:
   we were teased." Now they went home, they arrived at She said his elder
                                           home   sister:

19 "TakE kapE't atxuwā'Lįam."
   "Then enough we went visiting."

Translation.

There were Blue-Jay and his elder sister Iŏ'i. "Let us go visiting,
Iŏ'i," he said to his sister. "Let us visit the Magpie [?]." Early the
next morning they went. They came near his house and saw him on
the roof. They landed and went up to the house. Then they saw
Magpie on his house. After a little while he swept his house and
found one salmon egg. He put it into his topknot [made a fire], and
heated some stones. When they were hot he took a kettle, poured
water into it, and threw the dry salmon egg into the kettle; then he
boiled it. The kettle came to be full of salmon eggs. He placed it
before Blue-Jay and his sister and they ate. When they had half
emptied the kettle they were satiated. They carried away what was
left and started to go home. Iŏ'i said to her brother: "Let us go to

the beach; you go down first." Blue-Jay said: "You go first down to the beach." His sister went down. Then Blue-Jay said [to Magpie]: "Come to-morrow and fetch your kettle." Magpie said: "I shall go." Then Blue-Jay and his sister went home. Early in the morning Blue-Jay made a fire and went up to the roof of his house, where he staid. After awhile he said to his elder sister: "A canoe is coming." She replied: "It comes because you told him to come." Now Magpie landed and went up to the house. Blue-Jay arose and swept his house. He found a salmon egg. He put it into his top-knot. He finished sweeping his house and he heated stones. When they were hot he took his kettle and poured water into it. He took that salmon egg and threw it into the water. Then he threw the hot stones into the kettle and the water began to boil. Then he covered it. He imitated all Magpie had done. After awhile he uncovered it, but nothing was in the kettle. "Blue-Jay can do only one thing," said Magpie. He took the stones and threw them out of the kettle. He threw one dry salmon egg and hot stones into the kettle. When the water began to boil he covered it and when he uncovered it the kettle was quite full of salmon eggs. Then Magpie left them and went home.

After several days Blue-Jay and his sister became hungry. "Let us go and visit the Ducks," said Blue-Jay. "To-morrow we will go," said Iō'i. The latter had five children. On the following morning they started and went visiting. After awhile they landed at the beach of the Duck. They came up to the house. The Duck said to her five children: "Go and wash yourselves." They went to the water and washed themselves. They dived. [Soon they emerged again] each carrying a trout. Ten times they dived and their mat became full of trout. They went up to the house, made a fire and roasted them. Then they gave Blue-Jay and his sister to eat. Now the fish which they were roasting were done. They fed Blue-Jay, and he and his sister ate. They ate part and were satiated. Iō'i said to her brother: "You go down first, else you will talk ever so much." He replied to his sister: "Ah, you would always like to stay here, you go down first." His sister went down first [and as soon as she had left he said to the Duck]: "Come to my house to-morrow and get your mat." Now Blue-Jay went down to the beach. The Duck said: "We shall go to-morrow." Then they went home. They arrived at home. Early the next morning Blue-Jay arose and went up to the roof of the house. He said to his sister: "A canoe is coming." She remarked: "It comes because you invited them." Then the Duck landed [with her five children] and went up to the house. After awhile Blue-Jay said to his sister's children: "Go and wash yourselves." Then Blue-Jay and his sister's children went down to the beach. They tried to dive, but their backs remained over water. Ten times they dived and were almost dead with cold. They came up to the house empty handed. "Blue-Jay does one thing only" [said the Duck]. She told her children: "Go and wash yourselves.

We will give them food." The Duck's children went down to the beach and washed themselves. They dived ten times and their mat was full. They went up to the house. "That trout is thrown at your feet." Now the Ducks went home. After a number of days Blue-Jay and his sister became again hungry. "Let us go and visit the Black Bear," he said. The next morning they went. They arrived at the Bear's house. The Bear heated stones. Blue-Jay said to his sister: "What may he give us to eat, Iō'i!" When the stones were hot the Bear sharpened his knife and cut his feet here [all around the sole] and cut his thigh. Then he rubbed over the wounds, and they were healed. Then he cut [the flesh which he had cut from his feet and from his body] into small pieces and boiled it. When it was done he placed it before them, and after a little while they were satiated. Iō'i said to her brother: "You go down first, else you will talk ever so much." Blue-Jay said: "You go down first." His sister went, and then Blue-Jay said: "Come to-morrow and fetch your mat." Then he went home with his sister. They came home. Early the next morning Blue-Jay arose and made a fire. He went up to the roof of his house. He said to his sister: "A canoe is coming." [And she replied:] "It comes because you invited him." Then the Bear landed and came up to the house. Blue-Jay heated stones, and when they were hot he sharpened his knife and cut his feet. He fainted right away. They blew on him until he recovered. The Bear said: "You can do only one thing, Blue-Jay." The Bear took his foot and slowly cut it. He cut his thigh. Then he cut the flesh into small pieces. He boiled it. When he had finished cooking and it was done he threw it before them and went home. Blue-Jay's feet were sore.

After several days they again got hungry. Then Blue-Jay said to his elder sister: "To-morrow we will go and visit the Beaver." Early in the morning they started to visit him, and they arrived at the Beaver's house. The Beaver was in his house. After a little while he went out and carried willows into the house which he placed before them. He took a dish and went out. Then he carried it back filled with mud. Blue-Jay and his sister could not eat it and started to go home. As they set out homeward his elder sister said to him: "You go down first else you will talk ever so much." Blue-Jay said to his elder sister: "You go down first." She went to the beach first. Then Blue-Jay said: "Come to my house to-morrow to fetch your dish." The Beaver replied: "I will come to-morrow." Early the next morning Blue-Jay made a fire and went up to the roof of his house. He said to his sister: "A canoe is coming." "It comes because you told him to come." The Beaver landed and entered the house. Blue-Jay went out and when he had been away a little while he brought that many willows. He threw them before the Beaver, who began to gnaw and ate them all. Then Blue-Jay ran to the beach. He went to get some mud, which he put before the Beaver. He ate it all and went home.

Blue-Jay said again to his sister: "To-morrow we will go and visit the Seal." On the next morning they started and arrived at the house of the Seal, who had five children   The Seal said to her young ones: "Go to the beach and lie down there." They went and lay down at the edge of the water. The Seal took a stick and went down. When she reached her children she struck the youngest one upon its head. The others dived and when they came up again they were again five. Then she pulled up to the house the one which she had killed. She singed it. When she had finished singeing it she cut it. Its blubber was three fingers thick. She boiled it and when it was done she gave it to Blue-Jay and his sister. Soon they had enough. Then Iōʹi said to her brother: "You go down first." He replied: "You go down first, else you will always want to stay where they give us food." He said: "Go to the beach." His elder sister went to the beach. Then Blue-Jay said to the Seal: "Come to-morrow and fetch your kettle." " I shall come," replied the Seal. [They went home.] Early next morning Blue-Jay made a fire and went up to the roof of his house. He said to his elder sister : "A canoe is coming." She replied : "It comes because you invited him." The canoe came ashore. The Seal and her children landed and they came up to the house. Then Blue-Jay said to Iōʹi's children: "Go to the beach and lie down there." Then Iōʹi's children went and lay down at the edge of the water. Blue-Jay took a stick. He went down and struck the youngest one ; he struck it twice and it lay there dead. Then he said to the other children : "Quick, dive!" They dived, and when they came up again one was missing. Five times they dived, but the one [which was struck] remained dead. Then Iōʹi and her children cried: "Ä." The Seal said: "Blue-Jay knows to do one thing only." She struck one of her daughters and said : "Quick; dive!" And when they came up again all five of them were there. She singed her daughter. When she had finished singeing her she cut her and threw her down before Blue-Jay and his sister, saying : "You may eat this." Then they tied up and buried the dead child of Iōʹi, and the Seal went home.

After awhile they got hungry again. "Let us go and visit the shadows." "To-morrow we will go." Early next morning they started and arrived at the house of the shadows. They went up to the house. The house was full of provisions, and on the bed there were large dentalia. There were coats, blankets of deer skin, of mountain goat, and of ground-hog. Blue-Jay said : "Where may these people be?" His elder sister replied : "Here they are, but you can not see them." Blue-Jay took up one of the large dentalia. "Ahahaha, my ear, Blue-Jay," cried a person. They heard many people tittering. He took up a ground-hog blanket and pulled at it. "Ahahaha, my ground-hog blanket, Blue-Jay." He searched under the bed [for the person who had spoken] and again the people tittered. He took up a coat of mountain-goat wool. The person cried, "Why do you lift my coat, Blue-Jay?" He took a nose ornament and the person cried: "Ahahaha, my nose-ornament, Blue-Jay." Then a basket fell down from above. He took it and put it back. Then a salmon roe fell down. He put it back, and again he searched under the bed for persons. Then, again, the people tittered and laughed at him. His sister said to him: "Stay here quietly. Why should they be called shadows if they would not act as they do?" They looked around. There was a salmon roe [put up in a bag for winter use] and they ate it. Blue-Jay said again: "Where may these people be?" His elder sister replied: "Here they are, here they are; but you do not see them." When it got dark Blue-Jay said: "We will sleep here." Now they slept during the night. Blue Jay awoke and went out. He tried to urinate standing. It ran down his legs. Blue-Jay's elder sister went out. She sat down on the ground and urinated. There stood her urine. Blue-Jay spread his legs: "Look here, Iō'i, what became of me!" He pulled his groins and his sister cried much. "Ahaha, that hurts me, Squint-eye!" "Is it Iō'i's body, and it hurts her?" After some time she took revenge upon him. She pulled the penis; "Anah," cried Blue-Jay, "it hurts me, Iō'i." "Is it his body, and he feels sick?" Then they went to sleep again. Blue-Jay awoke early. Then he was a man again as before. His elder sister awoke. Now she was again a woman as before. She was well again. Thus they took revenge on Blue-Jay, because he had teased the people. "Let us go, else they will tease us again," said Blue-Jay. His sister replied: "You did not believe me and they teased us." Then Blue-Jay went home. He arrived at home. His sister said: "Now we have gone visiting enough."

17. CKULKULŌ'L ICTĀ'KXANAM.

CKULKULŌ'L   HIS MYTH.

A'lta cxēlā'itX Ckulkulō'L kᵢa-y- uyā'xk'un. A'lta agiō'lXam: **1**
Now there was a Salmon-harpoon and his elder sister. Now she said to him:

"Qō-i amxuxō'k'ulax iqᵢoanē'X tgiā'wulᶜ." A'lta nau'itka. Atci'ctax **2**
"Future you will imitate them steel-head they catch." Now indeed. He made it
salmon.

ckulkulō'L, a'lta atcLi'ckōLᵢ Ckulkulō'L. A'lta nē'ktcuktē, a'lta **3**
a salmon-harpoon, now he finished it Ckulkulō'L. Now it got day, now

akLōlā'pam uyā'xk'un. A'lta ia'xka ā'yō, nixēlalā'ko-imam. A'lta **4**
she went digging his elder sister. Now he he went, he went to catch salmon. Now
roots

atcLē'lukc ēXt iqoanē'X. A'lta nē'Xkō. A'lta ayō'yam gō tE'ctaqL. **5**
he speared it one steel-head Now he went home. Now he arrived at their house.
salmon.

A'lta nē'xēlktc. A'lta nō'ktcīqt ōk'u'ltcin. "TgEt!ō'kti agE'xk'un **6**
Now he roasted it. Now it was done its head. "Good my elder sister

nalᶜē'm Xak ōk'u'ltcin. Kᵢē, taua'lta agā'k'altcin naxā'lax. **7**
I give her this fish head. No, else her fish head comes to be
to eat on her.

TgEt!ō'kti iā'wan nialᶜē'm. Kᵢē, taua'lta itcā'wan ayaxē'lax. **8**
Good its belly I give it to No, else her belly comes to be on
her to eat. her.

Iqᵢē'qau nialᶜē'ma. Kᵢē, taua'lta itcā'qᵢēqau ayaxē'lax. TgEt!ō'kti **9**
Its back I shall give it No, else her back comes to be on Good
to her to eat. her.

LElē'ct nLalᶜē'ma. Kᵢē, taua'lta Lgā'lict aLā'xalax." A'lta ka'nauwē **10**
its tail I give it to her No, else her tail comes to be on Now all
to eat. her."

atctā'wulᶜ. Iā'wan atciā'wulᶜ, ia'ᶜēqau atciā'wulᶜ a'lta Liā'lict **11**
he ate it. Its belly he ate it, its back he ate it, now its tail

atcLā'wulᶜ. A'lta aya-ō'ptit. A'lta nā'Xkō-y- uyā'xk'un. NaXkō'mam **12**
he ate it. Now he went to sleep. Now she went home his elder sister. She came home

gō tE'ctaqL. A'lta iā'qxôiō Lgā'wuX. A'lta aLā'XiLq, a'lta **13**
to their house. Now he slept her younger bro- Now she heated stones, now
ther.

agiā'kxôpq itcā'kᵢEnatan. A'lta agē'lᶜēm Lgā'wuX. **14**
she roasted them her potentilla roots. Now she gave them her younger
to him to eat. brother.

A'lta nē'ktcuktē wiXt. A'lta nō'ya wiXt akLōlā'pam. A'lta lē'2lē **15**
Now it got day again. Now she went again she went digging. Now long

ka nixā'latck Lgā'wuX. Nixēlalā'ko-imam. Lē'lē, mank lē'lē ka **16**
and he rose her younger bro- He went to catch salmon. A long a little long then
ther. time,

atcLē'lukc iā'qoa-iL iqᵢoanē'X. "Anē'4 Ckulkulō'L! Tatc atcuwa' **17**
he speared it a large steel-head salmon. "Aneh Ckulkulō'L! See! [exclamation]

nēkct tcalᶜē'ma-y- uyā'xk'un." Ta'kE naxLō'lEXa-it uyā'xk'un: "Ō, **18**
not he will give it to [to] his elder sis- Then she thought his elder sister: "Oh,
her to eat ter."

ka'ltas qiaō'nim Liā'xauyam." A'lta nē'Xkō Ckulkulō'L. Ta'kE **19**
only he is made fun of his poverty." Now he went home Ckulkulō'L. Then

niXkō'mam. Ta'kE nē'xēlktc. Ta'kE nixgē'ktcikt. "TgEt!ō'kti **20**
he came home. Then he roasted it. Then it was done. "Good

agE'xk'un nalᶜē'm Xak ōk'u'ltcin [etc., three times as above.] **21**
my elder sister I give it to this fish head [etc., three times as above].
her to eat

A'lta aLā-iLā'kuX Lᶜā'tcau gō wē'wuLē. Ta'kE wiXt nē'ktcuktē. **22**
Now she smelled it grease in the interior of Then again it got day.
the house.

183

1 Ta'kE wiXt nō'ya akLōlā'pam. Ta'kE wiXt ā'yō nixēlalā'ku-imam.
  Then again she went she went to dig Then again he went he went to catch salmon.
                          roots.

2 Kä2-y- akē'x ka wiXt naxaltcā'ma: "Ē'yaa-itcLx iā'q¡oaniX
  Where she was and again she heard: "How large his steel-head
                                                        salmon

3 Ckulkulō'L." "O, Liā'xauyam Lō'nas aqiaō'nim." Ta'kE atcLē'lukc
  Ckulkulō'L." "Oh, his poverty perhaps he is laughed at." Then he speared it

4 iā'q¡oaniX, ta'kE nē'Xkō. NēXkō'mam gō tā'yaqL. Ta'kE
  his steel-head then he went home. He arrived at home at his house. Then
  salmon,

5 nē'xēlktc. Ta'kE nō'ktcikt ōk'u'ltcin. "Ō agē'xk'un, nalcē'ma
  he roasted it. Then it was done the head. "O my elder sister, I shall give
                                                                     her to eat

6 Xak ōk'u'ltcin. K·¡ē, taua'lta agā'k'altcin naxā'lax. TgEt!ō'kti
  this fish head. No, else her fish head comes to be on Good
                                                       her.

7 iā'wan nialcē'ma. K·¡ē, taua'lta itcā'wan ayaxā'lax. Iq¡ē'qau
  its belly I give it to her. No, else her belly comes to be on her. The back

8 nialcē'ma. K·¡ē, taua'lta itcā'q¡ēqau ayaxē'lax. TgEt!ō'kti LELē'ct
  I give it to her. No, else her back comes to be on her. Good the tail

9 nLalcē'ma. K·¡ē, taua'lta Lgā'lict aLā'xalax." A'lta ka'nauwē
  I give it to her. No, else her tail comes to be on her." Now all

10 atciā'wulc, iyā'eqau atciā'wulc, Liā'lict atcLā'wulc. A'lta aya-ō'ptit.
   he ate it, its back he ate it, its tail he ate it. Now he slept.

11 A'lta nā'Xkō uyā'xk'un. A'lta naXkō'mam. A'lta aLā'xEltq.
   Now she went home his elder sister. Now she came home. Now she heated stones.

12 Agiā'kxōpq itcā'k¡Enatan. Ta'kE ayō'ktcikt itcā'k¡Enatan, ta'kE
   She roasted them her potentilla roots. Then they were done her potentilla roots, then

13 agē'lcēm Lgā'wuX. A'lta L¡ap agE'Lax Lcā'tcau gō wē'wuLē. "Ō,
   she gave them her younger Now find she did it grease in inside of house. "Oh,
            to him to eat brother.

14 nau'itka, taL¡ Xōku ē'ka atcinā'xt Xōku nēkct atcinElcē'mEniL."
   indeed, look here thus he did to me here not he always gave it to me
                                                                   to eat."

15 A'lta L¡ap agE'Lax Lcā'pta gō iā'yacqL. A'lta akLugō'Lit gō-y-
   Now find she did it salmon roe in his mouth. Now she put it up on

16 ōmā'p kucā'xalē. Ta'kE agē'lcēm ik¡Enā'tan. Ta'kE akLō'cgam
   a board above. Then she gave them potentilla roots. Then she took it
                                                                    to him to eat

17 qō'La Lcā'pta, ta'kE akLē'lcēm. "Ō x·ilē'k aqLnē'lcēm." Ta'kE
   that salmon roe, then she gave it to him "Oh, this I was given it to eat." Then
                                                                to eat. •

18 atci'Lukct, ta'kE k¡wac nē'xax. "Ō, ta'kE taL¡ L¡ap agā'nax."
   he saw it, then afraid he got. "Oh, then behold find she did me."

19 A'lta nē'ktcuktē. Ta'kE naxE'ltXuitck. Ta'kE agiō'lXam Lgā'wuX:
   Now it got day. Then she made herself ready. Then she said to him her younger
                                                                         brother:

20 "Ni'Xua mE'pa." Ta'kE ayō'tXuit. "Ē'tsEntsEn imē'xal. Nēkct
   "Well go outside." Then he stood up. "Humming-bird your name. Not

21 qa'nsiX iq¡oanē'X miā'xo." Ta'kE nō'ya, naiE'ltaqL.
   ever steel-head sal- you will eat Then she went, she left him.
          mon it."

22 Nō'ya, nō'ya, kulā'yi nō'ya. Ta'kE agō'ēkEl t!ōL. Ta'kE
   She went, she went, far she went. Then she saw it a house. Then

23 nō'p!am. Ta'kE agiō'ci itcā'k¡Enatan iā'Lēlam. Ta'kE akLō'cgam
   she came in. Then she roasted her potentilla roots ten. Then she took it
            them in ashes

24 Lcā'pta; agE'Lax. AkLā'wulc. Ta'kE aLXaLgō'mam LgōLē'lEXEmk.
   salmon roe; she ate it. She ate it. Then he arrived a person.

25 Ta'kE aLgō'cgam aLkcā'nk¡o-iam. Ta'kE aLōlā'taXit qō'La Lcā'pta.
   Then he took her he struck her. Then it fell down that salmon roe.

26 Ta'kE naxEmā'tcta-itck, ta'kE nō'pa. Ta'kE wiXt nō'ya, kulā'yi
   Then she was ashamed, then she went out. Then again she went, far

nō'ya. Ta'kE wiXt agō'ēkEl t!ōL. Nō'ya, agixā'laqLē. A'lta pä2L   1
she went. Then again she saw it a house. She went, she opened the Now full
door.

qō'ta t!ōL tk¡ē'wulElqL, cka mEnx·i nō'La·it ka ayō'lEktcū ēXt   2
that house dried salmon, and a little while she stayed and it fell down one

iq¡oanē'X. Agiō'cgam agiuk'ō'n iā'kō. WiXt ayō'lEktcū. WiXt   3
steel-head salmon. She took it she put it up there. Again it fell down. Again

agiō'cgam, wiXt agiok'ō'n iā'kō. A'lta agiō'ci itcā'k¡Enatan   4
she took it, again she put it up there. Now she roasted her potentilla roots
them in ashes

iaLē'lam. A'lta agiōna'xLatck môkct. A'lta agiō'xtkin, agiō'xtkin,   5
ten. Now she lost them two. Now she searched for she searched for
them, them,

agiō'xtkin. K·¡ē, nēkct L¡ap agā'yax. A'lta aLō'lEktcu Lᶜā'pta.   6
she searched for Nothing, not find she did it. Now it fell down salmon roe.
them.

AkLō'cgam wiXt akLok'ō'n iā'kō. Lē'2lē ka aLXatgō'mam LE'kXala.   7
She took it again she put it up there. Long and he arrived a man.

Ta'kE L¡äk nā'xax ōᶜō'lEptckiX. TakE aLE'k·im: "Ā2!" Ta'kE wiXt   8
Then crackle it did the fire. Then he said: "Ah!" Then again

L¡äk nā'xax ōᶜō'lEptckiX. Ta'kE wiXt aLE'k·im: "Ā2. Ē, qa'da   9
crackle it did the fire. Then again he said: "Ah. Eh, why

qa nikct amiō'cgam agimElᶜē'mEniL! Môkct agiō'cgam ōq¡oyō'qxut   10
not you took it she gave to you to eat Two she took them the old woman
always?

imē'k¡Enatan. Amiō'Xtkin gō-y- ī'tcaqL. Amxa'LōX na   11
your potentilla roots. You searched for them in her mouth. You think [int. part.]

LgōLē'lEXEmk x·ix·iau amigā't'ōm! Ē'ltcap iā'xal x·ix· iāwunē'nEm."   12
a person this you met him! Fishhawk his this danger."
name

A'lta agā'wan uaxā'lax. A'lta nakxā'to; LE'kXala akLaxô'tō.   13
Now pregnant she got. Now she gave birth; a male she gave birth
to it.

A'lta aLE'tsax qō'La Lk¡āsks. ALix·E'lgiLxax. A'lta aksō'pEnax,   14
Now he cried that child. He put him on top of Now she jumped,
the fire.

akLō'sgamx Lgā'xa. "Anā', qa'daqa aLEmXE'lgiLx!" "Qa'daqa   15
she took it her child. "Anah, why you put him into the fire?" "Why

amLā'xcgamx ōq¡oyō'qxut; giLginā'o·i. Iā'ma iau'a tE'mᶜEcX   16
you take him from her the old woman; she looks after him. Only here wood

mtupiā'Lxa. Nēkct mō'ya iau'a mai'ēmē." A'lta nau'itka iā'ma   17
gather. Not go there down river." Now indeed only

iau'a nā'xElEmEqa. A'lta lē'2lē, a'lta k·¡ē tE'mᶜEcX iau'a kca'la,   18
there she gathered wood. Now long time, now no sticks there up river,

ta'kE aktō'tctXōm. A'lta nō'ya iau'a mai'ēmē. A'lta L¡ap agā'yax   19
then she finished them. Now she went there down river. Now find she did it

ē'mᶜEcX, iū'Lqat ē'mᶜEcX. A'lta LEkᵘ agā'yax. A'lta Lpil qigō   20
a stick, long a stick. Now break she did it. Now red where

LEkᵘ nē'xax. WiXt LEkᵘ agā'yax, a'lta Liā'qxauwilqt. Lō'ni   21
broken it was. Again break she did it, now its blood. Three times

LEkᵘ agā'yax, ka LE'xauwē Liā'qxauwilkt. A'lta nā'Xko.   22
break she did it, then much its blood. Now she went home.

NaXkō'mam, agixā'laqLē. A'lta yuqunā'-itX itcā'k·ikala. Lō'ni   23
She came home, she opened the door. Now there lay her husband. Three
times

Lq¡up ikē'x. A'lta Lgā'xa Lā'qxulqt wä, wä, wä. A'lta pō'pō   24
cut he was. Now her child cried wä, wä, wä. Now blow

ā'kxax ōᶜō'lEptckiX. A'lta tcXEp akē'x ōᶜō'lEptckiX. Ta'kE   25
she did it the fire. Now extinguished it was the fire. Then

akLō'cgam Lgā'xa, ta'kE nō'ya.   26
she took it her child, then she went.

Kulā'yi ta'kE nō'ya. Ta'kE tEll nā'xax. "TgEt!ō'kti nLxElkctgō'ya   27
Far then she went. Then tired she got. "Good I desert it

1 LgE'xa. Iā'xkayuk nL'Eltā'qLa." AgE'Lōtk gu itconā'k. Ta'kE
my child.   Here   I shall leave it."   She carried it   to   a maple.   Then

2 naL'ē'taqL. Nō'ya ta'kE kulā'yi. A'lta kā aLgiā'xoil ikanī'm
she left it.   She went   then   far.   Now   where   he was work-   a canoe
                                                          ing at

3 qō'La Lē'Xat LE'k·ala, ta'kE aLkLtcā'ma Lk¡āsks. Ta'kE
that   one   man,   then   he heard it   a child.   Then

4 aLkLō'Xtkin. Ta'kE L¡ap aLgE'Lax, ta'kE aLgE'Lnkᵘɪ qoā'p gō
he searched for it.   Then   find   he did it.   then   he carried it   near   to

5 t!ōL ka aLkLō'pcut. Ta'kE nē'Xkō x·ix· ē'k·ala. Ta'kE atcō'lXam
house   and   he hid it.   Then   he went home   this   man.   Then   he said to her

6 uyā'k·ikala: "L¡ap anE'Lax Lk¡āsks. Amē'wan mxolā'xo." Lā'xlax
his wife: "Find   I did it   a child: You are pregnant   you do."   Deceive

7 ctā'xōya-y ōctā'xa. A'lta acgō'lXam ōctā'xa: "Ā, Lmē'na ayi'tcātc!
they did her   their daugh-   Now   they said to her   their daugh-   "Ah,   your mo-   her sickness
               ter.   ter: ther

8 ayā'la-ot. A'lta Lō'nas akxtō'ma." Ta'kE nō'La-it ōctā'xa. Hē
is on her.   Now   perhaps   she will give birth."   Then   she remained   their   Heh,
                                                            there   daughter.

9 qoā'p ikteu'ktai ka ta'kE anaō'ptit. Ta'kE atcLugō'lEmam qō'La
nearly   it was going to   and   then   she fell asleep.   Then   he fetched it   that
         get daylight

10 Lk¡āsks. "AmxE'lᶜōkō; LEmē'wuX ta'kE aLtē'mam." Ta'kE
child.   "Rise;   your younger brother   then   he arrived."   Then

11 naxE'lᶜōkō uyā'xa. "Ō, Lgā'wuX," ta'kE nā'k·ēm. A'lta Lgā'wuX
she rose   his daugh-   "Oh,   my younger   then   she said.   Now   her younger
        ter.   brother,"   brother

12 Lā'qoa-iL aLE'xax. A'lta atcLā'lax Lkalai'tanEma. A'lta ka'nauwē
large   he got.   Now   he made them   arrows.   Now   every
                            for him

13 qā'xēwa ayō'yix k·¡imtʌ'-y- uyā'xk'un. Itcā'q¡atxal. "Nikct
where   he went   after   his elder sister.   Her badness.   "Not

14 iamā'wuX," agiō'lXam. "L¡ap aqā'max; LgE'mama L¡ap atcā'max.
you are my   she said to him.   "Find   you were done;   my father   find   he did you.
younger brother,"

15 Ē'tsōL iā'xa mai'k·a." Ta'kE nēxE'Lxa Lgā'wuX. Ta'kE acXgō'mam.
Salmon-   his son   you."   Then   he was angry   her younger   Then   they came home.
harpoon   brother.

16 "GEnā'xo-il, gEnā'xo-il, ē'tsōL LgE'mama." "Nā2xaxā'x! qā'daqa-y-
"She always says   she always   Salmon-   my father."   "Naxaxā'x!   why
   to me,   says to me,   harpoon

17 ē'ka-y- amiā'xo-il LEmē'wuX?" Aqiō'cgam ē'mᶜEcX,
thus   you always say to him   your younger brother?"   It was taken   a stick,

18 aqaxElqē'lEx·Lakō. A'lta ka'nauwē Lᶜalā'ma tEll ā'yamxtc. "Ō,
she was whipped.   Now   every   day   tired   his heart.   "Oh,

19 tgEt!ō'kti nuwā'ᶜô." A'lta nē'ktcuktē, wiXt ā'cto. A'lta tgā'maᶜ
good   I kill her."   Now   it got day,   again   they went.   Now   shooting her

20 atctā'lax. Nō'mEqt. Ayaē'taqL, gō'yē nē'xax, ā'nqatē agiā'wat.
he did it to   She was dead.   He left her,   thus   he did   already   she followed
her.   [turned round],   him.

21 A'lta iā'qoa-iL nē'xax, iq¡oā'lipX nē'xax. A'lta niXē'qauwakō:
Now   large   he became,   a youth   he became.   Now   he dreamt:

22 "Ma'nix muwa'ōᶜ, ka gō-y- ogō'kcia L¡EmE'nL¡EmEn mā'xō. Ka
"When   you will kill her,   then   at   her finger   broken to pieces   make it.   Then

23 tcopEnā'ya-y- i'kta lō'Elō ka iā'xka L¡kōp miā'xō. A'lta ō'mEqta.
it will jump   something round   and   that   squeeze   do it.   Now   she will die.

24 Qē'xtcē gEmolā'ma: 'Nai'ka mEnuwa'ᶜō!'" A'lta wiXt nē'ktcuktē;
Intending   she will say: 'Me   kill me!'"   Now   again   it got day;

25 a'lta ā'ctō. A'lta gō Lqā'nakc ka wiXt atcā'waᶜ. A'lta wiXt
now   they went.   Now   at   a stone   then   again   he killed her.   Now   again

26 Lq¡ōp ā'tcax ogō'kcia. A'lta-y- atcō'pEna-y- i'kta lō'Elō. A'lta
cut   he did it   her finger.   Now   it jumped   something round.   Now

Lᵢkōp atcā'yax. Qē'xtcē agiō'lXaɪn: "Nai'ka mEnuwa'ᶜō." A'lta   **1**
squeeze   he did it.   Intending   she said to him: " Me   kill me!"   Now

nō'mEqt. A'lta ayaē'taqL.   **2**
she was dead.   Now   he left her.

A'lta ā'yō kulā'yi. A'lta Liā'XēwicX iLā'kēmatsk Liā'XēwicX.   **3**
Now   he went   far.   Now   his dog   spotted   his dog.

~~A'lta ayagō'ēm tō'lx-ma tā'nEmckc,~~ ō'Xuitikc tā'nEmckc. "Anā',   **4**
~~Now   he reached them   people~~   women,   many   ~~women.~~   "Anah,

masā'tsiLx qō'La Lkē'wucX. Wu'ska LxLōcgā'ma." A'lta ~~qē'xtcē~~   **5**
pretty   that   dog.   [Exclamation] we will take it."   Now   ~~intending~~

aqakLxLē'mōL. Kᵢē, nickct akLō'cgam. A'lta ēXā'tka   **6**
it was called much.   No,   not   she took it.   Now   one only

ōLā'XakᵢEmana: "Ai'aq, ai'aq, LgE'lxēm." Lē'lē ka akLgE'lxēm.   **7**
their chieftainess: "Quick,   quick,   call him."   Some time   and   she called him.

ALaga'ōm ka akLō'cgam. Nō'Xōgō tā'nEmckc: "Ō, Lgē'wucX   **8**
He came to her   and   she took him.   They went home   the women: "Oh,   a dog

Lᵢap ancgE'Lax, ōntcā'xakᵢEmāna akLō'cgam." Ta'kE nē'k·im   **9**
find   we did him,   our chieftainess   she took him."   Then   he said

iqē'sqēs: "Ni'Xua, nLō'kctama." Ta'kE ayō'p! iqē'sqēs. Ta'kE   **10**
blue-jay: "Well,   I will go to see him."   Then   he entered   blue-jay.   Then

atci'LᵉElkEl Lgē'wucX. Ta'kE atciō'cgam ikamō'kXuk, ta'kE   **11**
he saw it   the dog.   Then   he took it   a bone,   then

atciLE'lᶜēm ikamō'kXuk qō'La Lgē'wucX. Nēkct aLgā'yaqc. Ta'kE   **12**
he gave it to him   a bone   that   dog.   Not   he ate it.   Then
to eat

atcLā'owilX. "Iā'c Lē'Xa LgE'XēwucX. Iā'c Lē'Xa, mLuwā'ᶜō."   **13**
he hit him.   "Letting   do him   my dog.   Letting   do him,   you will kill
        alone   alone   him."

Ta'kE nē'Xkō iqᵢē'sqᵢēs. Ta'kE atciō'lXaɪn iā'xk'un: "Kā'sa-it,   **14**
Then   he went home   blue-jay.   Then   he said to him   his elder brother: "Robin,

LgōLē'lᴇXEmk, nēkct Lgē'wucX." "Hō'ntcin, cka kᵢā mxā'xō.   **15**
a person,   not   a dog."   "Don't,   and   silent   be.

Mā'mkXa na mLā'qxamt?" "Hō'ntcin, iā'xka x·ix·ī'k iqᵢēyō'qxut,   **16**
You alone [int. part.] you see it?"   "Don't,   he   this one   the old one,

ā'Lqē iā'xka iā'nēwa i'kta ilā'xo-ila." Lē'lē Lō'nas Lōn LᵘaLā'ma ka   **17**
later on   he   he first   some-   he knows it."   Some   perhaps   three   days   and
                     thing   time,

wiXt ā'yō iqᵢē'sqᵢēs. Ayō'p!aɪn, a'lta tā'lalX Lxē'lax Lgē'wucX.   **18**
again   he went   blue-jay.   He came in,   now   gamass   he ate it   the dog.

Ta'kE atciō'cgam ē'mᶜEcX iqᵢē'sqᵢēs, atciLgE'lXcim. "Ē, ē,   **19**
Then   he took it   a stick   blue-jay,   he struck him.   "Eh,   eh,

Lā'xauyam LgE'XēwucX," nā'k·im qaX ōᶜō'kuil. Ta'kE nē'Xko   **20**
his poverty   my dog,"   she said   that   woman.   Then   he went
                                                     home

iqᵢē'sqᵢēs. Ta'kE atciō'lXam iā'xk'un: "LgōLē'lᴇXEmk kā'sa-it;   **21**
blue-jay.   Then   he said to him   his elder brother: "A person   robin;

tā'lalX Lxē'lax." Nō'pōnEm. A'lta atcō'lXam uyā'k·ika: "O,   **22**
gamass   he eats."   It got dark.   Now   he said to her   his wife: "Oh,

ta'kE tEll atcā'yax ē'tcamxtc iqᵢē'sqᵢēs. Ala'xti LEkᵘ tciā'xoyē   **23**
then   tired   he makes it   my heart   blue-jay.   Finally   break   he will do
                                                  them

itcE'xamōkuk. NLxE'lkctgōya Lkē'wucX Lā'ōk." A'lta pō'lakli   **24**
my bones.   I shall throw it away   the dog   his blanket."   Now   dark

atci'LxElukctgō. A'lta nē'ktcuktē, a'lta txalôi'ma Liā'ōk. A'lta   **25**
he threw it away.   Now   it got day,   now   another   his blanket.   Now

ayō'p!aɪn iqᵢē'sqᵢēs. "Ē2, anē'k·iɪn LgōLē'lᴇXEmk. TcnE'luwats   **26**
he came in   blue-jay.   "Eh,   I said   a person.   He did not believe
                                                  me

kā'sa-it." A'lta iā'xkatē ayō'La-it.   **27**
robin."   Now   there   he remained.

Translation.

There was Ckulkulō'L [the salmon-harpoon] and his elder sister. Once upon a time the latter said to her brother: "Do as the other people do and catch steel-head salmon." Now he did so. He made a harpoon. On the day after he had finished it his sister went digging roots. Now he went to catch salmon. He speared a steel-head salmon and went home. When he arrived at home he roasted it and when it was done he said: "I will give the head to my sister to eat. No, else she will get a fish's head. I will give the belly to my sister to eat. No, else she will get a fish's belly. I will give the back to my sister to eat. No, else she will get a fish's back. I will give its tail to my sister to eat. No, else she will get a fish's tail." Now he ate the whole fish. He ate the belly, he ate the back, he ate its tail. Then he lay down to sleep. Now his elder sister came home. Her brother was asleep. She heated stones and roasted the roots. Then she gave them to him to eat.

On the next morning she went again digging roots. After some time her younger brother arose and went to catch salmon. After some time he speared a large steel-head salmon. "Ah, Ckulkulō'L behold! he does not give anything to his sister," said the people. His sister thought: "Oh, they make fun of my poor brother." Now Ckulkulō'L went home. When he arrived he roasted his salmon. It was done. Then he said: "I will give the head to my sister to eat" [etc., three times, as above].

Now she smelled the smell of grease in their house. On the next morning she went again digging roots. Then her brother went again to catch salmon. Again she heard: "How large is Ckulkulō'L's salmon!" "Oh, perhaps they make fun of my poor brother." Then Ckulkulō'L speared a salmon and went home. When he arrived he roasted it. Now its head was done. He said: "I will give the head to my sister to eat. No, else she will get a fish's head. I will give the belly to my sister to eat. No, else she will get a fish's belly. I will give the back to my sister to eat. No, else she will get a fish's back. I will give its tail to my sister to eat. No, else she will get a fish's tail." Now he ate the whole fish. He ate the back; he ate the tail. Then he lay down to sleep. Now his elder sister went home. When she came home she heated stones and roasted her potentilla roots. When they were done she gave them to her younger brother. Now she found some grease in the house. "Oh, indeed! Behold how he acted against me. He never gave me anything to eat." Now she found a salmon-egg in his mouth. She placed it on top of a shelf. Then she gave him the roots. Then she took that salmon egg and gave it to him. "Oh, somebody gave this to me." When he saw it he became afraid. "Look, she found me out." On the next morning she made herself ready and said to her younger brother: "Leave the house."

Then he arose. "Your name shall be Humming-Bird. Henceforth you shall not eat steel-head salmon." Then she went away and left him.

She went and went. She went a long distance. Then she saw a house. She entered and roasted ten roots in the ashes of the fire. Then she took a salmon roe and ate it. Then a man arrived who took her and struck her [on the nape]. The salmon roe fell [out of her mouth]. She was ashamed and went out of the house. She went again a long distance. Then she saw another house. She went and opened the door. The house was full of dried salmon. When she had stayed a little while a steel-head salmon fell down. She took it and put it back. It fell down again. She took it and put it back again. Now she roasted ten roots in the ashes of the fire. She lost two of them. She searched and searched, but did not find them. Now a salmon roe fell down. She took it again and put it back. After some time a man arrived. Then the fire crackled. He said, "Ah." The fire crackled again, and he said once more, "Ah. Heh, why did you not take the food which she offered to you? She took two of your roots and you searched for them in her mouth. Do you think the man whom you met was a human being? Fish-hawk is the name of that danger." Now she became pregnant. She gave birth to a boy. Now the child cried and the man put it on top of the fire. She gave one jump and took the child. "Ah, why do you put our child into the fire?" "Why do you take it away from the old woman? She will look after it." He continued: "When you gather wood go only this way. Do not go down the river." Now she did so, and gathered wood only above the house. Now one day there was no wood above the house. She had taken it all. Then she went down the river. She found a long stick and broke it. It was red where she had broken it. She broke it again and it bled. Three times she broke it and it bled profusely. She went home. When she opened the door she saw her husband lying there. He had three [deep] wounds. Now her child cried. She blew the fire, but it was extinguished. Then she took her child and left.

After she had gone a long distance she became tired. "I will desert my child," she thought. "I will leave it here." She carried it to a maple and left it. Then she went far away. Now a man was working at a canoe [near by]. He heard a child crying and searched for it. He found it and carried it to a place near his house. Then he went into the house, and said to his wife: "I found a child. Feign to be pregnant." Thus they deceived their daughter. They said to her: "Your mother begins to be in labor. Perhaps she will give birth to a child." Then their daughter stayed there. But when it was almost morning she fell asleep. Then he fetched the child. [He said to his daughter:] "Arise, your brother has been born." Then his daughter arose. "Ah, my brother," she said. Now, the boy grew up, and [his father] made arrows for him. He went about following his sister. She was bad and said:

"You are not my brother. My father found you. You are the salmon-spear's son." Then her brother became angry. When they came home he said: "She always says the salmon-spear is my father." Her father said: "Naxaxā'x, why do you always say so to your brother?" He took a stick and whipped her. Now the boy became tired [of her teasing and thought]: "I will kill her." On the next morning they went again. Then he shot her several times and she was dead. He left her, but when he turned round she followed him again. Now he became a youth. One day he dreamt: "If you want to kill her, you must break her finger. Then a round thing will jump out of it, and that you must squeeze to pieces. Then she will die. She will say: 'Kill *me!*'" On the next morning they went again. Then he killed her at a stone. He cut her finger and a round thing jumped out of it. He squeezed it and she said: "Kill *me*"[but he squeezed the round thing to pieces]. Now she was dead and he left her.

He went a long distance. Now he [assumed the shape of] a spotted dog. He came to a place where there were many women. They said: "See, how pretty is that dog. Let us take him!" They called him often, but he did not allow himself to be taken. Now only their chieftainess [had not tried]. They said: "Now you call the dog." She called him. He went to her and she took him. Then the women went home. They said: "Oh, we found a dog; our chieftainess took him." Then Blue-Jay said: "I will go to see him." He entered her house and saw the dog. He took a bone and offered it to him, but he did not eat it. Then he struck him. [The chieftainess said:] "Let my dog go; you will kill him." Then Blue-Jay went home and said to his elder brother: "Robin, that is a man and not a dog." "Oh, be quiet, do you think you alone can see?" "Ha, he is the elder one, and he ought to know everything sooner than I," retorted Blue-Jay. After about three days Blue-Jay went again. He entered the house and saw the dog eating gamass. Then Blue-Jay took a stick and struck him. "O, my poor dog," said that woman. Then Blue-Jay went home and said to his elder brother: "He is a man, Robin, he eats gamass." When it got dark the dog said to his wife: "Blue-Jay makes me tired. He will break my bones. I shall throw away my dog-skin blanket." At night he threw it away. When it got day again he had another blanket. Now Blue-Jay came in. [When he saw him, he said:] "Eh, I said he was a man and Robin would not believe me." Now he remained there.

18. IQATSĒ'LXAQ IĀ'KXANAM.

THE PANTHER HIS MYTH.

A'lta iŏ'c iqatsē'lxaq, imŏ'lEkuma iă'k¡ēwula. Ka'nauwē 1
Now   there was   the panther,   elks   hunter.   All

LᶜaLā'ma atciā'wul imŏ'lEkuma. Lē2, ka L¡ap atcā'yax ipē'naLX ka 2
days   he hunted them   elks.   Some   and find   he did it   a twig   and
     time

atciXp¡enē'nakō ka atcē'xElukctgō gĕ'kXulē ilEmē'tk. Ŏ, masā'tsiLx 3
he twisted it   and   he threw it down   under   the bed.   Oh,   pretty

x·ik ipē'naLX: "Anā' LgōLē'lEXEmk tayaX mxā'tx!" Wax 4
that   twig: "Anah   a person   good   you become!"   On the next
     morning

ā'yŏ-y· imŏ'lak nē'kElōya. Tsō'yustē niXatgō'mam. A'lta Li'Xuc 5
he went   elk   he went to catch   In the evening   he came home.   Now   there was on
     it.   the ground

Luē'lōL. "Â, qā'xēwa Lx atgatē'mam tê'lx·Em¡ Iqā'lxal ōxucgā'liL." 6
cedar bark.   "Ah,   whence   maybe   they came   people¡   Disks   they played."

Wāx wiXt nē'ktcuktē. WiXt ā'yŏ-y· imŏ'lak nē'kElōya. Tsō'yustē 7
On the   again   it got day.   Again   he went   elk   he went to catch   In the even-
next   it.   ing
morning

niXatgō'mam. A'lta LE'Xauē Luē'lōL: "Qā'xēwa Lx atgatē'mam 8
he came home.   Now   much   cedar bark: "Whence   maybe   they came

tê'lx·Em¡ Iqā'lxal ōxucgā'liL gō tE'kxaqL." Wāx nē'ktcuktē 9
the people¡   Disks   they always play   in   my house."   On the next   it got day
     morning

iLā'Lonē. WiXt ā'yŏ. NiXatgō'mam tsō'yustē. A'lta pāL Luē'lōL 10
the third time.   Again he went.   He came home   in the evening.   Now   full   cedar bark

Li'Xuc gō tā'yaqL. A'lta ŏ'wa axŏ'ca. ILā'laktē ā'yŏ. Lāx ŏᶜŏ'Lax 11
it was on   in   his house.   Now   counters they were   The fourth   he went.   Afternoon
the ground   on the ground.   time

ka nē'Xkō. Q¡oā'p atctä'xōm tā'yaqL, ō'kumatk atcaltcā'ma. Ta'kE 12
and he went home.   Nearly   he reached it   his house,   batons   he heard them.   Then

nixE'LXa. "Qā'xēwa tê'lx·Em, ōxucgā'liL iqā'lxal gō tE'kxaqL." 13
he became angry.   "Whence   the people,   they always play   disks   in   my house."

Q¡oā'p atci'tax tū'yaqL, ta'kE k¡ā nā'xax ō'kumatk. Ta'kE 14
Near   he came to it   his house,   then   silent they became   the batons.   Then

niXkō'mam, ayŏ'p¡am. A'lta-y· ŏ'wa ä'xŏc gō-y· ōmā'p. "Wu'Xi 15
he arrived at home,   he came in.   Now   counters   lay   on   a plank.   "To-morrow

ka nxptcō'ta, qā'xēwa Lx atgatciā'ya." Wāx nē'ktcuktē. 16
and   I shall hide,   whence   maybe   they came."   On the next   it got day.
     morning

NixE'ltXuitck. Ayŏ'pa. Ayŏ'La-it gō tE'pcō. Nigē'qxamt, nigē'qxamt; 17
He made himself   He went   He stayed   in the grass.   He looked,   he looked;
ready.   out

k¡ē, nikct atci'LᶜElkEl LgōLē'lEXEmk. Ta'kE atcaltcā'ma ō'kumatk 18
nothing   not   he saw it   a person.   Then   he heard them   batons

gō wē'wuLē. Ta'kE nē'Xkō. Ta'kE atcickxā'nap¡ē. A'lta· iqā'lxal 19
in the interior of   Then   he went home.   Then   he looked into the house   Now   disks
the house.   through a hole.

Lxcgā'liL Lq¡oā'lipX. A'lta iŏ'kuk LE'Lapc uLā'Xematk ā'LgōtX. 20
be played   a youth.   Now   here   his foot   his baton   it struck it.

A'lta Lxā'xo-il: 21
Now   he sang:

Ē'pēnaLX   atsē'nkatXEl   Xiau   ē'tselXit   atsEnō'gutXap!

c [musical notation]

Twig   he gives me name   this   my brother   he twists me

ēnē'nankuL Xiau ē'tselXit.

2 [musical notation]

often   that   my brother.

Ta'kE ā'yup! iqatsē'Lxaq: "Ē2 Lgā'wuX, LgE'xauyam. Qa'daqa
Then he entered the panther: "Eh, my younger my poverty. Why
                                        brother,

4 ēmxanx'ā'l!" Ta'kE ayō'La-it Liā'wuX; nixemā'tcta-itck. Cka
you keep secrets Then he stayed his younger he was ashamed. And
before me?"   brother;

5 mä'nx·i nixemā'tcta-itck, ta'kE atciō'lXam Liā'wuX: "T!ā'ya
a little he was ashamed, then he said to him his younger bro- "Good
                                                        ther:

6 mE'La-it." Ta'kE ayō'La-it. T!ayā' ayō'La-it, ta'kE acxä'la-it. Ta'kE
you stay." Then he remained. Good he stayed, then they stayed. Then

7 atctē'lōt tiā'xalaitanEma. TgEt!ō'kti tiā'xalaitanEma. A'lta
he gave them his arrows. Good his arrows. Now
to him

8 tEmacā'nukc iā'k¡ēwula Liā'wuX. Ta'kE atciō'lXam Liā'wuX:
deer he hunted his younger brother. Then he said to him his younger
                                                        brother:

9 "Iā'ma iau'a mō'yima. Näkct iau'a mai'ēmē iLtā'yim." Ta'kE
"Only there go. Not there down stream go." Then

10 nau'itka iā'ma iau'a k^ucala' ayō'yim. Ta'kE iq¡oā'lipX nē'xax.
indeed only there up stream he went. Then a youth he became.

11 Ta'kE agō'n ō^ɛō'Lax, a'lta ā'yō iau'a mai'ēmē. Ayogō'om tEmɛā'ēnia,
Then one day, now he went there down stream. He reached it a prairie,

12 ta'kE ayoga'ōm ō'npitc. Ta'kE itcā'maɛ atciā'lax gō itcā'potē. Ta'kE
then he reached her a chicken Then shooting her he did it to on her wing. Then
                          hawk.   her

13 nōē'luktcu ō'npitc. A'lta nā'xankō, aksō'pEnän, aksō'pEnän
she fell down the chicken hawk. Now she ran, she jumped, she jumped,

14 nā'xankō. Ta'kE nē'xankō atcagE'ta. Kulā'yi atcagE'ta, ta'kE
she ran. Then he ran, he followed her. Far he followed her, then

15 atcō'ikEl t!ōL. Ta'kE iā'xkatē nō'p!a gō qō'ta t!ōL. A'lta Lawā'
he saw it a house. Then there she entered in that house. Now slowly

16 ā'yō. NixLō'lXa-it: "Ō, qEnuwa'ɛō. TgEt!ō'kti uXtā'kōya. Ō-y-
he went. He thought: "Oh, I shall be killed. Good I turn back. Oh,

17 ō'XalaitaEnEma tq¡ex näxt. Qā'doxuē nō'p!a." Ta'kE ā'yōp!. Gō-y-
my arrows like I do them. Must I enter." Then he entered. At

18 icE'q ayō'La-it. A'lta pāL tê'lx·Em gō qō'ta t!ōL. A'lta aqō'kumam
the door he stayed. Now full people in that house. Now it was looked at

19 uyā'Xalaitan. A'lta ka'nauwē tê'lx·Em atgō'kumam uyā'Xalaitan.
his arrow. Now all the people looked at it his arrow.

20 Ta'kE aqayā'lōt iq¡ē'sq¡ēs. A'lta atcō'kumam iq¡ē'sqēs. A'lta
Then it was given to blue-jay. Now he looked at it blue-jay. Now
him

21 nē'k·im: "Sai'anē, sai'anē, sai'agEq¡oē'Lnē, iq¡ē'sq¡ēs." "Nēkct
he said: "Give it to me, give it to me, my double-pointed arrow, blue-jay." "Not

22 mai'ka sE'm'ēq¡oēLnē, tEXu'l gimē'q¡atxala." Ta'kE wiXt aqō'kumam
your your double-pointed very you having badness." Then again it was looked at
arrow,

23 uyā'xalaitan. "La'ksta Lx Lkā'nax uLā'xalaitan! At!ō'k¡i-y-
his arrow. "Whose maybe chief his arrow? Good

24 ōkulai'tan." TakE wiXt aqayā'lōt iq¡ē'sq¡ēs. A'lta wiXt nē'k·im:
arrow." Then again it was given blue jay. Now again he said:
to him

25 "Sai'anē, sai'anē, sai'agEq¡oē'Lnē, iq¡ē'sq¡ēs." "Ni'Xua si'sgum."
"Give it to give it to my double-pointed arrow, blue-jay." "Well, take it."
me, me,

Ta′kE ayū′tXuit, atcū′ckam. Ta′kE tō′tō nē′xax. A′lta tktē′ma 1
Then   he stood up,   he took it.   Then   shake   he did.   Now   dentalia

pāL ā′yaLᵋa. Ta′kE nē′k·im iqᵢē′sqᵢēs: "Ā Lōwatskā′ Lkā′naxā′!" 2
full   his body.   Then   he said   blue-jay: "Ah,   follow him   the chief!"

Ta′kE nē′xankō iqᵢoā′lipX. Ta′kE agikE′ta ōᶜō′kuil. Ta′kE a′ctō, 3
Then   he ran   the youth.   Then   she followed him   the woman.   Then   they went,

a′ctō, a′ctō, a′ctō. Ta′kE ayō′pᵢam gō tE′ctaqL iā′xk′un. Ta′kE 4
they went,   they went,   they went.   Then   he came in   at   their house   his elder brother.   Then

nēxE′pcut. Ta′kE nō′pᵢam ōᶜō′kuil. K·ᵢē LgōLē′lEXEmk gō wē′wuLē. 5
he hid himself.   Then   she came in   the woman.   No   person   in   interior of house.

Ta′kE naxLō′lXa-it: "Qā′xēwaLx ā′Lō qō′La Lqᵢoā′lipX!" Lē ta′kE 6
Then   she thought: "Where maybe   he went   that   youth!"   Some then time

ɪsō′yustē niXatgō′mam iqats!ē′Lxaq. A′lta Lᵋā′gil Lōc. "Ō, ta′kE 7
evening   he came home   the panther.   Now   a woman   there was.   "Oh,   then

taLᵢ ē′wa mai′ēmē ā′yō." A′lta atcō′cgam qaX ōᶜō′kuil. NaxLō′lXa-it 8
behold   thus   down river   he went."   Now   he took her   that   woman.   She thought

qaX ōᶜō′kuil: "Qansi′x· aLXatgō′mam qi′La Lqᵢoā′lipX!" Agō′n 9
that   woman: "When   he came home   this   youth!"   The next

ōᶜō′Lax akLō′xtkin. Lak, Lak, Lak, Lak agā′yax ēecō′ma, 10
day   she searched for him.   Turn over,   turn over,   turn over,   turn over   she did them   skins,

ɪmō′lak iā′ecōma. Ta′kE nō′ponEm. Mȏkct Lᶜ aLā′ma, tā′nata t!ōL 11
elk   their skins.   Then   it grew dark.   Two   days,   one side of house

ka agiō′tctXōm. TE′gōn tā′nata t!ōL agiō′xtkin. Lak, Lak, Lak, 12
then   she finished it.   Next   the other side of   house   she searched.   Turn over,   turn over,   turn over,

Lak ēicō′ma agā′yax. Iā′kxȏiū. Ta′kE akLō′cgam Lᶜā′tcau, ta′kE 13
turn over   the skins   she did them.   He slept.   Then   she took it   grease,   then

aktō′cgam tqc′ō′cūtk. Ta′kE ataxE′lgiLx. Ta′kE naxō′LEla tqc′ō′cūtk. 14
she took them   hoofs.   Then   she made a fire.   Then   they got done   the hoofs.

Ta′kE LᵢEmē′nLᵢEmEn agE′tax. Ta′kE aktō′cgam tc!ō′wuLᵢ. Ta′kE 15
Then   broken to pieces   she made them.   Then   she took it   soot.   Then

akcxē′lakō kᵢa imō′lak ā′yaqcō gō ciā′ktcXict. A′lta aqcxē′lakō, 16
she mixed it   and   elk   its hair   at   its nostrils.   Now   she mixed it,

ka′nauwē aqcxē′lakō kᵢa Lᶜā′tcau, imō′lak Liā′qxatcau. A′lta wax 17
all   it was mixed   and   grease,   elk   its grease.   Now   pour out

aktē′lax gō ciā′ktcXict. Pō′lakli nixE′lᶜōkō. A′lta ē′ctatc!a 18
she did it to him   in   his nostrils.   At dark   he awoke.   Now   their sickness

ciā′ktcXict: "Ō, kā′pXō, kā′pXō, cgEmō′laktcXict cxanā′lax." "Ō, 19
his nostrils: "O,   elder brother,   elder brother,   my elk nose   comes to be on me."   "O,

au, cmē′mōlaktcXict cxamā′lax. QEqā′ta ayamā′xo." "Ō kā′pXō, 20
younger brother,   your elk nose   comes to be on you.   Unable to help   I do you."   "O elder brother,

kā′pXō, ō tgEqc′ō′cotk txauā′lax." "Ō au, tEmē′qc′ōcōtk txamā′lax. 21
elder brother,   oh,   my hoofs   come to be on me."   "O, younger brother,   your hoofs   come to be on you.

QEqā′ta ayamā′xō." Nē′ktcuktē ka nixēnā′Xit ēecō′ma, imō′lEkuma 22
Unable to help   I do you."   It got day   and   they stood up   the skins,   elks

nē′xax. Ka ayō′tXuit Liā′wuX. Ē′lEmiX nē′xax. Ayō′pa Liā′wuX. 23
they became.   And   he stood up   his younger brother.   ElEmiX   he became.   He went out   his younger brother.

Nixēnā′Xit imō′lEkuma ka′nauwē. A′lta ayō′ptck gō tqā′-itEma. 24
They stood up   the elks   all.   Now   they went inland   to   the woods.

A′lta atcō′cgam qaX ōᶜō′kuil itcā′potē. Ā′tcukᵘ ᴛ gō Lā′xanē. 25
Now   he took her   that   woman   her arm.   He carried her   to   outside.

1 A′lta tō′tō ā′tcax. Ka′nauwē tgā′Lwulē Laq atxā′xax. Atcā′xalukctgō:
   Now   shake he did her.   All   her flesh   come   it did.   He threw her down:
                                                     off

2 "Ō′npitc imē′xal. Näkct muXugō′mita tkanā′ximct. Qiā′x itcā′yau,
   "Chicken- your name.   Not   you will make them   chiefs.   If   a snake.
    hawk   unhappy

3 tcx·ī miā′xō. Imē′q atxala. Nai′ka iqats!ē′Lxaq itci′xal."
   then you will eat it. Your badness.   I   panther   my name."

Translation.

There was the panther. He was an elk hunter. Every day he went
hunting. One day he found a branch [of a spruce]; he twisted it and
threw it under his bed. It was a pretty branch. [Then he said:] "Oh,
I wish you would become a man!" On the next day he went again elk
hunting. In the evening he came home. Now he saw cedar bark lying
on the ground. "Where do these people come from? They have been
playing at disks" [said he]. On the following morning he went again
elk hunting. In the evening he came home. Now there was much
cedar bark [in his house]. "Where may these people have come from?
They always play at disks in my house." On the third day he went
again, and came home in the evening. Now the floor of his house lay
full of cedar bark and counters lay on the ground. He went out for
the fourth time and came home in the afternoon. When he reached
his house he heard batons. Then he became angry. "Where do these
people come from? They always play at disks in my house." He came
near the house, then the noise of the batons stopped. He arrived at
home and entered. Now counters lay on a plank. [He said:] "To-
morrow I shall hide to see where these people come from." On the
next morning he made himself ready and went out. He stayed in the
grass [near the house] and looked. He did not see anybody. Then he
heard the batons moving in the interior of the house. He went home
and looked through a hole in the wall of the house. Now there was a
youth who played at disks. He struck the rhythm with his foot and
sang: "My brother calls me branch of a spruce, my brother twisted me
often." Then the panther entered. "Oh, my poor brother, why did
you hide yourself before me?" Then the youth was ashamed. He
stayed there. The panther said to him: "Stay with me." Then he
remained there. Now the panther gave him good arrows, and the youth
went hunting deer. Then the panther said to his younger brother:
"Go only this way, do not go down the river." He obeyed and went
only up the river. He grew up. One day, however, he went down the
river. He came to a prairie where he found a chicken-hawk. He shot
it and hit its wing. It fell down and ran away jumping. He pursued
it a long distance. Then he saw a house. The chicken-hawk entered
the same. Now he went on slowly. He thought: "Oh, they will kill
me. I had better turn back. But I like my arrow [so well]. I must
go in." Then he entered and remained standing in the door. The house
was full of people who looked at his arrow. All the people looked at

it. Then they gave the arrow to Blue-Jay, who looked at it. Then the young man said: "Give me my double-pointed arrow, Blue-Jay." "It is not your arrow, you bad man" [, retorted Blue-Jay]. Again the people looked at the arrow and said: "To what chief may this arrow belong? It is a good arrow." Then they gave it again to Blue-Jay. Now the young man said again: "Give me, oh, give me my double-pointed arrow, Blue-Jay!" "Well, take it!" Then [the young man] arose and took it. He shook himself and his body was all covered with dentalia. Then Blue-Jay said [to the chicken-hawk, who on entering the house had assumed the shape of a woman]: "Follow the chief!" The youth ran and the woman pursued him. They went and went and went until he came to his elder brother's house. He hid himself [inside]. The woman entered and did not see anybody. She thought: "Where may that youth have gone?" In the evening the panther came home. Now there was the woman [in his house. He thought:] "Certainly he went down the river!" Then he married the woman. She thought: "When did that youth come home?" On the following day she searched for him. She turned over all the elk skins until it grew dark. She continued two days. Then she had finished all the skins on one side of the house. Now she searched at the other side of the house. She turned over all the elk skins. [Finally she found him] sleeping [under the skins]. She took some grease and [elk] hoofs. She made a fire and roasted the hoofs. When they were done she pounded them. She took some soot and mixed it with hair of an elk's nose. Now she mixed it all with elk's grease and poured it into his nostrils. When it grew dark he awoke. Now his nostrils felt sore. He said: "Oh, my elder brother, my nose is being transformed into an elk's nose." "Oh, my younger brother, your nose is being transformed into an elk's nose. I can not help you." "Oh, my elder brother, hoofs are growing on my feet." "Oh, younger brother, hoofs are growing on your feet. I can not help you." On the following morning the elk skins arose and became elks. The youth arose. He became Ē′lemiX* and went out. Then all the elks arose and went into the woods. Now [the panther] took the woman at her arm. He carried her out of the house and shook her, so that all her flesh fell down. He threw her down and said: "Your name shall be Chicken-hawk. Henceforth, you shall not make chiefs unhappy. When you see a snake you shall eat it. My name will be Panther."

* The tutelary spirit of the hunters.

BELIEFS, CUSTOMS, AND TALES.

THE SOUL AND THE SHAMANS.

1. Gitā′kikElal atgē′ix ē′wa tEmēuwā′lEma. Manix aLō′niks,
1. The seers go thus [to] the ghosts. When three.

2 Lā′nēwa aqLā′x pāt giLā′Xawôk. K¡imta′ aqLā′x pāt giLā′Xawôk,
first he is made a having a guardian Last he is made a having a guardian
strong spirit. strong spirit,

3 kā′tsEk aqLā′x gianu′kstX iLa′Xawôk. Ma′nix ala′ktikc atgē′ix
in the he is made a small one his guardian When four go
middle spirit.

4 gitā′kikElal, ä′ka amȯ′kctikc kā′tcEk aqtā′x. Lā′nēwa aqLā′x pāt
seers, thus two in middle are made. First he is made strong

5 giLā′Xawôk, LEk·i′mta aqLā′x pāt giLā′Xawôk. Aqē′ktaȯx
person having a last he is made strong a seer. It is pursued
guardian spirit,

6 iLā′Xanatē Lkā′nax, ma′nix ē′Latc!a Lkā′nax. Manix itcā′q¡atxala
his soul the chief's, when his sickness a chief. When its badness

7 ayā′xElax qaX uē′Xatk, aLktō′p!Ena Lā′ēwam qō′La Lā′nēwa.
comes to be on that road, he utters his song that first one.

8 Manix ē′wa k·¡imta′ itcā′q¡atxala ayā′xElax qaX uē′Xatk, ka qō′La
When thus behind its badness comes to be that road, and that
on it

9 iau′a k·¡imta′ aLktōp!Ena′x Lā′ēwām. Cka mE′nx·i nōpō′nEmx ka
there behind he utters it his song. And a little dark and

10 atōkoē′la-itx, tatc! ayu′ktEliL iō′itEt ka aqita′ȏm iLa′xanatē
they try to cure look! the morning star comes and they reach it his soul
him,

11 qō′La gē′Latc!a. Aqiō′cgam iLā′xanatē. Nuxutā′kux tgā′Xawôk
that sick one's. It is taken his soul. They return their guardian
spirits

12 gitā′kikElal. Ē′XtEmaē mȯ′kcti aLā′oix, ē′XtEma-ē ē′Xti aLā′o-ix
the seers. Sometimes two nights, sometimes one night

13 ka aqē′tElōtxax iLā′xanatē qigō nōxutā′kumx qō′ta tka′-uwôk.
and they give him his soul as they come back those spirits.

14 T!ā′ya aLxā′x gē′Latc!a.
Well gets the sick one.

2. Ma′nix aqiā′wax iLā′xanatē gē′Latc!a; atgē′x gitā′kikElal,
2. When it is pursued his soul the sick one's, they go the seers,

16 ma′nix aqiā′wax iLā′xanatē gē′Latc!a; iau′a qiq¡E′tcqta qaX
when it is pursued his soul the sick one's; there the left that

17 uē′Xatk aLō′ix; nōgō′go-imx gitā′kikElal: "O, Lō′mEqta, taL¡!"
trail it went; they say, the seers: "Oh, he will die, behold!"

18 Ma′nix iau′a qinq¡eama′ ayō′ix iLā′xanatē: "Ō, t!ā′ya qLā′xō!"
When there right hand goes his soul: "Oh, well he will be
made!"

3. Aqiga′omx qigō naLxoā′pē ilē′ē. Ia′xkatē aLkⱻEE′mcta-itx
3. It is reached where the hole [in] ground. There they drink always

20 tmēmElō′ctikc. Ma′nix aLkLā′mctx gē′Latc!a gō qō′La Ltcuq, a′lta
the ghosts. If it has drunk the sick one at that water, then

21 nēkct qa′nsix t!ayā′ aqLā′x. Qē′xtcē ka′nauwē tgā′qēwama
not anyhow well he is made. Intending all shamans

22 ataLgē′la-itx, näkct L!pāx aqLā′x.
they try to cure not well and he is made.
him, sound

196

4. L¡ap aqē'ax iLā'xanatē qō'La LkLāmctx Ltcuq. Aqiō'cgamx,   1
4. Find   it is done   his soul   that   having drunk   water.   It is taken,

iā'qoa-iL qix· ikanā'tē. Nuxotā'kux tgā'Xawôk gitā'kikElal. Iā'qoa-iL   2
large   that   soul.   They return   their spirits   the seers.   Large

qix· ikanā'tē. Aqiō'cgamx q¡oā'p iā'kua Natē'tanuē ka ianō'kstX   3
that   soul.   It is taken   near   here   the Indians   and   its smallness

nē'xElax. Nugō'go-imx qtōguilā'lē: "Lō'nas näkct Li't!ō-ix ka   4
comes to be   They say   those who cure   "Perhaps   not   one day   and
on it.   people:

Lō'mEqta." Niktcō'ktixē. Qē'xtcē aqē'tElōt iLā'xanatē. Aqā'tElōtx,   5
he will die."   It gets day.   Intending   it is given to   his soul.   It is given to him,
                                     him

q¡oā'p ka'nauwē ē'LaL'a ka aLō'mEqtx. NiLgEngā'gux iLā'xanatē.   6
nearly   all   his body   and   he dies.   It is too small   his soul.

5. Ma'nix atgē'ix gitā'kikElal, atgE'Lxamx tgā'Xawôk gō   7
5. When   they go   the seers,   they arrive seaward   their spirits   at

tEmēwā'lEma, kulā'yī gō-y· ē'lXam ikē'x iLā'xanatē gē'Latc!a, ka   8
the ghosts,   far   at   town   is   his soul   the sick one's,   and

nikct qLē't!ēmt, mgō'go-imx gitā'kikElal: "O, t!ayā' lxgiā'xō ka   9
not   he has been   they say   the seers: "Oh,   well   we shall   and
given food,   make him

nikct qiyī't!ēmt." Nau'itka, aqiō'cgam iLā'xanatē. Nōxutā'kux   10
not   he has been given   Indeed,   it is taken   his soul.   They return
food."

tgā'Xawôk gitā'kikElal. Qē'xtcē pāt ē'Latc!a, tatc! aqē'tElōt   11
their spirits   the seers.   Intending   really   his sickness,   look!   it is given to
                                                              him

iLā'xanatē, nau'i t!ayā' aLxā'x.   12
his soul,   at once   well   they make him.

6. Ē'Xtē wiXt qō'La aqLōngō'mitx; tEmēwā'lEma atkLōngō'mitx,   13
6. Once   again   that one   he is carried away;   the ghosts   they carry him away,

nau'i aLō'mEqtx. Nuxulā'ya-itx Lā'cōwīt. A'lta aqLElgē'mimtōmx   14
at once   he dies.   They tremble   his legs.   Now   they are paid

iLā'kikElal. A'lta aqugō'taox tEmēwā'lEma. ALqtā'qamitx qō'La   15
the seers.   Now   they are driven   the ghosts.   He sees them   that
                         away

aqLōngō'mitx qō'tac tEmēwā'lEma. Aqā'mxikc Lktō'kul, aqā'mxikc   16
he was carried away   those   ghosts.   Part of them   he knows   part of them
                                                                  them,

näkct aLktō'kulEqL'ax. Tā'mac qō'tac nikct ā'nqatē nuxo'La-it,   17
not   he knows them.   Only those   those   not   long ago   dead,

tā'cka aLktō'kulEqL'ax. Aqiktā'omx iLā'xanatē qō'La aqLōngō'mitx,   18
those   he knows.   It is reached   his soul   that   it is carried away,

aqLxlxēmē'takux. Nau'i atcElātā'kux, t!ayā' aLxā'x.   19
it is turned round.   At once   he recovers,   well   he gets.

7. Ma'nix tEmēwā'lEma atkLungō'mitx, manix k¡ē giLā'kikElal,   20
7. When   the ghosts   carry him away,   when   no   seer,

aLā'o-ix qō'La aqLungō'mitx, ē'Xtema ē'Xti aLā'o-ix ka aLō'mEqtx,   21
one day   that   he is [carried] away,   sometimes   one   night   and   he died

guā'nsum aLō'mEqtx, ē'Xtema mô'kctī aLā'o-ix aLō'mEqtx.   22
always   he is dead,   sometimes   two   nights   he is dead.

8. Ma'nix ayō'ix iLā'xanatē gē'Latc!a ē'wa tEmēwā'lEma, ma'nix   23
8. When   it goes   his soul   the sick one's   thus   ghosts,   when

atē'ktaòx gitā'kikElal atgE'Lktaòx tga'Xawôk, ā'nqatē aqiō'ktcx   24
they pursue it   the seers   they pursue it   their spirits,   already   it has been taken
                                                                          into the house

iLā'xanatē ka xā'oqxaL qa'da aqLā'x. Nōxoē'nimx tgā'Xawôk   25
his soul   and   can not   anyhow   it is done.   They cry   their spirits

gitā'kikElal. Nōxutā'kux. Môkct ikanā'tē aqtē'tElax; ma'nix Laq   26
the seers.   They return.   Two   souls   people have them;   if   take
                                                                   out

aqtE'Lxax qō'ta môkct, iā'xkatē ka aLō'mEqtx.   27
it is done   those   two,   there   and   he dies.

9. Ma′nix aqiE′lgElax ikē′utan, gō tEmēwā′lEma ikē′x. Ma′nix
9. When   it is seen   a horse,   at   the ghosts   it is.   When

nikct aqiō′cgamx, tcä′2xē ayā′o-ix ka ayō′mEqtx; ma′nix
not   it is taken,   several   days   and it is dead;   when

aqiō′cgamx ka näkct ayō′mEqtx. Ä′ka LgoLē′lEXEmk wiXt.
it is taken and not it is dead.   Thus   a person   also.

4. Ma′nix p!alā′ Lgō′cgēwal aqiE′lgElax iL′äxanatē gō tEmēwä′lEma,
When   well   some one goes   it is seen   his soul   at   the ghosts.

ma′nix näkct aqiō′cgamx, näkct iō′Lqtē ka aLō′mEqtx. Ä′ka
when   not   it is taken,   not   long   and he is dead.   Thus

wiXt ikanī′m. Ma′nix atgiungō′mitx tEmēwä′lEma ikanī′m,
also   a canoe.   When   they carry it away   the ghosts   a canoe,

ma′nix näkct aLgiō′cgam iLä′kikElal ka cä′ca nixä′x.
when   not   they take it   the seers   and smashed   it gets.

10. Ma′nix Lē′Xat giLä′kikElal ka-y- uts;ä′xō aLgä′x, ka
10. When   one   seer   and   shaking man- he does it,   and
                                   ikin

aLgä′tElutx nikct giLä′Xawôk. A′lta actō′ix ē′wa tEmēwä′lEma.
he gives it to one   not   having guardian   Now   they go   thus   [to] the ghosts.
                                   spirits.

ALkElgElgē′cgamx. ALktä′qamitx ka′nauwē tä′nEma gō
He helps him.   He sees   all   things   at

tmēmElō′ctikc ītä′lē qō′La nikct giLä′Xawôk. AkLō′kⁿᵢx ē′wa
the ghosts   their land   that one   not having guardian   It carries him   thus
                                   spirits.

tEmēwä′lEma qaX uts;ä′xō.
[to] the ghosts   that   manikin.

11. Ma′nix gō Natē′tanuē iLä′Xanatē ikē′x ia′mkXa ē′Xtka
11. When   at   the Indians   his soul   is   only   one only

Lāqᵘ nixē′lxax gē′Latc!a, aqiō′cgamx, nau′i t!ayā′ aLxä′x. Ma′nix
take out he did him   the sick one,   it is taken,   at once   well   he gets.   When

aqiō′cgamx qix· gianu′kstx iLä′xanatē gō Natē′tanuē aqē′tElōtx
it is taken   that   the one having   his soul   at   the Indians   it is given to
                    smallness   him

cka mE′nx·i t!ayā′ aLxä′x. TaL;, ēXt iLä′xanatē gō tEmēwä′lEma
and a little while well   he gets.   Look!   one   his soul   at   the ghosts

ikē′x, aqē′ktaôx qiX ē′wa tEmēwä′lEma iLä′xanatē iō′yama,
is,   it is pursued   that   thus   [to] the ghosts   his soul   arrives.

aqitElō′kⁿᵢamx iLä′xanatē, nau′i aqē′tElōtx nau′i t!ayā′ aLxä′x.
it is brought to him   his soul,   at once   it is given to him   at once   well   he gets.

12. Ma′nix Lkä′nax ayō′ix iLä′xanatē, ē′wa tkamilä′lEq ayō′ix
12. When   a chief   goes   his soul,   thus   [to] beach   goes

iLä′xanatē. Näkct ō′Xuitikc gitä′kikElal tgīō′kuētē. Ma′nix pät
his soul.   Not   many   seers   know about it.   If   a real

qLä′qēwama, tcx·ī Lgiō′kuētē ia′xkēwa ē′wa tkamilä′lEq.
shaman,   then   he knows about it   there   thus   beach.

13. Ma′nix ē′kta aLgiō′cgamx iLä′xanatē LgōLē′lXEmk
13. When   something   takes it   his soul   a person

tEmēwä′lEma ita′ktē, näkct qansi′x t!ayā′ aqLä′x.
the ghosts   their things.   not   ever   well   he gets.

14. Ma′nix Lō′mEqta gē′Latc!a guä′nEsum, qoē′t nixä′xoē.
14. When   he will die   a sick one   always   high water   it will be.

A′lta Lawä′ atgē′x qō′ta tkä′owôk. Ma′nix t!ä′ya qLä′xō
Now   slowly   they walk   those   spirits.   When   well   he will get

gē′Latc!a ka guä′nEsum q;ul nixä′xoē.
the sick one   and   always   low water   it will be.

15. Ma′nix aqiakLä′ētēmitx iLä′xanatē gē′Latc!a gō ikanī′m,
15. When   it is placed   his soul   the sick one's   in   canoe.

ä′qiukⁿᵢ ē′wa wē′kwa näkct qa′nsix t!ayā′ aqLä′x.
it is carried   thus   [to] ocean   not   ever   well   he gets.

16. Aqigä′omx iLä′xanatē gē′Latc!a. Aqiō′cgamx, aqiō′latcgux.
16. It is reached   his soul   a sick one's.   It is taken,   it is lifted.

Aqiō′kctx, ia′xka gō ikē′x. WiXt aqiō′cgamx, aqiō′latcgux; 1
It is looked at, it there it is. Again it is taken, it is lifted:

aqiō′kctx; a′lta k·ē qaxē′ qigō′ nikē′x, aLE′k·imx kLā′qēwam: 2
it is looked at; now nothing where as it was, he says the shaman:

"Ta′kE aniōc′gam." 3
"Then I took it."

17. Ma′nix Lō′mEqta, iLā′Xanatē qē′xtcē aqiō′cgamx, a′lta 4
17. When he will be dead, his soul intending it is taken, now

t!aqē′ qaX ŏ·ō′lEptckiX nutXui′tcax. Qē′xtcē aqiōmē′tckēnEnx 5
just as that fire sparks fall down. Intending he gathers it up

qigō ayutXui′tcax, aLE′k·imx kLā′qēwam: "Näkct taL· t!ayā′ 6
where it fell down, he says the shaman: "Not behold! well

nētx." 7
I make him."

18. Ma′nix Lō′mEqta, iLā′Xanatē ka-y- iā′pik nē′xaɬax. Ma′nix 8
18. When he will die, his soul and its being is on it. When
                                                   heavy

t!ā′ya qLā′xō giLā′Xanatē ka kullku′ll nēxā′x. 9
well he will be the one having a and light it gets.
    made   soul

19. Ma′nix tgigE′nXautē ikanā′tē tEmēwā′lEma, a′lta ēmā′cEn 10
18. When they watch it a soul the ghosts. then a deer

aLgiā′x Lā′qēwam. ALgiŏ′kux, nēxE′nkux. Atgē′kta-ŏx tEmēwā′lEma; 11
he makes it the shaman. He sends it, it runs. They pursue it the ghosts;

aqēē′taqLax qix· ikanā′tē. Ayoxoē′yumqtx tEmēwā′lEma qix· 12
it is left that soul. They forget it the ghosts that

ikanā′tē. Anā′L· lā′lax aLkLā′x Lā′qēwam. Lā′xlax aLktā′x 13
soul. Deceive he does them the shaman. Fool he does them

tEmēwā′lEma ka aLgiŏ′cgam qix· ikanā′tē. AtēE′ltaqL'ax, 14
the ghosts and he takes it that soul. They left it

tEmēwā′lEma. 15
the ghosts.

20. Ma′nix iā′q·atxala, aLk·kEm′Lō′lExa-itx, a′lta giLā′kikElal, 16
20. When he is bad, he is evilly disposed against him, now a seer,

a′lta aLXaLk·umLuwā′kōtsgōx. Alā′xti L·ap aLkLā′x Lā′qxŏio. Lāq 17
now he watches for him. Next find he does him sleeping. Take
                                                                    out

aLgē′Lxax iLā′xanatē. A′lta aLguipcō′tetEmx gō tmēmElō′ctikc 18
he does it his soul. Now he hides it everywhere at corpses

atgE′tgiX, ia′xkatē aLgiŏ′tkEX. Anā′2 gō igē′mEXatk ikanī′m; anā′ 19
they are, there he puts it. Sometimes at put up as burial canoe; some-
                                                                       times

gō iā′q·atxala ilē′ē aLgiŏ′tqx, anā′ gō kē′kXulē t!ōL, anā gō 20
in bad ground he puts it, some- at under house, some- at
                                  times   times

yumā′inx· tE′mcEcX. A′lta ē′Latc!a nixā′tElax qō′La giLā′Xanatē. 21
rotten wood. Now his sickness comes to be on that the one having the
                                            him   soul.

AqLElgē′mcimtōmx Lē′Xat qLā′qēwam. AqLgē′la-it gē′Latc!a, 22
He is paid one shaman. They try to cure the sick one,
                                            him

aqiE′lkElax iLā′Xanatē. "Ō′kuk Lā′qēwam ikē′x imē′Xanatē." 23
it is looked for his soul. "At that shaman is your soul."

A′lta aqiu′Xtkinax iLā′Xanatē. L·ap aqiā′x gō tmēmElō′ctikc. 24
Now it is searched for his soul. Find it is done at the corpses.

IxElō′ima L·ap āqiā′x gō iā′q·atxala ilē′ē. IxElō′ima L·ap aqiā′x 25
Another find it is done in bad ground. Another one find it is done

gō gē′gula t!ōL. Aqiō′cgamx. IxElō′ima L·ap aqiā′x gō yumā′inx· 26
at under the house. It is taken. Another one find it is done at rotten

tE′mcEcX. IxElō′ima L·ap aqiā′x, gō kⁿcā′xali ikē′x. Aqiō′cgamx· 27
wood. Another one find it is done, at above it is. It is taken.

Ma′nix iaXkiā′lkuil qix· ikanā′tē, t!ayā′ aqLā′x gē′Latc!a. Ma′nix 28
When its being well that soul, well he is made the sick one. When

1 ā′nqatē atcā′yax iLā′Xawôk kLā′qēwam, a′lta aLŏ′mEqt qŏ′La
  already   he ate it   his spirit   the shaman's   then   he dies   that

2 LgŏLē′lXEmk qŏ′La gilā′Xanatē.
  person   that   having the soul.

21. Ma′nix aqLgelŏ′kux qLā′qēwam LgŏLē′lXEmk, qantsī′x·
  21. When   it is sent to him   a shaman   a person,   how many

4 Lā′yana iqauwik¡ē′Lē, näkct La′kcta Lgē′tqEmt, aqLŏ′lXamx:
  fathoms   long dentalia,   not   who   knows it,   he is told:

5 "Iā′Xanate Lāqᵘ mēxā′xŏ x·ix·ī′x·." AqLŏ′gux qLā′qēwam,
  "His soul   take out   do it   this one's."   It is sent to him   the shaman,

6 aqLaLgelŏ′kux LgŏLē′lXEmk. Pā′nic aqē′tElax ēqauwik¡ē′Lē, anā′
  he is sent to him   a person.   Secretly   they are done   long dentalia,   some-
                                    paying   to him   times

7 Lᶜā′gil pā′nic aqLE′tElax qLā′qēwam. A′lta nau′itka Lāqᵘ aLgᵉ′Lxax
  a woman   secretly   she is done to   the shaman.   Now   indeed   take out   he does it
            paying   him

8 iLā′Xanatē qŏ′La aqLaLgelŏ′kux. ALŏ′mEqtx qŏ′La aqLaLgelŏ′kux.
  his soul   that one   to whom he was sent.   He dies   that one   to whom he was sent.

9 Ma′nix atauwē′xix·itx Lā′colal qŏ′La Lŏ′mEqtx, aqa′LgEloē′xax
  When   they learn about it   his relatives   that   dead one's,   somebody goes to take
                                                                    him

10 qLā′qēwam, aqLā′waᶜox, manē′x nôxŏ′x tkatā′kux. Ma′nix nēkct
   the shaman,   he is killed,   learning his   they do   their mind.   When   not
                                 secret

11 aqLā′waᶜox ka ŏ′Xuit Lā′ktēma aLktŏ′tx; ma′nix Lā′la-ētix·
   he is killed   and   many   his goods   he gives them   if   his slaves
                                           away;

12 qLā′qēwam ka Llaᵉ′ētix· aLkLŏ′tx ka näkct aqLā′waᶜôx. AqLŏ′lXam
   the shaman   and   his slave   he gives him   and   not   he is killed.   He is told
                            away

13 aLxalawi′tXuitx.
   he has not done it [it is
   forgiven].

22. Ä′ka wiXt pāt wuq¡ qLā′qēwam. Ma′nix xāx aLkLā′x
  22. Thus   also   really   strong   shaman.   When   observe   he does her

15 Lā′k·ikala gŏ Lqoā′lipx·, a′lta tqē′wam aLkLā′x. GiLā′kiLatEniL
   his wife   at   a youth,   now   sending disease   he does it.   He shoots much

16 tiŏ′LEma ttc¡ā′ma qlktuLā′tEniL. Ä′ka wiXt ma′nix aqLaLgelŏ′kux
   supernatural   sickness   who knows to shoot   Thus   also   if   he is sent to him
                              much.

17 LgŏLē′leXEmk, aqtä′tElŏtx tktē′ma. Pā′nic aqtE′tElax. Anā′
   a person,   they are given to him   goods.   Secretly   he is done.   Some-
                                                 paying   times

18 ēqauwik¡ē′Lē pā′nic aqē′tElax, anā′ Lᶜā′gil pā′nic aqLE′tElax.
   long dentalia   secretly   he is done,   sometimes   a woman   secretly   he is done.
                   paying   paying

19 Tqä′wam aLkLā′x LgŏLē′leXEmk. Manē′x nôxŏ′x tkatā′kux,
   Sending dis-   he does it   a person.   Knowing   they do   their minds,
   ease   his secret

20 aqLā′waᶜôx qLā′qēwam. AtkLā′waᶜôx Lā′cŏlal qŏ′La tqē′wam
   he is killed   the shaman.   They kill him   his relatives   that   sending dis-
                                                                       ease

21 kLkLā′x. Ma′nix L¡ap aqtā′x ttc¡ā′ma gŏ gē′Latc¡a aqLElgē′m′ētox
   who did it.   If   find   it is done   the disease   in   the sick one   he is paid

22 pāt qLā′qēwam. Lā′qLaq aLktā′x qŏ′ta ttc¡ā′ma. Qoā′nEm Lāq
   a real   shaman.   Take out   he does it   that   sickness.   Five   take out

23 aLktā′x qŏ′ta ttc¡ā′ma ka ēXt ē′Lan. L¡ pāq aLxā′x· gē′Latc¡a.
   he does it   that   sickness   and   one   rope.   Recover   he makes   the sick man.
                                                                 him

24 Ma′nix aqL¡Lā′tapax qŏ′ta ttc¡ā′ma, ma′nix ka′nauwē aqL¡Lā′tapax
   If   it goes through him   that   sickness,   when   all   it goes through him

25 qŏ′ta ttc¡ā′ma ka cka ŏqoā′kElax ka aLŏ′mEqtx gē′Latc¡a.
   that   sickness   then   and   it is discovered   and   he dies   the sick one.

23. Ma′nix Lāq aqiā′x qix· ē′tc¡a iŏ′LEma, a′lta aqLŏ′cgam gŏ
  23. When   take out   it is done   that   sickness   supernatural,   now   it is taken   in

Lā′kcia qLā′qēwam. Ōguē′ aLktā′x Lā′kcia, mā′nix L¡ux naxā′x Xak **1**
his hands / the shaman's. / Folded / he makes them / his fingers, / when / come out / it does / that

ōᶜōxgE′qxun uLā′kcia ayō′pax qix· iō′LEma. Ma′nix aLgiō′cgam qix· **2**
its eldest daughter (thumb) / his hand / it goes out / that / supernatural thing. / When / he takes it / that

iō′LEma qLā′qēwam, aqLō′cgamx gō Lā′ᶜowit, aqLō′cgamx gō **3**
supernatural thing / the shaman, / he is taken / at / his legs, / he is taken / at

Lā′potitk, aqLō′cgamx Xukᵘ iLā′kōtcX. A′lta aqLō′latcgux. **4**
his forearms, / he is taken / there / his back. / Now / he is lifted.

AqLā′lōtgax Ltcuq ōᶜōmē′cx. Q¡oā′p qō′La Ltcuq ka nixtckō′x qix· **5**
It is put into it / water / kettle. / Near / that / water / and / it escapes / that

iō′LEma. Gō atkLā′taxitx tê′lx·am. Tcā′2xē aqiō′kLx, a′lta L¡EmE′n **6**
supernatural thing / Then they fall down / the people. / Several times / it is carried to the water, / now / soft

aqiā′x, L¡EmE′n aqiā′x gō Ltcuq. Ts!Es nēxā′x iō′LEma. A′lta **7**
it is made, / soft / it is made / in the water. / Cold / gets / the supernatural thing. / Now

a¡iō′kumanEmx. Anā′2-y· ilā′q¡am, anā′2-y· uLxō′tē LElā′lax, anā′2 **8**
it is looked at. / Sometimes / a wolf, / sometimes / its claws / a bird, / sometimes

LgōLā′lEXEmk Lmē′mElōst iLā′Xamōkuk. Aqiā′x LgōLē′lEXEmk. **9**
a person / a dead one / its bones. / It is made / a person.

24. Ma′nix qoā′nEm uyā′k¡auk¡au qix· iō′LEma ka Lō′ni Lq¡up **10**
24. When / five / murderer / that / supernatural thing / then / three / cut

ē′wa ē′nata iā′pōtĕ, mō′kcti Lq¡up iau′a ē′natai. Ma′nix kstō′Xtkin **11**
thus / one side / his arm, / twice / cut / here / other side. / When / eight

uyā′k¡auk¡au iō′LEma, qoā′nEmi Lq¡up iau′a ē′natai; Lō′ni Lq¡up **12**
murderer / the supernatural thing, / five times / cut / here / on one side; / three times / cut

iau′a ē′natai. Ma′nix itcā′Lēlam uyā′k¡auk¡au, qoā′nEm ē′wa **13**
here / on the other side. / When / ten / murderer, / five times / thus

ē′nata iā′pōtĕ, qoā′nEmē iau′a ē′nata iā′pōtē. **14**
one side / his arm, / five times / there / on the other side / his arm.

Ma′nix Lāq° aqiā′x iō′LEma, Lāq° aLgiā′x qLā′qēwam. AqLō′cgamx, **15**
When / take out / it is done / the supernatural thing, / take out / he does it / the shaman. / It is taken,

aqLō′latcgux. Q¡oā′p qaX ōᶜōmē′cX Lā′kcia ka atcLō′kctx qō′La **16**
it is lifted. / Near / that / kettle / his hand / and / he sees it / that

Ltcuq x·ix· iō′LEma, L¡Ex acxā′lax ōᶜōmē′cX. WiXt aqō′cgamx **17**
water / this / supernatural thing, / burst / it does / the kettle. / Again / it is taken

ā′gōn ōᶜōmē′cX. Ma′nix tEll aLxā′x qLā′qēwam aqLō′lXam Lē′Xat **18**
another / kettle. / When / tired / he gets / the shaman / he is told / one

qLā′qēwam: "AngE′tcim Xau ōnā′Lata gō tgE′kcia." A′lta aLgō′cgamx **19**
shaman: / "Strike me / that / rattle / on my hands." / Now / he takes it

qLā′qēwam unā′Lata; aqaLgE′lltcim gō Lā′kcia qō′La iō′LEma **20**
a shaman / a rattle; / he is struck / on / his hands / that / supernatural thing

aqLiō′ktcan. L¡lE′pL¡lEp nôxō′x Lā′kcia, L¡EmE′n aLgiā′x qix· **21**
it is held. / Under water / they are / his hands, / soft / he makes it / that

iō′LEma gō Ltcuq. KauEmqoā′nEm Lāq aLktā′x. Nau′i nuxō′LElEx **22**
supernatural thing / in water. / Five together / take out / he does / At once / they burn them.

Lā′kcia. Ā′ĕlaxta ē′Lan Laq° aLgiā′x; a′lta aqLgElgē′cgamx, anā′2 **23**
his hands. / Later on / the rope / take out / he does it; / now / he is helped, / sometimes

aLō′nikc Lā′q° atgiā′x ē′Lan, anā′ amô′kctikc. Ma′nix ō′Xuitikc **24**
three / take out / they do it / the rope, / sometimes / two. / When / many

qtgā′qēwama ka alā′ktikc Lāq° atgī′ax ē′Lan. Lāq° aqē′Lxax ē′Lan **25**
shamans / then / four / take out / they do it / the rope. / Take out / it is done / the rope

1   qō'La tqē'wam kLkēx.   A'lta atgixk¡ā'x qix· ē'Lan qtgā'qēwama.
    that sending disease who did him. Now   they pull at that   rope   the shamans.
                                              both ends

2   AqLō'lXamk LgōLē'lEXEmk: "Ai'aq Lq¡u'pLq¡up ē'txa." ALō'tXuitx
    He is told   a person: "Quick   cut   do it."   He stands

3   nēkct giLā'Xawôk, aLgō'cgamx ā'qoa-iL ōqewē'qxē. Lq¡up aLgī'āx
    not   having a guardian he takes it a large   knife.   Cut   he does it
          spirit

4   gō nōxo-iā'yak tgā'kcia qō'tac tē'lx·am. Näkct ē'kta Lq¡up nēxā'x.
    at between them their hands those   people.   Not anything cut   he does.

5   Ma'nix Lᵉā'gil Lōc, iLā'Xawôk, aLgō'cgamx itcanō'kctX ōqēwē'qxē,
    When   a woman there is, her guardian she takes it its smallness knife.
           spirit,

6   cka goyē' aLgiā'x nōxo-iā'yak tgā'kcia qtgā'qēwama. ALgigē'Lq¡aôx
    and thus she does it between them their hands the shamans'.   She pierces it

7   qix· ē'Lan. Wax aLxā'x Lᵉā'owilqt. Tcä'2xē aLgigēLq¡aôx. Kopä'2t
    that   rope. Pour out it does blood.   Several times she pierces it.   At an end

8   wax   aLxā'x qō'La Lᵉā'owilqt. A'lta ōqo-iwē'qxē aqaLgE'lltcimxax
    pour out it does that   blood.   Now   knife   he is hit

9   qō'La tqē'wam kLkLāx LgōLē'lEXEmk. Ma'nix ōkulai'tanEma
    that sending disease who did it the person.   If   arrows

10 itca'k·ilx·tcō aqa-ilgā'maltEmx qix· ē'Lan ka-y- ōkulai'tanEma
    their heads   it is struck often   that rope   then   arrows

11 aqaLgE'lltcimx. Itcā'maᶜ aqē'tElax qigō aqLā'waᶜôx.
    it is hit.   Shooting him he is done as he is killed.

    25. Ma'nix tgE'Lqta tgā'Lan aqtā'wix qō'ta ttc!ā'ma ka
    25. When   long   their ropes are made those diseases and

13 iō'Lqtē nikct ē'Latc!a nixā'tElax, qō'La tqē'wam aqLā'x.
    long time not his sickness comes to be on that sending dis- is done to
                                 him,   ease   him.

14 Tcx·ī-y- ē'Latc!a nixā'tElax. Ma'nix tgE'tsk¡ta tgā'Lan aqtā'wix
    Then   his sickness comes to be on If   short   their ropes are made
           him.

15 qō'ta ttc!ā'ma, qoä'nEmi aLā'-ō·ix ka ē'Latc!a nixā'tElax,
    those   diseases,   five times sleeps and his sickness comes to be on him,

6   anā' txā'mē aLā'-o·ix.
    sometimes six times sleeps.

    26. Ma'nix aLō'mEqtx Lkā'nax Lā'Xa, a'lta aLkLō'gux Lā'qēwam.
    26. When   it is dead a chief his child, now he is sent for a shaman.

18 Gō Lē'Xat Lkā'nax Lā'Xa tqē'wam aqLā'x. Lkatō'mē aLkLā'x
    At one   chief his child sending dis- it is done. Taking revenge it is done
                              ease   on his relatives

19 Lē'Xat Lkak¡Emā'na Lā'Xa. Pā'nic aLkLā'x Lā'qēwam. Ma'nix
    one   chief   his child. Secretly he is done the shaman. When
                              paying

20 aLElā'xo-ix·itx Lā'XatakoX wiXt aqLE'nk¡ēmEnakox. Lā'wuX
    they know it   his mind   again it is taken revenge on him. His younger
                                                                   brother

21 tqē'wam aqLā'x qō'La Lkā'nax. Mā'nix atElā'xo-ix·itx qō'La
    sending dis- it is done that chief.   When   they know him   that
    ease

22 Lē'Xat Lkā'nax, anā' aqLā'waᶜôx qō'La qLā'qēwam. Ē'XtEma-ē·y-
    one   chief, . some- he is killed that   shaman.   Sometimes
                  times

23 aqLā'waᶜôx Lā'icX qō'La Lkā'nax. A'lta-y· ukumā'La-it naxā'x.
    he is killed his relative that chief's.   Now   a family feud it becomes.

24 Qiā'x iqagē'niak ayō'Xuix, tcx·ī-y- uxō't!aya nôxō'x. Atcä'2xikc
    If   paying blood they make each then at peace they become. Several
         fine   other,

25 aqtōtē'nax, tcx·ī-y- uxō't!aya nôxō'x.
    they are killed, then   at peace they become.

    27. Ma'nix acxtē'nax nikct giLā'Xawôk k¡a qLā'qēwām ka
    27. When they are angry not having guardian and shaman then
         against each other   spirits

Lqē′wam	aLkLā′x	ka	aqLā′waᶜôx	qLā′qēwam.	Ma′nix	ō′Xuē	1
sending disease	he does it	then	he is killed	the shaman.	When	many	

Lā′ktēma	ka	akLktō′tx	Lā′ktēma,	ō′Xuē	aLktō′tx	Lā′ktēma	ka	2
his dentalia	and	he gives them away	his dentalia,	many	he gives them	his dentalia	and	

näkct	aLā′waᶜôx,	aLxaluwE′txuitxax.	Ma′nix	aqLE′Lxcgamx	3
not	they kill him	they forgive him.	When	it is taken away	

Lā′k·ikala	pā′nic	aLkLā′x	qLā′qēwama.	Tqē′wam	aqṭā′x	qō′La	4
his wife	secretly paying	he is done	the shaman.	Sending disease	it is done to him	that	

LE′k·ala.	Anā′	qō′La	Lᶜā′kil	tqē′wam	aqLā′x.	Ma′nix	aqLō′cgamx	5
man.	Sometimes	that	woman	sending disease	it is done to her.	When	she is taken	

Lā′pLᶜau	gō	kuLā′yi,	pā′nic	aLkLā′x	qLā′qēwam,	aLō′mEqt	qō′La	6
a dead relative's wife	to	far,	secretly paying	he is done	the shaman,	she dies	that	

Lᶜā′kil;	anā′	qō′La	LE′k·ala	aLō′mEqtx.	Ma′nix	ō′Xuē	Lā′ktēma	7
woman;	sometimes	that	man	dies.	When	many	dentalia	

Lᶜā′kil,	aLō′mEqtx	Lā′xk'un,	pā′nic	aLkLā′x	qLā′qēwam,	8
a woman,	he dies	her elder brother,	secretly paying	she does him	a shaman	

aLkтE′tElutx	Lā′ktēma,	tqē′wam	aqLā′x	Lē′Xat	Lkā′nax.	9
she gives them to him	dentalia,	sending disease	it is done	one	chief.	

ALkLktō′mitx	Lā′xk'un.	Anā′	aLōlē′mxa-itx	Lᶜā′kil	gō	qLā′qēwam.	10
She takes revenge on a relative of his murderer	her elder brother's.	Sometimes	she is married	a woman	to	the shaman.	

Lxā′pEnic	aLxā′x.	Nau′itka	aLkLō′gux	Lā′k·ikala.	11
Giving herself in payment secretly.	she does.	Indeed	she sends him	her husband.	

28.	Ma′nix	nugō′tcxEmx	qtgā′qēwama,	ma′nix	aLE′k·imx:	"Nai′ka	12
28.	When	they sing	the shamans,	when	he says:	"I	

iā′qoa-iL	itci′Xawôk,"	ka	aqLō′k'uakctx	Lē′Xat	qLā′qēwam.	Ma′nix	13
a great one	my guardian spirit,"	then	he is tried	one	shaman.	When	

nau′itka	iLā′Xawôk	qē′xtcē	āqiLgE′ltcim	iō′LEma.	AqLō′kLpax.	14
indeed	he has a guardian spirit	intending	he is hit	supernatural thing.	He is missed.	

LE′gun	Lē′Xat	Lā′qēwam	aLkLō′k'uakctx,	wiXt	aqLō′kLpax.	15
Another	one	shaman	is tried,	again	he is missed.	

Atcā′xikc	tgā′qēwama	qē′xtcē	atkLō′k'uwakctx,	näkct	iLā′maᶜ	16
Several	shamans	intending	they try him,	not	shooting him	

aqā′tElax.	AqLō′lXamx:	"Ō	nau′itka	taLị	tiā′qēwam."	Ma′nix	17
it is done to him.	He is told:	"Oh,	indeed,	behold,	he is a shaman."	When	

kā′ltac	iLā′yuLị l	qLā′qēwam,	aqLō′k'uakctx,	ā′nqatē	iLā′maᶜ	18
to no purpose	he bragging	a shaman,	he is tried,	already	shooting him	

aqā′tElax.	Ma′nix	Ltị ō′xoyal	aLE′ktcxEmx,	qē′xtcē	tqē′wam	aqLā′x,	19
he is done with it.	When	a strong man	sings,	intending	sending disease	it is done,	

näkct	qa′nsix	iLā′maᶜ	aqā′tElax.	Ma′nix	aLE′k·imx:	"Nai′ka	20
not	ever	shooting him	he is done with it.	When	he says:	"I	

nt!ō′xoyaḷ,"	aLE′ktcxamx,	tqē′wam	aqLā′x,	ā′nqatē	aLō′mEqtx.	21
I am a strong man,"	he sings,	sending disease	it is done to him	already	he is dead.	

29.	Ma′nix	ē′Latc!a	atcē′tElax	iLa′Xawôk,	a′lta	aqLō′lXam	22
29.	When	his sickness	he makes it on him	his guardian spirit,	then	he is told	

qLā′qēwam:	"Ō	tgt!ō′kti	migEltcxEmā′ya."	AqLElgē′mimtōmx	23
the shaman:	"Oh,	good	you sing for him."	He is paid for it	

qLā′qēwam.	A′lta	aqLgE′ltcxamx	qō′La	gē′Latc!a,	iLā′Xawôk	24
the shaman.	Now	somebody sings for him	that	sick one,	his guardian spirit	

1 ē′Latc!a atcē′tElax. A′lta t!ayā′ aLE′ktcxamx. Ma′nix näkct t!ayā′
  his sickness   he made it to   Now   well   he sings.   When   not   well
  be on him.

2 aqiā′x ka aLō′mEqtx. Ä′ka Lᵉā′kil, ä′ka LE′k·ala.
  he is made   then   he dies.   Thus   a woman,   thus   a man.

   30. Ma′nix aLE′xk'uwôkctx qLā′qēwam, tqē′wam aLgā′x
   30.   When   he tries himself   a shaman,   sending disease   he does it

4 ōᶜlE′m. Nau′i LEX acxā′lax ugō′ᶜlEm. Kanauwē′² nutXo·ī′tcax
  bark.   At once   burst   it does on it   its bark.   All   it falls down

5 ugō′ᶜlEm. ALxLō′lExa-itx: "Ō̃ tgE′qēwam tEnxā′lax." Ma′nix gō′yē
  its bark.   He thinks: "Oh,   my shaman's   is on me."   When   thus
                                power

6 iā′ap ē′maktc ōc utcaktcā′k, tqē′wam aLgā′x Lā′qēwam. Nau′i
  on top of   spruce   is   an eagle,   sending dis-   he does it   the shaman.   At once
                              ease

7 noē′luktcux. PāL ē′tcaqL Lᵉā′owilqt. ALxLō′lExa-it: "Ō̃ tgE′qēwam
  it falls down.   Full   its beak   blood.   He thinks: "Oh,   my shaman s
                                       power

8 tEnxā′lax."
  is on me."

   31. Ma′nix iā′q¡atxala nē′xElax igō′cax, a′lta aqiLgElō′kux
   31.   When   its badness   comes to be on it   the sky,   now   he is asked

10 giLā′Xawôk it!ō′ktē, iau′a maLna′ giLā′Xawôk, a′lta aLgigE′ltcxamx.
  one having a   a good one,   then   seaward   having a guard-   now   he sings for it.
  guardian spirit   ian spirit,

11 ALE′k·imx iō′kuk ōᶜō′Lax ka tciumā′Lxa-ē, aLE′k·imx giLā′Xawôk.
  He says   there   sun   and   it will become   he says   the one having a
                         clear,   guardian spirit.

12 Ma′nix iō′Lqtē iā′q¡atxala ixElā′xō igō′cax ka aLE′k·imx: "Q¡E′lq¡El
  When   long time   its badness   will be on it   the sky   and   he says: "Too difficult

13 igō′cax, Lx xā′oqxaL ē′tolē ixā′xō. Lāx nikLā′ko-it."
  the sky,   probably   cannot   clear weather   it will   Unable   I am to do it."
                                     be.

   32. Ma′nix iLā′maᶜ nixā′tElax LgōLē′lEXEmk aqL'Elgē′mēmtōmx
   32.   When   shooting him   it is done to   a person   he is paid
                   him

15 Lt!ō′xoyal. "Tgt!ō′kti milmē′ctxa imē′Xawôk." A′lta nau′itka
  a strong man.   "Good   you loan him   your guardian spirit."   Now   indeed

16 wäx aLkLE′Lgax Ltcuq giLā′maᶜ. A′lta aL'E′llpax Lᵉā′qauwilqt,
  pour out   he does it   water   on the one who   Now   it squirts out   his blood,
                      is shot.

17 ka′nauwē Lāq° aLxā′Lxax. ALE′k·imx Lt!ō′xoyal: "Ma′nix t!ā′ya
  all   come out   it does.   He says   the strong man: "When   well

18 niā′xō, ka-y- ikEnuakcō′ma ixā′xoya." Nau′itka cka mä′nx·i k¡ā
  he will get,   then   thunder   it will do."   Indeed   and   a little   quiet
                                                   while

19 aLxā′x ka-y- ikEnuakcō′ma nēxā′x. ALE′k·imx: "Mô′kctē qiltcimā′ō·y-
  it is   and   thunder   it does.   He says: "Twice   it will be heard

20 ikEnuakcō′ma," aLE′k·imx Lt!ō′xoyal.
  thunder,'   he says   the strong man.

   33. Ma′nix naLē′La-itx ōkulai′tan giLā′maᶜ ka aqLō′cgam
   33.   When   it is in him   an arrow   the one who is   and   he is taken
                                 shot

22 qLā′qēwam kLgē′mēmtōmx giLā′XaXana, ka aLgiLgXā′naôX,
  a shaman   who is paid   one who sucks,   then   he sucks it out,

23 Lāq° aLgā′x ōkulai′tan giLā′XaXana.
  take out   she does it   the arrow   the one who sucks.

   34. Ma′nix iLā′maᶜ nixā′tElax Lt!ō′xoyal, aqLō′tXuitgux
   34.   When   shooting him   it is on him   a strong man,   it is made ready

25 Lk¡ā′ckc. Ōnuā′LEma aqa′tElax gō Lctā′xōst, anā′ Lqā′LXatcX
  a child.   Red paint   is made on it   on   his face,   some-   coal
                                       times

26 aqLE′tElax. K¡au aqLā′x LE′Laqcō gō·y- ōLā′tcpuX; anā′
  is made on it.   Tie   it is done   his hair   on   his forehead;   some-
                                                     times

amô′kctikc aqtō′tXuitcgux. Wāx aqLE′Lgax Ltcuq ɬ′Lā′maˢ 1
two   are made ready.   Pour out   it is done   water   shooting him

Lt!ō′xoyal, Lāqᵒ naxā′Lxax ōkulai′tan. Ma′nix amô′kctikc 2
the strong man,   take out   it is done   the arrow.   When   two

aLktā′qamitx, Lē′Xat Lᶜā′gil, Lē′Xat LE′k·ala. E′wa tā′nata 3
look after him,   one   a woman,   one   a man.   Thus   on one side of

t!ōL Lᶜā′gil aqLō′tx·Emitx; aLkLō′cgamx Lk̹ē′wax Lᶜā′gil; ē′wa 4
the house   a woman   she is placed;   she takes it   a torch   the woman;   thus

ē′nata iLā′potē igilxEmalā′lEm aLgiō′cgamx. Ē′wa tā′nata t!ōL 5
other side   her arm   a rattle   she takes it.   Thus   on other side of   the house

LE′k·ala aLkcō′cgamx [aq]cē′LōtElk. Gō kⁿcā′xali t!ōL aLō′La-it 6
a man   he takes it   a whistle.   At   above   the house   there is

LE′k·ala, Lā′xka wāx aLkLE′Lgax Ltcuq qō′La giLā′maˢ. 7
a man,   he   pours out   he does it   the water   [on] that   the one who is shot.

A′lta Lāqᵒ ā′Lxax Lā′qauwilxt kanauwē′2 giLā′maˢ Lt!ō′xoyal. 8
Now   come out   it does   his blood   all   the one who is shot   the strong man.

Ma′nix k̹ē Lt!ō′xoyal gō ēˡXt ē′lXam, ka aqLgē′mēmtōmx 9
When   no   strong man   in   one   town   then   he is paid

giLā′XaXana ka aLgiLkXā′nan′Emx giLā′maˢ. Lā′qLaq aLkLE′Lxax 10
one who sucks   and   he sucks him   the one who is shot.   Take out   he does it

Lā′qauwilqt. 11
his blood.

Translation.

1. The seers go to the ghosts [the souls of the deceased]. When three go, one having a strong guardian spirit is placed first, another one last. One having a less powerful guardian spirit is placed in the middle. When four seers go, the two lesser ones are placed in the middle. A strong seer goes in front, another one behind. They pursue the soul of a sick chief. When the trail [which they follow] begins to be dangerous, the one in front sings his song. When a danger approaches from the rear, the one behind sings his song. In the evening when it begins to grow dark they commence the cure of the sick person. When the morning star rises they reach his soul. They take it, and the guardian spirits of the seers return. Sometimes they stay away one night, sometimes two. Then they give the sick person his soul and he recovers.

2. When the seers pursue the soul of a sick person and it takes the trail to the left, the seers say: "Behold, he will die." When it takes the trail to the right they say: "We shall cure him."

3. The spirits of the seers reach the hole in the ground where the souls of the deceased always drink. When the soul of the sick one has drunk at that water, then he cannot get well. Even if all the shamans try to cure him they cannot make him well.

4. They find a soul that has drunk of the water. They take it. It is large. The spirits of the seers return. When they bring it near the country of the Indians it begins to grow smaller. Then these men who know how to cure people say: "Perhaps he will die to-morrow."

It gets day. They try to give him his soul. It does not fill his body and he must die. His soul has become too small.

5. When the seers go and their spirits arrive at the water in the country of the ghosts, and the soul of the sick one is still far from their town, and they have not given him food, then the seers say: "Oh, we shall make him well, the ghosts have not given him food." And indeed their spirits take the soul and return. Even if the person is very sick and they give him his soul, he revives at once.

6. Again the ghosts carry away a soul. The person faints at once; his legs tremble. Then the seers are paid and drive away the ghosts. The soul which they carried away sees the ghosts. He knows part of them; another part he does not know. Only those he knows who died not long ago. The spirits of the seers reach the soul which was carried away and turn it round. At once the sick one recovers; he gets well.

7. When the ghosts carry a soul away and no seer is present [to recover it], when the soul has been away a night, the person who fainted remains dead. Sometimes when it has been away two nights he remains dead.

8. When the soul of a sick person goes to the ghosts, the seers pursue it. If it has already been taken into the house, it cannot be recovered. The spirits of the seers cry and return.

9. When a horse is seen in the country of the ghosts and it is not taken back it dies after a few days. When it is taken back it does not die. Just so a person. When a person is well, but his soul is seen in the country of the ghosts and it is not taken back he must die within a short time. Just so a canoe. When the ghosts carry away a canoe and the seers do not bring it back it will be broken.

10. When a seer wants to shake his manikin [a figure made of cedar bark] he gives it to somebody who has no guardian spirit. Now they go to the ghosts. He helps him. Now this person sees everything in the country of the ghosts. The manikin carries him there.

11. When only one soul leaves the body of the sick person, when it remains in the country of the Indians and it is taken, then the sick person recovers at once. When the lesser soul of a person is caught in the country of the Indians and is given back to the person, he recovers after a short time. A soul is in the country of the ghosts; the spirits of the seers pursue it and reach it when it arrives at the ghosts. They bring it back, return it to the sick person, and he recovers.

12. When the soul of a chief leaves his body it goes to the beach. Not many seers know about it; only strong shamans know how it goes to the beach.

13. When a soul has taken anything that belongs to the ghosts, the sick one can not recover.

14. When a sick person will die, it is always high water. Then the spirits of the seers walk slowly. When the sick one will recover it is always low water.

15. When the soul of a sick person is placed in a canoe and this is carried out into the ocean, the sick one can not recover.

16. The spirits of the seers reach the soul of a sick person. They take it and lift it. They look at it and seize it again. They look again and it has disappeared; then the shaman says that he has taken it.

17. When they try to take the soul of a sick person and sparks fall down, he will die. It seems just like a firebrand. They try to gather the sparks up. Then the shaman says: "Behold, I shall not cure him."

18. When a person will die, his soul is heavy; when he will recover, it is light.

19. When the ghosts watch a soul then the shaman makes a deer. He sends it and it runs away. The ghosts pursue it and leave the soul. They forget it. Thus the shaman deceives them and takes back the soul which the ghosts had left.

20. When a seer is evilly disposed against a person, he watches for him. At last he finds him asleep. Then he takes out his soul and hides it near a corpse, in a canoe burial, in a thorny place, under a house or in rotten wood. Then the owner of the soul falls sick. A shaman is paid to look for the soul and to cure him. He says: "Oh, that shaman has your soul." They search for it and find it in the country of the ghosts, or in a thorny place, under a house, or in rotten wood, or somewhere in the air. He takes it. When the soul is still hale and well, the sick one will recover. When the shaman's spirit has begun eating it, the owner of the soul must die.

21. Somebody sends, unknown to anybody, a string of large dentalia several fathoms long to a shaman, and asks him [through his messenger]: "Take the soul of that person out of his body." He gives in payment to him, secretly, long dentalia or a woman. Then he takes out the soul of the person against whom he was sent. The person dies. When his relatives learn about it and come to know the secret they take the shaman and kill him. If they do not kill him and he gives away a large amount of property or slaves, he is not killed. Then he is forgiven.

[Numbers 1 to 21 were originally Chehalish beliefs and customs.]

22. It is the same with a very strong shaman. When he observes his wife with a young man he shoots disease against them. In the same way a man sends a person to the shaman, who gives him goods. He pays him secretly long dentalia or a woman. Then he sends disease to a person. When his relatives learn the secret, the shaman is killed. The relatives of the man against whom he sent the disease kill him. If the disease is found in the sick one, a strong shaman is paid, who takes out the disease. He takes out five diseases [pieces of bone around which hairs are tied] and one rope. He cures the sick one. When the disease has gone right through him before it is discovered the sick man must die. Man has two souls. If both are taken out of the body their owner must die.

23. When the supernatural disease is taken out, the shaman takes it into his hands. He folds his fingers [the thumb of the right hand being inclosed by the fingers of the left]. When the thumb comes out, then the disease-spirit escapes. When the shaman has taken the disease-spirit, one man takes him at his legs, another one at his arms, a third one at his back. He is lifted. Then water is put into a kettle. When they come near the water and the disease-spirit escapes, the people fall down (as though a resistance which they try to overcome were suddenly removed). Several times they carry him to the water. Then the disease-spirit is made soft in the water. It gets cold, and they look at it. Sometimes it is a wolf's or a bird's claw, sometimes a human bone. It is carved into the shape of a person.

24. When the disease-spirit has murdered five people, it has three cuts on one arm, two on the other. When it has murdered eight people, it has five cuts on one arm, three on the other. If it has murdered ten persons, it has five cuts on one arm, five on the other. When the shaman has taken out the disease-spirit, he lifts it. He brings his hands near the kettle. When the spirit sees the water, the kettle will burst. Then another kettle is taken. If the shaman gets tired, he asks another shaman: "Strike my hands with that rattle." Then a shaman takes a rattle and strikes the hands of the one who holds the disease-spirit. He puts his hands into the water and rubs the spirit. He takes out five at the same time and his hands become hot. Then he takes out the rope. Now others help him. Sometimes three shamans, sometimes two take out the rope. When many shamans are present, then four take out the rope. They take the rope out of the body of the man into whom the disease was sent. The shamans pull at both ends of the rope and ask somebody to cut it. When a person who has no guardian spirit takes a knife and cuts between the hands of these people, he does not cut [feel] anything. If there is a woman who has a guardian spirit, she takes a small knife and cuts between the hands of the shamans. She cuts through that rope. Then blood flows out. She cuts through it several times. Now all the blood has flowed out. Then the person who sent the disease is struck with the knife. If the rope was struck [cut] with an arrowhead, then he is struck with an arrow. He is shot and killed.

25. When the ropes [the hairs tied around the middle of the pieces of bone] of the disease-spirits are long, then the sickness will come upon the person after a long time. If the ropes of the disease-spirits are made short, then the person will fall sick after five or six days.

26. When a chief's child has died, the people send for a shaman. Disease has been sent to the child of a chief. Then he takes revenge on the relatives of the murderer [and selects] the child of [another] chief. A shaman is paid secretly. When these people learn about it, they take revenge in their turn. They send disease to the younger brother of that chief. When that chief knows the shaman [who has done so],

he will sometimes kill him. Sometimes they kill a relative of the chief. Then a family feud originates. If they pay a blood fine to each other, then they make peace again. They do not make peace until several are killed.

27. When a shaman and somebody who has no guardian spirit are angry against each other, and the shaman sends disease against his enemy, he is killed. When he gives away many dentalia, he is not killed; they forgive him. When the wife of a man is taken away, he secretly pays the shaman, who sends disease, sometimes to the man [who eloped with the woman], sometimes to the woman. When a deceased relative's wife is taken by a stranger, a shaman is paid secretly and the woman or the man is killed. When a woman has many dentalia and her elder brother dies, she pays secretly a shaman, giving him dentalia, and he sends disease to a relative of the one who killed her brother. She takes revenge on a relative of the murderer of her elder brother. Sometimes she marries the shaman. She gives herself secretly in payment and sends her husband [to kill her enemies].

28. When the shamans sing and one of them says: "I have a great guardian spirit," then the other shamans try him. When he really has a guardian spirit, one of them tries to hit him with a disease spirit, but he misses him. Another shaman tries him, but he also misses him. Several shamans try him, but they can not hit him. Then they say: "Behold! He is really a shaman." When he only brags, saying that he is a shaman, they try him and hit him at once. When a strong man sings and shamans try to send him disease, they can not hit him. When a person sings: "I am a strong man" [without being a strong man], and they send disease to him, he dies at once.

29. When somebody is made sick by his guardian spirit his friends say to a shaman: "Please sing for him." They pay the shaman who sings for the man whom his guardian spirit made sick. Then the shaman sings until he gets well. If he is not made well, he must die. This is the case with men and women.

30. When a shaman tries his power, he sends disease to the bark of a tree. The bark bursts at once and falls down. Then he thinks: "Indeed, I have the powers of a shaman." When an eagle sits on top of a spruce tree, the shaman sends disease against him. He falls down at once, his mouth full of blood. Then he thinks: "Indeed, I have the powers of a shaman."

31. When the weather is bad, the people ask a good person who has a guardian spirit of the sea to sing for good weather. He says: "When the sun stands there and there, it will clear up." When it will be bad weather for a long time, he says: "It is too difficult for me, probably it will not clear up. I can not do it."

32. When a person is shot, a "strong man" is paid. "Lend him your guardian spirit." Then they pour water [on the face] of the person who is shot. The blood squirts out; all the blood comes out. Then

the "strong man" says: "If he gets well it will thunder." Indeed, it is quiet for a short time and then it thunders. He says: "You will hear the thunder twice."

33. When a "strong man" is shot, a child is made ready. Its face is painted red or sometimes black. Its hair is tied up over its forehead. Sometimes two children are made ready. Then water is poured on the "strong man" who has been shot, and the arrow is taken out. When two persons look after him, one is a girl and one a boy. The girl is placed on one side of the house. She holds a torch in one hand and a rattle in the other. The boy is placed at the other side of the house and has a whistle. On top of the house is a man who pours the water on the wounded "strong man." Then all the blood comes out of the "strong man." If there is no "strong man" in a town, a shaman who sucks is paid and he sucks out the blood from the one who is shot.

HOW CULTEE'S GRANDFATHER ACQUIRED A GUARDIAN SPIRIT.

LgE′qacqac Liä′mama it!ō′xoyal tiä′qēwam. Atcō′ikEl tqē′wam 1
My grandfather · his father · strong man · his supernatu- · He saw it · supernatural
· · · · ral power. · · power

LgE′qacqac; atcē′ᶜElkEl ilē′q¡am; atcā′ᶜElkEl ō̆ᶜō′kuil ŏkuē′wucX; 2
my grandfather; · he saw it · a wolf; · he saw it · a female · dog;

atcē′ᶜElkEl ē′tcōyuct. A′lta iä′qoa-iL nē′xax; a′lta nixLō′lExa-it: 3
he saw it · the evening star. · Now · large · he became; · now · he thought:

"Tgt!ō′kti a′lta Lᶜā′gil nLucgā′ma, ta′kE ō′xoē tgE′Xawôk." 4
"Good · now · a woman · I shall take her, · then · many · my guardian
· · · · · · spirits."

Nōxoik¡ē′wulalEmam tä′nEmckc nōxo-ēwulā′yemam. Atgiō′lXam 5
They went digging roots · the women · they went camping. · They said to him

tiä′cikcnana: "TcuXoal xkxtä′wax Xō′tac ō′xoēwulā′yemam." 6
his friends: · "Come, · we will follow them · those · who went camping."

Nē′k·im: "Näkct, taua′lta aqenōmē′lax." WiXt atgiō′kō tiä′cikcnana; 7
He said: · "No, · else · I shall be scolded." · Again · they asked · his friends;
· · · · · · him

ka nixLō′lExa-it: "Qä′dox nxEltō′ma." A′lta atctä′wax qō′tac 8
then · he thought: · "Must · I go along." · Now · he followed them · those

tq¡ulipXEnä′yū. Aqugō′om qō′tac tä′nEmckc. ALgiō′lXam Lē′Xat 9
youths. · They were · those · women. · She said to him · one
· · reached

Lq¡ēyō′qxut Lᶜā′gil: "TcimElä′xo-ix na Lmē′mama Xukᵘ amE′tē?" 10
old one · woman: · "He knows about you · [int. · your father · here · you came?"
· · · part.]

"Näkct qa′da," nē′k·im. "Ā′Lqi iamuklē′tcgō." AtgE′qxoya iä′xkatē 11
"Not · anyhow," · he said. · "Later on · I shall tell him." · They slept · there

qō′tac tq¡ulipXEnä′yū, ka ia′xka aya′′qxôiē. Gō ō̆ᶜō′lEptckiX 12
those · youths, · and · he · he slept. · At · the fire

nixō′kctē, q¡oä′p ō̆ᶜōlEptckiX. Nä′ktcuktē ka nō′Xukō qō′tac 13
he lay down, · near · the fire. · It grew day · and · they went · those
· · · · · home

tq¡ulipXEnä′yū. NŏXugō′mam. 14
youths. · They came home.

A′lta kᵘLä′xanī ayō′tXnit, k¡oa′c nē′xax, ayō′p!a gō-y· ä′yam 15
Now · outside · he stood, · afraid · he was, · he entered · in · his father

tä′yaqL. Atca-ixä′laqLē. Ē′wa tä′natä qō′ta t!ōL lakt t!ä′lEptckiX, 16
his house. · He opened the door. · Then · on the one · that · house · four · fires,
· · · side

ē′wa tä′nata wiXt lakt. Kstō′xtkin tgä′kxalptckix qō′ta t!ōL. 17
then · on the other · also · four. · Eight · its fires · that · house.
· side

Nē′tp!a a′lta gō qix· ä′yam tä′yaqL. Ayagä′t!ŏm qaX aō̆′Xt 18
He came in · now · in · that · his father · his house. · He reached it · that · one

ō̆ᶜō′lEptckiX. NixLō′lExa-it: "Qantsī′x· Lx qa′da aqEnōlä′ma?" 19
fire. · He thought: · "How long · may be · how · I shall be spoken to?"

Ayagä′t!ŏm a′gŏn ō̆ᶜō′lEptckiX. Ayä′xatgō. Q¡oä′p ä′tcax aLä′Lōn 20
He reached it · another · fire. · He passed it. · Near · he came it · the third

ō̆ᶜō′lEptckiX. Atciō′lXam Liä′mäma: "Ia′xkati x·iau mE′tXuit. 21
fire. · He said to him · his father: · "There · then · stand.

Ta′kE na ka′nauwē tiō′lEma amō′ēkEl ka Lᶜā′gil tq¡ēx amLä′Xt?" 22
Then · [int. · all · supernatural · you saw · and · a woman · like · you do her?"
· part.] · · beings · them

211

1 Aqayi′nᶜoL   ōcō′yaL: "Ai′aq   igă′wulXt   x·ix·   ipā′k·al.   Qui′nEmi
   It was thrown   a cape: "Quick   climb   this   mountain.   Five times
   at him

2 maō′ya   ka   mXatgō′ya.   Ia′xkati   tmē′q̣ēyōktikc   utā′Xawȯk   nakē′x
   your sleeps   and   you come back.   There   your ancestors   their female   is
     guardian spirit

3 Ut!ō′naqan."
   Ut!ō′naqan."

     Agiō′lXam   uyă′Lak: "Ma′nix   mikwu′lx·tama   x·ix·   ipā′k·al
     She said to him   his aunt: "When   you have climbed   this   mountain

5 tE′qp!ȯp!   mtnElpiā′Lxa,   ma′nix   migwu′lx·tama   x·ix·   ipā′k·al.
   [a grass]   gather it for me,   when   you will have climbed   this   mountain.

6 Atcō′cgam   qaX   ocō′yaL̦.   A′lta   ā′yȯ.   Ā′yō,   ā′yō,   à′yō,   ā′yō,
   He took it   that   cape.   Now   he went.   He went,   he went,   he went,   he went,

7 kulā′yi   ā′yō,   ka   nō′ponEm.   Iā′xkati   ayā′qxȯyē.   Nē′xEltcu,   cka wāx
   far   he went,   and   it grew dark.   There   he slept.   He talked,   and in the
     morning

8 nē′ktcuktē.   Nēkct   i′kta   atciltcā′ma   ka   nē′ktcuktē.   A′lta   wiXt
   it grew day.   Not   anything   he heard   and   it grew dark.   Now   again

9 ā′yȯ,   ā′yȯ,   ā′yȯ.   Nigā′wulXt   qix·   ipā′k·al.   Q̣oā′p   pāt oᶜō′Lax,
   he went,   he went,   he went.   He climbed it   that   mountain.   Nearly   noon,

10 a′lta   q̣oā′p   igwu′lx·tama-ē.   A′lta   i′kta   atciltcā′ma.   Ā,   ōqo-ikE′muXLut
   now   nearly   he had climbed it.   Now   some-   he heard it.   Ah,   howling
     thing

11 atcaltcā′ma.   Nau′i   L̦′ă   ā′yaLᶜa   nē′xax,   cka   mE′nx·i   ā′yū,   ka   wiXt
   he heard it.   Hence   feeling   his body   became,   and   a little   he went, and   again
   of fear

12 ōqo-ikE′mXLut   atcaltcā′ma.   A′lta   mank   tc̦pāk   ōqo-ikE′muXLuL
   howling   he heard her.   Now   a little   really   howling

13 atcaltcā′ma.   K̦ă   nā′xax   qaX   ōqo-ikE′muXLuL.   A′lta   tc4
   he heard her.   Silent   became   that   howling one.   Now   [noise of fall-
     ing leaves]

14 nutXuā′yutc   ō′qxōca.   NixLō′lEXa-it: "Ō,   iqctxē′Laut   x·ik   L̦ap
   they fell   spikes of fir.   He thought: "O,   the monster,   that   find

15 aniā′xȯyē."   NixLō′lEXa-it: "Qā′dȯxoētcinuwu′lᶜaya,   i′kta   L̦aqē′nxaua."
   I shall do."   He thought: "Shall   he devour me,   what   they planned
     against me."

16 Ayō′La-it   gō   kᵘcā′xali-y-   ē′mᶜEcX   ka   na·ixE′lqamx.   ME′nx·i   k̦ă
   He was   on   above   tree   and   she howled.   A little   silent

17 nē′xax,   wiXt   ōqo-ikE′muXLuL   nā′xax.   A′lta   q̣oā′p   katē′   mank.
   it became,   again   howling   she became.   Now   near   very   little.

18 K̦ă   naxā′x   ōqo-ikE′muXLuL.   Tc4   nutXo·i′tcax   qaX   ō′qxōca.
   Silent   became   the howling one.   [Noise of fall-   they fell down   those   spikes of fir.
   ing leaves]

19 WiXt   na·ixE′lqamx.   A′lta   nē′Xtakō   ayō′itcō.   NixLō′lEXa-it: "A′lta
   Again   she howled.   Now   he turned back,   he went   He thought: "Now
     down.

20 niXkō′ya."   A′lta   agigE′ta   qaX   Ut!ō′naqan.   Kulā′yi   ayō′yam,   a′lta
   I go home."   Now   she pursued   that   Ut!ō′naqan.   Far   he arrived,   now
   him

21 q̣oā′p   gia′xt   qaX   Ut!ō′naqan.   NaxE′lqamx,   nau′i   Läk̦   ā′yaL′a
   near   she came to that   Ut!ō′naqan.   She howled,   at once   weak   his body
   him   [whispered]

22 nexā′x.   NixLō′lEXa-it: "Ō,   gEnuwu′lᶜaya,   taL̦."   Nē′lgaLx   ēXt
   became.   He thought: "O,   she will devour me,   behold!'   He thought   one
     of him

23 iā′Xawȯk.   Kulā′yi   ayaē′taqL.   A′lta   wä2Xt   tEll   nē′xax.
   his guardian   Far   he left her.   Now   again   tired   he got.
   spirit.

24 Atcā′xEluktcgō   qaX   ōyā′cōyaL̦.   Agaga′ōm   qaX   ōcō′yaL̦   ka
   He threw off   that   his cape.   She reached it   that   cape   and

25 naxLā′nukT,   naxLā′nukT.   Atcā′qxamt;   a′lta   wiXt   nē′xankō.   Qē′xtcē
   she went around it,   she went around it.   He looked at her;   now   again   he ran.   Intending

26 atciā′qxamt   ē′cgan,   kaxē′   tcēᶜElkElā′ya   ē′ckan   ka   iō-oLxē′wula.
   he looked for it   a cedar,   where   he will see it   a cedar   and   he will go up.

WiXt në'lgaLX iä'Xawôk ilë'q̣am. Kulku'll në'xax ä'yaL'a. Kulä'yi **1**
Again / he thought of it / his guardian spirit / the wolf. / Fresh / got / his body. / Far

ayaë'taqL. Ka wiXt tEll në'xax. Atcia'kEnanä'koXuē. A'lta **2**
he left her. / And / again / tired / he got. / He looked back at her. / Now

tkä'tōma iō'kuk itcä'wan. Ta'qē Lkë'wucX Lä'tōma. YukpE'tEma **3**
her teats / here / her belly. / Just / as a bitch / her teats. / Right here

takiltcë'mXEllt gō tgä'potē. Ma'nix noë'tcax mank Lawa', ma'nix **4**
they struck her often / at / her legs. / When / she went down hill / a little / slow, / when

ë'wa no-ë'wulXtxax a'lta aia'q. Q̣'oä'p agi'ax. WiXt në'lgaLX **5**
thus / she went up hill / now / quick. / Near / she got him. / Again / he thought of it

iä'Xawôk. Nai-E'lgaLX ōꞓō'kuil ōguë'wucX uyä'Xawôk. A'lta kulä'yi **6**
his guardian spirit. / He thought of her / female / bitch / his guardian spirit. / Now / far

ayaE'ltaqL. Gō lax ōꞓō'Lax ta'kE nä'xax, ta'kE Ḷap atcä'yax **7**
he left her. / There / afternoon sun / then / it became, / then / find / he did it

ë'qxēL; ianu'kstX qix· ë'qxēL, ḶiE'pē. Yukpä't nilō'tXuit qix· **8**
a creek; / its smallness / that / creek, / it was deep. / Up to here / he stood in the water / that

ë'qxēL q̣oa'p tiä'xEmalap!ix·. Ayaxä'LElta qō'La Ltcuq ë'wa **9**
creek / near / his armpits. / He walked in the water / that / water / thus

mai'ēmē ä'yō ka ä'yōptck. Aqō'lXamx Ut!ō'naqan itcä'ḳoacōmi **10**
down stream / he went / and / he went from the water to the land. / It is said / Ut!ō'naqan / her fear of

Ltcuq. A'lta atcä'qxamt nä'Lxam gō qix· ë'qxēL. Ma'nix nau'itka **11**
water. / Now / he saw her / she came down to the water / at / that / creek. / When / indeed

itcä'ḳoacōmi Ltcuq ka näkct atElō'tXuita. A'lta nä'Lxam gō qix· **12**
her fear of / water / and / not / she goes into water. / Now / she came down to the water / at / that

ë'qxēL. Aⁿ, aⁿ, aⁿ nä'xax. Xuë'Xuë agE'Lax qō'La Ltcuq. Nō'La-it **13**
creek. / Aⁿ,* aⁿ, aⁿ / she did. / Breathing on water like a drinking horse / she did / that / water. / She stayed

a'lta. Nō'La-it ka naxE'lqaₘx: "Wâ4!" ka ayō'mEqt ia'xka ka **14**
now. / She stayed / and / she howled: / "Wâ!" / and / he fainted / he / and

ayaō'ptit. Atcä'ꞓalkEl, a'lta LgōLë'lEXEmk. A'lta agiupalä'wul: **15**
he slept. / He saw her, / now / a person. / Now / she spoke to him:

"Nai'ka Xuk amcgEnō'lXamx, atgEnō'lXamx Natë'tanuē Ut!ō'naqan. **16**
I / here / you say to me, / they say to me / the Indians / Ut!ō'naqan.

Ē'wa kⁿcä'xali x·ik ilë'ē antë'mam. Q̣at ayä'max. NE'tqamt **17**
Thus / above / this / land / I came. / Like / I do you. / Look at me

Itë'tanuē!" agiō'lXam. Tkalai'tanEma utä'k·ilx·tcutk pāL Xak **18**
Indian!" / she said to him. / Arrows / their points / full / that

ōguä'mōkuē, pāL x·ik ë'tciḶꞓa. "Ē'ka mxä'xō-y· ä'Lqē gō Natë'tanuē." **19**
her throat, / full / that / her body. / "Thus / you will do / later on / at / the Indians."

Tgä'maꞓ x·itë'kik. "Ē'ka-y· ä'Lqē mxä'xō gō Natë'tanuē." **20**
Shot / here. / "Thus / later on / you will do / at / the Indians."

Ayaō'ptit. Wax në'ktcuktē, a'lta kⁿcä'xali-y· ōꞓō'Lax ka **21**
He slept. / On the next morning / it got day, / now / above / the sun / and

ɴixE'lꞓōkō. A'lta ḳē näkct qaxē' àtcä'ꞓElkEl. NixA'kxōt gō **22**
he awoke. / Now / nothing / not / [any]where / he saw her. / He bathed / in

qix· ë'qxēL. A'lta në'Xkō cka-y· ë'qakⁿtitx· niXkō'mam. Ā'yup! **23**
that / creek. / Now / he went home / and / naked / he arrived at home. / He entered

gō tE'LaqLē. Agiō'lXam uyä'Lak: "Tcōx tE'qp!ôp! amtEnilpä'yaLx?" **24**
into their house. / She said to him / his aunt: / "Well / grass / you gathered it for me?"

---

* Nasalized.

1 Atcō'lXam: "Näkct anō'yam ka anxā'takō." Lō'ni ayā'qxòya ka
He said to her: "Not I arrived and I turned back." Three his sleeps and
times

2 niXatgō'mam. Näkct qa'da atciō'lXam Liā'mama.
he came back. Not [any]how he said to him his father.

Translation.

My great-grandfather had the guardian spirit of the warriors. My grandfather had seen the shaman's spirit, he had seen the wolf, he had seen the bitch, he had seen the morning star. Now he came to be grown up and he thought: "I will take a wife. Now I have many guardian spirits." The women went digging roots and camped [on the beach]. His friends said to him: "Let us follow the women who are going to camp out." He said: "No, else I shall be scolded." His friends asked him again. Then he thought: I must accompany them. Now he accompanied those young men. They reached those women. An old woman said to him: "Does your father know that you came here?" He said: "No, I shall tell him later on." The young men slept there and he also slept there. He lay down near the fire. At daybreak the young men returned. They arrived at home. Now he stood outside. He was afraid to enter his father's house. He opened the door. There were four fires on each side of the house. Eight fires were in the house. Now he entered his father's house. He reached the first fire. He thought: "When will he speak to me?" He arrived at the next fire and passed it. He came near the third fire, then his father said: "Stay there! Did you find all your guardian spirits and do you want to take a wife?" He threw a cape at him: "Quick, climb that mountain and [do not] come home [until] five nights [have passed]. There is the female guardian spirit of your ancestors. There is Utᵢō'naqan." His aunt said to him: "When you reach the top of that mountain, gather some grass for me." He took the cape and went. He went, he went, and went a long distance. It became dark and he slept there. He lay down and it became day again. He had heard nothing and it became daylight. Now he went and went again. He climbed that mountain. When it was nearly noon he had almost climbed it. Now he heard something. He heard her howling. At once he was chilled by fear and he went on for a little while, when he heard her again howling. Now he heard the howling a little louder. Then it became quiet again. Now leaves fell down. He thought: "O, I shall meet the monster." He thought: "They intended that she should devour me." He was on top of a tree and she howled. For a short while it became quiet, then she howled again. Now she was quite near. The howling stopped again. Leaves fell down again. Again she howled. Then he turned back to go home. He thought: "I will go home." Now Utᵢō'naqan pursued him. When he had gone some distance she came near him. She howled and immediately he became weak. He thought: "She will devour me." Then he thought of one of his guardian spirits and he left her far behind. Then he became again tired. He threw

away his cape. She reached it and went around it often. He looked
at her and he ran again. He looked for a cedar which he intended to
climb. Then he thought of his guardian spirit, the wolf. At once he
felt fresh and left her far behind. Then he became tired again. He
looked back at her. Her teats were along her belly, like those of a
bitch. They reached down to the middle of her legs and struck them
often. When she went down hill she went a little slower; when she
went up hill she ran quickly. She approached him. Then he thought
of his guardian spirit, the bitch, and left her far behind. In the afternoon he reached a small but deep creek. The water reached up to here,
near his armpits. He walked down stream in the water. Then he went
ashore. It is said that Ut;ō'naqan is afraid of water. Now he saw her
coming down to the creek. If she was really afraid of the water, she
would not step into it. Now she arrived at the creek. She made a^n,
a^n, a^n, and blew upon the water like a deer that is about to drink. She
stayed there and howled: "Ua," and he fainted and fell asleep. Now
he saw that she was a human being. She spoke to him: "I am the one
whom your family and whom the Indians call Ut;ō'naqan. I come
from the top of that mountain. I like you. Look at me, Indian!" Her
throat and her body were full of arrow-heads. "You will be just as I
am [when you return to the country of] the Indians." Her body was
full of [arrows which had been shot at her]. "You will be just as I am
[when you return to the country of] the Indians." He slept. On the
next day he awoke when the sun was high up in the sky. Now he saw
nothing. He bathed in that creek and went home, and he came home
quite naked. He entered the house. His aunt said to him: "Did
you gather grass for me?" He said to her: "I returned before I
reached there." Three days he stayed away. He did not tell his father
[what he had seen.]

THE FOUR COUSINS.

1 Lō′nikc Liã′xk'unikc ixgē′s'ax qix· Liã′xauyam. Pā2L ō′yaqct
  Three   his elder cousins   the youngest   that   his poverty.   Full   lice
                        one

2 cka Liã′k¡ēk¡ē, nēkct Liã′naa. Qō′ctac cgE′kxun ciã′xk'un ictã′giL'ōl
  and   his grandmother,   not   his mother.   Those two   the eldest ones   his elder   they knew to
                                                cousins   win

3 iqã′lExal. Tcã′ko·i nēxã′xoyē ka naktgEmã′ya·itx uyã′k¡ik¡ē omō′tan
  disks.   Summer   it will become   and   she spun always   his grandmother   willow
                                                        bark

4 ogutgEmã′ya·itx. AqagElō′kux Lē′Xat LgōLē′lEXEmk agã′tElax
  she always spun it.   She was hired   one   person   she made for
                                                       them

5 ōLã′mōtan. Mänx· Laq° agã′x. Naxilē′ma-ôx, agaxō′pcam. WēXt
  their willow   A little   take out   she did.   She kept it for   she hid it for   Again
  bark.   herself,   herself.

6 Lē′Xat agã′tElax ōLã′mōtan; wiXt mänx· nixElē′ma-ôx. Alã′xti
  one   she made for   their willow   again   a little   she kept for herself.   At last
        them   bark;

7 gōyē′ itcã′xa iL nExLã′mEXitx. A′lta alō′ix Nitc¡xēElc. Gō
  thus   its largeness   she braided.   Now   they went to   Chehalis.   At

8 Ik¡aniyi′lXam ōxo·elã′itix· qō′tac tē′lx·Em. Ia′xkaku nō′xôx ka′nauwē
  Mythtown   they stayed   those   people.   There   they are   every

9 tcã′epa ē, ma′nix atōlō′Lxē iau′a·y· ē′maLē. A′lta alō′ix Nitc¡xē′Elc
  spring,   when   they go down   there   Columbia   Now   they went   Chehalis
                     stream   river.   to

10 qō′Lac Liã′xk¡unikc. Agiō′lXam uyã′k¡ik¡ē: "Mō′kᵘ Ta Xak ō′pcam,
  those   his elder cousins.   She said to him   his grandmother: "Carry   this   rope.

11 c'ulã′l mcx·t!ō′ya." A′lta alō′ix iau′a Nitc¡xē′Elc. Iqã′lExal
  ground-hog   you will ex-   Now   they went to   there   Chehalis.   Disks
  blanket   change for it."

12 alō′guix Liã′xk'unikc; alō′yam Nitc¡xē′Elc.
  they went to   his elder cousins;   they arrived   Chehalis.
  play   at

  A′lta Lē′Xat LgōLē′lEXEmk L¡ap aLgiã′x ē·elã′kē. Qē′xtcē
  Now   one   a person   find   he did it   a sea-otter.   Intending

14 aqitxamElã′lamx, qē′xtcē ēqawik′ē′Lē aqē′tElōt. K·¡ē, nēkct aLiō′tx
  it was bought,   intending   long dentalia   they were given   No,   not   he gave it
                                 to him.   away

15 qix· ē·elã′kē. Qēxtcē ikanī′m aqē′tElōtx. K·¡ē, nēkct aLgiō′tx qix·
  that   sea-otter.   Intending   a canoe   it was given to   No,   not   he gave it   that
                                 him.   away

16 ē·elã′kē. A′lta nacElã′xo·ix·itx qax ō′pcam. A′lta aLiga′ômx qō′La
  sea-otter.   Now   they two learned about   that   rope.   Now   he went to their   that
                    it   house

17 LgōLē′lEXEmk: "TgEt!ō′kti iamElō′ta x·ix· ē·elã′kē, manlō′ta Xau
  person: "Good!   I give it to you   this   sea-otter,   you give me   this

18 ō′pcam." A′lta acgi′cx·tqoax qaX ō′pcam k¡a ē·elã′kē. A′lta aLXgō′x.
  rope."   Now   they exchanged   that   rope   and   sea-otter.   Now   they went
                                                    home.

19 Nē′k·imx: "Nixcgã′ma x·ix· ē·elã′kē. Atcuwa [Lqi] qēxō′L'ayū,
  He said: "I shall take it from   that   sea-otter.   Certainly   [?]   it will be won from
              him   him in gambling.

20 tcil'ē′tcgama." Nē′k·im qix· kcx·LEmã′t ia′xk'un: "Cka iã′c mtgē′kXax
  he will lose it."   He said   that   next to the   his elder   "And   let   you two do
                              youngest   cousin: alone   him

21 Liã′xauyam. Qã′dôxoē qexō′L'aya. Ma′nix tän agē′lotx qaX
  his poverty.   Shall   it will be won   If   something   she gave it   that
                      from him.   to him

uyā′kِikِē ā′nqatē aqē′xōL’ax, ma′nix aLgixualō′ta-itx LgōLē′lEXEmk   1
his grand-   already   it is won from   if   he made him happy   a person
mother   him,

tān aLgE′lōtxax ā′nqatē aqē′xōL’ax.” ALXō′x. Gō Nē′max ka   2
some-   he gave it to him   already   it is won from him.”   They went   At   Nema   then
thing   home.

aLō′o·ix. A′lta nikct ā′yaqsō qix· imō′lEk·an iā′ok. Iā′qxo-im ka   3
they slept.   Now   not   its hair   that   young elk's skin   his   He slept   then
                                  blanket.

atcta·ō′yutcax tia′xalawēma qix· iā′xk’un. A′lta aqē′xcgamx qix·   4
he awoke them   his people   that   eldest brother.   Now   it was taken from   that
                                        him

ēᶜelā′kē. AqēLā′takL’ax, iā′kxôi-ē ka aqēE′ltaqLax. KawI′X   5
sea-otter.   He was left,   he slept   and   he was left.   Early

nixE′l’ōkux, a′lta k·ِē qō′tac giLā′ckēwal. NixLō′lEXa-it: “Ō,   6
he awoke,   now   nothing   those   travelers.   He thought: ·· Oh

aqEn′E′ltaqL taLِ !” K·ِē qix· ēᶜelā′kē. “Ō, aqinxE′cgam qē′auwa   7
. I was left   behold!   Nothing that   sea-otter.   ··O,   it was taken away   that
                                        from me

ēᶜelā′kē.” A′lta itcā′ēpa·ē. A′lta ayō′ix pE′nka. Nikgē′Xax·ē Nē′max;   8
sea-otter.”   Now   spring time.   Now   he went   afoot.   He swam across   Ne′ma;

ka′namôkct qō′ta t!ā′LEma ayugōguē′Xax. Ayō′ix pE′nka, niXkō′x.   9
both   those   creeks   he went across.   He went   afoot,   he went home.

Ayō′yamx gō Nē′lEqtEn ka LXaluwē′gōt. A′lta ayō′La-it mā′Lxolē.   10
He arrived   at   Nē′lEqtEn   and   it was ebb tide.   Now   he stayed   ashore.

NiXLō′lEXa-itx: “Qiā′x Lِuwn′n Lxā′xō Lik Ltcuq, tcx·ī anigElgē′xaxē.”   11
He thought: “If   slack water it gets   this   water,   then   I shall swim across.”

Ka iō′c Lō nē′xau. A′lta i′kta atciltcā′ma gō Ltcuq: “Qā′doxuē   12
Where he calm it became.   Now   some-   he heard it   in   the water: ‘ Must
was   thing

niā′qamita i′kta x·ik ixā′xō.” Tumm nē′xax gē′kulē gō Ltcuq. Kِā   13
I see   what   this   does.”   Tumm   it made   below   in the water.   Silent

nexā′x qigō tumm nēxā′x. Ka ala′xti nē′xax dEll. A′lta nō′ix qaX   14
it became   where   tumm   it made.   Then   next   it made   dEll.   Now   it went   that

ugō′lal iau′a ma′ēma: wā2. Qoā′nEm atciltcā′ma qix· ē′kta dEll.   15
wave   then   down stream: wā.   Five   he heard it   that something dEll.

WiXt qoā′nEm atciltcā′ma qix· ē′kta gumm gō gē′kXulē. Lāx   16
Again   five   he heard it   that something gumm   at   below.   Come out

nē′xax ēē′tcxōt, Lō′nas qantcē′x itā′Lqta tiā′ucakc. WiXt ē′gun   17
it did   a black bear,   I don't know   how much   their length   its ears.   Again   one more

Lāxᵃ nē′xax. Qoā′nEm Lāxᵃ nē′xax ēᶜē′tcXutEma. NiLgEnā′Xit   18
come out   it did.   Five   come out   they did   black bears.   They stood

gō Ltcuq. Lāqᵘ nē′xax iā′mōlkan. Atciugoā′na-it mā′Lxolē: 19
in   the water.   Take off   he did   his elkskin blanket.   He threw it   landward:

“Qā′doxoē nō′mEqta,” nixLō′lEXa-it. A′lta ayō′guiXa. Atcē′xkō-y-   20
“ Must   I shall die,”   he thought.   Now   he swam across.   He passed it

ēXt, igō′n ēXt atcā′2xkō; ē′LaLōn atcā′xkō qix· ēē′tcxutEma.   21
one,   another   one   he passed it;   the third one   he passed it   those   bears.

x·ix·ī′k iLā′lakt ka atcā′yukct. Aqā′yukct qix· Itē′tanuē cka   22
This   fourth one   and   it looked at him.   He was looked at   that   Indian   and

atcē′ᶜElkEl gō ciā′xôst. Kِē nō′xôx tiā′Xatakôx. A′lta aqā′yuktc!   23
it looked at him   in   his face.   Nothing became   his mind.   Now   he was carried

gō t!ōL, Itc!x·ia′n tā′yaqL. TaLِ Ic!x·ia′n x·ix·ī′x atcē′ᶜElkEl.   24
to   a house,   Itc!x·ia′n   his house.   Behold   Itc!x·ia′n   this   he saw him.

Tā′nata tā′yaqL qix· iō′LEma ōxoā′ēma tgāXipalā′wul, ē′wa tā′nata   25
On one side   his house   this   supernatural   other   their language,   thus   on the
                     being   other side

tā′yaqL ōxoē′ma tgāXipalā′wul. AtcawitcE′mᶜlē. Ōxoⁱi′ēma   26
his house   other   their language.   He understood them.   Other

tgāXipalā′wul ē′wa tcē′tkum t!ōL. “TEmē′nEmckc ā′Lqē x·itac   27
their language   thus   in middle   the house.   “ Your wives   later on   these

manitcE′mElē kanā′intEma x·ita t!ōL. Ē′ka mxā′xō gō Natē′tanuē.   28
you hear them   on both sides of   this   house.   Thus   you will do   at   the Indians.

1 x·ix·ī′gik   mkā′nax   tcEmā′xō."   Aqē′lot igō′matk,   ikamō′kXuk
This here   you chief   it will make you.'   He was given a bird arrow-head,   bone

2 igō′matk,   ōkulai′tanEma itcā′kXōmatk.   AqLē′kXōL¡ qō′ta tiō′LEma.
bird arrowhead,   arrows   their heads.   They were finished these supernatural beings.

3 NixE′lᶜōkō,   gō   mā′Lxolē   yuqunā′itx·   iau′a   ē′natai.   Nixā′latck.
He awoke,   at   ashore   he lay   there   on the other side.   He arose.

4 A′lta kawe′X.   Pāt ōᶜō′Lax qigō ayō′kuiXa.   Tatc¡au wiXt kawi′X
Now   it was early.   Noon   when he swam across.   Behold!   again   early

5 ka nixE′lᶜōkō.   Ayō′tXuit, nigē′qxamt.   Yuqunā′-itX iā′mōlkan q¡oā′p
and   he awoke.   He stood there,   he looked.   It lay   his elkskin   near blanket

6 gō iā′xka.   Ayō′tXuit.   Atcō′ckam iā′mōlkan.   A′lta wiXt ā′yō.
at   him.   He stood there.   He took it   his elkskin blanket.   Now   again he went.

7 Nē′xkō.
He went home.

Ayō′yam gō I′tskuil ciā′mict.   Nē′kgix·aē.   A′lta wiXt ā′yō kā
He arrived   at   Itskuil   its mouth.   He landed.   Now   again   he where went

9 iqā′lExal   ōxucgā′liL   gō   Ik¡aniyi′lXam.   ALE′k·ikct   Lē′Xat
disks   they played   at   Mythtown.   He looked   one

10 LgōLē′lEXEmk: "Ēē′tsxot x·ix· ēxE′nkōn gō x·ix· ē′L¡uwalkL¡uwalk."
person: "A black bear this   runs about   at this   mud."

11 Atgiā′qxamt qō′tac tē′lx·Em.   ALE′k·im qō′La Lē′Xat: "Ēē′tsxot na¡
They looked   those   people.   He said   that   one: "A bear [int. part.]¡

12 LgōLē′lEXEmk Xō′La qLō′itEt.   Iā′xkaLX x·iau aqcē′taqL x·ix·
A person   that   coming.   He, I think,   who   was left   this

13 iō′itEt."   Nē′k·im qix· ixgE′kxun iā′xk'un: "Ē′kta wiXt qtciā′wat¡
comes."   He said   that   eldest one   his elder cousin: "What   again   does he want to do¡

14 Iā′kimatctamē."   Nē′k·im qix· kcx·LEmā′t: "Qā′dōxoē Liā′xauyam.
He is one of whom we must be ashamed."   He said   that   the one next to the youngest: "Let him   his poverty.

15 Qa′da atciuntā′xt ka nēkct amtgigē′tx·ē¡"   Ayō′ptcgam gō qō′tac
How   he did to you   and not   you like him¡"   He arrived coming at   those up from the beach

16 tē′lx·Em.   A′lta iqā′lExal ōxocgā′liL.   Gō2 kE′mkXiti ka nixē′lōtcx.
people.   Now   disks   they played.   Then   at the end   and he looked at.

17 Atciuqoā′na-itx qix· atciō′ktcan igō′ma.   Iā′xkati wiXt Lē′Xat
He put it down   that   what he held   the bird arrow.   There   also   one

18 LgōLē′lEXEmk Lōc, Lxē′lōtcx.   Aqiō′lxam: "Masā′tsiLx igō′matk."
person   was,   he looked at.   He was told: "Pretty   arrowhead."

19 "A, L¡ap anā′yax," nē′k·im.   Lē′giL'Et qō′La Lē′Xat LgōLē′lEXEmk,
"Ah,   find I did it,"   he said.   He always won   that   one   person,

20 qLō′L'Et qō′La Lē′Xat LgōLē′lEXEmk ē′wa qigō ayō′La-it.   ALgiō′lXam
it was always that   one   person   thus where   he was.   He said to him

21 qō′La   Lē′Xat LgōLē′lEXEmk: "Txō′xot¡ēya,   yamgEmō′tga ēXt
that   one   person: "Let us bet,   I stake against you   one

22 igō′matk."   AtcLō′lXam: "Mai′ka tEmē′Xatakôx," ka mä′nx·i ka
arrowhead."   He said to him: "Your   your mind,"   and after a little and while

23 aLE′k·iL, a′lta kadi′x·   nē′k·iL qix· Liā′xauyam.   Lō′ni nē′k·iL, la′kti
he won,   now   this one   he won   that   his poverty.   Three times he won.   four times

24 nē′k·iL ka iā′Lēlam nē′xax qix· igōmā′tgEma.   Atcā′yuL.   Ayā′qxôi·a.
he won   and   ten   they be these arrowheads.   He won them.   He slept.

25 Ayax'algu′Litck uyā′k¡ik¡ē: "Aniō′mEl ē·elā′kē ka aqinxE′cgam."
He told her   his grandmother: "I bought it   a sea-otter and   it was taken away from me."

26 Nagä′2tcax uyā′k¡ik¡ē, agixuwalō′ta-it.   Nä′2ktcnktē.   "Tcōxoatc¡a, cikc,
She cried   his grandmother,   she pitied him.   It got day.   "Come on,   friend,

txcgā′ma iqā′lExal." Nē′k·im: "K·ȩē itci′lkotē." "Ē′Xtka itxā′lkotē."   1
let us play   disks."   He said: "None   my mat."   "One only   our mat.''

"K·ȩē nēkct itci′Lȷalȴal." ALgiō′lXain: "IamilEmē′ctxa iLȷalȴā′l."   2
"None   not   my disks."   He said to him: "I loan to you   disks.''

A′lta   ayō′pa.   A′lta   atci′LōL, atci′LōL, atctE′LxōL   ka′nauwē   3
Now   he went out.   Now   he won,   he won,   he won it   all

Lä′ktēma,   Lä′XalaitanEma,   iLä′LȷalȴalL   atcē′LxōL.   ALäcXōLȷ.   4
his property,   his arrows,   his disks   he won them.   They finished.

ALE′k·im Lē′Xat wiXt LgōLē′lEXEmk. "Kȷwan qiya′xt x·iau ō′yaqct   5
He said   one   more   person.   "Hopeful   he is made that   lice

pāL gō Lā′yaqtq. Wuxē′ nai′ka ntxcgā′ma." Kawē′X nē′ktcuktē   6
full   on   his head.   To-morrow   I   we will play."   Early   it got day

ka iō′c gō uyā′k·ȷik!ē tE′kXaqL. ALgixā′laqLē LgōLē′lEXEmk.   7
and he was   at   his grandmother   her house.   He opened the door   a person.

Ilgō′titk   aLgiō′ktcan: "Tca   txcgā′ma, cikc,"   aLgiō′lXam.   8
A mat   he held: "Come   we will play,   friend.''   he said to him.

AtcLō′lXam: "Ayā′qaa." Atciō′mEl ilgō′titk. A′lta wiXt atci′LōL   9
He said to him: "Well."   He bought it   a mat.   Now   again   he won over him

qō′La   Lē′Xat   LgōLē′lEXEmk.   AtctE′LxōL   Lä′xamōta   ka′nauwē;   10
that   one   person.   He won it   his property   all:

ka iLä′xanim atcē′LxōL. A′lta atci′LōL qō′tāc gitā′qȷatxalEma   11
then   his canoe   he won it.   Now   he won of those   common them

tē′lx·Em. Alā′xti ka ā′tElactikc qō′tac tkanā′Ximct. Alā′xti   12
people.   Next   then   they next   those   chiefs.   Next

LElā′itix· atci′LōL. A′lta ō′Xuitikc t!ē′ltge-u atci′LōL. A′lta   13
a slave   he won him.   Now   many   slaves   he won them.   Now

ikā′nax nē′xax. Ka′nauwē qō′tac tē′lx·Em tgā′ktēma ka atctō′xōL.   14
a chief   he became.   All   those   people   their property   then   he won it.

Ka′nauwē L⸨aLā′ma noxo-iLxE′lma-itx tē′lx·Em gō tā′yaqL. A′lta   15
All   days   they always ate   the people   in   his house.   Now

atciō′lXam ē′Xat iā′xk'un: "Atcē⸨ElkEl Lō′nas iō′LEina.   16
he said to him   one   his elder cousin: "He saw it   perhaps   a supernatural being.

Antxcgā′ma kLiā′XEmatk. Ntēxō′L'a ka′nauwē tiā′ēltke-u. Kȷwan   17
We will play   having batons.   I shall win them   all   his slaves.   Hopeful

qiā′xt tiā′ēltke-u." Acxēlgu′Litck: "A, emē′xk'un tcEmaxō′ēmōL."   18
he is made   his slaves.''   They told him: "Ah,   your elder cousin   he wants to play with you.''

"Iā′xka   iā′Xaqamt."   A′lta   acxE′cgam   iā′xk'un   Liā′Xamatk.   19
"He   his mind.''   Now   they played   his elder cousin   batons.

TcēxLx LpōL′ȷEma acxE′cgam kȷa iā′xk'un. Atctē′xōL tiā′ēltke-u,   20
How many   nights   they played   and   his elder cousin.   He won them   his slaves,
I do not know

atcā′ēxōL uyā′Xanim ka′nauwē. Ē′gōn ē′Xat wiXt iā′xk'un   21
he won them   his canoes   all.   Once more   one   also   his elder cousin

acxE′cgam; wiXt ka′nauwē atctē′xōL tiā′ēltke-u; ka tctā′nEmckc   22
they played;   also   all   he won them   his slaves;   then   their wives

atcti′cxōL. Atciō′lXam ē′Xat iā′xk'un: "Ā′nElaxta txcgā′ma."   23
he won them.   He said to him   one   his elder cousin: "I next   we will play.''

Atciō′lXam: "Kȷē yamXuwā′lot. Ē′ka qē ā′nqatē amā′nax,   24
He said to him: "No,   I pity you.   Thus   as   formerly   you did to me,

amEnXuwalō′tā-it, ka wiXt ē′ka yamXuwalotā′-ēta." Qē′xtcē   25
you pitied me,   and   also   thus   I pity you."   Intending

atgē′ix Gitā′tcxēElc, ka′nauwē atctā′xoL'ax tgā′ktēma. Atgē′ix   26
they came   the Chehalis,   all   he won it   their property.   They came

Tkwinaiū′LEkc, atē′gElo-ix iqā′lExal. Ka′nauwē atctō′xōL'ax   27
the Quenaiult,   they came to play   disks.   All   he won it

tgā′ktēmā, tga′ēltke-u. Ka′nauwē tē′lx·Em atcLauwitxā′uyama qix·   28
their property,   their slaves.   All   people   he made them poor   that

1 gā′yaqct. Gō Lkā′nax Lā′Xa, ä′nqatĕ ĕ′kx·it atcĕ′tᴇlax. Ēwā′
   lousy one.   Where a chief his child, at once buying as he did her. Thus
                                                    a wife

2 Tkwinaiū′Lᴇkc, ĕ′wa T!ilĕ′mᴜkc ĕ′wa kᵘca′la x·ik nĕ′maʟ, ĕ′wa
   the Quenaiult,   thus the Tillamook, thus up stream that river,   thus

3 Gitā′qauĕlitsk, ka′ᴜauwĕ nōxuexĕlā′kXᴜit tcā′nᴇmckc qix· gā′yaqct
   the Cowlitz,   all   they were mixed   his wives that lousy one

4 ä′nqatĕ. Qĕ näkct qigō aqixᴇ′cgam ĕᶜelā′kĕ qō′ctac ciä′xkʼun
   formerly. If not where it was taken from the sea-otter, those his elder
                            him   brothers

5 acgixᴇ′cgam ka iō′Lᴇma atcĕ′ᶜᴇlkᴇl. Itc!x·ia′n atcĕ′ᶜᴇlkᴇl.
   they took it from then the supernat- he saw it. Itc!x·ia′n he saw him.
   him   ural being

Translation.

There were three brothers and their younger cousin, who was very poor. He was full of lice. He had no mother, only a grandmother. The two eldest brothers knew how to win in the game at disks. When the summer approached the grandmother spun twine out of willow bark. The people hired her to spin bark. Then she kept a little for herself. At last she made a large rope. Now [the cousins] went to Chehalis. The people stayed [at that time] at Mythtown [at the most southern part of Shoalwater bay]. There they are every spring when they are going to Columbia river. Now the cousins went to Chehalis. The grandmother said to her youngest grandson: "Take this rope and exchange it for ground-hog blankets." Now they went to Chehalis. The elder cousins wanted to play at disks. They arrived there.

Now somebody had found a sea-otter. They wished to buy it and wanted to give long dentalia for it; but that man did not want to part with his sea-otter. They wanted to give him a canoe, but he did not want to part with it. Now they heard about the rope. Then that man went to their house [and said]: "I will give you this sea-otter if you will give me this rope." Now he exchanged the rope for the sea-otter. Then they went home. [The eldest one] said: "I shall take the sea-otter away from him. He will certainly gamble and lose it." Then the one who was next to the youngest said: "Let the poor boy alone. Let him lose. If his grandmother gave it to him, let him lose it; if somebody made him happy and gave him something, let him lose it." They went home. They slept at Nema. The elkskin blanket of the younger cousin had no hair. When he slept the eldest brother awoke his people. They took the sea-otter away from him and left him asleep. Early the next morning he awoke. Now the brothers had disappeared. He thought: "Behold! they deserted me!" The sea-otter had disappeared. "O, they took the sea-otter away from me." Now it was spring time. He went on afoot, going home. When he arrived at Nĕ′lᴇqtᴇu it was ebb tide. He stayed ashore and thought: "At slack water I will swim across." It grew calm. Then he heard something in the water. "I must see what that is." It made tumm under

water. Then it became quiet, and again it made tumm. Then next it
made dᴇll. Now a wave came down the river. Five times he heard
tʟe same noise, dᴇll, and five times he heard it, gumm, below the
water. Then five black bears came out of the water; their ears were
I do not know how long. They stood on the water. Then the youth
threw off his elkskin. He threw it ashore. He thought: "I must
die," and began to swim across. He passed the first one, the second
one, and the third one. When he reached the fourth one it looked
at him. It looked that Indian right in the face. He fainted. Now
Itc!x·ia′n carried him to his house. Behold! he saw Itc!x·ia′n. On
one side of the house of this supernatural being they spoke one language; on the other side they spoke another language. He understood
them. In the middle of the house they spoke still another language.
"Those women whom you hear now on both sides of the house will be
your wives. Thus you will live among the Indians. This will make
you a chief." Then they gave him a bird arrowhead made of bone.
The supernatural beings finished. He awoke and lay ashore on the
other side [of the water]. He arose. It was early now; while it was
noon when he began to swim across. His elkskin blanket lay near
him. He arose, took his elkskin blanket, and went home.

He arrived at the mouth of I′tskuil. He came ashore. Now he
went to the place where the people of Mythtown played at disks. A
person looked up [and said]: "A black bear is running about on the
mud." The people looked up and one of them said: "Is that a bear?
It is a man who is coming. I think it is the one who was left alone."
Then the eldest brother said: " What does he want here? We must be
ashamed of him." Then the next to the youngest said: "Let him
come, the poor one. What did he do to you that you do not like
him?" He went up to these people. Now they played at disks. He
stood at one end and was looking at them. Then he put down the
bird arrow which he held in his hand. One of the bystanders looked
at it and said: "How pretty is your arrowhead." "Ah, I found it,"
he replied. The one man was winning all the time the other was
losing. Then one man said to him: "Let us bet, I will stake an arrowhead against yours." He replied: "As you like," and after a little
while the poor boy won. He won three times, four times, and now he
had ten arrowheads. He had won them. He went to sleep. Then he
told his grandmother: "I bought a sea-otter and they took it away
from me." His grandmother cried; she pitied him. It got day. [Then
a person said:] "Come, friend, let us play at disks." He said: "I
have no mat." "We can use one mat." "I have no disks." "I loan
you my disks." Now he went out. He won and won and won. He
won all his arrows and all his property. He won his disks. When
they had finished, another person said: "That one with the lousy head
is getting hopeful. To-morrow I will play with him." Early the next
morning when he was still in his grandmother's house, that person

opened the door.   He held a mat in his hand and said: "Come friend, we will play." "Well," said the boy. He bought a mat. Now he won again all the property of that person. He won his canoe. Now he had won over all the common people. Next he won over the chiefs. He won first one slave and then many. Now he became a chief. He had won the property of all those people. Every day the people ate in his house. Now his elder cousin said: "Perhaps he saw a supernatural being. We will play with the accompaniment of batons. Then I shall win all his slaves. He is [too] hopeful." Then he was told: "Your elder cousin wants to play with you." "As he likes." Now the cousins played and the people beat time with batons. They played several nights. He won the eldest brother's slaves and all his canoes. Then he played with the next brother and he won all his slaves; then he won his wives. Now the next brother said: "I want to play with you next." "No, I pity you, as you pitied me formerly." Then the Chehalis came and he won all their property. The Quenaiult came to play at disks. He won their property and their slaves. That lousy boy made everybody poor. He bought the daughters of chiefs among the Quenaiult, the Tillamook, the tribes up the river, the Cowlitz. The wives of the man who had been the lousy boy were taken from among all these tribes. If his cousins had not taken the sea-otter from him, he should not have seen the supernatural being. He saw Itc!x·ia'n.

THE GILĀ'UNALX.

Ē'Xat giā'unaLX ik¡ā'ckc aqa-E'ltaqL uyā'k¡ik¡ē gō 1
One Gila-unaLX boy she was left his grandmother at

Soguamē'ts!iak. Tqā'metē nā'kxoya ka aqiō'lXam qix· ik¡ā'ckc: 2
Tongue point. Six times her sleeps and he was told that boy:

"Ā'kctam ōmē'k¡ik¡ē. PE'nka mō'ya." A'lta nē'te mai'ēmē· 3
"Go to see your grandmother. Afoot go." Now he came down the river.

Nē'xatco. Atcāꞓ'alkEl môkct ō'Lqikc. Atctō'ktcan tiā'xalaitanEma. 4
He walked down river. He saw them two fish-ducks. He took them his arrows.

NixLō'lEXa-it: "Näkct itā'maꞓ aniā'lax, taua'lta agō'kLx 5
He thought: "Not shooting them I do them. else they carry down to the water

ōgu'xalaitanEma." Atciō'cgam iqā'nakc. NakL¡ē'iwamEn qaX 6
my arrows." He took it a stone. They dived those

ō'Lqikc. Nē'xEngō mā'Lnē. Lā'xLax nā'xax qaX ō'Lqikc. 7
ducks. He ran seaward. Visible they became those ducks.

AtciagE'ltcim qix· iqā'nakc. Itcā'maꞓ atciā'lax gō-y- ē'tcaqtq· 8
He threw it that stone. Hitting it he did it at its head.

Lāq° nē'xax iā'ok. Ayaga'om. Yukpä'2t Ltcuq nitElō'tXuit ka 9
Take off he did it his blanket He reached them. Up to here water he stood in the water and

akcō'nguē qaX ō'Lqikc, nuwā'Xit. Ā'yōptck. Ā'tcukct. ŌXunē'n 10
they fluttered those ducks, they escaped. He went landward. He looked. They drifted

ē'kⁿcaxala itcā'wan. WiXt ā'yuLx. Ayō'guiXa. Q¡oā'p atcā'xōm 11
up their belly. Again he went to the water. He swam. Nearly he reached them

wiXt akcō'nguē. Ā'yuptck wiXt. Qoä'nEmi ayō'guiXa ka 12
again they fluttered. He went up again. Five times he swam and

atcō'cgam cka nixä'Lxigō ka k·¡ē nō'xôx tiā'xatakuX. A'lta 13
he reached them and he turned round and nothing became his mind. Now

iō'LEma atcēꞓ'ElkEl. Nixigā'lax Iqamiā'itx. NixE'l'ōkō. Gō mā'Lxolē 14
a supernatural being he saw it. He saw a supernatural being the fisherman's supernatural helper. He awoke. At landward

yuqunā'itX. Itcō'ktcan qaX ò'Lqikc. Ia'Xkatē ayäē'taqL qaX 15
he lay. He held in his hand those ducks. There he left them those

ō'Lqikc. A'lta ā'yō. Ayō'yam Sōkuamē'ts!iak. Q¡oā'p ä'tcax 16
ducks. Now he went. He reached Tongue point. Near he got

uyā'k¡ik¡ē. Tgā'Xtē qaxē' qigō aqaē'taqL. Ayō'yam gō-y· uyā'k¡hk¡ē. 17
his grandmother. Her smoke where when she was left. He arrived at his grandmother.

Atcō'lXam: "Imä'Xanatē, taL¡." Agiō'lxam: "Itcä'Xanatē." 18
He said to her: "You are alive, behold!" She said to him: "I am alive."

Qē'xtcē agē'lꞓēm. Atcō'lXam: "Näkct ō'lō genE'tx" Ayā'qxoyē 19
Intending she gave him food. He said to her: "Not hunger acts on me." He slept

iā'xkatē. Nē'ktcuktē, ātcä'gElEmqtcē uyā'k¡ik¡ē. Ō'Xuē tE'mꞓEcX 20
there. It got day, he gathered food for her his grandmother. Many sticks

atctupā'yaLx ka nē'Xkō. Ayaē'taqL uyā'k¡ik¡ē. Tsō'yustē 21
he gathered them and he went home. He left her his grandmother. In the evening

niXkō'mam. Aqiō'lXam: "Ō'lō na gEma'xt¡" Nē'k·im: "K¡ē; tEll 22
he came home. He was told: "Hunger [int. part.] acts on you?" He said: "No; tired

1 nkēx.″ Nixō′kctit. Kawī′x· nixā′latck. A′yō gō kulā′yi;
  I am.″ He lay down. Early   he arose.   He went to   far;

2 nixEmō′cXEniam. Tsō′yustē tcx·ī nē′Xkō. Ayō′p!am ska mä′nx·i
  be went to play. In the evening then he went He came in and a little
                                         home.   while

3 ayō′La-it ka wiXt nixō′kctit. Lōn Lpō′lEma Lōn LᶜaLā′ma nēkct
  he stayed and again he lay down. Three nights three   days   not

4 nixLxā′lEm. Tcx·ī nixLxā′lEm gō-y- aLā′lakt ōᶜō′Lax. Ayō′mEt.
  he ate.   Then   he ate   on   the fourth day. He grew up.

  A′lta ē′Xat iā′cikc iq¡oā′lipx·. Cq¡oā′lipx· aci′xɐx. QāxLx
  Now one his friend a youth. Two youths they two became. One

6 naᶜā′Lax ka ā′ctō tcakEnīma.′ Kā′tcEk actō′yam ē′maL. Atciō′lXam
  day   and they went in a canoe. Middle they arrived the bay. He said to him

7 iā′cikc: "I′kta imē′Xawôk!" "Iqamiā′-itx itci′xawôk. K¡a ē′kta
  his friend: "What your guardian spirit!" "Iqamiā·itx my guardian spirit. And what

8 mai′kXa imē′Xawôk!" Nē′k·im qix· ē′Xat: "Nai′ka wiXt Iqamiā′-itx
  you   your guardian   He said that one: "I also   Iqamiā·itx
        spirit!"

9 itci′Xawôk!" "Ē′kta miā′xōya ma′nix ō′lō aktā′xō txā′cōlal!"
  my guardian   "What will you do when hunger will act our relatives!"
  spirit!"   on them

10 Nē′k·im qix· ē′Xat: "Ē′Lxan niā′xō." Atciō′lXam iā′cikc: "K¡a-y-
   He said that one: "Smelt I shall make He said to him his friend: "And
                          it."

11 ē′kta mai′kXa miā′xō!" Nē′k·im: "Iguā′nat niā′xō ma′nix ō′lō
   what you you will do!" He said: "Salmon I shall make when hunger
                                                                it

12 aktā′xō txā′cōlal. Ni′Xua, L¡mEn, ē′xa imē′potē gō Ltcuq. Ia′koa
   acts on our relatives Well, under water do it your arm in water. Here
   them

13 wiXt nai′kXa L¡mEn niā′xō itci′potē." L¡mEn acgE′tax tctā′potē.
   also I   under water I shall my arm." Under water they did their arms.
             do it   them

14 Iā′nēwa qix· ē′Lxan giā′Xawôk atcLō′latck Liā′kcia. A′lta quL
   First he that smelt having guardian he lifted it his hand. Now hang
                         spirit

15 ā′elaōt ō′Lxan gō Liā′kcia. Lä′lē qix· ē′Xat, tcx·ī atcLō′latck
   it did to it a smelt at his hand. Long time that one, then he lifted it

16 Liā′kcia. QuL ē′laōt gianu′kstX iguā′nat. Atciō′lXam iā′cikc:
   his hand. Hang it did to it a small salmon. He said to him his friend:

17 "Nau′itka LEmē′Xawôk Iqamiā′-itx."
   "Indeed your guardian spirit Iqamiā·itx."

   Aci′Xkō qō′ctac cq¡oā′lipx·. AyuLE′mX̣a-it. qix· ē′Xat qix· ē′Lxan
   They went those youths. He married that one that smelt
   home

19 giā′Xawôk. A′lta ō′lō agE′tax tê′lx·Em GiLā′unaLX. Lā′mkXa
   having guardian Now hunger acted on them the people GiLā′unaLX. Only
   spirit.

20 LE′kXalᶜpō atkLā′xo-itx. A′lta ikā′nax nē′xax qix· ē′Lxan
   skunk-cabbage they ate it. Now rich he became that smelt

21 giā′Xawôk. Qä′xLxnaᶜā′Lax, a′lta uäLgElō′ya LE′kXalᶜpō uyā′k·ikal.
   having guardian One day, now she went to get skunk-cabbage his wife.
   spirit.

22 Tsō′yustē naXatgō′mam. A′lta aLā′xElEtq. Naxckō′mit. TsEs
   In the evening she came home. Now she heated stones. She warmed herself. Cold

23 akē′x qē′wa tcā′qElqlē. Naō′ptit qigō nō′cko-it. NaLgEnā′itix·it gō
   it was that winter. She fell asleep where she was warm. She fell down at

24 qaX ōᶜō′lEptckiX. Nā′Lxᶜō. NaxE′tEla gō tgā′potē. ALE′k·im
   that fire. She fell asleep She burnt her- at her arms. They said
              sitting.   self

25 GiLā′unaLX Lkanauwē′tikc: "Acā′lᶜyit ilxā′xak¡Emana uyā′k·ikal.
   the GiLā′unaLX all: "She is starving our chief his wife.

26 K¡ä-y- ōmcā′pōtcxan; ā′Lxᶜō-y- ōmcā′pōtcxan. Cā′lᶜēyit, cā′lᶜēyit,″
   Nothing your sister-in-law; she fell asleep your sister-in-law. She is starv- she is starv-
                              sitting   ing,   ing,″

nugō′kXo-im qō′tac tê′lx·Em. Nā′k·im qaX ŏcŏ′kuil: "AnE′Lxᶜō, 1
they said   those   people.   She said   that   woman: "I fell asleep sitting

x·ik giā′qamia-itx, hē-k·imx giā′qamia-itx." A′lta nixEmā′tcta-itck 2
this   having Iqamiā′itx,   he says   having Iqamiā′itx."   Now   he was ashamed

qix· itcā′k·ikal, ka′namŏket tgā′potē nuxŏ′LEla. Näkct ayaō′ptit 3
that   her husband,   both   her arms   were burned.   Not   he slept

qix· itcā′k·ikal. Ka′nauwē nuguē′witx·it qō′tac tê′lx·Em. Atciō′lXam 4
that   her husband.   All   they slept   those   people.   He said to him

Liā′wuX: "Mxā′latck!" Nixā′latck Liā′wuX. "Ā′cgam XaX 5
his younger brother: "Rise!"   He arose   his younger brother.   "Take it   this

ōLk¡′E′nLk¡′En." A′lta atciū′cgam qix· itcō′itk. Ā′ctŏ mā′Lnē 6
basket."   Now   he took it   that   dipnet.   They two   seaward went

tcā′xElqlē. Actigō′om qix· ēlā′itk. Actō′cgam qō′ta tiā′qxōn ēlā′itk. 7
winter.   They reached it   that   willow.   They took them   those   its leaves   willow.

PāL nā′xax qaX ōLk¡′E′nk¡′En. Ā′yōLq. YukpE′t niLē′La-it Ltcuq. 8
Full   became   that   basket.   He went to the water.   To here   he stood in the water.   water

Atciō′lXam Lia′wuX: "LxEluwē′gōt. Ē′wa kᵘca′la nai′kXa, 9
He said to him   his younger brother: "It is ebb tide.   Thus   up river   [from] me,

LgE′kᵘcala wax amtā′xax x·ita tE′kXōn. Ka amiucgä′mx x·iau 10
up river from me   pour out   do them   those   leaves.   Then   take it   this

itcō′itk. Amgē′ma: 'Ēhê̒;' amgē′ma: 'Niā′waᶜ itci′tsōitk.' Amiŏlā′tcgō 11
dipnet.   Say: 'Ēhê̒;'   say: 'I broke it   my dipnet.'   Lift it

imē′tcōitk. WiXt wäx amtā′xŏ ē′wa LgE′kᵘcala. WiXt amgē′ma: 12
your dipnet.   Again   pour out   do them   thus   up river from me.   Again   say:

'Ēhê̒, niā′waᶜ itsō′itk.'" Lō′ni wax atci′tax; wiXt nē′k·im: "Niā′waᶜ 13
'Ēhê̒,   I broke it   the dipnet.'"   Three times   pour out   he did them;   again   he said: "I broke it

itci′tsōitk." Atciō′latck iā′tcōitk. Atciō′lXam qix· iā′qk'un; aqiō′lXam 14
my dipnet."   He lifted it   his dipnet.   He said to him   that   his elder brother;   it was said to him

qix· iq¡oā′lipx·: "Ni′Xua, tE′kEman!" Atctō′kuman qix· iq¡oā′lipx·. 15
that   youth: "Well,   look at them!"   He looked at them   that   youth.

A′lta tä′kXōn gō tgā′lictEkc, ä′Lxan ē′wa tiā′qtqakc. Wax atci′tax 16
Now   leaves   at   their tails,   smelt   thus   their heads.   Pour out   he did them

ē′LaquinEmix·. L¡lEp, L¡lEp, L¡lep, nikqLā′yux. WiXt atciō′tipa 17
the fifth time.   Under water,   under water,   under water,   they jumped into the water.   Again   he dipped

ē′Latxamē. Wax atcā′yax. A′lta niLkᵘkLā′Xit Ltcuq qix· ē′Lxan. 18
the sixth time.   Pour out   he did them.   Now   they swam on the surface   water   those   smelts.

Atciō′lXam Liā′wuX: "Tca txgīucge′Lxa x·ix· iqicē′tix·." Acgiō′cgiLx 19
He said to him   to his younger brother: "Come   we will launch it   this   fishing canoe."   They launched it

qix· iqicē′tix·. Acgiō′cgam iqaLē′mat. A′lta nicxLē′u. Xuwē′t qix· 20
that   fishing canoe.   They took it   the rake.   Now   they fished with the rake.   Half full   that

ictā′xēcitix·. Atciō′lXam: "KōpE′t." Ta′kE acxē′gila-ē. "Ai′aq Lgā′lEmam 21
their fishing canoe.   He said to him: "Enough."   Then   they went ashore.   "Quick   fetch

Lkuē′Lx·Ema qoā′nEm." AtcLugō′lEmam qix· iq¡oā′lipx·. Ōgoē′witiū 22
large mats   five."   He fetched them   that   youth.   They slept

qō′tac tê′lx·Em. Acgiō′kuē qix· ē′Lxan. Acgiō′kctEptck ka′nauwē. 23
those   people.   They carried them ashore   those   smelts.   They carried them inland   all.

Atciō′lXam Liā′wuX: "Kawē′X mxElā′tcgō ka mxElgē′Lxa ka 24
He said to him   his younger brother: "Early   rise   and   make fire   and

mx'ō′tama. Mīōgonā′ya tE′lxaqL. Ia′xkatē kᵘcā′xalē mōtX ka 25
go to bathe.   Open the smoke hole   our house.   There   up   stand   and

1 mxElqE′mxaya.   Mgē′ma: ′Ā, GiLāunaLXā′ ta′kE   na amcxE′La-it?
  shout.   Say: ′Ah, GiLāunaLX   then [int. are you dead?
                                                part.]

2 Ā tqagElā′xElta′;′ mgē′ma. Mỏ′kcti mgē′ma, mxElqE′mxa.″ Nau′itka.
  Ah, the news;′   say. Twice say,   shout.″   Indeed.

3 Kawē′X nixā′latck Liā′wuX. Na-ixE′lgiLx. Nix′ō′tam. Nē′tptcga.
  Early he arose his younger He made a fire. He went to He went inland.
                   brother.   bathe.

4 Atciugōnā′maın tE′LaqL, na-ixE′lqamx: ″Ā, GiLāunaLXā′ takE na
  He went to open the their house, he shouted: ″Ah, GiLā′unaLX then [int.
  smoke hole   part.]

5 amcxE′La-it? Â, tqagElaxElta′.″ Mỏ′kcti na-ixE′lqamx. A′lta
  are you dead? Ah, the news!″   Twice he shouted. Now

6 nuxōlā′yutck qō′tac tê′lx·Em. Atktō′cgam tgā′XalaitanEma.
  they arose those people. They took them their arrows.

7 AtkLō′cgam Ltā′mEq̨aL; atkLō′cgam LmōL̨anē′. A′lta ā′tgē ē′wa
  They took them their bone clubs; they took them lances. Now they went thus

8 qō′ta tā′yaqL qix· iLā′Xak̨Ema-na. Nugō′kXo-im qō′tac tê′lx·Em:
  that his house that their chief. They said those people:

9 ″Ē′kta ē′xax? Qā′xēwa atgatē′mam tqagElā′xElt?″ Nē′k·im qix·
  ″What is it? Whence came they the news!″ He said that

10 iq̨oā′lipx·: ″x·itā′ō, x·itā′o tqagElā′xelt gō qō′La qoā′nEm
   youth: ″These, these news in those five

11 Lkuē′tx·Ema.″ A′lta ixē′nXat ē′Lxan. Ia′xka LkLXā′nak igē′l′ōtitk,
   large baskets.″ Now they stood smelts. That one he had it on elkskin armor,
                                     there

12 ia′xka aLgixaniā′kôx. Ma′nix c′ōlā′l LckLXā′nax, iā′xkati
   he carried it in the fold When a ground-hog he had it on, there
       of the skin.   blanket

13 aLgixk̨ē′niakux qix· ē′Lxān gō qō′cta c′ōlā′l. Ma′nix oᶜōnaᶜ
   he wrapped them up those smelts in that ground-hog When a raccoon
                                          blanket.   blanket

14 LkLXā′nak, qē′xtcē aLgixk̨ē′niagux, ayutXuī′tcuwa-itx gō qaX
   he had it on, intending he wrapped it up in it, they fell through in that

15 ōLā′kXanaᶜ. Ka′nauwē-y· ē′ka qō′tac tê′lx·Em nō′xôx. A′lta
   his raccoon blanket. All thus those people they did. Now

16 nōxo-iLXā′lEm qō′tac tê′lx·Em. Aqiō′tXEmit ēXt iqā′ētEma ē′wa
   they ate those people. It was placed upright one young spruce thus
                                                        tree

17 mai′ēmē. Aqiō′tXEmit ēXt iqā′ētEma ē′wa kᵘca′la. Lā′maka
   down river. It was placed upright one young spruce tree thus up river. Only they

18 GiLā′unaLX aLgiupā′yaLx ē′Lxan. Pā′LEma nō′xôx tE′LaqL.
   the GiLā′unaLX they gathered them smelts. Full became their house.

19 ÄLgiō′kcEm. Ka′nauwē tiā′lEXam atgiupā′yaLx.
   They dried them. All their people gathered them.

   Ä′gōn iqē′tak ka wiXt ō′lō agE′Lax GiLā′unaLX. Lā′mka
   One more year then again hunger acted on the GiLā′unaLX. Only
                                          them

21 LE′kXaᶜpa aLkLā′xo-itx k̨a-y- ōpE′nxaLX. NixE′ltcEmaôx qix·
   skunk-cabbage they ate it and rush roots. He heard about it that

22 iLā′Xak̨Emana. Ā, ta′kE pā′LEma nō′xôx t̨ōLē′ma gō Iqā′niaq.
   their chief. Ah, then full they were the houses in Rainier.

23 Qiā′wul ē′Lxan. Atctā′x tE′mᶜEcX ē′cgan ōgō′kXuix itā′Lēlam;
   They were smelts. He made sticks cedar made out of ten;
   made [caught] them

24 qoa′nEm ō′Lqikc, qoā′nEm Lpā′qxo-ikc. Atctō′lXam tiā′cōlal: ″Ai′aq
   five fish ducks, five shags. He said to them his relatives: ″Quick

25 amcxE′ltXuitck. Lxō′tctōla, lxōwā′L̨ama.″ ALē′gEla-itx ēXt
   make yourselves ready. We will go up now, we will go to get food.″ They were in a canoe one

26 ikanī′m pāL, iā′qoa-iL ikanī′m. ALō′tctōlax, aLō′yamx Sōguamē′ts!iak.
   canoe full, a large canoe. They went up the they arrived Tongue point.
                              river   at

27 Ē′ktcxEm alō′ix. AtcLō′lXam giLā′′cgēwal: ″Ma′nix
   He sang his con- they went. He said to them his companions: ″When
   jurer′s song

qElxEngē'waL¡'amita,   nēkct   amcxLxE'lEma."   ALō'yamx   ka   1
we are given food,   not   eat."   They arrived then [at]

Liā'ēcaLxē. ALqēgēlā'xē gō y- ē'lXam. ALō'ptck. Nē'gimx: "Gō qaxē   2
Liā'ēcaLxē.   They landed   at   the town. They went up. He said: "At where

aqiā'wul x·ik ē'lxan¡"   "Ā   mā'ema Iqā'niaq, iā'xkati aqiā'wul."   3
are made   these smelts!"   "Ah, below   Rainier   there   they are made
[caught]   [caught.]"

Qē'xtcē aqiō'lEktc ē'lxan; q¡oā'p ayō'ktciktx. Atctō'lXam   4
Intending they were roasted the smelts; nearly   they were done. He said to them

giLā'cgēwal: "Ai'aq lxō'tctōwula." AqLō'lXam qē'xtcē: "A'lta   5
his companions: "Quick we will go up."   They were spoken to intending: "Now

q¡oā'p iō'ktcikta x·ix· ē'lxan." Nē'k·im: "A'ntcxElxulama. Ā'Lqi   6
nearly   they are done those   smelts." He said: " We will go at once. Later on

wuX ntcxēxā'txama-i."   ALō'ix kᵘca'la. A'lta nau'itka aLogō'ōmx   7
to-mor- we shall go ashore for They went up river. Now   indeed   they reached
row   awhile."   them

tê'lx·Em, tgiā'wul ē'Lxān. Q¡oā'p aLktā'x qō'tac tê'lx·am.   8
people,   they made it smelts. Near   they got them those   people.
           [caught]

ALE'gimx Lē'Xat LgōLē'lEXEmk: "PāL ē'xax itci'tsōitk. Ala'xti   9
He said   one   person: "Full   is   my dipnet.   Soon

L¡EX ixā'xō. Atcuwa'-y- ō'lō Lix·Lā'it GiLā'unaLX." Iqamiā'itX 10
burst it will.   Ha!   hunger they starve the GiLā'unaLX." Iqamiā'itX

iLā'Xawôk atcLō'lXam giLā'cgēwal: "Lawā' msкᴛē'watcgō." 11
his guardian spirit he said to them his companions: "Slowly   paddle!"

Ka'nauwē aLgaxgō'c qaX ōkunī'm kā atoLō'lXam: "Amcкᴛē'watck 12
All   they passed those canoes then he said to them: " Paddle
          them

mā'Lnē." A'lta aLkᴛē'watck mā'Lnē. Ē'wa ē'natai qix· ikanī'm 13
away from Now   they paddled away from Thus on one side that   canoe
the land."   the land.

qoā'nEm atcuXō'tqoax qō'ta tElalā'xukc; ē'wa ē'natai qoā'nEm 14
five   he put them into the those birds;   thus   on the   five
         water   other side

qix· ikanī'm. Iū'Lqat itā'Lan. ĒXt itā'Lan qoā'nEm, wiXt ēXt 15
that   canoe.   Long   their rope. One their rope five,   also   one

itā'Lan qoā'nEm. Atctō'lXam tiā'cōlal: "Amcкᴛē'watck!" A'lta 16
their rope five.   He said to them his relatives: "Paddle!"   Now

nugukᴛē'watck giLā'cgēwal. T¡ā'qē nauē'tka-y- atxā'Lgōwa 17
they paddled   his companions. Just as   indeed   they swam

tElalā'xukc qō'ta tE'mᶜEcX ugō'kXuiXt tElalā'Xukc. Q¡oā'p 18
birds   those   sticks   made   birds.   Nearly

aLXgō'mam ka nē'ktcuktē. Qonē'2 tqonēqonē' gō Lā'maLnē. 19
they came home and it got day. Gull   gulls   at   seaward from
                                                       them.

Nō'pōnEm. Nē'k·im: "Ni'Xua, mci'Lxa! Nau'itka na x·iau ā'nitkᵘᴛ 20
It grew dark. He said: "Well, go to the water! Indeed [int. these did I carry
                                                       part.]   them

x·iau ē'lxan¡" A'tgELx giLā'lEXam, atE'kXukL utā'Xanim, ska 21
these   smelts!" They went to the people of his they launched their canoes, and
                 the water   town,   them

mä'nx·i ka pā'Lma nā'xax. ALgiō'kcEm ē'lxan GiLā'unaLX. 22
after a little and full   they were. They dried them the smelts the GiLā'unaLX.

Pā'Lma nō'xôx Lā'uLēma. Qē'xtcē aqiō'Xtkin gō kᵘca'la Qauilē'tcq. 23
Full   they were their houses. Intending they were at up river Cowlitz.
                                  searched

KōpE't atgā'yamx. K¡ē qix· ē'lxan. Nuxoē'tcEmaôx tê'lx·Em: "Ā 24
Enough they arrived. None these smelts. They heard   the people: "Ah

GiLā'unaLX, ta'ke pā'Lma nō'xôx Lā'uLēma. Atcā'yukᵘᴛ taL¡ 25
the GiLā'unaLX, then full   are   their houses. He carried them, behold!

x·ik ē'lxan qix· giā'xamia-itx." A'lta aqLōmē'lax qō'La 26
those the smelts that the one having Iqamia'- Now   they were angry that
                        itx."   with him

LgōLē'lEXEmk. Ia'Xka, x·ix·ī'x· nē'k·im: "Atcuwa' ō'lō LE'XLa-itt 27
person.   He,   this one he said,   "Ha!   hunger they starve

1 GiLā'unaLX, Iqamiā'itx iLā'Xawôk." A'lta ŏ'lŏ nuxŏ'La-it qŏ'tac
the GiLā'unaLX, Iqamiā'itx his guardian spirit." Now hunger they died those

2 tê'lx·Em, ê'wa kᵘca'la tê'lx·Em. Kᵢē nē'xax qix· ē'Lxan. A'lta
people, thus up river the people. Nothing became those smelts. Now

3 Lā'macka GiLā'unaLX aLgiupā'yaLX qix· ē'Lxan.
they only the GiLā'unaLX they gathered them those smelts.

A'lta qix· ē'Xat giā'xamia-itx atcLŏ'cgam Lᶜā'gil. Ō'lo agE'Lax
Now that one having Iqamiā-'itx he took her a woman. Hunger acted on them

5 GiLā'unaLX tsakᵢE'ē. Qē'xtcē aLxEnkᵢānXā'tēmamx, nēkct i'kta
the GiLā'unaLX in the spring time. Intending they caught in the dipnet, not anything

6 aLgiā'waᶜôx. Qiā'x ōguē'can aLgŏ'kᵘⁱx Tiā'kᵢēlakē kᵢa-y- ŏpE'nxaLX
they killed it. If fern root they carried it the Clatsop and rush roots

7 tᴉā'nuwa aLgā'x, tcx·ī mänx· axLEᴉᶜēmx ōkᵢuē'lak kᵢa ōxŏ'ca-ut
exchange they did it, then a little they were given dry salmon and dry food

8 tkalguē'EX. E'Xauētē tᴉā'nuwa aLxā'xumx ka aLE'k·imx
salmon skins. Often exchange they did it often and he said

9 Lē'Xat LgōLē'leXEmk: "Tcx·ī kᵢa Lx tᴉā'nuwa GiLā'unaLX
one person: "Then and may be exchanging the GiLā'unaLX

10 ma'nix wiXt Ltē'mama, ka Līx· lxkLā'xō," aLE'k·imx qŏ'La Lē'Xat
when again they will come, then cohabit we will with be said that one [their women],"

11 LgōLē'leXEmk Tiā'kᵢēlak. A'lta wiXt aLŏ'ix GiLā'unaLX tᴉā'nuwa
person Clatsop. Now again they went the GiLā'unaLX exchanging

12 aLxā'xEmx. Aqā'tElōtx ōkᵢuē'lak kᵢa ōxŏ'ca-ut tkalguē'êx·. ALŏ'Lx;
they did it. They were given dry salmon and dry salmon skins. They went to the water;

13 a'lta aLXgō'ya. WiXt Lā'xka qŏ'La LgŏLē'leXEmk: "Ai'aq amci'tē!
now they went home. Again he that person: "Quick, come!

14 LxkLkā'ō, Līx· lxkLā'xō." Lxeltcē'mElit qŏ'Lac GiLā'unaLX
We will follow them, cohabit we will do them." They heard it those GiLā'unaLX

15 Lā'nEmckc. Katē'X qaX uyā'k·ikal qix· giā'xamia-itx. ALXgō'mam.
women. Accompany-ing that his wife that having Iqamiā-'itx. They came home.

16 ALxgu'Litck: "QLEntcilqLā'lEtciL, aqEntcō'lXam Līx· qEntcā'xō."
They told: "We were insulted, we were told cohabit we will be done."

17 Nēxŏ'kctē qix· iguā'nat giā'Xawôk. NixEmā'tcta-itck. Qoä'nEmi
He lay down that salmon his guardian spirit. He was ashamed. Five times

18 ayā'qxoya nixŏ'kctē. Nēkct nixLxā'lEm, ka atciā'waᶜ iguā'nat
his sleeps he lay down. Not be ate, then he killed it a salmon

19 Liā'wuX. Nē'k·im: "LE'mcxEltEq!" ALā'xEltEq uyā'k·ikal.
his younger brother. He said: "Heat stones!" She heated stones his wife.

20 Aqtugā'lEmam tqᵢēyŏ'qtikc. Atgā'tpᴉam. NuxōiLŏ'lEXa-it qŏ'tac
They were fetched old people. They came in. They thought those

21 tqᵢēyŏ'qtikc: "Tgiā'xō qix· iguā'nat." ALŏ'ckuit qŏ'La Lqā'nakc ka
old people: "We shall eat it that salmon." They were hot those stones and

22 nē'ktcxEm qix· igōLē'leXEmk qix GiLā'unaLX. Aqŏ'cgam ōᶜmē'cX.
he sang that person that GiLā'unaLX. It was taken a kettle.

23 Aqugō'Lit gō kā'tsEk tᴉōL. ALŏ'ckuit qŏ'La Lqā'nakc. AqLā'LXatq
It was put in middle of house. They were hot those stones. They were put into

24 qaX ōᶜmē'cX. Aqiuqoā'na-it qiX iguā'nat gō qaX ōᶜmē'cX ka
that kettle. It was put into it that salmon in that kettle and

25 lŏ'Elŏ, nēkct aqā'yaxc. Omŏkct cXumElā'itX qŏ'ctac cqᵢēyŏ'qxut.
whole, not it was cut. Two they stood close together those two old men.

26 Aqiŏ'tctEmt qix· ē'Xat: "Qa'daqa-y- ē'ka aqā'yax x·ix· iguā'nat!"
He was pushed that one: "Why thus it is done this salmon!"

27 Cka: "Kᵢā amE'xaX; kᵢā amxē'x itxā'k·ackc. Ā'Lqi tEmElā'xo-ix-ita
And: "Silent be; silent be to our young people. Later on you will know it

qa'da qiā'xō x·ix· iguā'nat." Lĕ'lĕ aqigkįētkiɛ qix· iguā'nat, **1**
how   it is done   this   salmon."   Long time   it was covered   that   salmon,

aqiɛlgē'lakō. Atctō'lXam tiā'lXam: "Nĕkct lxgiā'xôx x·ik iguā'nat. **2**
the mat was taken   He said to them   his people: "Not   we shall eat it   this   salmon.
off.

Iō'ya gō mā'Lnĕ." Atciō'lXam qix· ĕ'Xat iqįēyō'qxōt qix· **3**
It will go   to   seaward."   He said to him   that   one   old man   that

qcXɛmɛlā'itX: "Amxauwu'tcatkō tatc! amxō'xo-il, qa'daqa-y- ĕ'ka **4**
standing close to-   " You hear   behold!   you talk much,   why   thus
gether:

aqā'yax x·ix· iguā'nat." Aqō'cgam qaX ŏɛmē'cX; amô'kctikc **5**
it is done   this   salmon."   It was taken   that   kettle;   two

cqįulipXunā'yu atgō'cgam. Ā'qxokⁿɪ mā'Lnē qaX ŏɛmē'cX. **6**
youths   they took it.   It was carried   seaward   that   kettle.

Aqiō'cgiL iqicē'tix·; aqakgō'Lit qaX ŏɛōmē'cX gō qix· iqicē'tix·. **7**
It was launched   a fishing   it was put into   that   kettle   in   that fishing canoe.
  canoe;   the canoe

ALagā'la-it Lā'kįaquinumikc, iā'xqix· iguā'nat giā'Xawôk kįa **8**
They were in   five in a canoe,   he that   the salmon   the one having   and
the canoe   guardian spirit

lā'ktikc tqįulipXɛnā'yū. A'lta ā'Lō mā'Lnē, ĕ'ktcxɛm ā'Lŏ. **9**
four   youths.   Now   they went   seaward,   he sang   they went.

Kulā'yi mā'Lnē aLō'yam ka aqō'cgam qaX ŏɛmē'cX. Wax aqā'yax **10**
Far   seaward   they arrived   and   it was taken   that   kettle.   Pour   it was done
out

qix· iguā'nat gō Ltcuq ka qō'La Lqā'nakc. ALxē'gēla-ē. Atctō'lXam **11**
that   salmon   into   the water   and   those   stones.   They went ashore.   He said to them

tqįulipXɛnā'yū: "Mcē'kɛlōya iqā'yĕtɛma." Aqē'gɛlōya môkct **12**
the youths: "Get   young spruce trees."   They were got   two

iqā'ĕtɛma, Laq aqā'yax uyā'aptcXa. Nĕ'k·im qix· igōLē'lɛXɛmk **13**
young spruce   take off   it was done   their bark.   He said   that   person
trees,

qix· Giā'unaLX: "Gŏ kᵘca'la mcgiŏ'tXɛmita ēXt, gō mā'ĕmē- **14**
that   GiLā'unaLX: "At   up river   you place it   one,   at   down river

y-ēXt." Ä'ka atgā'yax qō'tac tqįulipXunā'yū. Nō'pōnɛm nuXuikį **15**
one."   Thus   they did it   those   youths.   It got dark   they laid

anXā'tēmam GiLā'unaLX. Nĕ'ktcuktē. Pā'Lɪna-y- utā'Xanim **16**
their dipnets   the GiLā'unaLX.   It got day.   Full   their canoes

tguā'nat ka ixElE'l iguā'nat ayuXtkē'Xĕwa mā'LxôLē. Aqtōmē'tckin **17**
salmon   and   moving   the salmon   swam   landward.   They were picked up

qō'ta tguā'nat. Mä'nx·ē aLktōmē'tckĕnimx LgōLē'lɛx·ɛmk, pāL **18**
those   salmon.   A little   he picked them up   a person,   full

ikanī'm. Atcō'lɛXam tqįulipXɛnā'yū: "Tca lxō'ya ĕ'wa **19**
the canoe.   He said to them   the youths: "Come   we will go   thus

Tiā'kįēlakē." ALō'yam Nayā'aqctaōwē. Lįmɛ'ɴLįmɛn atci'Lax **20**
Clatsop."   They arrived at   Nayā'qctaōwē.   Rub   he did it

Lā'môptcX. Atcxē'la gō Ltcuq. AtcLō'lXam giLā'ckēwal: **21**
green paint.   He mixed it   in   water.   He said to them   his fellows:

"LxkᴛēĚ'watcgō iau'a mā'Lnē." Atkᴛē'watck mā'Lnē. Wax **22**
"We will paddle   there   seaward."   They paddled   seaward.   Pour out

atci'Lax gō Ltcuq qō'La Lā'môptcX. AtcLō'lXam: "Lxgō'ya," **23**
he did it   into   the water   that   his green paint.   He said to them: "We will go,"

giLā'ckēwal. ALXgō'mam. Pā'Lɛma nō'xôx Lā'uLɛma GiLā'unaLX **24**
[to] his fellows.   They came home.   Full   were   their houses   the GiLā'unaLX

ōkįuē'lak, ōxō'ca-ot tkalguē'êx. Atci'tax tguā'nat qix· **25**
dry salmon,   dry   salmon skins.   He made them   salmon   that

giā'xamia itx.
the one having Iqamia'itx.

Translation.

The grandmother of a GiLā'unaLX boy was deserted at Tongue
point. After six days the boy was told: "Walk [to Tongue point

and] look after your grandmother." He walked downstream and saw two fish ducks. He took his arrows but thought: "I will not shoot them, else they will carry my arrows away from the land." He took a stone. When the ducks dived he ran to the water and when they emerged he threw his stone. He hit the head of one. Then he took off his blanket [and went into the water]. He reached them. The water reached to his armpits; then the ducks fluttered and flew away. He went ashore. Then they drifted again, the belly upward. Again he went into the water and swam. When he nearly reached them they fluttered again. He went ashore. Five times he swam to get them. Then he reached them. He turned round and fainted. Now he saw a supernatural being; he saw Iqamiā'itx [the helper of the fishermen]. When he awoke he was on the shore and held the ducks in his hands. He left them and went on. Now he reached Tongue point. When he came near his grandmother he saw smoke rising where she was deserted. He reached her and said: "Behold! you are alive!" She said to him: "I am alive." She was going to give him food, but he said: "I am not hungry." He slept there. On the next day he gathered fuel for his grandmother. He gathered many sticks and went home. He left his grandmother. In the evening he came home. Then the people said to him: "Are you hungry?" He replied: "No, I am tired." He lay down. Early the next morning he arose and went a long distance. He went to play. In the evening he came home. After he had been there a short while he lay down. For three nights and three days he did not eat. Then on the fourth day he ate. He grew up.

Now he had a friend, a youth. They grew up. One day they went out in a canoe. When they were in the middle of the river he said to his friend: "Who is your guardian spirit?" He replied: "Iqamiā'itx is my guardian spirit, and who is yours?" The other one said: "My guardian spirit is also Iqamiā'itx." The one said: "What are you going to do when our relatives shall be hungry?" The other replied: "I shall let smelts come;" and he asked his friend: "And what are you going to do?" He said: "I shall let salmon come when our relatives get hungry. Put your arm under water; I shall put mine also under water." They put their arms under water. The one who had the guardian spirit helping him to obtain smelts lifted his hand first. Now a smelt hung at his hand. After some time the other one lifted his hand. A small salmon hung at it. Then he said to his friend: "Indeed! Iqamiā'itx is your guardian spirit."

The youths went home. The one who had a guardian spirit helping him to obtain smelts married first. Now the GiLā'unaLX were starving. They had only skunk-cabbage to eat. Then the young man whose guardian spirit helped him to obtain smelts became rich.

One day his wife went to gather skunk-cabbage. In the evening when she came home she heated stones and warmed herself. The winter was cold. When she was warm she dozed away and fell down at the fire. She fell asleep sitting there and burned her arms. Then all the GiLā'unaLX said: "Our chief's wife is starving. Your relative's wife will die, she fell asleep sitting. She is starving." Thus spoke the people. The woman said: "I fell asleep, and my husband says he has Iqamiā'itx [for his guardian spirit]." Now her husband was ashamed because both her arms were burned. He did not sleep, while all the other people slept. He said to his younger brother: "Rise!" His younger brother arose. [He continued:] "Take this basket." Now he took his dipnet and they went to the water. It was winter. They came to a willow and he took its leaves. When the basket was full they went to the water. He stood in the water up to his waist. He said to his younger brother: "It is ebb tide. Pour these leaves into the river above me. Then take this dipnet and say: 'Ēhê', I broke my dipnet.' Lift it and pour it out again above me. Then say once more: 'Ēhê', I broke my dipnet.'" Three times he poured it out and said: "I broke my dipnet." He lifted the dipnet. Then the elder brother said to the younger one: "Now look at them." The youth looked at them, now they were leaves at the tails and smelts at the heads. He poured them out the fifth time. They jumped into the water. He dipped them up the sixth time and poured them out again. Now smelts swam on the surface of the water. He said to his younger brother: "Let us launch our fishing canoe." They launched it and took a rake. Now they fished with the rake and the canoe was half full. He said: "It is enough." Then they went ashore. "Bring five large mats." The youth brought them. The people were asleep. They carried the smelts ashore and carried them all up to the house. He said to his younger brother: "Rise early, make a fire and go to bathe. Open the smoke-hole of our house. Stand up there and shout. Say: 'Ah, GiLā'unaLX! are you dead? News has come.' Thus speak twice." The younger brother did so. He arose early, made a fire and went to bathe. He went up, opened the smoke-hole of their house and shouted: "Ah, GiLā'unaLX, are you dead? News has come." He shouted twice. Now the people arose. They took their arrows, their bone clubs, and their lances. Now they went to the house of their chief. The people said: "What is it? Where did news come from?" The youth said: "There, in these five baskets is the news." Now the smelts stood there. One of the men wore an elkskin armor; he carried some away in a fold of the skin. Another wore a ground-hog blanket; he wrapped them up in his blanket. Still another wore a raccoon blanket; he wanted to wrap them up in it, but they fell through it. All the people did thus. Now they ate. Now one young spruce tree was placed downstream and one upstream. Only the GiLā'unaLX caught smelts. Their houses became full and they dried them. All the people caught them.

Another year the GiLā'unaLX were again starving. They had only skunk-cabbage and rush roots to eat. Their chief heard that the houses of the people at Rainier were full. They caught smelts. Then he carved ten pieces of cedar. He made five fish-ducks and five shags. He said to his relatives: "Make yourselves ready. We will go upstream to get food." They went in a large canoe. They went up until they arrived at Tongue point. He sang his conjurer's song while they went. He said to his companions: "If they should give us food, do not eat!" They arrived at Liā'ēcaLxē. They landed at the town and went up to the houses. He said: "Where are those smelts caught?" "Ah, they are caught below Rainier." They were going to roast the smelts and when they were nearly done he said to his companions: "Let us go up the river." The people said to them: "These smelts are nearly done." But he said: "We will go at once. To-morrow we shall stay for a while." They went upstream. Now they came to the people who caught smelts. They were near them. One person said: "My dipnet is full. It will soon burst. Ha! The GiLā'unaLX are starving." The one whose guardian spirit was Iqamia'itx said to his companions: "Paddle slowly." When they had passed all the canoes he said to them: "Paddle toward the middle of the river." They paddled from the land. He put five of those birds into the water on each side of the canoe. Each five were tied to a long rope. Then he said to his relatives: "Paddle." Now his companions paddled. These wooden birds swam just like birds. When it was nearly day they came home. Gulls were seaward from them. When it grew dark he said: "Go to the water. See if I did not bring the smelts." The people went to the water and launched their canoes. After a short time they were full. The GiLā'unaLX dried the smelts and their houses were full. The people upstream searched as far as Cowlitz, but the smelts had disappeared; there were none. The people heard: "Ah, the houses of the GiLā'unaLX are full. That one whose guardian spirit is Iqamia'itx carried the smelts away." Now they scolded that person: "Ha! this person said: 'Ah, the GiLā'unaLX are starving, although one of them says that he has Iqamiā'itx for his guardian spirit.'" Now the people upstream were starving. The smelt had disappeared. Only the GiLā'unaLX caught smelt.

Now the other man who had Iqamiā'itx for his guardian spirit married. In spring the GiLā'unaLX were again starving. They tried to catch salmon in the dipnet, but they did not kill anything. They carried fern (*Pteris*) roots and rush roots to Clatsop and exchanged them. Then they received a little dry salmon and salmon skins. They went often to exchange it. Then a person said: "When the GiLā'unaLX come again to exchange we will cohabit with [their women]." Thus said a Clatsop man. Now the GiLā'unaLX went again to exchange [roots for salmon]. They received dry salmon and salmon skins. They went to the water and went home. That person said again: "Quick, let us follow them. We will follow them and cohabit with the women." The GiLā'unaLX women heard it. The wife of the man who had Iqamiā'itx for his guardian spirit was with them. They came home and declared: "We were insulted; they told us they would cohabit with us." Then the one whose guardian spirit helped him to obtain salmon lay down. He was ashamed. For five days he remained in bed, and did not eat. Then his younger brother killed a salmon. He said: "Heat stones." Then his wife heated stones. They called the old people and they came. They thought: "We shall eat that salmon." When the stones were hot that GiLā'unaLX sang his conjurer's song. They took a kettle and placed it in the middle of the house. When the stones were hot they put them into that kettle. Then they put the salmon into the kettle whole; they did not cut it. Two old men were standing close together. The one nudged the other and said: "Why do they treat the salmon in that way?" The other said: "Be quiet, do not disturb our young men. You will learn in due time what they are going to do with this salmon." Now the salmon had been covered a long time. Then the mat was taken off, and he said to the people: "We shall not eat this salmon. It will be taken out into the water." Then the one old man who was standing close to the other one said: "Now you hear it. You said before, why do they treat the salmon in this manner." Two youths took the kettle and carried it to the water. A fishing canoe was launched and the kettle was placed in it. Five men were in the canoe—four youths and the one whose guardian spirit helped him to obtain salmon. Now they went seaward, and he sang his conjurer's song as they went. They arrived in the middle of the water. Then they took the kettle and poured the salmon and the stones into the water. They went ashore. He said to the youths: "Take young spruce trees." They took them and peeled off the bark. Then that GiLā'unaLX said: "Place one above and one below this place." The youths did so. When it grew dark the GiLā'unaLX set their dipnets. When it grew day their canoes were full of salmon and the fish swam toward the shore. They filled their canoes quickly. Then he said to the youths: "Let us go to Clatsop!" They arrived at Nayā'qcta-owē. He rubbed some green paint in his hands and mixed it with water. He said to his companions: "Let us paddle toward the middle of the water." They paddled away from the shore. Then he poured his green paint into the water. He said to his companions: "Let us go." They came home. The houses of the GiLā'unaLX were full of dry salmon and of dry salmon skins. Thus the man who had Iqamiā'itx for his guardian spirit obtained salmon.

THE ELK HUNTER.

Ē'Xat igoLē'lEXEmk iqᵢoā'lipx· guā'nEsum Lkā'waōt atcLā'xo-
One · · · · person · · · · a youth · · · · always · · · · traps · · · · he always

2 ilEma-itx. Atciutē'niLa-itx ēē'tcxōtEma. Á'gōn iqē'tak wiXt atcLā'x
made them. · · · He always killed them · · · bears. · · · One more · · · year · · · again · · · he made them

3 Lkā'waōt. Tcē'xēL atcLō'kctamx Liā'Xawaōt. A'lta Lā'qxulqt
traps. · · · Several · · · he went to see them · · · his traps. · · · Now · · · she cried

4 Lᵉā'gil gō qō'La Lkā'waōt. NiLga'ōmx. A'lta uLa'ksia Lagē'laktcūt
a woman · · · in · · · that · · · trap. · · · He reached her. · · · Now · · · her hand · · · it was caught

5 qō'La Lkā'waōt. Lt!ō'kti Lᵉā'gil. SquL LE'Laqcō, tE'Laskō ka'nauwē
that · · · trap. · · · A pretty · · · woman. · · · Brown · · · her hair, · · · her tattooing · · · all

6 Lā'ᶜo-it, tE'Laskō gō Lā'potē ka'nauwē qō'La Lᵉā'gil. ·AtcLō'latcgux
her feet, · · · her tattooing · · · on · · · her hands · · · all · · · that · · · woman. · · · He lifted it

7 qō'La Liā'Xawaōt, Lāqᵒ aLXā'x qō'La Lā'kcia qō'La Lᵉā'gil.
that · · · his trap, · · · take out · · · he did it · · · that · · · her hand · · · that · · · woman.

8 ALgiō'lEXamx: "Lāx amtā'xō, mōxōgō'kō x·itikc tē'lx·Em. Äka
She said to him: · · · "Pass · · · you will do · · · you surpass them · · · these · · · people. · · · Thus them,

9 nai'kXa aLEngē'luktcu LEmē'Xawaōt. Mōxogō'kō ka'nauwē tē'lx·Em.
I · · · it caught me · · · your trap. · · · You surpass them · · · all · · · people.

10 TEmē'xēqLax tEmxElā'xō." Nē'k·im qix· iqᵢoā'lipx·: "Iamō'kᵘτa gō
You a hunter · · · you will be." · · · He said · · · that · · · youth: · · · "I shall carry you · · · to

11 intcā'lXam." Atcō'lXam qaX uyā'Xawōk: "Iamuxōnimā'ya
our town." · · · He said to her · · · that · · · his supernatural helper: · · · "I shall show you [to]

12 Natē'tanuē." A'lta atcō'kᵘτx gō iā'lXam. AtgaᶜE'lkElax tiā'colal,
the Indians." · · · Now · · · he carried her · · · to · · · his town. · · · They saw them · · · his relatives,

13 ka'nauwē nuxō'La-itx, ka iā'xka ayō'mEqtx.
all · · · they died, · · · and · · · he · · · he died.

Qantsī'x Lxqētā'kEma ka wiXt LE'gōn aLgēᶜE'lkElax Lkᵢāsks.
How many · · · years · · · and again · · · another one · · · he saw her · · · a boy.

15 Nēkst Lā'mama qō'La Lkᵢāsks, nēkst Lā'naa, Lā'xauyam. Ka
Not · · · his father · · · that · · · boy, · · · not · · · his mother, · · · his poverty. · · · And

16 iLauu'kstX qō'La Lkᵢāsks. AkLō'lXamx, qēc mank mā'qoa-iL pōs
small · · · that · · · boy. · · · She said to him, · · · if · · · a little · · · you large · · · then

17 ka'nauwē amuxō'kukō tgā'xēkLax. Näkct ē'ka aniō'lXam qix·
all · · · you surpass them · · · the hunters. · · · Not · · · thus · · · I told him · · · that

18 iā'nēwa Itē'tanuē. Tatc! atcēnuxō'uēma tē'lx·Em. Manē'x
the first one · · · Indian. · · · Behold! · · · he showed me · · · the people. · · · When

19 migElō'yamx imō'lak, iā'ınkXa-y- ē'ıⁿᶜEcX miucgElē'Lx, ōnuā'LEma
you go hunting · · · elk, · · · only · · · a stick · · · you carry it in your · · · paint hand,

20 ma-ilā'xo-iē qix· ē'ıⁿᶜEcX." Iā'qoa-iL nē'xax qix· ikᵢā'sks. Iqoā'lipx·
you will do it · · · that · · · stick." · · · Large · · · he got · · · that · · · boy. · · · A youth

21 nē'xax. A'lta nē'ktcxam:
he became. · · · Now · · · he sang:

"Anē'ekctcē gō -y-ēeka -y-aniō'olXam qix· iā'nēwa;
"Not [int. part.] · · · there · · · thus · · · I told him · · · that · · · first one;

||: "Atā'tc!a atinaxā'tEnēma Natē'tanuē. ||
"Behold! · · · He showed me to them · · · the Indians.

234

"Anē′ekctcē gō-y- ē′eka-y- aniō′olXam qix· iā′nēwa. Atā′tc!a."

1

"Not   [int. part.]   thus   I told him   that   first one.   Behold!"

WiXt nē′ktcxam:
More he sang:

2

"Qēs   tī′axi′tk,   qēs   tī′axi′tk,   qik   ē′qēna,   qik   ē′qēna   pōs

3

"If   what he re-   if   what he re-   that   orphan   that   orphan   [then]
members of   members of   boy,   boy
olden times,   olden times,

xoā′o   aqiō′Lī′a."

4

shall   he is carried farther than others."

AqigEnō′tēn   a′lta.   Aqā′Luk^uɪ   Lq̣ēyō′qxut,   Lxōutcā′tkama·

5

He was helped   now.   He was carried   an old man,   he went to listen.
there

Lā′xēqLax   ā′nqatē   qō′La   Lq̣ēyō′qxut.   ALxuwu′tcatk   qō′La

6

A hunter   long ago   that   old man.   He listened   that

Lq̣ēyō′qxut,   aLxigEluwu′tcatk   qix·   iē′ktcxEm.   ALE′k·im   qō′La

7

old man,   he listened to him   that   singer.   He said   that

Lq̣ēyō′qxut: "Ō   amcgigEnō′tēn   ilxā′ḳackc,   atcē′ᶜElkEl   iō′LEma.

8

old man: "O,   help singing   our boy.   he saw it   a supernatural
being.

TqēqLā′x   atcō′ēkEl."   Qoä′nEmi   ayā′qxoya-ē   nē′ktcxEm.   AqLē′lax

9

The hunte   he saw her."   Five times   his sleeps   he sang.   It was put on
him

Lᶜuē′lōL.   LpE′lpEl   aqE′Lax   qō′La   Lᶜuē′lōL.   Aqē′lax   qix·   ē′mᶜEcX,

10

cedar bark.   Red   it was made   that   cedar bark.   It was put   that   stick,
on him

LpE′lpEl   aqā′yax   qix·   ē′mᶜEcX.   Ā′yo-y-   a′lta   iā′wa   k^uca′la,   gō

11

red   it was made   that   stick.   He went   now   there   up river,   to

kulā′yi   ā′yō.   Ē′ktcxam   ka   ā′yuptck.   A′lta   atcē′Xatoa   qix·

12

far   he went.   He sang   and   he went inland.   Now   he drove them   those

imō′lakEma.   Ia′koa   iLā′lXam   ka   oqoēlā′ētix·   tiā′cōlal.   ALE′k·im

13

elks.   There   his town   and   they were there   his relatives.   He said

Lē′Xat: "Imō′lak   x·ix·   ē′Lxam."   Atktō′cgam   tgā′XalaitanEma.

14

one: "An elk   this   it comes down   They took them   their arrows.
to the beach."

Igō′n   wiXt   nē′Lxam,   igō′n   wiXt   nē′Lxam,   igō′n   wiXt   nē′Lxam.

15

One more   again   it came down,   one more   again   it came down,   one more   again   it came down.

Aqiā′q^ula.   aqiā′q^ula   qix·   imō′lEkuma.   Si′namōkst   LāL   aqiā′q^ula

16

They were   they were   those   the elks.   Seventy   were counted
counted,   counted

ka   nicxE′l′iomEqt.   ALE′k·im   Lq̣ēyō′qxut: "Iā′c   mci′kXiX,   nēkct

17

and   they forgot [the num-   He said   an old man: "Let   do them,   not
ber].   alone

iā′maᶜ   mcktElā′xō.   Lō′nas   ia′xka   Xiau   ē′qtcxam,   tciXuā′t   Xiau

18

shoot   do them.   Perhaps   he   this one   who sings,   he drives   this one

imō′lEkuma."   Nixēnā′Xit   qix·   imō′lEkuma   gō   q̣oā′p   Ltcuq   cka

19

the elks."   They stood   these   elks   at   near   the water   and

pāL   nō′xôx   qō′ta   tEmᶜā′ēma   gō   mā′Lnē.   Ta′kE   nē′Lxam   qix·

20

full   got   that   prairie   at   seaward.   Then   he came down   that

ē′qtcxam.   Atciō′cgam   qix·   ē′mᶜEcX.   Goyē′   atcā′yax   ē′wa   mā′Lnē

21

singer.   He took it   that   stick.   Thus   he did it   thus   seaward

ē′wa   Ltcnq   ka   mE′nx·i   nixēnā′Xit   qix·   imō′lEkuma   ka   ayō′kuiXa

22

thus   water   and   a little while   they stood   these   elks   and   they swam

iau′a   mā′Lnē.   Ka′nauwē2   ayō′guiXa.   Mā′Lnē   ayō′yam   ka

23

then   seaward.   All   they swam.   Seaward   he arrived   and

1 na-ixE'lqamx   qix·   iē'qtcxam.   A'lta   nix·E'La·it   qix·   imō'lEkuma
   he shouted   that   singer.   Now   they died   those   elks

2 ka'nauwē2.   A'lta   aqigE'lxēm   ē'wa   maLxolā'   nxitcxā'x.
   all.   Now   it was called   thus   landward   the wind blew.

3 AtcigE'lxēm   qix·   ēiktcxā'm.   Ayō'miptck   qix·   imō'lEkuma,   cka
   He called it   that   north wind.   They drifted ashore those   elks,   and

4 pāL   nē'xauē   mā'Lne   gō-y-   ē'lXam,   Liā'maLna-y-   ē'lXam.   A'lta
   full   it got   seaward   at   the town,   seaward from it   the town.   Now

5 ā'tgELx   tiā'colal.   Qiā'x   ayā'pXula,   tcx·ī   ia'xka   aqiā'xcx.   Manē'x
   they went   his relatives.   If   its grease,   then   it   it was cut.   When
   to the beach

6 iō'L!ElExt   ka   iā'mka   iā'qcō   Lāq°   aqē'xax.   Pā'2LEma   nō'xôx
   lean   then   only   its skin   take off   it was done.   Full   became

7 t!ōLē'ma,   tgā'ōLēma   tiā'cōlaL.   A'lta   ka'nauwē   iqē'tak,   manē'x
   the houses,   their houses   his relatives.   Now   the whole   year   when

8 imō'lak   atcē'kElo-ix,   iā'mka-y-   ē'mᶜEcX   atciō'cgamx   cka
   elk   he went to hunt,   only   a stick   he took it   and

9 atca-iā'LEqEmax.   Ma'nix   niga'ōmx   imō'lak,   ā'nqatē   ayō'mEqtx.
   he shouted.   When   he met it   an elk,   already   it died.

10 Atcuxō'kokō   ka'nauwē   qtgā'xēqLax.
   He surpassed them   all   hunters.

Translation.

A youth was in the habit of setting traps. He always killed bears. One year he had set his traps [as usual], and when he went to look after them [he heard] a woman crying in a trap. He reached her. Her hand was caught in the trap. She was a pretty woman. Her hair was brown, her feet and her hands were tattooed. He opened the trap and took her hand out of it. She said to him: "You will excel all the poeple. You have caught even me in your trap. You will be a great hunter." The youth said: "I shall carry you to our town." Thus he spoke to his supernatural helper. "I shall show you to the Indians." Now he carried her home. His relatives saw her and all died. He died also.

After many years another boy saw her. He had no father and no mother. He was poor. He was a small boy. She said to him: "When you have grown a little larger, you will excel all hunters. I did not tell the first Indian [not to show me] and behold, he showed me to the people. When you go elk hunting carry only a stick in your hand and paint that stick." The boy grew up and became a youth. Then he sang:

"I did not tell him thus, the first one, and behold, he showed me to the Indians.
I did not tell him thus, the first one. Behold!"

He also sang:
"If the orphan boy remembers what is told of olden times,
If the orphan boy remembers what is told of olden times,
He shall excel all others."

The people helped him singing. An old man was brought there who came to listen. He had been a hunter. He listened to the singer and said: "Oh, help our boy sing; he saw a supernatural being. He saw the hunter spirit." He sang five days. Cedar bark was dyed red and put on him. A stick was painted red and given to him. Then he went up the river. He went a long distance. He sang when he was going into the woods. Now he drove the elks [toward the water]. His relatives had remained in the town. One of them said: "An elk is coming down to the water." They took their arrows. Another one came; again one and again one came. They counted them, but when they had counted seventy they lost the number. The old man said: "Let the elks alone; do not shoot them; perhaps the boy who sings is driving these elks." They stood near the water and the opening was quite full of them. Then the boy came down singing. He took that stick and pointed seaward to the water. The elks stood there a short while and then they swam seaward. When the boy came to the sea he shouted, and all the elks died. Now he called the wind to blow landward and a northerly wind arose. The elks drifted ashore, and the beach in front of the town was full of them. Now his relatives went down to the beach. They cut up only the fat ones. The lean ones were skinned merely. Then the houses of his relatives became full. Now, whenever he went to hunt elk, he carried only a stick, and shouted. As soon as an elk met him it died. He excelled all hunters.

PREGNANCY AND BIRTH.

1 **Ma'nix aʟā'wan Lᵉā'gil näkct iū'ʟqtē aʟaō'ptitx. Kawī'X ā'nqatē**
When pregnant a woman not long she sleeps. Early already

2 **aʟxɛl'ō'kux. Aʟxɛl'ō'kux, nau'i aʟɛ'xaluktcgux. Aʟgixɛlā'qʟ'exē.**
she awakes. She awakes, at once she rises. She opens the door.

3 **Ma'nix aʟō'pax näkct aʟō'tXuitx go iqē'p!al. Nau'i aʟō'pax.**
When she goes out not she stands in the doorway. At once she goes out.

4 **Mā'nix aʟō'La-itx gaʟā'wan, näkct aqʟgumō'tXuitx iau'a**
When she sits down a pregnant one, not they stand near her there

5 **ⁱLā'kōtcX. Ma'nix aʟō'La-itx gaʟā'wan, näkct aʟxō'kctitx**
her back. When she sits down a pregnant one, not he lies down

6 **Lgōlē'lEXEmk ē'wa aʟxtcē'qʟgux. À'ka nupō'nEmx. Ma'nix**
a person thus across. Thus it is night. When

7 **aʟxō'kctitx Lgōlē'lEXEmk ka iau'a-y- ē'ʟaqtq, iau'a-y- aʟā'ᶜwit**
he lies down a person then there his head, there her feet

8 **gaʟā'wan. Manē'x aʟigā'omx ē'qxēʟ gaʟā'wan, mō'kcti**
the pregnant one. When she arrives at it a creek a pregnant one, twice

9 **aʟksikpEnā'kux. Näkct kᵘʟā'xani LxātkᵘctElt gaʟā'wan;**
she jumps across. Not outside she lies down a pregnant one;

10 **tgā'k·iLau, taua'lta tqē'wam akʟā'x ōᶜō'Lax. Näkct qansi'x**
it is her taboo, else sending disease he does to the sun. Not anyhow
her

11 **iLak¡ē'Lxōt gaʟā'wan, taua'lta niʟēLxō'Xuitx iʟā'amcō Lā'Xa-**
her necklace a pregnant one, else it is often around its its navel- her child
neck string

12 **Näkct qansi'x LE'Lakoalē, taua'lta k¡au nixā'tElax iLa'amco gō**
Not ever her bracelet, else tied it is to it its navel-string to

13 **Lā'kcia. Näkct akLē'tqamt Lmē'mElōct gaʟā'wan, näkct i'kta**
its arm. Not she looks at it a corpse a pregnant one, not anything

14 **aʟgē'tqamt iō'mEqtEt. Tgā'k·iLau. Näkct iq¡oala's Lgē'tqamt;**
she looks at it dead. It is her taboo. Not a raccoon she looks at it;

15 **näkct inanā'mukc Lgē'tqamt; näkct i'kta Lgē'tqamt**
not an otter she looks at it; not anything she looks at it

16 **giā'atcEkc gaʟā'wan. Näkct Lkcitpē'XuniL ikcgō'matk**
stinking a pregnant one. Not she blows it up a bladder

17 **gaʟā'wan. Näkct i'kta iLxē'tElax gaʟā'wan, ma'nix L¡ap**
a pregnant one. Not anything she eats it a pregnant one, if found

18 **aqiā'x. Tgā'k·iLau. Näkct ō'q¡o-ix·inē aʟxē'tElax. Näkct**
it is. It is her taboo. Not trout she eats it. Not

19 **iq¡oanī'X aʟxē'tElax. Tgā'k·iLau. Näkct· aʟxē'tElax Lā'k·ikala,**
steel head sal- she eats it. It is her taboo. Not he eats it her husband,
mon

20 **ma'nix i'kta L¡ap aqiā'x. Näkct Lgituwa'qxēmEniL iq¡oala'c**
when something find it is done. Not he always kills it raccoon

21 **Lā'k·ikala gaʟā'wan. Näkct LgaLk¡atsXē'mEnīL ō'lEXaiū**
her husband a pregnant one. Not he singes it a seal

22 **Lā'k·ikala gaʟā'wan. Näkct Lkttē'niL tElalā'xukc Lā'k·ikala**
her husband a pregnant one. Not he shoots them birds her husband

23 **gaʟā'wan. Näkct LkLE'tqamt Lmē'mElōct. Näkct**
a pregnant one. Not he looks at it a corpse. Not

24 **Lgituwā'qxēminiL inanā'mukc, taua'lta igē'kckamē nexā'x. Ē'ka**
he always kills it otter, else obtaining sickness it gets. Thus
by sympathy [the
child]

25 **iq¡oala's. Ma'nix ē'Latc!a nixā'tElax Lk¡āsks, q¡oā'p aʟō'mEqtx**
a raccoon. When its sickness comes to be on it the child, nearly it dies

238

ka aLxEnō′yuwanEmx, ä′ka qigō nixEnō′yuwanEmx inanā′mukc. 1
then it has a hard struggle before dying, thus as it has hard struggle before dying the otter.

Ä′ka wiXt LElā′lax; ä′ka wiXt iq¡oala′c. Igē′kckamē nexā′x. Ma′nix 2
Thus also a bird; thus also a raccoon. Obtaining sickness by sympathy it gets. When

iā′xot Lk¡up nexā′x iq¡oala′s ka iLā′xanatē ka Lk¡up nexā′x iLā′xōt 3
its eye squeezed it gets the raccoon and its life and squeezed it gets its eye

qō′La Lk¡āsks. Ma′nix acixElqē′LxalEmx aqiā′owilXLx qix· iq¡oala′s, 4
that child. When it cries much it is struck that raccoon,

ē′ka aLxā′x qō′La Lk¡āsks qigō q¡oā′p aLō′mEqtx. Ma′nix aLgā′xō 5
thus does that child if nearly it dies. When she eats it

ōp!ā′lō gaLā′wan, aLE′ktcx Lā′Xa, nau′i aLō′mEqtx. Iō′Lqtē 6
trout a pregnant one, it cries her child, at once it faints. Long

aLō′mEqtx ka wiXt atctElatā′kux. Ka′nauwē LᶜaLā′ma-y- ē′ka. 7
it is in a swoon then again it recovers. All days thus.

Ē′XtEma-ē la′ktē aLō′mEqtx aē′Xt oᶜō′Lax. Ma′nix aLgaLk¡tsxē′max 8
Sometimes four times it faints one day. When he singes it

Lā′k·ikala gaLā′wan ō′lXaiū, ka′nauwē qō′La Lk¡āsks nixLE′lx 9
her husband a pregnant one a seal, all that child is burnt

ē′LaLᶜa. ALiLā′lētEmx Ltcuq. Ma′nix aLkcilpē′Xux gaLā′wan 10
its body. Then is in it often [under its skin] water. When she blows it up a pregnant one

ikcgō′matk, guā′nEsum acilpē′XuniL iLā′wan Lā′Xa. Ma′nix aLgiā′x 11
a bladder, always it is blown up its belly her child. When she eats it

gaLā′wan i′kta L¡ap aqiā′x, iā′xkati Lxoa′p nikē′x qix· i′kta L¡ap 12
a pregnant one something found it is done, there hole is in it that something found

aqiā′x, iā′xkatē Lxoa′p aLxā′x qō′La Lk¡āsks. Ma′nix aLaō′ptit 13
it is done, there hole is that child. When she sleeps

kᵘLā′xani gaLā′wan, q¡oā′p aLE′qxtōmx, pāL nexā′x iLā′wan 14
outside a pregnant one, nearly she gives birth, full it gets her belly

Lᶜā′owulkt. ALō′mEqtx. Ma′nix aLō′tXuitx iō′Lqtē gō iqē′p!al 15
blood. She dies. When she stands long in the doorway

aLgē′qEmitx iau′a kᵘLā′xanē, ä′ka aLxā′x qigō aLE′qxtōmx cka Lāx 16
she looks then outside, thus does when she gives birth and come out

aLxā′x Lā′Xa, iō′Lqtē Lāx aLxā′x Lā′Xa. Ē′XtEmaē aLō′mEqtx 17
it does her child, long come out it does her child. Sometimes she dies

qō′La gaLā′wan, ē′XtEmaē aLō′mEqtx qō′La Lk¡āsks. Ma′nix 18
that pregnant one, sometimes it dies that child. When

iō′Lqtē aLxō′kstitx gaLā′wan, ä′ka aLxā′x qigō aLE′qxtōmx. 19
long she lies down a pregnant one, thus she does when she gives birth.

Ē′Latc!a nixā′tElax iō′Lqtē. Ma′nix aLxō′kctitx LgoLē′lEXEmk 20
Her sickness is on her long. When he lies down a person

ē′wa Lā′ᶜcowit gaLā′wan, a′lta iau′a aLōtcē′qxLkuitx qō′La Lk¡āsks. 21
thus her feet a pregnant one, now then it lies across that child.

Manē′x aLō′tXuitx LgoLē′lEXEmk iau′a iLā′kōtcX gaLā′wan, ka 22
When he stands a person there her back a pregnant one, and

iau′a aLō′tXuitx qō′La Lk¡āsks ma′nix aqLā′xtōmx. 23
then it stands that child when it is born.

Ma′nix aLE′kxtōmx gaLā′wan, qoā′nEm Lā′xanakc goā′nEsum 24
When she gives birth the pregnant one, five her stones always

Lō′cko-it. Lxoa′p aLgī′ax ēlē′ē. Môkct Lqā′nakc aLgE′Lx·guix qigō 25
she heats. Hole she makes it ground. Two stones she throws into where

naLxoā′pē. A′lta aLxk¡ē′niakux ka′nauwē ē′LaLᶜa aLqk¡ē′niakux. 26
the hole. Now she ties it around herself all her body she ties it around herself.

A′lta aLxaLgE′m′apgux gō qō′La Lqā′nakc. Qoā′nEmi aLā′o-ix 27
Now she takes a steam-bath at those stones. Five her sleeps

aLxaLgE′m′apkax ka′nauwē LᶜaLā′ma, ka′nauwē Lpō′lEma. Ma′nix 28
she takes steam-baths all days, all nights. When

1 tsEs aLxā′x qō′La Lqā′nakc, a′lta Lāq° aLā′x, a′lta Lē′gŏn
cold get those stones, then take out she does now others them,

2 aqE′LXtkoax. Ka′nauwē LᶜaLā′ma-y- ē′ka, ka′nauwē Lpō′lEma-y-
she puts into it. All days thus, all nights

3 ē′ka. Ma′nix aLE′LXōL¡ax aLxaLgE′m′apgux aLkLō′kᵘ⌐x Lā′xanakc
thus. When she finishes she takes steam-baths she carries them the stones

4 gō mā′Lxolē gō nasp!ā′qē k¡a Lā′q¡ELxap k¡a Lctā′mtkct k¡a
to inland in hole of a tree and her coat and her tongs and

5 Lā′kXo-iluL kLlgē′luq. Aqtā′lutx tktē′ma qaX ōpō′nē, ōLā′ponē
her cedar-bark belt. It is given property that after-birth, her after-birth

6 kLE′qtōmx aqagEmgē′kᵘtix. Ēkupku′p aqiā′lōtx, tkamō′sak
the one who has it is paid. Short dentalia it is given, beads
given birth

7 aqLā′lōtx. Lt!ō′kti Li′cgo-ic aqLaxaniā′kux qaX ōpō′nē. Ma′nix
it is given. Good mat it is put into that after-birth. If

8 nēkct aqayamgē′kᵘtix qaX ōpō′nē ka mä′nx·i ka aLō′mEqtx qō′La
not it is paid that after-birth and a little while and it dies that

9 Lk¡āsks; aLExElaLā′tax qaX ōpō′nē qō′La Lk¡āsks. Ma′nix
child; it takes it back that after-birth that child. When

10 gaLā′wan, näkct aLkLā′amctx qLā′o-it Ltcuq. Lā′mkXa tcx·ī
a pregnant one, not she drinks it one day old water. Only then

11 aqLō′tēpax, taua′lta aLElgē′o-initx gaLā′wan.
it is dipped, else she is sick long the pregnant one.

12 Ma′nix Lkā′nax aLE′kxtōmx, aqLugō′lEmam Lē′Xat Lᶜā′gil,
When a chieftainess gives birth to a child, she is fetched one woman,

13 aLgiLgEnā′oxo-ē. Ē′Xtemaē amō′kctikc aqtugō′lEmamx.
she looks after her. Sometimes two are fetched.

14 AtkLō′cgamx Lk¡āckc ma′nix aqLā′kxtōmx. Iā′qoa-iL
They take it the child when it is born. A large

15 ikaLxE′lEmatk aqLē′l′ōtx Lk¡āckc. At!ō′kti-y- ōqoēwē′qxē Lq¡ōp
dish it is washed the child. A good knife cut

16 aqē′Lxax iLā′amcō Lk¡āckc. Aqokumagē′kᵘtēx qō′tac ta′nEmckc
it is done its navel-string the child. They are paid those women

17 amō′kctikc; anā′ Lē′Xat Lᶜā′gil. Ä′ka Lk¡āsks Lᶜā′gil, ä′ka
two; sometimes one woman. Thus child male, thus

18 Lk¡āsks LE′k·ala. ILā′Lēlam LᶜaLā′ma Lā′k·iLau, ma′nix Lᶜā′gil,
child female. Ten days her taboo when a female,

19 qoā′nEm LᶜaLā′ma Lā′k·iLau ma′nix LE′k·ala. Qoā′nEm LᶜaLā′ma
five days her taboo when a male. Five days

20 ma′nix LE′k·ala ka aLgiā′x ixgē′wal Lā′mama. Ä′ka Lā′naa
when a male then he eats fresh food his father. Thus his mother

21 wiXt. Ma′nix Lᶜā′gil giLā′Lēlam LᶜaLā′ma ka aLgiā′x ixgē′wal.
also. When a woman ten days and they eat fresh food.

22 Ā′ᶜeXt ōkLEmē′n aqLa′xtōmx ka aqō′xôktc!ax tē′lx·Em.
One moon it is born then they are invited the people.

23 ALgō′xôktc!ax Lā′mama qō′La Lk¡āsks. A′lta aqLkEluwā′yutcgux.
He invites them its father that child. Now they dance.

24 A′lta aqLgElgō′xo-iLx tqā′cocinikc Lā′Xawôk. Lxoa′pLxoap aqtā′x
Now he is asked to do [his children his guardian Holes are made
work] spirit.

25 Lā′-utcakc. x·igō NagaLā′mat gō tgā′kᵘLil qō′ta-y- ē′ka.
its ears. Here at Katlamat there their custom this thus.

26 AqLä′LgōL¡ax Lxoa′pLxoap aqtā′x Lā′-utcakc. Ē′natai mōkct Lxoa′p
They are finished holes are made its ears. On one side two holes

27 aqLā′x ō′La-utcan, ē′natai wiXt mōkct. Aqawē′makuq tē′lx·Em;
are made in its ear, on the other also two. Presents are dis- the people;
side tributed [among]

28 aqawigē′kxo-imx. ĒXt iqē′taq ka aLō′tXuitx Lk¡āsks,
they are paid for dancing. One year and it stands the child,

29 aLkcXō′tkakux. WiXt yuL¡ᴵ aLxā′x Lā′mama. WiXt aLgō′xuktc!ax
it goes step by step. Again glad he gets its father. Again he invites them

tê'lx·Em,	wiXt	aqLkEluwä'yutcgux	Lä'Xa.	WiXt	Lxoa'pLxoap	1
the people,	again	they dance for it	his child.	Again	holes	
aqtä'x	Lä'-utcakc.	A'lta	qoä'nEmi	Lxoa'p	a'ĕXt	ŏ'La-utca.	2
he makes them	its ears.	Now	five times	holes	one	its ear.	
Ia'koa	ä'nata	wiXt	qoä'nEmi.	Ä'ka	Lᵉä'gil,	ä'ka	LE'k·ala.	3
Here	on the other side	also	five times.	Thus	a female,	thus	a male.	
Lä'qoa-iL	aLxä'x	Lä'Xa	Lkä'nax.	ALksaxLĕ'x	uk¡otaq¡ĕ'.	4
Large	gets	his child	the chief.	It catches with the hook	suckers.	
WiXt	q¡oa'nq¡oan	aLxä'x	Lä'mama.	WiXt	aLgŏ'xuqtc!ax	5
Again	glad	gets	his father.	Again	he invites them	
tê'lx·Em.	WiXt nuxuiwä'yutckux.	WiXt aqawigĕ'kxo-imx ka'nauwĕ.	6
the people.	Again they dance.	Again they are paid for dancing all.	
WiXt	pät	Lä'qoa-iL	aLxä'x.	ILä'maᵋ	aLgĕ'tElax	LElä'lax.	7
Again	really	large	it gets.	Shooting it	does it to it	a bird.	
WiXt	aqŏ'xuqtc!ax	tê'lx·Em.	WiXt	ik¡uauŏ'm	aqĕ'Lxax.	8
Again	they are invited	the people.	Again	a potlatch	is made.	
Nuxuiwä'yutckux tê'lx·Em.	WiXt aqawigĕ'qxo-imx ka'nauwĕ.	9
They dance the people.	Again they are paid for dancing all.	

Translation.

When a woman is with child she does not sleep long. She awakes early in the morning and arises at once. She opens the door. She does not stay in the doorway, but goes out at once. When a woman who is with child sits down, nobody must stand back of her and nobody must lie down crosswise [at her feet]. It is the same at night [when she lies down]. When a person lies down near her, his head must point in the same direction as her feet are turned. When she comes to a creek she jumps across twice. She does not lie down outside the house, else the sun would make her sick. It is forbidden. She does not wear a necklace, else the navel-string would be wound around the child's neck. She does not wear bracelets, else the navel-string would be tied around the child's arm. She does not look at a corpse. She does not look at anything that is dead. It is forbidden. She does not look at a raccoon nor at an otter. She does not look at anything that is rotten. She does not blow up a [seal] bladder. She does not eat anything that has been found. It is forbidden. She does not eat trout nor steel-head salmon. It is forbidden. Her husband does not eat anything that has been found. He does not kill raccoons. He does not singe seals. He does not shoot birds. He does not look at a corpse. He does not kill otters, else the child would get sick by sympathy. It is the same with the raccoon. When the child should fall sick and nearly die it would have a hard struggle against death, like the otter. It is the same with a bird or a raccoon. It would obtain sickness by sympathy. When a raccoon's eye is squeezed out [by the husband of the woman who is with child] the child's eye would be squeezed out. When the raccoon cries much on being struck [with a stick] the child will do the same when it is near death. When a woman who is with child eats trout, her child will faint whenever it cries and recover

only after a long time.   This will happen every day, sometimes it may
faint four times a day.   When her husband singes a seal, the child's
body will be burnt all over.   It will have blisters.   When she blows
up a [seal] bladder, the child will always have winds.   When she
eats anything that was found and there is a hole in it [eaten by
birds or other animals], the child will have a hole at the same place.
When she sleeps outside of the house, and it is nearly time for her
child to be born, her belly will be filled with blood and she dies.   When
she stays a long time in the doorway and looks out of the house, the
child will do the same when it is being born.   It will take long for the
child to be born.   Sometimes the woman will die; sometimes the
child.   When a woman who is with child stays in bed long, she will do
the same when she gives birth to the child.   When anybody stands
back of her the child will be born feet first.

When she gives birth to the child, she always heats five stones.   She
makes a hole in the ground and throws two stones into it.   Then she
ties her blanket around herself and takes a steam-bath over these stones.
Five days and nights she takes steam-baths all the time.   When the
stones get cold she takes them out of the hole and puts others into it.
She does so day and night.   After she has finished her steam-bath she
takes the stones inland and places them in the hollow of a tree with
her coat, her tongs and her cedar-bark belt.   The after-birth receives
presents—short dentalia and beads.   If this is not done the child dies
after a short time.   Then the after-birth takes it back.   A woman who
is with child does not drink water that has been standing [in a vessel]
a day.   She drinks only water that has just been taken from the river,
else she will be sick for a long time.

When a chieftainess gives birth to a child a woman is called to look
after her.   Sometimes two are called.   They take the child when it is
born and wash it in a large dish.   They take a good knife and cut its
navel-string.   Then the two women are paid; sometimes it is only one
woman.   It is the same with a male and with a female child.   When
the child is a girl the taboos extend over ten days; if it is a boy, they
extend over five days.   When it is a boy the father and the mother
may eat fresh food after five days.   If it is a girl they may eat fresh
food after ten days.

One month after the birth of the child the people are invited by the
father of the child.   Now they dance.   Now a man who has a guardian
spirit [who helps him to understand] children, is asked to practice
his art on the child.   Then its ears are perforated.   This is the custom
of the Katlamat.   They finish perforating its ears.   Two holes are made
in each ear and presents are distributed among the people.   They are
paid for dancing [for the child].   After a year, when the child begins
to stand and to walk, the father becomes again glad and invites all
the people, who dance for the child.   Its ears are again perforated.
Now five holes are made in each ear.   This is done with both boys

and girls. When the chief's child grows up and [first] catches fish with a hook, the father is gladdened again and invites the people. They dance, and all are paid for dancing. When the child becomes really large and shoots [the first] bird, he again invites the people. He gives a potlatch, and the people dance. Again all are paid for dancing for the child.

Notes.

Other taboos and beliefs.—When a woman gives birth to a child out of doors, this will be a reproach to her child throughout life. Her husband is allowed to be present during her confinement.

The father must not go fishing for ten days nor do any work that requires his going out on the water. He must not go hunting, but he may gather wood. If the child is a boy this rule holds for five days only. If a sick person is in a house where a woman is about to be confined, his bed is surrounded with mats so that he cannot see the woman.

There is a certain guardian spirit which enables its possessor to understand the cries and the cooing of babies. The child may tell him where it came from. It may say: After four days I shall go home; then it will die after four days. This spirit informed us that the land of the children is in sunrise. If a child in a family dies and another one is born later on to the same family, it may be the same child which returned. Sometimes, if it died after its ears had been perforated, the new-born child will have its ears perforated. Old people cannot return as new-born infants.

PUBERTY.

Maʹnix Lᵉäʹgil LäʹXa Lkäʹnax, maʹnix guäʹnsum ēʹLatc!a Lkäʹnax
When a girl his child a chief, when always his sickness the chief

2 ka yugoēʹ iLäʹqa-iL LäʹXa Lkäʹnax, Lq¡ᴛäʹplix· LäʹXa Lkäʹnax,
then thus [about its large- his child the chief, an immature girl his child a chief,
10 years] ness

3 ka ik¡uanōʹm aLgēʹLgax, aqLgäʹxôL¡kux Lq¡ēlawulXäʹᴇm.
then potlatch he makes, she is pretended to be menstruant for the first time.

4 AqLgᴇluwäʹyutckux. Qoäʹnᴇmi atgäʹo-ix nōxuiwäʹyutckux ka
They dance. Five times their sleeps they dance and

5 aqawigēʹqxo-imx.
they are paid for dancing.

Maʹnix aLq¡eläʹwulax LäʹXa Lkäʹnax, aʹlta aqLōʹpcôtxax.
When she is menstruating his daughter a chief, now she is hidden.
for the first time

7 LäʹmkXa LēXäʹtka Lᵉäʹgil aLgiLgᴇnäʹoxoē. K¡auʹk¡au aqLEʹtᴇlax
Only one only woman looks after her. Tied it is to her

8 LᵉuēʹlōL gō Läʹpôtē, gō Läʹᵉowit, aqLEʹlgilʹôx LᵉuēʹlōL. ĒʹXtᴇmaē
cedar bark to her arm, to her leg, it is tied around cedar bark. Sometimes
her waist

9 qoäʹnᴇmi aLäʹo-ix, ēʹXtᴇmaē iäʹLēlamē aLäʹo-ix, ēʹXtᴇma-ē laʹktē
five times her sleeps, sometimes ten times her sleeps, sometimes four times

10 aLäʹo-ix, ēʹXtᴇmaē txäʹmē aLäʹo-ix nikct aLxLxEʹlᴇmax. Aʹlta
her sleeps, sometimes six times her sleeps not she eats. Now

11 aqōʹxuktc!ax tēʹlx·ᴇm. ik¡uanōʹm aqēʹLgax Lq¡eläʹwulX. Qoäʹnᴇmi
they are invited the people. Potlatch is made for her the one menstru- Five times
ating for the first time.

12 aLäʹo·ix aqLōʹpcutx. Aʹlta Läq aqLäx, aʹlta LäʹqLaq aqLEʹLxax
her sleeps she is hidden. Now take out she is done, now take off it is done

13 qōʹLa kᴛᴛgēʹluq. Aʹlta äʹtᴇlaxta tqōqoäʹitᴇla k¡auʹk¡au
that what is tied around Now they next strings of short dentalia tied
her waist.

14 aqtEʹtᴇlax gō Läʹpôtē k¡a gō Läʹᵉowit. Aʹlta it!äʹlᴇqama aqiLEʹlgilʹôx.
they are to them at her arms and at her legs. Now a buckskin strap is tied around
her waist.

15 Pōc aʹlta guäʹnᴇsum aqiLEʹlgilʹôx iäʹk¡amōnaqē iaōʹya, tcx·ī Läqᵘ
If now always it is tied around a hundred days, then taken off
her waist

16 nēʹLxax qix· it!äʹlᴇqama. Aʹlta aLkLomēʹnagux Lq¡ēyōʹqxut. Aʹlta
it is that buckskin strap. Now she washes her face an old woman. Now

17 LEʹgun LēʹXat Lq¡ēyōʹqxut ūnowäʹLᴇma aLgäʹtᴇlax. Aʹlta
another one old woman paint she does her with it. Now

18 aqLEʹltcamx; Lq¡eyōʹqxut aLkLEʹltcamx. AqLēʹLgoL¡ᴇx kaʹnauwē.
she is combed; an old woman combs her. It is finished all.

19 Aqawigēʹkxo-imx qōʹtac tēʹlx·ᴇm. Aʹlta aqägumgēʹkᵘtix qōʹtac
They are paid for dancing those people. Now they are paid those

20 tq¡eyōʹqtikc täʹnᴇmckc. Aʹlta wiXt aqLōʹtgᴇx qōʹLa Lq¡eläʹwulX.
old ones women. Now again she is put away that one menstruant
for the first time.

21 IxElâʹima ēLäʹxēpal. Gō kuläʹyi ēʹqxᴇL ka iäʹxkati aLxʹōʹLa-itx.
Another one her door. At far creek and there she bathes.

22 Quinum LäʹLē ayaōʹēxē näkct aLgīʹax ixgēʹwal. WiXt aLq¡eläʹwulax,
Fifty her sleeps not she eats fresh food. Again she is menstruant,

23 iLäʹmôkct aLk¡eläʹwulax. WiXt äʹka aqLäʹx. WiXt ik¡uanōʹm
the second time she is menstruant. Again thus it is done. Again a potlatch

244

aLgiā'x Lā'mama. Näkct qa'nsix aLxckō'mitx Lq¡ēlā'wulX. Nēkct   **1**
he makes her father. Not anyhow she warms herself the one menstruant for the first time. Not

qa'nsiX aLqtā'qamitx tê'lx·ɛm. Näkct qa'nsix igō'cax aLgiā'qamitx,   **2**
anyhow she looks at them people. Not anyhow the sky she looks at it,

näkct qa'nsix tgōxoē'ma aLktō'piaLxax. Tgā'k·iLau. Ma'nix igō'cax   **3**
not anyhow berries she gathers them. It is her taboo. When the sky

aLgiā'qamitx Lq¡elā'wulX, guā'nɛsum iā'q¡atxala nē'xɛlax igō'cax.   **4**
she looks at it the one menstruant for the first time, always its badness comes to be on it the sky.

Ma'nix tgōqoē'ma aLktō'piaLx Lq¡elā'wulX, guā'nɛsum ēmɛlā'lkuilē   **5**
When berries she gathers the one menstruant for the first time, always rainy weather

nēxā'x. Iā'xkatē Lā'qxoēluL quL aLkLā'owix gō·y· ē'maktc. Iā'xkatē   **6**
it gets. There her cedar-bark hang up she does it on it on a spruce tree. There

nē'xca-ôx. Iā'k¡amonaqē aLā'o-ix Lq¡elā'wulX, tcx·ī aLgiā'x ixgē'wal,   **7**
it dries. One hundred her sleeps the one menstruant for the first time, then she eats it fresh food,

tcx·ī aLktō'piaLxax tgōqoē'ma, tcx·ī aLxckō'mitx.   **8**
then she gathers berries, then she warms herself.

Ma'nix qā'xēwa nōgoLā'yax, aqLō'kᵘ¡x Lq¡elā'wulX. Näkct   **9**
When somewhere they move, she is carried the one menstruant for the first time. Not

aLqLē'watɛgux cka aqLō'ctxôx gō ikanī'm. Näkct aLaLō'tXuitx   **10**
she paddles and she is carried on the back into the canoe. Not she stands in water

Ltcuq, gō·y· ē'maL Ltcuq. Kā pō'lak¡i ka aLx'ō'tamx Lq¡elā'wulX.   **11**
water, in salt water water. And at night and she goes to bathe the one menstruant for the first time.

ALguxōgō'kux tɛlalā'xukc, ka'nauwē LᶠaLā'ma-y· ē'ka. Ma'nix   **12**
She is superior to the birds, all days thus. When

tā'newatikc tɛlalā'xukc noxo-eō'lɛguLx, aqLxgā'lɛguLx Lq¡elā'wulX,   **13**
they first the birds rise, they are superior to her the one who menstruates for the first time,

ka näkct iō'Lqtē iLā'Xanatē. Ma'nix ka'nauwē-y· i'kta t!ayā'   **14**
then not long her life. When all things good

aLgiā'x Lq¡elā'wulX, a'lta Lq¡ēyō'qxut aLxā'x, tcx·ī aLō'mɛqtx.   **15**
she does them the one who menstruates for the first time, now old she gets, then she dies.

Mô'kcti aLq¡ēlā'wulax ka aLɛ'LXōL¡ax. A'lta ma'nix aɪ.qLā'Xitx,   **16**
Twice she is menstruant for the first time then she finished. Now when she is menstruant,

nau'i kᵘLā'xanē aLō'-ix. Qoä'nɛmi aLā'o-ix LkLā'Xit ka wiXt   **17**
at once outside she goes. Five times her sleeps she is menstruant then again

aLō'p!x. Ka'nauwē LkLmēna'kc ē'ka aLkLā'Xitx nau'i aLō'pax.   **18**
she enters. All months thus she is menstruant at once she goes out.

Anā' lā'kti aLā'o-ix kᵘLā'xani. Näkct gLɛ'tqamt gē'Latc!a LkLā'Xit.   **19**
Sometimes four times her sleeps outside. Not she sees him a sick one a menstruant woman.

Ma'nix ē'Latc!a LgōLē'lɛXɛmk, gō kulā'yi t!ōL aLktā'x LkLā'Xit.   **20**
When his sickness a person, at far a house she makes it the menstruant woman.

Ē'ka Lq¡ēlā'wulX. Nēkct LkLē'tqamt Lk¡āsks Lq¡ēlā'wulX. Ma'nix   **21**
Thus one menstruating for the first time. Not she looks at it a child one menstruating for the first time. If

LkLā'Xit aLgiā'x itā'k¡ētenax nauwā'itk, a'lta pāx noxō'x;   **22**
a menstruant woman eats what he caught [in] net, now unlucky it becomes;

qē'xtcē itā'tuk¡tX nauwā'itk, tatc¡a pāx noxō'x. Ē'ka-y· ī'kXik.   **23**
intending successful the net, behold! unlucky it gets. Thus a hook.

Ma'nix aLgiā'x ēnā'qxōn LkLā'Xit, qē'xtcē iā'tuk¡tX ī'kXik,   **24**
If she eats it sturgeon a menstruant woman, intending successful the hook

1 tatc¡a pāx nēxā′x.   Qiā′x qui′nEmi aLā′oix LkLā′Xit tcx·ī aLgiā′x
  behold! unlucky it gets.   If   five   days   menstruant   then   she eats

2 ixgē′wal. Ma′nix iLā′k¡ēwulal LkLā′Xit näkct iLxē′tElax Lk¡ăckc; ē′ka
  fresh food.   If   the berries which   the menstru-   not   it eats them   a child;   thus
            she picked   ating woman

3 gē′Latc!a ma′nix iLā′k¡ēwulal LkLā′Xit, näkct iLxē′tElax gē′Latc!a.
  a sick person   if   the berries which   the menstru-   not   he eats them   the sick one.
             she picked   ating woman,

4 Ma′nix nikct Lā′mama Lkā′nax Lā′Xa, ka Lā′tata ik¡oanō′m
  When   not   her father   a chief   his daugh-   then her mother's   a potlatch
                        ter,   brother

5 aLgē′Lgax.   Anā′ Lā′mōtX ik¡oanō′m aLgē′Lgax; anā′ Lā′Lak
  he makes it for   Some-   her father's   a potlatch   he makes it for her;   some-   her father's
  her.   times   brother   times   sister

6 ik¡oanō′m aLgē′Lgax; anā′ Lā′q¡otxa ik¡oanō′m aLgē′Lgax
  a potlatch   she makes it for   some-   her mother's   a potlatch   she makes it
           her;   times   sister   for her ·

7 Lq¡ēlā′wulX. Ma′nix nēkct ō′xoē Lā′ktēma LgōLē′lEXEmk, a′lta
  the one menstruating When   not   many   dentalia   a person,   now
  for the first time.

8 cka   aLktugō′lEmamx tê′lx·Em.   Näkct nioxō-wā′yutckux cka
  and   they fetch them   the people.   Not   they dance   and

9 aqLā′qamitx Lq¡ēlā′wulX.   Aqawē′makux kanauwē′ qō′tac tê′lx·Em
  they look at her   the one menstruating · Presents are distrib-   all   those   people
           the first time.   uted among them

10 ktkLā′qamitx qō′La Lq¡ēlā′wulX. Näkct ō′xoē tktē′ma aqtawē′makux.
  who looked at her   that   the one menstruating Not   many   dentalia   are distributed.
                for the first time.

11 Ē′ka wiXt mō′kctē aLq¡ēlā′wulX, mō′kctē aqawē′makux tê′lx·Em.
  Thus   also   twice   she is menstruant   twice   presents are distrib-   the people.
              for the first time,   uted among them

Translation.

When a chief who is continually sick has a daughter about ten years old and not yet mature, he makes a potlatch and pretends that she is menstruant for the first time. The people dance five days and are paid for dancing.

When a chief's daughter is menstruating for the first time, she is hidden [from the view of the people]. Only an [old] woman takes care of her. Cedar bark is tied to her arms [above the elbows and at the wrists], to her legs, and around her waist. She fasts sometimes five days, sometimes ten days, or four or six days. Now the people are invited and a potlatch is made for the girl. She remains hidden five days. Now she is taken out [of her hiding place] and the cedar bark which is tied around her [arms, legs, and waist] is taken off. Then strings of dentalia are tied around her arms and legs, and a buckskin strap is tied around her waist. This remains tied around her for one hundred days, then it is taken off. Now an old woman washes her face. Another old woman paints her; still another one combs her. When this is finished the people are paid for dancing for her. Now these old women are paid and the girl is hidden again. She has a separate door. She bathes in a creek far [from the village]. For fifty days she does not eat fresh food. When she is menstruant for the second time her father gives another potlatch. She must not warm herself. She must never look at the people. She must not look at the sky, she must not pick berries. It is forbidden. When she looks at the sky it becomes bad weather. When she picks berries it will rain. She hangs up her [towel of] cedar bark on [a certain] spruce tree. The tree dries up at once. After one hundred days she may eat fresh food, she may pick berries and warm herself.

If the people move from one place to another, she is carried into the canoe. She must not paddle and is carried on the back into the canoe. She must not step into salt water. When it is night she must go to bathe. She must rise earlier than the birds. If the birds should rise first she will not live long. If she does everything in the right way she will get old before she dies. After her second menses [these customs] are finished. Later on, when she is menstruant, she goes out of the house and comes back after five days. Every month when she is menstruating she goes out at once. Sometimes she stays outside four days. No sick person must see her. When a person is sick she makes a house for herself far away. The same is done by a girl menstruant for the first time. The latter must not look at children.

When a menstruant woman eats fish that was caught in a net, the net becomes unlucky. If the people try to catch fish in the net, they find that it has become unlucky. It is the same with a hook. When she eats sturgeon, and the people try to catch sturgeon with that hook, they find that it has become unlucky. After five days she may eat fresh food. Berries which she has picked must not be eaten by children or sick persons.

When a girl who is menstruant for the first time has no father, then her mother's brother gives a potlatch for her. Sometimes her father's brother, or her father's sister or her mother's sister will make a potlatch for her. If anybody has not many dentalia the people are invited. They do not dance, but look at the girl. Presents are distributed among them. Not many dentalia are distributed. In the same way presents are distributed among the people when she has her second menses.

MARRIAGE.

Ma′nix ĕXt gitā′lEXam tqᵢĕx aLkLā′x Lᶜā′gil gō-y- ĕXt ē′lEXam,
When one people of a town like they do it a woman in one town,

2 **ka atktō′cgam tgā′Xamōta ka′nauwē Lā′cōlal LE′k·ala, ka atgē′x**
then they take it their property all his relatives the man, then they go

3 **ē′k·it atgiā′xômx̣. AqLō′kux LEunā′yucX. Aqtō′tgEx tgā′ktĕma**
buying they do. They are sent messengers. They are kept their dentalia
a wife

4 **tĕ′lx·Em; ka nuxō′gux. Nuxō′gux gā′tamEl. A′lta pā′apa atctā′x**
the people; then they go home. They go home they who went Now divide he does it
to buy.

5 **ē′tcam qaX ōᶜō′kuil qō′ta tkamō′ta ka′nauwē gō tiā′colal.**
her father that woman that property all to his relatives.

6 **A′lta t!ayā′ aktā′x tgā′ktĕma qaX ō′kXua ōᶜō′kuil. A′lta**
Now good she makes them her dentalia that her mother woman. Now

7 **nōxuē′tXuitcgux. A′lta aqō′kᴛx gō ĕXt ē′lEXam qigō**
they make themselves ready. Now she is brought to one town where

8 **aqōᴍElā′lEmx. Nuxuigē′qtc!amx. Aqā′ktc!amx qaX ōᶜō′kuil.**
she was bought. They bring the bride to the She is brought as bride that woman.
groom. to the groom

9 **WiXt aqaxiktcgō′mamx. Ma′nix mE′nx·ka qō′ta ē′k·it aqtā′x,**
Again she is brought to him. When [for] a little only that buying a it is done,
wife

10 **wiXt aqLō′kXux LEunā′yucX. WiXt aqagilgē′x·iwa-y- ō′mEl.**
again they are sent messengers. Again it is added to it purchase
money.

11 **A′lta wiXt atktō′tx tgā′ktĕma tĕ′lx·Em. A′lta ā′yip!ē. WiXt**
Now again they give their dentalia the people. Now it is right. Again
them away

12 **aqtō′tx atcē′xikē t!ē′ltkĕu. A′lta noxoē′la-itx tĕ′lx·Em kᵘLā′xanē.**
they are several slaves. Now they stay the people outside.
given away

13 **AtuXuʟx·ā′nakôx tgā′okkc. A′lta nuxuiwē′yutckux tgā′cōlal qaX**
They put them on their blankets. Now they dance her relatives that

14 **ōᶜō′kuil. Nugō′tcxamx. A′lta nuxō′wax tĕ′lx·Em ē′wa qō′tac**
woman. They sing conjurers' Now they run the people thus [to] those
songs.

15 **ē′natai ōxoēlā′-itx·. Augugē′Latatckō. Lā′qʟaq aqtō′xôx ka′nauwē**
on the they are. They are taken off [their Take off they are done all
other side blankets].

16 **tgā′okkc. Lō′nē aqugugē′Latatckux, ē′XtEmaĕ la′ktē**
their blankets. Three times they are taken off, sometimes four times

17 **aqugugēLatatckux. A′lta uē′Xatk aqā′x. Tktē′ma uē′Xatk**
they are taken off. Now a road it is made. Dentalia a road

18 **aqtā′x. Uē′Xatk aqā′x ē′wa x·ix· ē′k·ala tiā′colal. AqLā′goʟᵢEx**
is made. A road is made thus this the man his relatives. It is finished

19 **qaX uē′Xatk. A′lta aqō′ctxôx qaX ōᶜō′kuil. Aqankᵢē′Litcax,**
that road. Now she is carried that woman. A blanket is pulled over
on back her head,

20 **näkct ci′qōcx·ī cgā′xôct. Aqtōtcē′naôx t!ōkkc. Lōn aqtōtcē′naôx.**
not it is seen her face. They are laid down blankets. Three are laid down.

21 **Ē′XtEmaĕ môkct aqtōtcē′naôx. AʟGō′ctxôx Lᶜā′gil qaX ōᶜō′kuil.**
Sometimes two are laid down. She carries her on a woman that woman.
back

22 **A′lta aqʟgumgē′kᵘtix qō′ʟa qʟgē′ctxôx. Aqtä′tElutxax tktē′ma.**
Now she is paid that the one who carried They are paid to her dentalia.
her on her back.

248

Alā́ːtēwa kᵘcā́xali aLgā́x iLā́ctxul. Aqtä́ːtɛlotx t!ŏkkc. Alā́ːtēwa **1**
Again   up   she makes her   her load.   She is given   blankets.   Again

kᵘcā́xali aLgā́x. Ṓxuit tkamŏ́ta aqtě́ːtɛlōtx qṓLa Lgḗctxox. **2**
up   she makes her.   Much   property   is given to her   that   the one who carried her on her back.

Tcx·ī aLgōLā́ːētamitx gō qṓta t!ŏkkc, kᵘcaxalā́. A'lta aqtṓqLx **3**
Just   she puts her down   on   those   blankets,   up.   Now   they are carried to her

tktḗma. Atktŏ́qLx tgā́colal qaX o̯c̯ṓkuil. A'lta k¡u'tk¡ut aqtā́x **4**
dentalia.   They carry them to her   her relatives   that   woman.   Now   tear   they are done

gō LE'k·aqtq. Ṓqxuqst aqā́lax. AqtikXā́tkoax qix· ē'k·ala **5**
on   her head.   Her louse   is made on her.   They are put on his head   that   man

tktḗma. Tiā́cōlal atktikXā́tkoax. Ṓyaqct aqā́·ilax. A'lta **6**
dentalia.   His relatives   they put them on his head.   His louse   is made on him.   Now

aqtṓkuiptckax tk!ḗwulɛlqL. ALuxupṓnax tgā́cōlal qaX o̯c̯ṓkuil. **7**
it is carried up to her   food.   They carry it to her   her relatives   that   woman.

Tä́cka qṓtac ōXuigḗXiwax, tä́cka aqtā́witx qṓta tk¡ḗwulɛlqL **8**
They   those   they help,   they   they are fed   that   food

qṓLa Lgā́pōna. Pā́apa aqtā́x qṓLa Lgā́pōna. A'lta **9**
that   it is brought to her.   Divide   it is done   that   what is brought to her.   Now

nuxumayā́mitx tgā́colal qaX o̯c̯ṓkuil. Ma'nix itā́Lɛlam tpacī́ci·y **10**
they return the purchase money   her relatives   that   woman.   When   ten   blankets

uyā́wa, kstā́xtkin aLx·mŏ́yamitx. Ma'nix qoā́nɛm uyā́wa iLā́kit, **11**
her expenditure,   eight   they refund them.   When   five   her expenditure   her price of purchase

lakt uyā́wa niLx·mŏ́yamitx. Ma'nix ḗxauwit aLuXupŏ́nax, **12**
four   her expenditure   they refund it.   When   much   food is brought her,

a'lta wiXt ē'k·it aqiā́wix. WiXt aqtā́witx tkamŏ́ta. A'lta wiXt **13**
now   again   buying a wife   is done.   Again   they are given   property.   Now   again

nuxumayā́yamitx. **14**
they return it.

Lā́xka Lā́qôkcin, Lā́xka ḗk·it aLgḗtɛlax. Ma'nix Lᶜā́kil **15**
Those are   relatives of a married couple,   they   buying wife   they did it to them.   When   a woman

Lā́qôkcin, kanamŏ́kctikc tā́nɛmckc Lā́qŏqcin Lā́xka ḗk·it **16**
married couple's relative,   both   women   married couple's relatives   they   buying wife

aLgḗtɛlax. **17**
they did it to them.

Ma'nix aLE'kxtōx Lgā́cinɛma·iL; ma'nix aqLṓmɛqt Lā́Xa, **18**
When   she gives birth to a child   their relative married in a foreign village;   when   it dies   her child,

atcLlṓtx qaX o̯c̯ṓkuil ḗtcam LɛLā́-ētix·. Ma'nix nēkct LɛLā́ētix· **19**
he gives him to him   that   woman   her father   a slave.   When   not   a slave

ka ikanī́m atciŭ́tx. Lkā́nix·ē atcLā́x. Ma'nix aLŏ́ix **20**
then   a canoe   he gives it.   Paying indemnity for the loss of a child   he does him.   When   she goes

aLxɛlk¡ḗwulalɛmamx aLXgṓmamx, a'lta ka'nauwē aLgiŏ́makux **21**
she goes to gather roots or berries   she reaches her house,   now   all   she gives food in dishes

iLā́k¡ēwula. Tä́cka qṓtac tkLumɛlā́lɛmx, tä́cka ka'nauwē **22**
what she had gathered.   They   those   they bought her,   them   all

aLgauwḗēmx. Ka'nauwē Lqitā́kēma-y· ḗka, ma'nix aLxɛlk¡ḗwula- **23**
she feeds them.   All   years   thus,   when   she goes to gather roots

lɛmX qṓLa Lᶜā́kil.
or berries   that   woman.

Ma′nix aLō′mEqt Lā′k·ikala, a′lta gō Liā′wuX qiX ē′k·ala
When he dies her husband, now to his younger that man
brother

2 aqLō′cgam qō′La Lᵉā′gil. Ma′nix näkct Liā′wuX qix· ē′k·ala, ka gō
she is taken that woman. When not his younger that man, then to
brother

3 Liā′mama aqLō′cgam Lᵉā′kil. Ma′nix kᵢē Liā′mama qix· ē′k·ala, ka
his father she is taken the woman. When no his father that man, then

4 gō Liā′icX aqLō′cgam qō′La Lᵉā′kil. Ka ā′yip!ē tiā′cōlal ē′tamxtc.
to his relative she is taken that woman. Then right his relatives their heart.

Ma′nix ē′k·it aLgiā′x Lqᵢoā′lipX aqL′laguē′gux Lā′xamōta.
When buying a he does it a youth it is refused his property.
wife

6 Mō′kcti qē′xtcē-y· ē′k·it aLgiā′x aqL′laguē′gux Lā′xamōta. E′XtEmaē
Twice trying buying a he does it it is refused his property. Sometimes
wife

7 Lō′nē qē′xtcē-y· ē′k·it aLgiā′x. ALxaLkᵢEmLuwā′kutcgux. Tcä′2xēL
three trying buying a he does it. He hides for her in the woods. Several times
times wife

8 ka Lᵢap aLkLā′x gō kō′lx·ē. A′lta aLkLungō′mitx. ALaLgE′ldax,
and find he does her in in the woods. Now he carries her away. She leaves them for
his sake,

9 naxE′ldax qaX ōᶜō′kuil. AqLōnā′xLatcgux Lᵉā′kil. AtkLōnā′xLatcgux
she leaves that woman. She is lost the woman. They lost her

10 Lā′cōlal. NacElā′xo-ix·tx qaX ōᶜō′kuil nā′xElta. Atgē′ix tgā′cōlal.
her relatives. They learn about her that woman she left. They go her relatives.

11 Ma′nix tgā′xkᵢunakc, atgē′ix ka′nauwē. AqōLā′tamx. Atgā′yamx
When her elder brothers, they go all. They go to take her They arrive
back.

12 tgā′cōlal gō qaxē′ nakē′x. AqōLā′tax. Aqō′kᵘ₁x. NuXō′gux
her relatives at where she is. She is taken back. She is carried. They go home

13 tgā′cōlal. Aqō′kᵘ₁amx. Tcä′xēL aya-ō′ixē, ā′nqatē wiXt naxE′ltax.
her relatives. She is brought home. Several days, already again she leaves.

14 WiXt ia′xka n̊a-igE′ltax. WiXt aqōLā′tamx, atgē′ix tgā′cōlal.
Again to him she leaves for his Again they go to carry her they go her relatives.
sake. back,

15 Tcä′xēL aya-ō′ixē, wiXt naxE′ldax. A′lta iā′c aqē′x. E′XtEmaē
Several days, again she leaves. Now let alone she is Sometimes
done.

16 Lō′nē aLxE′ldax Lᵉā′kil ka iā′c aqLā′x. A′lta näkct ō′Xuē-y·
three she leaves the woman and let alone she is done. Now not much
times

17 ē′k·it aqēE′Lgax, mE′nx· ka tkamō′ta-y· ē′k·it aqtE′Lgax. WiXt
buying is done to her, a little only property buying a is done to her. Again
a wife wife

18 aqLaxo-iktcgō′mamx. Ka′nauwē tgā′cōlal atgē′ix qaX ōᶜō′kuil.
they are married. All her relatives they go that woman.

19 Aqaxiktcgō′mam. Ma′nix nēkct Lā′xamōta LE′k·ala cka kā′ltac
She is married. When not his property the man and only

20 aLō′p!x gō Lā′qcix·. A′lta aLgiōgonā′oxoē t!ōL gō Lā′qsix·.
they enter at his father- Now he looks after it the house at his father-
in-law. in-law.

21 ALgiagEna′ôx ōᶜō′lEptckix. ALxelalā′guya-itx gō ka′nauwē Lā′cōlal
He looks after it the fire. He always catches salmon to all her relatives

22 Lā′k·ikal.
his wife.

Ma′nix aqLE′Lcgamx Lā′k·ikal LgōLē′lEXEmk, a′lta-y· ō′Xuē
When she is carried away his wife a man, now many

24 t!ē′Eltkēu ēqā′tēm aqtē′tElax, ka it!ō′kti nē′xax ē′Lamxtc. Ma′nix
slaves paying in- it is done, and good gets his heart. When
demnity

25 näkct iqā′tēm aqä′tElax ka aLkᵢē′tēnax. Ma′nix nikct Lᵢap aLkLā′x
not paying in- it is done and he kills him. When not find he does him
demnity

qō'La Lā'k·ikal kLkLxE'cgam, ka Lā'icX aLLā'wa⸢ox qō'La LE'k·ala.   1
that   his wife   who carried her   and   his rela-   he kills him   that   man.
                      away,   tive

LE'k·Emaua aLxā'x.   AqLgE'nuax Lā'icX   qō'La   kLgōxogē'cgamx.   2
Taking revenge he does it.   A relative of an   his relative   that   who carried her away.
on a relative of   evil doer is killed
an evil doer   in revenge

A'lta-y- ōkumā'La-it nE'xax. Ē'ka wiXt Lā'pL⸢au aqLō'cgamx, wiXt   3
Now   a family feud   it gets.   Thus   also   a dead   she is taken away,   also
                                              brother's
                                                wife

iqā'tĕm aqē'tElax ka t!ayā' nē'xax ē'Lamxtc.   4
paying in- it is done   and   good   gets   his heart.
demnity

Translation.

When a man of one town likes a girl of another town his relatives take [part of] their property and go to buy her. They send messengers. The [girl's relatives] keep the dentalia [which have been sent them] and the messengers go home. Now the girl's father divides that property among all his relatives. Now her mother prepares her dentalia and the people make themselves ready. They bring her to the town where the people live who have bought her. They bring the bride to the groom. When they had given a small amount only in payment, they add to the purchase money, giving more dentalia and several slaves to her father. Now the [amount paid] is sufficient. The relatives of the girl stand outside the house. They put on their blankets, dance, and sing conjurer's songs. Now the man's relatives run to the other party and take off their blankets. This is done three or four times. Now a road is strewn with dentalia by the man's relatives. When it is finished a woman carries the girl over it on her back. A blanket is pulled over her head, so that her face can not be seen. Two or three blankets are laid down. The woman who carries her receives a payment of dentalia. When she lifts her load again, she receives blankets in payment. She lifts her once more. She receives much property for carrying her on her back. At last she puts her down on those blankets. Now the relatives of the girl bring her dentalia. They are torn over her head, and [they feign to] louse her. Dentalia are also strewn on the man's head by his relatives and they feign to louse him. Now the girl's relatives bring her food. This food is divided among those who helped [in the ceremonies]. Then the woman's relatives return the purchase money. When ten blankets are paid, they refund eight. When five were paid, four are refunded. When much food is brought to her, the man's relatives pay once more, and this purchase money is also returned.

The relatives of the married couple transact the purchase. [Male and] female relatives of a married couple are [called] Lā'qoqcin.

When the relative of a family who is married in another village gives birth to a child and the child dies, the woman's father gives a slave or a canoe. He pays indemnity. When [the young wife] gathers roots or berries, she distributes them among the people who bought her. This is done every year when she goes to gather berries. When her husband dies she is taken to his younger brother. If he has no younger brother, she is taken to his father. If he has no father, she is taken to one of his relatives. Then the relatives of her husband feel satisfied.

When a youth tries to buy a wife and his property is refused, he may try twice or three times. If he is still refused, he hides in the woods in order to wait for the girl. Often he meets her there and carries her away. She goes to him. Then her relatives have lost her. Her relatives learn where she is. If she has elder brothers, they all go to take her back. They arrive at the place where she is and carry her back home. After several days she leaves again and goes to the young man. Her relatives go again and carry her back. When she leaves a third time they let her go. Sometimes she is allowed [to stay with the man] after she has left three times. Now she is bought for a small amount of property. They are married. All her relatives go to [attend the marriage]. If the man has no property, they live with his father-in-law. He looks after his father-in-law's house. He looks after his fire and catches salmon for his wife's relatives.

If a man's wife is carried away, many slaves are paid to him as an indemnity, and he is satisfied. If he is not paid indemnity he kills [the abductor]. If he does not find him he kills one of his relatives. Then a family feud arises. It is the same when the wife of a man's deceased brother is taken away. Then, also, indemnity is paid and he is satisfied.

DEATH.

Ma'nix aLŏ'mEqtx ŏ'Xuē Lā'cōlal ŏ'Xuē Lā'ktēma LgōLē'lEXɛmk,
When   he dies   many   his relatives   many   his dentalia   a person,   **1**

ŏ'Xuē Lā'ēltgēu, a'lta ka'nauwē atkLk¡ē'niakux Lā'cōlal.
many   his slaves,   now   all   they tie it on to him   his relatives   **2**

Amŏ'kctikc aqtŏ'cgamx tê'lx·Em Lē'x·Lēx· atkLā'x tq¡ōlipx·Enā'yū.
Two   are taken   men   to prepare corpse   they do   young men.   **3**

Ma'nix it!ŏ'kti iLā'Xanīm ka ia'xka aqLē'nkana-itx ka aqiupō'nitx
When   good   his canoe   then   it   he is put into it   and   it is put up   **4**

qix· ikanī'm kⁿcā'xali. Ōnuā'Lema aqā'ēlax qix· ikanī'm. Mŏ'kcti
that   canoe   up.   Paint   it is done   that   canoe.   Twice   **5**

Lxoa'p aqiā'x gō iā'pōtc. AtgE'Lxamx tê'lx·Em ka noxoŏ'yutx,
hole   it is made   in   its stern.   They come down to the beach   the people   and   they wash themselves,   **6**

aLoxŏ'ēṭamx. LE'kaqcō Lqup atqLā'x. Ka'nauwē LE'kaqcō Lqup
they comb themselves.   Their hair   cut   they do it.   All   their hair   cut   **7**

atqLā'x tā'nEmckc, tkā'lamuks, tqā'cōciniks. ALŏ'XuL¡ax
they do it   women,   men,   children.   It is finished   **8**

LE'kaqcō Lqup atkLā'x. A'lta Lāqᵒ atcŏ'xôx tgā'xal. Ka'nauwē
their hair   cut   they do it.   Now   take off   they do them   their names.   All   **9**

tā'nEmckc Lāqᵒ atŏ'xôx tgā'xal, ka'nauwē tkā'lamuks Lāqᵒ
women   take off   they do them   their names,   all   men   take off   **10**

aLŏ'xôx tgā'xal. Oxoē'ma t'atoxup!Ena'x tE'kXala ka tqā'cociniks.
they do them   their names.   Others   they name themselves   names   and   children.   **11**

A'lta aqtā'maquq Lā'qtēma qŏ'La Lŏ'mEqtx. Ka'nauwē atktŏ'cgam
Now   they are distributed   his dentalia   that   dead one.   All   they take them   **12**

Lā'cōlal Lā'ēltgēu, uLā'Xanima. Ma'nix tq¡ēx Lā'icX, q¡oā'p
his relatives   his slaves,   his canoes.   If   like   his relative,   nearly   **13**

aLŏ'mEqtx aLkLŏ'lEXamx: "x·ix·ī'x tcucgā'ma ōgu'k·ikal, ma'nix
he dies,   he says to them: "This one   he will take her   my wife,   when   **14**

anŏ'mEqta." Ma'nix amŏ'kctikc Lā'nEmckc ka amŏ'kctikc têlx·Em
I die."   When   two   wives   and   two   persons   **15**

aLktŏ'lEXamx. A'lta iā'xkati aqtŏ'cgamx Lā'nEmckc gō Lā'cōlal.
he speaks to them.   Now   there   they are taken   the women   to   his relatives.   **16**

Ma'nix Lᶜā'gil tq¡ēx Lā'k·ikal qoā'p aLŏ'mEqtx Lᶜā'kil
When   a woman   likes   her husband   nearly   she dies   the woman   **17**

aLkLŏ'lEXamx Lā'xk'un: "Mai'kXa tcEmucgā'ma imē'p¡au." Ma'nix
she says to her   her elder sister: "You   he will take you   your brother-in-law."   When   **18**

Lā'wuX, ä'ka wiXt aLkLŏ'lEXamx. Qē'xtcō Lq¡ēyŏ'qxut, Lk¡āsks
her younger sister   thus   also   she says to her.   Intending   old,   young   **19**

Lā'pLaɥ, tatc!a Lā'Xk̊a aLkLŏ'cgamx. E'ka LE'k·ala, ē'ka Lᶜā'gil.
his widow,   then   to him   they take her.   Thus   a man,   thus   a woman.   **20**

Ma'nix Lkā'nax aLcx·p!Enā'x; aqiup¡Enā'x iLā'xal. ALx·p!Enā'x
When   a chief   he takes his name;   he is named   his name.   He takes his name   **21**

Lā'icX. Aqtŏ'lXamx amŏ'kctikc tê'lx·Em: "ME'taika amtiup¡Enā'ya."
his relative.   They are told   two   people: "You   name him."   **22**

A'lta amŏ'kctikc tê'lx·Em actiup!Enā'x. A'lta-y- ŏ'Xuē tqamŏ'ta
Now   two   people   they name him.   Now   much   property   **23**

253

1 aqtā'witx qō'tac tgiup¡Enā'x ē'qxal. Ē'ka LE'k·ala, ē'ka Lᶜā'gil,
they are given those they name him name. Thus a man, thus a woman,

2 ē'ka Lk¡āsks, ma'nix aqiup¡Enā'x ē'qxal.
thus a child, when he is named name.

NēxEltā'kōmxēa wiXt t¡ayā' aqLā'x Lmē'mEluct. Amō'kctikc
After one year again good it is made the corpse. Two

4 aqtō'kux tq¡ulipx·Enā'yu. T¡ayā' atkLā'x ka qix· ikanī'm wiXt
are hired young men. Good they make it and that canoe also

5 t¡ayā' aqiā'x. Ōnuā'LEma aqā'ilax.
good it is made. Paint it is done to it.

Ma'nix giLā'Xawôk aLō'mEqtx aqō'tXEmitk uLā'XEmatk gō
When a man having a guardian spirit dies it is placed his baton at

7 qix· ikanī'm. Ma'nix Lā'qēwam aLō'mEqtx aqLxē'nx·ax Lā'XEmatk
that canoe. When a shaman dies it is placed his baton

8 gō qix· ikanī'm. QuL aqā'wiX uLā'anaLaLa gō gō'qxôiamē qix·
at that canoe. Hang up it is done his bear-claws rattle at its stern that

9 ikanī'm. Ma'nix iLā'gilx·EmalaLEma Lā'qēwam, quL aqiā'wix
canoe. When his shell rattle a shaman, hang up it is done

10 iLā'gilx·EmalaLEma. Ma'nix ō'Xuē La'a Lā'qēwam, a'lta kō'lEXi
his shell-rattle. When many his children a shaman, now far into the woods

11 aqLō'kᴛx Lā'XEmatk. Ä'ka wiXt uLā'anaLaLa kō'lEXi aqō'kᴛx.
it is carried his baton. Thus also his rattle far into the woods it is carried.

12 Ma'nix Lt¡ō'xoyal aLō'mEqtx aqawik¡ē'ktuwElax Lā'k¡ôckEla gō
When a brave dies it is put on top of a stick his head-dress at

13 igē'mXatk. Ma'nix iLā'gilx·EmalaLEma Lt¡ō'xoyal, quL aqā'wix gō
canoe burial. When his shell rattle the brave, hang up it is done at

14 ikanī'm. Ma'nix Lᶜā'gil aLō'mEqtx, ä'mkXa-y- uLā'q¡ēLxap quL
canoe. When a woman dies, only her coat hang up

15 aqā'wix gō igē'mXatk.
it is done at the canoe burial.

Ma'nix Laq aqtE'Lxax Lāxigē'xo-il, LgōLē'lEXEmk Lāq aLktE'Lxax,
When take off it is done the corpse's dentalia, a person take he did them,

17 aqLā'wařôx LgōLē'lEXEmk. Ma'nix aqix·EnEmō'sXEmx iLā'k·emXatk
he is killed the person. When it is made fun of it his canoe burial

18 Lmē'mElōst, atcilā'xo-ix·itx, ma'nix nēkct aLktō'tx Lā'ktēma qō'La
a dead one, he learns about it, if not he gives them away his dentalia that

19 qLx·EnEmō'cXEm Lmē'mElōst ka aqLā'wařôx. Ma'nix ō'Xoē
the one who made fun of him the dead one then he is killed. If many

20 aLktō'tx Lā'ktēma ka näkct aqLā'wařôx.
he gives them away dentalia then not he is killed.

Ma'nix aLō'mEqtx Lā'Xa Lkā'nax, a'lta Liā'xauyam aLē'xElax
When it dies his child a chief, now its poverty comes to be on it

22 ē'Lamxtc. A'lta aLktō'lXamx Lā'côlal: "Tca lxō'ya gō-y· ēXt
his heart. Now he says to them his relatives: "Come we will go to one

23 ē'lXam gō Lē'Xat Lkā'nax." Ēlamxtc t¡ayā' qitElā'xō. A'lta atgē'ix
town to one chief." His heart good it will be made. Now they go

24 tē'lx·Em go-y· ēXt ē'lXam. Alō'nikc aqtE'tElōtx t¡ē'Eltgēu, ō'kunīm
people to one town. Three are given him slaves, canoes

25 aqā'tElōtx. Tktē'ma aqtE'tElōtx. Ō'Xuē tktē'ma aqtE'tElōtx.
are given him. Dentalia are given him. Many dentalia are given him.

26 Ka'nauwē aLktā'witx Lā'côlal qō'ta tktē'ma, qaX ōkunī'm. Cmôkct
All he distributes them among them his relatives those dentalia, those canoes. Two

27 ka cElā'itiX atcxēlē'maôx. Ma'nix nēkct aqtā'witx tktē'ma gō-y·
only slaves he keeps them. When not they are given to him dentalia at

ēXt ē'lXam ka a'lta nōxō'maqtx. Ō'Xuitikc aqtōtē'nax tê'lx·Em,
one town and now they fight. Many are killed people,   1

ka a'lta ōkomā'La-it naxā'x. Ma'nix aLŌ'mEqtx Lā'icX qō'La
and now feud it is. When he dies his relative that   2

kLktō'tx tktē'ma, aLgō'xuptct!ax Lā'cōlal, aLŌ'ix wiXt gō qigō
the one who dentalia, he calls them together his relatives, he goes again to where   3
gives away

ā'nqatē aLktE'tElōtx tktē'ma. A'lta wiXt ē'ka aqLā'x. AqtE'tElōt
before he gave them to him dentalia. Now again thus it is done. They are given   4

t!ē'Eltgēu, aqtE'tElōt tktē'ma, ōkunī'm aqā'tElōtx. T!ayā' nē'xax
slaves, they are given dentalia, canoes are given to him. Good gets   5

ē'Lamxtc.
his heart.   6

Ma'nix aLŌ'mEqtx Lgak¡Emā'na. A'lta ā'yatɛ!a nē'xElax ē'Lamxtc.
When he dies a chief. Now his sickness is on it his heart.   7

A'lta aLktō'kux Lā'colal. Nugōgē'staq¡oamx. AqLā'waᴇôx Lkā'nax
Now they tell his relatives. They go to war. He is killed a chief   8

gō-y- ēXt itā'lXam.
at one their town.   9

Ma'nix aLk¡ē'tēnax LgōLē'lEXEmk, aqLŌ'lXam Lq¡ēyō'qxut,
When he has killed one a person, it is said to an old man,   10

giLā'Xawôk Lq¡ēyō'qxut: "Mai'ka miaxō'tckia." A'lta aLkLŌ'cgam
having a guard- an old man: "You work over him." Now he takes it   11
ian spirit

Lqā'LXatcX Lq¡ēyō'qxut. A'lta Lᶜā'tcau aLqcēlā'kᴏx qō'La
coal the old man. Now grease he mixes it that   12

Lqā'LXatcX. ALkLE'tElax gō Lctā'xôst. ALgā'tElax ōkuk¡uē'tik.
coal. He puts it on on his face. He puts it on a headring of cedar   13
                                                                                                          bark.

Iuk Lā'ᶜowit k¡au aLkLE'tElax Lᶜuē'lōL, iō'kuk wiXt k¡au, gō
Here [at his legs tied it is done cedar bark, here [un- also tied, at   14
ankles] der knees]

Lā'pōtē wiXt k¡au'k¡au. Qoä'nEmi aLā'o-ix nikct aLkLā'amctx
his arms also tied. Five days not he drinks   15
[wrists]

Ltcuq, nēkct aLaō'ptitx, nēkct aLŌ'La-itx, guā'nEsum aLŌ'tXuitx.
water, not he sleeps, not he lies down, always he stands.   16

Pō'lakli aLgō'cgēwalEmx; aLkciLŌ'tElkEma-itx cE'qoalala aqcē'LōtElk;
At night he walks about; he whistles much bone whistles he whistles;   17

ē'nxēaxul aLgiā'xolEma-itx galā'k¡auk¡au. Oka wäx nē'ktcuktē.
he says ɪ ä ɪ he always says the murderer. And on the next it gets day.   18
                                                                                                          morning

Qoä'nEmi aLā'o-ix nikct aLxEmē'nagux. A'lta tcx·ī aLkLōmē'nagux
Five his sleeps not he washes his face. Now then he washes his face   19

Lq¡ēyō'qxut. Lāq aqLE'Lxax qō'La Lqā'LXatcX. Lāq aqē'Lax
the old man. Take off he does it that coal. Take off it is done   20

ē'Lamnukt galā'k¡auk¡au. Aqā'tElax ōnuwā'LEma galā'k¡auk¡au.
his blackened face the murderer. It is put on him red paint the murderer.   21

Menx· Lqā'LXatcX aqcx·Elā'kux. Lā'xka wiXt qō'La Lq¡ēyō'qxut
A little coal is mixed. That again that old man   22

aLgā'tElax ōnuwā'LEma. Anā' LE'k·ala Lq¡ēyō'qxut, anā' Lᶜā'gil
he puts it on him red paint. Sometimes man old person, sometimes woman   23

Lq¡ēyō'qxut. Lā'qLaq aqLE'Lxax qō'La Lᶜuē'lōL, qō'La k¡au'k¡au
old person. Take off it is done that cedar bark, that tied   24

qLE'tEla-ut. A'lta it¡ā'lEqEma k¡au'k¡au aqē'tElax gō Lā'pōtē k¡a
being to him. Now buckskin straps tied they are to his arm and   25

gō Lā'ᶜowit. A'lta aqLE'lᶜēmx Ltcuq gō qui'nEmē aLā'o-ix
to his feet. Now he is given food water at fifth his sleep   26

galā'k¡auk¡au. A'lta aqā'tElōtx ō'cgan LkLalᶜE'mcta. A'lta
the murderer. Now he is given a bucket out of which he drinks. Now   27

aqēxtElā'max ik¡ē'wulElqL. Qiā'x Lē'el nēxā'x, nixLE'lx, tcx·ī
it is roasted until it food. If black it gets, it is burned, then   28
is burned

1　agiLE′lᶜēmx. LōtX ka āLgiā′x. Qoä′nEmi aLgiā′wulax ka kapE′t.
he is given it to eat. He then stands. he eats. Five times he swallows and enough.

2　LōnLā′Li aLā′o-ix, ka wiXt ā′gon ōnuwā′LEma aqā′tElax. A′lta
Thirty his sleeps, and again another red paint is put on him. Now

3　at!ō′kti ōnuwā′LEma. A′lta aLgō′kтx uLā′Xak¡ ētik k¡a-y- uLā′cgan
good red paint. Now he carries it his head ring and his bucket

4　gō kᵘcā′xali-y-ē′maktcX. QuL aLgā′wix gō-y- ā′ap ē′maktcX. Näkct
to on top of a spruce tree. Hang he does it on top of spruce. Not

5　qa′nsix· aqā′Lxamêêx gaLā′k¡ auk¡ au, ma′nix aLxLxE′lEmax. Näkct
anyhow the people eat in his company the murderer, when he eats. Not

6　qansi′x aLō′La-itx aLxLxE′lEmax, guä′nsum aLō′tXuitx ma′nix
anyhow he sits he eats, always he stands when

7　aLxLxE′lEmax. Ma′nix aLō′La-itx ka ēXt iLā′ᶜowit aLcxtcawā′txn-itx
he eats. When he sits and one his leg he kneels on one leg

8　gaLā′k¡ auk¡ au. Näkct qansi′x aLkLō′kctx Lk¡ ăckc gaLā′k¡ auk¡ au.
the murderer. Not anyhow he looks at it a child the murderer.

9　Näkct qansi′x aLktā′qamitx tê′lx·Em noxo-iLxE′lEmax.
Not anyhow he sees them people they eat.

10　Ma′nix aLō′mEqtx Lᶜā′kil Lā′k·ikala LE′pLᶜau aLxā′x. A′lta
When he dies a woman her husband a widow she becomes. Now

11　aLō′ix gō kᵘca′la ē′qxĕL. Ē′XtEmaê mô′kctē aLā′o-ix, ē′XtEmaê
she goes to up river a creek. Sometimes twice her sleeps, sometimes

12　ē′Xtē aLā′o-ix. ALE′X′ōtx. LōnLā′L Lᶜalā′ma nēkct aLgī′ax
once her sleep. She bathes. Thirty days not she eats it

13　ixgē′wal. Ē′ka wiXt näkct akLE′tqamt Lk¡ ăckc, näkct akLE′tqamɪt
fresh food. Thus also not she sees it a child, not she sees him

14　gē′Latc!a. Ka′nauwē Lᶜalā′ma aLx′ō′toLa-itx. ALxēnē′nago-itx
a sick one. Every day she always bathes. She rubs on herself

15　gē′tak¡ EsEma gō-y- ē′LaLᶜa. Näkct qa′nsix· it¡ ō′kti iLā′ok Lᶜapᴇ′pLau;
good smelling things on her body. Not anyhow a good blanket a widow:

16　iā′q¡ atxala iLā′ok guä′nsum. ĒXt iqē′taq nēkct qa′nsix· hē′hē
its badness her blanket always. One year not anyhow laugh

17　aLxā′x. Qiä′x aLkLō′lXam Lā′pLau: "A′lta it!ō′kti ē′xa ē′mēmxtc!
she does. If he says to her her dead husband's relative: "Now good make it your heart!

18　TcEmucgā′ma imē′pL'au," a′lta niLx·Lx·ā′nagôx it!ō′kti iLa′ōk.
He will take you your dead husband's brother," now she puts it on good her blanket.

19　Ma′nix näkct iō′Lqtē LE′pL'au, ka guä′nEsum hē′hē aLxā′x ka
When not long widow, and always laugh she does and

20　nēkct it!ō′kti nē′xax ē′tamxtc Lā′pL'ōnan. Ma′nix ai′aq
not good get their hearts her dead husband's relatives. When quick

21　aLōlē′mXa-itx LE′pL'au ka aqLō′gux qLā′qēwam, tqē′wam aqLā′x
she marries a widow then he is asked a shaman, sending disease is done to her

22　LE′pL'au. ALō′mEqtx. Manē′x Lā′Xa LE′pL'au, iLanō′kstX Lā′Xa,
the widow. She dies. If her child a widow, its smallness her child,

23　ka näkct iō′Lqtē ka aLkLō′lEXamx Lā′pL'au: "T!ā′ya ē′xa
and not long and he says to her her dead husband's relative: "Good make it

24　ē′mēmxtc;" nau′itka t!ayā′ nē′xax ē′Lamxtc.
your heart;" indeed good gets her heart.

Translation.

When a person dies who has many relatives, much property, and many slaves, his relatives tie [dentalia] to his body. Two young men are selected to prepare the corpse. If [the deceased] had a good canoe, he is placed into it and it is put up. It is painted and two holes are made in its stern. The people go down to the beach and wash and comb themselves. They cut their hair—men, women, and children. After they have cut their hair, they take other names. Women, men, and children change their names. Then the dentalia of the deceased are distributed. His relatives take them as well as his slaves and canoes. If the deceased liked one of his relatives [particularly] he would say: "He shall take my wife after I am dead." If he had two wives he speaks in this way to two persons. Now the women are taken to his relatives. When a woman loves her husband and she is near her death, she will say to her elder sister: " Your brother-in-law shall marry you;" or she may say so to her younger sister. When an old man dies and his widow is young, she is taken to his younger brother. In the same way [when and old woman dies and her widower is young, he is given his wife's younger sister].

When there is a chief, he takes the [deceased chief's name a long time after the death of the latter]. His relative takes his name. Two people are told to name him. Now two people give him the name. They are given much property [for performing this service]. This is done when a man, a woman, or a child is named. After a year the corpse is cleaned. Two young men are hired, who also rearrange the canoe and paint it.

When a man dies who has a guardian spirit, his baton is placed next to the canoe. When a shaman dies, his baton is placed next to the canoe. His rattle of bear claws is hung on to the stern of the canoe. When he had a rattle made of shells, it is hung in the same place. When a shaman has many children, his baton is carried far into the woods. His rattle is carried there also. When a brave dies, his headdress is placed on top of a pole near his canoe burial. When he had a shell rattle, it is hung on to the canoe. When a woman dies, only her coat is hung on the canoe burial.

When anybody takes the dentalia away from a corpse, the person who took them is killed. When anybody makes fun of a canoe burial, and [the relatives of the deceased] learn about it, he must give away many dentalia, else he is killed. If he gives away many dentalia he is not killed.

When the child of a chief dies, he becomes very sad. He says to his relatives: "Let us go to the chief of that town." The chief tries to please him. Now the people go to another town. Then he is given three slaves, canoes, and dentalia by the chief whom he visits. He receives many dentalia. He distributes all these dentalia and canoes among his relatives. He keeps only two slaves. If [the chief of] that town does not give him any dentalia they fight. Many people are killed, and now a feud originates. When a relative [of the chief] who has given dentalia dies, he assembles all his relatives and goes to the

man whom he had given dentalia. Now the same is done [as before].
They give him slaves, dentalia, and canoes. His heart becomes glad.

When a chief dies, his relatives are sad. They speak to each other
and go to war. They kill the chief of another town.

When a person has been killed, an old man who has a guardian spirit
is asked to work over the murderer. The old man takes coal and mixes
it with grease. He puts it on to the face [of the murderer]. He gives
him a head ring of cedar bark. Cedar bark is also tied around his
ankles and knees and around his wrists. For five days he does not
drink water. He does not sleep, and does not lie down. He always
stands. At night he walks about and whistles on bone whistles.
He always says ä ä ä. For five days he does not wash his face. Then
on the next morning the old man washes his face. He takes off that
coal. He removes the black paint from his face. He puts red paint
on his face. A little coal is mixed with the red paint. The old man
puts this again on to his face. Sometimes this is done by an old man,
sometimes by an old woman. The cedar bark which was tied to his
legs and arms is taken off and buckskin straps are tied around his arms
and his legs. Now, after five days he is given water. He is given a
bucket, out of which he drinks. Now food is roasted for him, until it
is burned. When it is burned black it is given to him. He eats standing.
He takes five mouthsful, and no more. After thirty days he is painted
with new red paint. Good red paint is taken. Now he carries his
head ring and his bucket to a spruce tree and hangs it on top of the
tree. [Then the tree will dry up.] People never eat in company of a
murderer. He never eats sitting, but always standing. When he sits
down [to rest] he kneels on one leg. The murderer never looks at a child
and must not see people while they are eating.

When a woman's husband dies she becomes a widow. Then she goes
up the river. [There she stays] sometimes one day, sometimes two
days. She bathes. For thirty days she does not eat fresh food. She
also does not look at a child or at a sick person. She bathes every
day. She rubs her body with sweet-smelling herbs. She never wears
a good blanket. Her blanket is always bad. For one year she must
not laugh. Then her dead husband's relatives tell her: "Now be glad;
your brother-in-law will marry you;" then she puts on a good blanket.
When she laughs shortly after becoming a widow, her husband's relatives are not pleased. When she marries again quickly, they ask a
shaman to send disease to her and she dies. When a widow has a
child which is small, her dead husband's relatives say to her soon:
"Now be glad," and, indeed, she gets glad.

GiLā′pcōyi, ma′nix Lʲap aLgiā′x ē′kolē, aqLō′lXamx Lqʲoā′lipX: 1
The people of   when   find   they do it   a whale,   he is told   a youth:
Sealand,

"Amxklē′tcgum."   Ma′nix   ō′Xoētikc   Lʲap   atgiā′x   ē′kolē: 2
"Go and tell them."   When   many   find   they do it   a whale:

"Amxklē′tcgum gō ilxā′lEXam."   Ma′nix āLā′k·iLau, aqLō′lXamx: 3
"Go and tell them   at   our town."   When   one having taboos,   he is told:

"Iau′a mā Lna Lā′qLaq amxigā′max." A′lta Lā′qLaq atxē′xax iau′a   4
"There   seaward   going up and   do."   Now   going up and   they do   there
      down   down

mā′Lna. Ē′ka wiXt galā′pōL, iau′a mā′Lna Lā′qLaq aLxē′kEmax.   5
seaward.   Thus   also   one having co-   there   seaward   going up and   he does.
                habited the pre-   down
                ceding night,

Ma′nix nēkct Lā′qLaq aLxē′kEmax Lā′k·iLau, ka ayuXunē′x. Näkct   6
When   not   going up and   he does   the one having   then   it drifts away.   Not
           down   taboos,

atgiā′xcx qō′tac Lʲap qtgiā′x, aqLgE′mLa-itx Lkā′nax. Atgā′yamx   7
they cut it   those   find   who did it,   they wait for him   the chief.   They arrive

ka′nauwē tê′lx·Em gō qix· ē′kolē, ka aLgiō′cgamx ê′mᶜEcX qō′La   8
all   people   at   that   whale,   then   he takes it   a stick   that

Lkā′nax. A′lta aqigEmgē′k·amita-ôx qix· ē′kolē ka′nauwē, kopä′t   9
chief.   Now   it is measured   that   whale   whole,   enough
                                              [at]

Lā′yaqtEq, kōpä′t cia′lict. A′lta aqtō′lXamx tê′lx·Em: "Iō′kuk 10
its head,   enough [at]   its tail.   Now   they are told   the people: "Here

mai′ka miā′xca, iō′kuk x·ix·ī′x· tciā′xca." Ka′nauwē aqiäuwē′makux 11
you   you will cut,   here   this one   he will cut."   All   it is distributed among

qō′tac tê′lx·Em. Ma′nix gitā′qʲatxalEma txelā′yuwima, ka gō 12
those   people.   When   bad ones   common people,   then   at

ciā′lict atkcā′xc. Ka′nauwē aqiā′xc. A′lta atgiō′kuix ē′wa 13
its tail   they cut it.   All   it is cut.   Now   they carry it   thus

itā′lEXam qō′tac tê′lx·Em. Ka′nauwē atgiō′kᵘɹamx gō tgā′uLEma 14
their town   those   people.   All   they carry it   to   their houses

qix· ē′kolē. Ē′ka(ōku) ā′yaLqt ê′mᶜEcX, môkct ciā′kōtctk tagun 15
that   whale.   Thus   long   stick,   two   spans   others

qoā′nEm tkci. Môkct ciā′kōtctk ē′wa ā′yaxalx·t, aLE′gimx Lkā′nax 16
five   fingers   Two   spans   thus   wide,   he says   the chief
       wide.

aqigumgē′k·amita-ôx itā′kolē tê′lx·Em, ma′nix iā′qoa-iL iLā′kolē. 17
it is measured   their whale   the people,   when   large   their whale.

AqLō′lXamx iō′kuk Lqʲōp ä′xa. Lqʲoä′p aLgiā′x iLā′kolē. 18
They are told   here   cut   do.   Cut   they do it   their whale.

Ka′nauwē ē′ka aqiā′x itā′kolē. Ma′nix môkct ciā′kōtctk tagun 19
All   thus   it is done   their whale.   When   two   spans   others

qoā′nEm tkci, ka Lpaci′ci aci′xLa-itx; qoā′nEm Lāq iqauwiqʲē′Lē 20
five fingers   wide,   then   a blanket   they exchange   five   outside   dentalia
                            for it;

aci′xLa-itx. Ma′nix môkct ciā′kōtck ā′yaLqt, äka iawa ā′yaxalx·t, 21
they exchange   When   two   spans   its length,   thus   here   its width,
for it.

ka cᶜula′l aci′xLa-itx ma′nix aqiumElā′lEmx. 22
and   a ground-   they exchange   when   it is bought.
    hog blanket   for it

Ma′nix gitā′ckēwal Gitā′tsʲxēEls Lʲap atgiā′x ē′kolē, 23
When   travelers   Chehalis   find   they do it   a whale,

1 aqioxō'cgamx, aqioxōXuLā'tax. Ma'nix Wintciawu'ct L¡ap aqē'ax
it is taken from / it is asked back from / When / at Oysterville / found / it is done
them, / them.

2 ē'kolē, Lā'cka GiLa'pcō-i iLā'kolē. Ma'nix mEnx· mā'ēma
a whale, / those / the people at Sea- / their whale. / When / a little / down the river
land / [northward]

3 Wintciawu'ct ka GiLā'XuilapaX iLā'kolē. Ma'nix L¡ap aLgiā'x
Oysterville / and / the Willapa / their whale. / When / find / they do it

4 GiLā'pcō-i mā'ema Wintciawu'ct ka aqiLXaLā'tax. Ma'nix
the people of / northward / Oysterville / and / it is asked back. / When
Sealand

5 GiLā'XuilapaX iau'a kⁿca'la Wintciawu'ct L¡ap aLgiā'x ē'kolē
the Willapa / there up river south- / Oysterville / find / they do it / a whale
ward of

6 aqiLXaLā'tax.
it is asked back.

7 Ma'nix aLgēE'lkElax qLā'k·iLau, q¡oā'p iuxonē'ptcga, tatca
When / he sees it / one having taboos, / nearly / it drifts ashore, / behold

8 wiXt ayō'Lx, mā'Lnē ayō'ix. Ē'ka gaLā'pōl, ē'ka LqLā'xit, ē'ka
again / it goes sea- / seaward / it goes. / Thus / some one who / thus / a menstruating / thus
ward / has cohabited the / woman,
last night,

9 wiXt Lq¡elā'wulX, ē'ka wiXt gaLā'k¡auk¡au. Ma'nix Lā'k·iLau,
also / a girl who is men- / thus / also / a murderer. / When / their taboo,
struant for the
first time,

10 nēkct Lgā'tckēwal ē'wa tkamilā'lEq. Ma'nix aLgō'cgēwalEmx ē'wa
not / they go / thus / beach. / When / they go much / thus

11 tkamilā'lEq, a'lta näkct L¡ap aqeā'x ē'kolē. A'lta ō'lō aktā'x
beach, / now / not / find / it is done / a whale. / Now / hunger / comes to
them

12 tê'lx·Em.
the people.

13 Ma'nix gō Nitc¡xē'Els L¡ap aqiā'x ē'kolē, ka'nauwē atgē'ix
When / at / Chehalis / find / it is done / a whale, / all / they go

14 tê'lx·Em GiLā'lēlam, GiLā'XuilapaX, atgiumlā'lEmamx ē'kolē.
the people / the Nisal, / the Willapa, / they go to buy it / the whale.

15 Ä'ka wiXt Lā'pcō-i ma'nix L¡ap aLgiā'x ē'kolē, ka'nauwē
Thus / also / Sealand / when / find / they do it / a whale, / all

16 Gitā'tc¡xēEls atgiumlā'lEmamx ē'kolē.
Chehalis / they go to buy it / whale.

17 Ma'nix ō'lō aktā'x tê'lx·Em, ma'nix iLā'yuLEma LgōLē'lEXEmk,
When / hunger / comes to / the people, / when / his supernatural / a person,
them / helper

18 iau'a maLna' niō'LEma, a'lta aLgigE'ltcxEmx ē'kolē. Näkct
there / seaward / where his supernat- / now / he sings for it / a whale. / Not
ural helper is,

19 aLō'p¡x qLkLā'xElt, näkct aLō'p¡x Lq¡oā'lipX, taua'lta
she enters / a mature woman, / not / he enters / a young man, / else

20 aLkL̥E'lkElax LE'ktcxEm kaLā'pōl. Ä'ka wiXt qLkLā'xElt, taua'lta
he sees it / he sings / man who cohab- / Thus / also / a mature woman, / else
ited the last
night.

21 aLkLā'xitx gō wē'wulē kLE'ktcxEm Lⁿā'gil. Tā'mac tq¡eyō'qtikc
she gets men- / in / the interior of / the singer / a woman. / Only / old people
struant / the house

22 nuxoēxō'tēnema-itx, tā'mac tqā'cōciniks nuxoēxō'tēnema-itx,
they help sing, / only / boys / they help sing,

23 tqLapLxiXEnā'yu. Qoä'nEmi aLā'o-ix kLE'ktcxEm. AqLō'gux
girls. / Five / his sleeps / singing. / He is sent

24 Lqoā'lipX: "Amgē'kctam gō mā'Lnē." Qoä'nEmi aqLō'guX, a'lta
a youth: / "Go and look / at / seaward." / Five times / he is sent, / now

25 L¡ap aLgī'ax. Nau'itka iuquná'itix· ē'kolē. Ma'nix kaLā'pōl aLō'p¡x
find / he does it. / Indeed / it drifts / a whalh. / When / a man who has / enters
cohabited the
last night

gō qō'ta t!ōL qō'La qLE'ktcxam, nau'i k¡ā aLxā'x, ayuwā'xitx qix· 1
in *that house* *that* *singing,* *at once nothing* *it gets,* *it flees* *that*

iLā'yuLEma. Ä'ka wiXt LkLā'xit. Ma'nix aLō'p!x LkLā'xit nau'i 2
his supernatural *Thus* *also* *a menstruant* *When* *she enters* *a menstruant* *at once*
helper. *woman.* *woman*

k¡ā aLxā'x kLE'ktcxam. PāL ē'pqōn qō'La kLE'ktcxam. 3
nothing *it gets* *the singer.* *Full* *down* *that* *singer.*

ALgiō'tXEmitx ē'mᶜEcX gō wē'gwa, iō'Lqtē ē'mᶜEcX. ALE'k·imx: 4
He places upright *a stick* *at* *the ocean,* *a long* *stick.* *He says:*

"Yukpā' iuXunē'ptcga ē'kolē." Nau'itka ia'xkati ayō'Xuniptckax, 5
"Here *it will drift ashore* *the whale."* *Indeed* *there* *it drifts ashore,*

ma'nix qui'nEmi ayaō'ēxē aLE'ktcxEmx. ILā'kital iLā'xal qō'La 6
when *five times* *his sleeps* *he sings.* *Ikē'tal* *his name* *that*

iaua' mā'Lna giLā'Xawôk. 7
there *seaward* *having a guardian spirit.*

Ma'nix Lā'k¡ēlak ē'kolē L¡ap atgiā'x, ma'nix amō'kctikc, Lxoa'p 8
When *Clatsop* *a whale* *find* *they do it,* *when* *two,* *hole*

aLgiā'x, k¡au aLgā'elax ō'kuēma; ma'nix nēkct ō'kuēma ka-y- 9
they make it, *tie* *they do it to it* *a strap;* *when* *not* *a strap* *then*

ogō'cil. Akoapä'tikc Lā'cōlal, koapä't k¡au aLgiā'x. A'lta atgiā'xc 10
kelp. *As many* *his relatives,* *as many* *tie* *he does it.* *Now* *they cut it*

ē'kolē. Ē'xauwē atgiā'xc. A'lta aqLō'gux Lē'Xat, aLxkLē'tcgōmx 11
the whale. *Much* *they cut it.* *Now* *they send him* *one.* *he goes to tell them*

ē'wa-y- ē'lXam. A'lta atgē'ix tē'lx·Em. A'lta atgiā'xcx ka'nauwē 12
thus *the town.* *Now* *they go* *the people.* *Now* *they cut it* *all*

tē'lx·Em. Ma'nix k¡au akē'x ō'kuēma gō qix· ē'kolē, näkct qa'nsix 13
people. *When* *tied* *it is* *a strap* *at that* *whale,* *not* *anyhow*

Lq¡up aqiā'x iā'xkatē. Qiā'x aLō'yamx qō'La-y- ō'kuēma aqā'tElax, 14
cut *it is done* *there.* *If* *he arrives at* *that* *strap* *it is made for him,*

tcx·ī aLgiā'xcx gō qaX ō'kuēma k¡au ā'ēlaut. Manē'x Lq¡ōp aqā'x 15
then *he cuts* *at that* *strap* *tied* *it is.* *When* *cut* *it is*

nLā'kēma LgōLē'lEXEmk, Lxalō'ima Lq¡ōp aLgā'x, ka nuXuigā'yax 16
his strap *a person,* *another one* *cut* *he does it,* *then* *they fight*

tē'lx·Em. Tā'cga uXunā'cgapXitc, tā'cga qix· ē'gigula ē'kolē 17
the people. *Those* *they come too late,* *those* *that* *under it* *the whale*

kā'nauwē atgiā'xc tē'lx·Em. Ka'nauwētikc qō'tac tē'lx·Em tkilē'mak 18
all *they cut it* *the people.* *All* *those* *people* *sell*

atgiā'x itā'kolē. Iā'qoa-iL, kapä't iā'qoa-iL; näkct Lq¡up akē'txo-il. 19
they do it *their whale.* *Large,* *enough* *large;* *not* *cut* *it is done.*

Ianu'kstX, ka ianu'kstX. Ma'nix ianu'kstX a'lta näkct pāt 20
Small, *then* *small.* *When* *small* *then* *not* *very*

aqiumElā'lEmx. Ma'nix iā'qoa iL ka LäXt Lpaci'ci aci'xLa-itx. 21
it is bought. *When* *large* *then* *one* *blanket* *they exchange.*

Manē'x Lctā'xēlalak Lᶜā'kil ka tcēx uyā'giLq¡up ē'kolē 22
When *strong* *a woman* *then* *several* *its cuts* *whale*

aqiLgEmō'ktix aLgē'ctxōniLx. Gō aLō'nikc tē'lx·Em aLgugigē'cgamx; 23
she is paid *she carries them.* *To* *three* *people* *she helps them;*

anā' ala'ktikc tē'lx·Em ma'nix Lctā'xēlalak Lᶜā'kil. Ē'ka 24
sometimes *four* *people* *when* *strong* *a woman.* *Thus*

Lq¡oā'lipx· wiXt, ma'nix aLXElgē'cgElitx, aLgē'ctxonitx tcēx 25
a youth *also,* *when* *he helps,* *he carries on his back* *several*

uyā'giLq¡up ē'kolē aqiLgEmō'ktiX. Kawī'X Lā'k¡ēlak ā'nqatē 26
its cuts *whale* *he is paid.* *Early* *the Clatsop* *already*

nuxo-iLxE'lEmax. Ma'nix gatElō'pamē LgōLē'lEXEmk 27
they eat. *When* *jejune* *a person*

ka acxauwikLē'tcgumx nuxō'wax, ska mä'nx·i aLXE'ngux 28
and *they go to tell them* *they run,* *and* *a little* *he runs*

qō'La kLō'pamē kLkēx LgōLē'lEXEmk aLcxtcgā'nEmtcgux. 29
that *jejune* *being* *person* *he gets faint.*

1 ALxacᶜEʼluwaqLʼax. Aʼlta aLgiXEmōʼckapamx ēʼkolē. Aʼlta näkct
   They leave him behind.   Now   he arrives too late at   the whale.   Now not

2 ēʼxauē iLāʼkolē. AqiōʼtctXumx, tcx·ī aLōʼyamx. GuāʼnEsum
   much   his whale.   It is finished,   then   he arrives.   Always

3 uLāʼkima k¡a uLāʼqēwēqxē; cx·Elāʼwat uLāʼkima k¡a uLāʼqēwēqxē
   their strap and   their knife;   they are tied   their strap and   their knife
                                together

4 k¡a Lāʼckuic Lāʼk¡ēlak. Kaʼnauwētikc ēʼka.
   and their mat   the Clatsop.   All   thus.

Translation.

When the people of Sealand find a whale they tell a youth to go to the town and to inform the people. A person who has to observe taboos is asked to go up and down [in his canoe] below the whale. Then he goes up and down below the whale. Thus also a person who cohabited the preceding night goes up and down below the whale. If no person who has to observe taboos would go up and down, it would drift away. Those who found the whale do not cut it; they wait for the chief. All the people reach the whale. Then the chief takes a stick and measures the whale from the head to the tail. Then he tells the people: "You will cut here; you will cut there." It is distributed among those people. The common people cut from the tail end. When it is all cut, it is carried to the town into the houses. When the whale is measured, the chief tells the people to make the [measuring] sticks two spans and one hand width long, if the whale is large [; two spans wide if the whale is smaller]. The people are told: "You cut here," and they cut the whale. Everything is done this way. A cut two spans and one hand width large is exchanged for one blanket, or for a string of dentalia five shells longer than a fathom. When a cut two spans large is sold it is exchanged for a ground-hog blanket.

When travelers from Chehalis find a whale it is taken back from them. If it is found at Oysterville, it belongs to the people of Sealand; when it is found north of Oysterville, it belongs to the Willapa. When the people of Sealand find a whale north of Oysterville, it is claimed by the Willapa. If the Willapa find one south of Oysterville, it is claimed by the people of Sealand.

When a person who has taboos sees a whale nearly drifting ashore, it will drift out to sea again. This happens with one who has cohabited the preceding night, with a menstruating woman, with a girl who is menstruant for the first time, and with a murderer. People who have taboos do not go to the beach. When they go often to the beach, no whale will be found and the people get hungry.

When a whale is found in Chehalis all the Nisal and Willapa go to buy whale meat. When a whale is found in Sealand, all the Chehalis go to buy its meat.

When the people are starving, a person who has a supernatural helper of the sea sings to bring a whale. No woman who has her regular menses enters, no young man; else a person might see the singing

who has cohabited the preceding night. Therefore, also, no woman
must enter, as she might become menstruant in the house where they
sing. Only old people, boys, and young girls help sing. For five
days he sings. Then a youth is sent and told to look seaward. Five
times he is sent; then, indeed, he finds a whale adrift. When a man
who has cohabited the preceding night enters the house in which the
singing goes on, the supernatural helper vanishes at once. Thus also
when a menstruant woman enters. The singer is covered with down.
He places a pole upright on the beach and says: "Here a whale will
drift ashore," and, indeed, it drifts ashore there after he has sang five
days. The name of the supernatural helper of the sea is Ikē′tal.

When the Clatsop find a whale, and there are two people, they make
holes [in the skin] and tie their straps to it. If they have no strap
they take kelp. Each ties as many straps to it as he has relatives.
Then they cut the whale. They cut much. Now they send one man
to bring word to the town. Then the people go and all cut it. They
will not cut where a strap has been tied to it. When the man arrives
for whom the strap has been tied to the whale, he cuts at that place.
If one man cuts at the strap of another one, they will fight. Those who
come last take the lower side of the whale. All those people sell their
whale meat. The pieces are not cut—when they are large they are left
large, when they are small they are left small. Small ones are not
expensive. Large ones are exchanged for a blanket. If there is a
strong woman who can carry several cuts, she does so and is paid [for
her services]. Sometimes she helps three people; when she is strong
she may help four people. Thus also is a youth paid who helps the
people carrying several cuts of meat. The Clatsop always eat very
early. When a person has not yet eaten and they learn [that a whale
has stranded] and they run there, he gets faint and is left behind. He
comes too late to the whale and finds that only little is left. He may not
arrive until the cutting is finished. The Clatsop always carry their
straps and knives, which are tied together, and their mats. All do thus.

1 Ma′nix aLgiä′wa⸂ôx Lā′xēkLax imō′lak gō kulä′yi, ma′nix
   When   he has killed it   a hunter   an elk   at   far,   when

2 ē′k·ala imō′lak aLgiä′wa⸂ôx iLā′Lēlamiuks igō′n amô′kctikc
   male   elk   he has killed it   ten   others   two

3 atgiugō′lEmamX. Ma′nix ē⸂ē′kil imō′lak aLgiä′wa⸂ôx, akstuXtkē′nikc
   they go to fetch it.   When   female   elk   he has killed it,   eight

4 atgiôgō′lEmamx. Ma′nix môkct aLgiutē′nax Lā′xēkLax ka
   they go to fetch it.   When   two   he has killed them   a hunter   then

5 ôXô′ētikc atgē′ix, atgiugä′lEmamx imō′lak. Ma′nix ē′Xauē
   many   they go,   they go to fetch it   the elk.   When   many

6 aLgiutē′nax Lā′xēkLax ka iä′xka gō aqiō′kcEmx mä′Lxôlē
   he has killed them   the hunter   then   that   there   it is dried   inland.

7 Nē′x·caôx, tcx·ī nuxō′gux. Ka′nauwē aqiōwē′magux qō′tac
   It is dry,   then   they go home.   All   it is distributed among   those

8 tē′lx·Em. ALgiō′magux iLā′k¡ētēnax kLā′xēkLax.
   people.   He distributes it   what he has killed   the hunter.

9 Manē′x LqLa′xElt L⸂ā′gil, näkct Lgitcgä′liL ä′yaqtq, tgä′k·iLau.
   When   menstruating   a woman,   not   she takes it   its head,   it is her taboo.
   always

10 Näkct iLxē′tElax iä′mEmkunEmatk L⸂ā′gil, Lā′mkXa LE′k·ala
   Not   she eats it   its tongue   a woman,   only   a man

11 aLgiä′x. Näkct cä′ca LktEtx gō tiä′pōtē tiä′XamōkXuk. Gō2 kulä′yi
   he eats it.   Not   break they do it   at   its forelegs   its bones.   There   far

12 aqtō′k⸁x tkamō′kXuk, tauä′lta aLgoē′kElax LkLä′xit tkamō′kXuk.
   they are car-   the bones,   else   she sees them   a menstruating   the bones.
   ried   woman

13 Manē′x aLktä′x tqc′ō′cutk LkLä′xit, päx aLxä′x kLä′xēqLax. Ma′nix
   When   she eats   hoofs   a menstru-   unlucky he gets   the hunter.   When
                          ating woman,

14 aLkcikLkä′nanukLx imō′lak ä′yaqtq LqLä′xit, ō′Laaliqct nä′Lxalax.
   she steps across it often   an elk   its head   a menstruating   dropsy   comes to be on
                                       woman,   her.

15 Ä′ka Lq¡ēlä′wulX. Näkct Lgē′tqamt imō′lak, ō′Laaliqct nä′Lxalax.
   Thus   a girl who is menstru-   Not   she looks at it   the elk,   dropsy   comes to be on
   ant for the first time.   her.

16 Ma′nix aLx·cE′mgEmax Lā′xēkLax, nēkct qa′nsix aLō′Lx Lā′Xa.
   When   he is unsuccessful   the hunter,   not   [any]how   it goes to   his child.
                                                       the water

17 Mä′nix aLō′Lx Lā′Xa, a′lta ē′Latc!a nixä′LElax, nau′i aLō′mEqtx.
   When   it goes to   his child   then   its sickness   comes to be on it,   at once   it dies.
              the water

18 Ma′nix aLxugōmä′q¡auwôx ka cgapE′t nōxō′x Lā′aa k¡a
   When   he goes hunting   then   motionless   they are   his children   and

19 Lā′k·ikal. Näkct qä′xēwa aLō′ix Lā′k·ikal Lā′xēkLax. Ma′nix
   his wife.   Not   [any]where   she goes   his wife   the hunter.   When

20 acōxoē′nx·ax Lā′a, ka Lē′Xat ē′Latc!a nē′LxElax Lā′Xa
   they make noise   his chil-   then   one   its sickness   comes to be on it   his child
              dren.

21 ma′nix aLx·cE′mgEnax.
   when   he is unsuccessful.

Translation.

When a hunter has killed a male elk far away, then twelve men go to fetch it. When he has killed a female elk, eight go to fetch it. When a hunter has killed two elks, many people go to fetch it. When he has killed many, then it is dried in the woods [it is not carried away]. The people go home when it is dry, and the hunter distributes the meat among all the people.

A menstruating woman must not take the head of an elk. Women do not eat the tongue; only men eat it. They do not break the bones of the forelegs. These are carried far away, else a menstruating woman might see them. When such a woman eats the feet and hoofs, the hunter will be unlucky. When she steps over an elk's head, she will be sick with dropsy. Just so a girl who has just reached maturity. She does not look at an elk, else she will be sick with dropsy. When a hunter is unsuccessful, his child must not go near the water. When it goes near water, it will fall sick and die at once. When he goes hunting, his wife and children sit motionless. His wife must not go anywhere. When his children make noise, one of them will fall sick if the hunter is unsuccessful.

THE POTLATCH.

1 Ma'nix ik¡oanō'mɛm aLgiā'x Lkā'nax, a'lta atgē'ix, aqtō'knx
When potlatch he makes it a chief, then they go, they are sent

2 ā'k¡alaktikc, ē'Xtɛmaē·y· ā'k¡aquinumikc, ē'Xtɛmaē·y· ā'k¡atxɛmikc.
four in a canoe, sometimes five in a canoe, sometimes six in a canoe.

3 Ma'nix giLā'Xawôk, kadī'x· aqLō'gux. Q¡oā'p atgiā'xômx ē'lXam
When a man having a in company he is sent. Nearly they reach a town
guardian spirit,

4 qō'tac aqtō'kux, aLɛ'ktcxɛmx qō'La giLā'Xawôk. Noxo-ē'tcɛmaδx
those who are sent, he sings that one having a guardian They hear it
spirit.

5 gitā'lXam: "Ō qɛlXtgā'lɛmam," nugō'go-imx. Atxigēlā'mamxē
the people of "Oh, people come to fetch us," they say. They land
the town.

6 qō'tac tê'lx·ɛm qtktugō'lɛmamx. Nuxō'klitcgux gō-y· ēXt ē'lɛXam,
those people those who came to fetch They tell to one town,
them.

7 a'lta wiXt atgē'ix gō-y·ēXt ē'lɛXam; ka'nauwē tê'lx·anēma. A'lta
now again they go to one town; all towns. Now

8 nuXō'gux. A'lta nuXuē'tXuitcgux tê'lx·am. Tā'cka qō'tac kulā'yi
they go home. Now they make themselves ready the people. They those far

9 gitā'lXam, tā'cka aqugumā'La-itx. Qiā'x atgā'yamx, a'lta ka'nauwē
people of a town, they are waited for. If they arrive, now all

10 atgɛ'tctcax tê'lx·am. Ē'ka wiXt iau'a atgɛ'tctōlax, ma'nix gō
they go down the people. Thus also there they go up the river, when at
the river

11 kuca'la ik¡oanō'm aLgiā'x Lkā'nax. Atgā'yamx gō qigō
up river potlatch he makes it a chief. They arrive at where

12 aqtugō'lɛmamx. Q¡oā'p atgiā'xoē-y· ē'lXam, ka aqax'ō'yuL¡ɛx
they are fetched. Near they arrive the town, and they are put side
by side

13 ōkunī'm. Kā'tcɛk ōomā'p aqak·ā'tqoax, ē'wa nōtcē'qLkuitx qaX
the canoes. In middle planks are laid on top of thus they lay them across those
them,

14 ōomā'p. Ka'nauwē-y· ē'ka gō qaX ōkunī'm. A'lta iā'xkatē
planks. All thus on those canoes. Now there

15 nōxuēnā'Xitx, aLɛ'ktcxɛmx a'lta giLā'Xawôk, akuapā'tikc
they dance, they sing now those having guardian as many
spirits,

16 gitā'Xawôk, akapā'tikc nugō'tcxɛmx. AtkLilgā'mitaxoē aqtō'lXamx.
having guardian as many sing. They sing in the canoe they are told.
spirits,

17 NuXuiwā'yutckux gō qaX ōomā'p. Ka'nauwē-y· ōtā'nuwaLɛma
They dance on those planks. All their painted faces

18 qō'tac tê'lx·ɛm; ka'nauwē itā'pqōn. Tā'nɛmckc ka'nauwē pā'Lɛma
those people; all their down. The women all full

19 tktē'ma, itā'ckɛlal, tgā'qoxoalXta, itā'k¡ēLxōt. Ka'nauwē tgɛt¡ō'kti
dentalia, their ear their hair ornaments, their necklaces. All good
ornaments,

20 tga'okc. Ma'nix Lt!ō'xoyal Lɛ'k·ala ka Lā'2k¡ēckɛlal, ē'LamɛuukLt.
their When a brave a man then his head ornament, his blackened face.
blankets.

21 Ma'nix Lā'qēwam LgōLē'lɛXɛmk ka Lā'Xumatk aLkLō'kLx.
When a conjurer person then his baton he carries it.

22 Nugō'tcxɛmx cka atxigɛlā'xē. AqLō'lXamx Lɛā'gil: "Mai'ka
They sing and they land. She is told a woman: "You

23 ia'mitstkɛnɛma mxɛlā'xō." ALɛ'k·imx Lɛā'gil: "K¡ē tcxɛp nkêx."
you head dancer be." She says the woman: "No not daring I am."

266

Qiā′x giʟā′t!owil tcx·ī iā′ʟatstkɛnɛma nā′ʟxalax. Ē′ka ʟɛ′k·ala,   **1**
If   one who under·   then   she a head dancer   she gets.   Thus   a man,
stands it well

qiā′x giʟā′t!owil ʟɛ′k·ala, tcx·ī iā′ʟatstkɛnɛma nā′ʟxalax. A′lta   **2**
if   one who under·   a man,   then   he a head dancer   he gets.   Now
stands it well

atgiuxtā′maxē. Ma′nix lāx° aʟxā′x ʟɛā′gil, aʟō′ix ʟē′Xat ʟɛā′gil   **3**
they enter the house   When   bent [her   gets   a woman,   she goes   one   woman
dancing.   head]

t!ā′ya aqiā′x ē′ʟaqtq. A′lta aʟkʟgɛmgē′ktix,· t!ā′ya aqʟgiā′x   **4**
good   it is made   her head.   Now   she pays her,   good   it is made

ē′ʟaqtq. Ma′nix naʟkɛmk¡ā′pax ʟgōʟē′leXɛmk, aqʟō′cgaɪnx   **5**
her head.   When   he gets out of rhythm   a person,   he is taken

mā′ʟxolē, aqʟōʟā′ētemitx. Kapē′tikc tgā′Xawôk, kapē′tikc   **6**
up to the sides   he is placed up there.   As many   those having guardian   as many
of the house,   spirits,

nugō′tcxɛmx. Aʟō′Xuʟ¡′ɛx ēXt giʟā′lɛXam, a′lta wiXt tgō′nikc   **7**
sing.   They finish   one   people of a town,   now   again   others

ēXt gitā′lɛXam wiXt ē′ka. Ma′nix nēkct ō′Xuē tē′lx·ɛm ka môkct   **8**
one   people of a town   again   thus.   When   not   many   people   then   two

tgā′lɛXamema atgiuxtā′max. Nux·ix·auwā′Xitx. Ma′nix tā′qoa-iʟ   **9**
towns   they enter the house   They come together.   When   large
dancing.

t!ōʟ ʟōn tgā′lɛXamema nux·ix·auwā′Xitx, ē′Xti atgiuxtā′max.   **10**
house   three   towns   they enter together,   at one   they enter the house
                                time   dancing.

Aqcō′gux cmôkct cq¡oā′lipx, ma′nix mānx· ka ʟā′k¡ēwōlɛlqʟ   **11**
They are sent   two   youths,   if   a little   only   his food

ik¡oanō′mɛm qʟgiā′xo-il: "Tgt!ō′kti mtō′ya," aqtō′lXamx   **12**
the potlatch   the one who makes it.   "Good   you go,"   they are told

tq¡ulipx·ɛnā′ya; "mtgɛmā′nɛmama gō ʟā′icX ik¡oanō′mɛm   **13**
the youths,   "fetch food   at   his relative   the potlatch

qʟgiā′xo-il." Gō ēXt ē′lXam nugōmā′nɛmamx tq¡ulipx·ɛnā′ya.   **14**
the one who   At   one   town   they fetch food   the youths.
makes it."

A′lta aʟktō′kᵘ¡x ʟā′k¡ēwōlɛlqʟ qō′ʟa aqʟxɛmā′nɛmamx.   **15**
Now   they bring it to them   food   those   who were sent to bring food.

Aʟktō′kᵘ¡x ʟā′cōlal ka′nauwē; aʟktō′kᵘ¡x ʟā′k¡ēwolɛlqʟ.   **16**
They bring it to   his relatives   all;   they bring it to   food.
them   them

Nugō′tcxamx, wiXt atxigēlā′xē. WiXt atgiuxtā′maxē qō′tac   **17**
They dance,   again   they land.   Again   they enter the house   those
                                dancing

axuxōmā′nɛmamx. Manē′x ō′lɛXkul aquxōmā′nɛmamx,   **18**
who were sent to bring food.   When   dry salmon   is brought,

qui′nɛmikc ʟkā′lamukc atgā′qcx ō′lɛXkul. Atgiuxtā′max tgā′qcit   **19**
five   men   they hold it in   the dry sal-   They enter dancing   they hold it
                their mouths   mon.   in their
                                                           mouths

qaX ō′lɛXkul. Manē′x tcaxalē′at, aqui′nɛmikc itā′ctxtcōl   **20**
that   dry salmon.   When   edible roots,   five   they carry it
                                                   on back

atgiuxtā′max. Qoä′nɛmi atgā′o-ix nuXuiwā′yntckuX tē′lx·am,   **21**
they enter dancing.   Five times   their sleeps   they dance   the people,

a′lta aqauwigē′qxo-imx. ʟā′nēwa ʟkā′nax aqʟōp!ɛnā′x.   **22**
now   they are given presents.   First   the chief   is named.

Āqʟō′lXamx ʟē′Xat ʟgōʟē′lɛXɛmk: "Mai′ka amtōp!ɛnā′nɛma   **23**
He is told   one   person: "You   go and name them

tē′lx·am." Gō ēXt itā′lɛXam ʟē′Xat ʟkā′nax aqʟōp!ɛnā′x. Ma′nix   **24**
the people."   At   one   their town   one   chief   he is named.   When

giyā′yuʟ¡ʟ ē′ʟamxtc, eâ′k aʟgē′ʟelutx qō′ʟa kʟtop!ɛnā′n   **25**
liberal   his heart,   a blanket   he gives it to him   that   the one who names
                                                                  them

tē′lx·ɛm. Iqauwik¡ē′ʟē aqē′ʟɛlōtx qō′ʟa kʟtōp!ɛnā′n tē′lx·am.   **26**
the people.   Long dentalia   he is given   that   the one who names   the people.
                                                         them

1 Ēxt itā′lXam aqLō′gōL¡ax aqawigē′qxo·imx, wiXt ē′gōn ē′lXam
One   their town   is finished   is given presents,   again one more town

2 aqauwigē′qxo·imx. Lā′nēwa Lkā′nax aqaLE′lqEmax, aqLōp!Ena′x.
is given presents.   First   the chief   is called,   he is named.

3 Ma′nix aLgiuLā′tax Lā′gēqo·im, a′lta mō′kcti aqaLE′lgEmax.
When   he drags it   his present,   then   twice   he is called.

4 Ka′nauwē·y- ē′ka; ē′ka tā′nEmckc, ē′ka tkā′lamukc.
All   thus;   thus the women,   thus the men.

Nugō′go·imx gitā′k¡oanEmEm: "Nēkct Lā′kcta LguLā′ta·y-
They say   those at the potlatch: "Not   anybody   shoot

6 ōkulai′tan." Ma′nix ē′maqt atctā′x ēXt gitā′lEXam, aLguLā′tax
his arrow."   When   a fight   he makes to one   people of a town,   he shoots it
                      them

7 ōLā′Xalaitan ka nuxō′maqtx tē′lx·am. Atcā′xikc aqtōtē′nax.
an arrow   then   they fight   the people.   Several   are killed.

Iā′nx·ama ēkupku′p aqēauwē′makux· tā′nEmckc. Tā′mkXatikc
A fathom to   short dentalia   they are given as presents   the women.   Only they
each

9 tkā′lamukc iqauwik¡ē′Lē aqiauwē′makux; txElā′yōwēmā tkā′lamukc
men   long dentalia   they are given as presents;   common   men

10 ēkupku′p aqiauwē′makux. Ma′nix ō′Xoē Lā′ktēma Lkā′nax ka
short dentalia   they are given as presents.   When   many   his dentalia   a chief   then

11 mōkctE′mtga Liā′nx·ama ēkupku′p aLgiō′magux.
two to each   fathoms to each   short dentalia   he gives it to them
                    as a present

Translation.

When a chief intends to give a potlatch, four, five, or six men are sent out in a canoe [to invite the guests]. One man who has a guardian spirit is sent among them. When they approach a town the man who has the guardian spirit sings. The people of that town hear him and say, "Oh, we are going to be invited." The messengers land and tell the people to come. Then they go to the next town. After having visited all the towns they go home. Now the people make themselves ready. They wait for those who live farthest away. When they arrive they all go down the river together. Thus they do also when a chief on the upper part of the river has sent an invitation. They go up the river together. When they reach the town to which they were invited they put their canoes side by side and lay planks across. This is done with all their canoes. Now they dance, and those who have guardian spirits sing. The people dance on the planks. Their faces are painted red, their hair is strewn with down. All the women wear their dentalia, their ear and hair ornaments, and their necklaces. They wear good blankets. Braves wear their head ornaments and their faces are blackened. Shamans carry their batons. They sing and finally land. Then they tell a woman, "You shall be our head dancer." She replies, "No; I do not dare to do it." One who knows how to dance well is made head dancer, a man or a woman. Now they enter the house dancing. When a woman [while dancing] bends her head, another one goes and raises it. Then she pays her for having made her head straight. When a person gets out of rhythm, he is taken to the side of the house and must sit down there. All those who have guardian spirits sing. When the people of one town have finished, those of another town enter dancing. When there are not many people of one town, those of two towns enter together. When the house is large, the people of three towns will enter together.

If the host has too little food, two youths are sent and told, "Go and ask my relatives to bring food." The youths go to a town and ask the [host's relatives] to bring food. They all come and bring food. They also dance on the canoes and land. They enter the house dancing. When they bring dry salmon, five men hold it in their mouths while they enter the house dancing. When they bring roots, five men carry them on their backs when they enter the house dancing. After the people have danced five days they receive presents. One man is asked [to stand near the host and] to name the people. First he names the chief of one town. When the host is liberal, he gives the man who calls out the names a blanket. Or he is given long dentalia. After one town is finished, another one receives presents. Again first the chief is called. When he drags his present he is called back. Men as well as women are thus given presents.

The people are forbidden to shoot with arrows during the potlatch. If a man should want to fight against the people of a town and shoot an arrow, then the people would fight and several would be killed.

The women receive each a fathom of short dentalia. Only men are given long dentalia. Common men receive short dentalia. If a chief has many dentalia, then every one receives two fathoms of short dentalia.

1 Ma'nix nuguguē'saq¡oamX ka aLuXuilā'lamX. Ma'nix
  When   they go to war   then they sing.   When

2 aqLᶜē'kElax Lᶜā'wulqt, Lā'xka aqLā'waᶜôx qigō noxō'maqtx. Ma'nix
  it is seen blood,   that one is killed   where they fight.   When

3 amô'kctikc akLoē'kEla Lᶜā'wulqt tä'cka aqtōtē'nax. ALō'XuLEx
  two   they see it blood,   those two are killed.   They finish it

4 aLōXuilā'lam. Ma'nix aLō'Xuilā'lamx aqā'xtEqoax oōmā'p,
  they sing.   When   they sing   they are put down planks,

5 ō'Lqta-y· oōmā'p môkct inā'xEmo-ix. Akōpä'tikc t'ōxulā'yuwima,
  long   planks two   parallel.   As many   warriors,

6 kopä'tikc aLuXuilā'lamx. AtkcĩntEnā'xē. A'lta atgē'x
  as many   sing.   They kneel.   Now   they go

7 nugugē'staq¡oamx. A'lta nuxō'maqt. Ma'nix kanā'mtEmax
  they go to war.   Now   they fight.   When   both parties

8 aqtotē'nax tê'lx·am ka aLō'xoL¡ax. Iō'Lqtē ka iqagē'niak
  they are killed people   then they finish.   Sometimes then exchange of pres-
                                                                 ents after war

9 ayō'xo-ix. Kanā'mtEma iqagē'niak ayō'xo-ix, ka oxō't¡us noxō'x.
  it is.   Both   exchange of pres- it is,   then peaceful they become.
                            ents after war

10 Ma'nix näkct t¡ayā' naxā'x ōkumā'La-it, ka Lᶜā'gil aqLō'tx gō-y·
   When   not   good they make it a feud,   the a woman it is given to
                                                                      away

11 ēXt itā'lEXam ka t¡ayā' naxā'x ōkumā'La-it.
   one their town and good they make it the feud.

Translation.

Before the people go to war they sing. If one of them sees blood, he will be killed in battle. When two see blood, they will be killed. They finish their singing. When they sing, two long planks are put down parallel to each other. All the warriors sing. They kneel [on the planks]. Now they go to war and fight. When people of both parties have been killed, they stop. After some time the two parties exchange presents and make peace. When a feud has not yet been settled, they marry a woman to a man of the other town and they make peace.

270

Historical Tales.

WAR BETWEEN THE QUILEUTE AND CLATSOP.

A'lta ē'Xat iqįoā'lipx· gō Tiā'kįēlakē aqiō'gō nix'ō'tam iau'a   1
Now one   youth   at Clatsop   he was sent he went to there
                                                                 bathe

Nakōtįā't. Qoä'nEmi ayā'qxôiŏ ka nĕ'Xatgō. NĕXatgō', maLnā'   2
Nakōtįā't. Five times his sleeps and he returned. He returned, seaward

nĕ'Xatgō iau'a tkamilā'lEq. Tsō'yustē ka qįoā'p atci'txamē   3
he returned there beach.   It got dark then nearly he reached it

Tiā'kįēlakē, iau'a tstāX Tiā'kįēlakē. Nĕ'k·ikct ē'wa mā'Lxôlē.   4
Clatsop,   there around the Clatsop.   He looked thus landward.
                   point

A'ltā-y- ōkunī'm olā'ox; ā'Xoyĕ ōkunī'm. "Qā'xĕwa Lx natē'mam   5
Now   canoes they lay side many canoes. "Wherefrom may they came
             by side;   be

Xak ōkunī'm?" niXLō'lEXa-it. "NXtā'kō." NixE'Lxĕgō iXtā'kō.   6
those canoes?" he thought.   "I will turn back." He turned he will go
                                                              back.

A'lta atgiā'wat tĕ'lx·Em cka pāL tkamilā'lEq tĕ'lx·Em. Nĕ'k·ikct   7
Now they followed people and full the beach people. He looked
     him

ē'wa qigō ayō'yama. A'lta wiXt LgE'Lxat tĕ'lx·Em. Lqįōp tgixā'xo-ē.   8
thus where he will go. Now also they went down people. Cut off they did him.
                                    to the beach

A'lta atē'xLakō qō'tac tĕ'lx·Em. A'yō, ā'yō, ā'yō; a'lta atē'xLakō   9
Now they surrounded those people.   He he he now they sur-
     him   went, went, went; rounded him

qō'tac tĕ'lx·Em. Ka'nauwĕ cquiLįā'mukc akLō'ktcan. Aqē'lkikc,   10
those people.   All   spears   they held.   He was thrown,

atsō'pEna kⁿcā'xalē, aqiō'kLpa iau'a kĕ'kXulē ka'nauwĕ qō'La   11
he jumped up,   he was missed there below   all   those

cquiLįā'mukc. "Hahä'!" atgiō'lXam qō'Lac tĕ'lx·Em. AtkLē'lukc   12
spears.   "Hahä'!" they said to him those people. They threw him

iau'a kⁿcā'xalē qō'tac tĕ'lx·Em. TskįEs nĕ'xax. Aqiū'kLpa iau'a   13
there up   those people. Stoop he did. He was missed there

kⁿcā'xalē. WiXt atgiō'lXam qō'tac tĕ'lx·Em: "Hahä'!" A'lta atsō'pEna   14
above.   Again they said to him those people: "Hahä'!" Now he jumped

kā'tsEk gō qō'tac tĕ'lx·Em. Ayō'ipa qō'tac tĕ'lx·Em. A'lta atigE'ta   15
middle at those people. He went those people. Now they fol-
                            out of   lowed him

qō'tac tĕ'lx·Em. Qē'xtcē aqLē'lukc'ax atsōpEnā'x kⁿcā'xāli. A'lta   16
those people. Intending he was thrown he jumped up.   Now

ayo-ē'taqL qō'tac tĕ'lx·Em, ta'kE nitē'mam Tiā'kįēlakē. Kįē Liā'naa   17
he left them those people, then he arrived at Clatsop. No his mother

qix· iqįoā'lipx, aLō'mEqtx; kįē Liā'mama, aLō'mEqt; cka Liā'qacqac.   18
that youth, she was dead; no his father, he was dead; and his grandfather.

A'lta tsō'yustē ka niXatgō'mam Tiā'kįēlakē. A'lta ōxoē'nx·at   19
Now evening and he came back to Clatsop.   Now they stood there

T!ilē'mukc; oXuiwā'yutckō. "I'kta mcx·ē'lEx·alEm? Mckti'ckam   20
the Tillamook; they danced.   "What are you doing?   Take them

tEmcā'xalaitan. Stāqį qE'lxax. Tĕ'lx·Em pāL ikĕ'x tĕ'itē.   21
your arrows.   War is made on us. People full it is on land.

McxE'ltXuitck!" "Ēiā' LįEmē'nXut" aqiō'lXam. "TmĕmElō'ctikc   22
Make yourselves ready!" "Ēiā' lies" was said to him.   "Ghosts

271

1 x·itā′c tq̣ēx tciqtxīgElā′xō. Ayŏxŏtuwā′xit." Ta′kE atciŏ′lXăm
   these like he found them. He became afraid." Then he said to him

2 Liā′qasqas: "Ē′cgam ēmē′ok. Txŏ′ptcgaya txpcŏ′t′ama!" Ta′kE
   his grandfather: "Take your blanket. Let us go inland let us hide!" Then

3 ā′ctŏptck iā′qasqas. Acxpcŏ′tam. A′lta nuXuiwā′yul T!ilē′mukc.
   they went his grandfather. They went to hide. Now they danced the Tillamook.
   inland

4 Kā′tsEk ŏ′pŏl ka nukuē′witXit T!ilēmukc. Q̣oā′p ē′kᵘtEliL ta′kE
   Middle night and they lay down the Tillamook. Nearly dawn then

5 staqḷ akE′tax. Aqtŏ′tēna-y- a′lta T!ilē′mukc gŏ kᵘLā′xanī-y-
   attack they did them. They were killed now the Tillamook at outside

6 ŏgŏ′Lᶜaiŏ. Aqtŏ′tēna ka′nauwē qŏ′tac ŏgŏ′Lᶜaiŏ. A′lta stāqḷᵒ
   sleeping. They were killed all those sleepers. Now attack

7 agE′tax t!ŏLē′ma. AmE′nx·katikc aqtŏtē′na iau′a ci′tkum ē′lEXam
   they did the houses. Few only were killed there at the town
   them   [upper] half
                                            of the

8 ka noxo-ŏ′yokŏ ka′nauwē qŏ′tac tê′lx·Em. A′lta atktŏ′cgam
   and they awoke all those people. Now they took them

9 tgā′xalaitanEma Lā′kḷēlak. A′lta aqtā′ktuq tkā′cŏcinikc.
   their arrows the Clatsop. Now they were carried the boys.
                                     away

10 Ŏ′Xuitikc tkā′cŏcinikc aqtā′ktuq, Tkulē′yut!kc atktā′ktuq. A′lta
   Many boys were carried away, the Quileute carried them away. Now

11 aLE′xangŏ LgŏLē′lEXEmk aLxkLē′tcgŏm iau′a kᵘca′la gŏ-y- ēXt
   he ran a person he informed them there up river at one

12 ē′lEXam Kŏnŏ′pē. A′lta aLxawigu′Litck tê′lx·Em. A′lta
   town Kŏnŏ′pē. Now he told them the people. Now

13 atktŏ′cgam tgā′xalaitanEma ka′nauwē. A′lta nŏxŏ′tua qŏ′tac
   they took them their arrows all. Now they ran those

14 tê′lx·Em ia′koa mai′ēmē. Atktŏ′cgam nauā′itgEma; atktŏ′cgam
   people here down the river. They took them the nets; they took them
                                                   away

15 Tkulēyū′t!kc. A′lta noxŏ′maqt qŏ′tac tê′lx·Em. A′lta aqtā′wa
   the Quileute. Now they fought those people. Now they were
                                                  driven away

16 Tkulēyū′t!kc. Aqtŏ′tēna tcē′2tkum. Ta′kE aqtŏ′kᵘ ṭam gŏ-y-
   the Quileute. They were killed half. Then they were carried into

17 utā′xanim. Atgŏ′cgiLx utā′xanim Tkulyēū′t!kc, qāmx iā′xkatē
   their canoes. They hauled them their canoes the Quileute, part there
                    into the water

18 mā′Lxolē ataē′taqL. Atgŏ′cgam qaX ŏkunī′m Lā′kḷēlak, ta′kE
   inland they left them. They took them those canoes the Clatsop, then

19 atgŏ′cgiLx. Atagā′la-it Lā′kḷēlak qaX ŏkunī′m; Tkulēyū′t!kc
   they hauled them They were in the Clatsop those canoes; the Quileute
   into the water. the canoes

20 utā′xanima. A′lta aqtē′lua-y- ē′maL Tkulēyū′t!kc. Lap, Lap, Lap, Lap,
   their canoes. Now they were pur- the sea the Quileute. Shoot, shoot, shoot, shoot,
                   sued on the water

21 tgā′maᶜ aqtā′wix. Ta′kE aqa′Lxalukctgŏ Lkḷăckc. AqLā′owilX
   shooting they were done. Then he was thrown into the a boy. He was struck
   them   water

22 gŏ-y- ē′Laqtq. Iā′xkatē LḷEla′p ā′Lo. WiXt LE′gun
   on his head. There under water he went. Again one more

23 aqE′Lxalukctgŏ. AqLā′owilX ka LuXunē′n. AqLgā′ŏm, aqLŏ′cgam
   he was thrown into the He was struck and he floated. He was reached, he was taken,
   water.

24 aqLaQā′na-it. Ŏ′Xuitikc tkā′cŏcinikc aqto-a′lguiLx. Qāmx
   he was put into the Many boys were thrown into the Part
   canoe.   water.

25 itā′xanatē, qāmx Ela′p atgē′x. Iakoā′ aqaxatgŏ′mam
   their life, part under water they went. There it was passed

26 WalE′mlEm. AqtE′tua Tkulēyū′t!kc. Ē′maL aqtā′yitoa. A′lta
   Port Canby. They were pur- the Quileute. Sea they were pursued Now
              sued towards here.

ā2k̡aLō′nikc gō-y- ēXt ikanī′m. Ak̡ala′ktikc gō-y- ēXt ikanī′m. 1
three in a canoe in one canoe. Four in one canoe.

A′lta mE′nx·ka-y- utā′xanima Tkulēyū′t!kc, nēkct ā′Xauē; ka 2
Now few only their canoes the Quileute, not many; then

nē′k·im iLā′Xak̡Emana Lā′k̡ēlak: "Ā′lta lxtā′kō. Ta′kE 3
he said their chief the Clatsop: "Now we will return. Then

ō′Xuitikc alxktō′tēna." A′lta aLi′Xtakō Lā′k̡ēlak. A′lta nō′xogō 4
many we have killed them." Now they returned the Clatsop. Now they went home

Tkulēyū′t!kc. Atxigilā′2mam gō Kuē′naiyūL Tkulēyū′t!kc. 5
the Quileute. They arrived at Quenaiult the Quileute.

PāL tmēmElō′ctikc ūtā′xanīm. A′lta atktagElai′tamit qō′tac 6
Full of corpses their canoes. Now they placed them upright those

tmēmElō′ctikc. A′lta qu′LquL aqtā′wix tgā′xēLētcuwama. A′lta 7
dead ones. Now put on they were done to them their hats. Now

ā′tgEptck qō′tac gitā′Xanātē. A′lta aqawigē′waL̡amit. 8
they went up to the shore those who were alive. Now they were given to eat.

Nōxo-iLxā′lEm Tkulēyū′t!kc. Ā′lta tkutcā′-it atktā′wix qō′tac 9
They ate the Quileute. Now carrying food they did it to them those

tgā′cōlal. Tatc! uxō′La-itt qō′tac tgā′cōlal. Atō′xuxōi-oa qigō 10
their relatives. Behold, they were dead those their relatives. They lied because they were ashamed where

aqtō′tēna. 11
they were killed.

Translation.

A youth at Clatsop was sent to bathe at Nakōt̡ā′t. After five days he returned, going along the beach. In the evening he approached Clatsop and came around the point. Then he looked landward and saw many canoes lying side by side. "Where did these canoes come from?" he thought; "I will turn back." He was going to turn back, then many people pursued him. The beach was full of people. He looked in the direction where he wanted to go. Now there also the people went down to the beach. They cut him off and he was sur-rounded. They all held spears in their hands. They threw the spears at him. He jumped up and they missed him, the spears passing below him. "Ha, ha!" said the people. They threw their spears again and aimed higher. He stooped and they missed him, the spears passing above him. Again the people said "Ha, ha!" Now he jumped right through them and escaped. They pursued him. They threw spears at him, but he jumped high. He escaped and arrived at Clatsop. The youth had no mother and no father; they were dead. He lived with his grandfather. Now it was evening when he came back to Clatsop. The Tillamook stood there and were dancing. "What are you doing?" he said. "Take your arrows. We shall be attacked. The beach is full of people. Make yourselves ready." "Eia, he lies," said the peo-ple. "He wanted to see the ghosts and became frightened." Then the youth said to his grandfather, "Take your blanket. Let us go inland and hide ourselves." Then he and his grandfather went inland to hide. Now the Tillamook danced. At midnight they lay down. When the dawn of the day approached, an attack was made on the village. The

Tillamook who slept outside were all killed. Now they attacked the houses. Only a few were killed in the upper half of the town, when the people awoke. The Clatsop awoke. Now the [enemy retired and] carried away the children. The Quileute carried away many boys. Now a person ran up the river to inform the people at Konŏ′pē. Now he told them what had happened; they took their arrows and ran down the river. The Quileute took away the nets. Now the people fought, and the Quileute were driven away. One half of them were killed. Then [the dead ones] were carried into the canoes and they launched their canoes. Part they left on the shore.

The Clatsop took those canoes and launched them. They went into the canoes of the Quileute and pursued them. They shot their arrows at them. Then the Quileute threw a boy into the water. They struck him on his head and he was drowned. They threw another one into the water and struck him on his head. He swam, and the Clatsop took him into their canoe when they reached him. Thus many boys were thrown into the water. Part survived and part were drowned. Now they passed Point Canby. The Clatsop pursued them on the open sea. Now only three or four men survived in each canoe, and a few canoes only were left. Then the chief of the Clatsop said, "We will return. We have killed a great many." Now the Clatsop returned and the Quileute went home. They arrived at Quenaiult. Their canoes were full of corpses. They placed them upright and put on their hats. Then the survivors went ashore, where they were fed by the Quenaiult. The Quileute ate. Now the Quenaiult carried food to their relatives to the canoes. Behold, they were dead! The Quileute had lied because they were ashamed [that so many of their number had been killed].

Ayŏ′maqt qaX ă′eXat ŏqჍoĕyŏ′qXut itcā′xa. Goā′nEsum 1
It was dead   that   one   old woman   her son.   Always

naktcā′xa-it. ĔXt iqŏ′tax goā′nsum naktcā′xa-it, ka kჍā ɪɪā′xax. 2
she wailed.   One   year   always   she wailed,   and   silent   she became.

A′lta lĕ′lĕ ka nŏ′ya. Iau′a Niă′xakci nŏ′ya. Iā′xkatĕ naŏ′yEniL gō 3
Now   a long time   and she went.   There   to the slough at Seaside   she went.   There   she stayed at   always

Niă′xakci ka nā′xatgō. Nă′tĕ, nă′tĕ, nă′tĕ, nă′xatgō iau′a 4
Niă′xakci   and   she returned.   She came,   she came,   she came,   she returned   there

tkamĕlă′lEq. QჍo′ā′p agĕ′txamĕ Tiā′kჍĕlakĕ. A′lta i′kta agĕ′ᶜElkEl. 5
the beach.   Nearly   she reached it   Clatsop.   Now   something   she saw it.

NaxLŏ′lEXa-it ĕ′kolĕ. QჍoā′p agiā′xŏm. A′lta mŏkct tmā′ktcXEma 6
She thought   a whale.   Nearly   she reached it.   Now   two   spruce trees

tigE′nx·at. NaxLŏ′lEXa-it: "Ŏ nĕkct taLჍ ĕ′kolĕ. Eqctxĕ′Lau taLჍ." 7
stood upright near her.   She thought: "Oh!   not   behold   a whale.   A monster   behold."

Naigā′t!ŏm qix· ĕ′kta yuqunā′itX. A′lta iā′woxomĕ ka′nauwĕ ĕ′wa 8
She reached it   that   something   it lay there.   Now   its copper   all   thus

kⁿLā′xanĕ. A′lta tE′pa-it kჍau′kჍau tĕ′laut ka′nauwĕ2 gō qŏ′ta 9
outside.   Now   ropes   tied   they were to it   all   at   those

tiā′maktcx·Ema cka pā2L ĕ′qewiqĕma. Ta′kE Lāx nĕ′xax ĕĕ′tcxŏt. 10
its spruce trees   and   full   iron.   Then   come out   it did   a bear.

Iā′kuc gō qix· ĕ′kta qix· ĕ′kta yuqunā′itX. Ɏaqĕ ĕĕ′tcxŏt iā′lEkuilĕ. 11
He was on   on   that   something   that   something   lay there.   Just like   a bear   it looked like it.

Tatc!a LgōLĕ′lEXEmk gō ciā′xŏct. Ta′kE nā′xkŏ no′ya. Ta′kE 12
Behold!   a person   in   his face.   Then   she went home   she went.   Then

ayā′lEkaLx itcā′xa. A′lta nagE′tsax. Nā′k·im: "Ŏ qĕau itcE′xa. 13
she remembered him   her son.   Now   she cried.   She said: "Oh!   that   my son.

Ayŏ′mEqt qĕau itcE′xa ka tqigā′Lxol atxĕ′gela-ĕ." QჍoā′p agiā′xom 14
He is dead   that   my son   and   what is told about in tales   landed."   Nearly   she reached it

ĕ′lEXam. Ā′qxulqt. "Ā iqix·Enĕ′mat iŏ′itEt; Lŏ′nas ikჍĕ′tēnax 15
the town.   She cried.   "Ah!   a crying person   comes;   perhaps   struck

ĕ′xax." Nŏxui′tXuitck tĕ′lx·Em. Atktŏ′cgam tgā′xalaitanEma. 16
he is."   They made themselves ready   the people.   They took them   their arrows.

Ka′nauwĕ atktŏ′cgam tgā′xalaitanEma. "Ni′Xua amcxagEluwE′tcatk," 17
All   they took them   their arrows.   "Well,   listen,"

aLE′k·im LqჍĕyŏ′qxut. Ta′kE nŏxuwi′tcatk tĕ′lx·Em. A′lta xā′xo-il: 18
he said   an old man.   Then   they listened   the people.   Now   she said always:

"Ayŏ′mEqt qĕau itcE′xa ka txĕ′gela-it tqigā′Lŏl." Ta′kE 19
"He is dead   that   my son   and   it landed   what is told about in tales."   Then

nugŏ′kXuim tĕ′lx·am: "Ĕ′kta Lx ĕ′xax!" Ta′kE acxalgĕ′taqtamĕ; 20
they said   the people,   "What may be it is!"   Then   they went to meet her;

nŏ′Xua qŏ′tac tĕ′lx·Em. Aqŏ′lEXam: "I′kta ĕ′xax!" "A, i′kta 21
they ran   those   people.   She was spoken to: "What   is it!"   "Ah!   something

275

1 x·ix· iuqunā'itX ē'wa tctāx. Iā'kōc môkct ēitcxō'tEma na
   this lies there thus around the There are two bears [int.
             point. on it   part.]

2 tcu tê'lx·Em na." Ta'kE nō'Xua tê'lx·Em. Ta'kE aqigā'ōm
   or people [int. part.].'' Then they ran the people. Then it was reached

3 x·ix· ē'kta iuqunā'itX. A'lta atkLō'ktcan qō'tac tê'lx·Em na
   this some- lay there. Now they held them those people [int.
       thing   part.]

4 tcō·y· i'kta na môkct LtcgE'nEma ēwaxō'miqL Lkēx. Ayō'yam
   or something [int. two buckets copper it was. He arrived
             part.]

5 qix· ē'Xat iā'nēwa nicga'ōm. Ta'kE wiXt ē'Xat ayō'yam.
   that one first he arrived at them. Then again one he arrived.

6 A'lta gōyē' aLi'xax LgōLē'lEXEmk gō·y· i'LacqL. A'lta
   Now thus he did the person to his mouth. Now

7 aqLcā'lōt qō'La LtcgE'nEma. Lā'sEmilᵉks qō'La LtcgE'nEma.
   they were given those buckets. They had lids those buckets.

8 Gōyē' aqE'ctax aLxE'ntciyakᵘtē iau'a mā'Lxolē. Ltcuq aqcō'kō.
   Thus it was done to they pointed there inland. Water they were
       them   sent for.

9 Ta'kE aci'Xaua mā'Lxôlē qō'ctac cgōLē'lEXEmk. Gō LE'mᶜEcX
   Then they ran inland those two persons. At a log

10 ka aLkcō'pcōt. WiXt aci'Xtakō, aci'Xaua iau'a mā'Lnē.
   and they hid themselves. Again they returned; they ran there seaward.

11 AyōuLXē'wulX ē'Xat, ayayE'La-it. Nē'ltcō qix· ici'p. Nik'ē'x·tkin
   He ascended one, he entered it. He went that ship. He looked about
                              down

12 gō wē'wuLē, LEqcā'nukc pāL qix· ici'p. Lap atcā'yax ē'tcEltcEl,
   in interior of ship, boxes full that ship. Find he did them brass buttons,

13 gōyē'·y· ixk¡ē'Lē. Ayō'pa kᵘLā'xanē. Qē'xtcē qtcuguixē'ma
   that long [half strings. He went out outside. Intending he called them
   a fathom]

14 tiā'cōlal, ā'nqatē wax aqā'yax qix· ē'kta iuqunā'itx. Atcō'pEna
   his relatives, already set fire it was done that something lay there. He jumped
                    to it

15 iau'a kē'kXulē. A'lta kē'kXulē ckēx qō'ctac môkct
   there down. Now below they were those two

16 cgōLē'lEXEmk. Nē'xLXa qix· ē'kta ka acgE'tcax. Aqē'xLx·ama-y·
   persons. It burned that some- and they cried. It was burned
                       thing

17 a'lta ka'nauwē. Nē'xLXa qix· ē'kta t¡aqē Lᶜā'tcau aLxtx·ā'x.
   now all. It burned that something just as fat it burned.

18 Iā'xkatē atgiupā'yaLx qix· iqēwēkē'ma. Atgiupā'yaLx qix·
   There they gathered it that iron. They gathered it that

19 iuwāXō'mē, atgiupā'yaLx iqēk¡E'c Lā'k¡ēlak. Ta'kE noxoē'xiXt
   copper, they gathered it the brass the Clatsop. Then they learned
                              about it

20 ka'nauwē tê'lx·Em. Ta'kE aqcō'cgam qō'ctac môkct cgōLē'lEXEmk
   all the people. Then they were taken those two persons

21 gō iLā'Xak¡Emana Lā'k¡ēlak. Ta'kE nē'k·im gō·y· ēXt iLā'lEXam
   to their chief the Clatsop. Then he said at one their town

22 iLā'Xak¡Emana: "Gō nai'ka nk'ōniā'xō-y· ē'Xat," Lä2qc nuxō'maqt
   their chief, "At me I shall keep him one." Almost they fought

23 tê'lx·Em. A'lta aqiō'cgam gō·y· ēXt ē'lEXam ē'Xat. A'2lta
   the people. Now he was taken to one town one. Now

24 it!ō'ktē nē'xax ā'yamxtc qix· ē'Xat ikak¡Emā'na. Ta'kE noxoē'xiXt
   good became his heart that one chief. Then they learned
                              about it

25 Tkwinaiū'Lukc, ta'kE noxoē'xiXt Gitā'ts¡xēEls, ta'kE noxoē'xiXt
   the Quenaiult, then they learned about it the Chehalis, then they learned
                              about it

26 Gilā'xicatck ta'kE noxoē'xiXt Gitā'qauēlitsk, ta'ke noxoē'xiXt
   the Cascade, then they learned about it the Cowlitz, then they learned
                              about it

LE'qatat.   A'lta   ä'tgē   Tiä'k¡ēlake   ka'nauwē.   Tkwinaiu'ᴌukc ä'tgē,   1
the Klickatat. Then they went   to Clatsop   all.   The Quenaiult   went,

Giᴌᴀ'ts¡xēEls ä'ᴌö̆,   GiᴌᴀᴌᴀXuilapaX   ä'ᴌö.   Ka'nauwē tᴇlamē'ma   2
the Chehalis   went,   the Willapa   went.   All   towns

ä'tgē.   Giᴌᴀᴌᴀᴌᴀᴌᴀxicatck aᴌE'tctcō,   Gitä'qauēlitsk atgä'tctcō, LE'qatat   3
went.   The Cascades   they went down   the Cowlitz   went down the the Klickatat
                             the river,   river,

atgä'tctcō. Ka'nauwē iau'a kⁿca'la nē'maᴌ atgä'tctco. Atgatē'mam   4
went down the   All   these   up the river the river they went down. They came to
river.

Tiä'k¡ēlakē. Mö̆kct kcī iwaXö'mit Lä'Xat ᴌᴌä'ētix· ska nix·ä'ômx   5
Clatsop.   Two   fingers copper   one   slave   and   it met [goes
                      [wide]   around]

gö   iᴌä'potē. Gȫyē' ä'yaᴌqt iqēwē'qxē Lē'Xat ᴌᴌä'ētix·. Gȫyē'   6
at   the arm. Thus [half the long   iron   one   slave.   Thus
                length of the
                  radius]

iä'qa-iᴌ mö̆kct kci iqēk¡E'c Lē'Xat ᴌᴌä'ētix·. Aqiö'mᴇlx·ix·   7
large   two   fingers brass   one   slave.   They were bought
                   [wide]

itsusä'qama, qiä'x ct!ö'kti cpä'yix tcx·ī qantsē'x· aci'Xᴌa-itX.   8
nails,   if   a good   curried deer   then   some   they exchanged
                            skin   them for them.

AqE'x·ctgoax. Qiä'x iū'ᴌqta iqauwik¡ē'ᴌē, tcx·ī tcēx aci'xᴌa-itx   9
It was bartered.   If   long   long dentalia,   then several they exchanged
                                                            them for it.

qix· itsusä'qᴇma· Atgiö'mᴇl qö'tac tē'lx·ᴇm. Tkanä'Ximct nö'xôx   10
those   nails.   They bought those   people.   Chiefs [rich]   became
                    them

ᴌä'k¡ēlak. Ia'xkatē ka q¡atsE'n aqē'ᶜᴇlkᴇl iqēwiqē'ma. Iqēk¡E's   11
the Clatsop.   There   and for the first it was seen   iron.   Brass
                            time

iä'xkatē q¡atsE'n aqē'ᶜᴇlkᴇl. A'lta nä'kö aqE'ctax qö'ctac   12
there   for the first time it was seen.   Now   keep   they were done   those

cgōᴌē'lᴇXᴇmk, gö ē'Xat ikä'nax ē'Xat; gö·y· ayö'kt!itē   13
persons,   at   one   chief   one;   at   point of land

Tiä'k¡ēlakē ē'Xat nE'kö aqä'yax.   14
Clatsop   one   keep   he was done.

Translation.

The son of an old woman had died. She wailed for him a whole year and then she stopped. Now one day she went to Seaside. There she used to stop, and she returned. She returned walking along the beach. She nearly reached Clatsop; now she saw something. She thought it was a whale. When she came near it she saw two spruce trees standing upright on it. She thought, "Behold! it is no whale. It is a monster." She reached the thing that lay there. Now she saw that its outer side was all covered with copper. Ropes were tied to those spruce trees and it was full of iron. Then a bear came out of it. He stood on the thing that lay there. He looked just like a bear, but his face was that of a human being. Then she went home. Now she thought of her son, and cried, saying, "Oh, my son is dead and the thing about which we heard in tales is on shore." When she nearly reached the town she continued to cry. [The people said,] "Oh, a person comes crying. Perhaps somebody struck her." The people made themselves ready. They took their arrows. An old man said, "Listen!" Then the people listened. Now she said all the time, "Oh, my son is dead, and the thing about which we heard in tales is on shore." The people said,

"What may it be?" They went running to meet her. They said, "What is it?" "Ah, something lies there and it is thus. There are two bears on it, or maybe they are people." Then the people ran. They reached the thing that lay there. Now the people, or what else they might be, held two copper kettles in their hands. Now the first one reached there. Another one arrived. Now the persons took their hands to their mouths and gave the people their kettles. They had lids. The men pointed inland and asked for water. Then two people ran inland. They hid themselves behind a log. They returned again and ran to the beach. One man climbed up and entered the thing. He went down into the ship. He looked about in the interior of the ship; it was full of boxes. He found brass buttons in strings half a fathom long. He went out again to call his relatives, but they had already set fire to the ship. He jumped down. Those two persons had also gone down. It burnt just like fat. Then the Clatsop gathered the iron, the copper, and the brass. Then all the people learned about it. The two persons were taken to the chief of the Clatsop. Then the chief of the one town said, "I want to keep one of the men with me." The people almost began to fight. Now one of them was taken to one town. Then the chief was satisfied. Now the Quenaiult, the Chehalis, the Cascades, the Cowlitz, and the Klickatat learned about it and they all went to Clatsop. The Quenaiult, the Chehalis, and the Willapa went. The people of all the towns went there. The Cascades, the Cowlitz, and the Klickatat came down the river. All those of the upper part of the river came down to Clatsop. Strips of copper two fingers wide and going around the arm were exchanged for one slave each. A piece of iron as long as one-half the forearm was exchanged for one slave. A piece of brass two fingers wide was exchanged for one slave. A nail was sold for a good curried deerskin. Several nails were given for long dentalia. The people bought this and the Clatsop became rich. Then iron and brass were seen for the first time. Now they kept these two persons. One was kept by each chief; one was at the Clatsop town at the cape.

Reprint Publishing

For People Who Go For Originals.

This book is a facsimile reprint of the original edition. The term refers to the facsimile with an original in size and design exactly matching simulation as photographic or scanned reproduction.

Facsimile editions offer us the chance to join in the library of historical, cultural and scientific history of mankind, and to rediscover.

The books of the facsimile edition may have marks, notations and other marginalia and pages with errors contained in the original volume. These traces of the past refers to the historical journey that has covered the book.

ISBN 978-3-95940-195-1

www.reprintpublishing.com

www.ingramcontent.com/pod-product-compliance
Lightning Source LLC
Chambersburg PA
CBHW080326270326
41927CB00014B/3117